Multimedia Training

Developing Technology-Based Systems

D1716463

Series Title

In order to receive additional information on these or any other McGraw-Hill titles, in the United States please call 1-800-822-8158. In other countries, contact your local McGraw-Hill representative.

iN

Multimedia Training

Developing Technology-Based Systems

Angus Reynolds

Thomas Iwinski

McGraw-Hill
New York San Francisco Washington, D.C. Auckland Bogotá
Caracas Lisbon London Madrid Mexico City Milan
Montreal New Delhi San Juan Singapore
Sydney Tokyo Toronto

McGraw-Hill

*A Division of The **McGraw·Hill** Companies*

Library of Congress Cataloging-in-Publication Data

Reynolds, Angus, 1936-
    Multimedia training: developing technology-based systems/by
Angus Reynolds, Thomas Iwinski.
        p.   cm.
    Includes index.
    ISBN 0-07-912012-1 (hc)
    1. Multimedia systems. 2. Computer-assisted instruction.
I. Iwinski, Thomas, 1963-   II. title.
    QA76.575.R48   1995   95-32922
    658.3'12404--dc20   CIP

pbk 1 2 3 4 5 6 7 8 9 DOC/DOC 9 0 0 9 8 7 6 5

ISBN 0-07-912012-1

The sponsoring editor of this book was Jennifer Holt DiGiovanna, the manuscript editor was Michael Christopher, the associate managing editor was David M. McCandless, and the executive editor was Joanne Slike. The director of production was Katherine G. Brown. This book was set in ITC Century Light. It was composed in Blue Ridge Summit, Pennsylvania.

Printed and bound by R.R. Donnelley & Sons Company, Crawfordsville, Indiana

McGraw-Hill books are available at special quantity discounts to use as premiums and sales promotions, or for use in corporate training programs. For more information, please write to the Director of Special Sales, McGraw-Hill, 11 West 19th Street, New York, NY 10011. Or contact your local bookstore.

MH95
9120121

Contents

Part 3   Applying Your Skills to the World of Work

Part 4   Enhancing Your Lessons

Part 5   Case Studies of Successful Applications

Part 6 The Business of Technology-Based Learning

Acknowledgments

This book is the product of help and encouragement provided by many fine people. With the hope that we do not fail to recognize any of this help, we publicly thank the following people who gave us information, insights, advice, assistance, or courage.

Michael Allen, Steve Allen, Jim Angelo, Roberto Araya, Harold Bailey, Mustafa Balci, Donald Bitzer, Terry Breedlove, J.R. Brown, Cheryl Samuels Campbell, Laura Chesson, Richard Davis, Jim Ghesquiere, Brien Heisler, Hui-Chuan Cheng, Stan Cohen, Don Crippen, John Eldridge, Ray Fox, Joel Freeman, Robert Gagné, Jim Glish, Barry Granoff, David and Eleanor Iwinski, Leah Iwinski, Don Kirkpatrick, Malcolm Knowles, Richard Lamberski, Harvey Long, Jesse Maddox, Richard Mager, Flip Millis, Lynn Misselt, Len Nadler, Adrienne O'Brien, Joan Penrose, Carl Philabaum, Hallie Preskill, Susan Taylor, Stan Trollip, Dean Wade, and Roger West.

Even writing about what is in store for you in this book enervates us. We *know* you can succeed, as we have personally helped hundreds of others do. We are eager to guide you through the process and watch you grow in understanding and capability as you read and work your way through these chapters.

There are massive needs for you to meet in nearly every organization. The potential you bring will be overwhelming. Let's get started!

Angus Reynolds
Albuquerque, New Mexico

Thomas Iwinski
State College, Pennsylvania

Foreword

Interactive Multimedia is a metaphor for the technology-based simulation of a process that takes place between a learner and a collection of subject matter. The mental construct that represents the stereotypical model is that of the instructor lecturing to a selected group. The presumption is that the instructor will be successful in imparting the needed information for that session or group of sessions and that, if the learners fail, theirs is the responsibility. The instructor decides what to deliver, delivers it, and grades the result.

The key attribute in multimedia learning is its basic systems orientation to a cybernetic process. The problem lies in the design and implementation needed to accomplish this, which is what this book is all about. *Cybernetics* is a term coined by Norbert Weiner to identify the confluence of two significant branches of technology that developed independently in the first part of this century: communications, and control systems. The concept of cybernetics implies a control stimulus communicated to an operating system, a resultant system status modification, and feedback that describes a new status of the system. It is a process oriented concept. Instruction can be viewed as a process in which information is transmitted, a feedback is elicited, and analysis of the feedback is made that governs the further transmission of information. Further, a prescription for instruction can be developed that will include each of these actions and be specific to an individual sequence of instruction, such as integration of learning theory, specific application requirements, available technology, learner profiles, and terminal educational or training objectives. From a systems viewpoint, design should be so structured that a replicable result can be expected—which implies the use of technology. The analysis and subsequent design must incorporate the foregoing.

Of great importance is the orientation to the learner. Learning styles vary, so to reach learners successfully, the instruction should be tailored to the individual's style and not necessarily the preconceived notion of an instructor.

Individual differences could involved background knowledge, language comprehension or literacy, cultural background, biases and orientations, in addition to innate differences in mental and physical information intake and processing ability. For many years, it has been presumed that the classroom instructors can spot these differences and modify the instruction, or alter the presentation for information delivery. Today it is the job of the instructional designer to make provision for this diversity and do the diagnostic and prescriptive job necessary to accommodate to individual differences.

This book is one of the few that deals with this important point in describing how adults learn in the context of multimedia design.

In addition, one of the critical elements of any system is the ability to measure its own performance. Where reference criteria of performance are not defined, one can not impose effective measurements and hence will have no way of knowing how it is performing. Hence, measurement to specific criteria is required.

One of the attributes of this book by Angus Reynolds and Thomas Iwinski is that it encompasses many of the foregoing elements, as opposed to merely describing the mechanical issues of identifying content, organizing instructional materials, coding, programming, and assembling completed interactive multimedia systems. We are given information on how to assess learners as a part of the design process, given a rationale for the process, introduced to the issues of evaluation, and made knowledgeable about cost benefit issues

To the extent that they have developed a more comprehensive picture of the multimedia designer's considerations and described how to understand and accomplish implementation of these issues, they have enlarged upon prior knowledge. For this reason, I feel this book is a very positive contribution to the advancement of this important field.

Raymond G. Fox
President
Society for Applied Learning Technology

Introduction

There is no reason to find multimedia training baffling. Multimedia is defined in *The Trainer's Dictionary* as

> Integrated computer and audiovisual technologies that provide access to multimedia content formats.

Training is defined as

> In Human Resource Development, instructional experiences provided primarily by employers for employees, designed to develop new skills, knowledge, and attitudes that are expected to be applied immediately upon (or within a short time after) arrival on or return to the job.

Multimedia training that we present in this book is consistent with these definitions. The examples are computer programs that help an employee to work more safely and productively by supplying very specific training that is interesting and easy to use. Even being relatively new in organizations, the growth in the application of multimedia training has been amazing—even compared to the growth of simple one-media computer-based learning. We will explore the details of multimedia training, how to decide when it is useful, how to develop it (with hands-on practice), what major companies do with it, how to make a business of it, and much more in the remainder of this book.

Overview of this Book

We have planned and structured this book to serve a very wide range of readers. You will find that you can obtain an executive overview of each topic we present, the in-depth coverage desired by those who want to know this field inside out, and the hands-on practice needed by those who will build multimedia training applications for their organizations and clients. We also offer tips that will make your efforts more productive and trouble-free.

The book is divided into six parts. Together they provide a comprehensive look at the important issues facing people who seriously want to produce multimedia training. These parts are:

1   About Technology-Based Learning
2   Building a Technology-Based Lesson
3   Applying Your Skills to the World of Work
4   Enhancing Your Studies
5   Case Studies of Successful Application
6   The Business of Technology-Based Learning

Part 1—About Technology-Based Learning

Part 1 provides the necessary background and sets the stage for your involvement in later sections. It also serves as an executive overview of background information needed by people who do serious multimedia training development.

In Chapter 1 we describe what multimedia training is, explain its relevance to you, and provide an example. We also introduce the book's hands-on concept. The chapter also covers the software included with the book, as well as hardware and software system requirements needed to complete the practical exercises.

In Chapter 2 we explore the problems faced by people getting started with technology-based learning (TBL). This chapter provides the necessary definitions and covers the relationship of the components of TBL. The components of TBL and the differences between them are defined. Each mode of the components is explored, to provide a comprehensive picture of the setting in which multimedia learning operates.

Chapter 3 covers the experience of others in applying technology-based learning. We present its strengths and weakness. Then we introduce and review the details of performance-based training. We also explore contemporary use of technology-based learning in a variety of organizations, ending with a brief historical background of these systems.

In Chapter 4 we look at the human factor considerations, providing ergonomic suggestions. The cost of multimedia training solutions is compared to traditional (instructor-led) training. There are differing patterns of improved performance and we compare them to derive attendant costs to the organization.

In Chapter 5 we explore some of the things that instructional technologists have learned about the learning process itself. We have prepared the chapter to provide a useful review for those with a background in training, as well as an understandable introduction for those who don't.

Chapter 6 covers the essential elements needed to build good technology-based instruction. We explain how to write and use learning objectives and explore the differences between the cognitive, psychomotor, and affective domains of learning. We introduce the members of the technology-based learning development team and review the roles of each. Finally, we present the meat and potatoes of instructional developers, the systematic approach to instructional development.

Evaluation is an important part of the instruction. In Chapter 7 we explore the rationale, advantages and disadvantages, and techniques used to carry out evaluation. We do not mean testing, since evaluation is much more than that. We explore the ways to make the instruction better—the true purpose of evaluation.

In Chapter 8 we provide the basis of calculating cost benefits and review several of the most commonly used methods.

In the final chapter of Part 1, Chapter 9, we add the characteristics of multimedia training to the knowledge base created in the earlier chapters. We introduce ideas that may be new, even if you are already involved with multimedia efforts, such as the characteristics of the technology cycle. We look at the characteristics of digital-video training options, including its advantages and disadvantages. Finally, we try to be as accurate as possible in setting forth the various costs.

Part 2—Building a Technology-Based Lesson

Part 2 provides the basic grounding in multimedia training that our title promises. A series of short chapters, each devoted to a particular process, leads you step-by-step through a project to create a lesson for a factory worker to enable him or her to guide a large overhead crane. By completing the practical exercises you will actually build a lesson.

Chapter 10 is the first of a series of chapters that describe a case you will follow and use to develop your skills in building your first system. This chapter describes the settings in which technology-based learning is created. We examine the knowledge and skills, equipment, and other considerations in detail. The chapter presents you with the criteria to consider in selecting a work setting suited for improvements with multimedia training. Finally, we unveil the crane operator case that sets the scene for the remaining chapters in this part of the book.

Chapter 11 launches the design process. This is a typical case requiring the ideas for the instruction to be laid out clearly so that anyone involved in the process, especially those who must approve it, can see what will eventually be implemented. We provide deliverable Design Document for the crane operator project.

Chapter 12 explains how to make the design so explicit that we could send our PRMs to another state or another country for completion. We discuss alternative content and approaches to building the PRMs. Finally, we provide a deliverable Programmer-Ready-Materials for more practice.

In Chapter 13 we continue discussion of the problems of further organizing the information. We provide an opportunity for you to become acquainted with the tool you will use to build your lessons, Authorware Professional, which we simply call , Authorware. The welcome includes an introductory review of the software produced by Authorware's parent company, Macromedia. Finally, using Authorware, you create a simple mouse tutorial to provide practice for your learners who aren't yet familiar with using a mouse.

Chapter 14 continues to build the crane operator lesson, while providing introductory experiences in using Authorware to build useful instruction. We start by building a utility to capture the learner's name for use in your lessons, and to apply captured data in keeping records of study.

Chapter 15 is an encounter in building a sophisticated lesson as a first experience. We believe that you should, as far as possible, attempt always to create sophisticated lessons, and so we provide the first experience. This one is highly interactive and avoids all the flaws that you will hear about as you meet with people who were "turned off" by the technology-based lessons they saw or experienced somewhere along the line.

Chapter 16 introduces and explores the basic techniques for finding problems in software. We will introduce specific techniques for finding problems in technology-based learning and even more specific techniques for finding problems in Author-ware lessons. Finally, we will help you get assistance when you can't find the solution to the problem.

In Chapter 17 we show you how to evaluate technology-based learning, and how to design or modify tools for evaluating lessons. Then we explain how to use the results of your evaluation.

Part 3—Applying Your Skills to the World of Work

Part 3 provides a series of experiences in building the kind of lessons we hope you will continue to make and supply to your own learners. We have intentionally placed these chapters in diverse work settings. You can apply interesting solutions to the problems you meet in your particular environment. We think the practical exercises in Part 3 will help you think of new ways to help others learn.

Chapter 18 provides experience in leading the learner through Authorware's built-in, pull-down menu system. It addresses control over the computer interface and includes changing the on-screen type size, playing narration, altering the cursor's shape, and even using different languages.

In Chapter 19 we help you create a very visual lesson that provides a stimulation of the intellectual aspect of mixing concrete. You will build a lesson that enables the learner to see the differences in the concrete created by various combinations of its component parts.

Chapter 20 is another simulation. You learn to manipulate variables to teach a tractor-trailer driver how to balance the load on a truck to operate safely and legally. The same thing can be accomplished with a truck weigh station, tractor, trailer, and load. This chapter provides you with the experience to make expanded learning a possibility in many different organizations.

Chapter 21 shows how to build a lesson to teach electrocardiogram (EKG) technicians how to place the electrodes that will produce the EKG. This chapter also provides useful information on how to provide custom-learner feedback.

Chapter 22 will explore how to use arrays with Authorware. Specific applications include preparing study information in a tireless drill and practice helper in the form of familiar flashcards. Also, you will learn how to use the Authorware paging model to allow your learners to navigate within the lessons you build.

Chapter 23 shows you how to tie together what you have built in the preceding lessons into a unified whole for presentation to your learners. This includes custom scoring of various testing strategies, running separate lessons from a central menu, how to pass variables, and how to store student results in an external file. We explore how to use Authorware's answer judging power. Then, you make your program read data from the external file. In preparing a diploma for the learner and generating reports for training administrators you learn to send a screen image to a printer and to print an external file.

Part 3 finishes the job begun in Part 2. You will have already succeeded in making a "vanilla-flavored" basic advisory system. The chapters in Part 3 will help you add all the additional multimedia support components to complete a system of which you can be proud.

Part 4—Enhancing Your Lessons

Making a complete lesson is not all there is to providing learning. In Part 4 you will explore other things you can do to provide better lessons in ways that, at the start, you might never have dreamed.

In Chapter 24 we show you how to help your learner when he or she doesn't know what to do. We explore help techniques and examine standards for providing help, and how to meet them.

Chapter 25 rounds out the section on the multimedia components of technology-based learning. First, we explore characteristics of video formats for multimedia training. Then, we show you the ramifications of hardware-supported versus software-supported digital video. Also, we review the platform differences for video, what they might mean to you today and tomorrow, and consider directions for future video use.

Chapter 26 introduces the divergent characteristics of simulation and simulators. We review the advantages and disadvantages of each. Then we explore various simulation methods. You will learn how to rank the fidelity and determine the categories of simulations. Finally, we will explore the characteristics of different types of simulated time.

In Chapter 27 we look at the things to consider when translating materials into foreign language, and the considerations for culturalization. We suggest how to identify and avoid cultural bias, and how to estimate the cost of adapting multimedia training for foreign delivery.

Chapter 28 is a deeper look at the differences between the Authorware Working model and the full version. Here, we identify and discuss the advanced features of Authorware and other authoring systems, and how they are used. We look at how and why to package courseware for delivery, and how to convert courseware for delivery on another platform.

Part 5—Case Studies of Successful Application

You are not alone. Organizations in quite different business sectors are pursuing excellence in multimedia training. Part 5 tells the story of three such companies. Each provides a different perspective from which you can find ideas to apply in other companies in other sectors.

At Union Pacific, multimedia training put quality back on track. Chapter 29 introduces a program designed to revitalize a railroad. The venerable Omaha-based transportation giant has spent close to $100 million since 1989, when management committed to a five-year service reliability improvement program incorporating multimedia training. The results have been so impressive that Union Pacific is expanding multimedia training to other areas.

Chapter 30 describes an effort at Magnavox to build a CAI tutorial, to be available in the classroom to teach a new specialized military computer system and in the field to provide practice for users of the system. The project was delivered on a militarized Hewlett-Packard computer using the UNIX operating system, and was developed when development tools useful for UNIX were scarce to non-existent. The result was an outstanding tutorial program that can be used wherever in the world the equipment is deployed.

Chapter 31 showcases a performance-improvement approach based on simulation from Aetna. As insurance companies also become financial institutions their employee training resembles that of a bank. Aetna combines the strength of technology-based learning with performance support systems to improve human performance.

Part 6—The Business of Technology-Based Learning

In Part 6 we talk about how to become a true professional. We are quite serious about this point, since we see people who mean well, but lack the knowledge sets needed in business.

In Chapter 32 we consider the platform needed for commercial development. We examine the skills and competencies needed for multimedia training development. We explore the comparative advantages of buying or building courseware, explain how to select a development platform, and talk about how to work within differing delivery environments.

We also present a rationale for working with a formal system for courseware development, and explain why everyone uses the same system. Among other things, we also review how to work with a formal system in a practical way.

Finally, in Chapter 33 we look at the *learning* horizon to explore the near-future trends in multimedia training. We explore coping with technological change. Then we present the technology lifecycle and look at how to use it to predict future changes in multimedia for training.

About Technology-Based Learning

1

Getting Ready

In this chapter you will prepare to embark on a fantastic voyage. If all this multimedia training stuff is new to you we can compare you to the heroic seamen who completed the first voyage around the world. We respect your bravery and sense of adventure, for wanting to explore something new and intimidating. If this is all old hat to you we welcome you as a colleague and modestly suggest that you consider what we have to offer.

What You Will Learn in This Chapter

- What technology-based learning is
- How it can help your organization
- What an example course is like
- How you can apply what you read in practical exercises
- What software is included with this book
- What hardware you need for the practical exercises

What Is Technology-Based Learning?

First, let's demystify technology-based learning. Technology-based learning is just what it sounds like. It is the use of technology to help people learn. The technology involved is a computer of some kind. But we are now in a period in time when the computers we use will undergo a transformation. Some employees will eventually do their work with computers (or with computer-based devices) that do not look at all like the PC or Mac on today's desktop.

A good example is the automatic teller machine (ATM) for banking. The ATM is actually a computer terminal connected to a distant mainframe computer. If people had to use a standard computer terminal they would never use ATMs. By hiding the computer, the ATM focuses on what the person is doing. That is why we say *technology*, in preference to *computer*.

We will cover the technology itself in detail, but let's quickly dispel some possible misconceptions by presenting the results of research. We will show that:

- Technology-based instruction can be cheaper than instructor-led instruction
- Learners in many organizations report that they prefer technology-based instruction
- Technology-based instruction takes less time than instructor-led instruction

Technology-based instruction has disadvantages too, and we will explore them as well as we move forward.

Thinking about Technology-Based Learning

We can get a better idea about technology-based learning by conducting some thought experiments. Don't be turned off by exercises. This is not going to turn into a workbook. There are very few in the whole book, and they are there for good reasons. We earnestly suggest that you take the time to try these exercises, because we have seen them open people's eyes.

Exercise 1-1

Directions: First, make a list of all the applications you can think of for using computers. For example:

1. *Payrolls*
2. *Controlling spacecraft*
3. *Graphics*
4.
5.
6.
Etc.

If you take the time to actually write these down on a separate sheet of paper you will probably be surprised. You will find that there are many diverse uses for computers. Most people can generate a list of more than 50 items.

Now, make a list of *non*-applications for computers. Things they can't do or can't be used for might include:

1. *Expressing love or other emotions*
2.
3.
4.
5.
6.
Etc.

Exercise Analysis: If you take the time to complete this list you may be surprised again. This list will be surprisingly short. Invariably, it will contain things that are uniquely human—particularly human interactions.

The lesson in making these two lists is that there are definite limits to the things we can do with computers, including instructional things. There is no reason to fear that computers will replace human beings as the primary conveyers of instruction. We estimate that, at most, only about 50% of all instruction could be done using technology. Today, only about 5% of instruction in business and industry is done this way. We have a very long way to go to reach technology's potential.

Exercise 1–2

Directions:

1. *Take a separate sheet of paper*
2. *Draw My TBL System*

or

List Things That Must Be In My TBL System

We recommend that you carry out the exercise, because you will force yourself to commit to an idea. If you don't want to go to the trouble to draw or list these items, at least think about how you would complete this exercise before continuing.

Exercise Analysis: Some possible answers might look like one of those shown in Figure 1.1

Look closely at these representations. These are typical of what people produce in response to this exercise. First, you might notice that this brings out the graphic or textual preference of the person in making the representation, because numbers one and four are different than numbers two and three.

The really interesting responses are not the text or graphic representations, but the person's concept of what they want. We recommend asking a client to do this, because you can learn something about the person when you see the response—something besides its specifics, which are also valuable. The two possibilities are the *systematic* and the *component* representations. By responding to the approach the client took here, you will be "in synch" with that person's thinking and will be better able to communicate about the planned system.

Communicating clearly about the need is important, but what about understanding that need?

About This Book

Have you heard of *The Snark*? It is a story by Lewis Carroll, the author of *Alice's Adventures in Wonderland. The Snark* is also a child's story that you can read in a

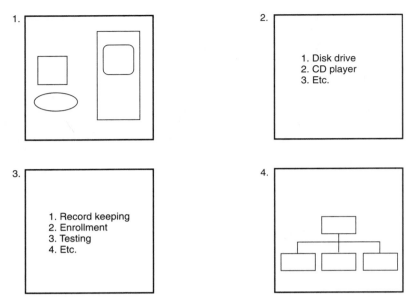

Figure 1.1 Four Possible System Concepts

few minutes. It tells of three Englishmen who set out on a hunt. Their prey is the Snark. What we soon see is that each hunter bases his hunt on a concept of the Snark colored by his own experience. One is ready for a ferocious beast like a lion; another seeks a tiny shy and reclusive species like a kiwi; the third expects and prepares to hunt a bird. The lesson for the reader is, "If you don't know what you're looking for you're not likely to find it." That is just as true in the world of work as in the world of Snark hunting. Unfortunately, we all too frequently meet people engaged in making multimedia training who should know a lot more about it than they do. They are essentially hunting the multimedia Snark. We will take care to ensure that you do not become a Snark hunter too.

Technology

In this book we will concern ourselves with instruction that is delivered to people via computers. Much good instruction is delivered by other means, but really good technology-based instruction can take your breath away.

We will present information that will enable readers who aren't yet familiar with technology to appreciate the differences and capabilities of various combinations, but we will not engage in deep theoretical or technical discussions. Our background and work make us practical people and we have written this book for other practical people.

How people learn

Strangely, some people are in the business of building instruction, yet they have no genuine grounding in how people learn at work. We don't think that should be the case and have included the information you need to make use of what is known for sure about how adults learn.

We believe we have succeeded in making this aspect of the book especially useful to you. Many old and new friends responded to our requests for people to try it out. You are the beneficiary of their efforts.

Secure funding

We devote a portion of this book to the very mundane prospect of funding your efforts. We believe that you can build beautiful training using the tools you develop and skills you acquire with this book. Still, you won't build any training at all if someone isn't willing to fund it. When we look at how to demonstrate that technology-based multimedia training is a good idea in your particular situation we will:

- Determine the requirements for resources and funding required to carry out the project.
- Estimate the level of effort involved in implementing a computer-based learning project.
- Estimate basic computer-based training cost/benefit.

The courseware production process

We are very serious about doing multimedia training right! Selecting the right project is important. There are many training wants and needs that do not lend themselves at all to technology-based instruction. Learning how to separate the appropriate from the inappropriate is as important as knowing how to develop the training itself. Some of the points we will cover include how to:

- Correctly use terminology common to technology-based instruction.
- Determine how CAI, CMI, or other methods can be used to advantage in a project, based on an understanding of each.
- Plan the development of a computer-based training course.
- Compare the advantages and disadvantages of different instructional systems.
- Identify implications of the use of computer-based learning in different situations or organizations, including your own.
- Determine which projects or portions of projects can effectively use computer-based learning methods.

Prepare the courseware development documents

We see people fail, while trying to build instruction that is very important, because they do not fully understand or use proven techniques that produce quality training. Recent failures are as common as historic ones. We know that you can do better, and therefore we provide the information and examples you need to do a first-rate job. We provide an example of a crane operator and follow it step-by-step. You will see the process used to develop the instruction, and will see the needed documents unfold. We will cover:

- How to prepare an Analysis Report to support the courseware development decision
- How to prepare a Design Document to set the design and limits for the courseware to be created
- How to prepare Programmer Ready Materials (PRM) to provide precise guidance to the courseware development team
- How to prepare a Management Plan to support the courseware development

Program lessons using Authorware Professional

We've seen people in organizations make almost every possible mistake in implementing technology-based learning. We know that, if you have a good background, you will be able not only to develop good learning materials, you will also be able to develop the ones that will solve the performance problems that cry out for solutions.

The programming can go wrong in many ways if it is not an integral part of a coherent courseware development process. Some people just sit down at the keyboard and hope that what they turn out fills a need. Other use strong programming techniques, or sophisticated video production knowledge, to build lessons that are still not instructionally sound. Others want to make solid, interesting instruction, but can't master Authorware sufficiently to do the things they want to do.

We believe that by showing you designs that are not like those that others call "page turners" or worse, you will be inspired to solve instructional problems without bad stereotypes to follow. The sample lessons that you will build as you follow the chapters will develop your understanding of how Authorware works, and how its structures lead to making things happen interactively for the learner.

TBL until now

Unfortunately, some companies have used computer-based learning because it is "new" or "the thing to do." We say "unfortunately" because that is not the correct reason and may be like building a house on sand.

Other companies set multimedia training to work solving trivial training problems because they want to run an experiment to "see whether it works." We will introduce you to the research that established the best reasons to use technology-based training.

Organizations should employ multimedia training to solve their knottiest problems, not waste it on trivia. Companies should adopt technology-based learning because it contributes to achieving the organization's goals. The improvements in the quality and quantity of performance can make an investment in TBL cost-beneficial.

Technology-based learning can help you and your organization

Whether you are a technician, scientist, manager, staff member, or a person studying for a career, a knowledge of technology-based training can make you more effective in both the short and long terms. If you are interested in training, it is because you are interested in helping individuals to perform better and to improve the organization's results. You don't have to be a computer whiz to follow the path we have laid out. We believe that, no matter which of these groups you belong to, you will learn something that you can apply for immediate benefit. We are glad you have decided to join us to improve human performance.

Introduction to the Hands-On Concept

We wanted to help others assist their organizations by building multimedia instructional systems. A theoretical book wouldn't go very far in that direction. For that reason, we determined to make it possible for you to have the complete confidence that only a person who has done something him- or herself can feel.

We have crammed this book with things that you can try for yourself on a work or home computer. Yet, this is not a software tutorial. Each chapter provides an introduction to a fresh aspect of putting multimedia training systems together. First, we present the topic overview for an executive reader. Simply reading the initial portion of the chapter provides the overall understanding needed to discuss projects, make decisions, and follow their progress. Then we describe how to implement an example selected from diverse work situations. Finally, we describe in detail how to implement the topic using the Authorware software.

The chapters and the practical exercises are graduated in difficulty. Mastering the material in earlier chapters will prepare you to consider quite sophisticated techniques. The result will be a thorough grounding in the whole realm of technology-based learning. Once you have that in your background, you will be ready to propose time- and money-saving solutions. Also, we strongly recommend that you carry out the Authorware exercises to fully appreciate how good instruction works.

Obviously, if you already have software other than Authorware, the exact procedures may vary. Even so, the principle of what you need to accomplish is the same. You may plan to implement your system on a totally different platform, such as a minicomputer or mainframe. If so, carrying out the practice exercise in Authorware will still help you to see the principles in action.

Introduction to the Software

This book includes the Authorware Professional Working Model and more than 100 other files that we have provided for your use in learning. You need the files to complete all the hands-on projects included as examples in the book. Let's look briefly at each component included.

Authorware Professional Working Model

Authorware Professional is a proven, sophisticated development tool for producing multimedia training. It is used by many of the leading technology-based training development organizations in the world today. Unfortunately for those who want to familiarize themselves with its capabilities and develop skills in its use, it is a multi-thousand-dollar package.

The Authorware Professional Working Model is a version of Authorware that has two distinct limitations. It is limited to 50 icons (typical lessons employ hundreds of icons), and it is not possible to package the developed lesson in a truly deliverable format. There are no other significant differences, yet the working model has sold in recent years for $25 or less. We have found that the working model is *not* too limited to provide a useful learning experience. The practice exercises in this book provide significant opportunities to stretch your Authorware wings using the working model.

Included with the working model is a Welcome lesson. It is useful to run this at any time. It acquaints you with the general makeup of Authorware and, in general, how each of its icons works.

Contents of the included compact disc

Files for Windows Users

ADA.APW	EKG.PAL
CONCRETE.APW	DISK.ID
CRANE.APW	MDCTRL.DLL
CURRICUL.APW	MEDIADYN.H
CU_TEST.APW	INSTALIT.EXE
EKG.APW	MDCTRLD.INF
FLSHCARD.APW	MDCTRL.001
MOUSEPR.APW	CONCBACK.BMP
SIGNON.APW	MBOX.BMP
TRUCK.APW	EKG_BACK.TIF
ADA_ALIC.WAV	MBOX.TIF
ADA_MOBY.WAV	(Plus Authorware WM files)

Files for Macintosh Users

ADA.APM	MOUSEPR.APM
CONCRETE.APM	SIGNON.APM
CRANE.APM	TRUCK.APM.1
CURRICUL.APM	ADA_ALIC.AIFF
CU_TEST.APM	ADA_MOBY.AIFF
EKG.APM	(Plus Authorware WM files)
FLSHCARD.APM	

Files for Both Platforms

ADAABOUT.PCT	CU_MSG.PCT
ADA_BKGD.PCT	CU_P_R.PCT
CONCBACK.PCT	CU_RPRTS.PCT
CONCEMT.PCT	EKGHEART.PCT
CONCHARD.PCT	EKGTORSO.PCT
CONCMARK.PCT	EGK_BACK.PCT
CONCMETR.PCT	EKG_BAD.PCT
CONCSAND.PCT	EKG_BODY.PCT

CONCSTRN.PCT   EKG_ELCT.PCT
CONGRAVL.PCT   EKG_GOOD.PCT
CONWATER.PCT   EKG_HINT.PCT
CRCONTROL.PCT   FLSHANSR.PCT
CRLNBMIN.PCT   FLSHBACK.PCT
CRLNBMOT.PCT   FLSHDISC.PCT
CRLNHSDN.PCT   FLSHNXCD.PCT
CRLNHSUP.PCT   FLSHQUES.PCT
CRLNSTOP.PCT   FLSHQUIT.PCT
CRLNTVET.PCT   FLSHSHUF.PCT
CRLNTVWT.PCT   MBOX.PCT
CRPSBMIN.PCT   MSHAPE_1.PCT
CRPSBMOT.PCT   MSHAPE_2.PCT
CRPSHSDN.PCT   MSHAPE_3.PCT
CRPSHSUP.PCT   MSHAPE_4.PCT
CRPSSTOP.PCT   SIGNQUST.PCT
CRPSTVET.PCT   TKBKGRND.PCT
CRPSTVWT.PCT   TKLDSLDR.PCT
CR_BKGD.PCT   TKLOAD.PCT
CR_LNSG.PCT   TKSLIDER.PCT
CUIPMENU.PCT   TKTANDEM.PCT
CUTESTBK.PCT   TKTKSLDR.PCT
CUTESTCK.PCT   TKTMSLDR.PCT
CUTESTO4.PCT   TKTRAILR.PCT
CUTETORS.PCT   TKTRUCK.PCT
CU_DIPLO.PCT   ADAALICE.TXT
CU_I_R.PCT   ADAMOBY.TXT
CU_MENU.PCT   FLSHTEXT.TXT
CU_MOUSE.PCT

System Requirements

Hardware requirements

All you need is:

- An IBM or IBM-compatible PC, with a 486 or Pentium chip, running at 33 MHz or faster
- At least 4 megabytes of RAM (8 megabytes is recommended)
- A VGA or SVGA color graphic display with 16 or more colors
- A hard disk
- A mouse
- Microsoft Multimedia Extensions (included with Windows 3.1)
- A sound card in the PC if you intend to do audio features

Software requirements

Your PC must have Windows 3.1 or higher versions, installed to run the Authorware software. Windows 3.1 is the version in common use today.

Moving On

Now that you are familiar with the basics of how we plan to approach technology-based learning, and know something of the Authorware software that is included, we are ready to begin. In Chapter 2 we will offer a much more in-depth approach to technology-based learning.

2

What Is Technology-Based Learning?

Aeschylus said, "He who learns must suffer." We don't know for sure about ancient Greeks, but if you are reading this book it is certainly not in the hope of making it even harder for your group of learners to achieve.

Many trainers have been working on this problem. Today, there is no excuse for making your learners suffer. You may have to learn to use some new tools to make their learning easier, but it needn't be painful.

This chapter addresses the problems faced by people getting started with developing technology-based training. It will provide the necessary definitions and cover the background of developing instruction to be delivered by technology. We also will define differences between the components of technology-based learning.

What You Will Learn in This Chapter

- The background of technology-based learning

- Basic terms used in technology-based learning

- Components of technology-based learning

- Modes of each component of technology-based learning

What Is Technology-Based Learning (TBL)?

Today, while technology evolves rapidly—sophistication increases exponentially. The training field is a busy area, often depending on the same "tried and true" techniques that have worked for years. Still, such techniques can pose problems. Sometimes they don't solve today's problem as well as they did yesterday's. Often nowadays, training must deal with a new environment of different systems and tools that are used (with ever increasing frequency) to boost various organizations' productivity. A "lecture," no matter how well designed and executed, cannot deliver immediate feedback, varying examples appropriate to each individual learner, and cease immediately when the student reaches mastery. Yet, these are not bad characteristics for instruction, are they?

Where did it come from?

Technology for learning has been around for almost four decades. It began in the late-1950s when the National Science Foundation awarded grants for computer-based education projects to the University of Illinois and Brigham Young University. Today, technology-based learning is no longer an experiment. We see many important projects using technology for learning in all sectors.

TBL is the practical use of computer technology for learning—and it works! Also, there is a trend to further integrate technology into the production and delivery of what we had previously considered "conventional" media. Raymond Fox, president of the Society for Applied Learning Technology, wrote:

> "There is an ever advancing body of knowledge pertaining to more effective technologies for development of interactive instruction systems. Coincident with this are technological advances in available hardware and software to support development of these instruction systems. The challenge for designing a course for communicating specific ideas or information is to understand how these new technologies can assist in that task and what changes to existing strategies and design must take place to capitalize on the benefits these technologies offer."[1]

How common is it?

One person's "Starship Enterprise" is another's daily workspace. This chapter is about technology-based learning—the training that utilizes the higher end of the technology spectrum for delivery. You may wonder how common TBL really is. A survey of the instructional media used in one organization produced a total of 21 different media. Of these, only four could truly fit our concept of TBL.

How can I use it?

The environment may be right for using technology-based learning in your situation, *yet it may not.* You have to determine that it *is* right before employing TBL. Careful needs assessment determines whether high-tech methods can accomplish training objectives better than conventional methods. Much training is the natural habitat of TBL because TBL is especially effective in showing motion, small detail, and providing realistic experiences in learning skills. On the other hand, if you must update your course materials frequently or rapidly, TBL may not be the best solution.

However, the important point is that when technology can help, it usually can help in a big way. Moreover, the toughest problems are the ones it solves best. Using TBL

---

[1]This text first appeared in an article entitled "Letter from the President," by Raymond G. Fox, president of the Society for Applied Learning Technology, in the *Society for Applied Learning Technology Newsletter*, Summer 1989, p. 1.

is an option worth any organization's consideration, and we hope you will join us in recommending TBL when it is the best solution.

Defining Technology-Based Learning Terms

Please refer to the Glossary for a full list of terms and their meanings. For an even more complete picture of the terms used in the training field, refer to *The Trainer's Dictionary*. This section will give you an introduction to a few of the terms we use, and also to the methods of providing training.

Hardware, software, and courseware

We often hear the terms hardware, software, and courseware during a discussion of technology-based learning. "Hardware" is a straightforward term. It describes the actual, visible, physical items involved. Hardware includes the learning station, computer disk drives of all kinds, printers, keyboards, cables, mice, and any other physical items.

"Software" refers to the programs written in computer languages that make the computer parts of a system work as they should. You may never see evidence of the "software" beyond the system's working properly.

Confusion can arise between the terms "software" and "courseware." In technical terms, some courseware is software. Both the technology (computer programs) and non-technology (texts, audiotapes, etc.) elements that support learning are courseware. We use the term courseware even when we are developing instruction with components of one type only, whether technological or non-technological. Courseware includes the computer-delivered CAI lessons and CMI tests, and the associated video, audio, texts, and other learning resources. These terms will be defined in this chapter.

The result of these distinctions is that course developers rarely refer to software. Our concern is with the *courseware*.

Changing technology and alphabet soup

Ron Anderson said that TBL has a "lexicon replete with jargon and acronyms apparently designed to baffle all but the initiated."[2] Unfortunately, he was at least partially right. TBL terms can be confusing. Here is a simplified short list to help with this chapter. Complete definitions appear in the Glossary.

TBL means Technology-Based Learning. It has several synonyms.

- CBL (Computer-Based Learning)
- CBE (Computer-Based Education)
- CBT (Computer-Based Training)
- CBI (Computer-Based Instruction)

---

[2]In Reynolds, A. & R. Anderson. 1992. *Selecting and Developing Media for Instruction*, 3rd Edition. New York: Van Nostrand Reinhold.

All of them mean exactly the same thing as TBL. TBL has three components:

- Computer Assisted Instruction (CAI)
- Computer Managed Instruction (CMI)
- Computer Supported Learning Resources (CSLR)

Variations in meaning can make terms confusing. Some people use "CAI" instead of TBL (or CBE or CBT) as the general descriptive term. Usually, the person using "CAI" is unaware that such casual misuse can cause confusion. The main reason for the too broad use of "CAI" is that many people think that CAI is the whole field. The same problem exists with CBT, which many people use to describe CAI lessons. Usually, people using the terms in this way are completely unaware of the full range of technology-based instruction!

Instructional technologists are quick to point out that not all technology is hardware—it includes systems and procedures. Not so with technology-based learning. It *will* break if you drop it. What people mean by "high-tech" changes with time and geography. Not that many years ago, the president of an Asian bank proudly told one of the authors that they had the "very latest training technology." He referred to an overhead projector. But, in the context of that time and place, he was right. In the year 2006, high-tech training will not include some of the things it does today, because by then these things will have become commonplace.

Why technology . . . not computers?

Today, all technology-based training is supported by some kind of computerized device. Technology-based methods also include performance support (helping people to work better, without necessarily training them), and TBL includes performance support systems (PSS). TBL media are generally ideal to use with self-teaching instruction, since they are all individualized, interactive, and competency-based.

Technology has a basis in computers. Today, there is a small computer chip in nearly all electrical equipment. It is becoming more difficult to separate the "computerness" of objects we use. Are your fuel injection system, or your fax machine, your VCR, and your video game all computers? It really doesn't matter. These items incorporate more processing power. We don't really care if the *technology* we use to improve our instruction is a "computer" or not.

Technology offers several advantages for producing audiovisual media. We can produce statistically accurate graphs and charts for a variety of visual media. Some computer-generated graphics systems can rapidly produce different views of three dimensional objects, offering a choice of images to the user. We rapidly produce attractive title slides, word slides, and graphics slides with computer systems at comparatively low cost. We use computers for precise editing and assembly of video and film productions. Today, computer-based word processing systems are commonplace in producing most print media.

We will look at the advantages and disadvantages of using TBL in detail in the next chapter. Right now, let's first consider a few important points.

The TBL good news

Technology brings significant capabilities to instruction that provide vast potential. Among them are to:

- Interact rapidly with individuals.
- Store and process vast amounts of information in a variety of forms.
- Combine with other media to display a broad range of audiovisual stimuli.

These features give technology the potential to become dominant in instruction. Although that is hardly the case today, it is rapidly becoming more common to use computers in a variety of instructional activities. Some of these include the production of graphics and other audiovisual media, as well as the development, delivery, and management of instructional materials.

The TBL bad news

The rapid advances in technology and more wide-spread application to instruction have not left TBL without some problems. Some problematic issues facing instructional personnel contemplating a technology-based approach include:

- Rapid obsolescence of costly hardware and software. The rapidly changing technology creates a high likelihood that equipment bought today will be obsolete the year after next, and outdated in about 5 years. (If you doubt this, look for the 386 computers bought in 1991.)
- Few generally understood administrative guidelines. We still debate questions such as: How much computer knowledge does a courseware developer need? Or, how best to interface the computer and instructional specialists on the development team.

TBL in General

Technology-based learning itself does not teach or manage the instruction. TBL makes learning easier, more appropriate, or more fun.

The *components* of TBL do the work. The components include computer-supported learning resources, computer-managed instruction, and computer-assisted instruction. Figure 2.1 shows the Technology-Based Learning Model.

University research pioneered the use of computers for learning. This origin led to use of the term computer-based *education*, or "CBE." When industrial organizations began to use so-called computer-based education, they substituted the more comfortable term "training" for the academically oriented "education." The result was CBT, a term in wide use today. Some organizations chose to use "instruction," resulting in CBI.

Still others, who preferred thinking in learner-oriented terms, preferred CBL. Computer-based learning is becoming increasingly popular, reflecting today's emphasis on learner-centered thinking. It is also appropriate to all settings: academic,

Technology-Based Learning

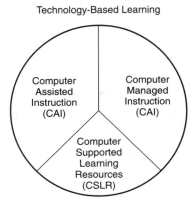

Figure 2.1 Technology-Based Learning Model

business, industrial, and even the home. The authors' bias is clearly learner-centered. Our perception that the technology used to deliver the instruction may not look so much like a computer leads us to replace the term "computer" with "technology." We favor Technology-Based Learning (TBL). In addition, the term Technology-Based Learning will remain appropriate for a long time.

Remember that CBE, CBT, CBI, CBL, and TBL are really synonyms. In this book, when we use TBL, it stands for all of them.

This sort of proliferation of terms does not cause confusion among experienced users, because they know the terms just mentioned are synonymous. Variations in meaning can make terms confusing. Unfortunately, that has happened with one term specifically. A closer look at what the major TBL-related terms mean will help. This is the "umbrella" term. It includes the activities described by the other terms. Our personal favorite is the definition given by a man called the "father of CBE," Donald Bitzer, of the University of Illinois. Bitzer said that CBE is:

> anytime a person and a computer get together . . .
> and one of them learns something.

Components of TBL

Each component of TBL is the subject of a separate section of this chapter. Briefly, they are as follows:

Computer Assisted Instruction (CAI)

CAI is the use of a computer in the actual instructional process. The various forms which CAI can take are called *modes*. The modes of CAI are:

- Tutorial
- Drill and practice
- Instructional game
- Modeling

- Simulation
- Problem solving

CAI includes the combination of computer and video called interactive video (IVD) and the more recent digital video. They are not separate modes, since any of the modes can incorporate IVD or digital video without becoming anything different. These technologies perform wholly within the function of one of the existing modes.

Computer Managed Instruction (CMI)

CMI is the management of instruction by computer. CAI always directly involves learning. CMI does not. The three modes of CMI are:

- Testing
- Prescription generation
- Record keeping

CMI is a potent technique. An investment of fewer resources in CMI can often produce a bigger result for the organization than CAI does. Because this is so, CMI may be the best way to begin use of TBL in an organization.

Computer Supported Learning Resources (CSLR)

CSLR provides access to information that we can use to learn. For example: a *library* is a non-computer learning resource. We use CSLR like a library. The difference is that a computer program supports a CSLR. CSLRs enable easier communication, retrieval, examination, and manipulation of the data. The modes of CSLR are:

- Data bases
- Telecommunications
- Expert systems
- Hypermedia

How to Use These Terms in Speech and Writing

A word on the use of these terms is appropriate. You will not find people with an extensive background in the TBL field saying or writing "a CBT" or "a CMI," when they mean a CBT course or a CMI system. Unfortunately, you do find those who recently discovered TBL making such mistakes. When the person new to the field is a college professor or practitioner with a newly minted Master's degree, such mistakes set even worse examples.

Computer Assisted Instruction

Let's take a look at CAI in detail. CAI is the use of a computer to interact directly with the student for presenting lesson content. Because of the flexibility and capability of a computer to provide branching instruction, it can assume the role of an infinitely patient tutor. Computers can also readily control other media and can provide learners with necessary reference materials, performance aids, and clerical services, and can simulate environmental or laboratory facilities, depending on the course.

CAI has produced some remarkable success stories and some dismal failures. However, most of the failures were caused by a lack of analysis and planning, resulting in a mismatch between instructional needs and computer system capabilities.

We used to debate whether computers were effective in presenting instruction. New organizations faced the question of whether they should use CAI. Many staged experiments to determine whether it really "worked" (long after that question had really been put to rest). Finally, research ended all this wasted activity. We will cover this in more detail in Chapter 3.

CAI continues to increase its impact in all areas of instruction. Whether this impact is positive depends on the amount of analysis given an organization's real instructional needs. Ignoring this analysis can often mean wasted energy. We have seen people trying to distort the world to fit it, somehow, into a computer for the sake of producing instruction. All effort devoted to determining the *proper* delivery system is well rewarded, no matter what that outcome may be.

Computer assisted instruction in general

CAI is a medium of instruction. It applies in appropriate learning situations. Film, videotape, and textbooks are other media. TBL, CMI, and CBLR are not instructional media. They are instructional methods.

The various forms in which we can apply CAI are modes. When you use CAI as a medium of instruction, it can be classed as one of these six modes. The modes of CAI are: tutorial, drill and practice, instructional games, modeling, simulation, and problem solving.

Tutorial

This is the mode most familiar to those new to the field. In a tutorial, the learner interacts one-on-one with the "program." The process in a good tutorial advances as the finest tutor would personally undertake the process.[3] A typical tutorial lesson presents some information, and then checks the learner's understanding. This process repeats throughout the lesson. Based on the learner's understanding, the learner's path continues to another point. If the learner did not understand, the tutorial presents the first point in a new way. The reinforcement process provides corrective comments to the learner.

A good tutorial uses "branching." It keeps the learner actively involved in the learning process. Figure 2.2 shows the general pattern of a tutorial branching structure. Its interactive nature involves the student in the lesson so that learning cannot be passive.

---

[3]Illustrations describing the methods used by Socrates are often used to explain the structure of a tutorial.

Poor tutorials are "linear." They are (derisively) called "page turners." Figure 2.3 shows the general pattern of a linear lesson. It is not very interactive. The contrast with a branching lesson is obvious. You may wonder why anyone would use the less effective design. The answer lies in the effort required to produce the branching lesson. The level of effort required is much greater. When CAI must be created "for a price" the result is often less interactive. It simply costs more to design and program the more interactive patterns shown in Figure 2.2 than the "page turner" patterns shown in Figure 2.3.

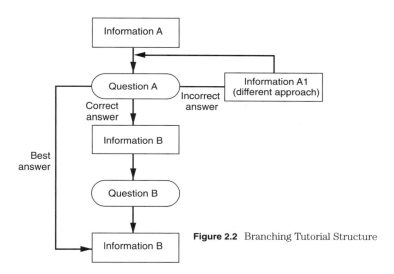

Figure 2.2 Branching Tutorial Structure

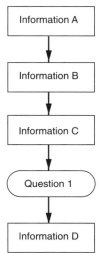

Figure 2.3 Linear Tutorial Structure

Drill and practice

Drill and practice is also a very familiar mode of CAI. One reason is that it takes less effort to produce than the other modes. This does not mean that it is not a valuable tool. It is. A well-developed concept of drill and practice existed well before there was anything called a computer. Drill and practice has repetitive presentations of problems to the learner. A drill and practice example is one which presents the learner a problem such as, "How much is two and three?" When the learner answers the question another follows, such as "How much is three plus four?" After a given number of problems, the system informs the learner of the total number of questions presented, and the numbers right and wrong.

The series of addition problems is a simple example of the drill and practice technique. It is not the only form of drill and practice. The drill and practice mode of CAI is successful with far more complex subject matter. Drill and practice is a good choice for learning terminology or the steps in a procedure. Figure 2.4 shows the drill and practice concept.

Sometimes, what appears to be a simulation is set up to provide drill and practice for a specific procedure. The "simulation" cannot actually simulate anything beyond the procedure to be learned. The learner repeats the lesson until the desired level of performance is reached. Another possibility is to use an actual full simulator to repeatedly practice one limited procedure.

Instructional games

The term "game" does not mean frivolous activity. In CAI, an instructional game is not always recognizable as a "game." The idea that they are "games" instead of in-

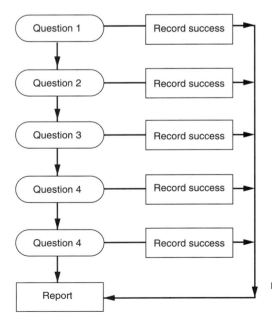

Figure 2.4 Drill and Practice Structure

struction created a problem in their use. However, it should be no surprise that instructional games often do contain an element of entertainment. In a CAI game, the
computer looks up the tables, calculates, and keeps score. The learners can concentrate on the events of the game. Unfortunately, the dividing line between amusement
and learning is not always easily discernible. It probably is unneeded anyway. Our
point is that learning while "playing" is, nevertheless, learning. Figure 2.5 illustrates
the game concept.

Instructional games are completely valid and "professional" ways to stimulate
learning. Historically, some individuals have had difficulty believing that learners
who enjoy the learning could be having a worthwhile experience. Because of this
prejudice, games are not used in all organizations. In fact, the use of games did
strike a mortal blow to several projects. There remains a real danger of project
cancellation because of what may be seen as a "trivial" use of the organization's
resources.

Selection of games still calls for discretion. However, today we have modified the
traditional position that games should not be included in the first phase of an organization's entry into TBL. We have found that once trust exists, multimedia instructional games can sell themselves to managers. This may be due, at least in part, to
the greater experience with games of new generations of managers. Such managers
may realize that playing "games" will help their people learn more painlessly than
other, less inviting learning experiences.

Models form the basis for many instructional games. The models used in games
have varying degrees of validity as related to the subject covered. An instructional
game has goals, scoring (usually), and an element of competition, which may also be
self-competition.

Modeling

The use of the CAI system to represent another system or process is modeling. The
learner can change values and see the effects of the change on the model. A model
is a non-realistic representation of the system (or, true representation may be un-
achievable). An example is a population model. The learner can change demo-
graphic variables such as birth rate, infant mortality, or death rate in the model. The
learner sees the results such changes would create, if they actually took place. They
may be displayed in a table or a graph. The learner can see the effects on the population over time. You can model population accurately by listing the numbers by gender, age, or other characteristics. At the same time, population does not lend itself to
realistic representation (by drawing all of the people). Figure 2.6 shows the structure of a typical model.

Simulation

Simulation involves a representation of a situation or device, with some degree of realism. The computer simulates the item of equipment, device, system, or sub-sys-
tem. Simulation enables the learner to experience operating that equipment. A
strength of simulation is that the learning can happen without destruction of the
equipment or harm to the learner or others. Simulation can be manual, in "hybrid"

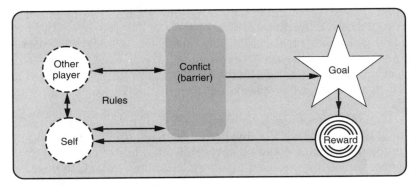

Figure 2.5 Instructional Game Structure

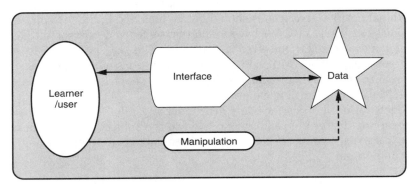

Figure 2.6 Model Structure

form using both manual and computer support, and solely with computer power. Figure 2.7 can be compared to Figure 2.6 to highlight the difference between simulation and modeling.

TBL simulation contrasts with the most familiar examples of simulation—simulators. Figure 2.8 shows the simulation model. Simulation is addressed in greater depth in Chapter 25.

Problem solving

Previously, problem solving was the mode of CAI seen least in industrial training (and other learning situations). Today, that has changed. In problem solving, the student uses the computer itself as a tool to solve a (work-related) problem. Any software may be used, depending on what skills the learner needs. Problem solving has always had good application in math and science instruction. The opportunities for appropriate use in typical learning situations grow as more employees use computers to do their work. Figure 2.9 shows the problem-solving model.

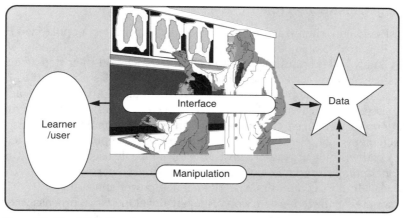

Figure 2.7 Simulation Structure

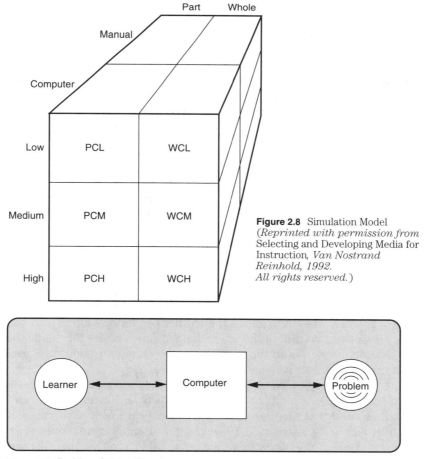

Figure 2.8 Simulation Model
(Reprinted with permission from Selecting and Developing Media for Instruction, *Van Nostrand Reinhold, 1992.*
All rights reserved.)

Figure 2.9 Problem-Solving Structure

Computer Managed Instruction (CMI)

John Buchanan, then training director of United Airlines, popularized *Buchanan's Law*. It states, "No amount of time and resources can teach someone what they already know." CMI offers the way to let people focus on their deficiencies while ignoring topics they have already mastered. CMI provides a method to be sure that each student's interaction is appropriate to his ability. CMI carefully tracks each student, assessing progress and learning resource effectiveness, and carrying out these functions with reduced clerical effort. CMI can be a robust and extensive learning-management tool. Central system CMI evolved exceptional sophistication in the past. On the principal systems, it was the most heavily used capability. Until recently, personal computers have lacked the processing power and storage to make CMI practical. Today's computers have the needed power and storage.

Computer managed instruction originally developed as a process to help instructors cope with growing clerical actions. As interest in self-paced instruction grew, so did demands on time and effort to score grades, maintain individual records, and summarize student and class results. These functions were often incremented using existing computer systems used for administrative and summary reports. Your CMI system should feature all three modes of CMI. These are: testing, prescription generation, and record keeping. In Chapter 24 you will construct a system with all these features.

Today the role of CMI has expanded. Added roles include supplying help in test building, assuring security of course materials, guiding students through lesson materials, and helping in analysis of both student results and segments of course content.

Using CMI

You break the instructional materials into content areas related to learning objectives (the rigorous objectives popularized by Robert Mager). Within each of these areas, the student alternates between the activities of testing, reviewing test results, selecting study materials assigned by the instructional prescription process, and studying. The computer managed instruction program directs the learner to learning resources. They may be presented by the computer system, by another media device, by any other method (such as laboratory exercise), or by all the above. The system automatically records the student's progress and maintains extensive records. The instructors may use them in helping the student learn, and for administrative purposes. The CMI system allows the learner to progress at his own pace. It makes management and control of the educational process easier for the instructor. It also provides feedback to both the learner and the facilitator about progress (or lack of it) and retention of knowledge.

Possibly because CMI received less fanfare and funding than CAI, less attention focused on its successes and failures. It grew slowly and steadily while staying so far in the background that many people have never heard of it. CMI can serve independently in support of instruction. However, it is often thought of only as a support system for CAI. Since the two systems are compatible, they are usually used in tandem.

CMI's value

CMI is as strong as it sounds. Several years ago, United Airlines proved very effective use of TBL solely through use of a CMI system. CMI, as carried out on small computers, continues to grow in sophistication. It will soon approach the power of the best central versions. Two problems delayed this evolution. One was the processing and storage capacity of PCs. The other was the effort necessary to develop a sophisticated learning management system. These barriers have now diminished.

An important consideration is the economy of effort typical with CMI use. A given amount of human or financial resources, if dedicated to CMI, can often have an effect on a larger training effort than would CAI. For example, if you have an entire videotape course that is satisfactory coverage for a given subject, you can make it even better with CMI. By relating the videotapes to objectives, and creating the appropriate learning-management structure, you can make the course accountable (the students will learn what you expect). You also reduce individual student effort. Comparable effort devoted to producing CAI lessons might only replace a single videotape. The benefits and potential of important savings possible through CMI will justify that extra effort and attention directed toward effective incorporation in the organization's TBL project.

CMI in general

It should come as no surprise that CMI is *truly* the management of instruction by computer. The term is not as familiar as CAI to many course developers. This surely does not reflect its inherent worth, or its frequency of use. It may reflect less romance in managing instruction well than in teaching with an "exotic" technology. The distinction is that CAI always directly involves learning, and CMI does not.

CMI has hidden in the shadow of CAI, at least for those not using TBL. This is a self-correcting condition. Since CMI offers the necessary power to apply considerable efficiency to learning, it will receive increasing recognition as more organizations begin to use the testing, prescription generation, and record keeping modes. These modes are illustrated in the conceptual diagram shown in Figure 2.10.

Testing

CMI testing is the TBL function that measures the learner's knowledge of specified objectives. Sometimes CAI includes quizzes called "progress checks" to determine the state of in-progress learning. These may branch the learner to various parts of the lesson. They are different from CMI. CMI testing offers learning efficiency by verifying the learner's mastery of the objectives. This determination is the foundation of CMI, since it accurately provides the information needed to prescribe learning activities.

This contrasts with the small progress checks used as mechanisms for minor "course corrections" in the tutorial presentation of instructional materials.

Prescription generation

In prescription generation, the CMI system generates an instructional prescription for each unmastered learning objective. Each separate learner receives an individual

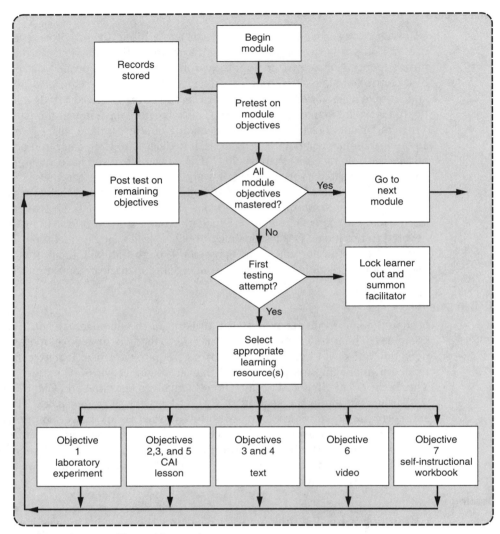

Figure 2.10 Computer Managed Instruction

prescription. Because, as you and I approach a new subject we bring different backgrounds and experiences. Each of us may know parts of the subject, but not all of it. Thus, individual prescriptions provide for more efficient assignment of resources and time commitment.

The test will show which different parts each of us does not know. Refer to Figure 2.10 to see a diagram of the prescription-generation process. You determine the prescriptions during the design of the instruction. Since individuals master different objectives, each will only study the materials needed. CMI directs each learner only to those learning resources that support the unmastered objective(s). This shortens the time each learner must study. The selectivity results in reduced time spent in instruction. This is the basis for instructional efficiencies associated with TBL.

Record keeping

The CMI system continuously generates and stores records of individual and group progress. An important feature is automatic generation of these records. They are then available to the learning specialist, as needed, on demand. You are free from statistics and records you really do not need to see. There is also no need to keep a closet with shelves piled high with old records and reports. We can see them when, and if we want them. Certain records, such as the individual grade book, are usually accessible to the learner.

Why is CMI attractive?

CMI is a compelling technique. It is typical that a smaller investment of resources can produce a bigger result for the organization with CMI than with CAI. An exclusively CMI solution can often successfully solve a given organization, project, or performance problem. It is also usual for CMI to be the best way for an organization to begin using computers in training. In the practical world of learning, CMI can often produce a concrete financial savings compared with traditional methods.

Computer Supported Learning Resources (CSLR)

CSLR is the least-often-seen component of technology-based learning. A possible point of confusion might exist between computer supported learning resources (CSLR) and the learning resources which CMI prescribes. CSLR is a completely separate part of TBL. Learning resources prescribed by CMI are predetermined to teach their associated learning objective(s). The learning resource prescribed by CMI may be a CAI lesson, videotape, textbook, audiotape, lecture, or any other form of learning experience. CSLR resources help the learner to master the content in more general ways, but do not teach directly (like the library). The Glossary included with many lessons is a form of CSLR. Figure 2.11 shows the relationship of the three components of TBL.

Thus far, CSLR has not come into its own. There are several factors that prevent more extensive use. Some need existing data bases. There are no specific CSLR "development tools" (as there are for CAI and CMI) to make their implementation easier, although each of the modes of CSLR has powerful development tools.

CSLR modes most often require more access to, and a bigger share of, the computer's power, memory, and storage. Like the library, they cannot promise direct realization of learning objectives. Their less clearly defined results and indirect connection to the planned learning make them a less sure investment for the organization.

CSLR in general

Computer supported learning resources do not teach, nor do they manage the instruction. They do make learning easier, more appropriate, or more fun. The modes of CSLR include data bases, telecommunications, expert systems, and hypermedia.

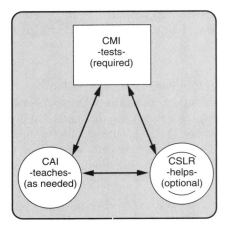

Figure 2.11 CSLR in Relationship to Other TBL Components

Data bases

You may be comfortable with the term "data base." The oldest form of CSLR is a data base. It is a good exemplar of the type. A data base is a pool of information, useful to a learner, but it does not itself teach. It only provides information that we can use to learn. For example, a library is a non-computer learning resource. We use a CSLR in the same way as a library, except a useful CSLR is always supported by a computer program. The computer program expedites the retrieval, examination, and manipulation of the data.

Communications

Another mode of CSLR is communications. Communications can take many forms. We can record comments and notes for later use. Files can help information sharing among users with like interests. Individuals and groups can exchange notes among themselves. Instantaneous communication is possible among users of a network of any size. Learning specialists use this capability to exchange information. The learner and a remote subject-matter expert can also communicate. Computers and communications networks also ease distance learning as video teleconferencing and computer conferencing. The access to remote sources of information offered by the Internet can be expected to give communications a big boost.

Hypermedia

A newer mode of CSLR is hypermedia. Hypermedia is what data bases have been waiting for! It provides a friendly front end to permit the user to move through the information in a relational way, based on words, objects, or relationships that the different pieces of data have with each other, as opposed to CAI's predetermined way. The computer program smoothes sophisticated retrieval, examination, and manipulation of the data.

Expert Systems and Performance Support Systems

Another mode of CSLR is expert systems. Expert systems are CSLRs because they are computer-based and don't teach. They are simply electronic job aids. Performance support systems employ expert systems along with text retrieval and CAI, to assist workers. These are often referred to as the consultant (expert system), instructor (CAI), and librarian (text-retrieval) functions.

What's in a Technology-Based Training System?

The issue for you at this point may be, "What is actually involved in a TBL system?" Let's consider these items.

- Technology-based learning
- Interactive multimedia
- Videodiscs and CD-ROMs
- Video and computer teleconferencing
- Simulation and simulators
- Virtual reality

Once on the "cutting edge," technology-based learning (most often seen as CAI, or computer-assisted instruction) is now the mainstay of high-tech training. Today's desktop computers are well-suited to CAI.

Interactive multimedia

Interactive multimedia (IM) is essentially CAI carried to its logical conclusion. It includes digital video, often requiring CD-ROM-size storage with a comprehensive mix of up to one hour of video, 7,000 still images, audio, computer text and graphics, and interaction capabilities. Because of the inherent advantages of the smaller disc, eventually these systems will replace the larger and more costly 12-inch videodisc.

IVD

Technically, IVD is only CAI controlling an added 12-inch laser-read player. IVD received separate attention, largely because of marketing efforts, as something new and better. Videodiscs hold 54,000 video images, or about one hour of playback.

Teleconferencing

Video teleconferencing is best for *classroom groups* located at a distance from the instructor. National Technical University courses are a good example. NTU transmits by satellite. Computer conferencing is for *individual* members of a group who will interact at separate times. It typically uses ordinary telephone lines.

Simulation

Simulation is one of the modes of CAI. Desktop computers can simulate complex systems, one part at a time. Simulation provides realistic practice without tieing up the real item. Simulators are dedicated, single-purpose simulation devices. They can simulate entire systems and are usually large.

Virtual reality

Virtual reality is today's "Buck Rogers" technique. It provides experience in a simulated environment, particularly one that does not actually exist in reality.

Technologies That Provide Training Support

What are the technologies used to support training? Here is a short list.

- Public (or private) data bases
- CD-ROM
- Hypertext
- Hypermedia

Data bases

Public (or private) data bases can also be accessed from the learning station via ordinary telephone lines. Examples are CompuServe and Dialog.

CD-ROM

CD-ROM is a commercial or in-house, 4.75-inch, 270,000-page compact disk designed to contain large amounts of text or picture data. A representative CD-ROM CSLR product is an encyclopedia. The learner can access information while studying.

Hypertext

Hypertext is a program that links text. The learner chooses a word such as "*gear.*" The program links to text that says "this equipment has *helical* gears." Further exploration of *helical* is possible, because the program will also recognize the hot word *helical.* It will perform a search to find any linked information.

Hypermedia

Hypermedia is a program that links different media under learner control in a way similar to hypertext. The learner can choose video when available, and can see a related video sequence, then return to the program.

Technologies That Provide Job-Related Support

Finally, there are the technologies that are not really intended to provide or even support learning. They exist to help the individual perform at a higher level. They are:

- Expert systems
- Performance support systems

Expert systems are programs that provide the captured knowledge of an expert to a less skilled person. They neither teach nor take control, but provide recommendations.

Performance support systems are integrated multi-program software that provides expert systems, hypertext, embedded animation, CAI, and hypermedia to a worker on an as-needed basis.

How Much Is It Going to Cost?

It is as difficult to create good technology-based lessons as it is to create conventional ones. As software vendors develop increasingly robust authoring systems, almost anyone will be able to generate courseware. In practical terms—it depends more on whether your organization formally carries out all the steps involved in development when developing training.

An organization with a strong instructional development capability should consider having their first course contractor-developed. They should participate in the process.

How much it will cost depends on what you want. The predicted savings resulting from any training should always far outweigh the cost. Buying is cheaper than making. An off-the-shelf CAI lesson could cost as little as $300.

Do you have skilled developers available to create the instruction? You could train your whole development staff to reliably produce expert systems for about $7,500. To train them to produce TBL could run about $12,000. To train them to produce IVD would add the video production component. To make an IVD development group capable of producing the more complex multimedia CD-I or digital video adds an additional level of complexity. To enable a competent traditional instruction development group to produce digital video is too great for a single step. Figure 2.12 shows these relationships.

The equipment and development cost range is enormous. A simple generic videodisc could cost around $10,000. A comparable, simple, custom-made IVD program can cost $30,000. A CD-I viewing system is about $700. An authoring system is about $10,000. The specialized hardware for IVD is about $3,000, but with needed computer equipment, the price goes to about $14,000. The downlink needed to access satellite video-conferences costs about $15,000. To transmit would cost $250,000 plus $500 per hour. Virtual reality is experimental and not needed for most technical and skills training. If you need it, it will be costly. At last count, a full, room-size, detailed simulator tops the list at about $12 million (without batteries).

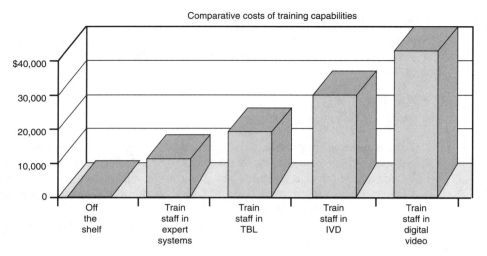

Figure 2.12 Approximate Costs of Various Training Solutions (or Comparative)

Understanding Your Own Project (And Organization)

Come up with three questions your manager's manager will ask after, "How much will it cost?"

1.

2.

3.

This is really an important question. You had better know the answers in advance, because they will surely be asked. We seriously suggest that you rehearse the answers to all possible questions before any presentation recommending a training solution to your management or client.

Be prepared to demonstrate your answers or proposal visually through points, charts, and graphs delivered by electronic presentation. This will demonstrate your ability to implement effective multimedia.

Starting Out

You can gradually increase your organization's capability, and diminish your dependence on external help in developing courseware, until the organization is self-sufficient in selected areas. Your staff can develop the skill needed to develop good courseware. If the organization is of adequate size, with a continuing need for new courseware, you can develop an internal courseware-development organization.

Why Now?

Now let's fill in some of the gaps in TBL. In Chapter 3 we will look at more TBL with yet more background and detail. Let's go after it now!

3

Why Technology-Based Learning and Why Now?

This chapter distills the experiences of companies large and small in applying technology-based learning. We will present the strengths and weakness of the technology-based learning concept and will provide examples of well-known early computer-based lessons. We will present a brief historical background of today's systems. Also, we will briefly explore contemporary use of technology-based learning in a variety of organizations.

What You Will Learn in This Chapter

- Advantages of technology-based learning
- Disadvantages of technology-based learning
- What performance-based training is
- The lineage of technology-based learning
- What the learning triangle is

The What, Why, Who, and How of Technology-Based Learning

Photography is an omnipresent part of our society. You may not realize that it lacked popular appeal for about fifty years in the United States. The reason was not the image-capture equipment. The camera was easy to handle. The problem was in the too complicated, time-consuming, and costly developing process. Photography came into popular use only after George Eastman developed a simplified, cost-effective way to produce a finished product for the public.

There is a similarity to today's situation with technology-based learning. That is, there are two ways to get courseware. You can buy it off-the-shelf (generic) or have it custom-made. Since generic courseware is ordinarily not available for most local training needs, it is not a good choice for those needs.

Courseware authoring is still like the early photo developing process. You can build custom courseware in two ways. You can write it yourself with an authoring system or a general-purpose programming language. Or, you can pay a courseware development organization to prepare it. Contracting for customized courseware is an added expense. This situation helps to explain why technology-based learning is not an even more widely used training method.

Vendors have devoted impressive amounts of time and money to writing courses for general use. Whether the specific course you want is already available depends on your area of interest. If you are working with specialized skills and technologies, you will probably have to produce your own courseware.

The computer environment

Here are the words of a TBL pioneer.

> "The past 30 years or so have produced a base of advancing technologies that have the power to revolutionize the quality, productivity, and availability of education.
> The technologies to apply are the electronic ones—television, radio, audio- and videotapes and disks, computers, computer conferencing, cable TV, microwave and satellite transmissions, and of course CBE.
> Some of those technologies have been applied individually—some with high success, others with less, but each contributing enough useful experience so that today we can begin to glimpse the education system of the future."[1]

If this sounds OK to you we agree, but this statement was made over 15 years ago! It was true then and it is still true, but it has taken 15 years for the technology to become as common and accepted as instructor-led delivery.

The questions

Organizations considering the use of TBL ask, or ought to ask, several questions. Two of them are:

- Why should we consider technology-delivered applications for training?
- Why are we focusing our attention on this particular issue now?

The answers

The answers to these questions center around your organization's key goals for training. They probably include some or all of the following:

- To reduce training costs
- To shorten training programs

---

[1]William C. Norris. Phi Delta Kappan. February 1977.

- To improve staff to student ratios
- To make training more timely
- To eliminate over- and under-training

To get right to the bottom line, properly applied TBL can achieve all of these goals. The reason we don't insert qualifications about this organization or that industry is that these goals match the characteristics of TBL. Only if it is misapplied will it fail to deliver these benefits.

Needs of trainers

Within the organization it is the courseware developers who organize the learning activities. We can derive the needs of the courseware developers from what we know about the organization. These may include:

- To provide more and better training
- To increase the total delivery of training in the same time period
- To reduce the cost of training
- To manage training better

Capabilities of trainers

The organization's courseware developers have skills and experiences. Among them we find these:

- To distribute training
- To support training tools
- To interact with the student in a meaningful way

The basis for the TBL solution

As mentioned in Chapter 2, in the early years of technology-based learning, many organizations set up projects to test whether a TBL solution would work in their industry, with their subject matter, or with their population of learners. Unfortunately, many of these were started well after the answers were known. In 1980 these concerns were laid to rest by three researchers, Kulik, Kulik, and Cohen. They published a study in the *Review of Educational Research*[2] that became very well known and was widely quoted. It was called "Effectiveness of Computer-based College Teaching: A Meta-analysis of Findings." A meta-analysis is a study of other studies. They examined over 70 other research studies and asked the question, "What does all of this research say?"

To appreciate why a meta-analysis was needed you should know that the studies had sought various results. In the early days, enthusiasts for the use of computers in train-

---

[2]Kulik, J., Kulik, C., and Cohen, P. 1980. "Effectiveness of Computer-Based College Teaching: A Meta-analysis of Findings" in *Review of Educational Research*, Vol. 50, pp. 525–544.

ing were convinced that their computer-based courses were superior to instructor-led courses, and the students learned "better." They set their studies up to prove that the students *did* learn better in a variety of ways. Most of these studies failed to show the expected findings. What Kulik, Kulik, and Cohen did was to examine exactly what the other studies *did* find. Basically, it was this:

> "There appears to be little doubt that students can be taught with computers in less time than with conventional methods . . . ."[3]

This was an enormously important finding. They also found that computer-based courses taught learners just about as well as an instructor, but not better. If the TBL worked as well as an instructor-led course, and if time is money, the advantage is obvious. Companies could expect similar results from the instruction, but the employees would spend less time away from their jobs. From that time forward, TBL has steadily grown and is an accepted method of delivering instruction.

More recently, a study that looked at what we can generally class as "multimedia" strengthened and expanded Kulik, Kulik, and Cohen's findings. Ruth Wienclaw, of the Institute for Defense Analysis, conducted another meta-analysis.[4] "Hold on," you may be thinking. "That's just something that applies *only* to soldiers." Not so. Wienclaw included related settings of industrial training and higher education in the study.

Since we had always considered Kulik, Kulik, and Cohen's findings that TBL is just as good, but faster, reason enough to apply it wherever it fits, even we were impressed. Wienclaw found that in all the settings combined, IVD improved achievement by about 0.50 standard deviations over less interactive, more conventional approaches to instruction. The non-statistically minded would say that this is roughly equivalent to raising the achievement of students by about 15 percentage points. Wow!

Wienclaw also found that the IVD was more effective when more interactive features were used, and that it was equally effective in both knowledge and performance outcomes. Also, it was *less* [our italics] costly than more conventional instruction (remember that today's digital video is less costly than IVD).

It should be no surprise to readers of this book, but in the first known study of its kind[5], Zenith Data Systems (ZDS) and Microsoft Corporation compared the performance of two different user interfaces. They compared character-based CUI (character user interface) and graphical user interfaces, (GUI) with novice and experienced users. Research results show that GUI provides benefits over CUI in office environments. Specifically, the research supports seven benefits of the GUI.

---

[3]Kulik, Kulik & Cohen, 1980. We should note that these researchers continued to round out their research with other studies that solidified their findings. This particular study became important because it was first.

[4]Wienclaw, Ruth. "Effectiveness and Cost of Interactive Videodisc Instruction in Defense Training and Education for the The Institute for Defense Analysis" (IDA Paper P-2372). Published by the US Department of Commerce, National Technical Information Service. July 1990.

[5]Reynolds, A. and Anderson, R. 1992. *Selecting and Developing Media for Instruction*, Third Edition. New York: VanNostrand Reinhold.

Jane Greiner reported a study carried out at NCR Corporation.[6] The numbers reported by recent research show that courses delivered by interactive multimedia instruction systems do as well or better in less time than courses given in traditional delivery settings. The review follows NCR practice and a four-level model of training evaluation: Reaction, Learning, Behavior, and Results. The findings show that students like interactive multimedia better and learn more from it than from more traditional delivery systems. Students probably also achieve more desired behavior changes when using interactive multimedia than when using traditional delivery systems, although there were too few studies to be sure. Also, although the return-on-investment outcomes are desirable to duplicate, most are inconclusive from a research standpoint because of design problems. Variables that are not controlled for make reliable and valid results difficult to achieve.

Shortening courses

Initially, conversion of existing instruction often delivered an 80% reduction in the time needed for instruction, or even more. There was a "sneaky" reason why TBL developers were able to promise such savings. The reason was that the older courses that were converted were developed using what we call "traditional" methods. Traditional methods are the same ones used in the middle ages. When the existing instruction was converted, it was also redeveloped using the ISD methodology that we will describe later in this part of the book, which is universally used by knowledgeable developers today. The ISD methodology alone typically resulted in radically shortened instruction, because all the unneeded content was removed.

The CMI described in Chapter 2 is responsible for other shortening. Remember *Buchanan's Law*? CMI is intended to avoid presentation of material the learner already has mastered. This avoidance shortens the instructional time and, as a side effect, produces a happier learner.

Improving student/staff ratios

An instructor can help only up to 30 learners or so, assuming that he or she actively helps them with problems rather than simply presenting the information. There is virtually no limit to the number of learners that can be served by a single instructor if presentation is considered sufficient, as is proven daily in the huge lecture halls of universities. Otherwise, more than 30 learners divide the instructor's time to the point that all are not helped effectively.

Since the technology carries the instructional load, the instructor (often called a *facilitator*) can handle the problems of many more learners, often up to 75 depending on the difficulty of the topic.

More satisfactory individualization

The branching tutorial model and CMI described in Chapter 2 hold the key to individualization. The CMI lets the learner avoid studying what he or she already knows,

---

[6]Greiner, Jane. *Interactive Multimedia Instruction: What Do the Numbers Show?* Presentation at 1994 NSPI conference.

and the branching tutorial adjusts to individual learner differences. No instructor, no matter how skilled, can match these accomplishments with individuals while working with a group.

Advantages and Disadvantages of Technology-Based Learning

By now the reasons why companies use technology-based learning should be obvious. They do it to save time, to avoid costs, and to provide instruction that can't be provided in any other way. Let's take a look at the good and bad points of TBL.

Advantages

TBL offers the following advantages:

- Can be available at the job site.
- Can be available on the job.
- Offers access to variety of media and resources that present the learning best.
- Trainees usually complete instruction in less time than with traditional (instructor-led) methods.
- Stimulating multimedia presentations with high interaction can make learning more enjoyable and engaging.
- Instruction can often be delivered when and where most convenient.
- Learner access to information can be on-demand rather than pre-scheduled.
- Students can show mastery of objectives at the outset, so an employee does not spend time studying already familiar material. Instruction is only presented if it is required. (Some organizations lack the courage to do this.)
- Can prevent a trainee from proceeding to more advanced materials until all prerequisites are thoroughly understood and performance is demonstrated.
- Implements criterion-referenced learning. Precisely measures student progress. Ensures mastery of prerequisites before proceeding to more advanced materials.
- Frees instructors from the lecture environment. They then have more time to counsel and provide individual help to individual trainees. They also have more time to maintain (update) the curriculum and keep it relevant to the requirements of the organization.
- Trainees usually have more accurate job performance, with benefits to productivity.
- Generic off-the-shelf courseware may be available, depending on the topic.
- Automated record keeping precisely measures student progress. Courses are presented in an orderly, logical progression. With accurate records, instructors can easily track where students are in their training prescriptions.
- Reduced loss of productive time away from the job, or readiness sooner for a new job.

- Can lead to more accurate job performance by learners, with benefits to productivity.

- The amortized savings realized should exceed the cost of the project within a reasonable time, such as a five-year shelf life or life cycle.

Disadvantages

TBL has the following disadvantages:

- Off-the-shelf software/courseware may not be available, depending on the topic.

- Generic off-the-shelf software/courseware may not meet local needs.

- Initial cost of technology-based learning development is high, compared to the cost of designing and developing a lecture-based course.

- Development requires skills that may not be available.

- Development of high quality instruction requires intense and extensive effort.

- May require investment in new equipment.

- Equipping equal numbers of simultaneous learners costs more for technology-based learning.

The History of Technology-Based Learning

Technology-based learning has a long history, stretching back almost 40 years. IBM started to try out CBL as a business, using their mainframe computers. Then, in 1957, the National Science Foundation (NSF) funded two very different projects, both at universities. These projects still echo back to us today, due to the hundreds of today's TBL experts who got their start in these pioneering projects.

The purpose of the University of Illinois project was to objectively determine which delivery techniques worked best. They ended with a system based on a super computer, with a communication network, with high resolution orange monochrome display, synthesized voice, and random access slide projection serving hundreds of users located at very distant points. It was called PLATO.

The other NSF-funded project was at Brigham Young University and was designed from the start to be based on existing technology—a minicomputer for computing and a Sony television set for display. It served a much smaller network of approximately 25 users up to 1,000 feet away and could deliver color video. This project was called TICCIT. The initial design for the planned community of Reston, VA called for TICCIT in every home, but it didn't happen.

In the 1960s and early 1970s, most of the basic research to see what worked was completed. Focus moved to cheaper delivery. The advent of the personal computer required a new focus. It is difficult for anyone who began their computing experience in the mid-1990s to appreciate just how weak the early personal computers really were. Initially, screen resolution, computing power, and storage were dismal. Improvement of these over time is truly remarkable.

In the 1980s personal computers became predominant in the delivery of TBL. Still, the screen resolution, computing power, and storage problems continued to prevent it from surpassing the by-then obsolescent PLATO system in technical achievement.

A new desire became important—to display video in conjunction with the training. The interactive videodisc appeared early in the 1980s, initially side-by-side with the computer, and by the end of the era the problems of using a single screen for both the computer-generated text and graphics and the video had been solved. The tools of the 1980s reflected these capabilities. There was a trend toward increasing numbers of authoring systems, and a product called PCD3 introduced the icon-based authoring system. PCD3 evolved into Authorware.

The early 1990s saw the advent of sufficient resolution, computing power, and storage. Digital video replaced the laser disc analog video, and programs became so large that CD storage was required. Faster CDs made delivery from the CD acceptable. By the mid-1990s all of these had reached amazing levels, setting the stage for truly fantastic things to come.

Figure 3.1 illustrates the development of TBL systems over time. Note the mainframe era and the personal computer era.

Intellectual origins of CBL

CBL is a fascinating amalgam of technologies, histories, theories, and more. You might ask, is it a discipline, science, art, or media? Where did it come from? Who were the key thinkers?

- Plato, Socrates, and Aristotle were great teachers who developed the tutorial method.
- Gutenberg advanced the technology of the day to make learning more affordable and accessible.
- Averrhoes (Abu-el-Walid ibn Rashid) was an Arab scholar who helped keep learning alive in the dark ages.
- Johann Amos Comenius, the bishop of Prague, introduced learning in the people's language (not Latin), used graphics to accompany text, and favored education for women.
- Edison invented motion pictures.
- DeForest invented the vacuum tube.
- Shockley invented the transistor.
- Bitzer and Bunderage developed the first practical computer-based learning systems.
- Gagné conducted the research that became incorporated into instructional systems design.
- Jobs and Wozniak popularized the personal computer.

How Technology-Based Learning Improved Performance at United Airlines

United Airlines (UA) didn't set out to make a significant contribution to the development of TBL, but they did so by implementing it in a major way. In the late 1970s, UA's

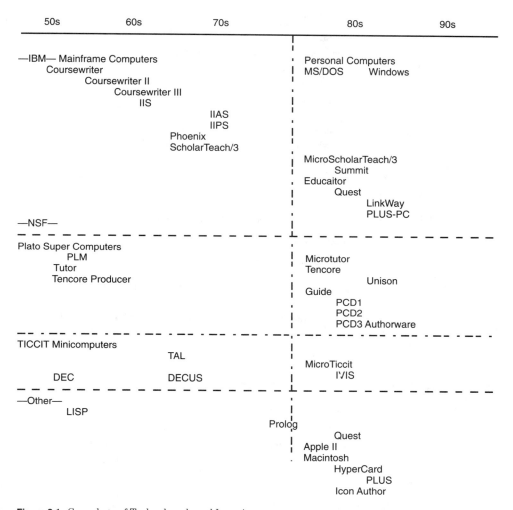

Figure 3.1 Genealogy of Technology-based Learning

training director, John Buchanan, decided to implement individualized training. They soon discovered that keeping track of the individual's training was overwhelming.

UA turned to the PLATO system's CMI capability, called PLM (PLATO Learning Management), to manage the record keeping. It also provided a criterion-based testing capability to ensure that the learners had mastered the content.

To test the CMI system, Buchanan selected the 30-hour new-hire pilot-training program. This training was required for all newly hired UA pilots, regardless of experience. As a result, master pilot-led classrooms included newly qualified pilots who had relatively few hours working alongside other pilots with multi-thousand hours of experience in the cockpit. It was an ideal selection and set the stage for resounding success.

The new system used CMI exclusively for testing, prescribing instruction, and keeping records. The results were that some pilots took less than 3 hours to complete the entire course. Some took as long as 18 hours, with the average being 11.5 hours.

Further, the master pilot who was asked to administer the CMI learning was dying of boredom, and his request to return to active service was granted. The replacement was a facilitator who could help with procedural questions.

Even further, the classroom (block) instruction tied up instructional resources for a fixed period of at least 30 hours. A new pilot would have to wait for the next session. The TBL version had continuous openings. Pilot learners who finished after only a few hours left a vacant spot for the next learner.

This may sound like it generated savings in every category. It did! Let's enumerate the categories.

- Non-productive study time was cut in half (average 11.5 instead of 30)
- Master pilot returned to duty
- No non-productive wait for new pilot learners

The project showed savings in the first year, even when including the cost of the new equipment.

There were other excellent projects, but the UA story was widely told and performed a service in demonstrating that TBL could be a cost-effective instructional method.

Technology-Based Learning in Other Organizations

Aviation

Dealing with some of the most complex and technically advanced products created by industry today, the largest airlines and largest manufacturers of commercial aircraft provide technology-based instruction for crew members. American Airline's training center near the Dallas-Fort Worth airport makes wide use of TBL. American, along with United Airlines and Boeing, are TBL pioneers. American Airline's TBL is not limited to pilots. Even new cabin attendants' training includes TBL. Tests are administered on the same computers.

Boeing has made wide use of technology-based training for over 10 years. The training on every system in the new 777 aircraft is supported by 40 TBL lessons.

Petroleum

The major oil companies use TBL to train their employees. Shell Oil, in Houston, makes extensive use of computers in providing training for a variety of corporate employees.

Food

Two of the largest companies in the food business have made extensive use of technology to train technical employees, those that operate, maintain, and repair the manufacturing equipment. This use of TBL is of long standing, and has produced the results that justified its use for a decade.

Manufacturing

The highly competitive automobile business have long provided the setting for the use of TBL. Auto makers GM and Ford are major users of technology-based learning. When new digital technology became a competitive necessity in manufacturing, major training programs were required to upgrade the knowledge and skills of the skilled tradespeople. TBL was the solution employed as each new high-technology plant opened.

Government agencies

The FAA was an early user of TBL. Unlike many other organizations, the FAA carefully selected only those projects where it made good economic sense. Even more unusual, the project leaders published annual updated reports to the training industry describing their progress.

Today, many U.S. government agencies use TBL in a wide variety of forms, for varied audiences, using differing delivery technologies.

Others

In Part 5 of this book, Chapters 30 through 33 examine the experiences of three organizations in detail. We have intentionally selected widely differing organizations: Aetna, an insurance company; Union Pacific, a railroad; and Magnavox, an electronics giant.

Now let's look at your own organization's readiness for TBL.

Exercise 3-1: Understanding your own project (and organization)

Directions: Fill in the organization's Technology Training Profile. Place an "X" in the Box that applies. Connect the X's.

	True				False
Accomplishment-Oriented Training					
Large Volume of Students					
Large Volume of Courses					
Course Content Stable					
No Strong Classroom Tradition					
Established Training Function					
Use ISD					

	True				False
Strong Development Skills					
Geographically Distributed Delivery					
Long-Term Technology Commitment					
Tied to Dynamic Technology					
Remote Delivery Possible					
Strong Administrative Control					
Company Economically Sound					

Analysis

Once you connect the Xs, a pattern may emerge that visually reveals your organization's or client's readiness for technology-based learning. The most "ready" pattern would go straight down the left column; the least ready would go straight down the right. If your connected line is pretty much to the right you may want to consider trying to change some of the factors before, or at the same time, that you institute a project.

A Good Reason

Soon the TBL solution will be a tool *you* can use to solve performance problems. You now have a considerable background knowledge of TBL. In Chapter 4 we will explore the environments in which we use TBL solutions today.

4

The Technology-Based Environment

Chapter 4 provides information about today's computer technology. This is not only a field-leveling chapter, but we plan to correct some misperceptions. Now that you understand the components of technology-based learning and are familiar with many of the definitions, we plan to dig deeper into the technology of lesson-making. By chapter end you will be familiar with some of the various collateral issues of technology-based learning and how they apply to solving training problems.

What You Will Learn in This Chapter

- Ergonomic factors related to technology-based learning
- Characteristics of various authoring tools
- Characteristics of various delivery systems
- Importance of display resolution and graphical user interface

Human Factors and Ergonomics

We are rightfully concerned about the people who learn from our technology-based systems. Sometimes people direct this concern at possible harmful effects of working at a computer. Today there is a trend to deter harmful effects of studying or working with video displays, and it is not unusual to hear some very legitimate questions about safety from the new technology-based learning users.

Most concerns center on the use of the display. Users worry that exposure to the video display terminal (VDT) might be harmful. Early, extensive research into the effects of exposure to VDTs in several countries did not identify any harmful effects. Some unions have negotiated provisions in their contracts that allow VDT users an immediate transfer if they become pregnant.

• Eye to screen distance	18–28"
• Keyboard height off floor	27.5"
• Seat height off floor	16"
• Screen centerline height off floor	39"
• Screen tilt	15°
(to reduce glare)	

Figure 4.1 Specifications for Human Comfort

Magnetic fields

More recently, VDT concerns have shifted to magnetic fields. Undetected, and possibly unsuspected in the earlier studies, these are called very low-frequency (VLF) and extremely low-frequency (ELF) electromagnetic fields. Research now shows that magnetic fields *are* harmful to humans. VDT manufacturers have turned to reducing the magnetic fields generated by their products, and VLF shields are incorporated in new monitor designs.

Physical stress

Carpal Tunnel Syndrome, and other repetitive strain injuries (RSI), did not become familiar business terms until the advent of computers. Typewriters were almost always placed on correctly designed typewriter stands. Computers didn't fit on the readily available typewriter stands and so were placed on the even more readily available, but higher, desks. Some workers have incurred disabilities from their improper posture while working at computers. We can avoid this problem through the use of wrist rests, ergonomically designed keyboards, and periodic at-the-desk exercises.

Stress is probably the most ubiquitous office problem, and the hardest to pinpoint. It's unclear if the stress comes from working at a VDT or from the tighter deadlines and stricter monitoring of using computers. Whatever the reason, the stress is real. The National Institute for Occupational Safety and Health found that clerical workers, working with VDTs in the insurance industry, had the highest stress level of any group it had studied. Their stress was higher than that of Air Traffic Controllers. An antidote for some stress is simply getting up and walking around. Thus, taking breaks is an effective cure for a case of the VDTs. Based on their human comfort research, Northern Telecom recommended the specifications given in Figure 4.1.

Results of studies will receive publicity as they become available. Watch for OSHA's national office to develop and release general industry ergonomic standards, including mandatory guidelines for computer use and workplace design. We can expect this area to be continuously monitored, and in the future additional guidelines may be released. Meanwhile, here are some easy tips on how to keep VDT users healthy :

- Be sure that your chair is not too high. Dangling feet reduce blood flow that can lead to swollen ankles. The chair should have an adjustable seat and back height, armrests, and swivel.

- Avoid any glare around the screen. Try to avoid direct light, whether from the sun or bright overhead lights. Light from a window, or from normal office lighting, can make eyes strain to see the screen.

- Place written material near the screen. Constant refocusing, from a VDT to paper, can cause extreme eye strain. There are many document holders on the market that let the user put papers wherever they want. The best place is near the screen.

- The keyboard and mouse should allow forearms to be horizontal. Keyboards that force arms or wrists to work at extreme angles are the cause of strained and even pinched nerves. Look for an adjustable height-and-distance set-up, one of the increasingly available ergonomic keyboards, and a wrist rest.

- The screen should tilt and swivel. It should be at or below eye level, and no more than 20 degrees below the line of sight. The more the head has to bend down, the greater the strain on the neck and back. The VDT should have a radiation shield or be a low-emission design. Some users prefer a screen filter to avoid glare.

There are other considerations that you should think about when you establish a technology-based learning environment. These include:

Acoustics

- Carpeting, low static (contributes to good acoustics)
- Acoustic ceiling
- Audio delivered to learners by headphones
- Administrative area separate

Light

- Indirect lighting (to reduce glare)

Physical

- Air conditioning (for human comfort, not equipment)
- Electrical power, stable (equipment must be protected against voltage surges)

Although learner's studying usually does not involve heavy keyboard use, all aspects of ergonomics remain important. We can expect improvements to continue, and to improve the physical aspects of technology-based learning.

Courseware ergonomics

There is a wide variation in the "learner friendliness" of courseware. Well-designed courseware has built-in consistency. This eases learning. Learners benefit from consistency in the courseware "infrastructure." In terms of making learning less painful, "Little things mean a lot." The learner should have planned support available, through the use of certain keys or always-available icons. "Help" should be available, to provide planned instructions. The best help is called context-sensitive help. It is more difficult to design and program, but significantly better. The "Help" function provides the learner with predetermined information on how to proceed. As technology-based learning becomes even more widely used, you can expect using organizations to demand courseware design that promotes ease of use.

Courseware Authoring

In a "Letter from the President"[1] to Society for Applied Learning Technology members, Ray Fox points out that the authors of courseware make the difference. We will have a look at how that is accomplished, through languages and authoring systems.

> A friend once described the inventor of the piano as an individual who felt that he had achieved a tremendous accomplishment and thereby secured his place in history. Contrary to his expectations, it is the accomplishments of Brahms, Beethoven, Bach, and scores of other composers which command historical notice. Few can identify the inventor of the instrument itself. As an analogy, there have been astonishing developments in the field of the technological components which constitute instruction delivery systems: the personal computer, the videodisc, CD-ROM as well as others. However, to realize the potential of this technology, the fame must accrue to the developers of interactive instructional materials. Achievement of this end is not without its challenges. . . .

Author languages

We have always been amazed at how people will use completely inappropriate tools, if they are all that are available. In the most recent case that has come to our attention, we found a major 1990 project in which a general purpose computer language[2] was used to write CAI courseware. Hardly anyone would try to calculate the shape of a new airfoil with a programming language intended for generating business reports. Even so, at least one organization did use COBOL to program courseware.

Strange as it may appear to those who haven't fallen into that trap, you can find people behaving similarly in technology-based learning. We call this the "Hammer Syndrome." The famous psychologist, Abraham Maslow is attributed with saying that, "If all you have is a hammer, everything will look like a nail." If all you know is the BASIC computer language, you will try to use BASIC for everything. We regularly see this in the world of courseware development. It should be no surprise that no one language is well-suited for everything. Languages are suited specifically for many purposes. Decades ago, people figured this out and created author languages. The author language, to be suitable for unreserved recommendation to any organization, must have the following characteristics:

- It must be high level
- It must be specifically designed for instructional computing
- It must be user-oriented

It should also be obvious that it must be a language specifically designed for instructional applications. TenCore is the principal language used for authoring today. It has the characteristics listed above.

---

[1]Summer 1989, p. 1.

[2]These are the fundamental languages, such as COBOL, Fortran, Pascal, BASIC, and C.

Programming is analogous to developing film. Some people will always want to do it. Most don't. Today there is no *need* for programming. Some organizations may continue to use appropriate authoring languages for their courseware due to the flexibility it offers, while others may move to authoring systems and others may attempt to eliminate the need for programming by using programmerless authoring tools.

Author systems

Authoring systems reduce the learning curve needed to be productive in any computer language. They make the things that an author wants to do, such as judging responses, tracking learner variables, and presenting multimedia, relatively easy to do. But there is a problem here, because the more power an authoring system has, the more complexity is involved. A system that was developed in the 1980s shall be nameless here. It was menu driven, and quite powerful. Some users said that learning where to find a feature, in the multi-layered nest of menus, was as difficult as learning a computer language.

Some authoring systems include access to a high level, user-oriented learning-specific author language. This reflected their development into a system from a language. Nowadays, possibly because many multiplatform computer applications are written in C, this tends to be replaced by the ability to insert a C routine.

Surprisingly large number of systems is available today. Commonly used authoring systems include, but are not limited to, Authorware, Icon Author, and Quest. The widespread use of such systems has significantly reduced the cost of lesson development. These useful author systems should also aid in the path to higher quality courseware.

Forms of Delivery Systems

Today's marketplace offers a fantastic variety of computers available for instructional purposes. You can assemble a very simple system and offer the least number of options. Other, more costly systems, offer a large range of attributes and options. Leasing is also possible, depending on the client's needs and budget.

Computer systems

Which of these computer types can be used to deliver instruction?

Which of these computers can be used for TBL? That is a trick question. Remember that the Problem Solving mode of CAI comes into play when a person uses a computer as a tool to learn something. Any of these computers could be used in that way. Additionally, many of the others could be used in more traditional ways. Although, to the best of our knowledge, a Cray has not been used to power a central TBL system, other super computers have been. IBM has long offered CAI on their mainframe systems. The PCs are the mainstay of today's TBL. Yet, even the tiny Timex/Sinclair 1000 had a CAI lesson written for it.

Historically, instruction has been delivered on large-computer-based networks, small-computer-based networks (LAN), and on desktop PCs. Today the big main-

Size	Cost	Availability	Usefulness
Macro (mainframe)			
IBM 4031	$1m	fewer	general
Mini			
DEC VAX Series	$100K	wide	flexible
IBM System 2	$100K	wide	business
IBM AS400	$100K	wide	business
Micro			
Apple II series	was $400	fewer	limited
IBM PC and compatibles	$1–5K	wide	flexible
Macintosh	$1–5K	wide	flexible
Super (and puny too)			
Cray	$10m	increasing	heavy computing
Timex/Sinclair 1000	was $100	gone	very limited
Newton	$400	increasing	limited

frame-based central systems have all but disappeared. However, the increasing availability of wide area networks (WAN) and growth of the Internet may replace them in concept.

Today, despite the brand or model, we can classify instructional computer systems into two general groups:

- Network systems
- Stand-alone systems

Network system

Typically, this system has student learning stations connected to a larger computer by a cabling system. These are local area networks (LANs). The computer (and system) may be a regular part of the work site. It may be a dedicated instructional system. The student stations may number in the hundreds and may be of varying configurations. Alternatively, the student learning stations may be dispersed. It is possible to connect with a LAN or even to connect several LANs in a wide area network (WAN). Further, although transmission over the Internet is slow, it offers tremendous possibilities for distributing training.

Advantages of Networks

- If the students will be working with computers on the job, the computer used for training is usually similar, needing little transfer of learning.

- The ability of the instructor to concentrate on instructor-related tasks is increased, allowing them to attend specifically to students who may be having problems.

- Excellent means for simulation situations that call for individualized yet coordinated task performance. For example, CAI networked crew coordination training allows each station to represent a specific flight task requirement where the host system monitors the coordination of the stations and provides appropriate response.

- Quick updating of course materials and records. Developers and instructors may access the processor from a learning station and revise materials rapidly.

- Learning stations can often interact with each other, even at long distances. This allows students or authors to communicate and leave messages for each other or to question an instructor about course material.

- Versions of software and courseware will be the same for all users. It is simpler to maintain current versions of the software than when separate software exists on each computer.

- The possibility of software piracy is reduced.

Disadvantages of Networks

- Dedicated instructional systems may be difficult to justify on a cost-effectiveness basis.

- Any breakdowns in the file server will affect every student on the network. Breakdowns elsewhere within the network *may* also affect all network users.

- Breakdowns in isolated parts of the network can cause delays in the instructional program.

- Network versions of software and courseware are often required at higher cost.

- Expense of network cabling and software itself is an additional cost.

- Network user interface may be somewhat different from what the user will experience with a PC.

- Network software requires extra steps to learn.

Stand-alone system

This hardly needs a description. Almost any PC can serve as a stand-alone learning station. It is a self-contained unit. Each unit is totally independent from others, providing maximum flexibility of curriculum.

Advantages of Stand-Alone Systems

- Normally, they are the least expensive systems to buy.

- Since there is no network, a breakdown of one PC will not affect all the students, and one student's PC cannot affect others.

- Response time may be faster than with network systems.

- A wide variety of commercially produced courseware is available for purchase.

- Network versions of software and courseware are not needed.

- Individual PCs are economically better for a small number of users.

Disadvantages of Stand-Alone Systems

- No centralized location for gathering, receiving, and updating data.

- Must distribute revisions in software materials to each student.

- Gathering test results and other management functions can be cumbersome and time-consuming.

- No communication links between students, developers, and instructors.

- No ability to share resources, such as a printer.

- Differences in individual computers or software installed can absorb considerable instructor time.

Graphical User Interface

In the first study of its kind that we know of, Zenith Data Systems (ZDS) and Microsoft Corporation compared the performance of two different user interfaces. They compared character-based CUI (character user interface) and graphical user interfaces (GUI), with novice and experienced users.[3]

Research results show that GUI provides benefits over CUI in office environments. Specifically, the research supports seven benefits of the GUI. GUI users:

- Work faster

- Work better (complete more of their tasks accurately)

- Have higher productivity than CUI users

- Express lower frustration

- Express lower fatigue after working with PCs

- Are better able than CUI users to self-teach and explore

- Learn more capabilities within applications

These findings support three conclusions. GUI generates:

- Higher output per work hour through higher productivity

- Higher output per employee because of lower frustration and fatigue levels

- Greater return on the technology investment because GUI users master more capabilities and need less training and support

Many of these benefits are linked to the "navigation theory." It holds that the intuitive icons and menus embodied by GUIs help exploration, use, and retention of applications' functions, making users more productive, self-sufficient, and confident in their computing. The navigation theory suggests that GUI is superior to CUI for all corporate microcomputer users: clerical, professional, and managerial.

Here is a summary of a Research Summary from a Zenith Data Systems news release, dated May 15, 1990.

(1) Work faster—On average, novice GUI users completed 42% more tasks than novice CUI users in the same time. Experienced GUI users completed 35% more tasks than CUI users.

(2) Work better—Experienced GUI users correctly completed a higher proportion of attempted exercises: 91% vs. 74%. And 69% of experienced GUI users completed all tasks correctly vs. 17% for CUI users.

---

[3]The study was developed and administered by Temple, Barker, & Sloane Inc., an independent research firm.

(3) More productive—Both experienced and novice GUI users accomplished 58% more correct work in the same time than CUI users.

(4) Lower frustration and (5) Lower fatigue—After two days of learning to use microcomputers and applications, GUI novices rated their frustration at 2.7 (out of 10), whereas CUI novices rated their frustration at 5.3. Experienced users' fatigue was rated at 4.3 for GUI and 5.8 for CUI.

(6) Better ability to self-teach and explore—GUI novices felt greater confidence than CUI novices in their abilities to explore an application's advanced features: 5.0 vs. 2.4 before a test, and 7.5 vs. 5.8 after.

(7) Learn more capabilities—GUI novices attempted 23% more new tasks than CUI novices.

We shouldn't have to convince you that GUI is better; it is intuitive. But what does this mean to you for developing TBL? If you combine this with the results of the research reported in Chapter 3 the answer should ring out clearly. It is better to use more GUI interactive features than less.

The display

Obviously, the graphical user interface depends on the display. How little text you can usefully place on one display may surprise you. Compared to a computer display, flipcharts, chalkboards, and handouts are all large-format. The information you can put on them won't fit on the screen. The display screen is a *finite* area. To offset this limitation, designers must adopt several new techniques. Hal Christianson of CES Training Corporation suggests these ideas:

- Repeat key concepts and ideas often
- Present information with spacesaving graphics, icons, and symbols in place of lengthy explanations or repetitions
- Use windows—small ones are best—to display material to which the learner must refer often

Following these procedures, you can break all instruction down to very small modules. As the screen is less flexible, our programs will become a series of small, discrete, self-contained modules. We assemble them to produce a coherent lesson. An interaction lies at the core of each module to ensure that the learner understands its content.

Resolving the question of graphic resolution

For most of the history of TBL, computer screen resolution was a major problem. Screen size isn't the same and doesn't matter. You cannot show more detail in the huge screens in stadiums; they are only monster television screens. Refer to Figure 4.2 to see the relative amount of information that can be displayed on a U.S. television screen. The figure also shows how much greater display potential the original square Macintosh and the 640 × 480 VGA have. The key is that this level of resolution was the threshold of acceptability for TBL to be flexible and effective.

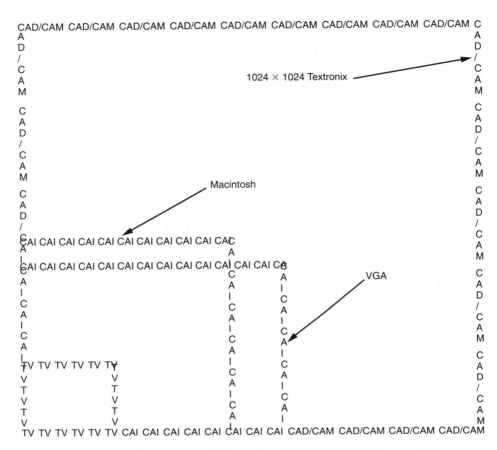

Figure 4.2 Computer Screen Resolution (© *Angus Reynolds, 1990. All rights reserved.*)

Today we are safely across that threshold. You do not see displays with less resolution for sale. The next threshold is 1024 × 1024 resolution that was needed for effective computer-aided design (CAD) and computer-assisted manufacturing (CAM). The trend is toward greater resolution for PCs. Since the CAD/CAM displays already exist, and have for many years, it is not a technological hurdle—it is a cost hurdle. You won't pay more for your display than you currently pay for your whole system, the price of true high resolution. Prices will fall, and someday we will have 1024 × 1024 resolution available on our desktop and for the TBL learning station. The point to remember about resolution is that the amount of information conveyed in any format remains constant. Making the learner's display or a projection screen larger does not change or improve its resolution.

Computer Software

Do you care what operating system your development or target computer uses? Here are some current operating systems listed in order of popularity.

- MS-DOS and Microsoft Windows (Windows 95)
- Macintosh
- PC-DOS and OS/2
- UNIX

The answer is that there are, and always have been, more tools available for more popular operating systems. You should also note that we cheated. UNIX may be more popular than suggested by the last position on the list. The problem is that course-ware authoring tools for UNIX have been very scarce. OS/2 is in a potentially worse position, but emulates Windows.

Applications software

No authoring tool that we know of is sufficient to develop high quality instruction without the use of other application software packages that are specialized in other areas. Here are some popular packages. The exact ones that you use may depend on many things, such as the platform you use, cost, software on hand, and other factors.

- Corel Draw
- Canvas
- Photoshop
- Autodesk
- Sound Edit 16 Pro
- Soundwave
- Videospigot
- Premiere
- Smart Video Recorder
- Splice
- Ready, Set, Go
- MacProject
- MS Project
- ABC Flow

Utilities/tools

You need these tools. If they are not built into the authoring tools that you use, you must use them separately.

- Spelling checker
- Grammar checker
- Dictionary
- Thesaurus

System Capabilities

For more than a decade, beginning in 1978, Angus Reynolds published an evolving list of desired development/delivery system capabilities. In some ways, for many years it was a wish list. Over the years, as the list evolved, it got much shorter because many of the older wishes have come true.

- A powerful authoring system with no requirement for programming
- A high level, user-oriented, education-specific author language with powerful authoring aids; or, ability to make calls to programs written in a general purpose language
- Flexibility in instructional strategy
- Courseware convertibility for delivery on other popular platforms
- A powerful instructional management system
- Excellent user support

The only addition to the list is user support. As more of the other needs were met, this basic need grows more important.

A comparison of authoring systems

Along the way, be sure that you look for different paths to the same end. On the other hand, be alert for "important" or "significant" differences. The flavor of a system will influence the projects you take on and how they appear. Are there flashes when graphics appear or video plays? Is the video in synch with the audio? Are animations done smoothly? Is the speed adequate for your learner's needs? How is judging accomplished? Will you be able to exercise your creativity within the vehicle being considered?

Don't be fooled

An old question to ask yourself when watching a demo of any kind is this: When you see an effect on the screen, can you really be sure what caused it? There is only one answer to this question, and it is no! You can't really be sure. The functioning could be rigged so that the demonstrator would get the same outcome no matter what he or she did. We have seen demos with something neat that actually took months for many people with special talents to bring about. You will be hard-pressed to achieve similar results. Beware of what you see.

Organizational Impact

Organizations resist change. You should consider how your own or your client's organization works and be prepared to work within its existing structure to the highest degree possible.

Formal and informal ways of operating

Use Figure 4.3 to compare how functions, structures, roles, and goals are formally and informally organized in your organization. For example, it may be that changes to procedures are formally posted in a document in a specific location, but employees actually learn of them through informal communications with their supervisor(s).

The supporting environment

Likewise, you may have to consider the existing and evolved training support structure. Figure 4.4 lists existing support structures. Consider how you will move from the existing to the evolved structure as you move from conventional to technology-based delivery.

Exercise 4-1: WOMBAT

Directions: The World Order of Machine-Based Automated Trainers (WOMBAT) has approached you to write the requirements for the next system they will procure. What will you recommend?

1.
2.
3.
4.
5.
6.
7.

If you have never thought about it before, it would be useful to try to write specifications for WOMBAT. The process of identification will stimulate your grasp of your needs.

Now, let's start to think about a project of your own that you might choose to try when you finish this book.

Exercise 4-2: Individual project—project definition

Directions: Answer these initial questions.

1. Select a project for training in your organization
2. Size—How large will this project be?
   - ~ Number of students?
   - ~ Who will be involved in the project? (What are the learners like in terms of current duties, likely familiarity with the topic, etc.)
3. Length
   - ~ Hours of estimated student effort (How many hours of sitting at the computer will it take the learner to finish the course?)

~ How long will one student's total involvement last? (Include non-study time, for example a learner that does a 4-hour course, one-hour per week, will have a total involvement of 4 weeks.)

4. Volatility of the material
5. Probable <u>total</u> project cost (it is important to make a guess even if you don't know at this point. We will use this number later)?
6. Biggest advantage of the project?
7. Biggest concern?

	Stated	Informal
1. Functions		
2. Structure		
3. Roles		
3. Goals		

Figure 4.3 Formal and Informal Means

	Existing	Evolved
1. Select students	–	
2. Distribute course info (market)	–	
4. AV– Media support	–	
5. Catalog/roster courses/students	–	
6. Media selection	–	
7. Distribute material	–	
8. Charge/billing	–	
9. Accounting	–	
10. Student aid	–	

Figure 4.4 Existing and Evolved Support Items

Analysis

Before you go on, let's make sure that your project is reasonable

Any project topic could be a good one, but there are several reasons to prefer a project with a large number of learners. One of our current projects has 4,000 learners a year. When you make a difference in delivery cost or time away from the job, and then multiply it by 4,000, it can add up. A small number doesn't automatically kill the project, but as the number shrinks to very small the criticality of the training must outweigh the cost per individual.

The estimated student hours should be relatively small. Remember development time is greater for technology-based learning and is often measured in hours of development time per hour of delivery time. When the delivery time becomes huge, the development time becomes astronomical.

Also:

- The lower the volatility of the topic, the less maintenance that will be needed.

- No project cost is necessarily too high. It must be compared to other considerations, as we will do in the next chapter.

- If you have a hard time thinking of an advantage, think of another project instead.

- The biggest concern should not be a sure project killer, only a reasonable uncertainty. But if it is too powerful, think of another project.

Adults Only, Please

This completes the pre-multimedia background of the technology. Now, it's time to turn our attention to the people. The big question is, how do people learn? Are there differences in preparing instruction for adults, compared to children? In Chapter 5 we will explore that. Let's move on!

5

How Adults Learn

You may not need to read this chapter. It depends on your formal background in the training field. We intend to level the *reading* field by providing information about what is known for sure about how adults learn. As you follow this chapter, you will find that the characteristics of technology-based learning match the characteristics of adult learners very closely.

What You Will Learn in This Chapter

- The events of learning
- The characteristics of adult learners
- The role of training in organizations
- The hierarchy of computer application

How People Learn

The truth is that scientists do not understand fully how people learn. Recently, much more has been learned, but there is still much that is not known. The information processing model provides an explanation that is sufficiently useful for our purposes. The information processing model links the environment to long-term memory through receptors, a sensory register, and short-term memory. Long- and short-term memories are linked back to the environment through a response generator and effectors. Human beings use long-term and short-term memories unconsciously every day. Figure 5.1 shows a representation of the information-processing model. Contributions were made to the information processing model by many people, including Georg von Békésy and Robert Gagné.

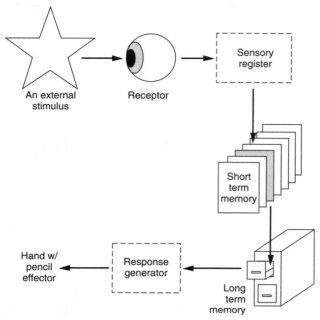

Figure 5.1 Information Processing Model

Short-term memory

Basically, stimuli that the learner acquires are placed in an area of memory called short-term memory. Short-term memory (STM) is limited to information of only approximately seven information items and is held in the brain for temporary use. For the learner to remember it later it must be moved to long-term memory, encoded, and stored there. When the learner places new items in STM, they displace the ones that were there, which are then forgotten.

Long-term memory (LTM) is information that is encoded, stored, and retained in the brain. All our memories of every kind are stored in LTM. Some of the information from short-term memory may be passed to long-term memory for later retrieval and use, but the rate of transfer is limited.

Long-term memory

The entire problem of training is managing to put all the wanted information into all of learners' long-term memories. You can think of the goal of training as to do just that. Jokes about implants and pills notwithstanding, as the percentage of wanted information approaches 100% it becomes much more difficult to reliably achieve success.

Domains of Learning

Instructional activities can be usefully placed into one of three *domains*. The domains are the:

- Cognitive
- Psychomotor
- Affective

Distinctly different instructional approaches are appropriate for each of the domains. Therefore, it is part of the instructional development process to categorize each instructional activity into one of the three domains.

Cognitive domain

The cognitive domain is the area of human learning associated with intellectual skills, such as assimilation of information or knowledge. We list the cognitive domain first because it is the most common in training and education. According to researcher Benjamin Bloom, learning in the cognitive area involves changes in knowledge, comprehension, application, analysis, synthesis, and evaluation. Cognitive learning objectives specify the acquisition of particular knowledge or information. Technology-based learning is well suited to, and powerful in handling, cognitive domain learning needs.

When matching cognitive objectives, TBL can control interactive self-instruction to teach concepts, rules, principles, steps and processes, and complex calculations. Combined with other media, computers can teach recognition or discrimination of applicable visual and audio stimuli.

Psychomotor domain

The psychomotor domain is the area of human learning associated with physical movement and skills. According to Bloom, the psychomotor domain involves the demonstration of some physical skill or the performance of some task. Examples include repairing a diesel engine or skating a triple Axel. Psychomotor objectives specify muscular coordination and movement, manipulation of materials and objects, or acts that require neuromuscular coordination. Technology-based learning can supplement, but can never fully satisfy, psychomotor domain learning needs. You can best use TBL to acquaint the learner with the cognitive aspects of activities that have a psychomotor component, and then including true psychomotor activities and testing.

TBL learning stations are an excellent "real world" device for teaching skills when students will work with terminals on the job in response to psychomotor objectives. When combined with simulated equipment, or facilities from the job environment, computers are excellent tools to create real world conditions.

Affective domain

We list the affective domain last, even though it is first alphabetically. This is the area of human learning associated with attitudes, feelings, interests, opinions, world views, and values. Perhaps it should not be the least commonly used, but it is. Some instructors fear attempting to change attitudes and have little idea how to approach this area. In the affective domain, outcomes are based on the development of attitudes or feelings rather than of knowledge, since this domain deals with the attitudes

Internal process	External instructional event
1. Reception	Gaining attention
2. Expectancy	Informing learners of the objective
3. Retrieval to working memory	Stimulating recall of prior knowledge
4. Selective perception	Presenting the stimulus
5. Semantic encoding	Providing learning guidance
6. Responding	Eliciting performance
7. Reinforcement	Providing feedback
8. Retrieval and reinforcement	Assessing performance
9. Retrieval and generalization	Enhancing retention and transfer of learning

Figure 5.2 Internal Processes and Their Corresponding Instructional Event

and motivation of the learner. Affective learning objectives, sometimes called attitudinal objectives, specify the acquisition of particular attitudes, values, or feelings. Video has always been a powerful tool in achieving affective objectives. Multimedia-technology-based learning has the same advantages, along with being able to provide the interactive activities and the measurement of change.

In response to affective objectives, TBL is very useful when used to cause the learner to interact and to display motion video illustrating the wanted behavior.

Designing for Learning According to Gagné's Internal Processes

Robert Gagné was one of the most prolific researchers in the area of training. His interest was in how people learn. He identified nine events of learning. Each of the events is characterized by an internal process that the learner experiences. You can ensure that these internal events occur.

There also are nine corresponding external steps that should take place, one for every objective during the course of the instructional activities. Figure 5.2 outlines these steps. The first three events are pre-instructional activities that serve to create the proper conditions for learning to occur. The next five (fourth through eighth) events coincide with the actual acquisition of knowledge. The ninth event occurs when application of the new knowledge takes place.

The following explanations reference a fictitious training program about a widget framis.

Pre-instructional activities

Research has proven that, for a desired behavior to occur, the proper conditions must exist. The first three steps involve preparing the learner for learning.

1. Gain Attention. The first and probably the most important step is to focus the learner's attention on the job of learning. Gagné suggests blinking text or audio tones to call attention to the computer screen. The use of video and graphics allows for more sophisticated methods of gaining the learner's attention. Your training module might begin with a colorful, eye-catching animation sequence of a hypothetical trip through the widget's "framis." The sequence ends on a graphic representation of a properly aligned framis. Behaviorally, the use of touch-driven responses to stimuli provides for hands-on involvement that helps to maintain the learner's attention.

2. Inform Learner of the Objective. An objective screen is at the beginning of each lesson. It describes what will be encountered and what the learner's performance must be upon completion. The objective helps to focus the learner's attention while initiating the internal process of expectancy.

3. Stimulate Recall of Prior Knowledge. It is vital that the learner evaluate the new material in the context of previous knowledge in order to encode new information as it is presented. The prior knowledge must be retrieved from long-term memory into working memory. A simple way to get the learner to recall concepts learned previously involves embedded questions. The embedded quiz provides at least two questions about the framis. These questions serve two functions. They test the learner's mastery of the prerequisite entry skills necessary for the lesson, and they stimulate the needed recall of prior learning.

Acquisition

The primary function of any training program is the acquisition of new knowledge by the learner. Steps to ensure that the acquisition takes place are described below.

4. Present the Stimulus. We present a brief tutorial in Lessons 1 and 2, and a simulation is used in Lessons 3 and 4. In this case, Lessons 1 and 2 are the expository segments for the simulation in Lessons 3 and 4. We tell the learner the generalities that apply to the operation of the widget. Rather than being shown an example of the generality, the learner is given the option to use prompts in Lessons 3 and 4, in an adaptation of the discovery method, to perform the example. Graphics are used in Lessons 1, 3, and 4 to help the learner visualize the physical results of the procedure being described.

5. Provide Learning Guidance. Supplying a suggested means of encoding new information is one of the most beneficial things that an instructional developer can do for a learner. Encoding has a tremendous influence on the ability to recall information from long-term memory. A well known example of an encoding suggestion is using the mnemonic HOMES to remember the names of the great lakes. During interviews with the job incumbents, we were told many times that one of the most difficult parts of learning their jobs was visualizing what was physically happening inside the widget's framis while they manipulated the controls. We decided on a high quality visual representation of what the framis was doing, as they performed the procedure, to help the learners encode and therefore remember the steps.

6. Elicit Performance. The internal process of responding (thinking about a stimulus and formulating a response) is a critical part of the learning process. We chose a simulation of the widget keypad and display to elicit performance in Lesson 3. The learner has now been told the generality and must practice the example procedure. The learner has the option to rely on guidance from the system at this point. We establish a series of prompts to take the learner step by step through an example; objective 3.0, "Set the 2nd Alignment to One Side." This task was chosen as an example because it is a subset of the next objective, "Align the 2nd Framis." An on-screen prompt asks the learner, "What key will return you to the CMD [command] level?" If the learner remembers the generality from the previous lesson, the RESET key will be selected. If the learner cannot recall, the HELP box must be pressed. The section on feedback gives a more detailed description of how helps and prompts are implemented.

7. Provide Feedback. Eliciting performance from the learner is only half of what must be done, it is essential to provide feedback to make the learner aware of the quality of his or her performance. When learning procedural tasks, feedback should be immediate for maximum learning efficiency. In addition to the timing, the type of feedback given is a critical factor in teaching procedures. You can use noises, illuminating lamps, changing displays, or even motion! For example, when the RESET key on the keypad is pressed, the display will always display CMD. This feedback is usually sufficient for simple tasks but does not provide enough information for complex tasks that require a chain of responses. Another example of feedback would be a prompt saying, "You need to use the left and right arrow keys." This is information supplied by the training device that the actual device would not supply. This type of prompting is sometimes called *pre-response* help. Reinforcement usually takes the form of encouragement. An example of this feedback would be an overlay, saying "Excellent, you breezed right through that!" Help is yet another type of feedback. When we feel that a particular step of the instruction is difficult, or the user may require assistance, we usually offer help to the user. Help may be offered by displaying an icon for the learner to touch to ask for assistance, or it may be displayed automatically after a predetermined elapsed time with no response.

8. Assess Performance. Sometime during the training the learner will feel confident that mastery of the skills has been attained. The learner should be able to demonstrate mastery of the procedure right then. In Lesson 3 the assessment is done with the simulation. All help and feedback is removed and the learner must perform the procedure. The computer easily keeps track of the learner's actions. The results will pinpoint the specific areas of weakness, if any, and will branch the learner to a remedial sequence that will address the specific weakness.

Application

Once mastery of an objective has been demonstrated it is important to apply the newly acquired skill in the context of previous knowledge. That is, the learner must be able to apply the new skill in a variety of new situations.

9. Enhance Retention and Transfer of Learning. Finally, the simulation is used to introduce learning activity 5.0, "Align the 1st Framis." For this procedure the learner must recall to working memory all the tasks learned thus far in the module, and must be able to apply them to the situation. Once again the learner will rely on the prompts and help. The systematic process of mastering a sub-task, and gradually building sub-tasks up to mastery of a larger task, is a behavioral approach known as *chaining*. This method will enhance retention and should improve transfer of learning. In general, it should instill in the learner a sense of confidence that the new knowledge can be applied to any procedure they might perform on the system.

Characteristics of Adult Learners[1]

Researchers have examined adults and, not surprisingly, found that they are different than children. We aren't making this up.

- The rate of learning varies between individuals.
- Adults enter the instructional setting with considerable previous experience and learning.
- Individuals have different learning styles and preferences.
- In a group, individual participants may have a variety of goals for learning.
- Adults need to feel that they are learning to meet their goals.

Let's examine each of these for its impact on technology-based learning. That the rate of learning varies between individuals is also true of children. Further, there seem to be differences by topic between individuals. The difference provided by TBL is that it can permit the faster learners to finish when they are done, not when everyone is done. Examine the branching tutorial structure in Figure 2.2. It illustrates how the faster learner can proceed to the end of the learning more quickly than the slower learner.

The characteristic of adults to enter the instructional setting with considerable previous experience and learning matches exactly with the capabilities of CMI to dramatically shorten the instruction. Consider the CMI structure in Figure 2.9. By measuring the objectives that the learner can master without instruction, the learning can proceed directly to those topics in which the learner does need instruction. TBL can produce amazing savings while meeting this adult need. On the CAI design side, because adults have significant previous knowledge of the content, presentation of known materials is irrelevant and often uninteresting to students. Try to provide options for learners to skip content that may be familiar within the CAI.

Individuals have different learning styles and preferences. There is very little we can do to directly address this need, because it would require providing learning resources matched to each individual's learning styles and preferences. That is prohibitively expensive. What we can do is provide for such differences in the design. For example, you can reinforce on-screen text with audio.

---

[1]For additional information see *The Adult Learner, A Neglected Species*, and other books by Malcolm Knowles.

It is true that individual participants may have a variety of goals for learning and that they need to feel that they are learning to meet their goals. As with learning styles and preferences, you can best meet these needs by considering them in the instructional design. If you provide options for learner control of content, adult learners are often able to make the choices based on their particular needs. Make sure that it is clear why the learners are being asked to learn the content and how it applies to their own goals.

The Role of Training

Training's role in the organization has expanded and shifted over the years as the organization's priorities have altered.

During the 60s, the emphasis was on educational psychology. If we had to characterize the quest of the period, it was for the "ultimate training manual." In an era before the real advent of computers, but anticipating them, the closest to TBL that could be achieved was programmed instruction and individualized instruction.

During the 70s, system analysis was the basis for much advance in TBL. The PLATO system best characterized the era, one during which cybernetics seemed the fruitful approach to progress.

During the 80s, an increase in management emphasis led to creation of automated environments for development and delivery of instruction. At the beginning of the 80s, TBL was not fully accepted nor considered a part of the average organization's training options. By the end of the 80s, it had achieved acceptance and was steadily gaining ground in terms of topics included and organizations using TBL approaches.

The 90s unveiled the technological maturity that had always been needed to make full use of TBL. The power to provide the best of TBL economically had arrived. Digital video made possible motion video on fairly ordinary learning stations without special hardware. Inexpensive hardware-assisted digital video provided full-screen, full-motion, high-resolution video by the early 1990s. CD-ROM provided access to the large files such video requires. The amazing growth of the Internet suggested that the very wide linkage of learner with expert begun with PLATO was at last universally at hand.

Technology-Based Training Characteristics

As was clear from considerations encountered in Chapter 4, technology-based delivery requires a different support structure. The characteristics of TBL are also different from what you may be accustomed to.

Computer applications hierarchy

What we can do with a computer depends on the amount of resources we are willing to pour into it. In TBL, the most difficult and rewarding activities require the greatest resources. Figure 5.3 shows the hierarchy of application of computers to TBL use. The simplest applications, requiring the least resources, are at the bottom. As we climb the pyramid the resources expand greatly, until we find the most difficult activity at the top.

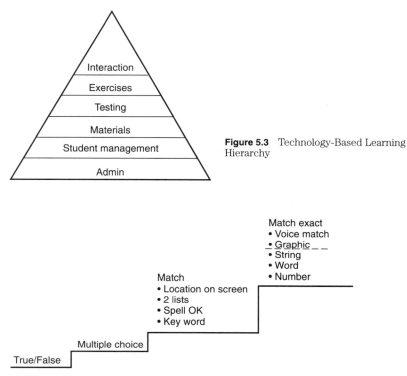

Figure 5.3 Technology-Based Learning Hierarchy

Figure 5.4 Hierarchy of Judging Strategies

Judging strategies

It is also increasingly difficult to do more complex interactions. The strategies used to judge the learner's response fall into this category. The judgment of whether the learner selected True or False is the simplest. Making exact-match judgments is the most complex. Figure 5.4 illustrates the Hierarchy of Judging Strategies. Those above the dotted line are not yet possible with ordinary equipment.

Outcomes of judging (or, How to make a type-2 error, CAI style)

When judging the learner's input you have to make certain that you have done so correctly. This leads us to the type-2 error. A type-2 error is one made in statistics. It can be compared to a double error. Statisticians draw a figure similar to Figure 5.5 to chart the type-2 error. We have borrowed the chart to explain the type-2 error you must avoid in TBL.

There is obviously no problem if the student is right and the system judges him or her to be right. Likewise there is no problem if the learner is judged as wrong when he is actually wrong. That leaves two other possibilities. You have a problem with the validity of your system if it judges the learner right when he or she is wrong. How-

	Student actually right	Student actually wrong
Computer judgment right	✔	
Computer judgment wrong		✔

Figure 5.5 Type-2 Error Chart

	Inputs	Outputs
Psychomotor physical		
Simulation		
Sight		
Touch		
Realia		
Graphic		
Random audio		
Synthesized sound		
Manipulanda		
Sensors (probes)		

Figure 5.6 Inputs and Outputs Devices

ever, if you make an error of the second type (the type-2 error), look out! The student is highly unlikely to be pleased with the lesson if it says, "You are wrong!" when he or she is right.

What about other inputs and outputs

We authors were both drawn to work at the same company (First EG&G, then Allied Signal) at least in part, because of a simulator developed there by our prospective work group. A device used to train security guards, it features a scene depicting a situation in which the security guard must use his or her weapon. The simulator can shoot at a guard that does not take cover, if it is available. The guard uses a real pistol, modified to shoot infrared beams, and the location of the hit on the screen is compared to the scene displayed at that moment. The whole thing can branch instantly, based on actions.

What impressed us was the group's ability to connect the computer to a gun, a screen, and vests worn by the learner, while bringing very meaningful training out of the combination.

We want you to think of ways you could do the same thing. Do not be limited by thoughts of only a learner sitting at a desk with a computer. What is the human performance problem? Brainstorm how it could be solved if anything were possible. You may find that you can make that "anything" happen. Figure 5.6 lists various input and output devices that you could use.

Realia are any real thing. We have seen a classroom (not an aircraft hanger) with an entire real helicopter inside for use in learning how to maintain the helicopter. The helicopter, or parts of it could have been connected to a computer to ensure that the maintenance is being performed properly. Never lose sight of this kind of possibility.

Exercise 5-1: Individual project step #1—Defining the project (continued)

8. If you already have a system in mind, or must use one system or another due to organizational constraints, what is it?
9. Label your project as CAI, CMI, or something else.
10. Does this replace *existing* training?
11. Where will the course be delivered to the learners. For example, will it be delivered at each employee's work place?
12. How many different delivery locations are there? Describe them geographically; for example, are they all in one city, all in one building, or all over the world?
13. Do the students have to communicate with the instructor in real time? This means must a learner's question be answered immediately or can an overnight delay (for example) work?
14. Will the course materials require frequent maintenance (change or update)? How much (in percentages)? How frequently?
15. What is the target number of simultaneous learners?
16. Will they all use the same system type to learn?
17. What is the computer going to do? Describe in detail what the learner is going to see and do on the terminal.

Exercise Analysis: Many of the questions help to decide just what is required in terms of a delivery platform. If you must use a particular system you may not be free to speculate on a full range of possible options.

This book can help you with a CAI or CMI solution. If you are considering performance support, we recommend that you consider *Building Multimedia Performance Support Systems* by Angus Reynolds and Roberto Araya. If you are considering a totally different solution, we remind you that the main way to help people learn, using technology, is CAI, and the best to help them perform is performance support systems.

If the planned training replaces existing training, much is known about the learners and the topic. The project will evolve very differently from one for a new but unfinished product or service currently under development. The latter will be much more difficult.

Currently, delivery at learners' workstations is impractical for multimedia because so few workers have multimedia-capable computers. This will change over time.

The larger number of delivery sites will require greater delivery assets than a single site. Also the mechanics of servicing the courseware may need attention.

If the learners have to communicate with an expert in real time, the best answer today for typical installations is an 800 number. We believe that the Internet will offer the truly worldwide connections that have been a dream of courseware developers for many years.

Some advocates prefer CAI because of the ease of updating the materials. The degree of change can make a big difference. If it is limited and predictable, you can arrange for the user to make changes in a simple file using a word processor. High percentages of changes required very frequently may make TBL a poor choice for the instruction.

Every simultaneous learner will require a separate learning station. This will be a factor in determining the finances of the project.

If your learners do not all use the same type system, you will have to do double development, or at least to convert the lessons. This requires effort and affects the project's resource requirements.

The last question is for your own understanding. You must have a very clear picture of what will happen. If your thoughts are vague you must think more carefully about what will happen before you are really able to plan the project.

Towards a Technology of Learning

This completes our look at the human dimension in which you will employ technology to help people learn. Now, it's time to turn our attention to the so called "soft" technology of how to build learning programs. In Chapter 6 we will explore the field of instructional technology. Let's go!

6

Instructional Technology

Can you imagine what it would be like to sit in on James Bond's special agent training classes? One day his instructor might have said "Double-Oh-Seven, after our training course, you will be able to draw your Walther PPK pistol from the standard shoulder holster and fire five rounds from the hip within three seconds. On the 15-yard range all rounds will hit the standard 'Goldfinger' target between the eyes." James would have known exactly what he would have to be able to do after training. He could also foresee exactly how he would be tested and appreciate its relationship to his job.

A well-known trainer, the late Dugan Laird, once said, "Understanding the objectives is sometimes called 'motivation.' Until the learner has ownership, little useful learning will result." Bond was well on his way to being a well-trained secret agent as the beneficiary of training based on instructional technology. No wonder he was a success!

What You Will Learn in This Chapter

- The goals of instructional technology
- How to write and use learning objectives
- How to use a systematic approach to instructional development
- The differences between cognitive, psychomotor, and affective domains of learning
- Roles in the technology-based learning development team
- Criterion vs. norm-referenced instruction
- Mastery concept
- Phased approach to development

Instructional Systems Development (ISD)

Instructional Systems Development is usually referenced in its abbreviated form—ISD. ISD is a term for a variety of orderly, but flexible, processes for planning and developing instructional programs that ensure learners are taught the knowledge, skills, and attitudes (sometimes called KSAs) essential for successful job performance in a cost-effective way.

The five phases of ISD are:

- Analysis
- Design
- Development
- Implementation
- Evaluation

In its complete form, ISD depends on a description and analysis of fundamental information, such as the tasks necessary for performing the job, and learning objectives. The test is clearly overviewed before instruction begins, evaluation procedures are carried out to determine whether the objectives have been reached, and solid information is the basis of methods for revising the process.

You may have heard people speak against ISD, or you may even have decided that it is not for you. If you don't like the ISD label, don't use it. However, if you are doing performance-based training, we suggest that you update your knowledge of what ISD is really all about. A sound knowledge of some of the details can help you do an even better job. Quite frankly, it works wonderfully well for producing high quality technology-based courseware, so we use it exclusively.

About Learning Objectives

Learning objectives are the key part of the instructional system. We base each on the job tasks. That way the job tasks establish the basis for the instruction, and the matching learning objectives describe what you expect the learner will be able to do after instruction. The objectives include how we expect learners to do it and how we will know if they meet our expectations. Good courseware developers routinely prepare "James Bond" quality training.

Our work force's job tasks may be many and complex. They must do the tasks correctly for the organization to survive in a competitive world. A good courseware developer will identify the knowledge and skills needed to enable the learner to do the tasks. We describe the knowledge and skills for training as *learning objectives*. Finally, we set clear testing criteria so we will know for sure that the trainee has mastered our objectives.

Magerian objectives

Bob Mager wrote a book that has endured for almost 30 years. *Preparing Instructional Objectives* has had a powerful effect on the training field. In it, Mager suggests why we should use objectives and teaches how to write them. Carefully written objectives will identify the sought-after behavior to trainers as well as learners. They must communicate in clear and precise language. In the system developed by Mager, a well-written and useful learning objective contains three elements. They are:

- Behavior (performance)
- Condition(s)
- Standard (proficiency or criterion)

Condition

Condition describes the environment the learner must function within during the test. It states what items or circumstances will apply, be provided, or withheld from the learner. The condition may include manuals or tools the trainee will have to work with.

Typical conditions include: without references (a withheld condition); given a circuit diagram; given three hearings of recorded bearing sounds; while wearing the standard tool belt; given a table of figures showing monthly sales; or wearing the firefighter's air pack.

Behavior

The *behavior*, sometimes called *performance*, is what the learners must show to prove that they have grasped the task. It must be written in action words that state the main intent of the objective. The behavior should match the job task, should be stated clearly, and should describe the simplest and most direct behavior possible. We accomplish this by *observable and measurable* action words. For example: choose, describe, write, identify, or solve. We use the following words. We avoid words open to many interpretations. The lists are taken from Mager (1977).

Words Open to Many Interpretations	**Words Open to Fewer Interpretations**
to know	to write
to understand	to recite
to *really* understand	to identify
to appreciate	to sort
to *fully* appreciate	to solve
to grasp the significance of	to construct
to enjoy	to build
to believe	to compare
to have faith in	to contrast
to internalize	to smile

To be useful, performance statements must tell plainly how we will observe the trainee's learning. Words we avoid are: to know or understand. Bad performance statements include: "understand the Operator's Manual, and know Ohm's Law." Examples of good performance statements are: be able to name the parts of the disconnector switch assembly, and assemble the Mark IV power assist unit.

Criterion

The *criterion* is also called *standard,* or *proficiency*. It is the benchmark by which we evaluate performance. A proper criterion allows the designer and learner to measure classroom success. You must state it clearly. We base the criterion on time limit, accuracy, or quality.

A time-limit criterion shows the time for the learner to do the task. For example, the learner must be able to assemble the gear box within ten minutes. A quality-based criterion states the variation from perfection that will be acceptable. Accuracy, for example, might be: the learner must identify seven of ten blueprint errors to pass the test. Rather than go into great detail, you might say, for example, "according to tech manual specifications"

James Bond's learning objective

Let's see whether Bond's learning objective had all the requisite elements. The condition includes many elements:

Distance	15 yards
Weapon	Walther PPK pistol
Holster	standard shoulder holster
Position	shoot from the hip
Rounds	five rounds

The behavior includes two action verbs: draw and fire. The criterion that he must meet is also clearly pre-defined in high performance terms. Bond must place all rounds between the eyes of the 'Goldfinger' target. M5 did a good job with the objective.

Writing Instructional Objectives

An instructional objective is a statement of the planned instructional outcome. It should be a clear statement for the intended learner behavior. The statement should describe the planned student performance at the end of instruction. The statement should be worded in terms of learner performance, as opposed to instructor performance.

The behavior is a statement of what the learner is to do. The conditions is a statement of the conditions under which the performance is expected to occur. The criterion or standard is a description of the level of performance that must be demonstrated to be considered acceptable.

Training is best when we can reach the same level in the classroom as is needed on the job. Figure 6.1 is an example of a job performance measure that can be equaled in the classroom.

Sample job performance measure

Task:	Set DVM alignment to subscale.
Performance:	Monitor the DVM aperture current and use the SBF keypad to align the beam in the subscale.
Conditions:	As described in terminal learning objectives 1.0 initial conditions, and 2.0, power-up procedure.
Behavior:	1. Selects "DVM" position on the monitor select switch and the "TGT/RST" position on the S/A/T switch. 2. Selects and presses the following keys in the given sequence: "RESET", "5", "ENTER", "2", "3". Selects and presses the up arrow key until the current reading is maximized.
Standards:	+ or −0.001 μA from maximum on the subscale.

Figure 6.1 Sample Job Performance Measure

---

1. Is the desired behavior clearly stated?
2. If the main objective is not announced to the learner (covert) is there an indicator behavior stated?
3. Is the behavior the simplest and most direct possible?
4. Are the items or circumstances that will apply or be provided or deprived described?
5. Is the standard to which learner performance will be compared, in order to be considered acceptable, stated clearly?

Figure 6.2 A Checklist for Objectives

From the job performance measures, the subskills and prerequisite knowledge are defined. Any prerequisite knowledge is included.

However, to enable higher order problems in a user, prerequisite knowledge not given in the step list is essential. For the example in Figure 6.1 the learner must understand a three-dimensional beam-targeting system. This is a good candidate for an entry skills pretest. The learner should also be able to explain what is meant by the term "align" in this context. That definition should be taught in an earlier segment of the lesson.

The performance is a statement of what the learner is to do. The condition is a statement of the circumstance under which the performance is expected to occur. The criterion or standard is a description of the level of performance that must be demonstrated to be considered acceptable.

An instructional objective is a statement of the planned instructional outcome. It should be a clear statement of the intended learner behavior. The statement should describe the planned student performance at the end of instruction. The statement should be worded in terms of learner performance, as opposed to instructor performance.

Figure 6.2 provides a checklist for drafting objectives.

We urge you to complete the two exercises that we present here. We know that, if you do, your skill in the important task of writing learning objectives will be sharpened.

Exercise 6-1: Behavior Identification

Directions: In this exercise you identify correctly stated behaviors. Place a Y or an N in the blank at the right of the objective statement

States a
Behavior
Yes or No

1. Understand the Operator's Manual.   ____
2. Be able to write three examples of the instructional   ____
   advanced organizer.
3. Be able to name the parts of the disconnector switch   ____
   assembly.
4. Understand the meaning of Ohm's Law.   ____
5. Know the needs for the maintenance associated with   ____
   the stresses of over-revolution and with normal operation.
6. Be able to really understand the principles of   ____
   aerodynamics.
7. Be able to identify (circle) objectives that include a   ____
   statement of desired performance.
8. Recognize that the practical application of participative   ____
   management requires time, adjustments, and continuous
   effort.
9. Appreciate the ability of others, and perform as an   ____
   intelligent spectator.
10. Be able to describe the indications for the use of a   ____
    Mark IV power assist unit.[1]

Exercise 6-2: Analyzing Objectives

First, circle the behavior. If there is no behavior, it is not necessary to continue the analysis. Then circle the condition and standard, if they exist. For your convenience, you can check each element that you find in the spaces to the right.

B = behavior
C = condition
S = standard

B   C   S

1. Without reference materials, be able to describe   ___ ___ ___
   three common points of view regarding mass
   marketing that are not supported by available.
   research.
2. Be able to write a description of the steps   ___ ___ ___
   involved in writing a computer program.

---

[1]Behavior Identification Answers: 1-N, 2-Y , 3-Y, 4-N, 5-N, 6-N, 7-Y, 8-N, 9-N, 10-Y

3. Without regard to subject matter or pay grade, be able to describe ten examples of work practices that promote learning and ten examples of work practices that retard or interfere with learning.   ___ ___ ___

4. Given an oral description of the events involved in an aircraft accident, be able to fill out a standard FAA accident report.   ___ ___ ___

5. Given twenty minutes of instruction and a lab exercise, be able to develop an understanding of the difference between power, indifferent, and affiliate personality types, as taught in class. Criterion: 80 percent correct.   ___ ___ ___

6. The student will learn the basic wiring standards for the plant, according to local and state codes.   ___ ___ ___

7. Given three hearings of recorded bearing sounds, beable to state whether a given sound, heard separately, was or was not one of the three heard previously.   ___ ___ ___

8. Given the sell price of two different-sized packages of a potential product and the quantity of the contained in each, be able to calculate the unit price product of each and state which is the most profitable. Assume equal quality of products.   ___ ___ ___

9. Given a list of descriptions of management behavior, be able to differentiate (sort) between those that reflect Theory A and Theory B.   ___ ___ ___

10. Given a table of figures indicating quantities which consumers will purchase at different prices, be able to draw a demand curve.   ___ ___ ___

11. Be able to locate correctly the following three robot joints: shoulder, elbow, wrist.   ___ ___ ___

12. Write all of the return privileges described in the standard sales contract.   ___ ___ ___

13. Demonstrate a knowledge of the principles of thermodynamics.   ___ ___ ___

14. Using any available reference materials, be able to name correctly every item shown on each of twenty blueprints.   ___ ___ ___

15. Be able to know well the cardinal rules of accounting.   ___ ___ ___

16. Be able to write a coherent essay on the subject "How to Write Objectives for Adult Instruction." Individual notes, as well as any class references, may be used.   ___ ___ ___

17. Be able to write an essay on supervision.   ___ ___ ___

18. Be able to develop logical approaches in the   _____ __ __
    solution of labor relations problems.
19. Be able to recognize correct and incorrect ways   _____ __ __
    of placing and removing power assist units for
    machines (a) that are under powered and
    (b) that are normally configured.

SAMPLE TEST ITEM
Look at the photographs in Envelope A and place
an X on those showing incorrect ways of placing and
removing power assist units.[2]

An objective need not be a single sentence. Often, several sentences are required to communicate the full intent of the objective clearly. This is especially true when the objective requires creative activity of the learner. For example:

- Given a practical problem, write a fully commented computer program with Aztec C, within two hours. The program must completely solve the problem, as written. You must apply at least three rules of good programming in the development of your program.

Another example of a longer objective shows psychomotor activity:

- On the apprenticeship mock-up, be able to feed and pull a 16-gauge wire for termination. The completed feed must meet state, community, and plant electrical codes.

The Development Process

The courseware development process most frequently used is the instructional systems development (ISD) or "systems approach." Whether they acknowledge the

---

[2]Analyzing Objectives Answers: 1-B=describe, C=without reference materials, S=3 and not supported by research; 2-B=write, C=not present, S=not present; 3-B=describe, C=without regard to subject matter or pay grade, S=20 examples (10 of one or 10 of another); 4-B=fill out, C=given an oral description, S=standard FAA accident report; 5-No performance. Understand is not a measurable performance.; 6-no performance. Learn is not a measurable performance.; 7-B=state, C=given three hearings of recorded bearing sounds, S=was or was not one of the three previous; 8-B=calculate, C=given the sell price of two different sized packages and the quantity contained in each and equal quality, S=unit price of each and most profitable; 9-B=sort, C=given a list of descriptions of management behavior, S=reflect Theory A and Theory B; 10-B=draw, C=given a table of figures indicating quantities, S=demand curve; 11-B=locate, C=not present, S-three specific joints; 12-B=write, C=not present, S=all; 13-no performance. Demonstrate a knowledge is not a measurable performance.; 14-B=name, C=using any available reference materials, S=every item shown on 20 blueprints; 15-no performance. Be able to know well is not a measurable performance.; 16-B=write, C=individual notes as well as class references, S=not present. Who can be certain what the professor will consider to be a coherent essay; 17-B=write, C=not present, S=not present; 18-no performance. Be able to develop logical approaches is not a measurable performance.; 19-B=place an X, C=photographs, S=correct and incorrect for 2 types of configurations.

heritage, almost all models of instructional development are based on the landmark Florida State University model produced in 1976.[3] Many organizations use a variant of the name, such as TSD, systems approach to training (SAT), or some other, but the content is the same. Some people glorify in announcing a new model, but the bulk of instructional technologists recognize that it is only a minor variant on the main ISD theme.

We use ISD (and you should) because the phased approach, emphasis on instructional objectives, and concept of "mastery" that characterize it match perfectly with many developers' own philosophies of instruction. In TBL this is especially significant. As we showed in Chapter 5, TBL matches very well with adult instruction. Its match with mastery learning makes it all the stronger.

The use of the ISD model results in the division of an instructional development project into distinct phases. The phases of a typical model used for training development, and the one we will refer to consistently in this book, include:

- Analysis
- Design
- Development
- Implementation
- Evaluation

Most activities in a particular phase are the same, regardless of the delivery method or media to be used. Let's look briefly at each of the phases.

Analysis

During the analysis phase, one of the tasks typically carried out is defining the needs and the constraints. Identifying the constraints can point up how the various restrictions can affect possible solutions in a particular case. The availability of funds and the delivery environment are two factors that could affect a training project. The basic analysis is of the job performed. During the analysis of the target population, factors such as learners' previously acquired knowledge and skills and present qualifications are identified. Geographic distribution of learners can favor various strategies. This phase also includes the analysis of the job involved and its specific functions. A key possibility of the analysis is determining that instructional activities will not solve the particular performance problem. Another possible outcome is the determination to develop a job aid rather than training. The product of the analysis phase is the Analysis Report.

Design

Regular chores included in the design phase include: specification of learning activities; and assessment, evaluation, and learning transfer systems. Determinations

---

[3]*Interservice Procedures for Instructional Systems Development* (Contract No: N61339-73-C-0150). Center for Educational Technology. 1976. Tallahassee, FL: Florida State University.

about the media best suited are made at this time. Learning activities may include a full spectrum of methods and media, called the instructional strategy. An internal and external search is conducted for appropriate existing instructional materials, since they are almost always cheaper than developing new instruction. The product of the design phase is the Design Document.

Development

The development phase is unique for any particular project. The activities, and the people involved, depend on the methods and media selected for the learning activities. Diverse development activities occur in multimedia instruction. An intermediate product of the development phase is the Programmer Ready Materials (PRM).

Graphic art is needed to enhance the screens and make the content clear. Video must be storyboarded, scripted, shot, edited, and compressed into digital files. The programmers complete the lesson code. Editors check everything and the subject matter experts ensure that the content has not become twisted.

Formative evaluation activities are conducted as a part of the development phase to ensure that the instruction works. The formative evaluation is conducted while the course is under development, via individual and small group trials, to try out and revise the course materials. The revisions made at this point make the materials better when they are put into general use. The actual production of the final materials is not begun until the formative evaluation is completed. Formative evaluation is (unfortunately) often omitted from development. This is done at great peril to the success of the project. Implementing unvalidated courses will nearly always result in unpredicted problems in the initial training environment. The final product of the development phase is the completed courseware.

Implementation

The implementation phase is the regular delivery of the instruction to the intended target population. All instructional activities are part of this phase, and generally include efforts towards delivery, support, and maintenance. Support may include a course "help" telephone hotline for remote learners. Maintenance includes upkeep of the instructional materials.

Evaluation

Evaluation comes in two parts, *formative* and *summative*. The formative evaluation part of the development phase was described in that section.

The summative evaluation is to measure the effectiveness of the course in solving the problem for which it was created. This phase is conducted while the course is in regular use. The relative ease of revising courseware already in use makes the summative evaluation a powerful technique, rather than an "empty" exercise. Evaluation is explored in greater depth in Chapter 7.

A Case Example of the Instructional Development Process

Suppose our "big boss," Joan Smith, is tired of seeing wads of bubblegum scattered over the floors in the company offices. She wants it stopped. The desks of employees are all ten feet from the wastebaskets, and she believes leaving a desk to dispose of a wad of bubblegum is a loss of valuable time. The boss calls you in and says, "Train all employees to hit the baskets! I want a training video made right now!" Analysis of the situation suggests that this is not a training problem. Someone should convince the boss that more, properly located wastebaskets would save time and money. They will also reduce hazards from sailing wads. The implication is that, during consideration of training needs, you may find solutions for important organizational problems. Unfortunately, there are many problems you should not solve by instruction.

Try to avoid needless training. Search for the problem, identify it, study alternative solutions, such as more wastebaskets. Don't train when you can find non-training solutions.

For our purposes, however, let's accept the boss's dictate. You must train the staff to hit wastebaskets. Here is a simplified approach to the instructional development procedure.

Step	Activity
Analyze the task	During this step you need to determine the difference between a good and poor performer. Why is a good performer good? What are the different conditions under which the staff throws "paper" or "bubblegum" wads? You note everything the staff must do, and under what conditions. For example: note locations of open windows, deflecting walls, and air ducts, and you list the differences between successful and poor performers. You are also determining possible alternatives to training, such as performance aids, and noting data for their design.
Prepare objectives and tests	Here, you determine what the boss has decided is acceptable performance. You prepare a performance test that will prove that the learners meet these standards. You also prepare the objectives that describe what they must be able to do, how well, and under what conditions. Your objective may read like this: Given ten various sized wads of bubblegum, learners will be able to sink at least eight of ten bubblegum wads in the wastebasket. The wastebasket is 12 inches in diameter, its rim is 20 inches off the floor, and it is placed 10 feet away against a plastered wall. Please note that you have already made some decisions regarding media—at least for the testing phase.

Step	**Activity**
Refine and sequence objectives, select media, design and prepare materials	Now you begin breaking the complete objective down into smaller objectives to teach those skills that separated the good throwers from the bad. Your lesson content may need to teach many things. These include how to check for open windows or hot air drafts. The lesson may also teach how to discriminate between the weights of different sizes of bubblegum wads, how to hold bubblegum wads, and how to judge distance to the basket and wad entry angle into it. Here again, we must make some media decisions to communicate the lesson content effectively. We must make decisions on how to distribute the material in the most practical manner. What media can best demonstrate, prompt, inform, provide practice, and give feedback to the students? It also must fit the constraints of your budget and facilities.

For maximum efficiency, design your lesson content as "lean" as possible to be sure you are not overteaching. You also prepare a set of pretests for the course and for each lesson unit. This step is critical. It prevents those who can already do some or all the tasks from having to take all the lessons, whether they need to or not. |
| *Test the materials and revise the content and media as necessary* | During this step you take your rough lesson and performance aids and test them with the cheapest materials, most flexible medium (or media) available on a small group of *representative* learners you have intentionally *undertaught* with the material. You can later add instruction in places where students do not perform to our standard. Remember, you can always find out what you didn't teach but you will never know what you overtaught.

The same principle holds true for the medium or media used to present the instruction. Too often we assume the lesson needs a more costly and exotic medium than it really needs.

So you revise and test, and revise again. You continue until the lesson finally works—the students complete the objective, at an acceptable level of performance.

Now you're ready to conduct the training and make the boss happy. During this phase you follow up on the lesson results frequently to make final adjustments. You also worry and pray a lot.

The boss was happy simply because you did the training, but for you to be happy it has to achieve its purpose. If missed baskets meant a loss to the company it would matter greatly whether the training worked. And, if the training was important enough to do, its outcome matters. You follow up to ensure that the learners can actually do what you trained them to do on the job. |

You have successfully solved the wastebasket performance problem. Now it is time to explain the process used in this guide to help you in selecting and developing media for instruction.

ISD and TBL

Let's look at a series of factors that explain why ISD is well-suited to business and industrial training.

Instruction—A Harvard case study

Every year at the high school graduation ceremony the student with the best grades makes the Valedictorian speech. Often that Valedictorian has received nothing but A marks since kindergarten.

In the fall, several hundred students, who include many of the high school valedictorians, arrive to begin their freshman year at Harvard University, the oldest and best-known university in the United States.

Sometime during the fall the first test is given and some of these former Valedictorians, who have received nothing but A marks since kindergarten, get Cs. How could this be? Let's forget any that spent their time partying; these are serious students who did their level best. Something must be very wrong for their formerly A work to drop to a C. What has changed in a system that gave them As regularly?

The normal curve

There is nothing wrong with the learners. The key to the surprising fall from grace of these students is that the system has not changed at all. The grading system in schools and universities works pretty much the same. The best work gets the As, the weakest work gets the Cs, and the people in the middle get Bs. It worked that way since kindergarten.

The big difference is that these former A students are playing in a bigger game. They were the best of their age in their home community, but Harvard is filled with people that are the best. In the newly formed group, some are better learners than others. As Ross Perot says, "It's that simple."

Figure 6.3 shows the common distribution of many natural phenomena. The speed of the 6th-grade students in running 50 meters could be plotted to reveal a similar configuration—some faster, some slower, most in the middle.

Using the principle of the normal curve, the best work in the group is marked A, the poorest is marked C, and the bulk is marked with a B.

Criterion vs norm-referenced instruction

The term used to describe the grading principles that the Valedictorians found at Harvard is norm-referenced instruction. Norm-referenced instruction compares the learners to each other to assign grades. Our entire educational system is based on it.

It has obvious flaws. In any year the true achievement of the learners may vary, because some classes are better than others. Nevertheless, the teacher gives the best learners As and the poorer learners Cs. All the rest get Bs. This is not happy news if

Placeholder for normal curve graphic

Figure 6.3 Normal Curve

your work would have earned an A last year, but in this year's competition you get only a B.

A norm-referenced system doesn't make any sense at all for training in business and industry. We don't really care whether one student is better than another. We want to and must know whether the performance is good enough to get the job done. This is called criterion-referenced instruction, because success is measured against a criterion or fixed standard.

Mastery learning

It is like drawing a line in the sand. All the learners whose results put them across the line have "mastered" the instruction. It isn't a competition. The instructors do everything possible to help the learners achieve mastery.

It is common practice to practice with test-like questions or the actual test. We're sure this would horrify medieval scholars, but it makes sense in today's world of work. If the test will be to install a programmable logic controller, we expect to have the learners make similar installations repeatedly in training. Harvard's tests are designed to separate the students. Training's tests are designed to measure a learner's readiness to perform on the job.

The Instructional Triangle

The instructional triad or triangle is the matching of an employee's on-the-job performance with the instruction to enable it and the test to ensure that it is learned. This simple concept is at the heart of all performance-based training. If even one of these three elements is missing, or is not matched with the other two, the result of the training effort may not meet your organization's needs.

Performance-based training is simple to describe, but a lot of work to do properly. It is the only reasonable way to do training when the outcome really matters. In it, learning activities are designed to provide the specific knowledge and skills required to perform the task on-the-job. It is exactly the same as "performance-based instruction" and "criterion-referenced instruction" (CRI). A complete system can be viewed as an "instructional triad" or an "instructional triangle." See the added information and figure on the next page. The three areas that require attention in performance-based training are the job, the instruction, and the assessment or test. They must match exactly to guarantee instructional success. Figure 6.4 illustrates the instructional triad concept.

The job

Often, attention is directed at a job because an imbalance exists. When there is a difference between *desired* and *actual* behavior for a specific work situation, we call the shortfall a "performance discrepancy." When you identify such a discrepancy and determine it can best be corrected through instruction, you bring your instructional system to bear on the problem. Whenever the job is new, or when it is not well understood by the training staff, its requirements may be determined through a task analysis. Otherwise, the specific discrepancy is the focus of your training action.

Performance objectives identify the capability the learner must demonstrate on the job. The instruction you develop is intended to enable this performance. The more familiar learning objective can be satisfied in the classroom, but the performance objective must equal the task at the job site.

The instruction

Learning objectives, also called *instructional* objectives, are the key parts of the instructional system. Carefully written objectives identify the sought-after behavior for the trainers as well as for the learners. Learning objectives must communicate in clear and precise language. Learning objectives are very well known and widely used components of instruction.

You must exercise extreme care to ensure that the learning objectives are as close to the performance objective that describes the task at the job site as possible. In some organizations, a weakness in this match means that the efforts expended to make the instruction good may be partly or wholly wasted because they focus on an earning objective that isn't tightly connected to the job.

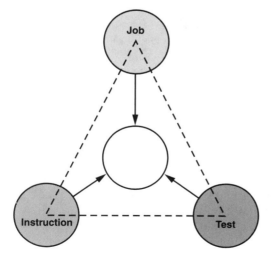

Figure 6.4 Instructional Triangle

The test

Organizing, delivering, and verifying instruction along the lines described here aims at "mastery learning"—evaluating a learner's performance according to a predetermined criterion. Mastery learning stands in contrast to norm-referenced learning, in which the learner is compared to other learners instead of to a fixed standard. Examples of norm-referenced learning are common in public school and college. The best score achieved on a test is graded A and so forth. Excellent examples of mastery learning are found in technical and skills training. The "best score" principle is replaced by a "go/no-go" standard. We don't want to compare learners with each other, but to a particular standard required for success on the job.

Since our learning objectives are as close as possible to the requirements of the job, we verify the learner's acquisition of knowledge and skill by observing actual performance whenever possible. We use performance measurement to determine if the learner's performance on a given task reaches the predetermined standard for that specific task. Meeting that standard is called "mastery."

Tests of this kind are called *performance* tests. Such a test involves performance of a task under test conditions to determine the achievement of the learning objectives by the learner. The performance checklist is used to carry out a performance test. The checklist includes a breakdown of each task into elements that must be correctly performed to indicate whether the learner satisfactorily meets the performance standards that are described in the objective. Performance tests are almost always evaluated on a go or no-go basis.

People in Technology-Based Instructional Development

The courseware development people consist of the different members of the instructional development team. Of course, in smaller organizations there may not be a team of six or more people. These are really roles, not people. One person often performs one or more roles. One person can perform all the roles when working alone. The six roles involved are shown in Figure 6.5.

Each of these courseware development process personnel and roles is described at the end of this chapter.

What About Quality Assurance?

This completes the core information you need to make a sensible design and carry it out. We will consistently apply the contents of this chapter throughout the book because the basics of ISD are applicable to every phase of every project that you carry out.

Sadly, some organizations do not even bother with tests. Without a check to ensure that the instruction was learned by the participants, we can't be sure that on-the-job performance will be up to snuff.

We all try our best, and our instruction is developed and delivered to bring the learner's performance up to par. But we have to apply quality assurance to our instruction just as we do to our processes. All the parts have to pass an instructional quality-assurance inspection.

• Analyst • Designer • Developer • Media specialist • Programmer/data entry person • Subject matter expert (SME)

Figure 6.5 Technology-Based Courseware Development Roles

The learning objectives must match the job performance as closely as possible in a classroom. The instructions must be designed to help the learner master the objectives. The tests must measure achievement of the objectives. Making all three match is a good bet for success!

Now, in Chapter 7, we will focus on one of the least understood parts of ISD, the evaluation. Time to move on!

7

Evaluation

Training is a costly way for organizations to solve human performance problems. Every company that we know of consciously avoids wasting money. Management has the right to expect that, when courseware developers expend resources, they've been well employed. Good training developers are in touch with the goals of their organizations, or clients, and are proud of what they do. We want our training to be as good as we can make it. These facts combine to provide us with good reason to do a top-notch evaluation of our training programs.

Remember, evaluation is not the same thing as testing. If that makes sense to you, this chapter may not be needed. You may be quite familiar with evaluating training and may realize that it is a comprehensive set of activities designed to improve it.

What You Will Learn in This Chapter

- How evaluation fits into the scheme of courseware development
- What formative evaluation is
- What summative evaluation is

In general

The evaluation is composed of activities you conduct to get ideas for improvement, to justify the use of training to solve the performance problem, or to help decide whether to continue offering a program. We use evaluations to decide who should participate in future programs, to determine whether a program is accomplishing its objectives, to gather data to assist in marketing future programs, and to identify the strengths and weaknesses in the training process.

Evaluation Procedures

We are tempted to call this section *formal* evaluation procedures, but that strikes us as potentially confusing. There are no *informal* procedures. Every evaluation is, or should be, a serious attempt to improve instruction.

Evaluation is one of the phases in the ISD process to determine weak areas in a course and to improve the instruction. The ISD phases are *analysis, design, development*, and *implementation*. We can consider evaluation as two separate activities. The first part you conduct using learners *during development*, long before the general implementation of the program materials. This part is called *formative* evaluation and is very important in technology-based learning. The second part, called *summative* evaluation, measures the effectiveness of the materials in solving the instructional problem that you identified in the analysis phase.

Formative Evaluation

Sometimes called *developmental testing*, formative evaluation is the evaluation of material, conducted during that material's early developmental stages, to revise materials before widespread use. Formative evaluation is conducted during the development phase of ISD and is applicable to all kinds of instruction, not only technology-based. Numerous articles and books have been written about formative evaluation, and it is impossible for us to cover all the recommended strategies here.

Purpose

The purpose is to ensure that the delivered instructional product is as valid and reliable as possible.

What it is not

Some courseware developers submit their work to an editor to identify and correct spelling and grammar problems. This is important, but it is not formative evaluation—or any other kind of evaluation. It is simply the needed developmental editing process of the material. It is *development*.

Some courseware developers submit their work to the SME to identify and correct any problems with the content—this is important, but it is not formative evaluation either. It is simply the required developmental content check made to ensure that the designer has not distorted the material in presenting it. It is *development*.

Some courseware developers ask a valued colleague to review their work to identify any weakness in the design and to suggest improvements. This is extremely useful, but it is also not formative evaluation. It is simply the developmental quality content check made (by those not working alone) to ensure that the material is as good as it possibly can be. It is *development*.

Only trials of the instruction under development, with genuine members of the target population (unless that is impossible), count as formative evaluation. Make sure that you don't confuse the various edits and quality processes with the critical step of trying the program under development with real learners.

Step 1: One-on-One Trials

One-on-one trials are conducted to determine how well the materials are likely to work. Developers often skip his step in the formative evaluation process, due to lack of understanding, laziness, cost-cutting, or its inapplicability to instructor-led instruction. This is a pity, since it is an extremely fruitful way of understanding the effectiveness of instruction that is under development.

The reason that developers omit this step from the instructional development process due to cost is that it requires the full time attention of a developer with a member of the target population of learners for even longer than the instruction itself is expected to take.

Here is how to conduct one-on-one trials. The instructional materials are in an early state of completion. In the case of technology-based multimedia instruction, the programmer-ready materials that represent each screen may be used to represent the lesson. You should spend considerable care in reassuring the learner that the session is in no way a measure of his or her knowledge and is purely to improve some instruction that will be delivered. Then, you explain the process to be followed. Tell the learner that he or she must read everything aloud and *think aloud*, and that since the learner is surely always thinking, you will remind the learner to voice those thoughts whenever there is a period of silence.

The learner then proceeds through the material, reading everything aloud. Learner thoughts may include: "I don't see how the underpin is connected to the pneumatic system" or "I'm not sure exactly what a Eurodollar is." Naturally, you thought that the learner would understand since you attempted to make it so clear. The learner's difficulty is an indication that further explanation of these points must be provided before the development is complete. You must never instruct the learner directly. Instead you must be prepared to intervene immediately with trial fixes, such as editing the materials on the spot with a pencil, or adding words or phrases intended to clarify the point.

On the basis of the first one-on-one trial, you modify the instruction and prepare an updated version for a similar session with a different learner. You repeat the same process and, if additional items are detected that require expansion or change, you complete the revisions. The one-on-one trial may be repeated a third time to ensure that all fixes work with real learners and that no undetected problems exist. It is rare to use more than three one-on-one trials in development of a single instructional product.

The learners that are selected to participate in the one-on-one trials must be average-or-below members of the target population. The reason for not using superior learners is that they may be able to make connections that are not really clear in the materials, indicating that the instruction works when it will surely fail as soon as it is presented to average learners.

Step 2: Small Group Trials

Small group trials are conducted to determine how well the essentially completed materials teach an increased variety of learners. We expect that we can learn something by trying out the instruction on small groups, and there is an expectation that the materials will be revised to reflect our discoveries.

Sometimes small group trials are conducted using quite polished materials. Other small group trials use fairly rough representations of the final materials. The typical case uses draft materials.

The procedure is to deliver the materials without interference, and particularly without help of any kind. The evaluator should only involve himself during the instruction if the learner becomes totally stuck and unable to go on (this can happen with technology-based instruction). Otherwise, he or she should observe the learners unobtrusively. The whole point of observing is to detect the learner's unexpected responses to stimuli, bewilderment, or other actions that indicate that the materials are not working as expected. Once the instructional session is completed the evaluator can interview the learners and/or ask them to complete a questionnaire.

It is possible to determine the correct size of the small group using statistical methods, but this is rarely done in the work environment. It is more often a case of "how many can we get" than of seeking optimum numbers. The total size of the small group is also affected by the size of the total training population, since we cannot eat up the whole population in testing materials. A colleague who works with a group of 13 learners performing highly critical tasks faces the problem of using nearly 10% of the eventual training population anytime she works with a learner to try out in-development materials.

Step 3: Field Trial or Pilot Tests

Field trials (sometimes called pilot tests) are conducted to answer the question: "How does the instruction work in real conditions?" Field trials use completed materials that are expected to be totally free of flaws and to meet the original need for instruction.

The delivery of the instruction in the field trial is completely normal. What is different is that it is monitored much more closely than would be the case for mature in-process instruction. Notes are taken for consideration in modification that might be required to "fine tune" the instruction.

Since real-world employees include a much wider variety of individuals than could ever be included in small group trials, pilot tests do sometimes reveal "glitches" in the instruction that were previously undetected despite the development team's best efforts to root them out.

Typical field trials include some unit of a total population. Groups constituting more than 15–20% of the total population are too large in the event that major problems are encountered. Groups that constitute less than 1% of the total population are unlikely to be sufficiently representative to ensure that all defects are completely identified. For example, American Express might initiate delivery of a new travel agent training program in one of its regional offices. Ford could use a particular assembly plant. Marriott could try a new program in a single hotel property, or in representative properties. On the other hand, an organization like McDonald's would not achieve the same assurance by using a single store. Only one store does not represent any significant fraction of the thousands of stores.

It would be better to adopt an attitude often associated with Japanese quality programs toward flaws uncovered in field tests. We are told that the Japanese are delighted to uncover a defect, to fix it, and to eliminate it from the product. The good news about a defect in instruction uncovered during a field trial is that it won't be seen by all the other employees who complete the revised version of the same training.

Summative Evaluation

Summative evaluation is the collection and interpretation of data to determine the value of training. It is the evaluation of instruction conducted during and after delivery to assess the instructional environment, learning, on-the-job use, and return on investment. Summative evaluation is conducted during the evaluation phase of ISD. Kirkpatrick's four-level model of summative evaluation is often used.

Don Kirkpatrick already did the hard work. He organized the evaluation process for management training. His series of four summative evaluation steps have proven themselves over time. They're widely used in good training programs in a variety of industries. They make much sense for your technical and skills training programs. These are the four steps to a good evaluation program. For further reading about evaluation, we suggest you try Donald Kirkpatrick's, *Evaluating Training Programs: The Four Levels* (1994, New York: Berrett-Koeher).

Purpose

The purpose of summative evaluation is to determine that the instruction has accomplished the purpose for which it was developed.

What it is not

Many people think that evaluation is tests. That is not an accurate way to think of evaluation. Testing is one aspect of a complete evaluation, but certainly not the only one, and not the most productive. Tests are one element in a comprehensive summative evaluation system.

Levels

Kirkpatrick described four levels of summative evaluation; each requires more effort than the one before, but provides a bigger reward for the effort expended.

Level 1: Reaction—How well did the learners like the program?

Reaction gathers the trainees' opinions about the instruction. We're all familiar with reaction sheets. They're known by many names and are a part of almost all training sessions. They tell how well you've managed the training environment.

Level 2: Learning—What principles, facts and techniques were learned?

Learning is usually measured by a performance or verbal test. The test measures how well the instruction succeeded. What you can really find out from a test is how well the learner has learned. To do so, you have to be closely matched to and measure the knowledge and skills you want the employee to gain from training. The basic point is that what you've decided that the employee will learn in training must really be what's needed to solve the basic problem. It's too bad that many organizations don't bother to test the knowledge and skills employees should have gained from training. This is especially true of supervisors' training.

Level 3: Behavior—What changes in job behavior resulted from the program?

Behavior usually takes the form of a survey sent to the trainee's manager 60 or 90 days after training. It asks the manager how well the training has enabled the employee to do what's needed to get the job done. Some courseware developers send a similar form to the trainee. It asks the trainee how well the training prepared him or her to do the job well. The use of this technique can be very valuable in maintaining the quality of training programs—even good ones. It helps to ensure that graduates continue to measure up in a changing environment. Many organizations don't bother to do this step. Those that do get good results.

Level 4: Results—What were the tangible results of the program in terms of reduced cost, improved quality, improved quantity, etc.?

Results produces a "bottom line" measurement. It measures the increased production, reduced scrap, or other benefit that was management's original goal for the training program. Most technical and skills training can be related to a measure of value. Measures such as reduced equipment down time, less scrap, and improved quality or productivity have a known value to the organization. If you pick the right things to train, and your programs work, you can measure their value. Sadly, most organizations don't bother with this step, but you can join the pros who ensure that training's results outweigh its cost.

What is wrong with this picture?

This is a strange list. Organizations do each step less often than the one before it, yet the steps most commonly used provide the least important information. To improve an organization's training quality, establish and maintain a complete summative evaluation system. Make it a point to use the more valuable techniques.

Market Evaluation

There is an "ultimate" evaluation that can be easily forgotten in zeal to complete the technical evaluation. The marketplace will be the ultimate judge of the value of a deliverable. If the learners dislike it for some reason it will not matter how many SMEs or Ph.D.'s pronounced it worthy. There are countless cases in which one or more engineers presented training on a machine to the plant where installed, as a part of the sales contract. We can recall hearing GM plant general mechanics tell of the training they received from the engineer, how little they were able to understand, and how they had to learn how the machine worked on their own in the days and weeks following. (Another part of the difficulty is that the manual is usually written by the same people, or same sort of people, that delivered the training.)

The lesson here for us is that we must be alert to ALL considerations that affect the lesson, and take them to heart.

Tips on Evaluation

- Use formative evaluation techniques
- Relate the results to the cost
- Make sure the problem is fixed by the training

What Does It Cost?

Other people will take a hard look at another side of your planned courseware, and you'd better be ready. Their decision may preclude you from ever developing the course you have in mind. You have to prove that developing the courseware is a good idea from the financial point of view. We will explore just that in Chapter 8. Let's move on!

8

Cost Benefits of
Technology-Based Learning

Do you know where your children are? We often hear this on radio and TV. The question is supposed to make parents aware of a potential problem. On the other hand, what we ought to hear in our organizations, but don't, is, "Do you know whether the money spent on training is paying off?" Too bad. Many companies should consider the question because the answer would make them aware of a potential problem that may or may not be under control.

Aetna's Stan Malcolm tells us that, in the life insurance industry, the average turnover in the sales force is 75% in the first 36 months. This means that, if it takes 18 months to develop a fully competent salesperson, and 75% of the new salespeople are gone within three years, the revolving door is very expensive. Everybody in life insurance already knows that. Stan asks a salient question, "What are the critical numbers for jobs in your business?" He follows with a suggestion that illustrates how experienced training professionals look at costs. "Don't think in terms of annual turnover. Look at the time it takes to at least break even on your investment in recruiting and developing people into competent performers."

In fact, managers often feel that they are on top of things because they know that training is happening. They actually think that learning is also happening, but that is not always true. Focusing solely on the activity per se, instead of cost and result, reflects this. Statistics that are kept on how many underwent training, and possibly how well they enjoyed it, are totally out of tune with the financial management successful companies apply to other areas. This emphasis is misplaced because it ignores the whole reason we are doing the training in the first place. The "golden rule" of training is that it shouldn't cost more than the problem it is intended to fix.

What You Will Learn in This Chapter

- To explain the basic concepts and terminology of cost-benefit analysis
- To describe the types of costs and benefits involved in technology-based instruction, and how they are measured
- How to formulate cost-benefit models
- How to conduct a cost-benefit study
- How to explain the factors involved in cost-benefit trade-offs

You Benefit, Too

Cost-benefit analysis is one more way to improve your understanding of your training system, and a very valuable tool at that. Don't fail to use it this way. Don't let the numbers get in the way of learning more about what is going on. Right from the beginning, you will hear what people say when you are gathering information. You'll have another chance when you present your results. For the real payoff, focus on new information, or newly understood relationships, about the problem you are studying.

Heavy-Duty Accounting?

It is only fair to point out that there are two levels at which you can do cost-benefit analysis. We focus on the basic methods used to gain an understanding about how well a training program is working. Accountants will be impressed if you present a case using the formulations and financial analysis techniques with which they are familiar. For example, including consideration of the time value of money and your organization's internal rate of return.

Brave the New Terminology

Don't be put off by the terms and concepts used in cost-benefit analysis. There is a difference between cost-benefit and cost-effectiveness. Cost-benefit is an attempt to weigh the costs of training against the outcomes achieved. Cost-effectiveness focuses on comparing the costs of two or more training alternatives, or examines ways to reduce an existing program's costs.

We will explore both. The benefits that we seek include, but are not limited to, *increases* or improvements in customer satisfaction, end-of-course achievement, job performance, productivity, quality, or sales. We will also be equally pleased to achieve *decreases* in equipment downtime, injuries, scrap or rejects, turnover, or other problems.

Cutting costs

One thing we are not even considering is taking a "meat cleaver" to the budget. That is called cost-avoidance. We want to look for benefits that create additional revenues or increase productivity. Simply cutting costs can never achieve that. It doesn't take brains or talent to spend less—anybody can do it except Congress. In other words, we want it (or should want it) better—not cheaper. Using cost-benefit analysis is a way to get more for less. It's like buying wholesale!

Opportunity costs are those costs or benefits other than labor, overhead, and outlay costs. Lost opportunity costs are benefits that are not being realized. For example, with improved training salespeople could increase the number of orders, or production employees could increase the output of finished products.

Counting (blessings) benefits

When you want to improve the effectiveness of training you will want to look at expected benefits. Let's say that you want to provide an equipment simulation on a desktop PC. Your new approach may cost more, but is justified by increased employee proficiency. Your benefits analysis must link the training program's features with the program's major goals, and with those of the organization. You can link each training system attribute with its payoff in training or operational outcomes. You can double the emphasis on "hands on" practice time. If you do, will the technicians be twice as proficient at maintaining equipment? Will the value of the reduction in downtime be more than the cost of achieving it?

Cost-Benefit Techniques

There are four methods ordinarily used to analyze cost-benefit. They are:

- Benefits
- Life cycle
- Productivity
- Resource requirements

These are well covered by Greg Kearsley in his chapter on *"Cost and Benefits of Technology Based Training"* in the *ASTD Handbook of Instructional Technology*. Briefly, here are the ideas.

Benefits

Quantifying benefits is a difficult task, because the outcomes of training are often intangible or difficult to translate into dollar amounts. Places you can look include salary, sales, and expenses. Job performance or organizational results can even be expressed in financial terms. Most technical training is much easier to quantify than most management training, because it is linked to processes and products with known or measurable value.

Life cycle

Often you can only determine true cost savings by considering the entire lifetime of the training project. The life cycle model is shown in Figure 8.1. The life cycle method's strong point is that you can evaluate the total costs of each of the planned program's phases to determine whether it will result in a net cost savings.

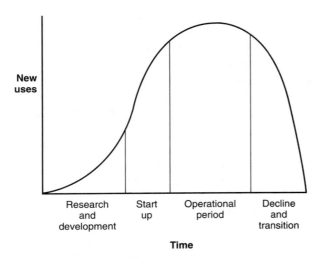

Figure 8.1 Technology Life Cycle

Figure 8.1 shows the expenditure profile for most training projects. Expenditure corresponds to new implementations. The figures show that some money must be spent before anything at all happens. We label these costs as research and development (even if no research is involved). The next phase is called startup and marks a sharp rise in money spent on the training technology since it has come of age. The operational period, sometimes called the "steady state," is the main time during which the program is active. This period is much longer for some technology than for others. Often a program that does its job well, and remains current, is delivered by an obsolescent technology for years. Finally, the aged program is phased out or eliminated during a phase called decline. At the same time there is a transition to a new program. In Figure 8.1 the new technology's start up phases coincide with the decline of the old and are shown with a dotted line.

For example, the desktop PC equipment simulation we considered may have high start-up costs compared with the current or a competing method, such as lecture. If we compare the costs for the current year's budget only we will never choose a training method that requires equipment purchase. However, when we are able to look at the whole picture (perhaps over five years) it may turn out that the cost savings that will be produced during the operational phase far outweigh hefty start-up costs.

Productivity

To use productivity you compare both a program's efficiency and its effectiveness. You can use this method to demonstrate that a proposed project reduces training costs or utilizes resources and produces increased training results. A productivity analysis can be complex, but you can use it to tell you when to switch from one training approach to another, or when further application of a particular approach will no longer produce cost-effective improvements.

For example, in our desktop PC equipment simulation case we would chart the cost of our planned program against the value of the improvements we expect to achieve. We explore possibilities, such as doubling the number of PCs or hours of practice, to determine if we will cut down time in half. If that looks promising, we explore whether doubling it again make a further reduction by half. Often it will not, because of the well known law of diminishing returns. Training must also obey that law! In a productivity analysis you determine how much equipment or training will produce the most payoff.

Resource requirements

The resource requirements method is the simplest and most direct way to compare the costs of two or more different training approaches at a given time. You determine the costs in four major categories for each ISD phase (analysis, design, development, implementation, and evaluation) of the training project. Use the cost categories *equipment*, *facilities*, *materials*, and *personnel*. The result of the analysis will be the total costs for each phase and category. Resource requirements work well in comparing a potential new method with an existing one, assuming that both approaches will be equally effective. To compare two possible approaches, you simply add the total costs of each for all phases and resource categories. Resource requirements are limited to training costs and cannot be used to compare effectiveness.

Technology-Based Training Costs

You have to know what things cost when done conventionally, and what they will cost if TBL is employed, in order to make reasonable and believable projections of savings from using a TBL approach. Here are three forms you can use to collect the information you need. Note that every item does not apply to both columns. Some of the costs are specific to either leader-led or TBL training. Figure 8.2 is a worksheet for comparing the development costs for instructor-led training with technology-based.

Development cost comparison chart Item	Instructor–led	TBL
Course development time • Conversion of existing course • New development Graphics • Animation • Drawings • Overheads Text production • Word processing • Reproduction Video production		
Totals		

Figure 8.2 Development Cost Comparison Chart

Figure 8.3 is a worksheet similar to Figure 8.2 and is used to make comparisons of delivery costs for instructor-led training vs. technology-based training.

Figure 8.4 is a worksheet similar to Figures 8.2 and 8.3. It is used to make comparisons of support and miscellaneous costs for instructor-led training vs. those for technology-based training.

Cost-Benefit Costs

What are the costs of training now? Here are the typical costs that you must consider.

Delivery cost comparison chart Item	Instructor–Led	TBL

Student costs × # of students
• Salary during travel time
  × # of students
• Salary during training time
  × # of students
• Airline costs × # of students
• Lodging costs × # of students
• Meal costs × # of students
• Rental car costs × # of students
Instructor costs × # of instructors
• Preparation time
• Salary during travel time
  × # of instructors
• Salary during training time
  × # of instructors
• Airline costs
• Lodging costs
• Meal costs
• Rental car costs
Delivery sites
• Data communications
  –Computers
  –Fax machines
• Equipment
• Facilitation support
• Material distribution
• Material storage
• Network (video/audio/computer)
  –Installation
  –Usage
• Room costs
• Training room redesign costs
• Telephones		

Totals		

Figure 8.3 Delivery Cost Comparison Chart

Support and miscellaneous cost comparison chart		
Item	Instructor–led	TBL
Advertising		
Developer training		
Development/delivery consultants		
Instructor training		
Meetings		
Research		
Student registration		
Studio		
Support team training		
• Project manager		
• Production manager		
• Other		
Training effectiveness measurements		
Vendor tuition × # of students		
Totals		

Figure 8.4 Support and Miscellaneous Cost Comparison Chart

Current costs

Typical current costs in most training include the following. What are these costs for your organization?

- Travel
- Time lost to training
- Performance gap (the cost of the failure to perform at standard)
- Loss avoidance
- Realia costs (the cost of using real things)

Cost factors in development

The costs that affect the development of most training include:

- Instructional strategy (technology-based strategies cost more than cramming everyone in a large room and talking at them)
- Existing or new course (new courses cost more to develop because everything must be unearthed to put the new course together)
- Amount of existing information
- Amount of individualization
- Type(s) of media used (in general, the higher technology media cost more than the simpler, older media)

Cost-effectiveness in organizations

Several considerations can be used to address cost-effectiveness. Each one done has good potential, but they are often found in combination(s).

- Improve training effectiveness
- Control costs
- Reduce cost
- Increase throughput (training volume)
- Simplify training administration
- Achieve consistency (this can be crucial for some tasks)
- Meet organizational needs

Cost-Benefit Benefits

After considering the costs you must look for benefits. These balance the costs in general. It is possible for several of the benefits to combine to make a case. In our experience, to find a highly successful project it is almost essential that one of these benefits overwhelm the costs.

Benefits

Look for tangible returns from one or more of the following, such as:

- Cost per student day
- Savings associated with skill-based performance improvement
- Reduced travel costs
- Increased sales associated with training
- Reduced time to market

There are also intangible returns that are not easily quantified with a dollar value. These include:

- Attitude change
- Access to subject matter experts
- Access to training/education
- Timing/consistency of training

Comparing Training Cost Patterns

One way to convince decision makers of a proposed course's benefits is to state the cost by the student hour. This walks away from the total cost of technology that might put a kink in decision making. Somehow, even though computer hardware is a small cost in terms of a whole project, decision makers often focus on it. Figure 8.5

Project cost per unit worksheet

Expenses:

      Purchase equipment
      ___ ea @ $ _____ $ __,__ .

      Maintenance
      $ ___ /ea × ___mos $ __,__ .

      Course development
      or purchase $ __,__ .

      Total development expense $ __,__ .

Unit delivery scale:

      Use 180 days/yr (or other _____ days/yr)

      × ____ hrs/day
      × ____ machines
      × ____ yrs

      =   __,__ hrs total use

Total expense/units of delivery = hourly cost per unit

      __,__ / __,__   = $ _____ . __ per hr

Figure 8.5 Cost Per Unit Worksheet

shows a worksheet for calculating the cost per student hour for technology-based projects.

Development example

First, let's practice using the worksheet as we consider an example based on the development of a new course of instruction. It really doesn't matter whether the instruction is to be contractor-developed or done in-house. In either case, you must roll the development cost up into a single figure.

This example is based on a high delivery volume over a five-year period. Let's assume that we have a very heavily needed course that will continue for as long as we can foresee. Any course that is required of all employees annually might serve as an example. Any of the required OSHA topics that you feel will remain relevant is a possibility. Figure 8.6 shows the example.

To deliver the course we will purchase five multimedia learning stations at $3,500 each, for a total of $17,500. This is a fair price, because they all include a special dig-

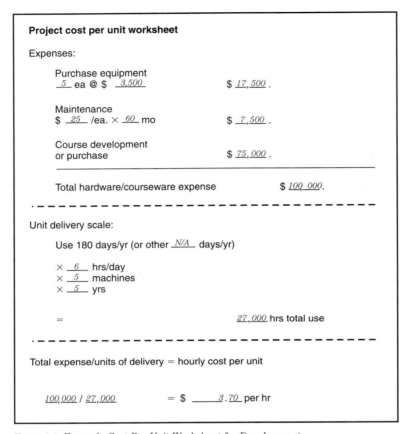

Figure 8.6 Example Cost Per Unit Worksheet for Development

ital video card and a CD-ROM drive. You will find, as you work the figures, that the cost of the delivery equipment doesn't matter very much to the overall finances of the project. You could easily spend more for each machine without changing the trust of the analysis.

You could buy a maintenance contract (probably costing more than shown) or simply budget for expected equipment maintenance. Believe us, there will be some, so don't leave this cost out. We calculated $25 per month per computer for five years ($25 \times 5 \times 60$) or $7500. Yes, it can cost almost as much to keep heavily used computers up as to buy them in the first place.

Add the $75,000 that we will pay a contractor to develop the course and the total cost is $100,000. It falls nicely at the $100,000 signature approval level.

Now let's look at delivery. There are about 220 working days in a year. It is not realistic to schedule every day. We have stepped back to 180 because we believe that, given the intent to fully schedule, it is possible to actually keep a learning center busy for at least 180 days per year.

A typical learning day is only six hours because of delays in checking in and out, travel time to the learning area, or a million other small reasons in many organizations. We purchased five computers and the project will run for five years. It does not matter whether you plan to continue the project for twenty years. No accountant will permit you to run a cost-benefit calculation for longer than five years. The total of the delivery calculation will give us 27,000.

Finally, let's see what the result is. You divide the cost, $87,000, by the number of hours the lesson will be in use, 27,000, to get the cost per hour, which is $3.22 in this case.

We are looking for a figure of $20 or less, depending on the target population. Technical training *can* cost $25 per hour or more, depending on the topic. A cost of $10 per hour is not at all unreasonable for general business and industrial training, and a cost less than $5 per hour is a bargain. These figures will be mightily persuasive to sell the project.

There are other projects that come up. Some include courseware that costs $250,000. Some involve only 100 people in all. The project we just worked was economical, in part, because there were 1,800 learners each year to participate. If we were doing the analysis for a company of only 500 people, the math would have worked out differently.

Purchase example

Let's work a different example. Let's assume that we want to upgrade the math skills of one of our skilled trades (craft) workers, the General Mechanic. There are only fifteen of them in the plant including all shifts, a small total number, and it will be impossible for all of them to attend training at once. Figure 8.7 shows this example.

Let's work the example. We start by making notations on the sheet to figure out how we are going to configure the project. We start by deciding that we can pay overtime (a cost not included in these calculations, but a price we're willing to pay for the increase in skill) for six hours to have each shift study the course's math content before their regular shift. That will give us a learner group of fifteen General Mechanics per day. The 300-hour multimedia math course, which we will purchase on the open market, costs $1,000 per copy. We need one copy per machine. The total hours spent on the project are 300 for each of the craftspeople, or 4,500 total hours. We plan on a 6-hour study day which is 750 days for the project. When we distribute the study over five computers, we can see that the whole project will be completed in 150 days—less than one year. Since the General Mechanics can apply what they learn to the job immediately, we should see benefits in less time than that. We divide the $24,000 cost by the 4,500 hours that we calculated to get a cost per hour of $5.33. Clearly this is trivial compared to the overtime, which will be the main cost of the project just described. Management's decision to upgrade the math skills is reduced essentially to the willingness to pay the overtime needed to make it happen.

Reporting Return on Investment

It isn't enough to work hard to make a good plan. Unless you work in a very small organization you must convince someone else of the merits of your idea. The presen-

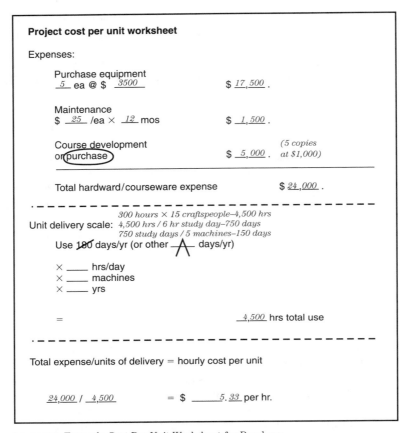

Figure 8.7 Example Cost Per Unit Worksheet for Purchase

tation of your case can make a big difference in how it's accepted and whether it ever gets implemented.

You may have to prepare a written report to justify your ideas. Figure 8.8 shows a possible table of contents of a report.

Figure 8.9 presents a checksheet you can use to work up some of the content for a written report. It uses data produced on the worksheet shown in Figures 8.2 through 8.7. However it is a start, not a finish. You should include whatever supports your idea. We suggest that you overcome any temptation to exclude points that are not favorable to your plan. Others will surely identify them and bring them up, possibly in an embarrassing way. It is more professional to present the cons along with the pros.

Don't let your right brain hibernate. Not only do you have to figure out which course of action is best, you have to convince others that what you are proposing makes economic sense. The straight numbers are important, but you can bring your ideas home quickly to decision makers by illustrating them with graphics. Here are three ideas.

```
┌─────────────────────────────────────────────┐
│            Executive summary                  │
│                                               │
│ Introduction                                  │
│         Initiating event for this study       │
│         Purpose                               │
│         Scope                                 │
│         Limitations                           │
│ Presentation of data                          │
│         Cost breakdown                        │
│         Comparison/analysis of alternatives   │
│         Additional factors for consideration  │
│ Conclusion/recommendations                    │
│         Summary of findings                   │
│         Conclusions                           │
│         Recommendations                       │
└─────────────────────────────────────────────┘
```

Figure 8.8 Table of Contents for Report

Cost comparison checksheet

	Estimated costs	
	Instructor-led	Technology-based learning

Cost comparison analysis
• Cost comparison data from the analysis
Forms indicates:
• On a comparison, using a base of anticipated
student days over the life of the project, the cost
comparison per unit is:

Knowledge change
• Knowledge gained as a result of training
• Number of trainees
• Assessment instrument
• Pre-test results
• Post-test results

Skill change
• Observable change in skills as a result of training
• Number of trainees
• Assessment instrument
• Pre-test results
• Post-test results

Attitude change
• Change in attitude as measured by a standard or
specially designed and validated attitude instrument

• Measure of individual performance
• Current actual individual performance:
• Anticipated post-training individual performance:
• Associated individual dollar savings: $ _____
× annual number of anticipated students = $
Project life student unit cost:
Technology-based learning: $_____ /hr
Leader-led: $_____ /hr
TOTALS

Figure 8.9 Cost Comparison Checksheet

Show how much is needed

Sometimes the point is that if a certain volume is reached, revenues will exceed costs. Figure 8.10 shows this situation and calls attention to a key feature of such analyses, the break-even point. This example compares a typical instructor-led to a TBL approach to training. Method A is a better choice if the volume of delivery is less than nine months. On the other hand, if the volume is greater than that shown for nine months, TBL becomes an increasingly better choice. This is a very typical pattern for this comparison.

In other cases, we want to compare two or more options. Obviously we might simply compare initial cost, but when we look over time the characteristics of one option may make it a superior choice. Figure 8.10 compares one method with low initial cost against another with much higher initial cost, but lower delivery costs. This is the typical pattern of comparing TBL against instructor-led training. Again we use a break-even point to highlight the project length for which Method B becomes the better choice.

Making a Simple Comparison

An extremely simple way to present the comparative costs of training (or any other) alternatives is called a *bridge scorecard* comparison. Figure 8.11 shows a bridge scorecard with the bridge We and They left in place. Replace these words with the specific labels appropriate to the precise comparison that you wish to make.

Confirm the Proposed Project's Cost-Effectiveness Envelope

When you think you have a winning idea, it is wise to compare it to the training that the organization is currently undertaking. It may be that an organization con-

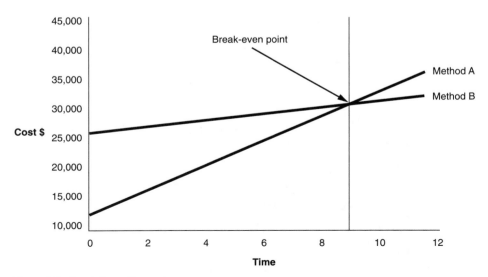

Figure 8.10 Break-Even Comparison

	WE (Computer-based learning costs/benefits)	THEY (Alternatives costs/benefits)
I N D I R E C T		
D I R E C T		

Figure 8.11 The Bridge Scorecard

ducts training of only three days or less. If you propose a 16-week resident course you will face many new problems that the organization has yet to learn to face, much less solve. Figure 8.12 provides a tool for making just this sort of comparison.

To use the cost-effectiveness envelope, first plot one dot for each of the training courses that are conducted by the organization over the course of a year, based on both the course length and volume. Then draw a trapezoid to contain all the dots. Make the upper and lower course limits parallel to the baseline. Draw straight lines for the development and delivery limits. When all this is done you will have enclosed the sort of courses the organization knows how to do comfortably. Finally, plot your proposed course. It either falls within the comfort zone or outside it. If it falls inside you can rest assured that there will not be objections based simply on the delivery dynamics of the course. If it falls outside the comfort zone you must examine how it is different and figure the ramifications of the planned course and be prepared to deal with the differences it creates. Figure 8.13 shows a completed example cost-effectiveness envelope.

In this example, the organization offers essentially ½-day, 1-day, and 3-day courses. The individual courses are never more than 20 per group, but are offered several times per year. A 10-day course with over 200 attendees would be completely out of keeping with the organization's experience.

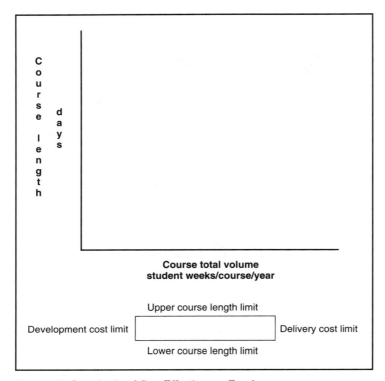

Figure 8.12 Organizational Cost-Effectiveness Envelope

Choose High Payoff Strategies

An obvious issue is that of how to justify the costs of technology-based learning when the issue is money, rather than benefit or payback. High payoff strategies may work. Three high payoff strategies should be tried. These strategies avoid cost and benefit calculations in favor of winning strategy. They are:

- Economy of scale
- Impossible without the computer
- Look for high risk-reward ratio

Economy of scale

The economy-of-scale strategy approaches the project on the assumption that a major-size project amplifies any benefit. A 1% savings on a project involving processes costing $ 10 million derives $ 100,000 in reward.

Impossible without the computer

A completely different strategy is effective in some cases. If the improvement is impossible without the computer it may offer a new chance to prepare learners. Simulations often fit into this category when the activity to be simulated has never been performed before, or cannot be performed safely in any other way. The importance of the task will determine the relative effectiveness of this strategy.

Look for high risk-reward ratios

This strategy is somewhat similar to the economy-of-scale strategy turned inside out. The difference is that high risk-reward ratio ignores the size of the project for a spectacular payoff. Large, or even small, payoffs of 1,000 % in savings on the cost of the intervention will get attention. This strategy is effective for getting attention and winning the opportunity to perform bigger projects, using the successful one as a model.

Capture Attention with a Sexy Presentation

You can make your point with drafting board-like precision. Nowadays, it is simple to convey a message with much visual force. Figure 8.14 shows a comparison of cost of two approaches.

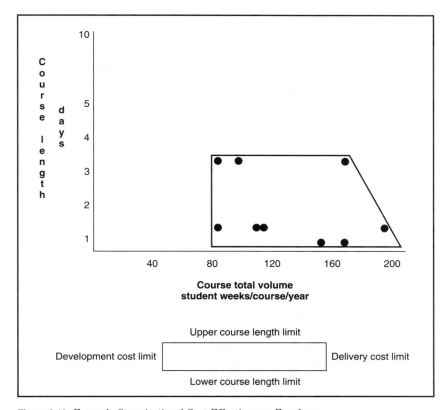

Figure 8.13 Example Organizational Cost-Effectiveness Envelope

Commonly available programs, such as Excel™, put the power to create sophisticated graphics easily in your hands. Figure 8.15 conveys exactly the same information as Figure 8.14, and is equally accurate. The visual effect will help convey your message more dramatically.

Get Off the Dime!

Some people mean to do a cost-benefit analysis, but turn off when they see that some costs aren't known. Don't let that get in the way of learning about your training from the technique. It is not unusual to start-up a cost-benefits analysis by estimating many costs and benefits when the actual figures are not available. Later on you simply refine your initial estimates based on expert judgments and the information you collect.

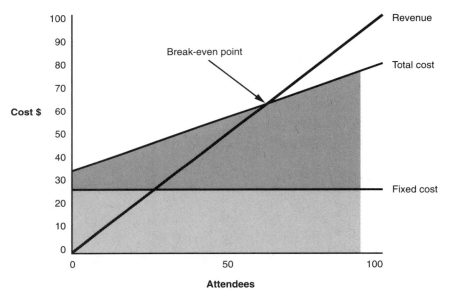

Figure 8.14 Break-Even Point

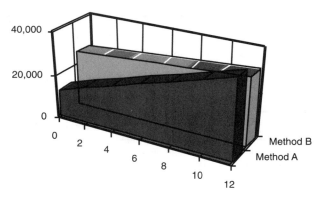

Figure 8.15 Graphic Comparison

On the other side, you have to translate benefits into dollar values. Technical training people have more data than those working in other parts of the field, yet some find it a difficult skill to acquire. Maybe you don't like to work with numbers. Obviously numbers form the critical part of cost-benefit analysis, so you have to lick this problem one way or another. Today there are a growing number of computer-based tools that save a bundle of time and make this part much easier. Just be able to justify any assumptions you make about costs or benefits, and give it a shot!

Cost-Benefit Practice

Now is the chance for you to consider your own project. What will be your strategy? Are you able to demonstrate economy of scale? Can you use the per-unit cost of the planned instruction to demonstrate the worth of your ideas? We suggest that you put your ideas to the test.

Exercise 8-1: Project Justification Exercise

Directions: On any sheet of paper, write the following three items:

1. Outline your plan for project justification.
2. What is the basis for cost-benefit?
3. Outline your cost-benefit ideas here.

Get on the Multimedia Express

You now have a very thorough and complete background upon which to place the multimedia technology. Now, it's time to turn our attention to the technology that makes it all exciting to be involved in training today. We will explore the multimedia technology in Chapter 9. Let's get interactive!

Chapter

9

Enter Multimedia

Sometimes we think about Jedi Knight training. From what we have seen, it includes a selection of media depending on the need. Yoda used stand-up tutoring methods to teach the aspirant Luke Skywalker about The Force. We can imagine that, when other strategies better fit the objective, C3PO and R2D2 can produce holographic virtual simulation or other technology-based learning solutions to match that need.

We see this as an extension of today's pattern, correctly employed. Today's sophisticated trainers use the best method for each case. They employ a light touch or supportive technology, or a heavy dose of the highest technology, depending on when each offers the best training solution.

In this chapter we will present information about multimedia technology to increase your familiarity with it. The information here will be considerably expanded as we look at the media in greater detail in Chapter 24.

What You Will Learn in This Chapter

- Characteristics of the technology cycle
- Characteristics of digital video training options
- Advantages and disadvantages of digital video training options
- Costs of digital video training options

Will the Real Multimedia Please Stand Up?

Trainers have used multimedia (more than one medium) training for many years. For example, audiotape, combined with slides and filmstrip, was widely used. From the earliest years computers have controlled and presented other media.

Interactive multimedia for training

The real power of interactive multimedia is *not* the often glitzy graphics shown, but the method "behind the scenes." It is the computer program that controls the graphics. It is the result of the coming together of two major technologies. Industrial-grade videodisc units can present simple programs entirely without any computer. Sometimes we use a small programming device to enter the program. Embry Riddle Aeronautical University of Daytona Beach, Florida, used this approach for much of their instruction. A more typical use of IVD, by Union Pacific Railroad, is described in Chapter 29, and an IVD-based simulation at Aetna is described in Chapter 31.

Educators and trainers have exploited this new entity quite effectively. Video specialists in education and training have been willing to put video under computer control because individualized interaction becomes possible this way. On the other hand, our computer specialists perceive that the realism of video enhances the capabilities of computer-assisted learning. The result has been a dazzling technology that places moving and still pictures under computer control with computer text and graphics. It combines them both with audio in a form of dynamic presentation previously unknown. The basic product of this technology is the laser-read, interactive videodisc (IVD).

Technically, IVD and interactive multimedia are only CAI. They receive separate identification in the public mind because of the different talent needed to create them, and the marketing efforts to "sell something new."

These advanced systems provide the same degree of control capability for auxiliary devices. The devices include random-access audio, random-access videotape, and videodisc. Use of these standard, or other unique, accessory devices begins to approach the full potential of the technology-based learning system.

An entertainment definition

Unfortunately, multimedia is being defined for the public by the entertainment industry. Is there plenty of marketing hype to sell multimedia as something new? Is multimedia the latest game machine? Is multimedia a user-controlled adventure distributed on a compact disk (CD)? Will multimedia be delivered by your cable or telephone company? The answer to each of these questions is yes! But none of these are about the multimedia that you can use to train employees in business and industry.

Entertainment can be a positive source of contributions and can inspire good training design. Unfortunately, we see some designers playing CD-ROM games for inspiration when they should read a book on human cognition. They become convinced that multimedia training design should permit the learner to skip around willy-nilly in the hope that the learner will eventually come across the essential information. This is whether or not the information has sequential content. The most useful lesson we can learn from today's best commercial products is to help the learner forget they're using a computer. The computer is the least important fact about the experience.

We are not picking on colleagues who consider themselves creative. We have seen that, in some instances, learners do not choose the most effective route through the instruction, and research bears us out. It *is* beneficial to provide the learner with information through active exploration of your program. In solving problems, learning through discovery promotes understanding and supports retention when fresh knowledge is linked to existing knowledge.

A valuable training tool

Today's multimedia can be used to teach cognitive objectives, particularly when it involves recognition or discrimination of applicable visual stimuli and audio stimuli. It is also an excellent tool to re-create (as closely as possible), real-world conditions for providing the non-psychomotor knowledge and skills that accompany the physical requirements of psychomotor objectives. Interactive multimedia is also very useful in the affective domain. It provides the power of detailed portrayals of situations and facilitates interactive learner participation to achieve affective domain objectives.

Development difficulties?

There is no free lunch. Developing excellent multimedia training requires high level skills in video, graphic art, computer authoring, and instructional development. Few individuals excel at all of these. A team is more likely to have the requisite skills in abundance. There is also a significant investment in equipment. Beyond these requirements, multimedia is currently the most difficult technology-based learning to develop. This doesn't mean you can't do it. It does mean that you have to be well-prepared and equipped.

Interactive Multimedia in General

In this chapter we will focus on video. Audio performance and availability continue to improve, and there are other technologies in this category. These are explored in additional detail in Chapter 25.

Hypermedia

Hypermedia have the power to "front end" other computer-based technologies. Hypermedia are described in Chapter 4 as computer-supported learning resources. This strength makes them the obvious choice to provide access to digital video-based programs. Hypermedia and interactive multimedia are synergistic but are not the same. In practice, the interactive multimedia may be one part of a single user interface. The user may have access to a package that includes an expert system, embedded animation, CAI, and hypermedia modules.

One kind of media—many flavors

The media we will discuss use optical disc video storage technologies. Both analog and digital optical disc media are in use today. The analog-based laser media is called interactive videodisc (IVD). The digital-based laser media include CD-ROM data storage media and WORM technology (write once, read many) and can be applied to produce CDs on your own desktop. Many organizations have this capability in-house already. We expect it to become very common.

Tactile input required

Today, computer systems do not make most learners feel threatened. However, some user groups appear to dislike typing. They respond much better to the use of the screen for input. Example groups include: managers, physicians, and aviators. Typing has nothing to do with most subjects learned on a multimedia system. Although we can conduct serious and successful instruction without such tactile input, we can use the screen for access to the computer in several ways. The most common and preferable screen input devices used in multimedia today are the light pen, touch-panel screen, and the much more common mouse. Using any of these access methods helps to avoid the need for typing. Today, there is little question that an organization's TBL systems should provide such a capability. This is, again, a question of using the right tool for the job.

Yesterday's Technologies

Multimedia is not new. Even during the development of the PLATO system at the University of Illinois there were several media associated with CAI delivery. The early terminals had built-in 35-mm slide carousels. Any of the images could be accessed randomly and overlaid on the computer display. There was also a special electro-mechanical sound generator that emulated speech. Using special codes, the programmer could make the emulator talk. American Airlines used the next step in audio technology. They used special audiotape that could be accessed randomly to play prerecorded sounds, such as the control tower giving the pilot learner takeoff instructions. Just before the videodisc was announced, Sony produced a random-access tape player. We have heard that this device was also used to associate video sequences with CAI lessons, but we never saw examples of this interim technology ourselves.

What makes today incredibly exciting for trainers is the increasing power of computers in small packages. The fantastic training that is now possible at reasonable cost fulfills the wildest dreams of many instructional technologists, and it just keeps getting better.

Interactive videodisc (IVD)

The first modern multimedia technology, by today's definition, is now about 15 years old. It combined moving and still video images with computer text and graphics and audio in dynamic interactive learning programs not previously known. Interactive videodisc was widely used and the best examples were dazzling. IVD technology places a permanently recorded 12-inch analog disc under computer control. There are three "levels" of interactive video. Level one provides control through a manual keypad. Level two uses a built-in microprocessor to permit limited programming and resident memory, and level three interfaces with a PC. This greatly improves programming possibilities and adds huge quantities of memory. Only level three is widely used in recently developed IVD training.

The three levels of interactive videodisc are shown in Figure 9.1

- Level 1–manually operated controls
- Level 2–built-in microprocessor
- Level 3–i nterface for PC

Figure 9.1 Levels of Interactive Videodisc

Videodisc, the best-known optical disk, is simply a storage medium much like a floppy disc. It stores video, similar to a videotape. The computer software controls the videodisc player. Videotape is a linear format meant to play from beginning to end. Videodisc yields random access to any of the frames of video stored on one side. Interactive simply means that the user's responses determine the sequence of the presentation. This medium supports motion visuals and accurate, repeatable instruction.

The capabilities of the basic videodisc technology are:

- Analog video and audio. This means that editing changes are severely limited.

- Twelve-inch platter. Holds about 30 minutes of linear play video on each side. It has synchronized dual channels of audio, or 54,000 still pictures with very limited audio per frame.

- Three "levels" of interactive video. Level one IVD provides control through a manual keypad. Level two IVD uses a built-in microprocessor. It permits limited programming and resident memory. Level three IVD interfaces in real time with a PC. This greatly improves programming possibilities and adds huge quantities of memory.

- Input devices. These include keypad, keyboard, joystick, mouse, trackball, bar code reader, touch panel, or light pen.

- Read-only technology. This results from a permanently recorded impression on the disc. No change is possible after the disc is mastered.

- Interactive learning programs. The programs use moving and still pictures coupled with audio and computer text and graphics.

- Authoring systems. These reduced (but did not end) the complexity of instructional design and development.

The capabilities of the classical videodisc proved to be its limitations. These attributes governed the videodisc as it emerged in the late 1970s. Over time, however, learning needs prompted new capability development. The most important of these were:

- Overlay of analog video images with computer-generated text and graphics. This called for more costly hardware and a growth in the power of authoring systems.

- Sound-over-still through the use of computer hard disks to play the audio.

- The coming of CD-ROM with its vast memory capacities.

The increase in memory greatly increased the amount of audio possible for each frame. This feature cut the costs of instructional program development. It made it possible to create interactive videodisc programs based increasingly on less expensive still photography instead of costly motion visuals. A single disc, combined with paper-based materials, can support many hours of instruction.

The interactive videodisc equipment has been a great medium to use with self-teaching instruction. It was the first technology able to carry CAI, carried to the logical end of its capabilities.

According to *Corporate Video Decisions* (October 1988), the chairperson of Phillips Petroleum, in talking about the company's 14-year-old internal corporate video department, said "Ten years ago, video was the stepchild to other ways to communicate—print and public speaking. These days, it's a regular part of our communications, and it's an essential part of most of our management, training, and sales jobs."

Technology life cycle

It wouldn't be fair to you to discuss DVI without also considering the life cycle of technology. The random-access videotape device had a truncated lifecycle because of the release of the videodisc. That is, as new technology appeared to replace it, demand went away and eventually the technology disappeared from the market.

Angus Reynolds was amazed to see a brand new filmstrip projector not long ago. In training, the device was replaced partially by 35-mm slides and finally by video tape by the middle 1980s. But in the public school setting, the brand new projector served to make use of a huge collection of still-useful film strips that had been amassed over the years.

The stages in the life cycle of technology were shown in Figure 8.1. IVD has reached maturity and is well into its operational period. There are many fine programs in the IVD format in use and available. Videodisc players are rugged, reliable, and will continue to be serviceable for a long time. However, we have always known that the analog laser disc was an interim technology that would eventually be replaced by digital video, as shown in Figure 9.2.

Today's (Compact Disc) Technologies

John Eldridge was the first trainer that we know of to recognize the potential of the compact disk for training. He provided valuable help in preparation of this chapter. The compact disk is ever more important for training, and is used in a variety of ways.

CD-audio

The first downsizing of the laser-read disc took it from 12 inches to 12 centimeters (4.72 inches). This was a joint effort in design by Philips of the Netherlands and Sony of Japan. CD-Audio is an entertainment medium, providing up to 74 minutes of high fidelity music. Introduced in 1979, these discs have been a monumental success because of the quality of the digitized music. The players are now ubiquitous and range from portables not too much larger than the disc itself to programmable "juke boxes" for the Hi Fi shelf that hold 100 CDs and provide hours of sound without further attention. DVD will replace the CD-audio format.

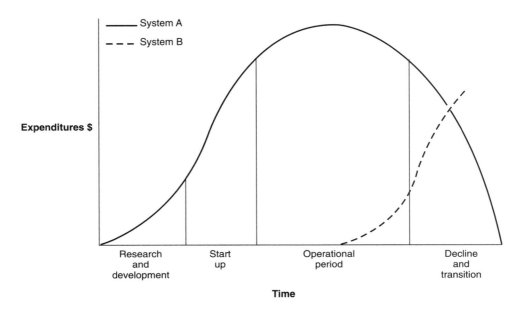

Figure 9.2 New Technologies Replace Old

Compact disc

With the success of the 12-inch videodisc and the coming of the compact disc, efforts to "downsize" the technology to the smaller platter were inevitable. There are significant technical differences between 12-inch IVD and a compact disc. To understand the capabilities, a trainer or a manager need only think of the interactive videodisc. As their larger counterpart, DVI, CD-I and the new DVD will deliver:

- Motion, and
- Still video, mixed with
- Computer text, and
- Graphics, and
- Audio, under computer guidance for interactive learning materials.

While the older videodisc technology also delivered the same assortment of learning tools, in the all-digital compact disc newer flexibility and capabilities emerge. They are:

- About 550 megabytes of digital information (computer files). These can be text, images, graphics, sound, and computer programs. All are integrated in a package created by an authoring system. Then they are used under the command of a computer just like computer files stored on the computer's own hard disk.
- Hardware and software compression of this digital information to make gargantuan storage possible. This provides rapid reading and use.

- On-the-fly editing of the information, reducing preproduction costs significantly. For example: a wipe or dissolve is achieved by computer code that modifies the image at the instant it appears in the digital stream for processing and display.

- Four levels of audio in mixtures of audio at a range of fidelities. The range is from 18–20 hours of AM radio quality to 72 minutes of CD-Audiodisc quality sound under the control of the computer program.

- Seven thousand still images.

- Up to one hour of full motion video, depending on the pixel density, display resolution, and number of colors.

- Digital still and motion images, sound, computer text, and graphics are all mixed and matched by the computer into an instructional program. It is not possible to store them all to maximum capacity on one disc. That is, there cannot be 7,000 stills and one hour of video stored on one disc. Everything (pictures, text, graphics, audio, and computer program) must be stored together and brought into the computer using a single-bit stream.

As John Eldridge says, "That it works at all is a triumph of electronics and computer programming."

CD-ROM

Not long after it was clear that CD audio was a tremendous success, Philips and SONY again presented a new hardware standard using the compact disc. CD-ROM used the same small disc, but the device added error-detection for the recording of information. The hardware results were literally astounding: 660 megabytes of information could be stored on its tiny surface. After formatting with a quickly established standard, the user was left with only 550 MB. To put that in perspective, that's equivalent to 27.5 20-MB hard drives, or 1,500 high density floppy disks. You can record 250,000 pages of text and that's equivalent to 625 volumes at the average size of 400 pages per volume.

There are two primary applications for CD-ROM. First, it is a publishing medium. Any organization with large quantities of information to disseminate or store should investigate the possibilities of CD-ROM. Second, the drive can be coupled to the computer to provide additional audio capabilities to interactive videodisc or computer-based training. The CD-ROM disc will hold 74 minutes of stereo Hi Fi sound, or up to 20 hours of AM radio sound limited to 4 KHz.

In fact, these capabilities have opened entire new markets. Arthur Andersen Company, the accounting and consulting firm, now uses CD-ROM discs to replace the manuals it formerly shipped to its consultants and customers by the ton on paper. The Corps of Engineers is replacing hundreds of manuals that were once stored in a 12,000 square-foot warehouse with CD-ROM discs. They found that, for this purpose, they could put 17,000 pages of text, plus graphics, on a single disc. That's roughly equivalent to 17 one-thousand-page technical manuals that weigh 68 pounds. The CD costs about 50 cents to mail as opposed to $23.37. NYNEX produced a telephone directory with about 10 million names and addresses that is a best-seller in the northeast to municipal governments, collection agencies, law enforcement agencies, and the like. Finally, Ford Motor Company and Mack Trucks are both using CD-ROMs for parts catalogs. They can find parts several times faster with CD-ROM than with microfiche or paper-based books. The CD offers speed, downsizing, accuracy, lower costs, and is easy to use. It is less destructible and longer lasting than paper or microfiche.

A CD-ROM drive can be added to your computer for about $300–500. To induce buyers to invest in hardware, many vendors throw in discs. After the initial purchase, you will find typical discs today costing $50 on up, depending on the disc. Some professional disks, such as the Encyclopedia Britannica, can cost thousands.

Prices to convert an existing database to CD-ROM are about $10,000. The work of compiling the database is an added cost. Developers have found that it is necessary to scan documents twice to make them easily usable. We expect to see CDs continue to grow as a major publishing medium. We also anticipate continued use as a source of sound in computer-based learning applications.

Digital Video Training

Digital video also delivers motion and still video, mixed with computer text, and graphics, and audio for interactive learning materials. Today, learning stations for digital video are much cheaper than for IVD, and new training projects are more likely to choose the digital video arena. Digital video is not tied to the vast storage of the 12-cm CD for delivery, but is often selected as the means of the physical delivery. This is true because an average lesson with full motion video is often up to 50 times larger than it would be without, swamping older, smaller hard disks.

The all-digital format offers important new flexibility and capabilities. The video, now a computer file, can be easily edited or updated. Because of their inherent advantages these systems will replace the larger and more costly 12-inch videodisc quite quickly.

Compact disc-interactive (CD-I), digital video interactive (DVI), and MPEG

Two products were the first to emerge: digital video interactive (DVI) and compact disc interactive (CD-I). DVI is offered to the market by Intel Corporation and CD-I is a Philips corporation product. CD-I capitalizes on Philips sponsorship of the CD-ROM and CD Audio standards. They use entirely distinct approaches. The result is two significantly different and incompatible systems. While both of the two product lines are based on the same basic technology, the two companies have radically different approaches to somewhat different commercial target audiences.

MPEG is a third compression standard. DVI and MPEG depend on computer peripherals: you buy a board and insert it into your old computer. CD-I is a separate box with its own built-in computer. DVI is aimed primarily at the professional and business market. CD-I is aimed at the mass consumer market. Philips hopes to attract the CD audiophile to interactive multimedia. In any case, we in the education and training world benefit. Although these products are completely incompatible, their success will lead to better products and lower prices for training.

The smaller size, flexible video, and audio capable of manipulation by program sources, are all advantages. This allows complete integration of video images, audio, and computer graphics. Computer controls foster individualized, interactive instructional materials. Simulations, serious games, tutorials, surrogate travel, are some of the uses.

Quality in these systems is comparatively low because of the enormous amount of data required to produce synchronized moving video, audio, and computer graphics in a single bit stream from the computer. CD-I is limited by the TV resolution that is often used.

Digital video boards cost approximately $300–$1,000. The CD-I player is currently being marketed at $400, with courseware and many entertainment discs below $50 each.

CD-I

Philips corporation's CD-I aims primarily at the consumer marketplace. CD-I comes in a simple box intended *not* to look like the powerful computer that it is. CD-I is a standard, not a product, so other manufacturers also produce CD-I machines. A plus for economy and convenience is that any TV can serve as the monitor. The corresponding minus is TV's poor picture resolution. CD-I offers lower unit cost than other technology-based approaches. Players currently retail for about $400. This low cost makes it perfect for new projects that must install hardware in huge numbers of locations. It also suggests that, like the 35-mm projector and the videotape player, it can jump from the home to the training room.

DVI

Intel and IBM developed DVI. When they did, they aimed squarely at the business marketplace. DVI is based on a personal computer and strives for highest resolution, full-motion video. It had the disadvantage of a costly board for the computer, which cost almost $1,000. Today, neither organization is enthusiastic about the DVI standard, and even though it met every expectation for highest resolution, full-motion video, most of its supporters are dropping away.

A side note is that full-screen is an important capability, first possible on DVI. Instructional developers often prefer quarter-screen video to permit combination with text and graphics.

MPEG

Other PC-based standards may eventually supplant DVI, but the goal of high-resolution, full-screen, full-motion video will remain. MPEG, described more fully in Chapter 24—is a likely successor. The MPEG card currently costs less than $300, making it a more likely choice than DVI. MPEG offers the same advantages as DVI, with the exception of frame-accurate editing. Play can only start at one of the pre-designated key frames.

Software digital video

Today, top-quality full-motion, full-screen video requires special hardware, but the direction is clear. There have been software standards for almost as long as the hardware ones. QuickTime for Macintosh/QuickTime for Windows is a single standard that plays on two platforms. Video for Windows is a Microsoft product, as is the less capable Indeo.

Two processes are proceeding in unison. The compression algorithms are improving and the computers are getting faster. Soon the newest PCs will have the power to do the necessary processing without special hardware.

Cost

All technology-based learning methodologies share a single cost pattern. Compared to conventional training, it is a pattern of high development expense with low costs. Multimedia is most appropriate when its combined development and delivery costs are less than those of other methods, when the criticality of the learner's performance justifies the method, or the training can't be accomplished any other way.

Today, a simple, custom-made IVD program can cost at least $30,000; a comparable generic videodisc's price is around $10,000. Many practitioners look at the real advantage of the technology—the ability to train for specific tasks—and wonder whether generic videodiscs can ever fit the bill for corporate use. Careful needs assessment to determine whether a generic videodisc can accomplish training objectives will help answer the "make or buy" question. For training managers, organizations can buy digital video systems in a smaller size with consequent savings in storage and handling, at lower costs. The major disadvantage is that these new systems reside on hardware and software that is different and incompatible with the older technology. CD-ROM drives, although cheap, were not included in the purchase of the installed base of PCs.

CD-I products for a viewing system only are about $400. Authoring capabilities add another $2,500 to the costs. Today, authoring systems have not reached a firm figure but promise to be several thousand dollars.

Advantages and Disadvantages of Interactive Multimedia

This book is about multimedia. Still, we are able to be level-headed in considering multimedia solutions for training problems. Here are the pluses and minuses:

Advantages:

- Possible to directly support on-job performance.
- Possible to access a variety of media and other resources easily.
- Possible to access information as wanted by the learner.
- Individual, self-paced instruction for individual students.

- The ability of the instructor to concentrate on instructor-related tasks, allowing them to attend specifically to those students who may be having problems.

- Excellent means for simulation situations that need individualized, yet coordinated, task performance. For example, networked crew coordination training allows each station to represent a specific flight task requirement where the host system monitors the coordination of the stations and provides appropriate feedback.

- Hardware may be same as for home use, with low cost.

Disadvantages:

- Does not teach or instruct.

- May not tie directly to particular learning objectives.

- Uncontrolled student access to the information depends on the student's interest and motivation.

- Development of lessons requires skills that may not be available.

- Development of high quality lessons requires extensive effort.

- Generic multimedia lessons may not be available to meet your needs.

Helpful hints in creating CD-I products

Kevin Gillen, President of Gillen Interactive Group, has been in the forefront of CD-I development from the beginning. As the author of many CD-I products, including some of the very first, he offers this advice for creating CD-I products:

- Have all involved know the Green Book Standards for their role in the production. The Green Book is the name for the set of books created by Philips and Sony that contain all the technical information about the CD-I Standard.

- Keep design and production separate. Get the design done first. Don't assume you can create assets while finishing the design. You don't start building a new building until the blueprints are done and approved.

- Optical rights are a new copyright issue. Sometimes it is cheaper and faster to create a new photo or sound effect, or re-record a piece of music, than to negotiate or haggle with a rights holder over reusing an existing asset.

- Always create images with CD-I resolution in mind. This means NTSC-384 × 240 or 768 × 480 PAL-384 × 280 or 768 × 560.

- Changes in the production process can create the dreaded "spaghetti effect." By changing one small element you may unknowingly affect other elements downstream.

- Authoring tools do exist. And authoring systems for non-computer programmers are coming. Meanwhile, Optimage, Script Systems and ISG have excellent hardware and software systems to help create CD-I productions, with the final steps being accomplished by a computer programmer or software engineer.

Where Do We Go from Here?

Although the current digital video products are completely incompatible, their success will lead us to better products and even lower prices for training use. Eventually, the best multimedia will run on most computers workers use. It will appear seamless to the learner, and play a role in performance-support systems.

The more things change, the more they stay the same. The future Jedi Knight Training Academy will use technology-based learning methods when they are the best solution, just as we do.

Let's Make a Lesson!

This completes the background needed to fully appreciate what you are doing when you develop technology-based training. Now, let's build that lesson. We will do just that as Part 2 unfolds, beginning with Chapter 10. You will follow the process used by the best commercial developers. Let's get at it!

Building a Technology-Based Lesson

10

Analysis

Analysis is the proper first step in developing training of any kind. The basic analysis approach is to determine the requirements of the job and the current capability of the employee. The difference or gap between these two is the training need. If we are considering technology-based training, there are unique considerations to ensure that we produce a good solution. You may recall a discussion of this in the section on criterion-referenced instruction in Chapter 6.

What You Will Learn in This Chapter

- Components of the analysis phase of instructional development
- Characteristics of analysis techniques
- Format for an analysis report

What Is Training Analysis?

For some courseware developers, the excitement of the microscopic attention called for in analysis ranks almost as high as watching cars rust. It may not be everyone's favorite part of developing good training, but everyone who tries can do a credible job.

We think that we can best answer the question "What is training analysis?" by providing you with a look at the analysis report completed during a project for a major U.S. automobile manufacturer. To retain the privacy of the information, we have replaced the name of the manufacturer with Jordan Motors (an early automobile manufacturer) and the location to Oshkosh (a real place, but distant from the actual location). Figure 10.1 shows the table of contents for the report and can represent the content for us.

Table of contents

Section	Page
Executive summary	1-1
Introduction	2-1
Why not me?	
Oshkosh operations training in perspective	
About training	
About non-training solutions	
About this document	
Problem identification and analysis	3-1
Identification of the problem	
The why not me problem	
Definition of the target population	
Quantitative description of the training need	
Past training	
Identification of other groups needs	
Identification of skill/knowledge discrepancies	
Analysis of discrepancies	
Identification of training needs	
Survey of existing training	
Solution identification and analysis	4-1
Specification of training needs	
Identification of constraints	
Training program specifications	
Organization of material	
The Oshkosh operations training pyramid	
Description of development approaches	
Training program effectiveness	
Recommendations	5-1
Non-training solutions	
Training solutions	

Figure 10.1 Table of Contents for Analysis Report

Custom reports

Not everyone was to receive training as a result of the project, which led to writing a short section titled "Why Not Me?" This illustrates the concept of customization and reinforces the fact that there is no standard format for an analysis report, because the situations being analyzed are so different. Appendix A includes an example analysis report.

Non-training solutions

Notice the attention given to non-training solutions. Angus has found that, over a large number of projects, the non-training solutions were as numerous as those requiring training. They are appreciated by the organization as much or more, since they usually cost less to implement and often can show an immediate improvement. You may be surprised to learn that the non-training solutions can be as simple as "install improved lighting in the work area."

Key elements

Important areas come through clearly. There is a focus on the learner, including their past training and existing training, both internal to the organization and commercially available. The solution is complete, will solve the problems identified, and its effectiveness can be measured.

The analysis report appendices provide further insight into what happened during the analysis. Figure 10.2 shows the appendices for the report.

The appendices provide considerable additional detail. Appendix E lists the tasks for each craft and Appendix G lists the detailed training needs by craft.

Job/Task Analysis

In job analysis you identify the complete set of duties that a person performs on the job. When instruction is needed, job analysis is often combined with task analysis. According to The *Trainer's Dictionary*, task analysis is, "a process of arriving at a step-by-step description of all the performance elements (tasks) that make up a job. Task analysis applies whether the steps of the task are mainly cognitive or psychomotor. Task analysis is done by questionnaires, observations of performance, and interviews with incumbents and supervisors. A term coined by Robert Gagné, it is also referred to as skills analysis. Task and skills analysis are subsets of the complete job." Also, task analyst is the role of identifying activities, tasks, subtasks and human resource and support requirements necessary to accomplish specific results in a job or organization.

Clarity

Let's clear up possible confusion with other analyses that trainers often talk about. The most often mentioned is needs analysis.

- Analysis is a step in the analysis phase of ISD.

- Front-end analysis is a needs analysis method named by Joe Harless.

- Needs analysis is a methodical process of collecting and evaluating information about on-the-job performance to determine the learning needs of the organization's employees. A performance deficiency can be related to equipment or procedures. Therefore, we most often conduct a needs analysis to confirm the existence of a learning need. Needs analyst is the role of identifying ideal and actual performance and performance conditions and determining causes of discrepancies.

- *Performance analysis* is another term for needs analysis.

How Is It Done?

One of the best ways to do the job/task analysis is a personal interview by a skilled analyst, although other methods are also used. We watch a job, question every observable act, and collect its prerequisite knowledge and skill, decisions, perceptions, and psychomotor activities that produce a result or accomplish a task. We look for a

```
Appendices

   A. Persons contacted                          A-1
   B. Written resources consulted                B-1
   C. Description of the target population        C-1
   D. Oshkosh operations automated systems
      and equipment                              D-1
   E. Oshkosh operations craft task lists         E-1
   F. Training completed                         F-1
   G. Training needs by craft                     G-1
   H. Existing training                          H-1
   I. Instructional considerations                I-1
   J. Training program specifications             J-1
   K. Instructional systems development (example) K-1
   L. Training program evaluation                 L-1
```

Figure 10.2 Appendices for Analysis Report

definite beginning and end and check interaction with systems, equipment, and other people. We watch and measure the results. We check written standards, manuals, and manufacturer's technical information. Everything is recorded.

A task may be of any size or degree of complexity. It can always be divided into a hierarchy of detail. The tasks are divided into subtasks and the subtasks into elements. It is possible to continue to analyze the task's components down to very small activities. We stop when it no longer makes sense to subdivide.

Are There Alternatives?

There are many variations on task analysis. One technique, intended to complete an entire analysis may include analysis of the task. The DACUM (developing a curriculum) analysis is almost always called by its acronym. DACUM is analysis conducted by bringing all concerned parties together. In the process, all analysis questions are addressed and resolved on-the-spot. The process moves more quickly than a conventional analysis, which is certainly true of analyzing the task. The chart used to record the DACUM process is often wall-size. You must exercise great care when you perform a DACUM analysis to be certain that you avoid superficial results.

What Is My Motivation?

Actors sometimes ask the director, "What is my motivation?" It should come as no surprise that there are organizations that *don't* do a job/task analysis when preparing training. In most of these cases, the organizations involved have decided what the training will be and don't want to invest the extra resources in analysis. Also, there are situations in which the job and task are not relevant. For example, in compliance training that mandates a certain amount of training with a pre-defined specific content. That training just has to be done.

When we want to do the best job of developing training it all starts with a job/task analysis. This step provides the solid information about what the learners do. If this thorough understanding is enough to help the learner to perform even a few percent more productively, the payback can be enormous. Examples exist where an improvement by a single employee can translate into millions of dollars. In short, we collect the job/task information to do the very best job we can of developing excellent training.

We expect to see detail about the organization of the job. Special data-collection sheets are often created to record the information as it is collected. They can add significant detail about a job, beyond that needed for the job/task analysis.

Figure 10.3 shows a portion of the data as reported for a skilled trade employee, a millwright.

The completed job/task analysis should also report other information needed to place the job and tasks in perspective. This is sometimes called prerequisite knowledge and skills.

Figure 10.4 shows a portion of the prerequisite knowledge and skills as reported for the millwright.

Introduction to Your CAI Project

This chapter initiates a project that you will carry through the remaining chapters of this section. You will build a complete lesson surrounded with the elements that an organization would want and expect to use in their training program. When you complete the lesson you will understand how to apply your learning to another organization and situation, because you have built the entire project and you know how it works inside and out. The focus of this project is, of course, the learner—in this case a crane operator. Figure 10.5 shows some of the findings.

Crane Operator Project—What Are Some of the Questions to Ask?

As you approach a project, you want to know as much about it as possible. Here is a set of questions you can use to examine the crane operator (or other) situation. Figure 10.6 shows the same analysis questions that we suggested you consider earlier when thinking about a project of your own.

```
Millwright
1. Fabricate
        1.1 Plan job
                1.1.1 Review job package
                      (if applicable)
                1.1.2 Determine sequence of jobs
                1.1.3 Determine needed tools and
                      miscellaneous materials
                1.1.4 Determine material handling needs
                      (if applicable)
                1.1.5 Plan safety considerations
        1.2 Obtain materials
                1.2.1 Obtain miscellaneous materials
                . . .
2. Install
        2.1 . . .
                2.1.1 . . .
```

Figure 10.3 Millwright Analysis Example

Operate
1. Personal (small) tools (as required)

        . . .
        1.6 Wrenches
                1.6.1 Box
        . . .
2. Basic power tools
        2.1 Snag grinder
        2.2 . . .
3. Precision tools
        . . .

4. . . .

Uses
        1. Mathematics
                1.1 Shop math
                        1.1.1 Whole numbers
                        1.1.2 . . .
                1.2 etc.
        2. Blueprints

                . . .

Figure 10.4 Millwright Prerequisite Knowledge and Skills Example

---

2.2 Present Performance

Recent audits of damage for some items provoked critism of Jordan Motors' deficiencies in materials handling. Corporate image cannot tolerate damaged materials. Therefore, it is extremely important that the materials handling function be performed properly by all operators including new ones.
The problems identified above suggest that the materials handling personnel responsible for crane operation lack knowledge in the following areas:

• Safety
• Operator maintenance
• Interpreting the meaning and purpose of each standard hand signal

The problems affecting overall operation performance are exacerbated by the turnover of personnel. It has been estimated that the current methods of on-the-job training can take up to one year before the employee has the necessary knowledge to operate the crane with complete efficiency. This period is similar to that needed to become a good candidate for a position elsewhere in the manufacturing organization. A combination of factors can cause some personnel who have accumulated the experience necessary to become increasingly effective at crane operation to leave the crane-operation-related position.

2.2 Desired Performance

Crane operators should be able to move loads quickly, accurately, and reliably. A significant reduction in small errors should be attainable, and time taken to train a new operator in crane operation should be measured in months rather than years.

Figure 10.5 Partial Findings

```
Topic
        1.      What is the need?
Size
        1.      How many learners are there?
        2.      What is the target number of simultaneous students?
Length
        1.      How many hours of estimated student effort are there?
        2.      How long will one student's total involvement last (including non-sturdy)?
Delivery
        1.      Where will the course be delivered to the learners (e.g., at the work place)?
        2.      How many different delivery locations are there? Describe them geographically.
                Will they be all in one city, all in one building, or all over the world?
        3.      Will they all use the same system type?
        4.      If you already have a system in mind, or must use one system or another due to
                organizational constraints; what is it?
Other Issues
        1.      Who will be involved in the project?
        2.      What is the probable project cost (it is important to make a guess even if
                you don't know at this point)? A related question is what is the available budget?
        3.      What is the biggest advantage of the project?
        4.      What is your biggest concern?
        5.      What strategies seem workable for the project? (Lecture, CAI, or whatever)
        6.      Do the (distant) students have to communicate with the instructor in real time?
        7.      Will the course materials require frequent maintenance (corrective updates)?
                If so, how much and how frequently?
```

Figure 10.6 Analysis Questions

Here are the answers we find for the crane operator:

Topic

Q1.   What is the need?

A1.   The company wants to train new operators safely and uniformly. The cranes are busy and cannot be diverted exclusively to extensive training, there is potential for injury to others if work is not stopped while students learn to operate the cranes, and their loads could be damaged or could damage other things if out of control.

Size

Q1.   How many learners are there?

A1.   There are over 100 learners now if training is consolidated for the company's five locations, bringing them to one location could be expensive. Newly hired workers must also be trained as they come on board.

Q2.   What is the target number of simultaneous students?

A2.   There could be five learners at one time, one from each plant, but there is no necessity of training the learners all at once.

Length

Q1.   How many hours of estimated student effort are there?

A1.   If it included classroom and practice on the crane the learner might spend one hour in the classroom, three hours with the crane, and four hours of supervised crane operation. The total is eight hours.

Q2.   How long will one student's total involvement last (including non-study)?

A2.   In this case, the total will also probably be eight hours.

Delivery

Q1.   Where will the course be delivered to the learners?

A1.   The training can be at the workplace. The regular cranes can be used once the new operator is sufficiently prepared to engage in supervised work.

Q2.   How many different delivery locations are there?

A2.   There are five, one in each plant.

Q3.   Will they all use the same system type?

A3.   Yes.

Q4.   If you already have a system in mind, or must use one system or another due to organizational constraints, what is it?

A4.   The training would not, alone, justify special computers. It must use the existing plant computers.

Other Issues

Q1.   Who will be involved in the project?

A1.   The learner, a coordinator (*not* instructor) at each plant, and a master crane operator to supervise the new operator's first four hours of operation.

Q2.   What is the probable project cost?

A2.   The cost is estimated at 100 hours for the development plus 8 hours for each new operator trained.
        A related question is, what is the available budget? No budget is reserved for this, but funds can be found if the project is reasonable.

Q3.   What is the biggest advantage of the project?

A3.   It will make training safer, consistent, and equally high in quality when only a single new operator needs qualification.

Q4.   What is your biggest concern?

A4.   Lack of experience in technology-based learning development.

Q5.   What strategies seem workable for the project? (Lecture, CAI, self study, or videotape).

A5.   CAI will work effectively.

Q6.   Do the (distant) students have to communicate with the instructor in real time?

A6.   No

Q7.   Will the course materials require frequent maintenance (corrective updates)?

A7.   If so, how much and how frequently? No. Once it is developed, the course will remain valid even if new cranes are installed.

Crane Operator Project—Analysis

The tool often used to collect data during an analysis is called, just as you might suspect, an analysis sheet. Again, because projects differ so widely there is really no standard analysis sheet. They are usually made up for each project. However, they have elements in common. Figure 10.7 shows a typical analysis sheet.

We know you would make up a blank analysis sheet form for the crane operator project and have done one to help you. It is shown in Figure 10.8.

The sheets are normally filled out in longhand. If the project is huge and analysis is likely to be extensive, they may be redone using word processing capability to improve legibility for many project member and subject matter experts.

Crane Operator Project—Job Analysis

We learn that there are a total of 29 hand signals in use in the 5 company plants, if we include outside mobile cranes. Figure 10.9 shows a representative portion of the crane operator analysis.

Service Representative

Duty C. Complete orders and forms for service and equipment

Task 01 Complete new connect service

Page 72 of 378

Revised: 18 April 1995

Subtask	Assumptions/ Rules/Principles/ Policies/Operating practices/References/ Coordination requirements	Input conditions	Terminating events/ Contingencies/ Potential corrective action	Standards/ Outputs/ Products	Frequency/ Time factors	Importance	Skills/ Knowledge/ Attitudinal requirements
0111 Enter due date	Assumptions: Some locations colocated with business offices are able to determine available due dates. Other locations must call the business office. Operating practices: There are local variations in when service is provided and when access can be scheduled. Enter °date °code Enter °access (if applicable)	Triggering event: Completing new service agreement Location: Store Tools: None Materials (including job aids): Form/: 5229 GPX Service representative handbook	Termination: Behavior complete Contingencies: Some customers want service "today" or tomorrow when tomorrow is already scheduled. Such requests can be accommodated in some cases	Standards: Without error or omission Outputs: Due date entered Products: None	Frequency: As required	Semi-critical Domain (check one): Cognitive y n Psychomotor y n Affective y n 3. Due date code (available in service representative handbook).	Knowledge: 1. Local practice for service activation and access scheduling. 2. Variations and exceptions to local practice.

Figure 10.7 Sample Analysis Sheet

	Crane operator							
Duty: Task:						Page of Revised:		
Subtask	Assumptions/ Rules/Principles/ Policies/Operating practices/References/ Coordination requirements	Input conditions	Terminating events/ Contingencies/ Potential corrective actions	Standards/ Outputs/ Products	Frequency/ Time factors	Importance	Skills/ Knowledge/ Attitudinal requirements	
	Assumptions: Operating practices:	Triggering event: Location: Tools: Materials (including job aids):	Termination: Contingencies:	Standards: Outputs: Products:	Frequency: Domain (check one): Cognitive y n Psychomotor y n Affective y n			

Figure 10.8 Sample Blank Crane Operator Analysis Sheet

```
Crane operator
1. Operate crane
        1.1 Recognize hand signals
                1.1.1 Recognize hoist signals
                1.1.2 Recognize traverse signals
                1.1.3 Recognize travel signals
        1.2 Operate controls
                1.2.1 Operate hoist
                1.2.2 . . .
2. Perform operator maintenance
        2.1 . . .
                2.1.1 . . .
3. Practice safety
        3.1 . . .
                3.1.1 . . .
```

Figure 10.9 Crane Operator Analysis

The completed job/task analysis should also report other information needed to place the job and tasks in perspective—the prerequisite knowledge and skills. The prerequisite knowledge and skills for the crane operator do not apply to the portion of the project that we will follow, although some are related to preventative maintenance.

Crane Operator Learner Analysis

The learners, new operators, are typically high school graduates, higher than might be the case in some instances. They have no other training or skills that are relevant to crane operation. They vary widely, but unlike some organizations, all of them have English as a first language. They have never had formal training in any aspect of their jobs (this is not too uncommon).

Crane Operator Organizational Constraints

One constraint is the lack of multimedia learning center computers for delivery. The existing computers in each plant must be used. However, they are sufficient for the lesson that you will design and program. No suitable existing training, internal to the company or an external commercial product, is identified for the topics that we need to cover.

Crane Operator Analysis Report

The whole training curriculum for crane operators includes lessons on orientation, operation, operator maintenance, and safety. The analysis report can be much simpler than the Jordan Motors example discussed earlier. Still, using a format based on the example you can produce a professional looking report, even for a small project.

We will follow the operation lesson. It has two units—signal recognition and control functions. In the remaining chapters we will focus on the signal-recognition unit, the unit you will develop, and the supporting components.

Non-Training Solutions

It is usual to find improvements that address the problem but have no training element. These should be included in the report. For example, management can take action on your recommendation to increase the foot candle of lighting in the machinist area.

Job aids should always be identified and developed whenever they can be implemented. Performance support systems are included in this category. In the case of the crane operator, we did identify a job aid that can be installed as a plate on the crane itself.

Tips on Analysis

- Be curious
- Identify job aids wherever possible
- Use the snowball technique to gather data
- Say yes to opportunities to see processes and to interview additional people

Designing Men and Women

In the analysis we found out all the information that we need to decide whether training is an appropriate solution, what the training should include, the readiness of the learners, and the ability and willingness of the organization to support such training.

Now let's move forward to plan just how we will solve this training problem. We will become designing men and women as we produce a design plan and produce a design document.

11

The Design Document

The Design Document is the key to a successful development process. It just isn't possible to produce technology-based learning in a businesslike way without producing good design documents as a matter of course.

Our problem is not simply converting training needs to creative ideas for the instruction of the learner. This is true even though there is little doubt that creativity can go a long way toward making the ultimate courseware enjoyable and interesting to the learners. We devote an extra measure of effort to doing just that, but that's not the whole story. There are many creative people in the world, yet training that is only creative may not be sound. We've seen many such unsound training products, and we continue to meet people who are in the process of developing training but really don't know how.

Our problem is also to structure the whole project for success, manage the customer's expectations, and build in a procedure that the customer may not ever have heard of. In this chapter we will suggest a specific document format for presentation of the design to the training's sponsor.

What You Will Learn in This Chapter

- Considerations for design of a learning sequence
- Application of design possibilities to training needs
- A format for a design document

Context

The Trainer's Dictionary defines the design document as:

> "A formal courseware development document required to ensure that all parties understand accurately what the planned CAI lesson (module, course) will be once developed."

As in the preceding chapter, we will begin by showing you the end product. In this case, it is the outline from which you can prepare a design document for any project. Figure 11.1 shows a suitable outline.

Let's look at the problem. What are we trying to accomplish? Taking the definition from what we wrote in the introduction to this chapter, we want to accomplish several things. They include:

- Demonstrate an understanding of the problem, organization, and instructional setting
- Set expectations of what the planned instructional product will be once it is developed
- Build in a procedure
- Structure the whole project
- Manage the customer's expectations

We rely on the design document to accomplish all of this.

Differences in format

The design document may also vary somewhat between projects. The reason for that is that we may have additional goals for the document and the structure of the entire project may vary.

If the project is solely analysis and design (there are such projects), the design document will be the principal deliverable of the entire project. In other cases, the statement of work may be complete and detailed or virtually nonexistent.

All these differences can be summed up as a need for structure and information because they are not provided elsewhere in the project. For example, your organization may have a detailed process document outlining how you will perform instructional development projects (not unusual). The customer probably isn't going to read it and you can't point to it later and say, "Well it says in here that we can't make changes at this point." It will prove much more effective to point to a signed copy of the project's design document that includes such verbiage, and to point to the signature and say exactly the same words. Don't think you will never have to do this.

Let's look at each of our goals in a bit more detail.

Demonstrate an understanding

Even though you have been engaged to do this work it is necessary to demonstrate that you didn't just emerge from a lifetime spent in a cave. This is accomplished by outlining the background of the project with sufficient description of the organization to build the customer's confidence that you understand the organization and setting in which the learning is needed.

Remember, you don't know who or how many people in the client organization don't want the project, you, or both. Your arrogance or naiveté can play into their hands, bringing your project to an untimely end. This is something to remember well beyond writing the design document.

```
Design Document Outline

1. Introduction
1.1 Background
1.2 Statement of need
1.3 Target population

2. Approach
2.1 Goals
2.2 Objectives
2.3 Existing materials
2.4 Instructional strategy(ies)
2.5 Assessment plan
2.6 Evaluation plan

3. Constraints and requirements
3.1 Equipment
3.2 Software
3.3 Entry behaviors

4. Course structure
4.1 Organization
4.2 Schematic representation
4.3 Design standards
4.4 Proof of concept

5. Lesson content narrative(s)
5.1 Title
5.2 File name
5.3 Length
5.4 Instructional objective(s)
5.5 Overview
5.6 Learning activities
5.7 Assessment
5.8 Content reference(s)

6. Execution
6.1 Programmer-ready materials (PRMs)
6.2 Final courseware development
6.3 Roles and responsibilities
6.4 Deliverables
```

Figure 11.1 Outline for Design Document

Set expectations of what the product will be

To do this, include a very complete word picture of what will happen in each part of the product, lesson-by-lesson in multiple lesson products. The learning objectives, instructional strategy, and a narrative summary of each element is included.

Also include a flowchart of the overall operation of the product. Usually this can be done in a flowchart covering a single page, but if greater detail is needed you must provide it.

This is a very important stage of the project. You must clearly convey your ideas and answer all potential questions that the training's sponsor may have, to avoid expending big efforts in the wrong direction.

Build in a procedure

Don't expect the customer to know the ISD process or how you plan to carry out the project's lesson development. They may, but more often they don't. In fact, they may have a concept that is totally wrong. Include as much explanation of your process as the document can stand. This provides advance notice of what you are doing at any stage, and can provide a reference to what the customer is expected to do, when, and on what schedule. In practice this is the beginning of an educational process involving your customer. If you teach the process to the customer as it unfolds you will avoid potential misunderstandings.

Structure the whole project

This is not too different from the preceding point. We are concentrating here on the aspects of the project beyond the instructional development. Include milestones, PERT and Gantt charts, and schedules. Use a program like Microsoft Project or MacProject to easily produce professional looking schedules. Figure 11.2 shows a typical PERT chart and Figure 11.3 shows a Gantt chart for the same project.

Include designations of who is responsible for what. Identify who will sign for the customer. The design document should be received, reviewed, and approved by the customer, so have the person named in it who will sign for the customer. Sign it just above the words "Approved by" with a date. The same design document in this chapter shows a separate signoff sheet that can be used to formalize customer approval and acceptance.

Manage the customer's expectations

You will have succeeded if, when you show the customer the programmer-ready materials (PRM) that implement the design you described in the Design Document, they are not surprised.

We've never seen a case quite this bad, but imagine a design document that says a symbolic figure, representing the organization, will introduce each of the lessons. Three different readers may all say they like it, but one of them pictures a ballerina, another sees a clown, while the third imagines a pirate! If you mean to include a pirate as the symbolic figure, say so.

Typical Instructional Content

Figure 11.4 lists the elements that are often a part of a typical complete instructional presentation. Note that it includes CMI elements. There may be a separate CMI system to accommodate the testing, prescription generation, and record keeping functions. When that is the case, typical lessons would have solely instructional content.

Flowchart

Produce and include a flowchart that makes it clear how the instructional, and possibly administrative, elements will connect and what can be accessed from where. Figure 11.5 is a sample of a flowchart for a lesson.

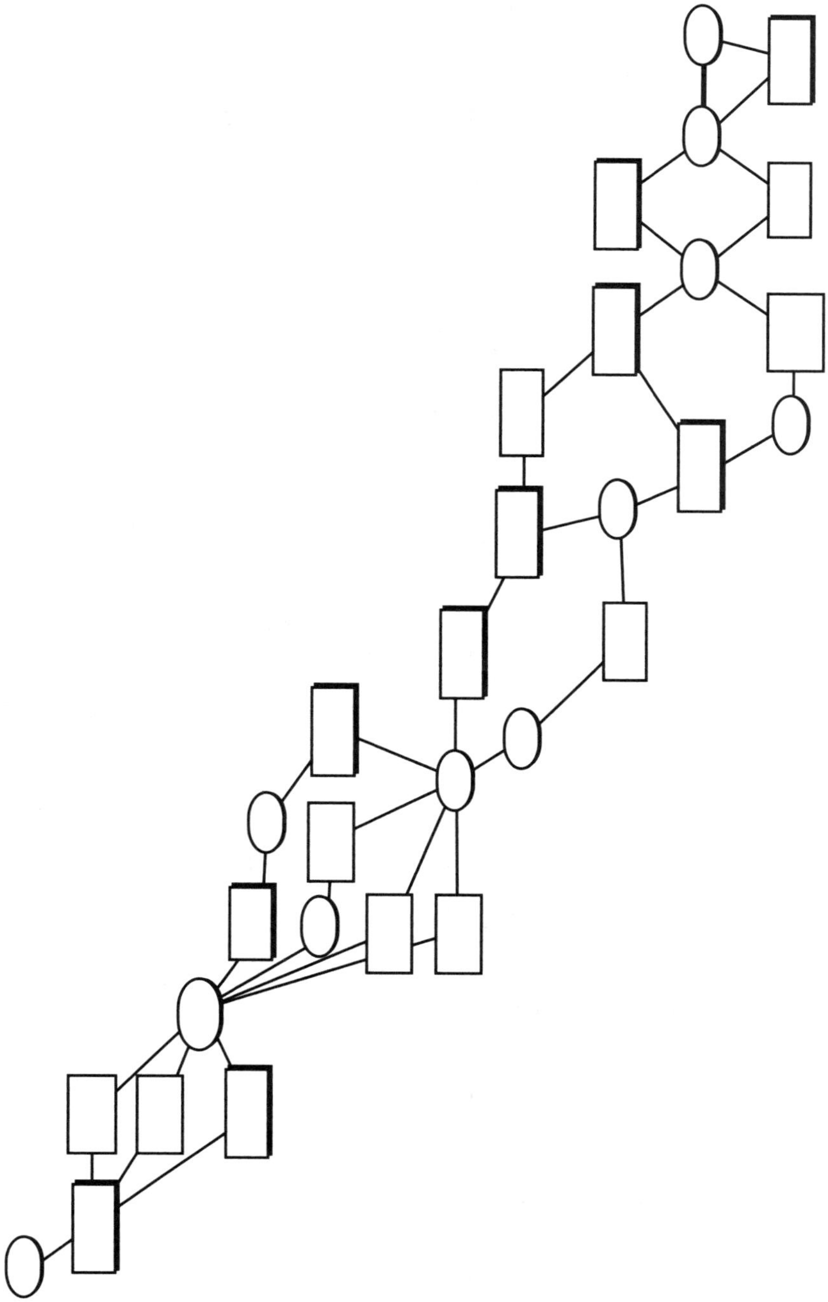

Figure 11.2 Sample structure of a Project PERT Chart

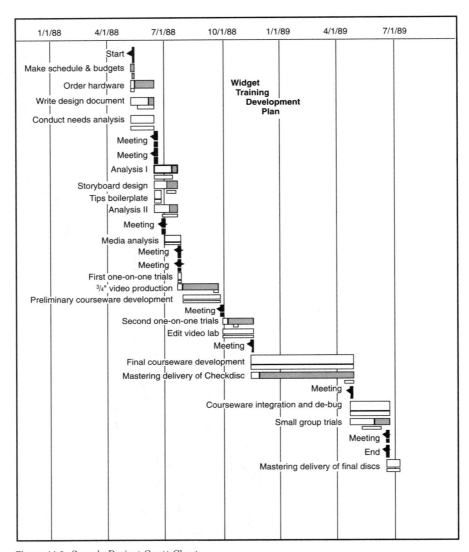

Figure 11.3 Sample Project Gantt Chart

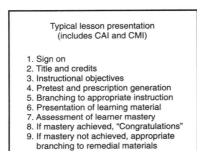

Typical lesson presentation
(includes CAI and CMI)

1. Sign on
2. Title and credits
3. Instructional objectives
4. Pretest and prescription generation
5. Branching to appropriate instruction
6. Presentation of learning material
7. Assessment of learner mastery
8. If mastery achieved, "Congratulations"
9. If mastery not achieved, appropriate
   branching to remedial materials
10. Appropriate records stored

Figure 11.4 Typical Instructional Structure

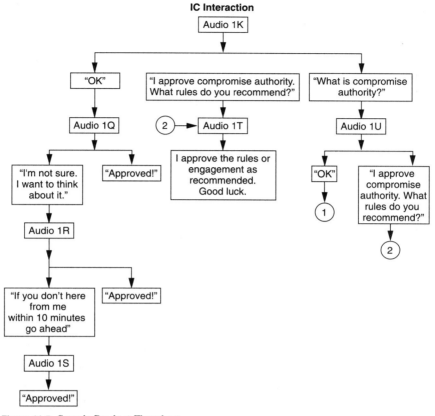

Figure 11.5 Sample Product Flowchart

Narrative

As we indicated earlier, the document must make it clear what will be developed. Many elements contribute to the needed clarity, but this is accomplished principally in the content narrative of the element's description.

Crane Operator Design Document

Now let's look at the design document that we prepare for the Crane Operator course. It is based on the outline shown in Figure 11.1. The whole Crane Operations Curriculum includes a mouse practice utility for those learners who need it, lessons on orientation to the crane, operation, operator maintenance, and safety. We will limit this book to following part of the operation lesson. It has two units—signal recognition and control functions. You will develop the mouse practice in Chapter 13, a sign-on utility for the whole Crane Operations Curriculum in Chapter 14, and the crane operator's signal-recognition lesson in Chapter 15.

We will use the example, practice, test paradigm to present the crane information to the learner. An additional possibility that will not be included in this lesson is to provide easy and hard versions of each of the three: example, practice, and test. We

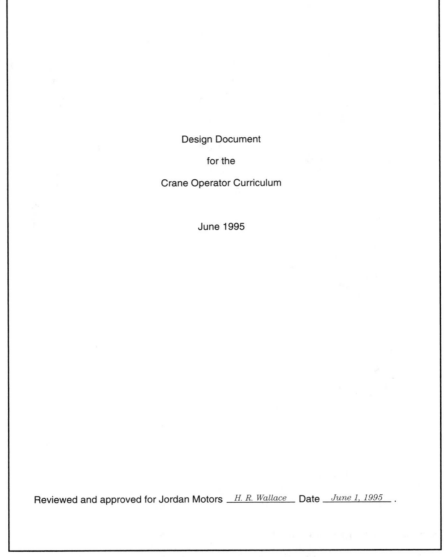

Design Document

for the

Crane Operator Curriculum

June 1995

Reviewed and approved for Jordan Motors _H. R. Wallace_ Date _June 1, 1995_ .

Figure 11. 6 Crane Operator Curriculum Design Document Cover Sheet

also think hands-on practice with a real crane is of maximum importance in the whole curriculum. As we focus ever inward toward the portion you are going to develop, the hands-on practice will fade into the background. That is because of this book's emphasis on programming. Never let such a need fade from the forefront of your thinking when involved with your own projects.

Since you do not need the entire design document for the crane operator curriculum, we will detail only the portion that relates to your first Authorware programming experience, a mouse-practice utility. Notice that we do not call it a lesson. The following figures are highlights from the Design Document for the Jordan Motors Crane Operator Curriculum. Figure 11.6 shows the cover sheet with the signature of the Jordan Motors manager who is designated to review and approve project documents.

We would start each section on a fresh page, but in the interest of saving a few trees, we present each one right after the other in this chapter. Here is the design document itself. Information deleted to avoid redundant information is indicated by an ellipsis (...). Our comments are shown in brackets ([]). Figure 11.7 shows the Table of Contents and Figures 11.8 to 11.19 show the rest of the document.

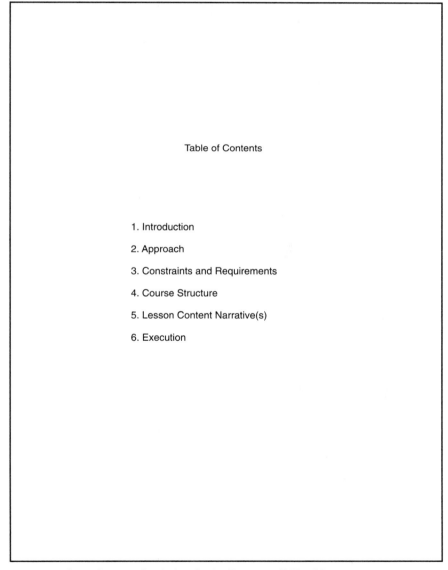

Table of Contents

1. Introduction

2. Approach

3. Constraints and Requirements

4. Course Structure

5. Lesson Content Narrative(s)

6. Execution

Figure 11.7 Crane Operator Curriculum Design Document Table of Contents

1. INTRODUCTION

Background

Meetings were held in Oshkosh, Wisconsin during the weeks of January 13–15 and 17–21, 1995. In these meetings, Jordan Motors subject matter experts and representatives of some of the organizations concerned with manufacturing training and multimedia project team members discussed requirements for the planned crane operator curriculum development. In Oshkosh, newly hired members of the training target population also were interviewed and observed at their jobs. The design for the crane operator course presented in this document is based on analysis of the information obtained from the Oshkosh visits as well as supplementary information gained from discussions with the Jordan representatives and subject matter experts (SMEs) in-person or over the telephone. This document presents the design of the proposed course, as well as the lessons that comprise it, and the course development plan.

Statement of Need

When a non-palleted item must be moved within the manufacturing area, it must be rigged and lifted and moved to the desired location accordingly.

Specific standard hand signals are used by the machinists and line workers to signal the crane operator, who often cannot directly see the load and/or its destination. When a load is moved there is possibility of injury to a worker or damage to the load, other equipment, or the structure itself. There are a variety of controls for cranes, depending on the size, type, and manufacturer. Safety considerations and operator maintenance is similar for all types of cranes.

This course is being developed to provide crane operators with the knowledge required to perform their job effectively. Although the overall crane operation process involves other related tasks, this course will focus on the specific task of operation and operator maintenance, the procedures for doing these tasks and what the operators need to know to ensure the safety of crane operations.

At the end of training, the Crane Operator must be able to safely and accurately operate Jordan Motors cranes.

– 1 –

Figure 11.8 Crane Operator Curriculum Design Document, Page 1

Target Population

The personnel involved in crane operation include manufacturing technicians, machinists, operators, and plant general mechanics. All personnel have at least a high school education. Some are college graduates, or are enrolled in college. Few have completed a formal course of study in mechanics. All complete OSHA training as required by Federal laws and regulations. Specifically, all have completed Lockout Tagout training with 12 months.

[Be as thorough as possible in describing the target population.]

2. APPROACH

[This is a new section. We would start it on a fresh page.]

Goal

Manufacturing operators and technicians involved in crane operation will become thoroughly familiar with the procedures and methods for safe movement of materials within the manufacturing area as well as proper operator maintenance of the equipment.

Learning Objectives

After completing this course the student will be able to:
1. Given representations of standard hand signals, identify the crane movement associated with each.
2. Given a standard hand signal, indicate the crane control operation necessary to carry out the motion indicated by the signal.
3. . . .

Existing Materials

There are no existing Jordan Motors materials to support crane operator training because the training has always been conducted by on-the-job training.

[You should attempt to identify existing materials. Any suitable material will reduce the total development cost.]

Instructional Strategies

There are no existing Jordan Motors materials to support crane operator training because the training was always conducted by on-the-job training in the past.

– 2 –

Figure 11.9 Crane Operator Curriculum Design Document, Page 2

Preliminary analysis of the information obtained at the meetings in Oshkosh, and of other efforts for Jordan manufacturing courseware development, has led to the following conclusions:

1. The main focus of the crane operation course will be on enabling the student to move loads safely.

2. New crane operators can be assisted in their work effectively by a course that provides clear step-by-step learning. For this, we propose the example, practice, test instructional paradigm.

3. Crane operators should not be overwhelmed with information that is not necessary for the effective performance of their jobs. However, when access to the concepts and principles involved can make the procedures more easily understood and remembered, they should be included.

4. The operators must know when, why, and how to undertake operator maintenance.

5. Novice crane operators cannot be expected to memorize all the information and procedures immediately, and will need a reference accessible to them while performing their work.

The recommended approach follows.

Consultant analysts, together with Jordan Motors subject matter experts, have observed and interviewed crane operators performing their work at the Oshkosh plant and have gathered detailed information about the operating process. Consultant instructional technologists will analyze this information to identify the specific tasks and problem areas, and develop lesson content.

A multimedia TBL course will be developed. This will be delivered on CD for installation to run from the hard drive of the corporate standard microcomputer.

Assessment Plan

Tutorial lessons will include progress checks as appropriate. Assessment will be at the curriculum level, as well as in supervisor sign-off.

Evaluation Plan

There will be formative and summative evaluations. The formative evaluation will occur during the development. Selected candidates for the crane operator course will be identified by Jordan. One will work with a designer to review the programmer ready materials. Later, another will review the completed programmed lesson. The summative evaluation will consist of post on-line assessments delivered at the curriculum level.

– 3 –

Figure 11.10 Crane Operator Curriculum Design Document, Page 3

3. CONSTRAINTS

Equipment

Each of the Jordan Motor's plants have corporate standard 486DX66 workstations consisting of a high-resolution terminals, a hard drive, one or two disk drivers, and a CD-Rom drive.

[Be specific. You may later be asked why your course doesn't run on a 386.]

Jordan would like to retain the current 486 VGA learning station capabilities and so it has been decided that all new courseware would be designed for the standard workstation. There remains the future possibility of upgrading the existing microcomputers to faster, state-of-the-art models. In that event, the courseware could be downloaded ready for use on these computers without extensive redesign.

Software

It is understood that a courseware hour will be the equivalent of 30 frames. Lessons will be indexed and self-paced, will utilize graphics, and will provide exercises to ensure understanding of the content. Pre- and post-testing will be compatible with, and will use, the to-be-developed corporate CMI system.

[This quantification is inserted at the insistence of Jordan Motors purchasing. They insisted on something to count to prove they got what they paid for. You may encounter this on some projects. You will develop the CMI system in chapter 23.]

Entry Behaviors

The learners who require the crane operator training have no previous background in crane operation.

[Unlike the target population description, this is a specific statement of what prerequisites, if any, must exist in learners and without which they cannot be expected to master the instruction.]

– 4 –

Figure 11.11 Crane Operator Curriculum Design Document, Page 4

160   Building a Technology-Based Lesson

4. COURSE STRUCTURE

Organization

We currently envision the course to consist of five lessons and an integral Job Aid. The lessons are:

1. Introduction of crane operation
2. Safety
3. Signals and controls
4. Operator maintenance
5. Supervised on-the-job practice

A significant feature of the course is the inclusion of a Job Aid for the operator to use both during the course, and at any time later and while performing his or her work. This Job Aid will include a visual representation of hand signals and a list of operator maintenance items. This will permit the operator to access summarized information to avoid error.

The estimated course length will be approximately four hours of instruction, plus the integral Job Aid which will consist of approximately one label. The instruction will be supplemented by four additional hours spent operating a crane under the supervision of a master operator.

[This level of quantification is desirable. This is the minimum.]

Descriptions of this course and the lessons are contained in sections 9 and 10. The Job Aid is described in section 11.

Schematic Representation

The Jordan Crane Operator Course will consist of approximately four hours of CBL courseware with integrated job aid. The course emphasis will be on teaching the student how to operate cranes safely. The example, practice, test paradigm will be used throughout the course to present the information and provide reinforcement to ensure proficiency in applying it. A schematic diagram of the course structure is shown in fig. 1.

Schematic Representation

This course will follow the Jordan Motors corporate design standards for technology-based learning (JMTS03-94).

– 5 –

Figure 11.12 Crane Operator Curriculum Design Document, Page 5

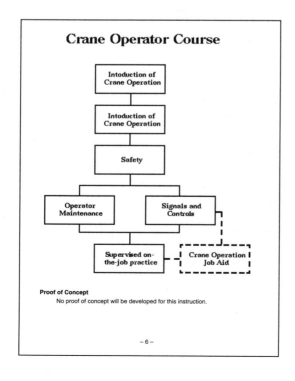

Proof of Concept

No proof of concept will be developed for this instruction.

– 6 –

Figure 11.13 Crane Operator Curriculum Design Document, Page 6

5 LESSON CONTENT NARRATIVE

Curriculum Utilities

Lesson Title: Mouse Practice

Length: Five minutes or less

Description:

This utility will provide an opportunity for learners, who want it, to learn the operation of the mouse. It will be offered as a curriculum level option. This lesson will present the learner with three challenges that must be mastered to operate a mouse in Jordan Motors technology-based lessons: move the mouse accurately, click and double-click on a screen object, and drag a screen object.
The following topics will be included:

• Move the mouse accurately
• Single click and double-click on a screen object
• Drag a screen object

Lesson Purpose:

After completing this activity, the student will have gained or reinforced an understanding of:

1. Mouse skills required to interface with Jordan Motors' lessons.

Instructional Objectives:
None.

Content Narrative:

The learner will be presented with a screen showing the numbers 1 through 5 arranged in separate locations. Directions will instruct the learner to move the cursor over each number in sequence. Only the number 1 will be active at first. When the learner moves the cursor over the number 1, it will be covered by an object. Each time the learner moves the cursor to one of the remaining numbers, in sequence, it will also be covered until all the members are replaced with objects.
When all the numbers have been replaced, the screen message will direct the learner to click on a specific object. Only the specified object will be active. When that object is clicked on, it will disappear with an effect and the message will change to direct the learner to click on a second specific object.

– 7 –

Figure 11.14 Crane Operator Curriculum Design Document, Page 7

After the second object has been clicked and removed the screen message will direct the learner to double-click on the third specific object. Only the specified object will be active and it will not respond to single clicks. Each time the learner double-clicks on one of the remaining objects, as directed, it will also be removed with an effect until all the objects are gone.
When all the objects are gone a screen will appear with pieces of a jigsaw puzzle. Screen directions will tell the learner to drag the pieces into an empty frame. A Continue button will also be available. The puzzle pieces are movable and may be dragged as the learner chooses.
When the Continue button is clicked the screen directions will disappear and be replaced by two buttons. Quit and Repeat Mouse Practice. The Quit button will return the learner to the curriculum. The Repeat Mouse Practice will present the practice again from the beginning.

6. EXECUTION
[This section should start on a new page.]

The following outlines the activities for the development of the Jordan Crane Operator course.

a. Task Analysis and Content Gathering
Consultant instructional design analysts and designated subject matter experts (SMEs) met in Oshkosh to perform a task analysis and collect data related to lesson content. This task analysis involved interviewing and observing personnel who are responsible for operating Jordan cranes to obtain increased knowledge of the specific tasks related to crane operation for use in lesson design. The analysis report was formally approved by Jordan Motors.

b. Course Design
The design document has been written to reflect the findings of the task analysis and content gathering meeting. A meeting will be held with representatives from Jordan to review this document and formally approve it as the design baseline.

– 8 –

Figure 11.15 Crane Operator Curriculum Design Document, Page 8

The design baseline document will clearly define the training requirements and the development plan and will constrain the scope of the lessons. Any deviations from the scope of effort defined by this document will clearly identified and presented during the requirements review.

c. Lesson Content

Meetings between Consultant personnel and Jordan Motors SMEs have resulted in completion of the content gathering. Consultant analysts have prepared lesson content reports in the form of this design document describing each lesson in the course in accordance with the guidelines set in the design report. The reports will be reviewed by Jordan SMEs to ensure that the following criteria have been met:

• The lesson structure, topics, objectives, and lengths are within the constraints specified in the approved design report.
• All relevant and necessary instructional objectives have been included.
• All topics necessary to meet the stated instructional objectives have been included.
• All references are complete and are correctly designated.

Any changes or corrections required will be clearly conveyed to Consultant. The reports will be revised and resubmitted for review and approval. Project development will not continue until the Design Document has been formally approved by Jordan Motors.

Programmer Ready Materials

Using the information gathered during the analysis and design, typed or hand-written PRMs representing the screen displays for each lesson, narration, and video scripts will be developed in accordance with the design report and content report. The PRMs will reflect the structure and content, including the graphics, of the TBL lesson, and will provide specific programming instructions concerning the displays, branching, judging, and feedback.
The design analysts and SMEs will perform a page-by-page review of the PRMs to ascertain that the following criteria have been met:
• The PRM is written in accordance with the design report and content report.
• The information presented is accurate and complete.
• The proposed instructional activities achieve the instructional objectives.
• Questions and feedback are unambiguous and clearly presented.
• The displays contain no grammatical or typographical errors.

– 10 –

Figure 11.16 Crane Operator Curriculum Design Document, Page 10

Any changes or corrections required will be clearly conveyed to Consultant. The programmer ready materials will be revised and resubmitted for review and approval. Programming will not continue until the Programmer Ready Materials have been formally approved by Jordan Motors.

Final Courseware Development

Consultant TBL programmers will develop the lessons according to the approved PRMs using the selected authoring tool, Authorware Professional. The lessons will be delivered on compact disk to run on the Jordan standard microcomputer in the Oshkosh training center.
As the programming for each lesson is completed, the lesson will be made available for Jordan review for the following:

• The lesson content and structure is in accordance with the approved PRM.
• All text and graphics are legible, and questions and feedback function as specified by the PRM.
• There are no typographical or mechanical errors.

After the lesson has been reviewed, Jordan will clearly convey any requests for corrections or changes to Consultant.

Job Aid Development

Consultant analysts will design an integrated Job Aid (for use both during and after course study) and will submit the design to Jordan for review. Jordan will review the design to determine if it properly serves its purpose of providing operators with a handy reference for performing their tasks. The design will be for a decal or plate suitable for mounting on or near each crane.
Jordan will discuss any desired changes with the analysts, who will revise the design accordingly and resubmit it for Jordan's approval. Once the design has been approved, the Job Aid will be designed constructed in the final format for production, and submitted for review of the following:

• It conforms to the design.
• The information and instructions are clear, technically correct, and complete.
• There are no grammatical or typographical errors.

After the Job Aid has been reviewed, Jordan will clearly convey any requests for corrections or changes to Consultant. The Job Aid will be revised and resubmitted for review and approval.

– 11 –

Figure 11.17 Crane Operator Curriculum Design Document, Page 11

Course Consolidation
When all lessons and the Job Aid have been programmed and reviewed, the Job Aid will be secured to each crane in a prominent occasion. Jordan will review the lessons for the following:

• The lessons and routers function with the CMI system as specified.
• All lessons are present and complete.
• There are no mechanical errors.

Any requests for corrections will be clearly conveyed to Consultant. The programmers will make the changes and load any corrected files for final review and approval. When approved, an archival CD will be delivered to Jordan with all course files and layout artwork for the Job Aid.

8.0 ROLES AND RESPONSIBILITIES
The Consultant project team will consist of the following team members:

Project Manager (Alexander Stakhanovich)
• Acts as the main point of contact between Jordan-designated personnel and Consultant personnel.
• Creates project plans, schedules, and checklists.
• Assigns specific tasks to Consultant personnel and monitors activities.
• Prepares monthly status reports.
• Participates in reviews of all deliverables.
• Coordinates travel arrangements and meeting schedules.

Design Analyst (Joycellen C. Clever)
• Works with Jordan subject matter experts to determine instructional goals and objectives, constraints, and scope.
• Collects and organizes subject matter.
• Develops instructional design strategy.
• Prepares design documents and content reports.
• Prepares lesson scripts and study guides and designs job aids.
• Performs quality assurance evaluation of disks and printed material.
• Interfaces with Jordan personnel to exchange technical information.
• Assists Jordan personnel in review of all deliverables and demonstrates disk usage.

Programmer (Paula Begay)
• Designs the programs and writes programming specifications.
• Translates scripts into CBL micro code.
• Checks and corrects programming code.
• Downloads code to CDS.
• Performs quality assurance testing of CDS.

– 12 –

Figure 11.18 Crane Operator Curriculum Design Document, Page 12

Jordan will designate personnel to the project to fulfill the following roles:

Project Manager (Gail Flowers)
• Acts as main point of contact between Jordan and Consultant project teams.
• Performs requirements assessment (with guidance from Consultant).
• Designates subject matter experts and other team members, as appropriate.
• Approves project plans and schedules.
• Monitors schedule compliance by Jordan personnel.
• Participates in reviews of all deliverables.
• Coordinates travel arrangements and meeting schedules.
• Signs approval and acceptance forms.

Subject Matter Expert (SME) (Winston Greer)
• Identifies existing documents and training courses.
• Provides Consultant analysts with all relevant course material and information sources.
• Creates forms, documents, and case studies where none exist.
• Answers questions relating to course content in a timely manner.
• Reviews all deliverables.

9. CONTENT REFERENCES
A partial list of references for lesson content follows.

• Hercules Crane Technical Manual.
• Jordan Crane Memorandum of July 27, 1991.

– 13 –

Figure 11.19 Crane Operator Curriculum Design Document, Page 13

Content Narratives

Each part of the entire curriculum would be described in detail in the content narrative portion of the design document. Only Mouse Practice is included in our example.

Tips on Design

We could write a whole book about design. Here are some ideas that we think you will find beneficial.

Chunk

One of the techniques that is part of the design process is called "Chunking ." To chunk the content, break it into small pieces and build in questions if a chunk is not otherwise interactive. Provide feedback on the questions, periodic reviews, and summaries for each segment. Chunking forces the learner to interact with the program more frequently than might be the case otherwise. The concept of chunking is also based on research about how people learn. If you chunk, you will not produce a page turner.

Blend

"Blending" the instruction you develop with practice will reduce boredom at the same time that it facilitates learning. If there is anything to practice in the content you are presenting up to that point, let the learner loose to try it! Blending practice into your lessons will give the learner an early chance to try out what he or she has learned up to that point. This is far better than making the learner wait an extended period to become involved.

Provide Feedback

Use on-screen feedback to inform the learner about the accuracy of a response. When used properly, feedback can help learners learn and can enhance their retention. Provide feedback for both correct and incorrect responses. Use the feedback to correct possible student misconceptions about the material. Otherwise, it may not be clear to the learner why the response was correct or incorrect (yes, even if they got it correct). To add to the learner's knowledge of results, feedback should provide specific information about the response the learner made at that point.

Never provide punishing feedback. Our experience in working with adults in business and industry reveals that they have often had negative experiences with learning and dislike "school." They are overjoyed (not an exaggeration in many cases) when they are praised for getting something right. They like TBL because it is fair and provides individual praise. Angus recalls vividly a 40-year-old repeating a sequence, because, at the end, it provided the on-screen reinforcement, "Super job Fred" with his own name. We avoid, and urge you to avoid, punishing wrong choices in any way.

Provide the feedback immediately after the response is made. Knowledge of the accuracy of their perceptions is important to the learner. Remember, we want the right information to go into long-term memory. Delay in providing feedback can confuse the learner. Provide feedback on the same screen where the learner made his or her response. Moving to a different screen increases the memory load for the student.

We don't often offer more than one try at a question, either in a progress check or on a test. If you decide to offer the learner more than one try at the same question, we think you should give a hint when you say "Try again." If the learner first thought A was the answer, he or she is obviously missing something. Since the learner does not have the information right, and certainly hasn't studied in the few seconds since the first attempt, without a hint he or she may fail again. The hint helps the learner recall the relevant information (you are helping the learner retrieve the information from long-term memory). The hint will help avoid frustration in the learner.

Example, practice, test

If you do not have a background in training you may not have seen good examples of instruction in your own experience, and you may not have any good instructional paradigm as a base to work from. In that case we can suggest one that is "tried and true." The example-practice-test model is instructionally sound, and you can tell how to use it just by hearing its name. Provide the three activities as you unfold your lesson. The main difference it is likely to make is that inexperienced developers may just use practice-test, or worse just examples. It isn't instructionally sound to test someone when they have not had an opportunity to practice. Remember, small progress checks for interactivity do not count as tests.

Example, practice, test is *not* always the best to use in every situation. However, if you lack an idea how to proceed, it is a good bet to start.

Meaningful interactivity

Research has shown that it is important to design as much meaningful interactivity as possible into your lesson. The ARA study quoted in Chapter 3 is not the only such study. At least a half dozen studies report similar findings. If the opportunities for interaction occur less than every three or four screens or, alternatively, less than about every minute, learners will not consider your lesson interesting.

Meaningful media

We could have called this section *gratuitous* media, the reverse of the same coin. When many computers were monochrome, it was disappointingly common to see color everywhere on platforms with that capability. We don't mean to suggest that it was tasteful or artistically pleasing; it wasn't. The overuse of the new color capability was the gratuitous use of color—using it for its own sake, rather than in a meaningful or instructionally related way. There are also gratuitous uses of audio, graphics, and video.

If you turn off the sound you will find that the movie *Jaws* isn't as scary. The music always gives clues of how we should feel. You can use sound effectively to provide cues. Audio can be very effective, but don't just play music because your computer now has a SoundBlaster card. Once the link between a sound and a specific event is established (i.e., a tune is associated with fixed events in the lesson), the sound can serve as an efficient navigation aid. For example, you can introduce all progress checks with a short but pleasant musical piece.

Use narration to provide continuity to your lesson. Do so even when you use video. Professional narrators are quite inexpensive and make a big difference in the outcome. If you haven't any idea where to start, contact an announcer at your local radio station. If you live in a metropolitan area you can always try a talent agency. When we use male narrators we seek a deep voice. When using a female we look for a pleasing tone. One idea you might try in a lesson that is sufficiently long is to alternate male and female narrators consistently, based on activity type. This can provide variety and retain the learner's attention.

Use narration to make the transitions from one concept to another clear. Keep narration short and simple and always provide a corresponding visual to accompany the narration. If the narration is too long, learners may become bored as they remain passive for an extended time.

We disagree with some experienced developers about the use of audio to warn students that they've done something incorrectly. They do this with a beep or an "oh-oh." As we stated when discussing feedback, our experience in working with adults in business and industry reveals that they have had enough negative learning experiences to last a lifetime already. Don't add to them.

We are frankly tired of seeing certain clip art that is supplied with popular art programs. We see the same images in presentations, in handouts, and in lessons. The issue isn't whether it should never be used; it should be. What disappoints us is that it is used by organizations that could easily afford the improved appearance that comes with original art.

We also think that video should serve some purpose. There is no point in using video unless it can add something of its power to show detail, motion, or model human behavior. Currently, the extra cost associated with including video keeps it from being used where it makes no sense at all. We believe that it will become more common as it becomes cheaper to include, resulting in more gratuitous use of video.

Learner vs. program control

We find many opportunities to combine program control with learner control of sequence, as you will find yourself doing as you develop the lesson in this and the next section of this book. Basically, we use program control when we know that material covered in lesson parts is sequential. When pieces of the instruction must be completed by the learner without a specific sequence, we maintain learner motivation and interest by giving them the choice of the order in which to pursue topics.

Get Ready

Well, you have your design document signed and approved by the customer. The next step is to make the design even more clear. To do that you have to produce programmer ready materials (PRM) that illustrate exactly how you plan to execute the design word picture that was just approved. We'll get to that right now. Let's move on to Chapter 12 to get the details.

12

Programmer Ready Materials (PRM)

This is a true story. A big corporation had a one-hour videotape professionally made, at a cost of $60,000 in 1980. When the completed tape was shown to a corporate vice president for approval, he said "No, that's not it at all." Due to the great cost of redoing the videotape, it was left undone. The multimedia course that contained it was never completed. There may be other true stories of even more stupid bungling out there, but we don't know of them personally. The whole reason for following a three-step approval process is to ensure that the ultimate customer for the program understands exactly what is being developed. There should never be a surprise. If there is, it is the result of poor project management.

In this chapter we will examine programmer ready materials (PRMs), the technique we use to advance the ideas described in the design document without risking programming something the customer didn't expect and possibly doesn't want.

Sometimes simply called simply "scripts" or "storyboards," complete programmer ready materials may include more than that. PRMs include any other documents needed to convey the details of the completed courseware. We prefer to avoid the term storyboard, because that term is used in video production to describe a document that has a different format. Likewise the term script suggests a totally text document, used in broadcast radio, video production, and the theater.

The goal for PRMs is to be so complete that they can be shipped to a competent programmer in another city who could complete the lessons without any additional information. This is not only a goal; it's good business because it happens all the time when overflow-level work requires it.

PRMs are a formal prerequisite to the programming of CAI, IVD, Hypermedia, and multimedia courseware. If you are a hobbyist developing a lesson for your sole use, and are also the subject matter expert or are able to survive a large number of successive reprogrammings of your lesson, you probably don't need to bother. Otherwise, if you are involved with normal courseware development, we simply advise you that this is the proper way to do business. As far as we know, all professional developers prepare the complete PRMs required to support their planned lessons. We would never be a customer for, or work with, a subcontractor that didn't.

What You Will Learn in This Chapter

- Importance of paper development
- Format for programmer-ready materials
- Techniques for producing programmer-ready materials

Programmer Ready Materials—Storyboards

The programmer ready materials (PRMs) used for multimedia courseware development consist primarily of a form that conveys complete information about what will happen at a given instant in the finished program, and what will happen depending on what the learner does next. Let's not delay in providing you with as clear an idea as possible of what we are talking about. Figure 12.1 shows a blank form used for developing storyboards for the PLATO and modular Macintosh systems. Note the square display format.

Format

We can't say use *this* or *that* storyboard format. There is no absolute standard for a storyboard. It is best to customize them so that they match the workings of the authoring system that you plan to use and the eventual delivery platform. This was formerly much more important due to the limited space for text on the screen (at one

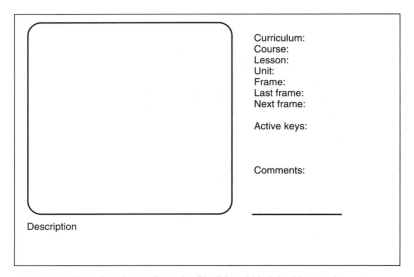

Figure 12.1 Blank Storyboard Form for PLATO and Modular Macintosh

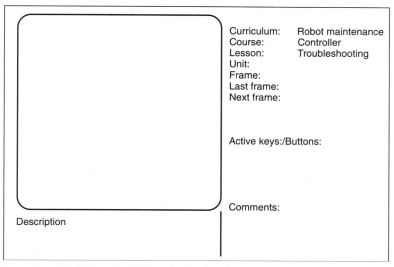

Figure 12.2 Blank Storyboard Form for the 3 × 4 Platform

point 40 characters per line with a maximum of 20 lines). All the lines and spaces weren't filled. It just clarified exactly what could go in what space to use a form that had a 40 × 20 grid.

We suggest that you develop a custom storyboard for your lesson, even if the only customization is to preprint the course name on each blank form. There are a variety of ways of automating the task. Figure 12.2 shows a storyboard format for Windows programming, customized for a Ford Motors lesson.

Appearance

Before we describe some of the ways to automate the storyboard development process, we want to deal with the issue of appearance. Some highly qualified, experienced developers insist that the storyboard present a very finished appearance, with text entirely in fonts and with graphics prepared on a computer before placement in the space representing the screen on the storyboard. Other designers, with equally impressive credentials believe that storyboards can be completed in pencil, with the graphics done as a sketch approximating the appearance and location of the final graphic. The better-looking storyboards do take more time and resources to produce, but that is not the sole reason some prefer to work manually. They believe that manually prepared storyboards suffice.

Presumably there are still other qualified developers who take various positions between these extremes. Hybrid storyboards are partially done using a word processor, and combined with graphics done separately, using scissors to literally cut and paste them together. Faster even than 100% manual, the hybrid method is still the most productive method we have seen for producing storyboards under time pressure.

You will have to decide for yourself, but here is our advice. Match the PRMs to the project. If you believe that the client expects a finished appearance, that fact deserves consideration at a minimum. If the project has time and resources to make the storyboards attractive, the freedom to take the time makes it possible. On the other hand, if the project is either underfunded, on a short fuse, or both, you might want to consider manual storyboards.

Automate the storyboard development

The combination of Authorware and the Macintosh altered our development process. Authorware was the first significant CAI authoring system available for the Macintosh. Until the time both were available in the late 1980s, we used the manual method. The easy interchangeability of graphics within the Mac made it possible to develop the screens once on the computer, in PageMaker-based storyboards and, when the storyboards were approved, copy and paste them into the Authorware display. This is probably about as simple as it gets.

Using the same tools, you can do it the same way on the PC. Here are a couple of other methods we have used successfully on various PC projects. Using WordPerfect, create the formatted text portion of the storyboard. Use an art program to produce the graphics. Since WordPerfect may balk at the graphics being pasted directly into it, print, cut (with scissors), and paste the graphics into their positions in the printed text storyboards. This is essentially the hybrid method.

A second method is similar to the first, except that it uses Authorware. Use Authorware as the pasteboard for on-screen text and graphics. Print each screen and cut and paste it into the separately developed text portion of the storyboard. The advantage is that a portion of the displays that do not require editing are essentially finished. The disadvantage is that this method does not support the built-up screens that we often use in Authorware, necessitating some additional on-screen cutting and pasting.

Yet another method is to develop the entire storyboard in the art program. We have done this in Windows Draw, and then, when approved, have copied and pasted the finished content into the Authorware display. This method has the disadvantage that the art program does not handle text as efficiently as a word processor, and the total transfer of content to Authorware is tedious.

Storyboarding systems exist. But none have yet come to our attention that seem to offer a distinct advantage over methods such as those just described. The storyboarding system provides menus for input of various elements that will eventually make up the program, storing them in a data base. The elements are added to storyboards more or less automatically and can then be printed. The storyboarding systems we have seen to date seem to require more effort to enter information than is the case in directly storyboarding as already described. Also, the area available to represent the eventual screen is too limited in size to include all the wanted content for a what-you-see-is-what-you-get view.

PRMs—Other Media Drafts

The PRMs *may* consist solely of the storyboards, but if there are project deliverables using other media they will take other forms. If there is video, as is often the case with multimedia training, the video script is part of the PRM. If the video is more complex than simply a visible narrator, the video storyboard should also be included. You may also use an audio narrator, someone whose image never appears. In that case the audio scripts should be included in the PRMs.

Audio and video scripting

A standard two-column script is used for video and audio scripts. These also include familiar terms such as "pan." They also include industry-specific abbreviations, such as MS for "medium shot." Figure 12.3 is an example of a portion of a video script illustrating the video script format.

Figure 12.4 illustrates the format for an audio script. If you are unfamiliar with producing these documents, the details of how to do it are explained in *Selecting and Developing Media for Instruction* in Chapter 7.

Tips on Writing PRMs

If it is clear what every screen looks like, how it operates, and what will happen no matter where the learner clicks or what key is pressed, you can consider your PRMs successful. Here are some ideas:

- Include all paper documents for media that will be part of the lesson
- If instructions do not fit on the storyboard sheet for a particular screen, use another as an attached sheet
- Preprint as much common information   (such as lesson name) as possible, to speed development

Scene 5B Security - M/CU sitting at EOC table. Already facing camera after getting the viewer's attention.	None.
Scene 5C Security -	All secure!
Scene 5D Security - "	We have a reporter from the local TV station at main gate.
Scene 5E Security - "	I recommend that we close the main gate to non-emergency traffic // There is a downside // Some of the employees will be outside and some inside // It'll complicate accounting for everyone.
Scene 5F Security - "	Look, if we don't close the gate we're going to have a nightmare of people in the way// It's my best professional opinion.
Scene 5G Security -	We'll continue to maintain close coordination with external law enforcement.

Figure 12.3 Example Video Script

Scene 10A
Soap Opera - CU of male and female in
nondescript location with potted palm.

John speaks softly	"You know you're the only woman for me."
Marsha replies	"How could you do this to me?"
John speaks with more feeling	"I never wanted to hurt you!"
Marsha replies in kind	"All you ever wanted me for is my money!"
SFX - Banner passes by on the bottom of the screen: "Action news mobile team on the way to a breaking story."	News station's audio tune interrupts

Figure 12.4 Example Audio Script

Crane Operator Programmer Ready Materials

After careful study of the design document, you come up with the following programmer ready materials for the signals lesson of the crane operator course. Figure 12.5 shows the customized version of the storyboard that we have made for the crane operator. Notice that the lesson is listed as Mouse Practice in this template. We will make custom variants with the names of the other lesson parts.

Now we fill them in to complete the programmer ready materials. This lesson does not use narration or video, so there are no other documents to make up the whole PRM. Don't be mislead by this simplicity. We *always* include whatever additional documents are required. The following figures show the completed storyboards for the mouse practice portion of the crane operator project.

Notice in Figure 12.6 that we have given the storyboard a name rather than a number. Former authoring systems sometimes assigned a number like NZ1234—not very user-friendly to anyone involved.

The storyboards cannot remain sequential, another reason not to number them as their name. For example, we may have a storyboard called "Main Menu," showing a menu with five choices. Only one of the choices can possibly follow the Main Menu. The storyboards related to the second menu choice will have to follow somewhere later in the stack. There will be only one set of (one or more) storyboard(s) for the glossary. Let's call it *Glossary*. Many storyboards will refer to it, but it can follow only one of them.

We will show the storyboards to a colleague for review as a part of our development process. He or she may suggest that something must be expanded to be clear, and in response we must create a new storyboard. If we had numbered them, we would now have to create a non-sequential number. As it is, we just change the names of the storyboard before and after the new one to reflect insertion of the new one into its spot.

Even though Quit is not available, it isn't forgotten. Because Quit, Glossary, and other choices may be designed to be consistently available, we remove possible programmer confusion by stipulating its availability. The screen depiction provides a reasonable idea how we expect it to be laid out.

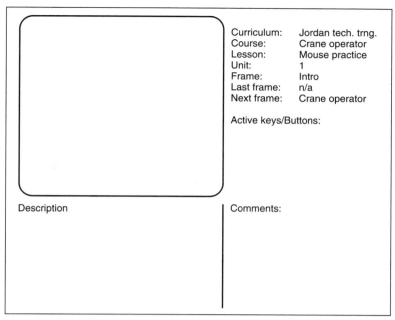

Figure 12.5 Template for Mouse Practice Utility

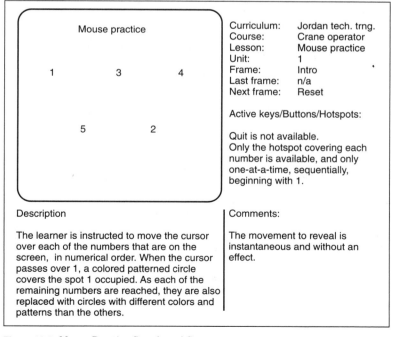

Figure 12.6 Mouse Practice Storyboard Start

The Comment shown in the Reveal shown in Figure 12.7 is a clue to the programmer that there is no significance to the move to the next storyboard in terms of lesson flow or structure.

In Figure 12.7 you can see that we are still in Unit 1. Remember that a unit is the portion of the lesson that covers one learning objective. There are no learning objectives set for this utility, so Unit 1 will be the only unit.

Again, the Description describes things that are not shown on this single screen. We think that the programmer (you, in this case) will be able to follow it and thatit describes the design clearly enough. If we had any doubt, we would insert a new storyboard showing the screen after the first circle had been clicked.

We have done our best to describe what is happening thoroughly and the text is a bit crowded, especially in Double-Click in Figure 12.8. Crowding is not unusual when you attempt to be thorough.

In Figure 12.8 the description was too long to fit in the Description section, so we have continued it in the Comments section. It happens that the description may be so long that it simply won't fit. In that case we say in Description, "See Double-Click2." Double-Click2 is a separate sheet that we place in our stack of storyboards just behind Double-Click. We take as much space as needed to explain what is happening on the screen, and how the learner will interact with it.

We do not provide separate storyboards showing the appearance of the screen after the upper left circle is clicked. The next storyboard may or may not represent a new section of program code. You should be interested in providing a clear idea

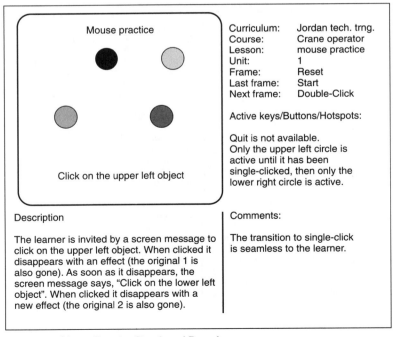

Figure 12.7 Mouse Practice Storyboard Reveal

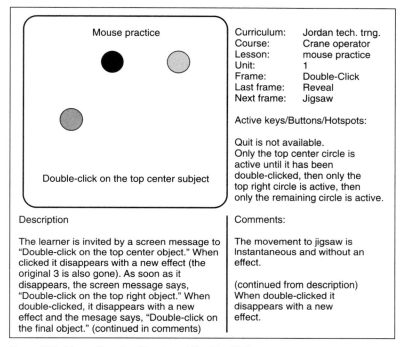

Figure 12.8 Mouse Practice Storyboard Double-Click

of what happens, rather than in matching the storyboards to the structure you expect the code to take. If you provide the idea clearly, the programmer will be able to follow your direction. If you try to outguess the programmer you may actually create confusion.

Figure 12.9 is an example of a storyboard written when we know who our programmer will be. In this case, of course, it will be you. We have specified that the shapes do not have specific targets, and nothing at all will happen if they are moved to the wrong location. We know this will be our programmer's first Authorware experience and we don't want to get into complexity. So, for now at least, the mouse practice will be a bit less polished than we would really like.

Figure 12.10 shows how we combine clarity and brevity when we know which authoring tool will be used to prepare the program, and are familiar with that tool. We specify that the Quit button will be **Quit(0)**, the specific Authorware function that produces the effect we want. In this case it is not outguessing the programmer, because it is a succinct statement of exactly the type of Quit we want, to return to Windows. It is preferable to specify exactly what the design calls for, as programmers have a tendency to solve programming problems in ways they find more interesting, rather than more direct. This is sometimes called eloquent rather than brute force. If brute force works equally well and will use less project resources (such as the programmer's time) we want brute force.

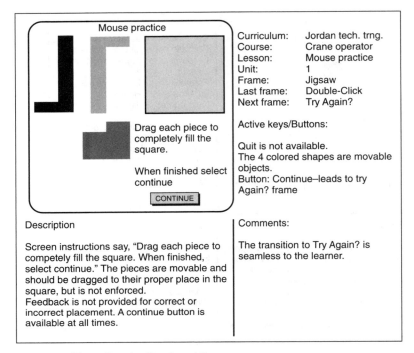

Curriculum:	Jordan tech. trng.
Course:	Crane operator
Lesson:	Mouse practice
Unit:	1
Frame:	Jigsaw
Last frame:	Double-Click
Next frame:	Try Again?

Active keys/Buttons:

Quit is not available.
The 4 colored shapes are movable objects.
Button: Continue–leads to try Again? frame

Description

Screen instructions say, "Drag each piece to competely fill the square. When finished, select continue." The pieces are movable and should be dragged to their proper place in the square, but is not enforced.
Feedback is not provided for correct or incorrect placement. A continue button is available at all times.

Comments:

The transition to Try Again? is seamless to the learner.

Figure 12.9 Mouse Practice Storyboard Jigsaw

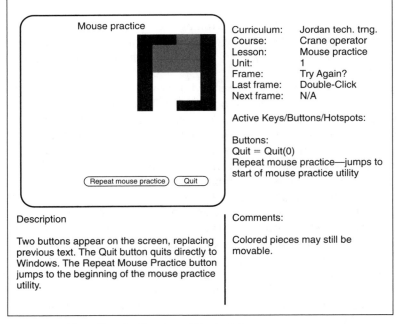

Curriculum:	Jordan tech. trng.
Course:	Crane operator
Lesson:	Mouse practice
Unit:	1
Frame:	Try Again?
Last frame:	Double-Click
Next frame:	N/A

Active Keys/Buttons/Hotspots:

Buttons:
Quit = Quit(0)
Repeat mouse practice—jumps to start of mouse practice utility

Description

Two buttons appear on the screen, replacing previous text. The Quit button quits directly to Windows. The Repeat Mouse Practice button jumps to the beginning of the mouse practice utility.

Comments:

Colored pieces may still be movable.

Figure 12.10 Mouse Practice Storyboard Try Again?

Eeek, a Mouse

You are ready to roll in more ways than one. You have the programmer ready materials in hand for the crane operator course and you are about to start working with Authorware.

You will begin your Authorware experiences with the mouse practice utility for your learners. We think that you will find it fun to make and it is within your capability as a beginning Authorware programmer. In addition, you will be able to use it with real learners who haven't yet conquered the mouse.

13

Welcoming the Learner

Now we turn to actually making things happen on the computer. This chapter establishes the basic Macintosh or Windows computer skills needed to follow the practical exercises in the succeeding chapters. We invite you to gain initial familiarity with the program by trying out the Authorware Welcome Lesson. We discuss the differences between authoring on the respective platforms and explore computer set up and the concept of rapid prototyping.

We devote the remainder of the chapter to a graded experience in building a useful module, using Authorware. We carefully cover each new learning point as you meet it, building experience and confidence in your ability as we go. By the end of this chapter you will have built a simple mouse practice module for your learners to use, if needed, before beginning the lessons that you will create.

What You Will Learn in This Chapter

- Primary differences between authoring on the Windows and Macintosh platforms
- How to set up the computer
- Concept of rapid prototyping
- How to use Authorware's calculation, display, erase, interaction, map, and wait icons
- How to import graphics
- How to use system functions

Programming

It is wise to establish programming standards before beginning to storyboard the content. Issues surrounding such standards are discussed in Chapter 32. We suggest that you proceed with this chapter, rather than exploring programming standards now.

Documentation

The ability to update material is an advantage of technology-based learning. Therefore, it is important for you to document the content. This problem is widely recognized. Unfortunately, learning specialists sometimes do not create or retain documentation of the process used to develop their instructional materials. This can make future revisions difficult.

Documents that you should retain include course specifications, learning maps, grouped and sequenced instructional objectives, test items, learning activity descriptions, lesson designs, assessment, evaluation, and a plan for the transfer of learning system. Among the most important documents are programmer ready materials—those that guide programming. You will refer to your PRMs to build the mouse practice lesson.

We will encourage you to continue to document your work as you move into the use of software.

Entry Level Skills

This book won't teach you how to manipulate the Windows or Macintosh interfaces. We must assume that you are already comfortable in the interface that you use.

Unfortunately, at least at present, you can't make the same assumption about the users of your lessons. We still come across people who might be called technological illiterates. They have yet to use any program requiring mouse control and haven't any notion how to use one. Also, in the same population of learners, are people who have been using a mouse for years. You will probably find that *your* target learners include both groups.

To be able to handle both groups you must find a way to provide *optional* mouse practice for those who want or need it. If you can't be present when they sit down to learn, then practice must be offered with the lesson.

Mac vs. PC

This book is intended to serve you, whether you develop on a Windows or a Macintosh platform. Authorware's working model 2.1's appearance is very similar in these two versions, making you ready to go on to the other version once you have mastered the first.

The biggest potential difference is that the mouse used with Windows computers has more than one button, while the Mac mouse has only one. Actually, the right button is used only rarely in Windows applications. Authorware makes use of the right mouse button principally to preview the contents of an icon without opening it. One potential further complexity is that some individual computer users may have configured their Microsoft computer for left hand use. This inverts left and right mouse button functions on that computer. If you or your learners have made this reconfig-uration, it can create some potential for confusing instructions that involve the right mouse button, or specifically states "left mouse button."

There are some other differences between the platforms. However, because we feel you would find it confusing at this point, we will present them in later chapters, where you can consider them in context.

Windows Descriptions

We show the Macintosh version of Authorware in the examples found throughout this book. We also describe the procedures that you will follow exactly as needed for development on a Windows computer. Sometimes the Macintosh interface is differ-ent in structure, procedure, or terminology. If the Mac-related difference is small, we simply point out the difference in parentheses. When it is significant, we point it out by including a Mac Difference sidebar similar to the one shown here.

 Mac Difference: The difference is described in a paragraph or more to the right of the Mac Difference icon.

File setup

If you haven't already done so, you must move the Authorware Working Model from the compact disk to your hard drive. To do this, use the file manager to find the SETUP.EXE file on the CD. Double-click SETUP.EXE and it will process the files and install them on your main hard drive (probably the C:\ drive on Windows systems) in a directory named MLTMEDIA, and will create a Multimedia program group with an Authorware program item for the Authorware Working Model. It also creates a MY_WORK subdirectory in which to store the lessons that you will create as you complete each of the chapters of this book. (On Macintosh computers it will create icons and folders.)

Time to feel welcome

If you have been patient enough to wait until now without running the Authorware-provided *Welcome* lesson, it is now time to do so! If you are unfamiliar with these fea-tures it can easily take 30 minutes or more to explore them thoroughly. Use the File Manager to find *welcome.apw* (*Welcome* on Macs). Double-click on it and explore the lesson. When the lesson opens it will look similar to Figure 13.1.

To run it you must do as the small icon at the top of the window's name suggests. Please select "Run" from the Try It menu. Look near the top of your screen for Try It. It is on the menu bar. When you click on it a pull-down menu will appear offering Run among other choices. Select Run.

This Authorware-provided overview will facilitate a general understanding of the purpose and potential of each of the Authorware development tools. Examine each one. Doing so will help you to quickly follow our suggestions and speed your under-standing of how to make the most of the capabilities of that development tool in cre-

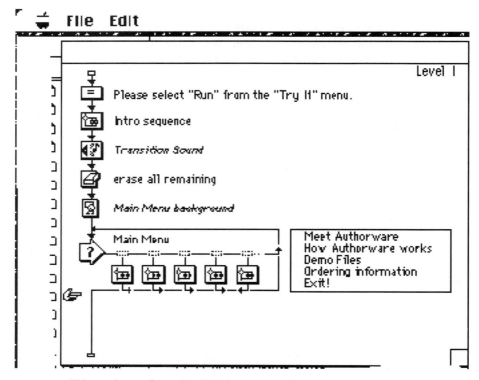

Figure 13.1 Welcome Lesson Opened for Running

ating useful and interesting lessons for your learners. Here is a checklist you can use to ensure that you have looked at each feature:

- Flowline
- Display icon
- Animation icon
- Erase icon
- Wait icon
- Decision icon
- Interaction icon
- Calculation icon
- Map icon
- Start and stop flags
- Sound icon
- Movie icon
- Video icon

- Libraries pull-down menu
- Attributes pull-down menu
- Try It pull-down menu

Time to mouse around

Since you already appreciate that your learners may not know how to use a mouse, you will start by developing a simple mouse practice module. You will create a scalable mouse practice module that will start with positioning the cursor on the screen, then single and double-click on objects, and finally click-and-drag objects to complete a puzzle. These are the three skills that people need to use a mouse-controlled computer program, such as the lessons you will develop. While you are building the mouse practice you will gain familiarity with the display icon tool box.

Rapid Prototyping

Rapid Prototyping is the term used to describe the process of quickly producing a small sample of a planned project. An early look at what you might develop often results in refinements, or a better understanding of how to make best use of the planned formats. Most of the lessons that we provide in this book can, with adjustment and adaptation, serve as rapid prototypes of the future lessons that you may develop. In this chapter, you will make a mouse practice module that may *look* crude, but works. After seeing how it works you could generate ideas to improve its looks.

Preview mousepr

To better understand the mouse practice module that you are about to create, we recommend that you run the sample *mousepr.apw* (*mousepr.apm* on the Mac) lesson that is included in this book's CD. Use the File Manager to find it and open it as you did *welcome.apw*.

Preview Lessons

We suggest that you try each sample lesson before you begin to build your own from scratch. This is the interactive version of Confucius saying, "A picture is worth one thousand words." Run the file from the CD now, and it will open revealing the icon structure that you will construct as you follow this chapter. It will take 3–4 minutes of simple effort to complete. Doing so will ensure that you have a clear understanding of the module you are about to create.

Double-click on the *mousepr.apw* icon to run the program from the CD. First, you will receive a warning that you cannot save the file. This is logical because you are running it from a compact disc that is a read-only device. The program will open to the first presentation screen, with directions prompting you to move your mouse to each number in sequence. As you encounter each number, a circle graphic will appear. After you reveal all five circles, the directions will change to tell you to single-click on the upper left circle. When you click on that circle it will disappear and new instructions will advise which circle to click next. As you continue to the third circle, you are directed to double-click. After you have removed all the circles, four puzzle pieces and a square frame will appear. The directions will prompt you to arrange the puzzle pieces within the square. When the puzzle is complete, select the Continue button. Finally, you are asked whether you want to repeat the mouse practice or quit the program. You may want to try the mouse practice several times, so you will be familiar with it as you build the same lesson from scratch. When you are finished, close Authorware.

Authorware Tip: You must be cautious in clicking. The *mousepr* program is in editable form, so that you can explore how the icon structures were originally created. In this form, the program will stop and open for editing if you double-click anywhere on the screen where only a single click is expected. This is convenient for authoring but can cause confusion for new authors. If you see "handles" appear on the screen objects, you can restore the program to running by choosing Proceed from the Try It pull-down menu. Don't worry about spoiling the sample program itself. Because it is on a CD you will not be able to change it.

Motivation

Actors often ask "what is my motivation" before rehearsing a scene. If your motivation is to learn Authorware, here it is.

We have written this book to help course designers and developers build sophisticated lessons using Authorware Professional. If you really are interested in developing your skills in using this software it is necessary to complete the exercises and follow the process yourself. If you only examine the sample code that we provide and work the exercises, you can expect to simply gain limited skill and knowledge of the functionality of Authorware.

You may remember Professor Harold Hill from *The Music Man*. He fraudulently told his band members that they could learn to play their instruments by the "think" system. We want you to know that to truly learn Authorware, you must use the "do" system.

Mouse practice creation

Mouse practice generally must include several different activities to prepare a learner for running most lessons. These are:

- Cursor movement practice
- Click and double-click practice
- Drag-and-drop practice

Now you will re-create the program you just tried. First, you will create the practicing cursor movement portion of the mouse practice module.

A word to the wise

We have done everything we can to make this first step one you can take without falling. We have reworked it many times, trying it each time with people new to Authorware and programming. Still, we know from these trials that some readers can find it a bit confusing. We offer this advice:

1. Read the chapter through before starting at the computer.
2. Note the numbered steps. They are what you are supposed to do.
3. Carefully read the teaching/telling text material to understand the what and why of what you will be doing to build the lesson.

Open Authorware

You will open a new Authorware file, start a new lesson, and save it as *mousepr*. To do this:

1. Double-click on the Authorware Working Model icon to open Authorware.
   When Authorware loads, it will display a menu from which you can either select an existing lesson to edit or generate a new lesson.
2. Select New.
   Your new file, named *untitled*, will open immediately. First, save your new file.
3. Select File from the menu bar at the top of your screen. When the pull-down menu appears, select Save. (On the Mac, you will be asked for your new file name immediately.) When asked the file name, type *mousepr*.
   Remember the DOS convention limit of 8 characters for your file name. (Mac users should use the same name to avoid confusion.) Before you select **OK** (**Create** on the Mac) you must consider where you will locate the file. The Authorware program will always attempt to save the file in its own current location, but that may not be where you want it.
4. Use the menu to move to the location where you want to store your new creation. We suggest that you place this and other files in the directory **my_work** on your local drive. This will probably be **C:\my_work**. (On the Mac it should be a folder titled **My Work**.)
   Once you have created the new file you will see the window with the lesson flowline as shown in Figure 13.2. You can tell where you are working because the window is titled *mousepr.apw* in the title bar at top center. Authorware added the .apw file extension for you. (No file extension is needed on the Mac.) The long vertical line that extends from the top to the bottom of the window is called the *flowline*. The flow of the lesson and flowline are very important in programming in Authorware.

 Mac Difference: When you select *New* you must immediately enter a name for the file and choose where you want to save it. On the Mac you have up to 31 characters for the file name.
   Figure 13.3 shows a map icon.
5. Drag a map icon from the icon palette to the flowline and release it.

The map icon will assume a place at the top of the flowline and its name, *untitled*, will appear at its right side. Authorware presents the names of all icons on their right side. The icon and name will be highlighted.

6. Immediately type the name you wish to give the icon. In this case, name it *intro*. Now, one by one, drag four more map icons to the flowline. As each is dropped, label it.

To follow along best, name the icons *intro*, *move cursor*, *single & double-click*, *drag pieces*, and *wrap up*.

Figure 13.4 shows how the screen should appear. When finished, save your work.

7. Save from the File pull-down menu. (We will not continue to remind you to save.)

Development Tip: You can name the icons more quickly than by selecting each with the mouse. If you press the return key, you will be able to advance to the next lower icon associated with the interaction icon. The next icon's name will be highlighted and ready for you to title.

Development Tip: It is always wise to save frequently. Almost everyone has lost work because they didn't save. Some application programs, including some other authoring systems, provide periodic automatic backups as a system feature. Authorware does not include this feature. **Wise programmers save frequently!**

Go With the Flow: Observe the flowline in Figure 13.4. It shows that the program progresses from top to bottom, passing through first *intro*, then *move cursor*, then *single and double-click*, then *drag pieces*, and finally the *wrap up* icon. As it passes through each icon on the flowline it executes the contents of the map icons.

Developing the intro

8. Double-click the *intro* map icon to open it.

Inside you will find another flowline that looks very much like Figure 13.2. Notice that in the upper right corner it says level 2. This indicates that you are working within an icon that is nested within another level of icons. Figure 13.5 shows a display icon.

9. Drag a display icon from the icon palette to the flowline inside the *intro* level 2 window and release it.

If you drop the icon into the level 1 window by mistake, you can simply grab it and drag it into the level 2 window because it is a simple matter in Authorware to drag icons between windows.

As before, it will assume a place at the top of the flowline and be called *untitled*, and both the icon and name will be highlighted.

10. Immediately type the icon's new name, *title*. Drag another display icon from the icon palette to the flowline and release it in a position below the *title* icon.

If it assumes a position above the *title* icon, simply drag it to a lower position until it stays there when you release it. You must persist until the icon is properly placed, because placement determines the functionality of the program.

11. Type this icon's name, *background*.

The completed structure for *intro* will look like Figure 13.6.

12. Double-click the *title* icon that you just named to open it for editing.

The window will open, showing the screen as your learner will see it (full screen on the Mac, and partial screen in Windows). Figure 13.7 shows the empty display. Currently, the blank display is like an empty canvas where you can create contents, using text and graphics. You will also see the Display Icon toolbox with the pointer tool highlighted. The pointer tool looks like an arrow.

Graphics toolbox

Recall the Authorware Welcome lesson. (If you have not run that lesson, it is still not too late to benefit from it.) The graphic toolbox includes the following tools: pointer, text, straight line, diagonal line, oval, rectangle, rounded rectangle, and polygon. Together, they provide the means to place text and shapes in your display without resorting to external software. Briefly, each tool provides the following capability:

- Pointer—Selects an object or text field.
- Text—Creates text fields, sets tabs and margins, specifies a scrolling text field.
- Straight line—Draws horizontal, vertical, or 45° lines.
- Diagonal line—Draws a line between any two points.
- Oval—Draws ovals and circles.
- Rectangle—Draws rectangles and squares.
- Rounded rectangle—Draws a rectangle with rounded corners.
- Polygon—Draws multisided objects.

---

13. Click on the text tool (the tool that looks like the letter A). Then click in the upper center of the screen and type **Mouse Practice**.

Don't be distracted by Authorware's text block length marker. Just type **Mouse Practice**. You will begin to see how the text block length marker works to control the line length of text in each text block as we move along.

14. Click in the small square in the upper left of the toolbox (called the close button) to close the *title* icon. Double-click the *background* icon to open it for editing.

The window will open, showing a blank screen and Display Icon toolbox as depicted in Figure 13.7.

15. Again select (click on) the text tool, then click in the upper left portion of the presentation window, and type **1**.

At this point, your screen should look like Figure 13.8. The text line may be very long.

If you click in multiple places, you will see new text lines in each of them replace the old. This can be disorienting to new authors, but persevere. You will get used to it. You can grab the small button at the end of the line with the text cursor to shorten the line if it bothers you. If you finish the text you can use the arrow cursor to select the text and change its dimensions, by dragging the buttons on the corners of the text box.

16. Continue to place five numbers as shown in Figure 13.9, in the same way that you placed the 1. Then type the direction "Move the cursor to touch each number in sequence" at the bottom of the screen.

    This will complete the display shown in Figure 13.9.

17. Close the Presentation Window by selecting the Close Box located in the upper left corner of the Display Icon toolbox.

    If you haven't been doing so on a regular basis, now would be a good time to save your work. We won't continue to remind you, but you should continue to save regularly in this lesson and all the others that follow.

    You are now inside the *intro* map icon and have finished work on this section of the mouse practice.

18. Close the *intro* map icon by double-clicking the close button located in the upper left corner of the active window (single click on the Mac).

    You are now at the *mousepr.apw* main flowline (level 1) showing the original five map icons.

About learner control

Authorware provides learner control through the interaction icon and its differing response types. Figure 13.10 shows the interaction icon. In this lesson you will work with the *text entry* response type.

The opposite of learner control is program control. We will introduce you to the program control function in Chapter 15.

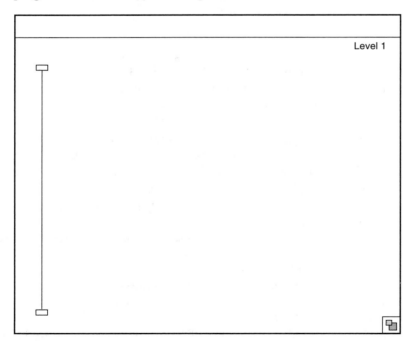

Figure 13.2 New mousepr File Window

Figure 13.3 Map Icon

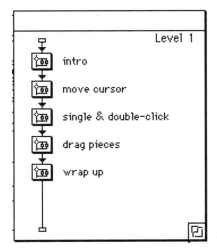

Figure 13.4 Design Map

Figure 13.5 Display Icon

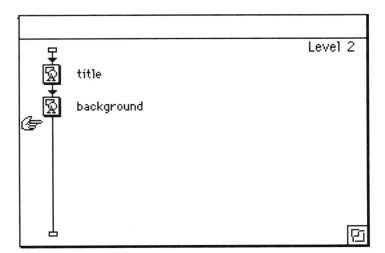

Figure 13.6 Intro Structure

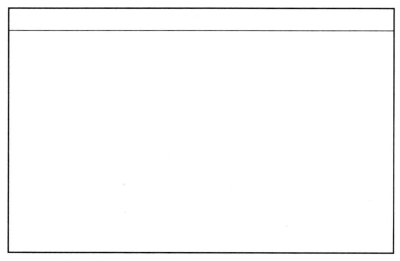

Figure 13.7 Display Icon Presentation Window

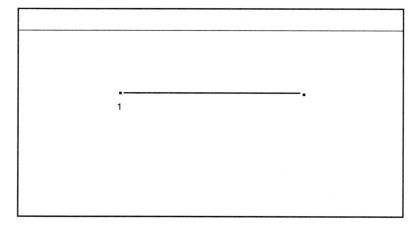

Figure 13.8 Beginning of Mouse Practice Display

Learner control

We define learner control as the ability of the learner to affect the outcome of the instruction. Learner control is accomplished through the interface tools provided by the system. In general, interface tools can include the light pen, touch screen, and voice activation. In this book we will confine our focus to the interface tools you are most likely to have—the keyboard and the mouse.

Through the tools provided by the computer, the authoring system (in this case, Authorware) will facilitate unique interfaces for inputting information. The practical effect of your interface choice is that the only way the learner can interact with the program is through these interfaces.

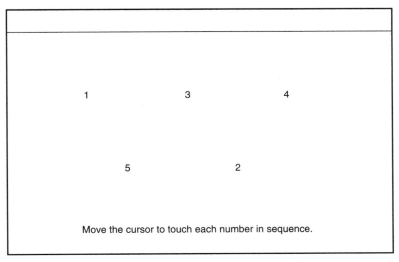

Figure 13.9 Mouse Practice Display with Numbers

 Figure 13.10 Interaction Icon

The mouse-related interfaces are:

- Pushbutton
- Click/touch
- Clickable object
- Movable object
- Pull-down menu

The keyboard-related interfaces are:

- Text
- Keypress

Authorware calls these interfaces *response types*. You will become quite familiar with them as you proceed through the rest of this book.

Developing the Move Cursor

19. Double-click the *move cursor* map icon to open it. After it opens, drag an interaction icon to the flowline.

   The icon will assume its proper position on top of the empty flowline, regardless of where on the flowline you release it.

20. Name it *hotspot 1*. Double-click directly in the center of the *hotspot 1* icon to change its default functionality.

Figure 13.11 shows the dialog box that will appear when you do.

21. Click on the small box called On Exit (Upon Exit on Macs) under Erase Interaction. This will activate the drop-down menu choices. Select Don't Erase.

Make sure that when you release the mouse the drop-down menu shows Don't Erase as the selected option.

22. Click on OK to close the dialog box. Now drag a display icon and drop it to the right of *hotspot 1*.

If it misses and drops to the flowline above or below *move cursor*, just drag it to the right of *hotspot 1* again until it "sticks." When it lands in the correct position it will cause an Interaction response type dialog box, as shown in Figure 13.12, to appear.

Notice that the response type default is Pushbutton. You are going to create a "hotspot" as the interaction's name implies, so:

23. Select Click/Touch. Then select OK to close the box. Name the display icon *shape 1*.

Figure 13.13 shows the appearance of the completed interaction.

Go With the Flow: Follow the flowline in Figure 13.13. As always, the flowline starts at the top, then it falls down into the *hot spot 1* interaction icon. Then it "looks" out of the arrow tip, checking to see whether any responses have been matched. In the case of *hot spot 1*, it continuously checks to see whether your learner has matched (in this case, passed the cursor over the top of) the *shape 1* hot spot. When the learner moves the cursor over the *shape 1* hot spot, the flow falls down into whatever icons are appended. If a map icon were appended to the *shape 1* hot spot there could be several icons, or an entire structure, in it to execute. In this case, it en-

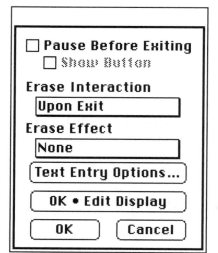

Figure 13.11 Interaction Icon Dialog Box

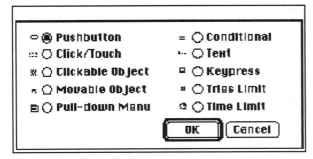

Figure 13.12 Interaction Response Type Dialog Box

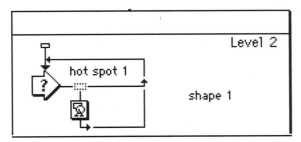

Figure 13.13 Hotspot 1 Interaction

counters a display icon that contains a graphic of a circle. It displays the circle on the screen and continues around to the top of the interaction icon.

Response Types

Response types are essentially the transitions between an interaction icon and any other icon on the flowline. If the requirements of a response type are not met, that branch of the interaction will not be executed. It is possible to include multiple response types in any combination in the same interaction. The response types and their functionalities are:

- Pushbutton—Displays a pushbutton that can be resized and repositioned.
- Click/Touch—Creates an invisible hotspot that can be resized and repositioned.
- Clickable Object—Turns a display object into a hot area the user can click.
- Movable Object—Creates a target area and a specified object to be moved to it.
- Pull-down Menu—Generates menus that the user can pull-down from the menu bar.
- Conditional—Creates a condition which must be matched.
- Text—Creates a learner text entry area.
- Keypress—Specifies a key the learner must press (frequent secondary response type).

- Tries Limit—Requires a specified number of times through an interaction.
- Time Limit—Sets a time limit on the learners inactivity in an interaction.

You will have the opportunity to practice using most of these as you complete the exercises in later chapters of this book.

Next you will change the Ease Feedback type to On Exit from the default of After Next Entry.

24. Carefully select the response type symbol (the small dotted rectangle) above the display icon *shape 1*.
    Refer to Figure 13.14 if you aren't sure. It shows the dotted line clearly.
    This will open the dialog box for the click/touch area.

25. *Carefully* double-click on the small response type symbol above the *shape 1* display icon and to the immediate right of the *move cursor* interaction icon.
    When you succeed, you will see the Click/Touch dialog box shown in Figure 13.15.

26. Click the Match With drop-down menu (button on Macs) to select Cursor in Area.
    This selection will permit Authorware to branch to the display icon when the learner moves the cursor over the number 1 that you placed on the screen. Soon you will position a click/touch area over the number to make this possible.

27. Next, click on the drop-down menu under Erase Feedback that reads After Next Entry.
    You will then see four options for erasing in the drop-down menu. They are:

Windows	**Macintosh**
After Next Entry	Before Next Entry
Before Next Entry	After Next Entry
On Exit	Upon Exit
Don't Erase	Don't Erase

These options control when Authorware erases any display icon attached to that particular feedback branch. For your *shape 1* display choose Don't Erase.
    Now you must change the default branching. The bottom drop-down menu under Erase Feedback controls branching. The default is Try Again. If you click on

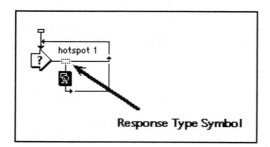

Figure 13.14 Click/Touch Dialog Box

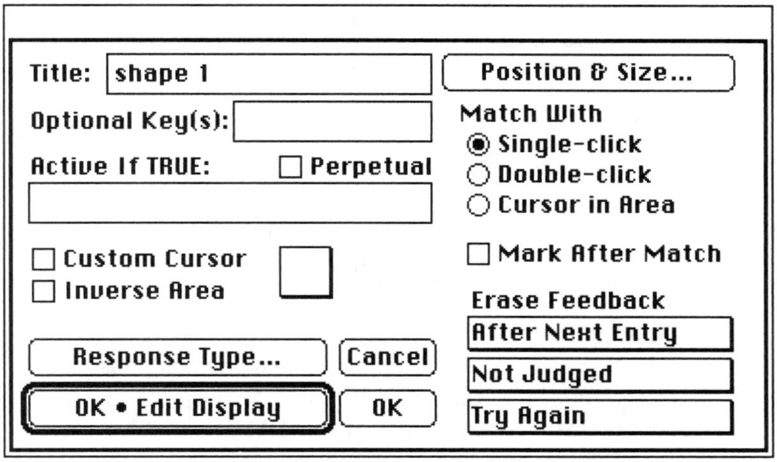

Title: [shape 1]   [Position & Size...]

Optional Key(s): [   ]   **Match With**
                               ⦿ Single-click
Active If TRUE: ☐ Perpetual   ○ Double-click
                               ○ Cursor in Area
[   ]
                               ☐ Mark After Match
☐ Custom Cursor   [   ]
☐ Inverse Area   **Erase Feedback**
                               [After Next Entry]
[Response Type...] [Cancel] [Not Judged]
[OK • Edit Display] [OK]   [Try Again]

Figure 13.15 Click/Touch Dialog Box

Try Again you will then see 2 more options (3 on Mac) for erasing in the drop-down menu—Try Again and Exit Interaction. There can be more under some circumstances. They are:

Windows	**Macintosh**
Try Again	Continue
Continue	Try Again
Exit Interaction	Exit Interaction
Return	Return

28. Change the setting to Exit Interaction.

     This will cause the flowline to drop out of the bottom of the icon and return to the main flowline, as you will soon see. By setting these features of the interaction now you will be able to copy this interaction and maintain all these settings in the copies.

29. Select OK (not OK-Edit Display) to close the dialog box.

     The completed icon will look like Figure 13.16.

30. Now select Run from the Try It pull-down menu.

     When the display with five numbers appears, the computer will pause. If the mouse practice were finished, this would be to let you place the cursor over the number 1. Because you have set the branching response to Cursor in Area, Authorware will automatically branch to the display icon that is next in the flowline below the click/touch area selected.

     At this point, the click/touch area is in its default position, not over the number 1. You want to position the click/touch area associated with the *shape 1* display icon to coincide with the number 1 on the *background* display icon.

31. Now select Pause from the Try It pull-down menu.

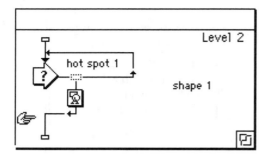

Figure 13.16 Move Cursor Structure

A dotted rectangle should appear in the upper left corner. This is the click/touch area. You can see it now because the program is paused. The click/touch area is invisible when the program is running.

You will move, resize, and reshape the click/touch area by dragging or stretching its borders.

32. Try to select the click/touch area by its top, bottom, or sides to move it without reshaping. Drag it to the 1 on the display. Now select one of its corners and drag to both resize and reshape the area as a square surrounding the 1.

    The position of the *shape 1* click/touch areas should be approximately as illustrated in Figure 13.17 on page 198.

33. Select Proceed from the Try It menu (it will be where Pause was earlier, because they are the two states of a toggle). Now pass the cursor over the number 1.

    Because the display icon is empty (no text or graphics), Authorware automatically opens the *shape 1* display icon's presentation window for creation of content. You can tell what you are editing because the name of the icon is shown on the toolbox. We want to have a graphic for display when the learner moves his or her cursor over the number 1.

34. Start by selecting the circle tool from the display toolbox. Use this tool to draw a circle, approximately the same size of the click/touch area you created earlier.

    The exact *location* of the circle doesn't matter. You will place it properly later.

 Authorware Tip: When drawing graphics within displays, you can maintain an equally proportional image (perfect square or perfect circle) by holding the shift button down while drawing the graphic. This is a standard convention used by many other graphic applications.

We want you to explore the variety of graphics Authorware is capable of creating. After you have drawn your circle, make sure it is still selected and:

35. Choose Fills from the Attributes pull-down menu. Pick a fill that you like, then click on OK to close the Fills option box. Close the presentation window by double-clicking in the upper left corner to return to the *move cursor* icon at Level 2.

Attributes

Attributes are qualities that you can specify that lend interest or appropriateness to displays. You can only apply them when you are editing a display in the presentation window, provided that the graphic toolbox is visible. There is an exception for the Effects attribute, which you can apply to a display or interaction icon that is selected. Attributes are:

- Effects—Specifies the way a display is shown; includes moveability, erasing features, and updating displayed variables and layers.
- Lines—Specified line types and thickness.
- Fills—Creates patterns for any object except text, bitmap, and line.
- Modes—Determines the effect of overlaying one object on another, or a background.
- Color—Set pen, foreground, and background colors.

You will employ many of the attributes in creating the mouse practice module. You will continue to expand your experience with them in later chapters.

Now you want to populate the *move cursor* icon with a total of five hot spot structures, one for each of the five numbers. Before you begin:

36. Maximize the application window. Then, using the standard Windows or Macintosh conventions, expand the size of the *move cursor* window so that it extends to the bottom of the screen. Copy the entire *shape 1* icon set by drawing a selection box around the entire set of icons while holding the mouse button down. (Click in the space to the upper left of what you want to group and drag to the lower right until everything you want is included in the rectangle created, then release the mouse button and the items in the rectangle will be selected.)

    The icons will indicate that they are selected by becoming highlighted. If all the icons are not selected, repeat the process drawing a larger box until you have selected them all. Use copy from the Edit pull-down menu to copy the icons.

37. Move the cursor to a location below the entire set, and click.

    You will see that the small hand (called the "paste hand") moves to indicate where your paste will occur.

38. Select paste from the Edit menu and the set of icons will be duplicated below the original set. Repeat this four times to create a total of five repeating interactions. Then click on the icon names and rename them to *hotspot 2*, *shape 2*, etc.

    The result will look like Figure 13.18 on the next page.

 Development Tip: We would never program Authorware in the way shown in Figure 13.12, and in the future you won't, either. We use this simple structure here to painlessly introduce you to the basic features of Authorware. As we move into later chapters you will become acquainted with more sophisticated icon structures that will be more efficient and elegant.

Move hotspots

We want to point out in advance that the procedure we will lay out for you at this point is *not* the way we would accomplish the same thing, nor is it how you will accomplish similar things in later chapters. We *do* believe that it is a way that you can follow easily at this point in your Authorware authoring experience.

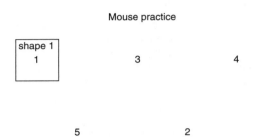

Move the cursor to touch each number in sequence.

Figure 13.17 Final Click/Touch Area

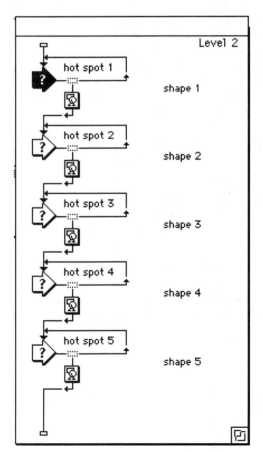

Figure 13.18 Five Hotspot Interaction Icons

Now we want to position the click/touch areas associated with the remaining four interaction icons to coincide with each of the five numbers on the *background* display icon. Assuming that you have not opened a display since you drew the circle, you can continue by:

39. Double-clicking on the *hotspot 2* response type symbol (refer to Figure 13.14 to refresh your memory of where to locate a response type symbol).

   Authorware will retain in its memory the screen image of the last display or combination of displays. This capability will aid you in positioning the next four click/touch areas.

 Authorware Tip: If you have stopped and are only now continuing to finish this lesson, you can place the background in memory by running your program only until you see the display with numbers and then selecting Jump to Icons from the Try It menu. You can use this technique if, by mistake, you click on OK-Edit Display instead of OK.

   When the response type opens the click/touch area will be shown, along with the icon name inside the rectangle that defines its size and shape.

40. Position the *shape 2* click/touch area by dragging it to the proper location. Try to select the click/touch area by its top, bottom, or sides to move it without reshaping, because it is already the proper shape. Drag it to the 2 on the display.

 Authorware Tip: Now you realize that you can resize and move a click/touch area in one operation by selecting a corner and dragging it to its ultimate location, then selecting the opposite diagonal corner and dragging it to its location.

   If the click/touch options dialog box covers the portion of the screen where you want to work, drag it to a new location.

41. Reposition the click/touch area over the number 2, in the same way you accomplished the same action for number 1. Then click on OK to close the dialog box and presentation window. Now repeat this process for each of the remaining three click/touch areas associated with shapes 3 through 5.

Edit Circles

Now you want to position each of the circles over its corresponding number and hotspot. To simplify the process and minimize the potential for confusion we want to edit each of the displays separately. To accomplish this:

42. Run the program again. When the background screen appears, move the cursor to the location of 1 in the upper left portion of the screen.

   When the cursor passes over the *hotspot 1* click/touch area it will cause the *shape 1* display icon to appear. Since you previously didn't position the circle precisely, it will appear wherever you left it. To move your circle over the number 1 on the screen:

43. Select Pause from the Try It Pull-down menu. Double-click on the circle and you will find that you are editing the *shape 1* display icon.

You can tell you have achieved this when the toolbox appears with the name of the display icon you are editing. When the display opens for editing, all objects in the display will be selected. In this case there is only one object in the display.

44. Drag the circle to cover the number 1 in the background.

In the future, when you have created displays with several objects it may be very important to de-select those objects you do not wish to move.

Mac Difference: When the display opens for editing, no objects in the display will be selected.

45. Next select Lines from the Attributes pull-down menu. Select a thicker line for your circle.

Note the difference this choice makes to your graphic object for this and the following choices. Make certain that the circle is still selected (showing the buttons on the corner of the circle graphic).

46. Now select color from the Attributes pull-down menu. Choose a red to suit your taste.

47. Lastly, select mode from the Attributes pull-down menu. Select the inverse mode.

48. Proceed (select Proceed from the Try It pull-down menu).

The screen will change somewhat, as it moves to the presentation window and becomes active to continue running.

49. Move the cursor to the number 2 in the display and the *shape 2* display icon circle will appear.

It will appear in the same location as it did when you created it. Remember, it is a copy of *shape 1*. In fact, it might even cover *shape 1*, but you can see it is there because it looks like *shape 1* reverted to its old attributes whereas the new object actually has those attributes.

50. Pause the program (Select Pause from the Try It menu). Position this circle over the number 2 in the display. While the *shape 2* circle is still selected:

Mac Difference: Authorware on the Macintosh allows you to have multiple floating palettes open simultaneously. Therefore, you are not required to close each palette after you have made a selection. Authorware on the Macintosh will allow you to close the authoring window with any or all of the palettes open. The next time you open a display for editing, the palettes will appear in the same location with the same features selected. If the palettes obscure each other you can easily drag them to a new location, or close them until needed.

51. Select Lines from the Attributes pull-down menu. Select a different line for your *shape 2* circle. Then select Color from the Attributes pull-down menu. Choose a green to suit your taste. Finally, select mode from the Attributes pull-down menu. Select the transparent mode.

52. Proceed (Select Proceed from the Try It pull-down menu).

Authorware Tip: You can select default settings for the line thickness, fill, color, and mode by making these selections without any object being selected. The same principle applies to the text options: font, size, justification, and style.

53. Repeat this process three more times to create a graphic object for each number on the screen. Each time, select a different combination of line thickness, color, fill, and mode.

    This should result in five somewhat different graphics—one for each number. You have finished this part of the effort.

54. To close the display, select Jump to Icons from the Try It pull-down menu.

Test Drive

Now is the time to enjoy the fruits of your labor.

55. Run your new mouse practice module. Your lesson should perform as the first part of the sample you ran from the CD. If it does not, re-read each step in the process and check to identify a difference you may have introduced.

Erasing the Background

To complete the *move cursor* section of the module you must create a transition to the next section. For a transition we want to erase the numbers that were displayed by the *background* display icon.

Figure 13.19 on the next page shows an erase icon.

56. Drag an erase icon to the bottom of the flowline of the *move cursor* Level 2 flowline. Name it *erase background*.

    When you open the erase icon it will demand to be told what you want to erase. We want to have the background itself displayed at that point, so that when you are asked what you want to erase you can click on the background.

57. Close the *move cursor* Level 2 flowline (by selecting the close button located in the upper left corner of the active window) to return to the main flowline (Level 1) showing the original five map icons.

58. Open the *background* icon (double-click on it) in the *intro* map. Immediately close it.

59. Now open the *erase background* icon. (Remember, it is in the move cursor wrap icon.)

    Your display will look like Figure 13.20.

60. Click on one of the numbers that are part of the background icon.

    When you do, the *background* display will disappear and a small representation of its icon will appear in the erase icon dialog box to indicate that this erase icon will erase the *background* display icon. This would be the time to select an effect for the erase, but this erase does not require an effect so we will leave it at the default None setting.

61. Close the erase dialog box by clicking the OK button.

Figure 13.19 Erase Icon

Click Object(s) To Erase

Effect   None

☐ Prevent Cross-Fade
☐ Erase All Icons Except:

OK

Cancel

Replay

Remove

1   3

5   2

Move the cursor to touch each number in sequence.

Figure 13.20 Erase Icon Dialog Box

Developing the Single- & Double-Click

Now, create the single- and double-click practice portion of the mouse practice module.

62. Double-click the *single & double-click* map icon to open it for editing.

63. Drag an interaction icon to the flowline and name it *single-click*.

64. Now associate a new erase icon with the interaction (by dragging it to the right of the interaction icon). The response type dialog box shown previously in Figure 13.12 will appear.

65. Select Clickable Object, then select OK to close the dialog box.
    You will run the program to associate one of the circles as the clickable object and as the object to be erased.

66. Now double-click the small clickable object response type symbol above the erase icon.
    Figure 13.21 shows the clickable object response type dialog box that will open. The title, *untitled*, is highlighted.

67. Type in the new title, *erase 1*.

Although you are being prompted to click on an object, wait until you run the program to make this choice uniquely for each of the icons involved.

68. Select the Try Again option under Erase Feedback to reveal the drop-down menu. Change it to Exit Interaction and select OK to close the dialog box.

Notice that the erase icon is now named *erase 1*. There will be an interaction icon for each of the objects, just as there were in the *move cursor* map.

69. Copy the entire *single click* interaction icon, including the *erase 1* icon, and paste it four times just as you did in the *move cursor* section. The first two interaction icons are both named *single click*. Rename the third, fourth, and last interaction icons to *double-click*. Then rename the erase icons *erase 1* through *erase 5*.

 Development Tip: Applications can consist of thousands of icons. To search effectively for multiple changes, adopt a naming convention. Icons with similar or identical content can be given similar or identical names. Icons with unique content or functionality should be given unique names.

Because the final three interactions will require the learner to double-click we must edit the clickable object options box (shown in Figure 13.21) for each.

70. Double-click the small clickable object response type symbol above the *erase 3* icon. Click on the Double-click choice under Match With and select OK to close the dialog box.

71. Repeat this for the *erase 4* and *erase 5* icons.

Figure 13.22 shows the completed *single- & double-click* map flowline.

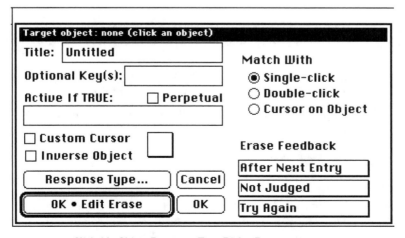

Figure 13.21 Clickable Object Response Type Dialog Box

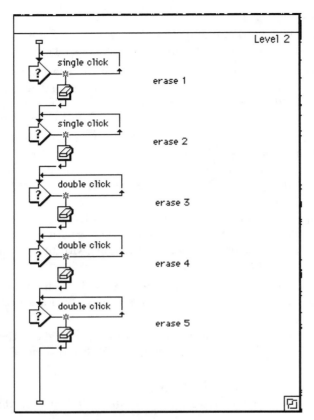

Figure 13.22 Single- and Double-Click Map Flowline

Adding Instructions

Now you want to add instructions, so the learner will know which icon to click on and whether the click should be single or double.

72. Open the first (top) *single-click* interaction icon (double-click on it). Select OK - Edit Display to open the interaction icon's presentation window.

73. Select the text tool from the toolbox and click near the bottom of the window. Type the clicking instruction the learner will see first:

```
Click on the upper left object
```

When this is done:

74. Select the arrow tool. This will cause the text to become a selected object (not selected on the Mac). You can now use the arrow tool to move the text to a pleasing position near the bottom of the screen. You can have the text appear in the same spot on all the screens by copying it now.

Authorware Tip: You can precisely align objects in different displays. By copying from one display and pasting in another the object is pasted in the exact position it held in the source display. Beware that the objects' orientation can be spoiled by clicking in the presentation window before pasting. A stray click will cause the object to paste near the spot where you clicked (a possible advantage in other circumstances).

 Mac Difference: When you open the second icon, nothing will be selected. You must click on the object you want to edit or move. If you are not careful, you can select and change the wrong icon's content. Often you will want to reference one display icon's graphic while editing another.

75. Copy the text as an object (select Copy from the Edit pull-down menu). This will place the text object in the Clipboard memory of your computer, ready to be pasted elsewhere. Now close the presentation screen (by clicking its close box).

76. Now open the other *single click* interaction icon all the way to the presentation window. Then paste the text you have copied by selecting Paste from the Edit pull-down menu. Select the Text tool and modify the text to read:

```
Click on the lower right object
```

If you find that the text wraps to the second line because it is longer now, grab the "handle" at the right of the text entry field. Drag it to the right to lengthen the line. Reposition the text if necessary.

77. Close the icon. The original text is still in memory and accessible to you for additional pasting.

 Development Tip: If you doubt your ability to correctly find the center by "eyeball," in almost any software you can have the computer do it for you. As in this text, change the justification characteristic of the text to centered. Then drag each end of the text object to opposite sides of the screen (in other cases, there may be closer objects to use as a guide). You will find that the computer will center the text.

 Mac Difference: The Macintosh version of Authorware offers Show Grid and Snap to Grid features under the Attributes pull-down menu. You can use these to judge the position of objects.

78. Open the first *double-click* interaction icon (third from the top) to reveal the presentation window. Paste the text by selecting Paste from the Edit pull-down menu.

79. Again select the Text tool to modify the text. Change it to read:

```
Double-click on the upper center object
```

Adjust the text if necessary.

80. Then select the arrow tool. Choose Copy from the Edit pull-down menu to change the clipboard to the new "Double-click" wording.

81. Close the icon.

82. Repeat this process for the final two *double-click* interaction icons. Change the wording to read:

```
Double-click on the top right object
```

and

```
Double-click on the lower left object
```

Set the Objects to Erase

Next you will associate which circle will be erased, and in what order.

83. Run the lesson. You will proceed through the first section just as you have done before, revealing each unique circle. After you have revealed all the circles, the instructional text will appear at the bottom of the screen, prompting you to click on the upper left object. The Clickable Object Options dialog box will appear on the screen and will request an object to be associated with the Clickable object response type that you have programmed for that interaction. It says: "Target object none (click an object)." Refer to Figure 13.21. Move it if necessary to access the circle.

84. Click on the upper left object just as your screen directions prompt you. The clickable object response type will associate itself with that object. The message will change to "Target object shape 1." Be careful to click on the appropriate circle. If you accidentally click on the wrong circle you can easily change your selection be clicking on the correct one. The Clickable object response type can have only one association. If you select a different object, Authorware will reassociate to the new selection, eliminating the previous one. Once this is correct:

85. Select OK to close the Clickable Object Options dialog box. Now that you have assigned a clickable object, you must click on it to continue. Do so now.

    As soon as you click on it the program will continue along the flowline to the erase icon attached to the interaction icon. You have not previously associated a display with any of the erase icons in this section of the lesson. An erase icon dialog box will appear, prompting you to Click an object to erase. Refer to the dialog box in Figure 13.20.

86. Again, click on the upper left object just as your screen directions prompt you.

    The Erase icon will associate itself with that object and erase it. Authorware offers a variety of erase effects that can be applied to the object being erased.

87. Select an effect of your choice from the effects pull-down menu.

    If you missed the effect being applied to your erase you can select the Replay button and watch it again. This allows you to preview the different effects.

Mac Difference: The erase effects available in the current Mac version of Authorware do not precisely duplicate those available in the Windows version, in features and performance.

88. Select OK to close the Erase Dialog box.

     As soon as you close this dialog box the program will continue along the flowline to the next interaction icon. You were probably wondering why you didn't click on the message to erase it as well. Authorware will automatically erase your instruction to the learner as it leaves the single-click interaction.

     A second Clickable Object Dialog box will appear, along with the new instructions you have previously pasted. Go ahead and:

89. Carefully repeat this process for each of the five interactions.

     You will finish with the presentation window still open.

90. Close it by selecting Jump to Icons from the Try It pull-down menu.

91. Close the *single- and double-click* Level 2 flowline (by selecting the close button located in the upper left corner of the active window) to return to the main flowline.

Test Drive

Once you have completed setting the erasures:

92. Run the program again to see that it works as you expect.

     These simple steps have taken considerable time to explain and for you to do for the first time, but soon they will become routine. If you are like most people, you will run the program several times for the satisfaction of seeing your efforts at work!

Developing the drag pieces

Finally, add the drag-and-drop practice portion of the mouse practice module. To do this:

93. Open the *drag pieces* map icon.

94. Drag five display icons to the flowline.

95. Title them *box*, *piece 1*, *piece 2*, *piece 3*, and *piece 4*.

     Figure 13.23 on the next page shows the *drag pieces* map as it will appear when you finish.

     Now you will import a separate graphic for each display icon. Start with the box graphic.

96. Open the *box* display icon and select Import Graphic from the Authorware File pull-down menu.

     The operating system's standard directory dialog box will appear.

97. Search for the *mbox.pct* file by opening directories and changing drives as you would to search for any other file. When you find it, double-click on the file name to load it into your program.

You may find that the window you have been working in is too small. If so, maximize your screen.

Mac Difference: You will be presented with a dialog box similar to Figure 13.24. Select Load to import the graphic into your program.

98. Move the imported box graphic to the right side of the screen. Then type the onscreen directions for this display. Under the positioned box graphic, type:

```
Drag each piece of the puzzle to
completely fill the square.

When finished, select Continue.
```

The completed display should look like Figure 13.25.

99. Repeat the import graphics procedure for each of the remaining display icons. The shapes files are named *piece_1.pct* through *piece_4.pct*. Once that is completed, place the shapes to fill the learner's screen as shown in Figure 13.26. You may recall how, earlier in the chapter, you were able to view a graphic displayed previously and closed in order to erase it. You can achieve the same thing to place the three additional shapes in relationship to the first one.

100. Open the display icon that you want as a reference; for example, box. Immediately close it.

101. Then, *while holding the shift key down,* open the display icon that you want to place relative to the *box*; in this case, the *piece 1* display icon.
    You will see both the *box* and *piece 1*. Once the piece has been placed:

102. Select the Attributes pull-down menu and click on Freely under Movable.
    This will cause the shapes to "remember" their initial position after they have been moved by the learner.

Authorware Tip: Often you will want to reference one display icon's graphic while editing another. In Authorware, you must first open the graphic that you want to reference. Then you open the graphic that you want to edit by depressing the shift key. You will see both display icons' images, but be set up to edit the second one.

103. Follow the same procedure to place the remaining three graphics. Use Figure 13.26 as a guide to placement.

Authorware Tip: Your lessons will be run in the Authorware working model, and movable objects will behave differently than when packaged. When running the unpackaged version of your file the graphics are movable by the learner. When you package a file using the full version of Authorware its graphics will become fixed, unless you specify them as movable.

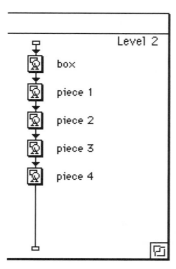

Figure 13.23   Drag Pieces Map Icons

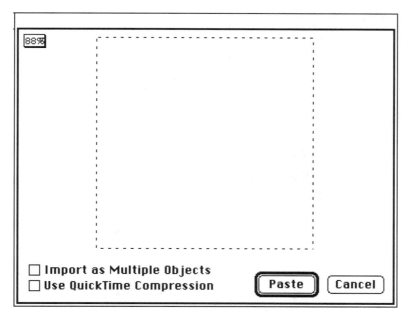

Figure 13.24   Macintosh Import Graphics Box

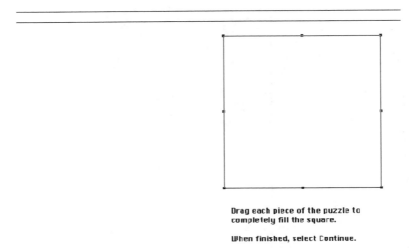

Drag each piece of the puzzle to completely fill the square.

When finished, select Continue.

Figure 13.25 Box Display

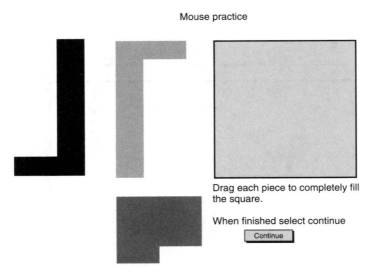

Mouse practice

Drag each piece to completely fill the square.

When finished select continue

Continue

Figure 13.26 Completed Drag Object Display

Test Drive

Run your nearly finished mouse practice module to test it. Once you see the improvements that you have made, continue.

Developing the Wrap Up

Finally, let's add the touches you might expect to find in a completely developed module. You will erase the text that gave instructions for dragging shapes and provide buttons for the learner's use, to either quit or run the practice again. If you are not at the Level 1 flowline, close the other windows now to reveal the *wrap up* map icon.

104. Double-click the *wrap up* map icon to reveal its flowline.

You want to ensure that the learner is finished with the drag-and-drop practice before offering him the opportunity to quit or try again. If you simply created the interaction containing the buttons the program would follow the flowline and would display the buttons as soon as the learner moved into the drag-and-drop section of the lesson. To separate this functionality of your lesson you will use a wait icon. Figure 13.27 shows the wait icon.

The wait icon has several features that stop the program or allow it to continue. They can be used individually or in combination. These features are mouse click, keypress, show button, and time limit (in seconds). Refer to Figure 13.28.

105. Drag a wait icon to the *wrap up* map icon flowline.

Unlike other icons in Authorware, the wait icon does not have a default name of *untitled* when placed on the flowline. It appears with no title at all.

106. Double-click on the wait icon to open the Wait Options dialog box.

The default selection is Keypress and Show Button (just Show Button on the Mac).

107. De-select the Keypress by clicking in its selection checkbox.

108. Select OK to close the dialog box.

The Continue Button that is generated by the wait icon will appear in a location other than the one you want. You will have to move it to the correct spot, but you can do that later.

 Figure 13.27 Wait Icon

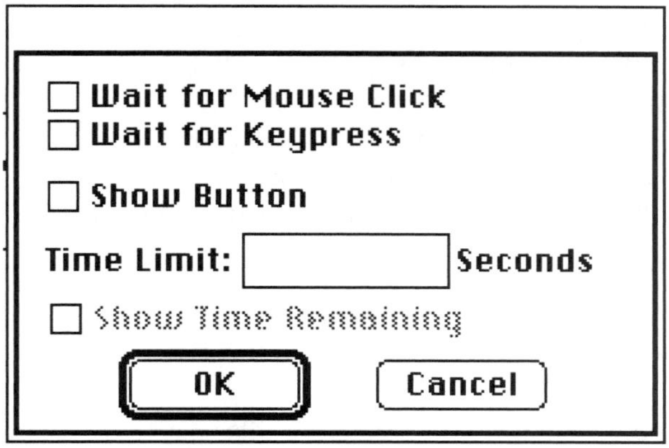

Figure 13.28 Wait Icon Option Box

Before the learner is provided the buttons to quit or try again you will need to erase the instructions from the screen that were used for the drag object section of the lesson.

109. Drag an erase icon to the flowline below the wait icon. Title it *erase text*.

110. Double-click on *erase text* to open it, and select the on screen text instructions from the previous section to be erased. You can also select any erase effect of your choice.

111. Close the *erase text* icon.

To create the two buttons for quit and try again:

112. Drag an interaction icon to the flowline below the erase icon.

113. Name it *choices*.

The functionality of quit and try again will come from Authorware functions that you will place in calculation icons. Figure 13.29 shows a calculation icon.

114. Drag a calculation icon to the right of the *choices* interaction icon.

Again the default response type is Pushbutton.

115. Select OK to approve this, because the response type you will be using is push-buttons.

116. Drag a second calculation icon to the right of the first.

The name you give a pushbutton will become the name of the on-screen button. If you want your on-screen buttons to have capitals, use capitals in their icon names.

117. Title the two calculation icons *Quit* and *Repeat Mouse Practice*.

The completed structure is shown in Figure 13.30.

To make the buttons work you have to place a written expression called a function, that will be executed by Authorware, inside each of the calculation icons. Another type of instruction is called a variable. A variable can hold or assign values; for example, the learner's name or score. You will use variables in the next chapter.

To place the function in the calculation icon:

118. Double-click *Quit* to open it.

You can type expressions directly into the icon, but to avoid clerical mistakes it is generally preferable to let Authorware do the typing.

119. Under the Data menu select Show Functions to open the Functions dialog box. The General function category is the default and includes the function we want—Quit. Scroll down to display the Quit function and select it.

It will look like Figure 13.31.

  Figure 13.29 Calculation Icon

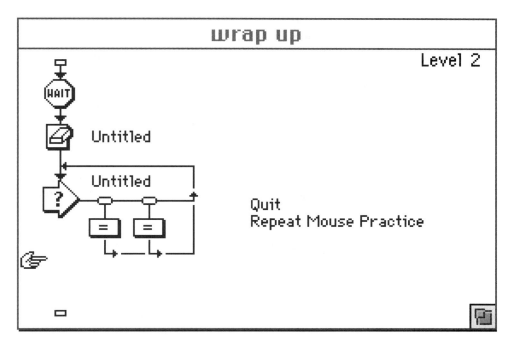

Figure 13.30 Completed Wrap Up Structure

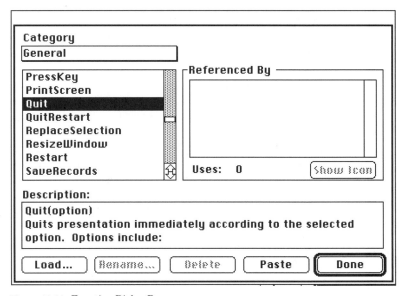

Figure 13.31 Function Dialog Box

120. Read the function Description.

    The Description provides useful information about the various ways in which you can use the function. We suggest that you always read descriptions until you have used each several times.

121. Select Paste.

    The dialog box will close and paste the Quit function into the open calculation window. The text pasted will be:

```
Quit(option)
```

    As you recall from the Description, there is more than one way to quit. The design document and programmer-ready materials for this lesson are quite specific about which type of quit is wanted.

122. Replace the word option with the option you choose. In this case replace it with 0 (zero).

    The edited expression will be:

```
Quit(0)
```

123. Select OK to close the calculation window.

Functions

Much of the power in authoring programs lies in the use of built-in and custom variables and functions. A function performs a specific task. It is also possible to import external code as custom functions to perform other tasks. Functions are used in:

- Calculation windows (as you will do in this chapter)
- Condition fields
- Option fields
- Display text

They control some action of the program; for example, running an external program or jumping to another location in the program. You can give any name to a custom function that you create, except the name of a system function. It is possible to buy custom-developed functions that permit Authorware to do more things.

    In Authorware, system function names always begin with an uppercase letter, may include more than one word, and are without spaces.

Mac Difference: You cannot embed functions in display text in the Macintosh version.

    To close the calculation window:

124. Click the close box. You will be prompted to "Save Changes?" with yes, no, and cancel options. Select yes to finish the edit.

Now you will perform a similar edit for the *Repeat Mouse Practice* calculation.

125. Double-click the Repeat Move Practice calculation to open the calculation window and select Show Function from the Data pull-down menu.

The Function dialog box opens with the General category showing. The default is the last category used, so it will open to General now.

126. Click on General to access the Category pull-down menu. Select the Jump category. The top function is GoTo. Select it (preselected on the Mac).

We remind you to read the description of each new function that you use.

127. Select Paste to place the function directly into the open calculation window.

The pasted text will be:

```
GoTo(IconID@"IconTitle")
```

When the program flow reaches this icon, this GoTo statement will cause the program to go directly to the icon (IconID) that is between the quotation marks, where "IconTitle" currently is.

128. Use the cursor to select only the words IconTitle and type **background**, the name of the second icon in the program.

We will have no problem in this case, but in the future you could find yourself renaming icons. Authorware will allow only one icon in a program to have the name referenced in a calculation. When you have completed the edit, the text in the icon should read:

```
GoTo(IconID@"background")
```

Once you have completed the edit:

129. Close the calculation icon.

Test Drive

The mouse practice module is now complete with icons, but requires some cleanup to be finished. It is efficient and very acceptable to run a program to complete placements. You may recall that earlier we decided to wait to make a placement of the Continue button. Run the program to attend to that detail.

When you reach the drag object portion of the module you will see that the continue button is not in the proper place.

130. Select Pause from the Try It menu. Select the Continue button and drag it to a spot directly below, and centered on, the text. Select Proceed to return the program to a state of running.

The Continue button is active, so:

131. Click it to activate the Quit and Repeat Mouse Practice buttons. Use the same procedure to stop (pause) the program, and then move these two buttons to a location centered on, and under, the box. When you select Proceed, both buttons are ready and the module is finished.

We think you will want to try *Repeat Mouse Practice* to experience your completed work.

Troubleshooting

If you experience problems, re-read the chapter to identify where you have omitted a step or misplaced an icon. If you cannot easily find the problem, refer to the *mousepr.apw* file included on the book CD and make an icon-by-icon comparison.

If these procedures don't solve your problem, you may want to skim through the more extensive troubleshooting ideas in Chapter 16.

Ideas for Expansion, Enhancement, and Evolution

We limited this mouse practice because it would be your first exercise in programming Authorware. We think it could be improved in several ways after you have more experience. Here are some of them:

- A pleasing background and custom fonts
- Feedback to the learner if he or she fails to click on the target circle
- Feedback to the learner if he or she single clicks when a double click is required

Meet the Learner

You have created objects; e.g., five circles of differing sizes that all have unique attributes. Each circle has a different color, mode, line thickness, fill and effect (layer) and is erased with a different effect.

You now have familiarity with many of the different attributes that Authorware has, and also have gained familiarity with the Display Icon toolbox. You have done a lot and already used six of the eleven types of icons: map, display, interaction, erase, calculation, and wait. Look at how much you can achieve using only thirty-nine icons (since you are using a version limited to only fifty icons). In our work we may use as many as 500 icons in developing a complex lesson.

All this provides you with the basic tools to build your first real lesson. You are now ready to carry out the design that we evolved for the crane operator course. Let's move on to build the lesson sign-on.

14

Getting to Know Him and Her

In this chapter we will continue to include hands-on computer activities, starting from scratch.

On the oft-proved premise that the sweetest sound anyone hears is his or her own name, this chapter provides you with the ability to capture and use the student's name to personalize your instructional products. The content is simple and you will get an added, immediate sense of achievement in authoring. You can incorporate this "sign on" with any of the later chapters of this book, or with any other lessons you build.

What You Will Learn in This Chapter

- How Authorware facilitates learner control
- How to capture and use the learner's name to personalize instruction
- How to make extensive use of a captured variable
- How to generate simple graphics using Authorware's graphic toolbox
- How to use system variables

In this lesson

In this lesson you will continue your exploration of response types by using the text entry response type in an application that allows the learner to enter his or her name. The text entry response type will capture the learner's name, typed into the computer, in a system variable. You will use the variable to display the learner's name at any later point you choose.

Establish Initial Interaction

First, open Authorware, start a new lesson, and save it as **signon**. Drag an interaction icon to the flowline. Call it *what is your name?* It will provide the question and structure to capture the learner's keyboard input. To have any practical use in the lesson, the learner's name must be stored in a variable. Authorware assigns its variables inside calculations. The first variable you will use stores the learner's name. It is a *system* variable, which means that it is built into Authorware. In later chapters you will create your own *custom* variables.

Open the *what is your name?* interaction icon by double-clicking on it. You will see the Interaction dialog box. Figure 14.1 shows the box. To open the interaction icon's display window, select the OK • Edit Display button.

Mac Difference: This box is slightly different on the Mac but will not cause a problem for you in this lesson. Follow the directions as given for Windows.

When the display window opens it will be blank, but it will contain a graphics toolbox. Ignore the toolbox for now. You will use it often later in this chapter. Pull down the File menu from the menu bar. Select Import Graphic. Now find and select the **signqust.pct** graphic provided in your book CD, to place it inside the display icon. Select Import Graphic from the File pull-down menu as you did in the previous chapter. The operating system's standard directory dialog box will appear. Search for the **signqust.pct** file by opening directories and changing drives as you would to search for any other file. When you find it, double-click to load it into your program. (On Macs you will be presented with a dialog box similar to Figure 13.24. Select Load to import the graphic into your program.) When you import the graphic, its overall location may not be exactly where you think looks most pleasing. It will be selected when it is placed. Before you close the display, move the image to the center of the screen. You may want to increase the size of the presentation window by dragging its corners.

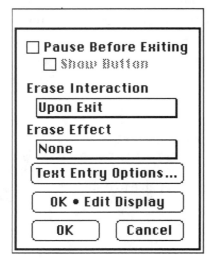

Figure 14.1 Interactions Dialog Box

Mac Difference: Also, DOS and Windows users are limited to eight characters for a file name. To make this book as similar as possible for users of both platforms, we will use the same eight-character file names with extension for both platforms. Although the Mac files require no extension, we will use the same extension for both. *This difference will apply throughout the entire book.*

Now you will see the beginning of your sign-on module. Figure 14.2 shows the imported graphic in place.

Close the interaction display window by selecting the close button in the upper left corner of the floating toolbox.

 Authorware Tip: If you click on a display after either importing or pasting an image, all or part of it may become deselected. If this happens, you can use Select All from the Edit menu to restore the image with all objects selected.

Capturing the Learner's Name

To make *what is your name?* work, drag a calculation icon immediately to the right of the interaction icon.

 Development Tip: Notice that all icons have the default name of "untitled." It is a poor programming practice to leave them that way. Good programmers will not leave a single untitled icon in a finished product. It is one simple form of documentation—something that is very important. We suggest that you name your icons exactly as shown in the book to simplify comparison. When creating your own courseware, try to give your icons meaningful names so that you know what they contain without the need to open them. If you supervise or contract with Authorware programmers, *insist* that they name every icon.

You may find at first that you "miss" and the calculation icon ends up on the flowline above or below the interaction icon *what is your name?* If this happens, just select the calculation icon again and drag it carefully to the right of the interaction icon.

Now the response type option dialog box (as shown in Figure 14.3) will open. Select the text button and OK to close the dialog box. It should create the feedback response structure shown in Figure 14.4.

Carefully double-click on the small response type symbol (a triangle and three dots) above the calculation icon and to the immediate right of the decision icon. When you succeed, you will see the Text Response Options dialog box shown in Figure 14.5.

Response options dialog box

The area at the top of the Text Response Options dialog box is unique for each response. The Xs in the checkboxes near the top of the dialog box indicate that certain features will be operational as default selections. You will change two elements in this box before closing it. The interaction icon will cause the screen to request a text input. These checkboxes control how the program will deal with what the learner

Figure 14.2 Imported Sign-on Question Graphic

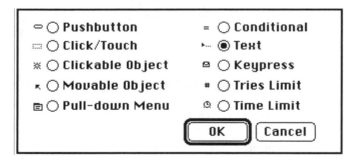

Figure 14.3 Response Type Dialog Box

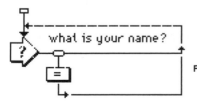

Figure 14.4 Feedback Response Structure

enters. In this case, under Ignore, Capitalization is checked. That means that capitalization will be ignored, so the learner can type with initial caps, or in all uppercase or all lowercase, or in any combination of upper- and lowercase letters without causing a problem. Extra Punctuation is also checked. That means that any stray commas, periods, or the like will be ignored when judged, as though they were never entered. All Spaces isn't checked as a default. You would check it if you wanted judging to ignore spaces. For example, either "data base" or "database" will be judged as the same. As it is, spaces are relevant. You want to differentiate between the learner's first and last names, so the space is important. Extra Words means that the program will ignore words other than those expected while looking for the anticipated word(s). For example, if the program is set to anticipate "washington" as an entry, if the learner enters "george washington" a correct match will be made. Word Order means that the program will accept the expected input in any order. For example, if the question asked for three primary colors, the learner could type "red," "blue," "green" in any order and the program would accept it. We think you will agree that these options provide a wide array of useful control mechanisms for text input.

The large initially highlighted text field is for entering the anticipated response for the learner-entered text to be judged against. You will learn more about this area soon.

The Match At Least __ Words section expects a number. For example, in the primary color example mentioned above, you could enter "3" in the Match At Least __ Words section. The program will look for three matched responses. This requires careful handling in some cases. For example, when there are six colors, but you only demand that the learner enter three, you must enter the names of all six possibilities in the text field above to enable the program to recognize three correct matches.

Incremental Matching remembers the words the learner types in each try. For example, if Incremental Matching is selected and the learner enters "washington" on the first try, and "george" on the second, it will match the anticipated "george" "washington" even though the learner didn't type "George Washington" on either attempt.

The area at the bottom of the Response Options dialog box is similar for all response types. The buttons for Response Type, OK • Edit, Cancel and OK are always the same. The pop-up menus under Erase Feedback are always the same, but the choices they hold differ among the response types.

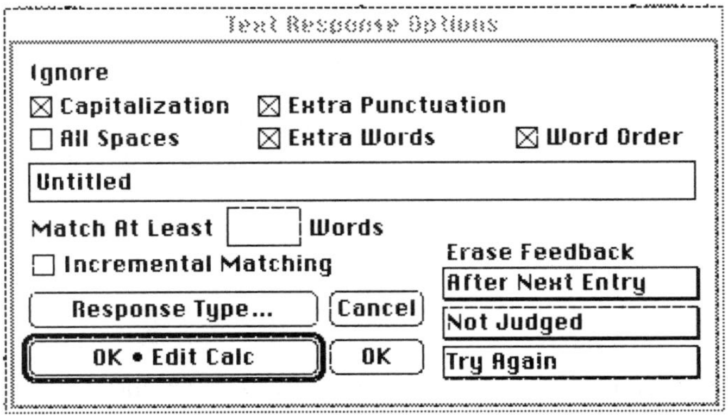

Figure 14.5 Text Response Options Dialog Box

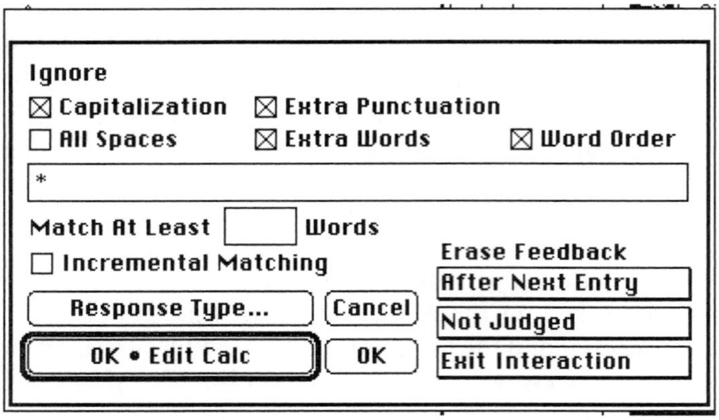

Figure 14.6 Text Response Options Dialog Box after Changes

Your response options

First, you enter the text to be matched in the highlighted *untitled* text field. In this case, you want to accept (or match) any possible name the learner has. You will do this by using the wildcard character. Enter the wildcard character, an asterisk (*), in the highlighted *untitled* text field. This becomes the name of the icon.

Next, to avoid an endless loop of asking the same question, you will change the branching direction from Try Again to Exit Interaction. Figure 14.6 shows the Text Response Options dialog box as it should be when you have completed these steps.

Select OK to close the Text Response Options dialog box. The feedback response structure was changed by your selections. The new structure is shown in Figure 14.7. Compare it to the structure as it was before editing, shown in Figure 14.4.

Your first system variable

Open the calculation icon with a double-click. An empty calculation window will open, showing the asterisk as its name. In this window you will enter a simple argument that will store the name the learner types, in the system variable User-Name. To assign the variable UserName with the value typed in by the learner, soon you will type UserName = EntryText. In this statement, EntryText is the system variable that temporarily holds the value of the most recently typed words. In principle, this variable updates with the text the learner enters when the program encounters a text response type on the interaction flowline. The system variable UserName holds the value you assign it. It does not automatically update or change.

Variables

A variable represents a changeable value. As you might suppose, a variable's value varies with the program. There are two types of variables: predefined system variables and custom variables. Variables are used in:

- Calculations windows
- Condition fields
- Option fields
- Display text

You can give any name to a custom variable that you create, except the name of a system variable.

In Authorware, system variable names always begin with an uppercase letter, and may include more than one word, without spaces.

Documentation

Documentation of Authorware calculations can be facilitated by typing two hyphens in front of your comment that describes the issue. For example:

```
This controls branching to the beginning of the program.
```

is a valid comment. It will not be allowed by Authorware as it is, because Authorware does not recognize that you mean it to be a comment rather than an argument. If you add the two hyphens, the comment is ignored when Authorware runs the program. For example:

```
--This controls branching to the beginning of the
--program.
```

Note that a multiline comment requires hyphens on all lines.

 Development Tip: We cannot overemphasize the importance of documentation. It only takes a few seconds longer and, in some cases, can save hours of frustration. All good programmers document their work.

Enter

```
-- Store the user's name in the system variable UserName and
-- capitalizes initial lower case characters
UserName = Capitalize(EntryText)
```

This describes what you are doing, and then does it. Even though you are typing it in, you should find it and read the description. Capitalize is in the Character category, under Show Functions, in the Data pull-down menu. You can use it to either capitalize all initial letter of words, as in a title—or the first word only, as in a sentence.

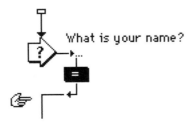

Figure 14.7 New Feedback Response Structure

Before you close the text box, verify that the syntax of your equation is *exactly* as shown in Figure 14.8. That is, the N in UserName and the T in EntryText *must* be capitalized. This format tells the system that you want to use the system variables called UserName and EntryText. If you do not type them correctly, the system will assume that you want to create new custom variables with the (similar) names that you do type. If that happens, select cancel when a new variable dialog box opens and carefully type the names of the system variables that you want. Figure 14.8 shows the completed calculation window, including the documentation. Select the OK button to close the calculation window.

 Authorware Tip: When you close the calculation window, Authorware will prompt you for an initial value when you have created a custom variable. When you use a system variable you will not be prompted.

 Mac Difference: On the Mac, the calculation text box closes differently than it does in Windows. When you click on the close button, a dialog box will ask whether you want to save the changes to the calculation.

Displaying the Learner's Name

Let's quickly create a way to see the results of your work. You can create a display that shows the learner's name as it was entered by the learner. Drag a display icon to the flowline below the interaction. Name the icon *show learner name*. Figure 14.9 shows the flowline with the new *show learner name* icon.

Double-click *show learner name* to open the display icon. Initially it will be empty except for the floating toolbox. Now you will embed the system variable in the display. When the program runs, the text variable you embed will show whatever value it was assigned in the previous calculation. Or, if none was assigned, it will show its initial value.

Select the text tool from the toolbox and click a little to the left of center of the screen. This will open a text field in which you will paste the system variable. When you paste a system variable it will automatically be displayed with brackets. Brackets represent embedding the variable. With the text field still open, pull down the Data menu and select Show Variables. The variable dialog box will open with the General category selected as the default. Scroll down until you reach the UserName variable. Select this variable so it is highlighted, as shown in Figure 14.10. Read the description, then click on the Paste button. The variable dialog box will close automatically.

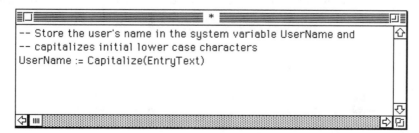

Figure 14.8 Completed Calculation Window

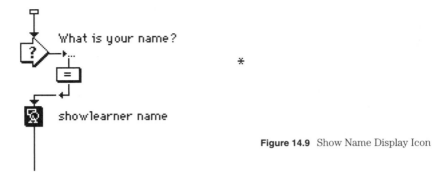

Figure 14.9 Show Name Display Icon

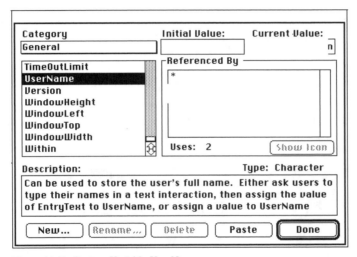

Figure 14.10 System Variable UserName

{UserName}   **Figure 14.11** Embedded Variable

When the dialog box closes, the variable will have been pasted on your screen where you had opened a text field. The spot in the display where it is pasted will now look like Figure 14.11.

Test drive

There is hardly anyone who doesn't like to see some progress as a program is built up. It is also a good practice. Pull down the Try It menu and select Run. When you run your sign-on module, you will see the basic question graphic and a text-entry field. The text-entry field will almost certainly not be located in the part of your screen where it will eventually go. We want to move the text-entry field to the white box in the question graphic, near the center. Pull down the Try It menu and select Pause. This will enable you to move or change screen objects. It will appear as a white box. Click in the middle of the white box and drag it to the appropriate area of your graphic. Then select Proceed from the Try It menu and the program will continue to run.

Now you are ready to try the text functionality of the sign-on. At the question, enter your name. Your screen should look similar to Figure 14.12, except that your own name will be entered in the text-input field.

Now that the text-entry field is properly placed, and you have entered your name, press the Return key. This will store your name in the variable UserName. In the next screen, you will see your name displayed in the embedded variable. You will also find yourself stuck.

If your name is not all on one line, you can fix it now. Double-click on your name and it will open for editing. Six "handles" will define it as an object. Grab the middle handle on the right side and drag to the right until it all fits on one line.

Since there is nothing you can do to advance or exit, press Control-J (hold down the Control key and press the J key) to jump to the icons and escape from the final screen. This "quicksand" is temporary and you will remove it soon.

Mac Difference: In general, the Mac uses the Command key (the one with the flower-like scrolling symbol) where Windows uses Control. Even if your Mac keyboard has a Control key, it will not work in these cases.

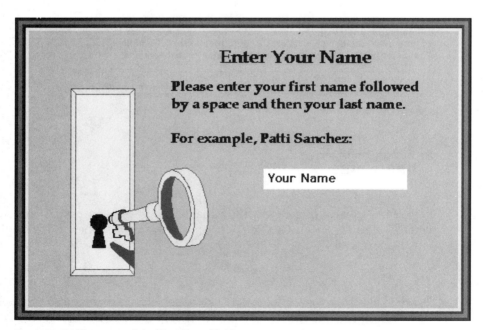

Figure 14.12 Placement of the Text-Entry Field

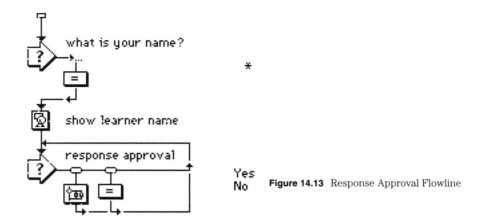

Yes
No   **Figure 14.13** Response Approval Flowline

Error Trapping

First you want to add a bit of user friendliness to ask whether the name has been correctly entered and interpreted. Double-click to open the *show learner name* display icon and, using the text tool, enter the following in the screen just above the embedded variable:

```
Is this correct?
```

Don't worry about placement right now; you will have an opportunity to make adjustments later. Close the presentation window by clicking the close button on the toolbox.

Next you will set up buttons for the learner to indicate yes or no. To do this, drag an interaction icon to the flowline below the *show learner name* display icon. Name it *response approval*. Then drag a map icon to the right of the interaction. A Response Type dialog box will appear with the Pushbutton selected as the default. Click OK to close the dialog box. Then drag a calculation icon to the right of the map icon. It will automatically pick up the response type of the icon to its left; in this case, another pushbutton. With the cursor, select the *untitled* names one at a time and replace them with *Yes* for the map icon and *No* for the calculation icon. Your flowline will now look like Figure 14.13.

Test drive

Now Run the program as you did earlier. Enter your name and press **Return**. You will see the question "Is this correct?" and the embedded UserName variable, showing the learner's name (in this case, your name). The buttons will be in the upper left of the screen.

Press Control-P to pause the program. Now, *carefully* select one of the buttons and drag it to a position under the embedded variable currently showing your name. Do not double-click the buttons at this time. Move both buttons and place them nicely aligned with the other screen elements.

The next step is to eliminate the quicksand that trapped you when you ran the program the first time. You will alter the flow of the program so that if the learner's name is approved as correct the module ends. If the learner indicates that the name is not correct it will recycle to permit the name to be entered again. Start by double-clicking on the Yes button. This will open the Pushbutton Options dialog box. Under Erase Feedback, select the Try Again pull-down menu and change it to Exit Interaction. The results should look like Figure 14.14.

Select OK to close the Pushbutton Options dialog box. Now do the same thing for the *No* button. Double-click on it. Remember that *No* is a calculation icon. Its dialog box is almost identical to the one you saw for *Yes*. The difference is that the Pushbutton Options dialog box for the calculation icon has an OK • Edit Calc button rather than an OK • Edit Map button. Click on the OK • Edit Calc button now. A calculation text box will open. Type the following exactly:

```
GoTo(IconID@"What is your name?")
```

GoTo is a system function. If you had preferred, you could have made this entry by pulling down the Data menu and selecting Show Function. **GoTo** is found in the Jump Category. Once Jump is selected, paste from the system function **GoTo** and substitute the correct name of the icon that you wish to jump to, as shown just above.

Close the calculation icon and select Jump to Icons by using Control-J. Your sign-on module flowline will now look like Figure 14.15. It is important that the yes icon flowline extend down and to the bottom of your screen and not loop around to the right with the no flowline. If it does not, reread the directions for the yes icon and follow them carefully.

The program lacks one feature. You can't quit. There is more than one way of setting up the quit. At this stage, we think it will better illustrate the flow if you add a

Figure 14.14 Pushbutton Options Dialog Box

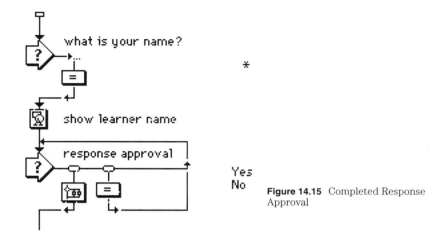

what is your name?

show learner name

response approval

Yes
No

Figure 14.15 Completed Response Approval

calculation icon with a Quit function to the bottom of the flowline. To do that, drag a new calculation icon to the very bottom of the flowline. Name it *quit*. Open the *quit* icon for editing. You used the menus to paste the Quit in Chapter 13. Just type it in this time. Type:

```
Quit(0)
```

Remember, it is a zero and not the letter "O." Close the calculation icon. The completed flowline is shown in Figure 14.16.

You could have used a calculation icon for *Yes*, rather than an empty map. We are unlikely to title the icon Quit, because it will almost surely go on to another program or part of a program rather than really quitting. Next time you have this situation you may want to try the other approach.

Test drive

Now Run the program as you did before. Enter your name and press return. Try approving your name as entered. Then run it again and insist on making a correction.

Go With the Flow: If you approve your name the system will continue; in this case, ending. If you attached this sign-on to the beginning of a program, Authorware would retain the value in UserName and display that name anywhere you placed the embedded variable UserName. If you disapprove your name as entered, the system will GoTo the icon at the beginning of the module and begin again by asking you to enter your name.

Troubleshooting

If you experience problems, re-read the chapter to identify where you have omitted a step or misplaced an icon. If the program does not start over when No is selected, verify the *No* calculation. It may have been canceled instead of OK'd. Did you put an argument on two lines because the displayed text field was too short to see it all at once? If so, fix it. You can always maximize the calculation window to see better.

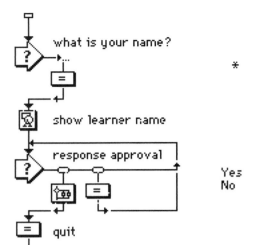

*

Figure 14.16 Completed Flowline

If you cannot easily find the problem, refer to the **signon.APW** file included on the book CD. First, check your flowline carefully to see that it conforms to our example. If that check does not reveal the difference, make an icon-by-icon comparison.

Ideas for Expansion, Enhancement, and Evolution

Most utilities that collect learner's names are similar to the one you have just made. Here is one idea for use of this lesson in a new way:

- Some organizations prefer to store training records by employee number. You collect the learner's employee identification number instead of, or in addition to, the name.

Up, Up, and Away!

Now you have a little module that you can copy and paste in front of any Authorware lesson, to capture the learner's name. Remember, we try to have our instruction make sense. There is no point in collecting the person's name if you have no intention of using it in some way.

You may choose to use the name to personalize your lesson. You may also, or instead, plan to execute the CMI function of record storage by placing a record of that person's studies in a file. In fact, that is the use we have planned for. In a later chapter you will continue development of this sign-on to do just that.

Now, with your knowledge of and experience with variables in hand, you are ready to move on to complete the instruction we have planned and developed in this part of the book, the crane signals lesson. When you are ready to go up, up, and away, move on to Chapter 15.

15

Crane Operator

This lesson is the implementation of the final planning and paper lesson documentation produced for the crane operator curriculum designed and developed in Chapters 7 through 10. You will finally create the lesson that teaches hand signals used to direct a crane operator. You will increase the fidelity as the lesson builds from simple to more elaborate, and as the learner applies the signal to the proper crane control. You will also be introduced to buttons that are always available, such as Quit. They are called perpetual buttons and will enhance your Authorware development capabilities. You will learn how to exercise program control to round out what you learned about learner control capabilities in Chapter 13.

This lesson uses a valid instructional strategy—learn, practice, test. The structure of the lesson reinforces the strategy. You will be quite aware which portion you are creating as the development process unfolds.

What You Will Learn in This Chapter

- How to use Authorware's decision icon
- How to create and use system variables
- How to create drill and practice lessons
- How to create and use perpetual buttons

Achieving Fidelity

We have selected an overhead crane. Unless you are familiar with factories, it is more likely that your image of a crane is the type called a boom crane. A boom crane is a mobile type used in construction, and they are the ones you see lifting components to build skyscrapers.

An overhead crane is fixed to a set of rails that allow it to travel from one end of the shop to the other (let's call this North-South). The hoist can also move from one side to the other (we can call this East-West). Finally, it can be raised and lowered (which we will call Up-Down). One more control is needed. When the crane starts moving in any of these three dimensions (the six directions), it will continue to do so until it is halted. We need a control for stop.

We would argue that crane operators must use the actual crane to be considered competent in its use. However, we can teach a combined activity, such as interpreting the hand signals into crane movements and operating the crane. In this case we will complete the intellectual practice portion of the training first—the lesson you are about to build. Later, more elaborate, realistic screen representation and actual operation of the target equipment would round out the needed training.

Limitations of an Interface

It is difficult to achieve high levels of fidelity. We could have the real and complete crane control set hooked to our computer. Or, we could simulate them very closely, showing the multiple and combined actions (on screen) triggered by the mouse or keyboard. Many things are possible. What you will do here is carry out the designer's intent as expressed in the Design Document and Programmer-Ready Materials.

Create the Main Menu Structure

First, create the main menu in relationship to the major components of the lesson— learn, practice, and test. The learner will access each component through a push-button labeled with these names.

Now, let's create the basic structure for the lesson. Open a new file and drag an interaction to the flowline. Label it *crane operator*. Next, associate a map icon with the interaction (drag a map icon to the right of the interaction icon and release). The response type dialog box will appear automatically with the default Pushbutton response type selected—exactly what is needed here. Simply select OK to approve the default. At this point, *Untitled* is highlighted. Type *Learn* to replace *untitled* as the icon's title. It will automatically become the button's name, so be sure to use a capital L.

This, and the other level 1 icons will be perpetual.

 Authorware Tip: You can create Perpetual responses that will always be available in your lesson (unless you specifically make them inactive with a variable). This feature is often used to make the Glossary and Quit buttons available throughout a lesson, except in quizzes where they are specifically turned off. Remember, the perpetual interactions are only activated if they have been "read" in the flowline to make them active. Therefore, they are usually placed near the top of flowlines that are extensive. Perpetual interactions are available for all response types except: Text, Keypress, Tries Limit, and Time Limit.

You are going to create three buttons to provide access to the three units. We want the learner to be able to jump directly from any unit to any other. The way we will achieve this is to make this button *perpetual*. A perpetual button is always active, unless specifically made inactive. To make the Learn button perpetual, select the small Pushbutton response type symbol just above the *Learn* map icon. Double-click the symbol. The Pushbutton Options Dialog Box will appear as shown in Figure 15.1. Select the Perpetual checkbox located in the upper right corner (left center for the Mac). We will leave the Active If TRUE box empty, for now. Later we will modify it so that it is not available during a test. Then use the mouse to select OK to close the dialog box. Do not use the Enter key or click on OK•Edit Map. If you do so by mistake, and find yourself inside the map, close it to return to Level 1.

Drag one more map icon to the right of the *Learn* map icon and title it *Practice*. Remember that, when you drop an icon to the right of another icon attached to an interaction icon, it will assume the properties of the icon to its left. For that reason, *Practice* is now also a perpetual pushbutton.

If you drop it to the left of *Learn* it will not be perpetual. If this happens, delete the new *untitled* icon and try again.

 Authorware Tip: An icon placed to the right of another icon will assume the same characteristics as the first icon. There are exceptions, but for now this generalization can serve as your guide.

Now drag a calculation icon to the right of *Practice*. It will also assume the pushbutton and perpetual characteristics of *Practice*. Name this icon *Test*.

Quit (Perpetual Button)

Finally , activate the Quit pushbutton. This will make Quit available to you as you develop the lesson. To do this, drag another calculation icon to the right of *Test* and label it *Quit*. Open the Quit calculation icon for editing. Now, open the Data pull-down menu, select Show Functions, and under the General Category find and select Quit. Read the Description, then select Paste. The Quit function will be pasted into your calculation window.

```
Quit(option)
```

Figure 15.1 Pushbutton Response Type Dialog Box

The option called for in the design is zero, to Quit to Program Manager (Quit to Finder on Macs) or return to file if jumped to from another file. Highlight "option" and type a zero (0). It should now read:

```
Quit(0)
```

Close the calculation window. Your completed overall structure for the three units of the crane operator lesson will look like Figure 15.2.

 Authorware Tip: When naming several icons, use the Enter (Return on Macs) key. You will automatically advance to the next icon on the flowline with its name already highlighted for easy modification.

Using File Setup

Now we want to place the background for the menu. Before we can do this we must adjust the way Authorware displays the lesson. Let's have a look at how Authorware displays the Presentation window on your computer. Double-click the interaction icon, then select OK•Edit Display. You will most likely see a display that is smaller than your total screen. We want to force the computer to use the full screen.

Pull down the File menu from the menu bar and select File Setup. You will see the File Setup Options Box. In the upper right-hand corner of the box you will find a pull-down menu to use to select your computer's display type.

Since the graphics we have provided are for a VGA (640 × 480) display, select VGA. De-select the User Menu Bar, Overlay Menu Bar (not present on Macs), and Title Bar. The User Menu Bar will still appear when you return to the graphic, but it will only be present when you are in author mode. It will not appear when the learner runs the lesson. The File Setup Options Box will now look like Figure 15.3. Select OK to close the box to return to the display, which is now full screen. From now on, make these selections for all of your lessons as soon as you create the lesson file.

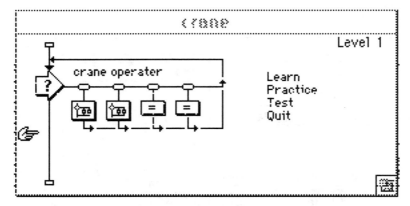

Figure 15.2 Crane Lesson Structure

Memory : 3,230K   File : 2K in 4 icons 0 variables

Title:
Crane

Wait Button Title:
Continue

Content Search Path:

┌When User Returns:─────────
◉ Restart at Beginning   ○ Resume

┌Presentation Window Size:──────
UGA
☐ User Menu Bar ☐ Use UGA Palette
☐ Title Bar   ☐ Desktop Pattern
[Background Color...] ☐
[Chroma Key...] ■

[OK]   [Cancel]

Figure 15.3 File Setup Options Box

Mac Difference: As with many other dialog and option boxes, the Mac version is slightly different. In this case it does not offer the palette choices found in the Windows version. The Authorware Professional for Windows default palette most closely mirrors the Macintosh palette. If you know in advance that you will develop the same lesson for the Windows platform, select the Use VGA Palette box.

Mac Difference: To toggle the menu bar from hide to show while authoring, press Command Backslash (⌘ \ ).

You will return to the Presentation window. Close it by clicking on the close button on the toolbox to return to the icons.

Using the Signals

Let's finish the interaction icon. The background graphic in the interaction icon will provide the scene for the three-part program. Double-click the *crane operator* interaction icon. The Interaction Option dialog box (shown in Figure 13.11) will appear. Change the Erase Interaction from the default setting of Erase on Exit to Don't Erase, by clicking on Erase on Exit to reveal the other choices and selecting Don't Erase. Then, click on the OK - Edit Display button to open the *crane operator* interaction presentation window.

Import the cr_bkgd.PCT graphic. Click on the file pull-down menu selection from the menu bar and choose Import Graphics. The operating system's standard directory dialog box will appear. Search for the cr_bkgd.PCT file by opening directories and changing drives as you would to search for any other file. When you find it, double-click to load it into your program. (On a Mac you will be presented with a dialog box similar to Figure 13.24. Select Load to import the background graphic into your program.) Center this full-screen background in the presentation window, and also position the pushbuttons in their appropriate places. Figure 15.4 shows this screen as it looked to us when we placed the cr_bkgd.PCT graphic.

Close the display once you have made the necessary edits.

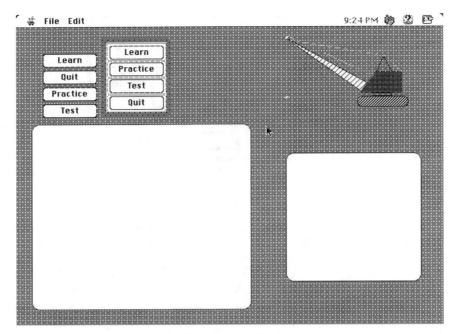

Figure 15.4 Developer's View of the Crane Operator Display

Create the Learn Instructional Unit

This lesson will provide instruction on seven different hand signals, displaying a graphic of each signal with its corresponding description. Double-click the *Learn* map icon to begin creating the crane operator instruction. Drag an interaction icon to the flowline and label it *learn signals*. Next, drag a display icon to the right of the *learn signals* interaction. Select the Click/Touch area response type and close the Response Type Dialog box (click OK). Name the display icon *stop*. Double-click the small Click/Touch response symbol above the *stop* display icon. This will open the Click/Touch Options dialog box. Select the check boxes for Mark After Matched, Inverse Area, and Use Custom. When you select the Use Custom checkbox a standard directory dialog box will appear with several available cursors. For this lesson, choose the hand by double-clicking on it. The hand will be loaded and associated with the lesson as the cursor that appears over this specific individual Click/Touch area. Note that it does not become the cursor in general use in the entire lesson. Close the Response Type dialog box. You have established the characteristics for each of the icons that will be associated with this interaction.

Scrolling Interaction window

Drag four more display icons to the right of *stop*. Label them *boom in, boom out, hoist down*, and *hoist up*. As we stated earlier, you are going to provide instruction for seven hand signals. You will have to place two more displays on the *learn signals* interaction. *Carefully* drag a display icon to the immediate right of the *hoist up* icon. Authorware only displays five icons associated with an interaction at any one time. The other icons are accessible by scrolling up or down in the Scrolling Interaction window. When you placed the new untitled icon on the interaction flowline, the Scrolling Interaction window was created and the *stop* icon scrolled off the top of the scrolling display, and the *stop* icon itself disappeared. Figure 15.5 shows the newly formed scrolling interaction window.

The dotted lines to the left of the leftmost display icon indicate that there are more icons in that direction. The same principle holds true if the dotted lines are seen to the extreme right of the rightmost icon. Title the new icon *travel east*. Now place another display icon to the right of *travel east,* and name it *travel west.*

Place learn graphics

Now you will import the appropriate graphics, one-by-one, into the seven displays of the *learn signals* interaction. Recall how, under *More Hotspots* in Chapter 13, you opened a background display and then closed it to set the stage for viewing the background while you placed graphics. Do this now, by opening the crane operator interaction icon and immediately closing it. Now, double-click on the *learn signals* interaction icon. When the Interaction Options dialog box appears, hold the shift key down and click on OK-Edit Display. The background will be displayed. Ignore the click/touch areas for now.

Now import the *cr_lnsg.PCT* graphic just as you did for the *cr_bkgd.PCT* earlier in this chapter, and place it in the *learn signals* interaction in the large square

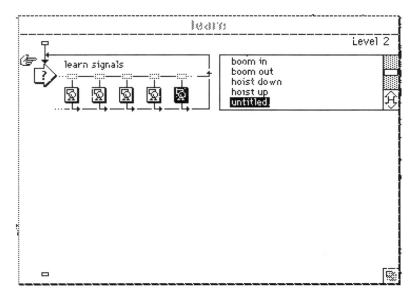

Figure 15.5 Scrolling Interaction Window

space, so that the hand graphics are nicely centered. Then import the remaining seven graphics as follows:

Icon Name	Graphic File to be Imported
stop	**crlnstop.PCT**
boom in	**crlnbmin.PCT**
boom out	**crlnbmot.PCT**
hoist down	**crlnhsdn.PCT**
hoist up	**crlnhsup.PCT**
travel east	**crlntvet.PCT**
travel west	**crlntvwt.PCT**

Be very careful that you import the correct files! For example, the *learn*-associated file **crlntvet.PCT** could be confused with the *practice*-associated file **crpstvet.PCT, that has a similar but nonidentical content.** Don't worry about their position. You will place them in their proper locations soon.

Place *Learn* Click/Touch areas

Open the *learn signals* Interaction display. Select, resize, and place each of the Click/Touch areas appropriately over the corresponding graphic. You should make the click/touch area a bit larger than actually needed to cover the hand, so that the Mark After Matched boxes are outside of each graphic to its left. When you have completed the placement in *learn signals*, your display should look like Figure 15.6.

Run the program and select Learn. You are asked to select a hand signal. Eventually, you will select all the signals. Let's start with stop (the clenched fist). When you

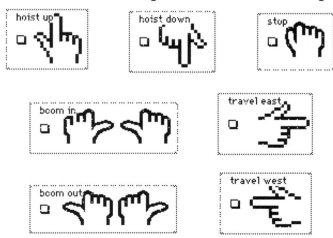

Figure 15.6 Click/Touch Area Placement

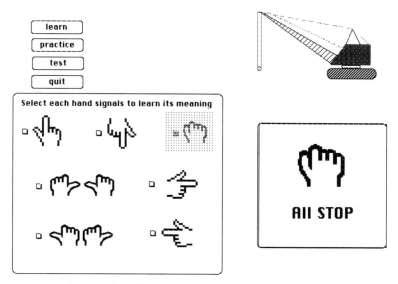

Figure 15.7 Stop Feedback Placement

select stop, the Mark After Matched square beside the hand will become filled in. Also, the feedback graphic and an associated colored highlight will appear somewhere on the screen. Carefully select the feedback graphic (*in a spot not among the hotspots you just placed*) and drag it to its proper position on the background. You should try to click the hand or the text. The correct position will place the colored highlight over the corresponding signal. Be careful not to double-click, which will pause the program. If you do, simply select Proceed from the Try It pull-down menu. The finalized display will look like Figure 15.7.

Repeat this process by selecting the *hoist down* hand signal. When you do, the feedback from *stop* will disappear and the feedback for *hoist down* (down-pointing finger) will appear somewhere on the screen. Make the necessary placements, just as you did for *stop*. Continue placing each of the remaining feedback graphics over the background in the appropriate location. The highlight area will move with it to fall directly over the hand signal the learner has just selected. When you have completed the placement, use Control-J to jump to the icons.

Test drive

Now test your work. Run the lesson from the Try It pull-down menu. Check out the Learn unit that you have just completed. You can Quit, and then Run the program again. When you are ready to continue, read on.

Mac Difference: Authorware automatically resets the Marked After Matched buttons on Windows machines. On the Mac they will remain selected as you click on the Learn button to try again. You can avoid this by simply selecting Quit, and then Running the program again.

Create the Practice Instructional Unit

The second part of the crane operator lesson is the opportunity for the learner to practice what was learned in the Learn section of the lesson. Remember, in the Practice section, hand signals will be displayed randomly to the learner, who must identify each one by selecting the appropriate button on the crane controller. Feedback is provided immediately, based on the learner's selection. The learner will indicate when he or she is ready to proceed by clicking on a Continue button.

Program Control

We discussed learner control in Chapter 13. Now let's look at the other possibility. Program control is the ability of the system to make decisions resulting in a different outcome in the learner's use of the program. Program control is the result of information that the computer uses that can be either predetermined or generated by the learner during the program. In practical terms this means that when the learner takes an action, it affects a subsequent result of that action. In this lesson, the program controls when and where the learner's name is displayed. There are more complex forms of program control and we will explore them in greater depth in Chapters 20 and 22.

Develop the practice present stimulus

You will now work with the decision icon. Figure 15.8 shows the decision icon.

Double-click the *Practice* icon to open it for editing. Drag a decision icon to the flowline and label it *practice signals*. Now drag a display icon to the right of the *practice signals* decision icon. Name it *hoist up*.

You may recall that the first icon in the learn interaction was named *stop*. We have purposefully selected another icon to begin the decision sequence, just to illustrate that there is no necessary connection between the sequences of icons in the *learn signals* interaction icon and the *practice signals* decision. Double-click *hoist up*. The Decision Options dialog box will open. (You may recall that a display icon attached to an interaction opens directly for editing.) The default Erase Displayed Objects choice is Before Next Selection. Change the Erase Displayed Objects choice to Don't Erase. Figure 15.9 shows the box after editing. Select OK to close the dialog box.

We want to provide the practice hand signals in a random order. The decision icon default setting is to present the icons associated with it sequentially, moving across the associated flowline icons one-by-one, from left to right. You will have to change the branching characteristics of the decision.

Double-click the practice signals decision icon to access the Decision Options dialog box. Select the Random w/o Replacement branching option. The difference be-

Figure 15.8 Decision Icon

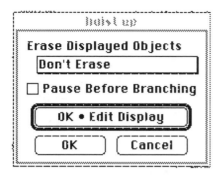

Figure 15.9 Attached Decision Options Dialog Box

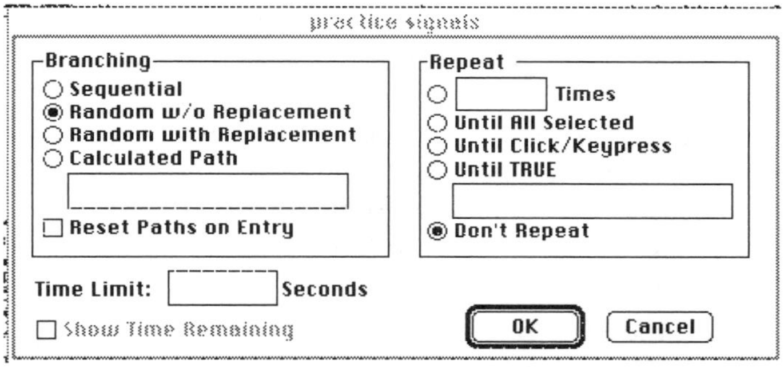

Figure 15.10 Decision Options Dialog Box

tween Random w/o Replacement and Random with Replacement is that when Authorware selects the icons associated with the decision, it does so randomly in both cases. But on a later selection, if the option is Random with Replacement, it will reuse a previously selected icon if the same one comes up again. Remember, it would be random if the same icon were selected twice in a row, just as heads can come up twice in a row when you flip a coin. Your selection will look like Figure 15.10.

Close the Decision Options dialog box. You will be presenting seven different signals for practice, the same seven you presented in the Learn section. Drag six more display icons to the right of *hoist up.* Label them *hoist down, boom out, boom in, travel west, travel east*, and *stop* respectively. The icons will automatically pick up the characteristics of *hoist up.* You will notice that, after five icons on the decision branch, Authorware provides a Scrolling Decision window, as in the Learn interaction you previously created. Figure 15.11 shows the completed *practice signals* decision as it should appear on your screen.

Place *practice* graphics

Now you will add the graphic content for each of the *practice signals* display icons. This is exactly the process that you have performed with the *learn signals* interaction and its displays earlier in this chapter. In fact, place the hand signals in exactly

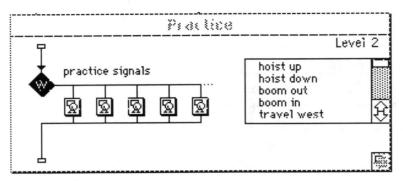

Figure 15.11 Practice Signals

the same location as you placed them in the learn section. Open and close the *crane operator* interaction icon, which contains the lesson background, to establish "landmarks" for your placement. Be sure to hold down the shift key as you open each display icon. If you forget to do so, just close it and repeat the process of opening and closing the *crane operator* icon. Import the *crpshsup.PCT* graphic (finger pointing upward) and place it in the *hoist up* display icon. Then import and place the remaining six graphics as follows:

Icon Name	Graphic File to be Imported
hoist down	**crpshsdn.PCT**
boom out	**crpsbmot.PCT**
boom in	**crpsbmin.PCT**
travel west	**crpstvwt.PCT**
travel east	**crpstvet.PCT**
stop	**crpsstop.PCT**

As you import the second graphic following these instructions, you will see the previously imported graphic where you placed it. This is how the shift key is supposed to work. It holds all the previous displays in memory for simultaneous viewing. This can be a very useful feature. Simply place your newly imported graphic over the previous one. It will cover it.

Again, be careful to ensure that you are importing and placing the correct graphic. Read the file names carefully.

Develop the practice provide response

Now you will add the crane controller that the learner will use to translate the stimulus of the hand signal to movement of the crane. On the basis of the controller choice you will judge the accuracy of the learner's action.

Drag an interaction icon to the flowline below the *practice signals* decision icon set. Name it *controls*. Soon you will place the crane controller in it. Right now, drag a map icon to the right of the *controls* interaction icon. The Interaction Response Type dialog box will open. It should be familiar, as you have seen it many times. It will look exactly like Figure 13.12. Click the Click/Touch button to change the response type. Click OK to close the dialog box.

Next open the Click/Touch Options dialog box (double-click on the small response type symbol above the *hoist up* map icon). You will want to provide an indicator to the learners that they have made a selection, so you should set the Click/Touch area to inverse when it is selected. Select the Inverse Area check box. Then select the drop-down menu set at Try Again under the Erase Feedback. Change it to Exit Interaction. When you have finished these steps the dialog box will look like Figure 15.12. Close the dialog box by selecting OK.

Name the map icon *hoist up*. Now drag six additional map icons to the right of *hoist up*. Name them *hoist down, boom out, boom in, travel west, travel east*, and *stop* respectively. Your completed *controls* interaction should look like Figure 15.13.

 Go With the Flow: This is an excellent chance to practice reading the flowline. Understanding it here will make everything that follows simpler to grasp. The flow enters at the top of Figure 15.13 and falls into the *practice signals* decision icon. It will be instructed to randomly select one of the seven branches (path), with a notation

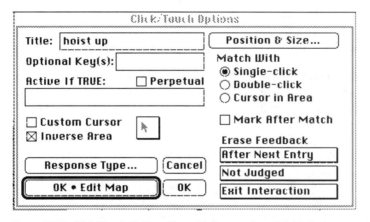

Figure 15.12 Click/Touch Options Box with Inverse Area Selected

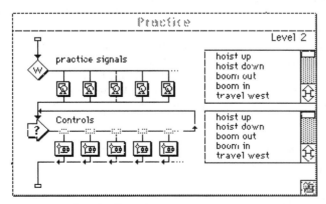

Figure 15.13 Practice Controls

not to repeat that path until all the others have been used once. Let's assume that Authorware randomly selects the third branch, *boom out*. The flow draws the graphic in the display and falls through to the main flowline entering the *controls* interaction. The *controls* interaction waits for the learner to interact with the program by clicking on the hot spot that covers the corresponding crane control graphic. It falls through the map (which is empty) and back to the main flowline.

Next we will place a graphic into the controls interaction. This graphic will be a crane controller with selectable buttons for this practice session. First, you must generate the background image so you will have a reference for placing the crane controls. Open the *crane operator* interaction icon, and close it. Then, while holding down the shift key, double-click the *controls* interaction icon. The Interaction Options dialog box will appear (as in Figure 13.12). Select Don't Erase from the drop-down menu under Erase Interaction. Select OK•Edit Display to prepare for importing the graphic.

Now import the crane controller into the *controls* interaction icon. The process is quite familiar by now. The file to import is: *crcontrl.pct*. If you have difficulty remembering, refer to when you imported the *cr_bkgd.pct* graphic.

When you have the controller placed properly, look at the Click/Touch area hot spot indicators, each named appropriately. Reposition and resize them to occupy appropriate positions over the crane controller buttons. Close the *controls* presentation window.

As it is, the control will flash as it is automatically erased and redrawn when the learner wants to select another practice question. To head off this development right here, select *controls* to highlight it, if it isn't already highlighted. Then select the Attributes pull-down menu, and select Effects. When the Effects dialog box appears, click in the Prevent Automatic Erase check box. Select OK to close the dialog box. The automatic erase will create a different problem of its own that you will deal with later in this chapter.

Your next activity will be to set up judgment of the selection the learner makes in this practice. Now you will create a calculation to compare the randomly selected and displayed hand signal with the learner's identification of them on the crane controller. Drag a calculation onto the main flowline below the *controls* interaction icon. Name it *judge response*. The extended flowline should now look like Figure 15.14.

Double-click the *judge response* calculation icon to open it. The calculation window will open, allowing you to enter a scripted line of text that will report the judgment of the learner's selection. Earlier we showed you how to paste functions and variables but, since completing this calculation would require many steps, you will simply enter it directly into the calculation window.

Type :

```
IF(PathSelected@"practice signals" = ChoiceNumber@"controls", feedback :=
"Correct", feedback := "Incorrect")
```

The calculation you have just entered in the *judge response* click/touch area compares the value of the system variable **PathSelected** in *practice signals* with the

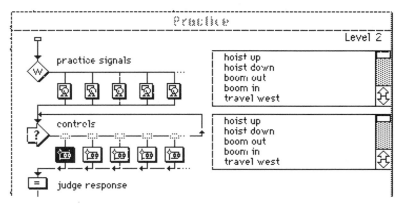

Figure 15.14 Flowline Showing Judge Response

IF(PathSelected@"practice signals" = ChoiceNumber@"controls", feedback := "Correct", feedback := "Incorrect")

Figure 15.15 Open Calculation Box

number of the learner's choice number (**ChoiceNumber**) in *controls*. They either match (True) or not (False). *Feedback* is a variable that you created. There are two sets of *feedback* after the comma. The first represents what the computer should do if the IF is True (set the variable feedback to equal "Correct"); the other indicates what the computer will do if the IF is False (set the variable feedback to equal "Incorrect"). The completed entry (which must be all on one line to work properly) will appear as in Figure 15.15.

If your calculation window is too small to easily work, maximize it.

IF then

Much of the power in authoring programs lies in the use of built-ins. Authorware system function names always begin with an uppercase letter, may include more than one word, and are written without spaces.

When you close the calculation box you will be asked for the initial value of the variable *feedback*. By entering an unknown string into a calculation you have created a new custom variable. Authorware asks for the initial value of the variable when the calculation box closes. Your program assigns a value before one is needed, so you can click OK to close. (Mac users, refer to the Mac Difference.)

Authorware Tip: No, Off, 0 (zero), and False all hold the same value. If a variable has no value, Authorware makes it False. This can create a problem sometimes. If a displayed variable (like the one you are about to create) was assigned a value of False by default, Authorware will display a zero ("0"). If, for example, the variable is new user, but Peggy has not yet entered her name, a spot on the screen that you proudly expect to show "Peggy" will show only the zero. To avoid this, assign an initial value of no text by typing two quotation marks (""). Do not use four apostrophes ('). You could also enter something that *would* display, such as "John Doe" or "Anonymous."

 Mac Difference: Yes, On, 1, and True all hold the same value. Mac users must correctly identify the type of variable. This will be a character variable, so click on the character button. Notice the default value of two quotation marks that the system writes for you.

Develop the practice present feedback

Now you want to display the feedback that you have just entered in the *judge response* calculation, so it is presented to the learner. Also, you will create a button to offer the learner a different signal to try.

Drag an interaction icon to the flowline below the *judge response* calculation. Name it *provide feedback*. Now drag a calculation icon to the right of the *provide feedback* icon. The response type dialog box will open. The default settings are just what you want, so select OK to close the dialog box. Name the calculation *Try Again?* Be sure to use leading capital letters because the name of the icon will appear on-screen as the pushbutton's name. This completes the look of the entire practice flowline. It is shown in Figure 15.16.

Now you can place the feedback. Open and close the *crane operator* icon to provide "landmarks" for placement. Then, while holding the shift key down, open the *provide feedback* interaction icon all the way to edit its display. Select the text tool

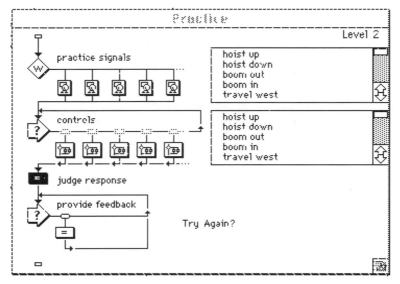

Figure 15.16 Completed Practice Flowline

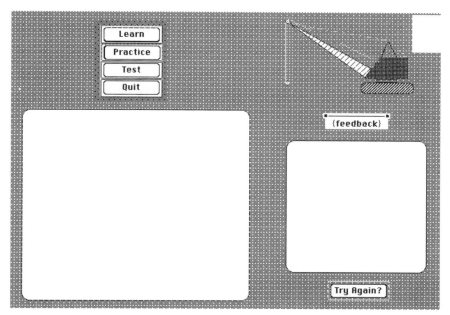

Figure 15.17 Embedded Variable

from the toolbox, place the cursor in the proper feedback location, and click once. The text field will open. Type in:

```
{feedback}
```

Be sure to type it in lowercase, as custom variables are case-sensitive and you initially entered your variable as all lowercase. Now click on the selection tool and move the *Try Again?* pushbutton to its proper location. The completed display will look like Figure 15.17. Click the close button to close the display.

Now you will arrange for Authorware to branch to a particular location when the *Try Again?* button is selected. We want to repeat the practice, so the instruction will be to go to the first icon in *Practice*.

Double-click the *Try Again?* calculation icon. When the calculation appears, select Show Functions from the Data pull-down menu (Figure 13.31 shows the functions dialog box). Select Jump from the Categories drop-down menu. GoTo is the first function (and will be highlighted by default on Macs). Select Paste to paste the function in your open calculation. The pasted function will be:

```
GoTo(IconID@"IconTitle")
```

Edit it to read:

```
GoTo(IconID@"practice signals")
```

Close the calculation window.

So far in this lesson you have created some perpetual options for branching. While the learner is in Practice he or she may select Learn, and while in Learn he may select Practice. You may recall that the interaction in the learn group was simple in design and programming (refer to Figure 15.5). The displays in *Learn* erase automatically when the learner selects Practice. However, the programming of Practice was more extensive and its construction prohibits automatic erasing (remember setting Prevent Automatic Erase in the *controls* interaction icon?). You must use an erase icon to overcome the Prevent Automatic Erase to permit the same clean appearance when the learner moves from Practice to Learn. Drag an erase icon to the top of the main flowline in the *Learn* map and title it *erase practice*. Figure 15.18 shows the correct position.

Run the program. You must use a specific sequence. When the program opens, select Practice from the on-screen menu, NOT Learn. The reason for this is that you will bring up the Crane Controller when you select Practice. Then it will be present when you are asked what you want to erase. If you choose Learn first you will be asked what to erase, but the Crane Controller won't be on the screen.

If you select Practice, just let the Practice display open. Then select Learn from the on-screen menu. When Learn opens, an erase dialog box will appear, saying Click Objects to Erase. Click on the Crane Controller, then select OK to close the erase dialog box.

Test drive

You are now ready to try the completed Practice and see that both Learn and Practice are fully functional. When you are satisfied, read on.

Reusable Code and Models

It is possible to save work within a single program by copying sets of icons and pasting them in a new location, making minor changes to account for differences. You could copy the *Practice* group, paste it, and rename the new group *test,* make some

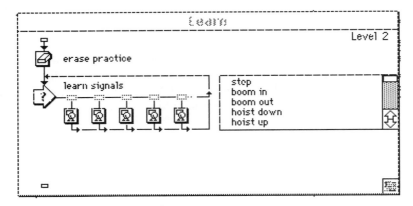

Figure 15.18 Learn with Erase Practice

changes in how it works, and have a lesson "test." You could, that is, if you had the full version of Authorware. Your version of Authorware is limited to 50 icons, preventing you from considering a wholesale copy and paste.

The same concept can be applied to save work within multiple programs by saving the icon groups as models that can be called when needed, and will reside out of sight in the meantime. Likewise, if we had the *Practice* module saved as an Authorware Model, we could paste it. In the current circumstance, we must come up with another solution. There is also the problem of file size. Pasting *Practice* again would nearly double our file size. In large programs, doing this could swell the program considerably.

Create the Test Instructional Unit

After the learner has completed the learning section and practiced to a degree of confidence, he or she will be ready for a test. This test will be similar to the practice, except it will not be possible to select Practice or Learn during the test, each signal will be displayed to the learner only one time, and at the end of the test the test results will be posted. You will make the test in two steps: entering the *test* calculation and revising the *practice* group.

Develop the test calculation

Open the *test* calculation. You will enter four lines of calculations. They will turn the test on, count the number of correct responses the learner takes, count the number of signals given during the test, and branch to practice upon completion of the test.

Enter the following in the *test* calculation icon:

```
test = ON
x = 0
signals = 0
GoTo(IconID@"practice signals")
```

Test, x, and signals are all new variables. When you close the calculation window you will be asked for initial values for each one, one at a time. Since the default value of zero is the value you want, you can select OK for each.

Authorware Tip: If you open the calculation again after you have closed it, you will see that Authorware has inserted colons before the equals signs. The calculations now look like this:

```
test := ON
x := 0
signals := 0
```

It is undesirable to type colons in the places you see them, although in most cases it would do no harm. If you enter the colon in some cases, Authorware will assign a value rather than comparing the values. For example, IF(test = on, Display IconID@"question_1") is the appropriate form. If you were to type the colon before the equals sign then Authorware would assign the value of "on" to the variable test rather than compare it. Spaces are not important in the expression, except in variable names. You can make the expressions much easier to read if you add them. Place the lines in the order you want then executed, since Authorware will read them from the top down and execute each before moving to the next.

Revise the practice group

Open the *Practice* map icon. The first thing you must do is make the embedded variable "feedback" have a null or blank value. This is necessary so that, if the learner is in the practice section and he selects the Test button, the previous feedback will disappear. To accomplish this, you will soon assign a blank value to the variable "feedback." A blank value is formed by two quotation marks with nothing between them.

To track test questions you will want to increment a variable each time the learner enters a question. The typical format programmers use in all computer languages to do this is: variable = variable + 1. In this case, we will call this variable "signals." Therefore, you will soon enter an expression: signals = signals + 1.

Not all calculations are inside calculation icons. It is possible to append calculations to other icons. When the flowline reaches the icon in question, the calculation is read and executed *before* the icon contents.

To enter the calculation, select (single-click only) the *practice signals* decision icon. Open the Data pull-down menu and select Calculations (it is at the bottom of the menu). This will open a calculation window that is exactly the same as one opened from a calculation icon. Enter the following expressions and close the calculation window.

```
feedback = ""
signals = signals +1
```

Figure 15.19 shows the appearance of the *practice signals* decision icon, with its newly appended calculation indicated by a small equals sign.

Now you must make an adjustment to keep score. You will write the code to track the number of correct responses the learner makes. Later, this number of correct responses will be used to calculate a percentage score for the learner at the end of the test. To do this you will use the same condition that you wrote to evaluate the learner's response and display the Correct or Incorrect feedback.

Open the judge response calculation icon. Copy the complete argument, press the Return key once or twice, and paste it on a line below, creating two identical lines. Then, over in the second line, select **feedback := "Correct", feedback := "Incorrect"** and type x=x+1 to replace it. The resulting new line should read:

```
IF(PathSelected@"practice signals" = ChoiceNumber@"controls", x=x+1)
```

When your new argument is correct, close the calculation. If there is no error it will close without complaint.

Now you will enter the feedback that the learner will see, and will establish the reactivation of the Learn and Practice buttons (for which you will soon establish the deactivation) after he or she is finished testing on all seven of the signals.

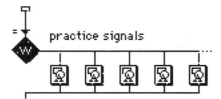

Figure 15.19 Appended Calculation

Drag a wait icon to the flowline to the right of the *feedback* interaction icon, *but to the left of* the *Try Again?* calculation icon. The response type dialog box will appear with the default of Pushbutton preselected. (Macs require you to click on the pushbutton response type symbol, and to select Response Type from within the Pushbutton Options dialog box.) You want this icon to activate after all the questions have been completed, but to be inactive when the learner is not in the test. The appropriate choice is the Conditional response type, so select Conditional. The Conditional Options dialog box shown in Figure 15.20 will open. Enter **signals = 7 & test** in the Match if TRUE field and click on OK to close the dialog box. Notice that the new icon is named *signals = 7 & test*.

Now you will create the expression that generates the end-of-test feedback and restores functionality to the Practice and Quit buttons. Select the *signals = 7 & test* icon. As you did earlier to append a calculation, open the Data pull-down menu and select Calculations. The calculation window will open. Enter the following expressions.

```
feedback = "Your score is "^Round(x / 7 * 100,0)^"%."
test = OFF
```

Be certain to type a space after the **is**. It will provide the proper spacing between the word and the score that will be inserted by the program. Now close the calculation window. Figure 15.21 shows the completed Practice flowline as you have modified it to control the test.

You are almost, but not quite, finished modifying Practice. As the flowline stands now, the learner would never see the post-test feedback. This is because the feedback exists in the embedded variable displayed from inside the *provide feedback* interaction icon. Let's look at the flow.

Go With the Flow: Follow the flowline in Figure 15.21 as it leaves the *judge response* icon and enters the *provide feedback* interaction. For the first six tries, the provide feedback icon displays the feedback "Correct" or "Incorrect" and waits until one of its responses is activated. Since signals do not equal 7, the *signals = 7 & test* icon is ignored. Once the learner clicks on the Try Again? button the flow moves to the *Try Again?* icon and the GoTo(IconID@"practice signals") returns the flow to the *practice signals* icon. On the final question (number 7), the *signals = 7 & test* icon is active and the flow drops into that icon (executing the actions that you just programmed) and waits there until Learn, Practice, or Quit is selected. The problem is that, since it waits at the *signals = 7 & test* icon, the feedback embedded variable inside the interaction icon will not change to provide the total score "feedback." For

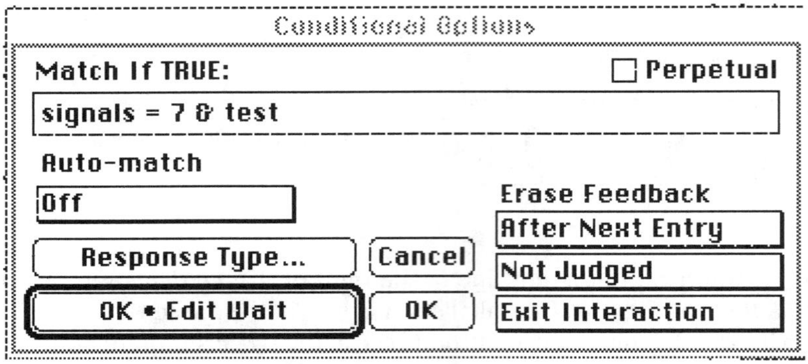

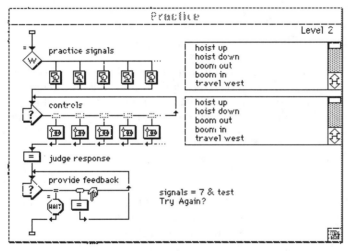

Figure 15.20 Conditional Response Type Dialog Box

Figure 15.21 Completed Practice Flowline Modified for Testing

tunately, you can overcome this problem by directing Authorware to continuously update the display of the embedded variable "feedback."s

Select the *provide feedback* interaction icon to activate the Attributes pull-down menu. Select the Effects choice from the Attributes menu and click the Update Displayed Variables checkbox. Then close the Effects dialog box.

Test drive

Run the program to see the test. As you do this you will notice that the Learn and Practice buttons remain active during the test. This does not meet the design specifications of the lesson.

Deactivate buttons

You can deactivate those buttons using the existing variable "test." It has the values of either TRUE or FALSE, and the test is only active when the "test" variable is TRUE.

Go to the level 1 menu and select the *Learn* pushbutton response type symbol to open the dialog box. In the Active if TRUE field, type **test = false**. Figure 15.22 shows the box after this entry.

Now the Learn pushbutton will be active only when the value of test is FALSE. Note that you are not declaring that test *is* False, you are establishing a comparison. Now repeat this procedure in the same field of the *Practice* Pushbutton Options dialog box. Your lesson is complete!

Test drive

Run the program again. Try everything. It should all work as advertised. When you select the Continue button at the end of the test the Learn and Practice buttons should become active. You are in the practice mode. It may look the same as the test, but you will find that Practice continues as far beyond seven questions as you care to go.

Nothing done later should have hurt the functionality you established earlier. Not bad, huh?

Troubleshooting

Now you can use some of the advanced features of Authorware as you edit on the fly. Text that was imported with a graphic may create a white rectangle that covers areas that it should not. This is because it is in the wrong Attributes Mode. Go to the icon that contains the text. Open it and select the offending text with the arrow cursor. Select Mode from the Attributes menu and choose Transparent.

The highlight that is associated with hand signals in Learn is supposed to be transparent to let the hand that it covers show through. If one of yours should be solid, select the transparent mode as described above.

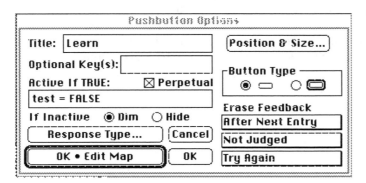

Figure 15.22 Active If TRUE Entry

In Practice, the Correct and Incorrect text block may be too short to display those words on one line. When it is displayed, double-click directly on the word Correct or Incorrect. It will open *provide feedback*, where the variable lives. The displayed feedback variable also provides the feedback of test result, which is even longer than either word. Complete the test to ensure that your text block is long enough to accommodate the test results. Fix it if it is not. Select the Text pull-down menu, select Justification, and choose Center to center the text in the text block. Finally, you should change the displayed variable text to transparent mode as described in the paragraphs above.

Ideas for Expansion, Enhancement, and Evolution

Here are some ideas for use of this lesson in new ways:

- You could use audio to call out the names of the hand signals, so the operator could select the matching signal. Conversely, the audio could be used to reinforce the correct identification of a hand signal by calling out its name when the learner identifies it.

- Video could be employed to display the image of a worker in a real shop floor setting, giving the hand signals at the distance and angle they would be seen by the crane operator in a cab.

- You could use Hide instead of the default Dim display attribute associated with the variable that controls the Learn and Practice buttons. Figure 15.23 shows the Dim and Hide choices. You may want to experiment with them to see the effect of their use.

That's Cool

Long before the movie of the same name, in Jamaica *Cool Runnin'* meant that everything is OK and under control. Unfortunately, everything doesn't always go right. You may have the intention to make a change near the end of the day. When you start up again the next day, you think that you made the change the day before and may move on. Then the lesson doesn't run right and you have to fix it.

Chapter 16 is about finding those errors of omission and commission, routing them out, and making your lessons smooth. You can have cool runnin' lessons from now on.

Chapter

16

Troubleshooting

We wish that we could tell you that all there is to troubleshooting is to give your computer a romping, stomping look straight in the display, go to the code, see the problem, and fix it. Unfortunately the only part of that we can be sure will work right away is the part about going to the code. A romping, stomping approach may work for some things, but not troubleshooting. Neither can we be sure that we, you, or anyone else will see the problem right away. It may take considerable patience to find it.

What we will do is provide you with some proven techniques to use when moving beyond this book's exercises to create your own unique courseware for your own organization or client. You will be able to use some of them right away. Others will not be useful until you attempt more complex lessons. Refer back to this chapter as you complete the exercises in later chapters of this book.

What You Will Learn in This Chapter

- Basic techniques for finding problems in software
- Specific techniques for finding problems in technology-based learning
- Specific techniques for finding problems in Authorware lessons
- How to get help when you can't find the solution to the problem

Basic Techniques

Some techniques are universal, in that they work with any type of computer application. They form the backbone of your problem-solving efforts because you apply them at any time and in combination with other Authorware-specific troubleshooting techniques.

Add temporary variables

You may set initial values at the beginning of a program. When you are running from the flag deep within the program, the variables would not be assigned their initial value. You can place a variable temporarily to assign the value you want within the flag boundaries. It is removed when the problem is resolved. For example, if part 3 of a course is only available after parts 1 and 2 are complete, and is controlled by variables, you could set the variables

```
part1=done
part2=done
```

so that you can troubleshoot part 3.

Comment-out variables and functions

If you have a dysfunctional, incomplete, or missing portion of your program, you can prevent it from appearing or working by commenting-out functions that call it. There is an example of this in Chapter 23, when the argument to display the diploma was written, yet diploma itself had not yet been created. The argument was commented-out to avoid an Authorware objection.

You can use variables to provide the opportunity to repeatedly check the functionality of an icon structure. For example, if a variable increments as in question_number = question_number +1, it forces you onward to the next question after trying the one in which you are interested. If you comment-out the line with the variable, you can check all the feedback responses to a multiple-choice question without rerunning the question.

Use descriptive titles in the icon names

This is an obvious idea that we have used throughout the example chapters of this book. It is much easier to troubleshoot a program when the icon's names indicate what they do.

An absolute nightmare occurs when a programmer leaves almost all the icons untitled. We know people who do this! It takes much longer to make sense out of what is happening and, because they may have to revisit locations more than once, many troubleshooters will provide them with names as they go through the lesson.

The way to fix this (comparatively) quickly is to use the Find/Change option under the Edit menu. Figure 16.1 shows a Find effort underway to locate the untitled icons among the icon groups that are selected at the time.

Use comments to explain how things work

Place comments in calculations to explain what a particular line does. You can forget this amazingly quickly. For the same reason, fill in the Description box for custom variables you create that tell what each variable is used for.

Place a READ ME calculation icon at the top of your flowline. In it, write comments about the progress of the program and things that still need doing. Remove the READ ME icon when you have finished the lesson.

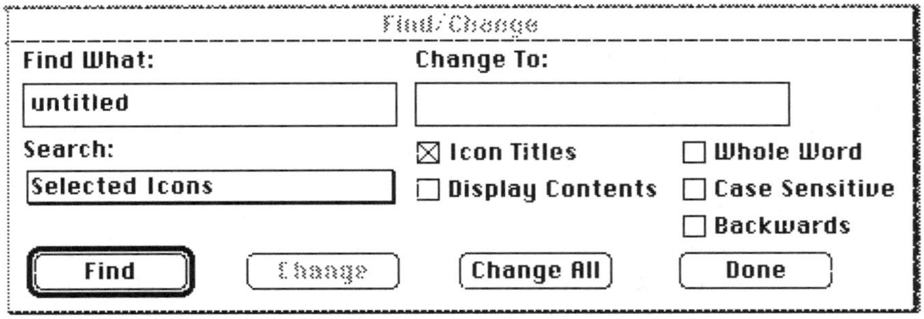

Figure 16.1 Find/Change Dialog Box

Use sounds

Use a sound to tell you that your program has reached a particular point. In some cases, you will have difficulty in making things happen in sequence. The sound will tell you where the flow is at that moment. Authorware has a built-in sound among its functions. It is Beep under the General Category. You could place a calculation with the function:

```
Beep()
```

at a spot on the flowline just before or after an icon you are having trouble with. Hearing the beep will announce that the flow has reached the Beep calculation's location without disrupting the visual display of the program.

You can use any sound as a placeholder when the final sound you need is unavailable. For example, in Chapter 18, when preparing narration of the readings, you can test the functionality of the program before the narration exists. We did this with two amusing sounds that were on hand—a cow's moo and a dog's bark. These represented the two narrations to ensure that the program's sound was operational and accurate.

Use video

You can use temporary video as a placeholder in the same way described for sound. You may have many video clips in a lesson. You can take an existing video clip, copy it, and rename each copy to substitute for video. All your uses of video can be placed and tested using these placeholders before the actual video is available.

You can use a video clip that is quite short as a "stand-in" for actual lengthy video. When the testing is over, you can overwrite the stand-in with the real video file.

Use displayed variables to track functionality

You can place an embedded displayed variable to enable you to see what has happened to help you understand how your program is working. For example, in Chapter 23, to test the development of the prescription, you can embed the variables obj_1_correct through obj_4_correct in the *Instructional Prescription* display. When you run the

Pre-Test, they will tell you what values have been passed back to the curriculum from the test. Figure 16.2 shows how the variables look when placed on the screen.

Figure 16.3 shows the embedded variables as they look when displaying their values. You can use this information to see whether the test questions are updating the variables appropriately. In the testing and prescription generating aspects of the curriculum, many variables must correspond to each other.

The learner's success (answering the question correctly) on a particular test question must relate to mastery of a particular objective. Figure 16.4 shows the test grades in response to a question on the test, and how that is reflected in the obj_1_ correct variable. This mastery must be reflected back to the curriculum and must result in an appropriate prescription.

The random variable shown in Figure 16.5 lets you see that the test question associated with a branch of a decision is being activated (tells you that the question related to an objective is being used for that objective). You can also use it to track that questions are not being reused when other questions have not yet been asked.

Figure 16.6 illustrates a displayed variable that tracks that the question being displayed is really the question that relates to Objective 2. This can be difficult to follow when there are many questions being displayed randomly.

Troubleshoot like an expert

You may not be aware of it, but experts troubleshoot differently than novices. Basically, novices go down a list of possibilities, trying each in sequence to see whether it could be the culprit.

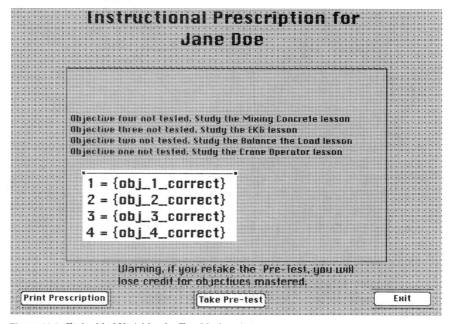

Figure 16.2 Embedded Variables for Troubleshooting

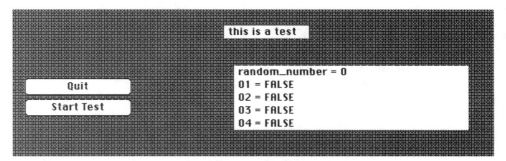

Objective two not tested. S
Objective one not tested. S

1 = FALSE
2 = FALSE
3 = FALSE
4 = FALSE

Warning, if you
lose credit for

Figure 16.3 Embedded Variables as Displayed

this is a test

Quit

Start Test

random_number = {random_number}
01 = {obj_1_correct}
02 = {obj_2_correct}
03 = {obj_3_correct}
04 = {obj_4_correct}

Figure 16.4 Embedded Variables to Check Initial Values and Randomization

this is a test

Quit

Start Test

random_number = 0
01 = FALSE
02 = FALSE
03 = FALSE
04 = FALSE

Figure 16.5 Display of Embedded Variables to Track the Values

Experts work very differently. After only a bit of fact-finding, experts draw a tentative conclusion as to the nature of the problem. Then they try to confirm they have the right solution by eliminating other possibilities, or performing tests that can confirm the diagnosis. Research supports these different approaches and you can observe them in action. Medical doctor's training leads them to follow the expert problem-identification methods. You can hear this process at work by listening to Click and Clack, the Tappet brothers who are on the amazingly popular radio program *Car Talk*.

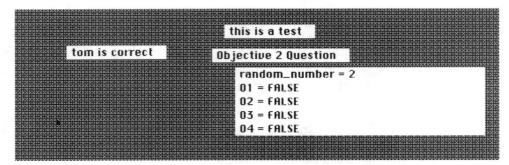

Figure 16.6 Embedded Variables as Markers to Observe Proper Functioning

Read the manual

Yes, even *you* should read the manual. In particular, check out the function or system variable that you are working with. It may work a bit differently than you remember.

Better than the manual

We highly recommend Joe Ganci's *Authorware System Variables and Functions*. It covers both Macintosh and Windows and is an invaluable resource for every Authorware developer. It is a super tool for understanding Authorware's variables and functions.

The currently offered Third Edition is a three-volume set with accompanying disks. It contains hundreds of complete examples covering all Authorware variables and functions, internal and external, for all versions and platforms. The new edition thoroughly illustrates UCDs, DLLs, and XCMDs. To obtain a copy, contact:

Successful Multimedia
12471 Dillingham Square, Suite 122
Woodbridge, VA 22192
Phone / Fax 703-878-2555
e-mail: MrMulMedia@aol.com

Look deeper

You *can* get your lessons under control. It just takes patience. Work methodically. When looking for problems that new programmers cannot find in their code we often find that they have not looked where the problem lies. That is, they have tried looking, but not *deeply* enough. For example, look inside the dialog box for an interaction, even though the interaction itself has nothing in its display. The erase there may be the cause of the problem.

Take a break

Sometimes, you are just blinded by your own efforts. You are making a troubleshooting logic or procedural mistake, but aren't aware of it.

You begin to think that you've tried everything when you really haven't. You may find the problem much more quickly if you turn away from the code for a while. If it is the end of the day, go home. If not, turn to some other work. If you must finish the lesson, take a walk. If you are gone long enough, when you come back your head will be clear. At that point, do not resume where you were. Start all over with a clean perspective. You will not be likely to repeat the same mistake.

Start over

Many things can happen. Somehow code, icons, and files can become corrupted. Sometimes, when you can't find a problem because things look OK but just don't work, consider that your code may be corrupt. In some cases you can retype it. In others you must replace it with fresh.

Also, you may not be able to recreate the sequence in which you built your code, because options may be presented in a different way for completed code, compared to how it unfolded initially. This is true of Authorware, making repetition of initial steps less helpful than one might hope. In such cases, select the smallest segment that seems connected to the problem and recreate it from scratch.

Network problems

If you deliver training over a LAN, the network can make troubleshooting more complex. The big test is to run the application outside of the network. If it works there the problem is related to the network, although the lesson itself may require a change to fix the problem. Network problems may lie with network cards, servers, server's utilization, and possibly with inherent hardware or software problems within the network itself.

Specific Techniques

Now let's look at Authorware-specific troubleshooting techniques. These are used in conjunction with the basic techniques to find the problem.

 Mac Difference: The Mac has a running man on the menu bar when the program is running. The man changes to the shape of the icon at which the program is awaiting an action. There is no equivalent feature on the Windows version.

Use wait

Insert a temporary wait icon to stop the action. This will keep activity at a standstill, before something different occurs when the flow falls through to other icons.

Use the start and stop flags

Use the Run from the flag feature to isolate a portion of the code. Use the stop flag to stop the action before something occurs when you fall through.

Use erase

When you have multiple layered displays you can use an erase icon to erase a specific icon, at a specific point in the flow-revealing object behind the icon, to make sure the proper ones are there then. Remove the erase once its troubleshooting function is performed.

Use show links

You can find the broken links to multiple libraries. Broken links can cause graphical problems with the program.

Use show variables

You can find the variables that have become unneeded by looking in the Referenced By window of the Variables dialog box and scrolling through the variables one by one. The Referenced By window will be blank for the unused variables.

You can also use the Referenced By window to find variables that are only referenced once. Only one reference is valid when you want to change an initial value only one time. Otherwise, you should suspect variables that are referenced only once. You are probably using a variable where one is not needed. Find the reference and look for a way around. An example can be found in Chapter 23 of this book, where you nested functions rather than assigning variables. If the variables were used instead, they would have been needed only in that one spot in the entire curriculum lesson.

The Referenced By window tells only what icons use that variable. To find out *how* it is used, select the Show Icon button to follow-up.

Use Get Info

Use Get Info to find the size and content of an icon. This will typically identify a huge imported graphic that is slowing your program. Converting the graphic to screen capture will speed up the program.

You can use Get Info to find the original library icons. This can be especially useful when using multiple libraries.

Use Jump to current icon

This feature will often take you to the icon at which you observe a problem. Unfortunately, programming patterns in Authorware often make the current icon a wait, because the flowline has reached it and is waiting for the learner to make a selection.

Use Pause

Use the Pause function of the Try It menu to reveal the existence and placement of hotspots. You may wonder why a hotspot isn't working and find that it is not in the right place, or that it isn't showing up at all.

You can use Pause to display the position of target areas for movable objects.

Use it to check the current values of system and custom variables. This is especially valuable when you have a large program using many variables. In this case, if you were to try to embed them on your screen, you could easily end up with your screen covered with variables.

On the Macintosh, Pause will show which pushbuttons are active. Active pushbuttons are surrounded by a dotted line.

Use layers

You can use Authorware's layers to see a path completely, when part of that path is obscured by higher-level objects. To do this, temporarily assign the object you want to see a higher level in the Effects menu. This will make it possible to see exactly what that object does.

Use sequential versus random in the decision icon

You can make a decision, that will eventually be random, easier to work with in the troubleshooting stage by changing it to sequential. For example, imagine a test bank of 100 questions. If you were to try to make sure each question worked properly while the decision was set to random, you would go crazy trying to track which question you had seen. Further, when you made a change and wanted to retry the question, it would be presented at an unknown point. If you make the questions sequential, each will appear at its expected point in the series for checking. Change it to random when you have completed troubleshooting all of the questions.

Use IconTitle as a displayed embedded variable

By embedding the IconTitle variable in a display at the head of your program, or a section that you want to test, you can tell where you are. Three setting characteristics are important, and must be turned on. They are:

- High layer
- Prevent automatic erase
- Update displayed variables

This will generate a text display that tells the name of the icon that you are currently in. Figure 16.7 shows an Effects dialog box with the needed settings.

This is not always as helpful as it sounds, because Authorware's flowline often is paused at an interaction, waiting for a response, running a loop in a decision waiting for a condition that will cause a path to be selected, or sitting in a wait icon waiting for a learner action that will cause the program to move on. All of these are typically not the icon that you are interested in. Nevertheless, the IconTitle gives a general idea of what is happening.

Beware of mistyped icon titles

If you get the message "Syntax error: The icon 'iconnamehere' does not exist. Please correct your expression" when attempting to close a calculation, look for a mistyping. Assuming that you do have an icon by the name you used, you probably have typed a leading or trailing blank space when you typed the icon's name. Find the icon and correct the typing of its name.

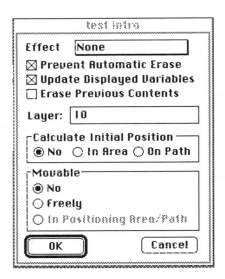

Figure 16.7 Effects Dialog Box for IconTitle

Use the IOMessage and IOStatus variables

Authorware will not ordinarily advise you of the failure of a function that is not critical to its own operation. For example, if you attempt to write a file you won't know if it was written or not. If you intend to write a file to the hard drive, but in fact your code attempts to write it to a CD (a read-only medium), Authorware will not complain even though nothing was written.

IOStatus holds numerical values. Zero indicates that there is no error. Other values report errors, with the number depending on what operating system is involved.

If you embed a variable to report IOMessage or go to the File Category and look at the current value of IOStatus, it will hold a Current Value that tells if the input/output you want is working properly. You want to see the message "no error." A current value of "no such file or directory" would result from attempting to write to a CD.

Use the IconLog variable

Authorware will store a list of up to 100 icon names that represent the most recent icons you have encountered. By assigning the value of this variable to another variable, or embedding it on the screen, you will have a list of the sequence in which icons were encountered when running the program. You may be interested in the absence of an expected icon, or its appearance in an unexpected sequence.

Use FALSE to deactivate interactions

To prevent an interaction from interrupting your examination of a portion of your lesson, you can make the interaction FALSE. You simply type FALSE in the Active If TRUE variable field of the interaction options dialog box for many of the response types. Then that interaction will be unavailable and effectively removed from the flowline, until restored by removing the FALSE.

If an interaction has a variable that controls when the interaction is available, but you want to effectively remove it while not deleting it from your code, you can type FALSE, along with the two hyphens to comment-out the remainder of the line that holds the expression. Figure 16.8 shows an example. The *Start Test* pushbutton would be available when the variable registered becomes TRUE. By entering FALSE - - in front of the variable name in the Active If TRUE field, it will remain dimmed.

Reading the Flowline

This is a useful technique. See Chapter 13 for a discussion of reading the flowline. If you followed the flowline reading suggestions in Chapters 13 through 23 you have a very good idea what we mean. We have observed that programmers who can read the flowline better can solve problems in the code better. If you are going to spend much time with Authorware, we suggest that you try to sharpen this skill.

Understanding Erasing

This is a thorny problem. Getting the erases right can occupy much of your troubleshooting efforts. Erases are activated through:

- Attributes preventing automatic erase
- Decision branches
- Erase icons
- Feedback branches
- Interactions
- Jumping
- Layers of graphics that resemble true erases
- Multiple erase functions
- Perpetual interactions

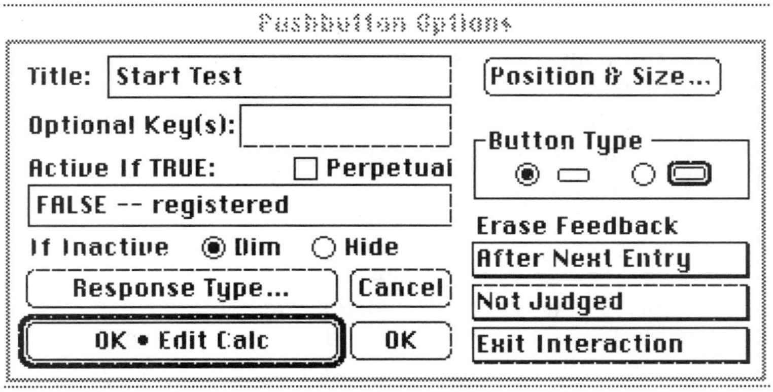

Figure 16.8 Active If TRUE Made FALSE

All these combine in ways that may seem mysterious to beginning Authorware programmers. Identifying and fixing erase problems requires patience, an understanding of Authorware's flow, and a willingness to thoroughly explore the guts of the structure instead of merely the surface. We suggest that you use the bulleted list as a checklist for debugging erases.

As with the flowline, we have observed that programmers who can follow the myriad erase combinations can eliminate these problems much faster. And again, as with the flowline, we suggest that you try to sharpen these skills.

Graphics

When you import graphics, the border comes in with the graphic. There are varying effects with different colors. For example, a white border can be made transparent by selecting Matted Mode. If it is any other color, Matted will not work.

Opaque graphics draw much more quickly (twice as fast) than matted. You may want to change the type to speed up your program.

Authorware uses 8-bit color. Therefore, 24-bit true-color images cannot be displayed as you might like. When imported, they are converted to 8-bit, 256-color images. For better image color you can use a custom palette with such images.

Switching palettes in a program will cause the screen to flash. A solution is to use the same palette for an entire program. Jumping to another program will cause a flash if the two lessons' palettes are different.

Resizing graphics can create problems. When you resize a vector graphic image (see Chapter 4 for a description), Authorware may distort the image so that it appears to "fall apart."

Computer Differences

You might prepare a program that works perfectly, but when given to your client it crashes or runs "like a dog." If the delivery computer has too little memory it can crash; with slightly more memory (but still less than the optimum amount) it will just be slow.

Also, you may have a super-duper development platform and everything looks great to you. Yet, when you place your work on the target machines, it runs unacceptably slow. This may happen because you have used gigantic graphics that only your machine can handle, or you may have introduced processor-intensive activities that your whiz-bang computer flies through but the learner's machine has to huff and puff to complete. The obvious answer to these problems is to periodically run your program on the target machine.

Controlling Text

A lesson that looks fine on your development computer may appear strange on the learner's computer because you used fonts that are installed on your computer. The number of fonts that you can count on being installed on a Windows computer may only include Arial and Times Roman.

The way around this problem is to design and create the display as you want it to look. Then do a screen capture (Alt-Print Screen) and paste the bit-mapped image that you created into the display.

You may need to leave room to avoid problems when converting to a foreign language. Refer to Chapter 27 for specific references.

Technical Support and Other Assistance

Technical support is the ultimate answer to bail you out when you get totally stuck. However, there are limitations. The Macromedia company does not provide technical support for the Authorware Working Model included in this book's CD. Currently, owners of the full version receive one year of telephone-based technical support, but must pay additional fees for continuation.

Do not contact McGraw-Hill for assistance.

You might consider joining a support group. The less experienced you are, the more likely that you can find others who have already faced and solved the problems you experience. Other companies that are not competitive with yours may be a source of friendly help.

We may not always be able to diagnose your problem at a distance, but we will be glad to help you with problems. You are welcome to contact us via e-mail. You can reach Angus at:

    areynolds@kcp.com

or Thomas at:

    tmi107@psu.edu

The Internet and electronic bulletin boards are also potential sources of help.

Blame the Computer

There is a tendency to assume absolutely that whatever is wrong is caused by the programmer. Frankly, if you *must* make an assumption, that's a pretty good one. But it isn't always right.

Sometimes your computer can *think* that its free memory is getting used up. If this happens, even though there is enough memory to handle the demands you are placing on it, it will begin to fail. One symptom is "artifacts" in the display—small squares may not erase properly.

The price for discovering whether the problem lies in the computer is very small. Just shut it down gracefully by turning a PC off from DOS prompt or Quitting from the Macintosh Special drop-down window. Wait 30 seconds, and start up again normally. This will clear your computer's head and eliminate the memory-related problems. Do not use Control-Alt-Delete, since the soft reboot that it causes will not clear the memory.

Check It Out

You have to fix the mechanical problems with your courseware. However, as you can appreciate, that isn't enough. You have to make sure that it does the job it was designed to do. If it doesn't, the whole project is a failure. In Chapter 17 you will continue the exploration of evaluation that you began in Chapter 7. You will explore more deeply into the evaluation steps that are performed when the courseware is fully developed. It's time to check out the learning and the success of the course.

17

Evaluating
Technology-Based Training

Every project should include the formative evaluation processes to make it as good as it can be, and the summative evaluation ones to ensure that it did the job it was originally assigned.

Unfortunately, this step is too often omitted because training sponsors see it as an additional cost. This helps to explain why some training is poor. To be a fully knowledgeable TBL developer, you also must know how to conduct an evaluation. As we described in Chapter 7, before completing an interactive multimedia training program, you might observe learners using prototype versions of the lesson. When you believe that it is completely ready to go, you would run a pilot test before making a general release.

Most evaluation activities are relatively simple in concept but require skillful application. The purpose of this chapter is to describe the concepts of evaluation that you must carry out to make your evaluation efforts more skillful.

What You Will Learn in This Chapter

- How to evaluate technology-based learning
- How to design or modify tools for evaluating lessons
- How to use the results of evaluation

What Kinds of Evaluation Are Important?

Bill Reeves, from the University of Georgia, suggests categorizing the different kinds of evaluation according to the types of questions you will want to answer before making decisions about the technology-based learning product under development. Here are four major questions that you should address in a product development context:

1. What resources (personnel, time, etc.) are used in developing a product?
2. How can the product be improved?
3. What is the immediate effectiveness of the product?
4. What is the impact of the product?

Each of these questions leads to a separate aspect of evaluation. As illustrated in Figure 17.1, adapted from Reeves, different types of subquestions arise when you attempt to answer the main questions, each of which can help alert you to one or more decisions about the courseware.

Formative Evaluation

We have already discussed formative evaluation in Chapter 7. After you have developed an entire curriculum, you should look at it again. Almost anything about a technology-based learning product can be improved at one or another point.

Reeves suggests several basic questions that must be addressed about technology-based learning products. Here are our adaptations of those questions:

- Do learners understand what their options are at any given moment?
- Does the lesson maintain the learners' attention?
- Do learners like the lesson?
- Do learners accomplish the objectives of the lesson?
- Is it feasible to implement the lesson as designed?

The earlier you ask the questions and make changes based upon the responses, the more efficient your overall development effort will be.

Never lose sight of the fact that the most valuable information is always derived from real learners during the various trials of the lesson. With that said, let's take a look at some other ideas.

Expert review

An expert review occurs when a (usually external, impartial) instructional expert evaluates the learning dimensions of the lesson. This process is normally done by

---

Subquestions decisions
Is the user interface clear? Should you redesign the icons?
Do learners stay attentive? Should you shorten video sequences?
Do learners pass skill quizzes? Should you add more practice?
How quickly do learners finish? Should you expand the product scope?
Do learners possess new skills? Should you market the program?
What are the learners' attitudes? Should you advertise learner comments?

Figure 17.1 Sample Impact Questions and Decisions

large organizations, who often call on a local professor to review the instruction. The expert reviewer can provide a useful perspective on the critical aspects of your lesson. For example, these aspects include:

- Accuracy
- Aesthetics
- Completeness
- Effectiveness
- Efficiency
- Feasibility
- Instructional validity
- Motivational strategies
- User-friendliness

You can use internal resources if they exist. If they do not, don't hesitate to use external experts.

Figure 17.2 is an expert review checklist prepared for use by an external expert, to review and critique an interactive multimedia training lesson.

Supervisor involvement

Although not an evaluation technique in itself, we include this idea here with the other processes. It is important to the success of training for supervisors of employees receiving the training to view it favorably. Mary Broad, of the Defense Communication Agency, has pioneered studies that examine *transfer of training*. When there is no transfer, the learner will not use the training on the job. Again we suspect that you are surprised that this could be the case. The leading cause of transfer failure is lack of supervisor's support, or their active hostility. The evaluation process is an ideal time to involve supervisors, even if it is gratuitous to the needs of the project from the point of view of the instruction. Ask them to review the lesson and provide input. If you do this, be certain to consider their input carefully.

Alpha tests

Alpha and beta tests are terms borrowed from the software development process followed by commercial software companies. Alpha tests are those that you make internally before involving anyone outside the development group.

Materials for the alpha test include prototype screens presented on either the intended delivery system or some easy-to-program alternative. In Chapter 32 you will read of how the developers at Magnavox used the Macintosh's excellent rapid prototyping environment to develop lesson layouts for Unix implementation. Some developers use paper scripts, story boards, sketches, and other draft documents to represent elements of the eventual program. We believe that the "look and feel" of the eventual program is better represented by graphics, with cartoonlike "balloons" that tell what would be happening if the program really worked.

Expert Review Checklist

Review conducted by:_____
Date:_____
Title of project:_____
Directions: Circle your rating and write comments on each aspect of the TBL package on the scale. 1 represents the lowest, most negative rating, 3 represents an acceptable rating, and 5 represents the highest rating. Choose N/A if the item is not appropriate or not applicable to this course.

NA=Not applicable 1=Strongly disagree 2=Disagree 3=Neither agree/nor disagree 4= Agree 5=Strongly agree

Part 1 - Instructional design review

1. This lesson provides the learner with a clear knowledge of the learning objectives.   N/A12345

2. The instructional interactions are appropriate for the objectives.   N/A12345

3. The instructional design is based on sound learning theory   N/A12345

4. The feedback is clear.   N/A12345

5. The pace is appropriate.   N/A12345

6. The difficulty level is appropriate.   N/A12345

Part 2 - Cosmetic design review

7. The screen design follows sound principles.   N/A12345

8. Color is appropriately used.   N/A12345

9. The screen displays are easy to understand.   N/A12345

Part 3 - Lesson functionality review

10. This lesson operated flawlessly.   N/A12345

Part 4 - Comments

(Use the reverse for additional comments.)

Figure 17.2 Sample Expert Review Form for Interactive Multimedia Product

During the alpha test you can evaluate the lesson's comprehension, interactivity, and appeal. If your work has progressed far enough, you can observe whether, at critical junctions of the lesson, the learners know what to do and how to do it.

Beta tests

Beta tests are conducted with more-or-less complete versions of the lesson, in trial versions, to identify bugs before general distribution. A simple principle that must be observed before any beta test begins is, if it doesn't run when you try it, it isn't going to work with a learner at the keyboard, either!

It is best to conduct beta tests at multiple sites, if possible. Individual test sites may have differences that you do not anticipate and may not perceive.

Summative Evaluation

You might want to review the description of Kirkpatrick's four-level summative evaluation method that we described in Chapter 7. As with formative evaluation, we will expand on those ideas now that you have completed a number of lessons and may have a different perspective on the development process.

The evaluation plan

We recommend that you develop an evaluation plan. It is a document that spells out the whys and hows of an evaluation effort in considerable detail. It can be a boilerplate document that you can use as a template for every project that you undertake, modifying it as needed. You may want to include an abbreviated form of the plan in the design document, if that document is serving multiple roles as we described in Chapter 11. Remember, too, that some projects exist solely to evaluate training.

One advantage of an evaluation plan is that you can present it to your clients to review and approve. We advise you to have your clients indicate their approval of the plan on a sign-off form, as described in Chapter 34 . Figure 17.3 shows the outline of an evaluation plan.

On-line course evaluation

As an Authorware programmer of growing skill, you might consider programming an on-line course evaluation. Like many of the ideas suggested in this chapter, it could become a template that you could reuse with many of your projects. Basically, you would ask the learner important objective evaluation questions, such as, "Objective 3 states that you will be able to recognize a crane hand signal and operate the correct crane control to effect the signal. Rate your own ability to do this." Figure 17.4 shows an on-screen evaluation.

You can collect the data in a file and use a spreadsheet to accumulate it and represent it in graphic, as well as text, form.

Collect data

You may be asked to provide a collection mechanism to record the learner's paths through the modules, choices among the instructional options, progress check scores, and test scores in all the tutorials, quizzes, practice exercises, and mastery tests that you will create in the lesson.

You can do all of this. However, we observe that only rarely are training organizations prepared to do anything with the results that are recorded. When we receive such a request for data collection, we suggest the measures that we feel will be most useful if reviewed as an initial set of data. We have never been asked to implement the remainder of the items from the original list.

Evaluation Plan

1. Introduction—Introduce the major parts of the plan and the principal people involved in writing the plan. Demonstrate that the assessment is tied to on-the-job requirements.

2. Background—Provide and information that is needed to describe the background of the lesson, course, or curriculum that is being evaluated.

3. Purposes—One evaluation plan can address several purposes, but all must thoroughly describe the purposes of the evaluation. Remember that evaluation can be a political process, and all parties must accept its purposes if it is to be successful.

4. Limitations—Specify the limits of the evaluation. Describe potential threats to the reliability and validity of the evaluation design and instrumentation, and to the interpretation and generalizability of the results.

5. Audiences—Specify each primary and secondary audience for the evaluation.

6. Decisions—List the decisions that can be influenced by the evaluation. Anticipate potential negative outcomes.

7. Questions—Specify clearly and in detail the questions to be addressed by the evaluation design and data collection methods.

8. Methods—Describe the evaluation designs and procedures. Specify who will interpret the scores, and on what basis. Specify who will have access to the scores, and how they will be sent and retrieved. Specify how feedback will be used to maintain and update courses. Specify how you will provide security for the test itself, and for the scores.

9 Popuation—Specify exactly which learners, trainers, and other personnel will participate in the evaluation.

10. Instrumentation—Describe the instruments to be used in the evaluation. Provide copy of the instrument for review and approval.

11. Logistics—Specify who will be responsible for the various implementation, analysis, and reporting aspects for the evaluation.

12. Time line—Provide a schedule for implementation, analysis, and reporting.

13 Budget—Provide sufficient detail for cost-of-evaluation activity.

Figure 17.3 Elements of an Evaluation Plan

That doesn't mean that you can't collect and use data meaningfully. We recommend that, if possible, you perform an item analysis for each course. Examine the responses of the initial learners, question by question. Look for items that give learners trouble. Determine whether the concept is difficult, or the question is poorly worded, tricky, or unfairly difficult. Check whether your answer-judging structure is correct.

Examine the data

Are the mastery tests within the lesson anchored to real-world competencies? Bill Reeves describes his evaluation of an infant neuromotor dysfunctions diagnosis lesson comparing two groups. The learners taught by traditional means scored 6.6, but the learners using the TBL system scored 7.9. That is quite a difference, but he didn't just accept it at face value. He looked deeper. He says, "My concern is not whether the difference between the two groups is significant, but whether the learners completing the TBL training program have mastered the diagnosis of infant neuromotor assessment. I want to know how expert pediatric physicians would score on such a test." Bill is interested in performance, not normative comparisons.

Doing Things Right

It troubles us that so many organizations ignore evaluation. Their reluctance is always based on not seeing the benefit, yet the benefit of both formative and summative evaluation is so strong we don't understand how it can be ignored. We hope you will help us do a better job of selling the evaluation concept.

The bottom line is that, like all business decisions, training decisions should be based on the most timely and accurate information available. In the absence of sound information, the decision-makers will fall back on habit, intuition, prejudice, and guessing.

We hope that you will join us in urging that every project include the processes to make it as good as it can be (formative evaluation), and those that ensure that it did its job (summative evaluation).

Get Ready to Provide Special Help

This represents the conclusion of a finished courseware development effort. The process of analysis, design document, programmer-ready materials, and programmed

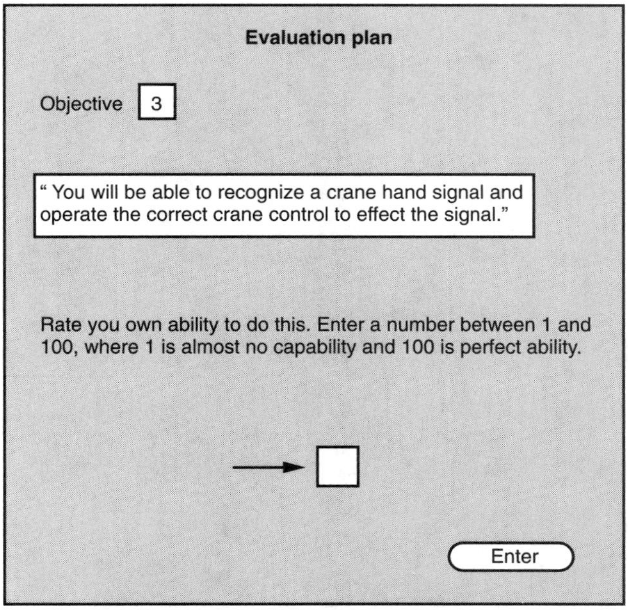

Evaluation plan

Objective 3

" You will be able to recognize a crane hand signal and operate the correct crane control to effect the signal."

Rate you own ability to do this. Enter a number between 1 and 100, where 1 is almost no capability and 100 is perfect ability.

⟶ ☐

Enter

Figure 17.4 Example of On-Screen Evaluation Question

lesson is followed by in-house and commercial development. In other chapters of this book we will pick up the action with programming to illustrate particular ideas. Remember, we would never jump straight to programming in the business environment, nor should you.

Now we will move on to Part 3 of the book, focused on more experience in programming with Authorware to achieve results. You will become competent as you explore different ways of meeting learner needs and learn how to program them. To start, you will learn more about Authorware while providing special features for disabled learners. Let's move on.

Applying Your Skills
to the World of Work

Chapter

18

ADA-Compliant Instruction

In this chapter, you will explore the wide range of control that you have over the presentation of your lessons. This will provide useful as you develop your own lessons in the future. For now, you also will learn more about Authorware.

How could you adjust your products for the visually- and hearing-impaired, as well as those with learning disabilities? This chapter addresses providing your learners options for adapting the look and feel of lessons to meet their own limitations. You will build a lesson that permits the learner with moderate vision impairment to select the size of the text on the screen, control the use and speed of a supporting narration, and change the cursor, based on the principle that some cursors may be easier to see than others.

What You Will Learn in This Chapter

- How to create pull-down menus
- How to use Authorware's sound icon
- How to control the menu bar
- How to create a scrolling text field
- How to incorporate sound into your lesson
- How to read an external text file into your lesson
- How to provide learner control over the multimedia user interface

The Americans with Disabilities Act

The principal law covering the disabled in the United States is Public Law 101-336, the Americans with Disabilities Act, called ADA. Along with Section 504 of the Rehabilitation Act of 1973, the historic ADA legislation sent the message that the intentional segregation and exclusion of people with disabilities would no longer be tolerated.

Assistive technology, already recognized in numerous federal laws as a component critical to leveling the playing field for people with disabilities, has become one of the critical vehicles for achieving the purpose of the ADA.

One of the remarkable achievements of the age of technology is the invention of devices to help many people with disabilities perform functions they would ordinarily be unable to do on their own. Available now are machines that "read" typed materials automatically, devices that "speak" text for blind or learning disabled individuals, and machines that "hear" and "understand" speech for persons who are severely disabled and who are unable to move their fingers.

Braille printers are now capable of printing in both braille and ink on the same sheet for use by persons who are blind and work in a "sighted environment"—that is, with sighted coworkers. The latest breakthrough in technology for the deaf is telecomputing. People who are deaf can use an ordinary telephone by using a voice synthesizer that speaks their typed-in words. The person at the other end uses the telephone's buttons to spell out words that then appear on the deaf user's screen. In addition to being much faster than the old-style telephone devices for the deaf (TDDs) , telecomputing is more advantageous because very few hearing individuals have teletype machines, while the number of persons with computers and modems is booming.

For those persons who have very limited control of their hands and arms, pointers that are held in the mouth or worn on a headband can be used to depress the computer keys. For persons who are unable to use their hands or a mouthstick or headwand, several devices can be operated with the eyes, eyebrows, or chin. For example, a person who is quadriplegic can use an infrared pointer on a headband to "type" on a special keyboard mounted above the computer. All of these devices already exist, and many of them permit people with disabilities to work.

This chapter only scratches the surface of possibilities. Hopefully, it will whet your appetite to explore further, and to consider the possibilities for incorporating the ideas of assistive technology into the lessons that you develop.

Provide Choice of Reading Material

First you will provide a pull-down menu for the user to choose one of the reading selections that you will furnish. It will always be available and accessible by use of a key combination. You will also add the quit option at this point.

Start by opening a new file, and saving it as *ada.apw*. Then, open File Setup under the File pull-down menu, just as you did in Chapter 15. The dialog box is shown in Figure 15.3. Under Presentation Window Size, select VGA. Deselect the Overlay Menu Bar and Title Bar checkboxes. Do not deselect the User Menu Bar. It is needed to display pull-down menus.

Now you will create the background on which everything will rest. Drag a display icon to the flowline and name it *background*. Open *background* and import the *ada_bkgd.pct* graphic. To import, click on the File pull-down menu selection from the menu bar and choose Import Graphic. The operating system's standard directory dialog box will appear. Search for the *ada_bkgd.pct* file by opening directories and changing drives as you would to search for any other file. When you find it, select Paste or double-click to load the *background* graphic into your program. (Select Load on the Mac.) Center this full screen *background* in the presentation window.

Because this background should always be displayed when the lesson is running, you have to prevent it from being erased as the user's actions make the flow jump to new locations, which would ordinarily erase the screen's contents. Select the Attributes pull-down menu and choose Effects. The effects dialog box will open. Click on the Prevent Automatic Erase checkbox and select OK to close the Effects dialog box. Then click on the toolbox to close the display.

Drag an interaction icon to the flowline and name it *File*. The icon name will be the title of the pull-down menu, so be sure to use capital "F." Now drag a map icon to the right of *File* to associate it with the interaction. The response type dialog box will automatically appear. Select the Pull-down Menu button and click OK to close the response type dialog box.

Now double-click on the Pull-down Menu response type symbol to open the Pull-down Menu Options dialog box. You can enter the name of the icon now by typing Open (remember to use a leading capital) in the Title field. Then check Perpetual to make this choice available throughout the program. Finally, in the Optional Key field, type o (upper- or lowercase letter o; it is not case-sensitive) to establish the Control-o combination as the alternative keystroke for the menu choice. (Enter o on the Mac to establish Command-o as the key combination.) (If you preferred the Alt-Q combination for this capability, you would enter Alt Q.) When you finish, the dialog box will look like Figure 18.1. Select OK to close the dialog box.

Authorware Tip: If you don't use the name "File" for your first interaction with pull-down menus, Authorware will create a default pull-down menu in the first position with only the Quit choice available. (Authorware will not create the icons on the flowline; it will only display the menu.)

Now drag a calculation icon to the right of *Open* and label it *Quit*. It will assume the perpetual status of the *Open* icon to its left. In order to give it a keystroke equivalent you will have to edit it. Open the small pull-down menu response type symbol above *Quit* to edit it. Type **Q** in the Optional Key field to establish the combination of Control-Q as the alternative keystroke for Quit. Select OK-Edit Calc to enter the Quit function. You did this in Chapter 15. When the calculation window opens, select Show Functions from the Data pull-down menu. As you know, the category last used will be selected, or General will be selected as the default if you have not used the Show Functions option since opening Authorware. Select Quit from the General category, then select Paste. This action will paste the Quit function in your calculation window. Change the Option to zero and close the calculation window.

Mac Difference: The Mac offers the ability to use the Command key in the same way as Control in Windows. There is no equivalent to the Alt combinations that occur in Windows.

Now drag a display icon to the flowline below the *File* interaction. Name it *story* and double-click to open it for editing. (Mac users drag a calculation icon and refer

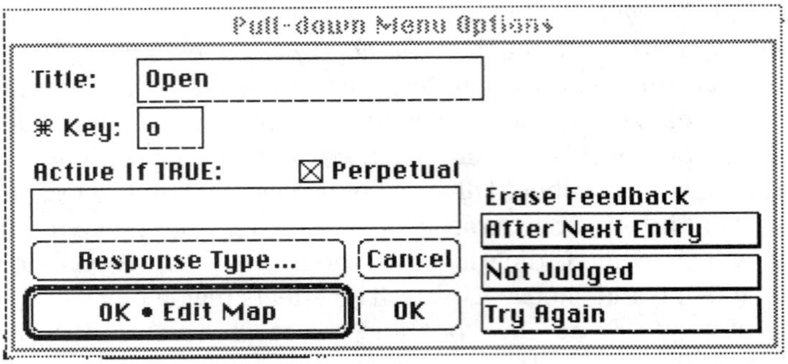

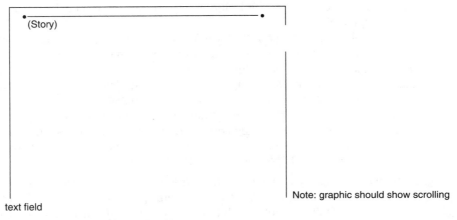

Figure 18.1 Pull-Down Menu Options

(Story)

text field
Note: graphic should show scrolling

Figure 18.2 Embedded Story Variable

to the Mac Difference sidebar below.) You will embed a variable in the display to show the story to the user. The reason for using the variable is to provide the option to use many different stories. You will activate two stories in this lesson, but you could expand it to include others. Select the text tool and click near the top left of the background graphic. Type:

```
{story}
```

While you still have the text tool, select the entire text **{story}** and then open the Text pull-down menu. Select the Font option and choose Times, or your favorite font if you have one, then pick a font size that looks good. We chose 12-point. If you didn't select every letter of **{story}**, only those you did select would have the new font and size attributes. Finally, select Scrolling Text. You will see the text field change to a rectangle with a scrollbar. At this point, your display should look similar to Figure 18.2.

Mac Difference: The Mac doesn't offer the scrolling text field choice under the Text pull-down menu. To establish a scrolling text field in the Mac, you must load the ScrollEdit XCMD that was provided with your Authorware program. Open the Load Functions menu under the Data pull-down menu. Locate the file (in the Authorware Program Files folder). Select the file. Another box will open, showing the file with Load dimmed. Select ScrollEdit and then select Load. Then you will find the new function ScrollEdit in Find Function under the Data menu in a category of functions that are unique to your own lesson. Since your lesson file is named ADA, there will be a category at the bottom of the list called ADA. The ScrollEdit function will be the only one in that category. Paste ScrollEdit into your open calculation window as shown here:

```
CloseWindow("storyhere")
ScrollEdit("R","storyhere","25,100,600,460","","","Times",12)
SetProperty("storyhere","text", story)
```

Click on the close box to leave the display and initialize the variable. The New Variable options box will appear. Enter an initial value of :

```
"Select Open under the File pull-down menu to activate story choices"
```

Be sure to include the quotation marks. This is different than your previous experience, in the feedback of the Crane Operator lesson, of initializing a text variable as blank quotes.

Let's work on documenting your work for future reference. Fill in a Description something like this:

```
Contains the text of the story to be displayed
```

Close the Variables dialog box. Figure 18.3 shows the flowline as it appears at this point. (Mac users will have a calculation *story* rather than a display.)

Now you will provide the stories to be displayed by the **{story}** embedded variable. Double-click the *Open* map icon to begin editing. Drag an interaction icon to the flowline and name it *pick a story*. Then drag a calculation icon to the right of *Select Story* to associate it with the interaction. You want the Pull-down Menu response

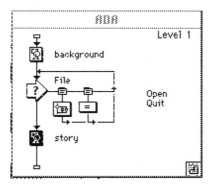

Figure 18.3 ADA Flowline

type, so select it when offered. Then double-click on the response type symbol. When the Pull-down Menu Options dialog box appears, select the Perpetual checkbox and then select OK to close the dialog box. Drag another calculation to the right of the first. It will assume all the properties that you have just established. Now name the two pull-down menus *Moby Dick* and *Alice in Wonderland*. Be sure to use appropriate capitalization since these names will be shown to the learner in a pull-down menu.

Copyright

You will use two short selections as readings for the learner: *Moby Dick*, the 1851 epic masterpiece by Herman Melville, and Lewis Carroll's famous 1865 children's story *Alice's Adventures in Wonderland*. The latter includes characters such as the Cheshire Cat, the March Hare, and the Mad Hatter. You might be concerned that in using these selections you might be breaking the copyright law. This is an important concern that will be very important in multimedia work. Copyrights protect written works of various kinds from unauthorized use. The reason you can use these famous works is that the exclusive rights for publication, sale, or production of works is for a specified time period. You might have liked to use *Atlas Shrugged* or *Catch-22*, and you might someday want to include Charlie Brown, Mickey Mouse, or the Beatle's music, but you can't. They are all protected, and protected vigorously in most cases. In general, you are safe in using works created before 1921.

The default branching is Try Again, which shows the flowline wrapping around counterclockwise and returning to the flowline above the interaction. Often you'll need to change the branching of perpetual icons to Return, but in this case Try Again is what you want. The completed structure is shown in Figure 18.4.

Now you will enable the calculation to get the text of the *Moby Dick* reading from the *adamoby.txt* file that was included in your CD. Double-click the *Moby Dick* calculation icon to open it for editing. You will paste a function in the calculation window. Can you remember how to do that? Go to Show Function. It will open to the General category (or the last category used). Try to find the Read External File function that you need here. If you can't find it refer to the footnote at the bottom of this page.*

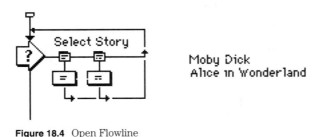

Figure 18.4 Open Flowline

---

*You will find it under the File category. The whole procedure is to click on the Data pull-down menu and select Show Functions. When the functions dialog box opens, select the File category drop-down list.

Paste ReadExtFile into your open calculation. Now type the remainder of the expression as follows:

```
story = ReadExtFile(FileLocation^"adamoby.txt")
```

Authorware will interpret it like this: "I will replace the content of the story variable that is embedded in the *story* display icon with an external file that I must read. The file is located in the same place as this program and is named adamoby.txt." `FileLocation` is a system variable that you could have pasted, but can also type. The concurrency operator (^) is on your keyboard as Shift 6. It concatenates (links) separate character strings or variables, so that Authorware will associate the `File Location` variable with the **adamoby.txt** string in the expression.

You need a similar expression in the Alice in Wonderland calculation to include the content of the story variable to load that reading. Now copy the whole expression that you just completed, just as you would any text, and then close the *Moby Dick* calculation. Open the *Alice in Wonderland* icon and paste the expression into it. Change the name of the text file to be read from "adamoby.txt" to "adaalice.txt" and close the window.

Place files to be read

This will only work if you have the two text files in the same subdirectory as the ADA lesson. Use the File Manager to move them to that directory now (called my_work, if you named it as we suggested).

Test drive

Now run your program to test it. You can select either reading by using Open, and can switch between them. Quit is always available from the pull-down menu and ends the program.

 Development Tip: Once the program is runable you can benefit from running it after each addition or modification. Then a problem can be related to whatever you did. If you do several things before testing, the problem may be more difficult to identify.

Create the Print Size Option

Now that you have tested your program to ensure that it will read the external text files and display their contents on the screen, you will enhance the program for readers with low visual acuity. You will accomplish this by providing the reader an option in choosing type size. Since you have already begun programming this lesson with pull-down menus, you will provide the type-size option from a pull-down menu.

You will modify the structure of ADA to install the choosing type size option. You will accomplish this through the use of a decision structure that contains a different text size in each of its branches.

Drag a decision icon on the bottom of the level 1 flowline and name it *display size*. Now drag the already created *story* display icon (calculation icon on Macs) to the right of *display size*. This will be the small text-size branch. Rename *story* to *small text*. Because you will end up with three different text-size display icons which will branch according to a pull-down menu choice, you will assign effects to each icon. (Macintosh developers will not assign these effects. Skip to the end of this paragraph.) Do this by double-clicking the icon to open the decision branch erase effects dialog box. Choose Don't Erase from the drop-down menu. Select OK to close the dialog box. Now, select the *small text* icon, if it is not already selected, then select Effects under the Attributes pull-down menu. Select the Prevent Automatic Erase checkbox. Also, because you will erase this icon before the *medium text* icon is displayed, you will assign an effect of Mosaic. Close the Effects dialog box.

The small text icon is still selected. Copy it, click to the right of it (the paste hand will appear where you clicked), and paste. The hand will move over one position, ready for you to paste again. Go ahead and paste a second time. You have now established the three text size displays. Select the center icon and name it *medium text* and then name the icon to the extreme right *large text*.

Open the decision icon to change the branching decision from sequential to calculated path. When open, it will look similar to Figure 15.11. Select the Calculated Path button. Then enter a variable to control which branch path will be chosen by the decision. Type:

```
size_branch_number
```

in the calculated path variable field. Figure 18.5 shows the completed dialog box.

Select OK to close the dialog box. Authorware will prompt you for the initial value of the new variable. Type 1 in the initial value text field and enter the description. Select OK to close the dialog box (Default Numerical variable type on Mac is correct).

Open the *medium text* display window to increase the point size of the text it displays. When the icon opens, everything is selected, but the only object in this icon is the displayed variable **{story}**. Immediately open the Text pull-down menu and se-

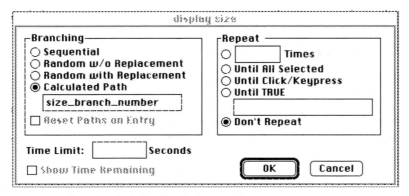

Figure 18.5 Completed Display Size Decision Options

lect 18 from the Size choice. Close the display and repeat this process for the *large text* icon, choosing 24-point this time.

Mac Difference: Open the *medium text* calculation. At the end of the argument for the ScrollEdit function, change the 12 to 18. Close *medium text* and repeat this process for the *large text* calculation, choosing 24 point.

You will establish an erase to remove each text display icon when another is selected (not on the Mac). Since you have just edited the *large text* display, it is already in memory. Now add the other two by holding down the shift key and opening the *medium text* display. Close it and open the *small text* icon, also while holding down the shift key. Close *small text* as well. These images will stay in memory until you set up the erase icon.

Next you will learn to group icons. You will now establish a map icon with more than one icon in it where each of the displays is. (Mac users skip to the next paragraph.) Select the *small text* icon if it is not still selected, open the Edit menu, and you will see Group about half way down. Select Group. The menu will close and the *small text* display icon will have become the *small text* map icon. Your *small text* display icon is inside the *small text* map icon right now. To avoid confusion, rename the map icon to *small* and then open it. Verify that *small*'s Erase Displayed Objects drop-down menu shows Don't Erase and select OK-Edit Map. The screen will show the level 2 flowline with *small text*, to which you will add the erase icon to erase each text display. Drag an erase icon to the flowline above the *small text* display icon. Name it *erase text* and the resulting display will look like Figure 18.6.

Open *erase text* to establish the erases. All three {**story**} variables are present in three different font sizes, but do not show simultaneously because they are layered on top of each other. The embedded variable says "Select a story to read from Open under the File pull-down menu." Click on the text and the one on top will erase, and its icon will appear in the erase list. Click again on the text to erase the second one. Finally, click again to erase the last one. Now choose Mosaic from the erase dialog box Effects drop-down list. You will see a repeat of the erase with the mosaic effect.

Authorware Tip: If you select two matching effects, Authorware will make the transition seamlessly. For example, if you erase one display with the mosaic effect and set the next display to open with the mosaic effect, one will appear to mosaic into the other. Anytime that the effects do not match, or one of them does not exist, the effects will be processed independently. For example, if you erase a display with a mosaic, but put no effect on the display of the next item, the first will mosaic out and the new display will appear all at once.

Close *erase text*. (Mac users skip to the next paragraph.) It will be selected, so copy it to place these erases in the computer's memory. If needed, resize and reposition the level 2 window on your screen to see and access the icons beneath. Now group the *medium text* display icon and rename the map *medium* just as you did for *small text*. Open it and paste the erase icon at the top of the flowline. Now repeat the whole process for the *large text* display icon. The resulting structure will look like Figure 18.7.

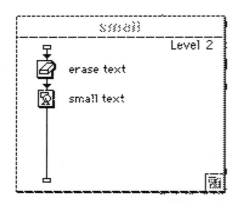

Figure 18.6 Small Icon Contents

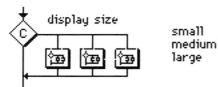

Figure 18.7 Display Size Decision Structure

On level 1 of the flowline, construct the Print Size pull-down menu. Just as before, drag an interaction icon to the flowline just below the File icon, but above the story icon. Title this icon *Print Size*, and take note to use leading capitals. This will be the pull-down menu's name. Save some time creating these menu selections. You have gone through the process of giving the icon the proper associations and characteristics (perpetual pull-down menu) through menu choices. To create another, just drag a new calculation icon onto the flowline to the right of the *Quit* icon in the *File* interaction. It will assume the perpetual pull-down menu characteristics of Quit. Immediately select and drag this new *untitled* calculation to the right of the *Print Size* icon. You will see that it retains the pull-down menu response type and no dialog box will open. Name it *Small*.

Authorware Tip: Generate feedback icons of the same type at an interaction icon by dragging them to the right of another icon of the desired type. This is quicker even if they must later be relocated to another position on the flowline.

Open the *Small* icon to enter the expression that will control the displayed text size. Type:

```
size_branch_number = 1
--comment-this will cause the decision to branch to the first map.
```

Select the expression text and copy it. Now close the *Small* calculation and drag another calculation icon to the right of *Small*. Name the new icon *Medium* and open it. Paste the expression **size_branch_number = 1**, change the 1 to 2 and the comment to second map, and close it. Repeat this process with a third calculation icon you will call *Large,* changing the 1 to 3 and the comment to third map so that *Small* has a 1, *Medium* has a 2, and *Large* has a 3. Close the calculations. The completed display size will look as shown in Figure 18.8.

Test drive

Run ADA to check that you have a pull-down menu called Print Size, with Small, Medium, and Large selection options. Cycle through, selecting each print size, and observe the text mosaic to the new size. (There will not be an effect on the Mac.)

Create Cursor Choice Option

Now you will add a feature that will allow the reader to choose a different cursor. You can use an even bigger shortcut in building this section than the one you used previously.

Select the entire *Print Size* interaction structure, including all the attached icons, by clicking to the left and above it and dragging to the right and below, then releasing the mouse. Copy the selection, click immediately below it and above *display size* to establish the paste hand, and paste. You will now have two identical *Print Size* interaction structures. You may want to enlarge the Level 1 window if you haven't done so already.

Rename the interaction icon *Cursor*. Rename the *Small, Medium*, and *Large* icons *Arrow, Plus*, and *Hand* respectively. Figure 18.9 shows the new *Cursor* structure.

Now, open the *Arrow* calculation icon and delete the contents. Then find the SetCursor function in the same way that you found FileLocation. If you can't find it,

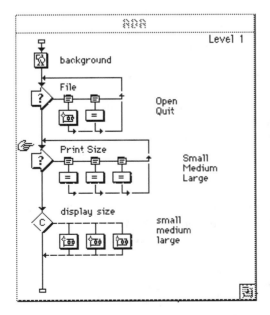

Figure 18.8 Completed Display Size

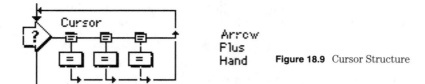

Figure 18.9   Cursor Structure

check the footnote at the bottom of this page.* Read the descriptions, and make note of the various cursors and the option numbers associated with each. Paste SetCursor, the dialog box will close and

```
SetCursor(type)
```

will have been pasted in your open window. Replace **type** with zero (**0**) so that it reads

```
SetCursor(0)
```

Close the *Arrow* calculation icon and open *Plus*. The SetCursor function is still on the clipboard ready to paste again. Paste it with a keystroke or Edit menu choice and replace option with 3, so that it reads **SetCursor(3)**. Repeat this process for the Hand icon, replacing the option with 6, so that it reads **SetCursor(6)**. Close the icon. Figure 18.10 shows the program completed to this point.

Test drive

Run the program again, making sure that you have a new pull-down menu from which you can select the cursor type. (On the Mac the cursor will change to the text I-beam when you pass over the scrolling text field. Don't worry that the learner can rewrite *Moby Dick*. You set one of the arguments within the SetCursor function to "R," which is read only. Melville's work is safe.)

Meet Multiple Learning Styles with Audio

The next step is to provide the learner with narration to accompany, or even replace, the screen text of the readings. You will add another menu bar selection with capabilities to play, or turn off, a sound. To implement this capability, you will create a new structure and make several changes to icons that you completed earlier.

Create narration pull-down menu structure

Let's get started by dragging a fresh interaction icon to the flowline between *Cursor* and the *display size* decision structure. Name it *Narration*. Now repeat the shortcut

---

* To find the SetCursor function, click on the Data pull-down menu and select Show Functions. It is under the General category. When the functions dialog box opens, select the General category drop-down list. SetCursor is in the list. Select it, read the Description, and then select Paste.

that you just used in building the *Print Size* structure, drag a calculation icon to the right of the *hand* icon in the Cursor interaction, and drop it there. It will assume the perpetual and pull-down menu characteristics of *hand.* Then move it and associate it with the *Narration* interaction. No dialog box will open. Name it *Play.* Now drag four more calculation icons and drop them to the right of *Play.* Name them *Slow, Normal, Fast*, and *Hush.* Your completed *Narration* icon structure will look like Figure 18.11.

Control the sound

Now you will enter the necessary expressions in each of the icons. Open *Play* and enter a new custom variable by typing:

```
sound = on
--comment-activates the story narration.
```

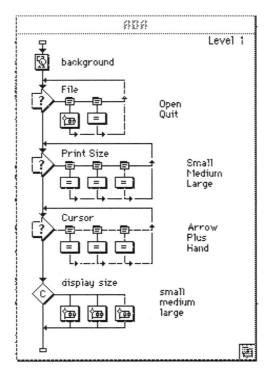

Figure 18.10 ADA with Structure Complete as Far as Cursor

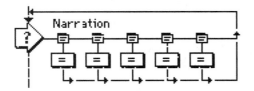

Figure 18.11 Narration structure

Then close the calculation window and, when the variable options dialog box appears, give **sound** an initial value of off. (You will have to change the default value of true to off. Mac users must change the type to Logical.) This will turn the Narration on when the learner selects the Play menu choice. Then click in the Description box and type:

```
Turns the Narration on when the learner selects the Play menu choice and off
when they select Hush.
```

Close the dialog box. Now go to the *Hush* icon, open it and enter:

```
sound = off
--comment-This will turn the Narration off when the learner selects the Hush
menu choice.
```

Since the variable sound has already been accepted by the system, the variable options dialog box will not appear.

Now open the *Slow* icon and enter:

```
speed = 80
--comment-sets the speed for sound to 80% of normal.
```

This creates a new custom variable that sets the speed with which the sound will be played. The normal speed is 100 (based on 100%), so 80 represents a somewhat slower speed for the narration. Macs support variable-speed playback, but for Windows users not all sound cards support variable-speed playback, so if you do not hear a difference the problem may lie there. Close the calculation window and, when the variable options dialog box appears, change the default value to 100 (so that the narration will start at normal speed). Then click in the Description box and type:

```
Sets the speed with which the sound will be played.
```

Now open the Normal and Fast calculations one by one, setting them respectively to speed = 100 and speed = 120 and modify the comment accordingly. This completes the sound control with the ability to turn the sound on and off, as well as to adjust the speed to faster and slower than normal.

Implement Authorware's sound features

Open the *Open* map icon (it is shown in Figure 18.4). Select the *Moby Dick* calculation icon and group it to create the *Moby Dick* map. Repeat the process for the *Alice in Wonderland* icon. Open the *Moby Dick* map to modify its contents to add functionality. Rename the *Moby Dick* calculation icon to *load Moby Dick text*. Drag a sound icon to the flowline below the calculation and title it *read Moby Dick*. The *Moby Dick* map structure will now look like Figure 18.12.

Open *read Moby Dick* and select the Load button. A Load Sound window will open. Search for the **ada_moby.wav** file and double-click it. (The Macintosh file is

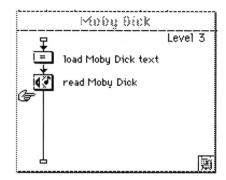

Figure 18.12 *Moby Dick* Icon Contents

ada_moby.aiff.) Play it now to verify that you have the correct sound. This file is shorter than would be the case if it were the narration of a whole chapter; nevertheless, you may want to click on Stop to terminate the play.

Next you will make this sound perpetual. This is so you can load the narration when the user selects the *Moby Dick* story, but not play it until, if, and when Play is selected from the Narration pull-down menu. Click on the concurrency drop-down list that reads Wait Until Done and select Perpetual.

You also will provide user control over speed. To do this, overwrite the default of 100 with the variable name *speed* in the Speed (% of Normal) field.

To prevent the sound from playing until the user selects the Narration pull-down menu, place the custom variable *sound* in the Start Playing When TRUE field.

Finally, select the Play Sound Until TRUE button and enter the condition of sound = off. This will stop the sound when the value of the sound variable becomes off, which will happen when the user selects Hush because you placed sound = off there. (Remember that you should not type the colon. This is the place where doing so can create problems.) Figure 18.13 shows the completed read *Moby Dick* sound options dialog box.

Close the *read Moby Dick* sound icon, copy it, and paste it into the *Alice in Wonderland* map underneath the *Alice in Wonderland* calculation icon. Rename that icon to *read Alice in Wonderland*. Then rename the *Alice in Wonderland* calculation icon to *load Alice in Wonderland text*.

Double-click *read Alice in Wonderland* to load the proper sound file. Locate and load the file *ada_alic.wav* (*ada_alic.aiff* on the Mac) just as you did for *ada_moby.wav*. The settings will be the same because you copied the icon, so there are no other changes to make. Its appearance will be identical to Figure 18.13 (except for the header bar) since the name of the loaded sound file is never visible.

Controlling multiple perpetual sounds

As it is now, each narration sound is loaded with its corresponding text. If you select one and then the other, both would be loaded. Then when you select play, Authorware will attempt to play both sounds sequentially, but the effect will be that one sound starts and then is replaced by the other.

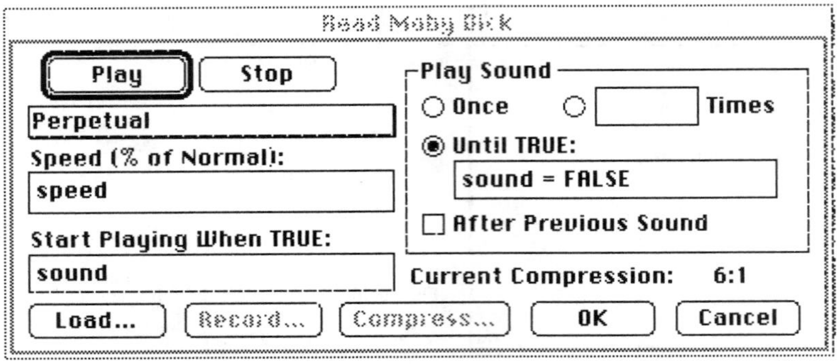

Figure 18.13 Read *Moby Dick* Sound Options Dialog Box

You can bring this under control by the use of a system function. An interesting feature of Authorware is that sounds are affected by erase features ("erased" by them). Open the *load Alice in Wonderland text* calculation icon. It already has the `ReadExtFile` expression in it. You will add the `EraseIcon` system function to it. Click at the end of the expression and hit the Return key. Then, find the `EraseIcon` function as you have earlier in this chapter* (If you have difficulty, refer to that footnote). Paste it into the calculation. It will look like this:

```
story := (FileLocation^"alice.txt")
EraseIcon(IconID@"IconTitle")
```

Change `IconTitle` to the name of the icon that plays the other sound, `read Moby Dick`. The resulting expression will look like the following:

```
story := (FileLocation^"alice.txt")
EraseIcon(IconID@"read Moby Dick")
--comment-erases (turns off) Moby Dick narration.
```

Close the *Alice in Wonderland* map and open the *Moby Dick* map to make similar changes there. Modify the *load Moby Dick text* icon to provide an erase icon function to negate the Alice narration. When you complete the process it should look like the following:

```
story := ReadExtFile(FileLocation^"mobydick.txt")
EraseIcon(IconID@"read Alice in Wonderland")
--comment-erases (turns off) Alice narration.
```

Close the *Moby Dick* map. Because you know that erases can affect the way sounds are handled by Authorware you will understand that, if there are erase features currently in effect, they can cause problems with your narration. In fact, there are several such erase features that you must attend to.

Open the *Select Story* interaction icon and, at the interaction options dialog box, change Erase on Exit to Don't Erase. Close the box by selecting OK. Now open the

Moby Dick response type symbol to open the pull-down menu options dialog box. Change the Erase Feedback to Don't Erase. Close *Moby Dick* and make the same change in the *Alice in Wonderland* pull-down menu response type symbol.

You also have to get rid of some other erase features that would affect the sound. Open the *File* interaction and, at the interaction options dialog box, change Erase on Exit to Don't Erase. Close the box by selecting OK. Then open the *Open* pull-down menu response type symbol to open the pull-down menu options dialog box. Change the Erase Feedback to Don't Erase. Close *Open*.

Test drive

Run ADA now to check your work. Notice that all the options under the Narration pull-down menu are always available. You can fix that!

Using variables to control availability of pull-down menus

The set-up for sound is essentially OK as it is, but you can add a nicety. As you saw, the Play pull-down menu choices are always active, even if no sound file had been loaded and therefore could not be played. You can fix this by making the Play pull-down menu inactive unless a sound is already loaded. Open the *Moby Dick* map icon. Drag a calculation icon to the flowline below the *two existing icons* and name it *sound loaded*. Open *sound loaded* and enter:

```
sound_loaded = true
```

Click in the Description box and enter the following documentation:

```
When True, activates the Play pull-down menu
```

Close the custom variable dialog box. Select OK to close the calculation window and, when the variable dialog box appears, make its initial value off. (Mac users select Logical.) Figure 18.14 shows how the *Moby Dick* map structure looks after you initialize the *sound loaded* variable. Copy the *sound loaded* icon, close the *Moby Dick* map, open the *Alice in Wonderland* map, and paste the sound loaded icon below the two existing icons there.

Now you must place the sound_loaded variable in the *Play* pull-down menu to make it work. Open the *Play* pull-down menu response type symbol. You will now join two variables to create a joint condition. Type:

```
sound = off & sound_loaded
```

in the Active if TRUE field. This means that *Play* will be active *only when both* sound is off *and* a sound file has been loaded. Figure 18.15 shows the completed *Play* pull-down menu options dialog box.

Close *Play* and open the *Slow* pull-down menu response type symbol. Type **sound** in the Active if TRUE field. This means that *Slow* will be active *only* when

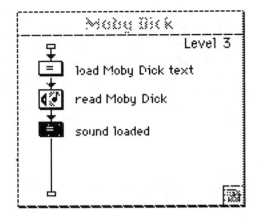

Figure 18.14 Modified Open Icon

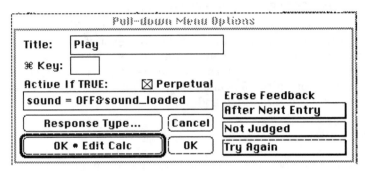

Figure 18.15 Play Pull-Down Menu Options

sound was turned *on* by the user selecting the Play pull-down menu. Figure 18.16 shows the completed *Slow* pull-down menu options dialog box. Repeat the same steps you implemented in *Slow* in the *Fast, Normal,* and *Hush* icons.

Test drive

Run ADA now to check your work. Check to see that the options under the Narration pull-down menu are not available unless a text file has been loaded.

Providing a choice of language

You can probably see now that you can make a variety of options available in a similar way. For example, you could offer a choice of Spanish or English text and/or audio.

Help

Finally, you will add a Help menu to the menu bar. It will provide basic information about the ADA program in a display icon.

Make room to work by grouping some icon structures to reduce the size taken on the screen. Group *Print Size* and *Cursor* (you have done this before in the Crane Operator lesson). The resulting map will be *untitled*. Name it *printsize and cursor*. Now drag an interaction icon to the flowline below the *Narration* structure and above the *display size* structure. Name it *Help*. Take the same shortcut as previously to capture the perpetual pull-down characteristics. Drag a display icon to the right of *Quit* at the first interaction of the flowline and drop it. Immediately move it to the right of *Help* and drop it there permanently. Name it *About ADA* and open it for editing. Select the Import Graphics choice from the File pull-down menu and import **adaabout.pct**. The screen will look similar to Figure 18.17. Close the display.

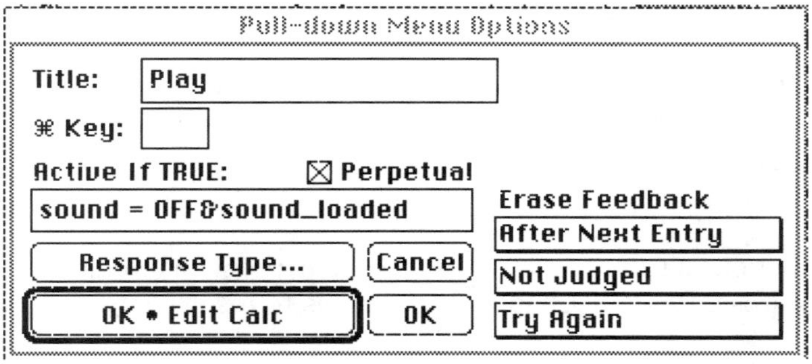

Figure 18.16 Slow Pull-Down Menu Options

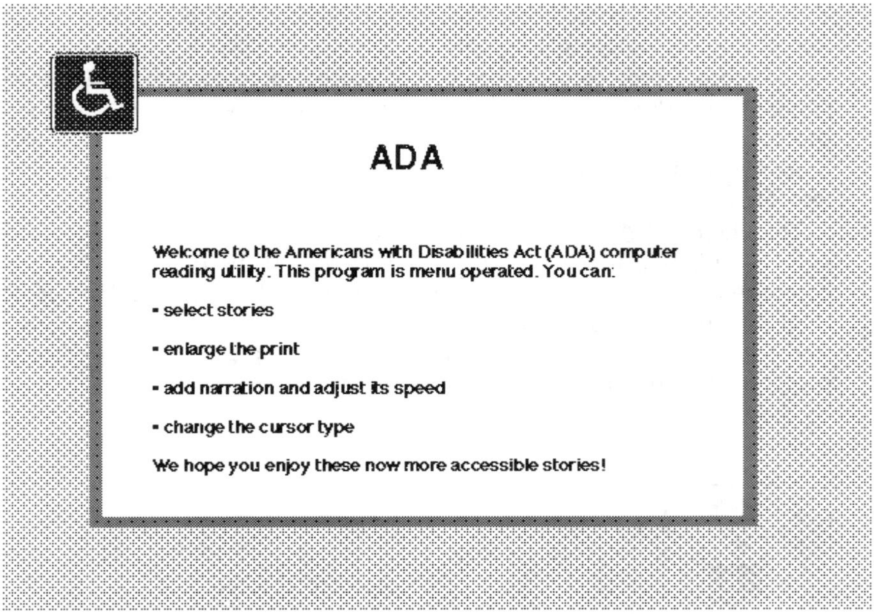

Figure 18.17 Help Contents

The *Help* is essentially complete but would not work properly as it is. It requires a wait to stop the flow to enable the user to read the display. As it is, it will erase immediately after displaying.

Group the *About ADA* icon by selecting it and choosing Group from the Edit menu. The Help structure will resemble Figure 18.18.

Now open *About ADA for* editing. The content of the display is OK but it is better to rename the *About ADA* icon inside to *ADA info* to avoid confusion with the *About ADA* map icon in which it resides. Drag a wait icon to the flowline below *ADA info*. Open it and change the checkbox selections to leave only Show Button active. Close the wait icon and close the Level 2 flowline. The completed ungrouped ADA structure is shown in Figure 18.19.

Test drive

You've done it again! Another lesson is completed. Now run the lesson and thoroughly go through every aspect to ensure that it works as planned.

Troubleshooting

Since you have done a test drive after each section, problems would have been identified as they arose. Refer to Chapter 16 for ideas to resolve any problems encountered.

Provide Reading Material Search Capability

You probably realize that you could add additional stories or change to other stories. Substituting a different content, such as Homer's *Odyssey*, in the *adamoby.txt* would immediately cause the new text to display when *Moby Dick* is selected. You could change the icon title *Moby Dick* to *Odyssey* everywhere it appears, using Authorware's Find/Change option under the Edit menu. This will not work for the contents of calculations. You would have to open each of them and manually change the new file name.

The choice of stories is controlled by buttons in the pick a story interaction. To add the *Odyssey* to the existing *Moby Dick* and *Alice in Wonderland* you could copy the entire *Moby Dick* map and paste it to the right of *Alice in Wonderland*, then rename it to *Odyssey*. You would have to rename the icons consistently, load the appropriate sound file to provide the *Odyssey* narration, and modify the read external file function to load the text file that contains the story.

About ADA

Figure 18.18 Help Structure

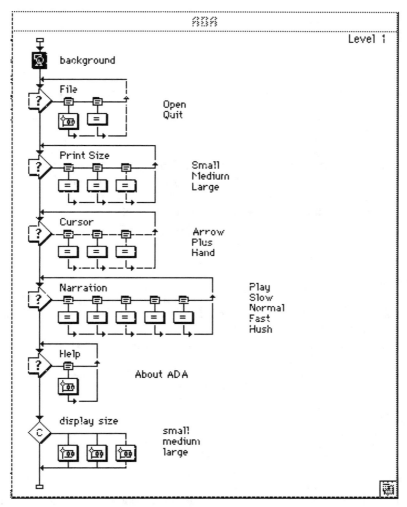

Figure 18.19 Completed ADA Lesson Flowline

A third possibility is to provide a search mechanism to look in specified directories for either specific files or all available files. If you had a large number of stories available, this would provide the ability to choose among them. The system function **Catalog** would perform this task.

Ideas for Expansion, Enhancement, and Evolution

Here are some ideas for use of this lesson in new ways:

Stopping narration on text change

At present, if you are reading a text accompanied by narration and you change the text, the narration of the newly selected text will play immediately. You might decide that it would be better to have the narration stop when a different text is selected. To do this you would enter a

```
sound = off
```

expression in each calculation icon that opens a text file. Don't forget to include a comment indicating what the variable is doing.

Displaying external text files

Displaying external text offers many possibilities. One of the most interesting possibilities involves giving your client the ability to change content. Any text anywhere in your program can be provided by an external text file in exactly the same way as in ADA. This permits the display of changing information and can get much more sophisticated. The content, such as current stock prices, can be obtained from another source.

Adaptive technology

You can consider providing additional adaptive technology capabilities. Many of these are special hardware that already exists in the marketplace. It can be purchased and integrated into a disabled person's workstation.

Here are some common devices that can provide access to the computer:

- Joystick
- Switch
- Mouse speed
- Voice activation

Get It Set in Cement

You have completed another lesson, gained a good understanding of pull-down menus, perpetual interactions, use of sounds, advanced erase features controlling events with variables, loading external text, custom cursors, and scrolling text. If you are a Mac user you learned to use an XCMD. Not bad at all!

Now you are ready to tackle an even bigger challenge. The contractor has arrived to pour your new concrete driveway but has forgotten how to mix cement and other materials to ensure a strong concrete. You can move on to the next chapter to build a lesson that will refresh his memory. This will really be "just in time" training!

19

Mixing Concrete

This chapter is another illustration of how you can eliminate sterile and boring instruction. Learning can be interesting and efficient. Technology-based instruction has no excuse to be anything else.

In this chapter you will build a lesson that teaches the learner how to mix concrete from sand, cement, gravel, and water. When your learner is guided to mixing in differing ratios to achieve distinct results the characteristics of the concrete are displayed.

Concrete is a hard, strong building material composed of a cementing material, such as Portland cement, and an aggregate of minerals (sand and gravel or broken rock) mixed with water. Reinforced concrete is a type of strong concrete used widely in bridge construction. The concrete is hardened onto embedded steel rods, bars, or mesh, that add tensile strength. Reinforced concrete can sustain heavy stresses over wide spans. Our lesson assumes that the concrete is for a driveway.

What You Will Learn in This Chapter

- How to employ clickable objects
- How to employ objects in layers
- How to use custom variables

Establish Initial Graphics

First, start a new Authorware lesson and save it as **Concrete**. Go to File Setup under the File pull-down menu to deselect the Title and Menu Bars. Then set the Presentation Window to VGA.

To begin work, let's establish the raw materials. Drag a display icon to the flowline.

Name it **background**. It will set the scene for the learner and will provide a basis for the actions we plan. Associate the graphics with *background* as follows:

Icon Name	Graphic to be Imported
background	**CONCBACK.PCT**

Now place the graphic provided in your book CD inside the display icon. When you import the graphic, its overall location may not be exactly where you think looks most pleasing. It will be selected when it is placed. Before you close the display, move the image to the center of the screen. It should look like Figure 19.1 when you do. Then close the *background* display.

Create the Basic Structure

The action of the lesson is provided by a loop that provides repeated chances to carry out the basic activities of the lesson. Drag a decision icon to the execution line and label it *loop*. Place a map icon to the right of the decision icon, so it creates a decision branch structure. Name the map icon **measure components**. Notice that the *loop* decision icon flowline branches back to the main flowline. We want to create the loop structure that reflects the functionality of the **loop** decision icon's name. Double-click the decision icon to work inside its options dialog box. The default setting for the Repeat option is Don't Repeat. We want to create a loop that will continue forever, or at least until we take a specific action to stop it. Click the **Until TRUE** Repeat option and enter **false** in the text box. This resulting configuration is shown in Figure 19.2.

Close the box by selecting **OK** or by using the **Enter** key. Your display should now look like Figure 19.3. Notice that the *loop* flowline now does create a loop by returning to the flowline above the decision icon.

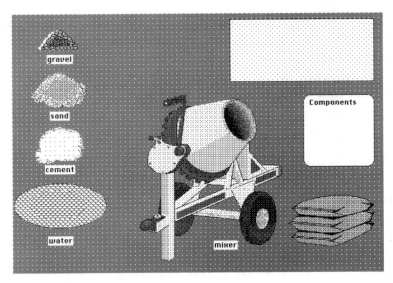

Figure 19.1 Background Image

loop

┌─Branching────────────────┐   ┌─Repeat──────────────────┐
○ **Sequential**   ○ [   ] **Times**
○ **Random w/o Replacement**   ○ **Until All Selected**
○ **Random with Replacement**   ○ **Until Click/Keypress**
◉ **Calculated Path**   ◉ **Until TRUE**
                                         false
☐ Reset Paths on Entry   ○ **Don't Repeat**

Time Limit: [   ] **Seconds**

☐ Show Time Remaining   [**OK**]   [Cancel]

Figure 19.2 Configuration Box for Loop

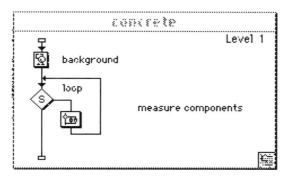

Figure 19.3 Initial Icons for Concrete Lesson

Creating a Loop

Double-click the *measure components* map icon. An erase options box for *measure components* will appear. The default setting, Before Next Selection, is shown in Figure 19.4. Select the **Erase Displayed Objects** pull-down menu and choose **Don't Erase**. Then select **OK–Edit Map**.

Drag four display icons to the flowline. Name them *sand, gravel, cement,* and *water*. These are the components of concrete. The sand and gravel are the aggregate, a construction material used to form concrete by mixing with cement. It provides desirable qualities, such as volume and resistance to wear. Examples of aggregates include sand, crushed and broken stone, pebbles, and boiler ashes. Fine aggregates are used to make thin and smooth structural members; coarse aggregates are used for more massive elements.

The displays will be movable objects on the screen and the learner will drag them to simulate mixing a batch of concrete. Portland cement, our binding material, is used in both concrete and mortar. It is made by heating mixed crushed chalk and clay to form a "clinker." The clinker is crushed and packed into bags. When you add

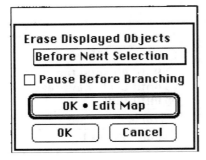

Figure 19.4 Erase Options for Decision Branch

water to cement it recrystallizes, and the interlocking crystals of calcium silicate and calcium aluminate form a hard mass when dry. Notice that cement is the name of a specific part of concrete. Some folks say "cement" to refer to concrete itself. You will import graphics as follows:

Icon Name	Graphic to be Imported
sand	**CONCSAND.PCT**
gravel	**CONGRAVL.PCT**
cement	**CONCEMT.PCT**
water	**CONWATER.PCT**

Now place the graphics provided in your book CD inside each icon. Match the icons and files as listed above. Each file contains a graphic matching its name. You may have difficulty in seeing some of the graphics because of the similarity of colors to the background, but they exist in their respective files.

The learner will drag these items into the concrete mixer. They must be so-called movable objects. For each of the four components, one at a time, select the icon then pull down the Attributes menu and select Effects. Under Movable, change the default No to Freely.

Make some objects unmovable

Because we will have movable objects in this lesson, we need to "nail down" anything that shouldn't be moved by the learner. Select the *background* icon and select Data from the menu bar. Select Calculations under Data to open *background*'s calculation window. You will select a system variable to prevent the background from moving when the learner moves objects. Open the Data pull-down menu to access the Variables. Under the General category, scroll down to Movable and select it. When you do so, it will become highlighted and its description will appear. Read the description, as it will tell what the choice does and how to employ the variable. It will also advise of options that you may choose, to provide alternate methods of operation. Figure 19.5 shows the Variable dialog box after you have selected Movable.

Now select Paste. The dialog box will close and Movable will be pasted into your Calculation window.

Authorware Tip: If Paste is not available in a Variable dialog box, it is because you do not have an open calculation window. It is best practice, if you intend to insert a variable, to open the calculation window first.

Your calculation will show:

```
Movable
```

Now assign the value FALSE to the variable movable. Your completed calculation should look like this:

```
Movable = FALSE
--comment-This nails down the background display.
```

Close the calculation window. Your confirmation is the small equal sign near the display icon. Now it looks like Figure 19.6.

This calculation makes the *background* image immovable in the unpackaged version of Authorware Working Model. If you have access to a full version of Authorware, you will package your finished lesson as described later in this book. The image will not be movable in the packaged lesson, so it will not be necessary to use this calculation. If you were to package the calculation you have just created, no harm would be done; it is simply redundant.

 Authorware Tip: It is more efficient to simply select an icon with a single click to assign attributes or append a calculation. Double-clicking will open the icon with some delay, depending on its complexity and your computer, but you will be no closer to making the change you want. When you select Calculations for the Data menu or Ef-

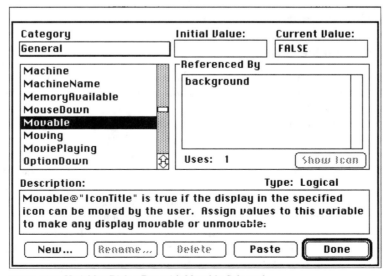

Figure 19.5 Variables Dialog Box with Movable Selected

Figure 19.6 Display Icon with Appended Calculation

fects from the Attributes menu, Authorware will display *the last icon image that was open*. Do not be confused! You will get what you want. For example, if you select the background icon, you will be assigning a calculation to it even though you see another icon displayed on the screen. If you are a new user this may seem confusing, but if you work regularly with Authorware it will not be a distraction.

Establish object initial locations

Now that the background graphic is immovable, you can place each of the (movable) imported graphics in its initial position. When you loaded each image it was placed arbitrarily. Now you must move each to its initial position. It will be necessary to reference the *background* display icon's graphic while editing each of the others. First open the *background* icon, then close it. Depress the shift key as you double-click the *sand* icon. Both display icons' images will appear, and (on the PC) the *sand* image will be selected. You will see a display something like Figure 19.7. Move the *sand* image to the middle of the pile of sand shown on the background. When you have positioned it well it will "fade" into the sand pile. Close the display.

Repeat this procedure for *gravel*, *cement*, and *water*. Hold down the shift key as you double-click on each next display. All of the preceding display icon's images will appear, but only the most current will be selected (on the PC).

Authorware Tip: When editing one display icon's graphic while also viewing another, you can switch the icon image you are editing by double-clicking on an element of the other icon's image. You can reference the name of the icon being edited by its name in the display window's toolbox.

Creating Targets for Movable Objects

Now you will establish the mixer as the place to which the learner will drag the components of the concrete. To do this, you will create targets for the movable objects: sand, gravel, cement, and water.

Drag an interaction icon to the flowline below *water* in the *measure components* map. Label it *target areas*. Drag a map icon to the right of the interaction icon. It will cause an Interaction response type dialog box, as shown in Figure 19.8, to appear. Select Movable Object. Then select **OK** to close the box. Name the map icon *leave at mixer*.

You must provide "error trapping" to handle those cases in which the learner does not do the expected; in this case, drags a material to a location other than the mixer. To achieve this, a second movable target area must be created to cover the situation when the concrete components are not dragged to the mixer. Now, drag another map icon to the right of *leave at mixer*. It will assume the same response type as the icon to its right. Name it *put back*.

Specify target areas

Since you must identify the mouth of the mixer as the target for the concrete components, you have the *background* in view as you place the target area. Open the *background* display icon, and close it. (If you are following the chapter instructions in a single session, it will already be the last icon opened and not require reopening now.) Double-click the small arrow above *leave at mixer*. This is the movable object response type indicator. Do not open the *leave at mixer* map. If you open the map by mistake, close it and select the small arrow more carefully. When you succeed, you will see a display similar to Figure 19.9. If the Movable Objects Options dialog box covers the mouth of the mixer, drag it by the title bar to another location. On our computer we moved it to the position shown in Figure 19.9.

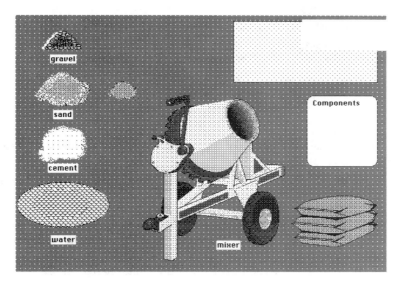

Figure 19.7 Display Icon with Appended Calculation

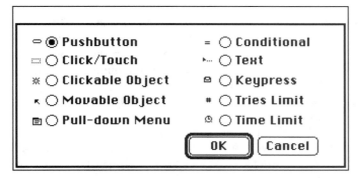

Figure 19.8 Interaction Response Type Dialog Box

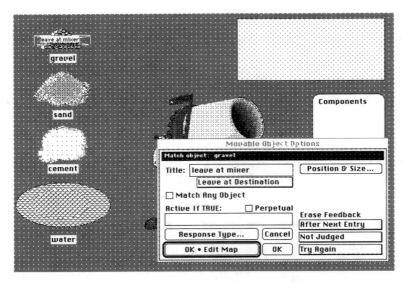

Figure 19.9 Default for Movable Object

You want the learner to be able to choose any of the concrete components, in any order, to place them in the mouth of the mixer. To enable this, select the **Match Any Object** checkbox.

Also, you want the learner to be able to repeat this a varying number of times to generate different component ratios. The ability to repeat is the function of the loop structure you created earlier. Now you want the flow to continue to loop, so it must exit the *leave at mixer* interaction and the *measure components* map to complete the loop. You can accomplish this by selecting the Try Again drop-down menu and choosing Exit Interaction.

Now, finish the target for the mixer's mouth. First, change the Leave at Destination pull-down menu to Snap to Center. Doing this causes the object to move to the exact center of its movable object target area. In your lesson, this is the center of the mixer's mouth.

The last step is to place the target itself. Initially, the target area appears in the upper left corner. Because this target area will define the mouth of the mixer you must move it there. Grab the movable object position box by the X in its center. Later, you will resize it. For now, just move it. When the box is in position over the mouth of the mixer, use the handles to resize the box to the same dimensions as the mouth. The result should look like Figure 19.10.

Select **OK** to leave the dialog box. Your display will look like Figure 19.11.

Now you will complete the error trapping that you began when you created the *put back* map icon. Double-click on the small movable object response type symbol (arrow) on the flowline above the *put back* icon. When you do this, the dialog box might hide the *put back* target area. If you don't see the target area, move the dialog box.

You want to capture the learner's inappropriate placement of components, so that only attempts to put the materials in the mixer will succeed. You do this by making the target cover the whole screen. The icons do not conflict with one another because the icon on the left is "seen" first by the program, because that is the direction in which the flow is traveling. If the learner selects the mixer mouth, the program won't consider *put back* at all.

You can place the target using the same technique that you used with *leave at mixer*. You can also use another method of placing targets. To do so, carefully select

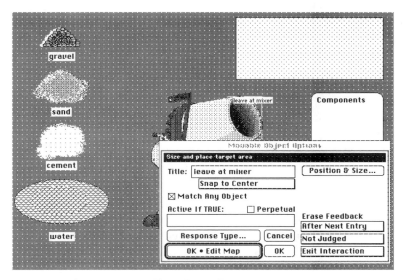

Figure 19.10 Completed Mixer Target Dialog Box

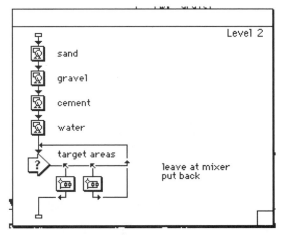

Figure 19.11 Leave at Mixer Complete

the upper left handle (located exactly in the upper left corner of the target) and drag it to the upper left of the screen. If you succeed, the box will expand to cover the area from its initial position to the upper left corner. If the whole target moves without changing size, you have missed the handle. Let go and try again with greater care to touch only the handle. To complete the error trap target, grab the lower right handle and drag it to the lower right corner of the screen.

When the target is placed, change the Leave at Destination pull-down menu to Put Back. This will return the misplaced component to its original pile. We want the error trapping to apply to any of the concrete components. To enable this, select the **Match Any Object** checkbox. The result of your effort should look like Figure 19.12. Select **OK** to leave the dialog box.

 Go With the Flow: You can think of target areas that overlap as though they were located on various levels. Target areas are "on top" of those to their right. In this case, the *leave at mixer* target area is on top of the *put back* target area. If you drop the object (one of the components of concrete) on the mixer's mouth, it is "caught" by the *leave at mixer* target area. It never can drop onto the other target area below. But, when you drop it in a spot other than the mixer's mouth, it falls onto the *put back* target area.

Test drive

There is hardly anyone who doesn't like to see some progress as a program is built up. At this point your program is runable, even though not complete. Save again and then select the Try It menu and choose Run. Your bare bones screen doesn't have instructions, but you can use the cursor to select and move each of the components to

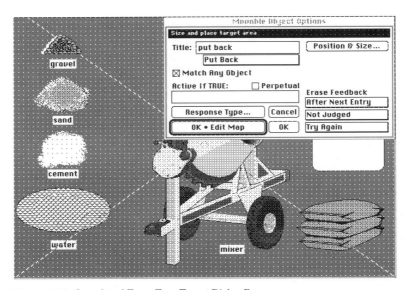

Figure 19.12 Completed Error Trap Target Dialog Box

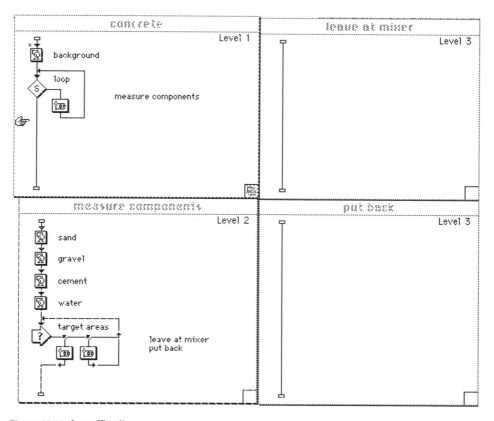

Figure 19.13 Loop Flowline

the mixer mouth. The component will appear to drop in and disappear. This is caused by your program loop. When you are satisfied with your work, move on.

 Go With the Flow: Follow the flowline in Figure 19.13 to examine the loop. As it leaves the *leave at mixer* map it is automatically erased. It follows the flowline out the bottom of *measure components*, reenters the loop, and enters the *measure components* map at the top and redraws each component.

Troubleshooting

 If the component won't go into the mixer, the problem may be that you reversed the destination target areas when you created them. For example, placing the mixer target as the whole screen. To check this, Pause the lesson when it is running at that point. The target areas will be shown with their names.

If the item does not erase at the mixer mouth, or if it will not restore again on top of the pile of raw materials, the problem might be that the components are not labeled as movable objects. To check that, select the component icons, and open Effects under the Attributes pull-down menu. Freely should be checked under

Movable. If the component does not restore, you may not have exit interaction branching. Check Figure 19.13 to be sure that the branch from *leave at mixer* is the same as the figure.

It is less likely, but you might have specified the component icon (sand, for example) as movable = false. If you did this the icon would have the small equals sign, like *background*.

If the item graphic isn't on the pile of materials at all, you probably canceled the Import Graphic operation. Repeat the Import Graphic.

 Development Tip: If you have a full version of Authorware, it will be wise to periodically package and run the in-progress version for verification. Problems can show up in the packaged version that are not apparent in the authoring version. This is a good policy with any development software.

Providing Feedback

Now that your program runs you can finish the practical side of it. You have to know how much of each component has been placed in the mixer to determine the kind of concrete that would be produced by that mixture.

Count components

First, count the components. Double-click the *leave at mixer* map icon to open it. Drag a calculation icon onto the flowline within *leave at mixer*. Label it *count components*. Double-click the *count components* calculation icon to open its calculation window.

Under the Data menu select Show Functions. The General function category, which includes the function you want, will appear by default. Scroll down to display the IF function. It will look like Figure 19.14. Read the Description. Then select Paste and the dialog box will close and paste the IF function into the open calculation window.

The text pasted will be:

```
IF(condition,TRUE expression,FALSE expression)
```

This follows a typical computer logic formulation: IF, THEN, ELSE.

IF, THEN, ELSE

IF, THEN, ELSE tells the computer what to do if a certain condition exists, and what to do if it doesn't. For example, "If it's cold outside wear a sweater, otherwise don't wear one" uses the same construction as the IF statement you are going to use in this lesson. Enter your sweater example in the IF structure.

```
IF(condition,TRUE expression,FALSE expression)
IF(cold outside,wear sweater,don't wear sweater)
```

Based on the value of the condition "cold outside" being TRUE or FALSE we would wear the appropriate clothing. If cold outside is TRUE we will wear the sweater. If cold outside is FALSE we will not wear the sweater.

```
                              Functions
  ┌────────────────────────────────────────────────────────┐
  │ Category                                                 │
  │ ┌──────────────────────────────────┐                    │
  │ │ General                          │                     │
  │ └──────────────────────────────────┘                    │
  │                              ┌─Referenced By──────────┐  │
  │  EraseIcon                ▒  │                        │  │
  │  FlushKeys                   │                        │  │
  │  IconTitle                   │                        │  │
  │  IF ·······················  │                        │  │
  │  Initialize                  │                        │  │
  │  LayerDisplay                │                        │  │
  │  MoveWindow                  │                        │  │
  │  Preload                  ◈  │ Uses:  0    (Show Icon)│  │
  │                              └────────────────────────┘  │
  │ Description:                                              │
  │ ┌──────────────────────────────────────────────────────┐│
  │ │ IF(condition,TRUE expression,FALSE expression)        ││
  │ │ Evaluates the specified condition and if it is true, evaluates ││
  │ │ TRUE expression; if it is false, evaluates FALSE expression.  If ││
  │ └──────────────────────────────────────────────────────┘│
  │  (Load...) (Rename...) (Delete) (Paste)   ( Done )       │
  └────────────────────────────────────────────────────────┘
```

Figure 19.14 Completed Error Trap Target Dialog Box

Applying this to your program, the calculation will look for a match of the expected name of a movable object display icon. It will deal with it whether there is a match or not. You can make this comparison with Authorware system variables. Do it now. Highlight the word "condition" within your IF statement. Under the Data menu select Show Variables. The General variables category will appear by default. Change the category to Interaction. Scroll down to display the ObjectMatched variable. It will look like Figure 19.15. Select Paste and the Variables dialog box will close and paste the ObjectMatched variable to replace the word "condition" in your calculation window.

At this point your IF statement should look like this:

```
IF(ObjectMatched,TRUE expression,FALSE expression)
```

The condition of the IF statement must have a logical value of either TRUE or FALSE. The variable that you just pasted holds the name of the icon that will be matched in the mouth of the mixer target area. You must modify the condition of the IF statement to look for sand. Later you will add more lines that look for the other components. Type

```
= "sand"
```

after the variable **ObjectMatched** and before the first comma (,). This statement will be either TRUE or FALSE depending on which component was matched in the target area. Now your IF statement should look like this:

```
IF(ObjectMatched = "sand",TRUE expression,FALSE expression)
```

 Authorware Tip: If you are in the middle of a calculation and want to quit authoring, or to refer to another section of your program (if, for example, you have forgotten the name of an icon that you must reference) you can do so by commenting-out the argument. Just type two hyphens at the beginning of a new line to comment it out.

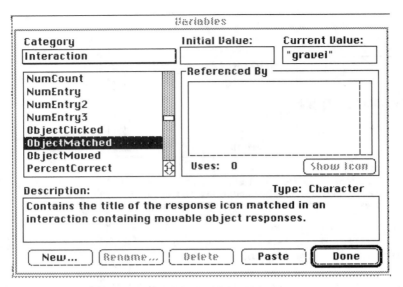

Figure 19.15 Variable Dialog ObjectMatched Selection

Next you will tell the computer what to do if the learner moves sand to the mouth of the mixer. To do this you change **TRUE expression** to what you want to occur if the ObjectMatched is sand. This will count the number of times sand is matched. You will use a simple expression to increment (add 1 to it) a custom variable that you will call number_sand_matched. The expression you will use is number_sand_ matched equals number_sand_matched plus one. Highlight **TRUE expression** in the IF statement and type the following:

```
number_sand_matched = number_sand_matched + 1
```

If the object matched isn't sand, nothing will happen. Because you do not want to act upon a FALSE condition, you will simply remove the FALSE expression from the IF statement. Highlight **,FALSE expression** (be sure to include the comma) and delete it. The resulting IF statement will be as shown below:

```
IF(ObjectMatched = "sand", number_sand_matched = number_sand_matched + 1)
--comment-This counts the unity added to the mixer.
```

Close the calculation. This isn't strictly necessary at this point, but we suggest closing it now to ensure that the contents of the calculation are correct. Because you plan to copy it you want to be sure there are no errors. For example, if you did not remove the comma, a syntax error would be reported when you attempted to close the calculation.

The new variable dialog box will appear. Click in the Initial Value box and enter the initial value of 0 (zero). (Select numeric on the Mac.) Then, enter a description something like:

```
Increments the number of times sand is matched
```

The completed New Variable box will look like Figure 19.16

Development Tip: It is much better to use descriptive titles for your variables if the authoring system that you use will allow it. This will make it much easier for you or someone else to look at the program and determine how it works. Also, it is better to make the name one long string of characters by using underlines to connect words. This ensures that the variable's name will always be recognized as one (long) name.

Authorware Tip: If you have made a syntax error in your calculation, Authorware will not let you close the Calculation window. If you cannot resolve the issue quickly, you can get out of the calculation window by making the offending line into a comment. Just type two hyphens at the beginning of the line.

Authorware Tip: Always enter equals signs. Authorware will add a colon to create an *assignment operator* (:=). If you reopen a calculation where you have included an equals sign in the TRUE expression, it will be altered by the program. It is not wise to type the colon yourself, since you could do so where it doesn't belong. The program will then not operate properly, and the cause could be difficult to identify.

Once you have successfully closed *count components*, reopen it and maximize the calculation window. Now you must handle each of the remaining components. The easiest way to do this is to copy the **ObjectMatched = "sand"** IF statement and press return to open a new line to paste it into. Paste it three times to create four identical lines. Then modify each of the three additional occurrences of "sand" to **gravel**, **cement**, and **water** to create an IF statement with unique variables for

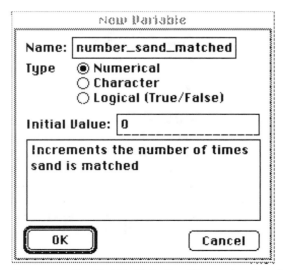
Figure 19.16 New Variable Dialog Box (Mac version shown)

each component. When you have completed this, your calculation window should contain the following IF statements:

```
IF(ObjectMatched = "sand", number_sand_matched := number_sand_matched + 1)
IF(ObjectMatched = "gravel", number_gravel_matched := number_gravel_matched + 1)
IF(ObjectMatched = "cement", number_cement_matched := number_cement_matched + 1)
IF(ObjectMatched = "water", number_water_matched := number_water_matched + 1)
--comment-count objects in mixer
```

Select OK in the calculation window to close it. When you do, Authorware will detect the new variable **number_gravel_matched** and you will be asked for information about it. Click in the Initial Value box and enter the initial value of 0 (zero). Then click in the comment box to document the variable. For this one, enter "Increments the number of times gravel is matched."

 Mac Difference: The Mac has a default of Numerical. If you want to change the variable to character or logical you must click on a button.

Click OK to close the gravel New Variable dialog box. You will be presented with the same New Variable box for each custom variable you have created.

Display the count

Now that you are able to count the number of components the learner will place in the mixer, you must provide feedback to help the learner keep track of the quantities of each component. At construction sites mixing small batches of concrete, a chalk board is used to keep track of how much of each ingredient has been added to the batch. Your lesson will do the same thing with numbers rather than hashmarks. To do this, you will embed variables in the *background* display that tell how much of each component has been added. They will be updated as the learner adds each additional portion of a component.

Double-click the *background* display icon. Select the text tool from the ToolBox, place the cursor in the small white box on the right, and click once. This will open a text field. Type the following:

```
gravel =
```

Be sure to type a space after the equal sign. Then select the Data menu and Show Variables under it. Change the default General category to the custom variables for Concrete. The variables for your file are always at the bottom of the list, with a category name the same as your file name. You will see the new custom variables in the selection window. Select **number_gravel_matched** and, when it is highlighted, select Paste. The variables dialog box will close and the variable will have been pasted into the text field at your cursor position. Authorware will add the brackets needed for a variable, and the line of text will read:

```
gravel = {number_gravel_matched}
```

You will see that your text wraps to more than one line. To see how it will look when in use, click on the arrow tool. The value of the variable is now displayed, taking only one space. Unless the learner adds thousands of portions of gravel the text will fit on the board. To continue, reselect the text tool, click on the text, and use the arrow key to move to the end. Now press **Enter** and type

```
sand =
```

Repeat the process that you used for gravel to embed the **number_sand_matched** variable in the text field. When you have embedded **number_sand_matched**, follow the same procedure for **number_cement_matched** and **number_water_matched**. When you have finished, your four lines of text will appear as follows:

```
gravel = {number_gravel_matched}
sand = {number_sand_matched}
cement = {number_cement_matched}
water = {number_water_matched}
```

It will look something like Figure 19.17. Click on the arrow tool to see the final appearance. (Mac users may have to adjust the size of the text field to fit the chalkboard.)

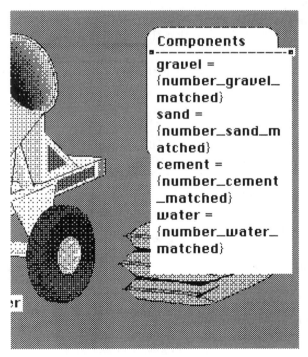

Figure 19.17 Embedded Variables

As it is, dragging materials to the mouth of the mixer would increase the values of the four component variables. However, the chalkboard would not be updated. The flowline in this lesson does not loop to the background each time it is activated. This is because we do not want to repeatedly draw the background. Another way to approach this would have been to place the variables in another display inside the loop (they would appear on top of the background). They would update every time the loop encountered the display.

While you have the background open, select Effects under the Attributes pull-down menu. Click the Update Displayed Variables checkbox. Then click on OK to close the Effects dialog box. Then close the background.

Test drive

Save again and select the Try It menu and choose Run. Now, when you use the cursor to select and move each of the components to the mixer mouth, it will appear to drop in and disappear and the number of measures of that component will increase by one. When you are satisfied with your work, move on.

Troubleshooting

 There are several potential problems that you may encounter when you run your lesson. Here they are, with suggestions for correcting each problem.

- If a component won't go in the mixer, it is probably a target problem. (Depending on the speed of your computer, the component may pause before disappearing.) Open the *target areas* icon to ensure that the target area falls over the mixer's mouth.

- If one or more values are blank, check that the embedded variables exist in the *background* icon.

- If a value fails to increment, it is probably a calculation problem. Check that the calculations in the *count components* icon match those shown on page 315.

- If a value fails to increment more than once, it is probably a loop problem. Check the *loop* decision icon. Make sure Repeat is set to Until TRUE, and the value compared is FALSE.

- If part of the variable shows in the image, it is probably mistyped rather than a pasted variable. Replace it by highlighting and repeating the process of pasting the variable from the Data pull-down menu.

Generating and Displaying Test Results

On bigger construction projects, samples of each batch of concrete are tested in a laboratory. Your program will submit the learner's concrete to a test and will report the results immediately on a custom meter.

You will create a working meter that will report the strength and hardness of the concrete just mixed to the learner. Open the *measure components* map and drag a map icon to the immediate right of the *target areas* interaction icon and to the left of the leave at mixer map. The Response Type Option dialog box will open, already set to pushbutton, which is what you want. (On Macs, it will assume the pushbutton response type.) Name it *Run Mixer*, taking care to use initial capital letters.

It has a branching characteristic of Try Again. This causes the whole bottom of the *target areas* interaction to look like a solid line. To see the flow at a glance you can now drag *Run Mixer* to the right of the other two icons. Open the *Run Mixer* Map to edit it.

Now you will create a meter to graphically show the results of the learner's most recent mix of concrete. Place three display icons on the run mixer flowline and name them *meter, strength,* and *hardness*. Import graphics for each of them as follows:

Icon Name	Graphic File to be Imported
meter	**concmetr.pct**
strength	**concstrn.pct**
hardness	**conchard.pct**

To place the meter and two needles in the proper orientation, Open the background icon (remember, it is in Level 1 of the flowline) and immediately close it. Now, while holding the shift key down, open the *meter* display icon. The background graphic will display with the meter on top of it. Drag the meter to cover the mixing instructions. Then close the *meter* display icon. The instructions are inappropriate while viewing the test results. The meter will erase when the learner tries a new mixture.

Again, while depressing the shift key, open the *strength* icon. Now move the *strength* marker (markers such as these on scales are usually called needles) to the left end of the meter's strength scale and close the display. Repeat this procedure to place the *hardness* needle to the left end of the scale. Figure 19.18 shows the portion of the display as it should appear after you place the hardness needle.

While the *hardness* icon is open, select the Effects option from the Attributes pull-down menu. Select On Path under Calculate Initial Position. When you do, additional elements will be displayed in an expanded dialog box as shown in Figure 19.19.

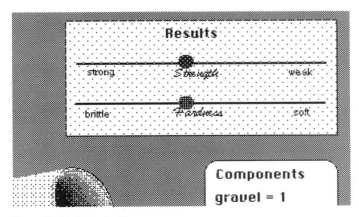

Figure 19. 18 Meter in Place

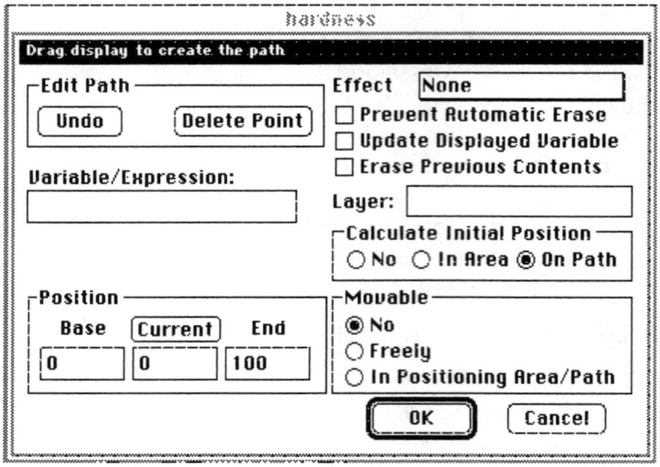

Figure 19.19 Initial Effects Dialog Box

The message at the top of the dialog box says, "Drag Display to Create Path." Move the dialog box as needed to see the hardness needle. It will have a small triangle in it. Click on a part of the needle, but not the triangle, and drag it to the right end of the scale. *Do not drag the triangle.* A line will be created that is the path for the animation of the needle to show the hardness of the concrete. You can adjust the path by moving the triangles. If at any time the path seems totally wrong, click on the Cancel button and repeat the process from the beginning.

Once the path is OK, enter a new variable name "hardness" in the Variable/Expression box. In order to give the scale more precision, under Position change the End to 200. Your results should look like Figure 19.20. When you are satisfied, click OK to close the dialog box.

A New Variable dialog box (shown in Figure 19.16) will appear to set the initial values for the new variable "hardness." The variable is numerical, with an initial value of zero. Enter a description. We entered:

```
Reflects the hardness of the cement on scale of 0 to 200.
```

Select OK to close the New Variable dialog box. Now repeat this procedure for *strength*. Create a path on the strength line of the meter and use the new variable name "strength."

Make the formula

Now you must create a formula to control the meter. The count of the raw ingredients are included in the formula, so that when the learner hits the Run Mixer button he or she will see the results of testing the concrete just created.

The real formula is complex. You are going to use a simplified formula. To create the formula, you will append the calculation to the *meter* icon. It would be possible to simply create a calculation icon for this purpose, but we want to provide you with practice in appending the calculation to an icon.

Select the *meter* icon. Use Control-W (or select Calculations from the Data pull-down menu) to open the calculation window. Type the following expression:

```
hardness = number_gravel_matched/number_cement_matched * 100
strength = number_sand_matched/number_water_matched * 100
--comment-This calculates the quality of the batch of concrete.
```

Select OK to close the calculation. You should not be provided with a New Variable dialog box, because these are existing variables. If you do see that box, you have spelled the variable's name differently.

Create try again

This is the final step in creating this lesson. You should provide a way to essentially empty the mixer and allow the learner to add new components from scratch. Quit is included in this choice.

Drag an interaction icon to the flowline below *hardness* and name it *recycle*. Then drag a map icon to the right of *recycle* and call it *Try New Mixture*. Accept the pushbutton option when offered in the Response Type Option dialog box. Then drag a calculation icon to the right of *Try New Mixture* and label it *Quit*.

Open *Quit* and enter:

```
Quit(0)
```

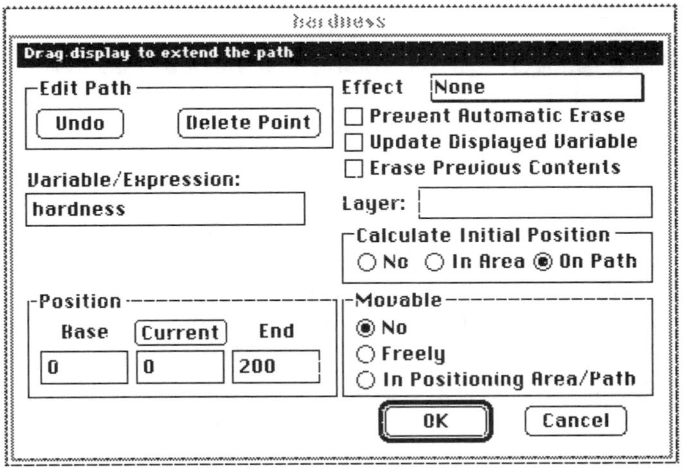

Figure 19.20 Completed Effects Dialog Box Choices

to make it function to quit from the lesson to Windows when the lesson is packaged.

Now you will provide the functionality of emptying the mixer and erasing the results of the test that are displayed in the meter. Open the *Try New Mixture* map and drag a calculation icon to the flowline. Title it *reset counter to zero*. Open the calculation and enter the following:

```
number_cement_matched = 0
number_gravel_matched = 0
number_sand_matched = 0
number_water_matched = 0
--comment-This initializes the component tally.
```

Close the calculation icon. As before, you should not be provided the New Variable dialog box because these are existing variables.

Drag an erase icon to the flowline below the *reset counter to zero* calculation and title it *Xmeter*.

Developmental run

This is a start flag. (See Figure 19.21.)

Place the start flag at the top of the Level 3 Run Mixer icon. Now select Run from Flag under the Try It menu. You will see only the meter and your two buttons, *Quit* and *Try New Mixture*. Click the *Try New Mixture* button. The erase icon will open to allow you to select the elements that it will erase. You may have to reposition the Erase Options dialog box to see the objects. Click on the meter and the two needles. They will disappear, and their icons will be placed in the dialog box's erase displayed objects drop-down list. Click OK to close the Erase Options dialog box.

Shift-click in the *Try New Mixture* icon's branching indicator to change it to Exit Interaction. The completed structure is shown in Figure 19.22.

It is a good practice to replace the flags in their original places. Just click in the spot where the Start Flag goes, and it will return there.

Authorware Tip: It is not critical that you replace the Start Flag in the icon palette. However, you must replace the Stop Flag because it will absolutely, positively, *stop the program* whenever the flow reaches it. You can use the Return key to get past it, but it is better that it not be there at all unless you want it.

Finally, you must place *Run Mixer, Try New Mixture,* and *Quit* buttons. Run the program from the Try It menu. You will see the *Run Mixer* button in the upper left corner of the screen. Pause the program by using Control-P, or by selecting Pause from the Try It menu, and move the button centered between the gravel pile and the meter. Then proceed by using Control-P or by selecting Proceed from the Try It menu. The meter will appear, along with the *Try New Mixture* and *Quit* buttons. Pause the program and place the buttons below the *Run Mixer* button, which will be grayed out. You have now completed the lesson's development.

Figure 19.21 Start Flag

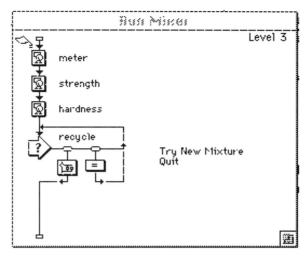

Figure 19.22 Run Mixture Structure

Test Drive

That's it! Run the program to test out the results of your programming prowess.

Ideas for Expansion, Enhancement, and Evolution

Here are some ideas for use of this lesson in new ways:

- Assign particular concrete mixtures to be made, such as mortar for laying brick, concrete for a driveway, and concrete for a steel-reinforced structural pillar
- Refine the formulas to provide greater accuracy in the mixtures
- Use the pail as the cursor for adding water to the concrete, and use the shovel for adding the solid components

Bring on the Load!

We can't help feeling that you are pleased with what you can do after completing the concrete-mixing lesson. There is much more to come. The key is NOT to copy the lessons you have been asked to complete over the years. Simply decide what is needed and how it can be made as interesting and challenging as possible.

Now we are ready to move on to another example of how you can make learning fun, as we devise a learner-controlled experiment. Let's weigh in!

20

Tractor-Trailer Weight Distribution

Sometimes we want to teach the learner something that must be done with real objects, but is based on an intellectual understanding of what is happening. In this case we want to teach tractor-trailer operators how to balance their loads for good operation and to meet legal requirements. The same thing could easily be done with a large truck scale, a tractor-trailer rig, and a large load that could be shifted about on the trailer. But think about the time it would take to shift the load, axles, and fifth wheel for the learner to witness the various outcomes. We can do this on a computer much faster and better.

In this chapter you will build a lesson that will allow the learner to simulate weight distribution appropriately across several axles of a tractor trailer. You will build this simulation including a movable load and a slider to control the wheel placement. The learner can place the load anywhere on the trailer, adjust the location of the tractor's fifth wheel, and move the trailer's axles.

Before you start, run the Authorware lesson called *truck.apw*, included in your book CD. This will give you an idea what the completed lesson is about and how it should look when you complete your effort.

What You Will Learn in This Chapter

- How to construct screens from separate objects
- How to use Authorware's animation icon
- How to permit the learner to animate screen objects
- How to use perpetually updated variables

Establish Lesson Graphics

Open a new Authorware file and name it *truck*. Open File Setup under the File pull-down menu. Set the presentation window size to VGA, deselect the Title Bar, User Menu Bar, and Overlay Menu Bar (no Overlay Menu Bar on the Mac). Select OK to close the dialog box.

In this lesson we will proceed in a more commercial way, based on the idea that you have all resources at hand. You will establish the icons' structures, place all the graphics at once, and then make it all work.

First you will establish the long sequence of display icons needed to paint the scene with its movable parts. Start by creating seven display icons for the essential lesson parts. Name them *background, truck, load, tandem, truck slider, trailer slider,* and *load slider.* When you are finished your structure should look like Figure 20.1.

Now begin placing the graphics provided in your book CD inside the icons. Begin with the icon that will form the background for the lesson. It also includes the trailer. Open the background icon and place *tkbkgrnd.pct* using the Import Graphics choice under the File pull-down menu. Since you won't want to move things around later, make sure your background is exactly placed. Use Control-spacebar (Command-backslash on the Mac) to hide the menu bar. Then carefully move the graphic until it fits exactly in all corners of the screen.

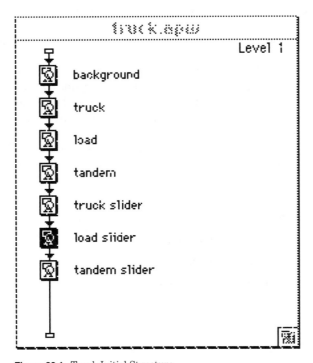

Figure 20.1 Truck Initial Structure

Icon Name	Graphic to be Imported
background	*tkbkgrnd.pct*

Figure 20.2 shows the *background* graphic.
Now continue to import the remaining graphics.

Icon Name	Graphic to be Imported
truck	*tktruck.pct*
load	*tkload.pct*
tandem	*tktandem.pct*
truck slider	*tkslider.pct*
trailer slider	*tkslider.pct*
load slider	*tkslider.pct*

Match the icons and files as listed above. Note that you reuse the same external graphic file as the basis for the three sliders.

Place graphics

Run the lesson now. The graphics will all be in various places on the screen, not where you want them to be. You must now place them so that they look like Figure 20.3.

You may also want to look at the finished truck lesson provided on your book CD, to confirm placement. Here are some guidelines to help you establish the graphics in the best relationship.

WARNING: If at any time during your placement efforts you move the background or distort the shape of a graphic, cancel using Undo under the Edit pull-down menu or Control-Z (Command-Z on the Mac).

If the imported graphics are in a pile, double-click on the pile to reveal the toolbox with the name of the selected object. It is likely to be one of the sliders, since they were drawn last because of their position at the bottom of the flowline. If so, you can place it in its initial position in the right side of its scale. Place all three sliders to the right end of their matching scales. If the graphic is a tractor-trailer component, you are better off to pull it aside to clear the area of the scale for precision placement of the components.

Place the tractor, aligning its front wheel directly over the "l" in Steer Axle and with its wheels one pixel above the edge of the steel plate that is the weigh station scale. Use your keyboard's arrow keys for final placement, so that a sliver of gray shows between the wheel and the scale.

The tandem is the set of two wheels that are attached to the trailer about three-quarters of the way to its rear. Place them so that the center between the two wheels is approximately above the "d" in Tandem, just below the roadway dotted line. Raise or lower them until they are the same distance above the scale as the tractor's wheels.

Place the load (it is a load of adobe bricks) in the absolute rear of the trailer. Do not allow it to overhang the end. Raise or lower the bricks until they are just above the gray line that runs the length of the trailer.

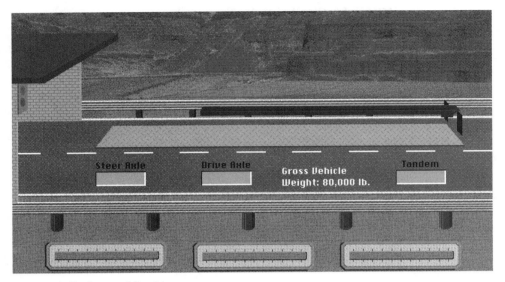

Figure 20.2 *Background* Graphic.

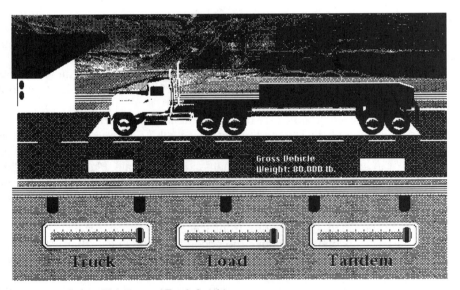

Figure 20.3 Screen Placement of Truck Graphics

Make objects immovable

In the regular version of Authorware, your final packaged lesson will automatically lock each graphic in place unless you specifically make it a movable object. In the Working Model you will not be able to package, and when you run the lesson, the graphics are potentially all movable unless you prevent it. That is what you will do next. The following four icons should be made *not* movable:

- background
- load
- tandem
- truck

CAUTION: *Do not* make the three sliders not movable. The learner will move them to manipulate the tractor-trailer load weight distribution.

To make the truck icon fixed, select it. Then proceed to the Data pull-down menu and select Calculations to bring up the calculation window. Enter the following inside the calculation window:

```
Movable=false
--This nails down the image
```

Close the calculation window. Note the small equals sign near the upper left corner of the truck icon indicating that a calculation has been appended. Setting Movable=false will not hinder your authoring, and will not prevent you from moving an object by mistake when authoring.

 Authorware Tip: You need not capitalize **Movable**. It is the Authorware system variable **Movable**, and is a reserved word. You cannot create your own custom variable named **movable**.

Now enter the same calculation in the same way in both of the other icons, to make them not movable. When this is complete you have all of the components needed to build the lesson. The result should look like Figure 20.4.

Establish Movable Object Structure

Your screen, as you can see, is essentially complete. Now you will make it functional. You will set up the sliders as movable objects and set up the truck, load, and tandem as animated objects with the animations correlated to the position of their respective sliders. We will hang the animations on an interaction icon.

Drag an interaction icon to the bottom of the flowline and name it *calculate weights*. Its name suggests its eventual function, but for now we will focus on the animation. The animation icon is shown in Figure 20.5.

Now, drag an animation icon to the right of *calculate weights*. The response type dialog box will open. Change the response type to Movable Object and select OK. The small arrow response type symbol that you see above the untitled icon reinforces your selection. Name it *animate truck*. Drag two more animation icons to the right of *animate truck*. Name them *animate load* and *animate tandem*.

Now you will associate each animation icon's movable object target area with the corresponding slider. The target will be placed relative to the scale shown on the background.

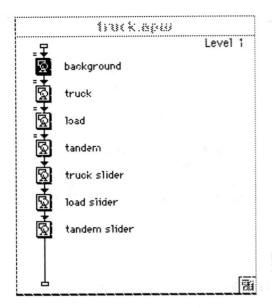

Figure 20.4 Initial Icons for Tractor-Trailer Lesson

Figure 20.5 Animation Icon

Open and close the *background* to place it into memory. While holding the shift key down, double-click on the truck slider display icon to open it and then close it to add it to memory. Finally, double-click the *animate truck* icon's response type symbol. A Movable Object Options dialog box will appear. Click on the truck slider as requested by the message at the top of the dialog box. Then move and resize the animate truck target area to conform with the size and shape of the slider scale above the word Truck.

At some point, when you are performing this edit, you may see the target area jump to the center of the screen. If this should happen, it is because you have accidentally clicked on the background. Authorware interprets this as your selection of the object to be moved and jumps the target area to the center of mass of the background. If this happens, just click on the slider to restore this relationship and continue moving and resizing as needed.

The dialog box will look like Figure 20.6. Select OK to close it.

Now carefully repeat this process for the load and tandem. If you continue immediately, the *background* will remain in memory. Open and close *load slider* while holding the shift key down, then double-click the *animate load* response-type symbol. Note that you do not have to hold down the shift key, as the response-type symbol will bring up everything in memory. After finishing the necessary placements, click OK to close the Movable Object Options response type dialog box. Then complete the same actions for the *tandem slider* and the *animate tandem* response type symbol. Figure 20.7 shows the whole *truck* lesson structure at this point.

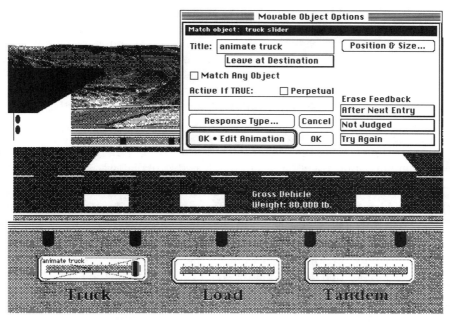

Figure 20.6 Movable Object Options Dialog Box

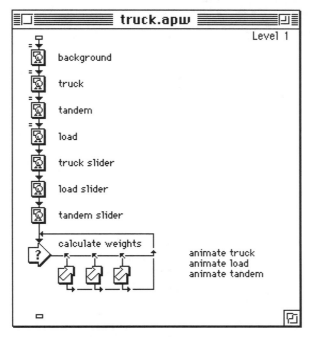

Figure 20.7 *Truck* Lesson Structure

Next, you will establish the paths of the animation for the truck, load, and tandem. Let's start with the truck. If you are continuing from establishing the target areas, everything will already be in memory. If not, open and immediately close the *background* and *truck*. Now double-click the animate truck icon. You will see a dialog box that looks like Figure 20.8. It is the default fixed destination animation type, suitable for a simple animation from one spot to another.

Select the Change Type button. You will see a dialog box that looks like Figure 20.9.

Each of these animation types offers different control and possibilities for on-screen effects. For the tractor-trailer lesson, select **Scaled Path**. This will convert your animation selection box to the Scaled Path dialog box shown in Figure 20.10.

Authorware Tip: You could have used the scaled x-y animation in this case. You would have to use it when the path is convoluted and you want the animated object to follow the path; for example, a blood cell animating through the heart-lung system.

The next step is to follow the instructions on the dialog box, which is Click display to be moved. You may want to move the dialog box to get it out of the way of the truck. Its position doesn't matter when you are setting the path.

To set the path, click once on the truck. A small black triangle will appear in the center of the truck graphic, and the message in the dialog box will change to Drag display to create path.

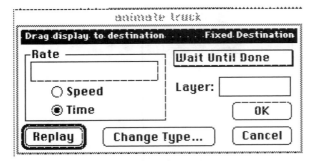

Figure 20.8 Fixed Destination Animation Icon Dialog Box

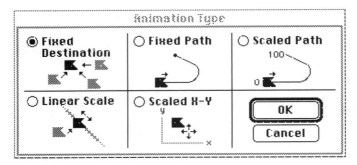

Figure 20.9 Animation Type Dialog Box

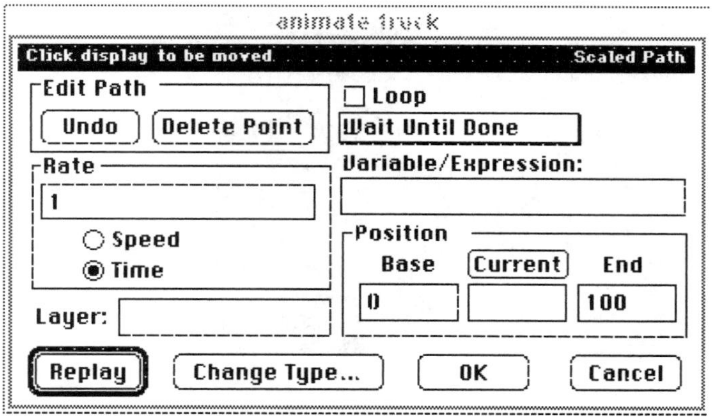

Figure 20.10 Scaled Path Dialog Box

To create the path, drag the truck to the other end of its path. Move it forward until the front tire is approximately over "ee" in Steer Axle. A line that is as long as the distance you moved the truck will appear, with a new triangle at its right end. Figure 20.11 shows the truck and path.

Now complete the animation by setting the parameters in the animation dialog box. Change the Wait Until Done drop-down list to Perpetual. This will make the animation perpetual, so that its location on the flowline does not affect its operation. Change the rate to a Time of 4, which will make the animation last four seconds. You will find that, the slower the animation, the smoother it will be.

Finally, you will set up a method to control the position of the three objects: truck, load, and tandem. You will create a variable that will determine the position in which to animate. Later you will create a path for the sliders, and they will communicate their positions through the variable to cause the objects to animate proportional distance.

Click the cursor in the Variable/Expression entry field. It is a simple expression, but we suggest that you go to the Data pull-down menu and select Show Variables. Then, from the General category, select PathPosition. Read the Description and then Paste PathPosition. Next time you can just type it, but you will have read the description already. Type the remainder of the expression so it is as follows:

```
PathPosition@"truck slider"
```

Figure 20.12 shows the completed animate truck scaled path animation dialog box. Select OK to close the dialog box.

Complete the remaining animation icons as follows. Carefully repeat the process for the tandem. Open the animation icon. Click on the tandem to establish the zero point. Then drag it to the left until the center of the two tires is approximately over the "b" in 80,000 lb. Then set the scaled path animation icon to Perpetual, with a Rate of 4 seconds. Finally, enter:

```
PathPosition@"tandem slider"
```

in the Variable/Expression entry field.

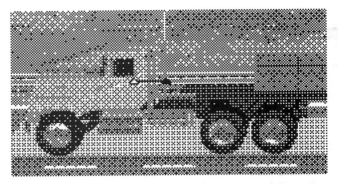

Figure 20.11 Truck after Path Is Established

animate truck

Drag display to extend the path.   Scaled Path

Edit Path   ☐ Loop
[Undo] [Delete Point] | Perpetual |

Rate   Variable/Expression:
| 4 | | PathPosition@"truck slider" |

  ○ Speed   Position
  ● Time   Base   [Current]   End
                                    | 0 | | 100 | | 100 |
Layer: [   ]

[Replay] [Change Type...]   [OK   ]   [Cancel]

Figure 20.12 Completed Animate Truck Scaled Path Animation Dialog Box

Now complete the animate load icon. Open it and click on it to establish the zero point. Then drag it to the left until the front of the load is approximately at the front end of the trailer. Do not let it overhang the front end of the trailer. Then set the scaled path animation icon to Perpetual, with a Rate of 4 seconds. Finally, enter:

```
PathPosition@"load slider"
```

in the Variable/Expression entry field.

You have completed the animation icons that will control the movement of the truck, tandem, and load. Next you will activate them to function by defining the sliders' paths.

Create Paths for Sliders

There is more than one way to create the paths. We recommend that you run the program to access them. Otherwise, you must open icons, close them, open the animation, and make the associations.

Run the truck program now. Then double-click on the truck slider. When the tool-box appears confirming your selection, open Effects under the Attributes pull-down window. Click on the On Path button under Calculate Initial Position. The box will enlarge and your screen will appear similar to Figure 20.13. To make your screen match the figure, click on In PositioningArea/Path under Movable.

Note the small triangular path indicator on the truck slider. The Effects dialog box is requesting that you click on the object for which you want to create a path. Care-fully click on the red needle that you placed in the right end of the truck slider scale in the lower left-hand corner of your screen. Drag the slider to the left end of the scale. A second path indicator will appear connected to the first by a path. When you finish, your screen will look like Figure 20.14. It is possible to adjust the path by care-fully moving the triangular path indicators. Click on OK to close the Effects dialog box.

Figure 20.15 shows the slider in greater detail.

Finish your paths by following the same process for the tandem and load slider.

Test Drive

You can try your handiwork at this point. Move each of the sliders through its full range. The smoothness of the animation will be partially related to the power of your computer. Try various combinations of positions. Each object should respond pro-portionally to its slider. If you move the load slider to its midpoint, the load should animate to its midpoint.

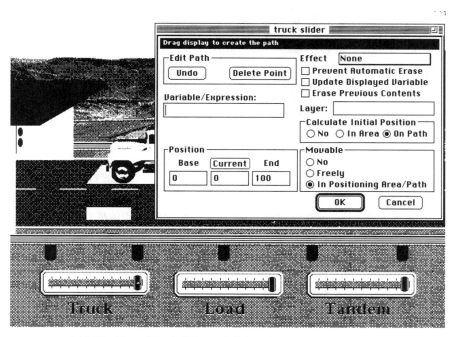

Figure 20.13 Initial Position of Truck Slider with Effects Dialog Box

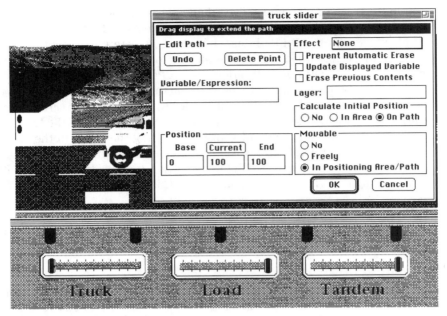

Figure 20.14 Truck Slider Path

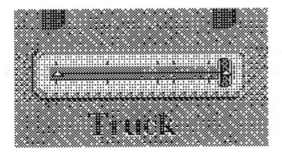

Figure 20.15 Path Detail

Embedding Variables

The next activity needed to make the lesson functional is generating the variables which will display the weight of each axle. You will enter each custom variable into its position in the pavement on the background. Be sure to enter each one separately into its own placeholder.

Open the *background* icon. Select the text tool and click near the Steer Axle weight placeholder. Type:

```
{steer_axle_weight}
```

Select the arrow tool. When you do, you will be presented with the New Variable dialog box.(Mac users must select Numerical and assign an initial value of 0 (zero).)

We suggest that you enter a Description similar to:

```
Displays the weight of the steer axle.
```

Figure 20.16 shows the result.

Select OK to close the New Variable dialog box. The variable will become an object with handles. Use the arrow tool to make further adjustments. Select Mode under the Attributes pull-down menu and set the mode to Transparent. Select Center under the Text pull-down menu, and finally, use the object's handles to adjust the size of the object box to conform neatly within the steer axle weight placeholder. Once you are satisfied you are ready to set the next variable.

Repeat this whole process for the two other embedded variables. They are:

```
{drive_axle_weight}
```

with a Description of:

```
Displays the weight of the drive axle.
```

and

```
{tandem_axle_weight}
```

with a Description of:

```
Displays the weight of the tandem axle.
```

Be sure to set each to center justification and transparent mode.

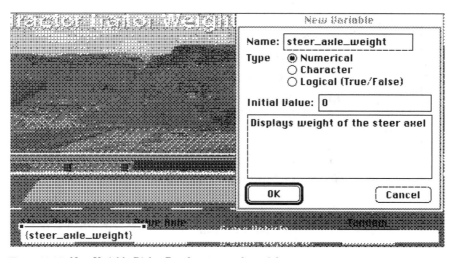

Figure 20.16 New Variable Dialog Box for steer_axle_weight

Development Tip: You can save time and effort by copying the first embedded variable and pasting it in the two other locations. This will give you embedded variables of the right size that are already transparent and centered. Then select each and edit its contents to the new variable name. When you select the arrow tool you will proceed just as though you had typed the variable in from scratch.

Now is a good time to set the format in which the weights will be displayed. These are large numbers, reflecting a portion of the weight of an 80,000-pound gross-weight vehicle. You will want to display whole numbers with a comma at the thousand mark. To do this, select all three displayed variables at once. Hold down the shift key on your keyboard and click on each one in turn. Do not release the shift key until all three are selected. Now click on the Data pull-down menu and select Number Format. The Number Format dialog box will open. Figure 20.17 shows the default setting in the dialog box.

Click in the check box under Decimal called Show Numbers After Decimal. This will result in showing only whole numbers. The example will provide feedback that the outcome will be as you expect. (There is no example shown in the Mac dialog box.)

Finally, before closing the *background* icon, you must ensure that the changing weights on each axle are shown to the learner dynamically as they change. To do this, select Effects under the Attributes pull-down menu and click on the Update Displayed Variables checkbox. When you finish, select OK to close the Effects dialog box and then close the *background* icon.

Mac Difference: Authorware on the Macintosh works differently for Number Format. There are three levels of text formatting: Default, All Text, and Selected Text. The Default includes two decimal places. In this lesson, by selecting three text fields

Figure 20.17 Number Format Dialog Box Default

that were the embedded variables, you were selecting All Text. If you had selected the text of one of the embedded variables before choosing Number Format, you would have been working at the Selected Text level.

Set Up Weight Calculations

The next activity needed to make the lesson functional is generating the calculations which will control the animations and values for display of the distributed weight.

You will set up relationships that assist in the calculation of the weight on each of the axles. We have generated values and relationships that approximate the actual distribution of weight based on an 80,000-pound gross-vehicle weight for a tractor and trailer, carrying a load of 60,000 pounds.

Select the *animate objects* interaction icon. Append a calculation by selecting Calculations from the Data pull-down menu to open a calculation window. Enter the following text:

```
load_placement := PathPosition@"load slider" * 60000
trailer_distribution := load_placement * PathPosition@"tandem slider"
tandem_axle_weight := 8000 + trailer_distribution
truck_distribution := 60000 - trailer_distribution
drive_axle_weight := 6000+(truck_distribution*PathPosition@"truck slider")
steer_axle_weight := 6000+(truck_distribution-(truck_ distribution*PathPosition@"truck slider"))
--Comment-These expressions determine the weight distribution based on Slider placement.
```

Click OK to close the calculation. As the calculation box closes, you will assign initial values as follows:

Variable	Value	Description
load_placement	0	determines distribution of weight on trailer
trailer_distribution	0	determines distribution of weight between tractor and trailer
truck_distribution	0	determines distribution of weight between steer and drive axles

Figure 20.18 shows the structure of the flowline at this point.

The next thing that you will do is to modify the base and end position values for each of the sliders, based on the percentage of the weight carried by that axle. Here are the values that you will enter soon:

Icon	Base	End	Variable/Expression
truck slider	.6	1	.6
animate truck	.6	1	
load slider	.9	.6	.9
animate load	.9	.6	
tandem slider	.5	.8	.5
animate tandem	.5	.8	

The Variable/Expression will control where the slider is shown on the path before the learner has moved it. You will set them all to the same value as the Base position. This will prevent the slider from adjusting its position as the lesson starts up.

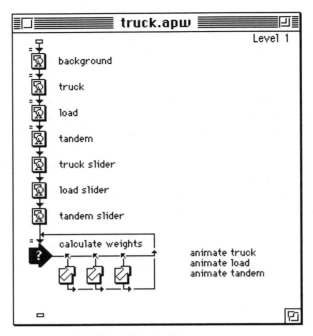

Figure 20.18 Final Truck Flowline Structure

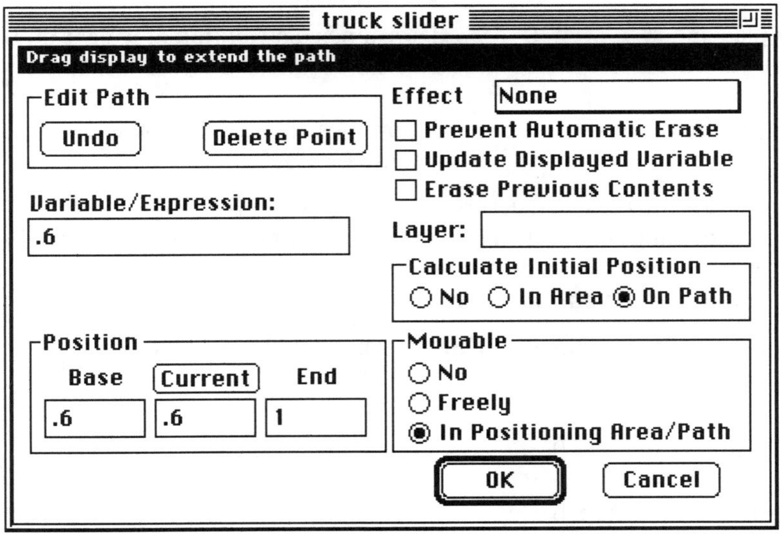

Figure 20.19 Truck Slider Effects Dialog Box

Authorware Tip: If you don't take special care to prevent it, objects will first be displayed in their actual position in the display or interaction from which they emanate, then move to their base positions if they are designated as Movable. Finally, if they are under program control they may move to yet another position. All this jumping around can be confusing and look messy. Avoiding this is our motivation for setting the Variable/Expression value.

Now select the *truck slider* icon (no need to open it) and choose the Attributes pull-down menu. Then select Effects. This box is shown in Figure 20.19. Now modify it as follows. In the position box, under Variable/Expression, enter the value .6. Then enter the Base value as .6 and the End value as 1. Figure 20.19 shows the truck slider Effects dialog box with the values entered. Select OK to close the dialog box.

Setting Up Equations

As you produce lessons you will find many occasions in which you will have to generate mathematical relationships to make your lessons work properly. By examining the rationale that underlies the truck weight distribution problem of this lesson, you will be more ready to tackle your own problem in a lesson of your own design.

The truck and the tandem bear weight placed on them by the trailer. The weight is not fixed in location because the load can be in various locations on the trailer, the trailer can bear on the truck in a variety of locations, and the tandem itself can move.

The ratio of weight distribution of the trailer is affected by the load position. The ratio of weight distribution between the drive and steer axles of the truck is affected by the position of the fifth wheel (the sliding part that connects the trailer to the truck). There is no ratio of weight distribution for the tandem since it is a single point for weight to bear.

In setting up equations and Authorware calculations you may find that you can get excellent results without using the precise and often complex equations taken from the real world. An example of this is in determining the trailer distribution. Rather than calculate both of the weights that bear on the tractor and tandem, we simply calculate the weight on the tandem and determine that the weight on the truck is the trailer's total weight, minus the portion on the tandem.

Here's how to derive the values for each axle. The empty weight of the tractor trailer is 10 tons, or 20,000 pounds. We use a simplification to ignore differences in weight distribution with an empty trailer. In practical terms of learning to balance the load, this won't matter. We decide that, regardless of positioning of truck or tandem, the empty weight distribution is: steer axle 6,000, drive axle 6,000, and tandem 8,000.

The load is 30 tons, or 60,000 pounds. When the load is at the extreme rear of the trailer, potentially 90% of its weight can be on the tandem. When at the extreme front, it will potentially place 60% of its weight on the tandem. These assumptions explain the expression load_placement := PathPosition@"load slider" * 60000, since the path is .9 (or 90%) at its base and .6 (60%) at its end. You can see that as the load is moved forward, more of its weight is borne by the truck.

The position of the tandem affects the distribution of the trailer and load between itself and the truck. The tandem bears only 50% of the weight when all the way to the rear, its base position, and up to 80% when fully forward. These are reflected in the .5 base value and .8 end value of the tandem slider. We use the value already derived for the load_placement in the expression trailer_distribution := load_placement * PathPosition@"tandem slider" and apply the position of the tandem slider. When multiplied, these give us the value for the weight on the tandem, which we call trailer_distribution, because when we subtract this value from the weight of the load we get the value of the weight on the truck. At this point, we know the weight on the tandem. This explains both the expression tandem_axle_weight := 8000 + trailer_distribution and the expression truck_distribution := 60000 − trailer_distribution.

We know the weight on the truck is the total weight minus whatever is on the tandem, but we don't know yet how it is distributed between the steer and drive axles. Remember that the truck's fifth wheel can be positioned forward or back, essentially shifting the position of the truck relative to the trailer. Our calculations are set up based on the concept of the truck's movement, not that of the fifth wheel, which moves in the opposite direction (when the fifth wheel moves forward the truck moves back). When the truck is at its base position (all the way to the rear), the drive axle will bear 60% of the weight on the truck. When the truck is at its end position, all the way forward, the drive axle will bear 100% of the weight on the truck. This explains the expression drive_axle_weight := 6000+(truck_distribution*PathPosition@"truck slider"). We get the steer axle weight by subtracting the weight on the drive axle, explaining the calculation steer_axle_weight   :=   6000+(truck_distribution−(truck_distribution*PathPosition@"truck slider"))

You will need to change the base and end positions of the load and tandem, also. Enter the values shown below just as you did for the truck slider.

Open the other sliders and replace the default base and end values as follows:

Slider Name	Base	End	Variable/Expression
load slider	.5	.8	.65
tandem slider	.6	.9	.75

Test Drive

Run your completed lesson. All animations should work, and weights should dynamically change based on the position of the objects. The weights shown should appear reasonable and should always total 80,000 pounds.

Be a good driver! A good driver will always balance the load over the axles so that the truck is within state weight regulations. Balance your load so that the steer axle has 12,000 pounds and each of the drive and trailer tandem axles bear 34,000 pounds.

You will discover that there are many combinations that can achieve this distribution. However, the rig's dynamics will be affected by your choice of positions. With the tandem fully back, the turning radius is much wider, but the ride is smoother. If you were in a city, a short turning radius would be better. Another point to consider is dealing with different load types. The adobe bricks are spread out. Some loads concentrate their weight in a small area of the trailer. In that case it is better to have the tandem under it.

Troubleshooting

 If the tractor-trailer weight distribution lesson does not work properly, you have an excellent opportunity to review Chapter 16 to identify the fix. One likely place to look is the setup of the animations—make sure that the parts move as expected. With practice, you can edit the faulty animations to place them and have them animate as desired. Without practice, the process can get frustrating. If you cannot get the icons to work, it is a completely honest troubleshooting technique to delete the offending icons and rebuild them.

Ideas for Expansion, Enhancement, and Evolution

We can think of any number of ways to make this lesson more glittery, including gratuitous audio and video. Here are ideas for enhancement of this lesson:

- Randomly assign the weight of the load to provide practice in balancing differing loads.
- Create a unique load or loads that distribute the weight differently than the adobe bricks. For example, watermelons, steel coils, electric transformers, or heavy machinery.
- Add a point scoring mechanism that will deduct points when one of the movable components is moved in the wrong direction.
- Add a timer that will deduct points as time passes before the load is well balanced.
- Determine what will be an acceptable balance. Then the truck horn might sound when balance is achieved, or you can set the stoplight to change from red to green, or to flash when the load is well balanced.
- One thing that would probably never work well is for the truck to drive away. It is difficult to get larger objects to animate smoothly. Even if the trailer were not part of the background, the trailer would probably have to stay put.

Lets Drive On!

You can see how powerful the lessons you create can be if you let your imagination run free. Learners will appreciate such lessons and your reputation will grow. Now, let's move indoors to a completely different work environment. You will learn more about movable objects and target areas as you help learner EKG technicians place electrodes on a patient. Let's apply some lubrication and get started!

21

EKG Electrodes

This chapter illustrates how subjects might be presented to trainee medical technicians. The lesson you are about to generate is about the familiar electrocardiogram (EKG). In your lesson, the learner places one electrode in the appropriate torso location. Then the learner receives feedback on the electrode placement by "recording" the EKG to produce a representation of the report graphic. Context-sensitive help is available in the form of a "hint" where to place the electrode. Considerations for expansion of the lesson to include other capabilities is also covered in this chapter.

An electrocardiogram is a graphic tracing of the infinitesimally small electric current that is generated and discharged by the sinus node of the heart muscle during a heartbeat. It is used to identify the existence of an abnormality. This tiny current can be recorded from the surface of the body as it traverses the heart muscle. The EKG is made by creating an electrical circuit between the heart and the electrocardiograph. Electrodes are placed on various parts of the body and, as these sites are varied, the "view" recorded also varies. Electrodes are attached to other parts of the body, including the wrists and right ankle, which functions as an electrical ground. The instrument remained essentially unchanged for many years, and once produced pen recordings on paper strips. Today, computerized electrocardiograms are in use in most large hospitals.

Standardization is important to electrocardiography. Nevertheless, sometimes technicians do attach the electrodes to the wrong limbs, smear excessive electrode paste, allow respiratory motion, introduce 60-cycle artifacts, and loosely attach the electrodes (that produces a recording resembling atrial fibrillation).

The lesson that you will build focuses solely on placement of the precordial electrode at location V_e. Location V_e is at the extreme tip of the xigmoid process (at the end of the sternum just above the stomach).

What You Will Learn in This Chapter

- How to use nested hot spots
- How to use animation
- How to provide learner feedback
- How to provide graphic feedback
- How to work with a background color

Establish the Structure

As you know now from experience, it works well to drag the icons needed in a structure and then to make them functional. Let's follow that practice for the EKG lesson.

After you open a new Authorware file, save and name the file *ekg*, drag a map icon to the flowline, and name it *welcome*. Now drag a second map icon below *welcome* and name it *lesson*.

Open File Setup under the File pull-down menu. Change the Presentation Window to VGA and deselect Title Bar, User Menu Bar, and Overlay Menu Bar (User Menu Bar and Title Bar on the Mac). You will establish a background color for the lesson. To do this, select the Background (Background Color on the Mac) button to reveal the palette.

Click on the Palette button. Then click on the Load button. The Windows search window will appear. Find the ekg.pal palette file that was included with your book. Click on the Preserve System Colors checkbox. You will see the 16 standard Windows VGA colors being replaced. Generally, you will want to use a palette that has the standard colors, so click again to restore them. Choose a pink flesh tone color for the background. (Mac users will not have the option to import a custom palette, and should click on the pink in the upper right corner of the standard palette.) Your confirmation will be a black square surrounding the color you select, and the sample square in the upper right corner of the palette display window will fill with the color you selected. Select OK to close the palette display window.

Replace Continue in the Wait Button Title text field. Type a space, followed by:

```
Begin
```

followed by another space. You must add the spaces to both sides of the word Begin to make it appear normally on the button face. Now, every time you drag a Wait icon to the flowline it will generate a button called Begin. Select OK to close the File Setup dialog box.

Building the Title Page

Open the *welcome* map icon. Drag a display icon to the flowline and name it *title screen*. Open *title screen* and select the rectangle tool. Draw a rectangle to fill about three-quarters of the screen. While the rectangle is still selected and the eight handles are showing, double-click on the rectangle in the toolbox. The Fills dialog box will open automatically. The default fill is None. Select the solid white fill below the

None selection and select OK to close the Fills dialog box. The rectangle should still be selected. Double-click on the Lines tool and the Lines dialog box will open automatically. Select one of the thicker lines to create a border for the white rectangle.

Next, import the graphic *ekg_body.pct*. Select the arrow tool and drag the body to the left side of the white rectangle. Resize the body using the standard shift-mouse drag combination method (click on a corner handle and press shift, then drag to make the image larger or smaller). Refer to Figure 21.1 for the approximate size of the image. Select the text tool and type:

```
EKG Lesson 1
Electrode Ve
Placement

by

Your Name
```

Select Justification from the Text pull-down menu and choose Center to position the text. Then select all the text and then pick Font from the Text pull-down menu, and follow the menu to choose a good looking font, such as Arial. (Mac users might choose Helvetica.) Now use the text tool to select only the first three lines, and select Color from the Attributes pull-down menu to choose the brightest red. Because the text is on a white background the default mode of opaque is satisfactory, so you needn't change it. While the text is still selected, choose Size from the Text pull-down menu and use the menu to choose 24-point.

The name of the placement location is V_e, not Ve. Select only the "e" and then choose Style from the Text pull-down menu to pick Subscript. When you do, you will

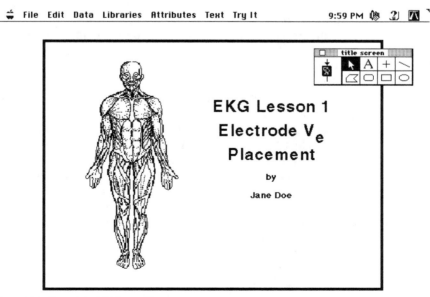

Figure 21.1 Completed *Welcome* Screen

see that the e is now a subscript letter, but the spacing between lines is uneven. To make them even, use the text tool to select the space between the n of lesson and the figure 1 to highlight only the space. Now repeat the process of subscripting to make the space a subscript. When you finish, the result will be that the lines are equally spaced. Figure 21.1 shows the completed *welcome* screen.

Close the title screen by clicking the close button on the toolbox. Now add control to the display. Drag a Wait icon to the flowline below the *title screen* and double-click to open it. Deselect the Keypress checkbox. (Mac users do not have to open the icon at all.) Now, to place the Continue button, Run the program from the Try It pull-down menu (or use Control-R). When the screen is displayed, Pause the program from the Try It pull-down menu (or use Control-P). You will see that the Continue button is displayed with the name you gave it, Begin. Then drag the Begin button to the bottom center of the screen in the portion that shows the background color. Now use Control-J to jump to the icons. The title page is complete, so close *welcome*'s Level 2 window by double-clicking on its close box.

Building the Lesson Structure

Now you can begin work on the lesson itself. Double-click on the *lesson* map icon to open it to Level 2 for editing. Drag a display icon to the flowline and name it *background*. It will obviously hold the background image for the lesson.

Then drag another display icon below *background* and name it *electrode*. It will hold the electrode that the learner will place on the patient to record an EKG.

You will create two buttons that the learner will use to control the learning experience. To do this, drag an interaction icon to the flowline below *electrode* and name it *place electrode*. Drag a map icon to the right of the *place electrode* interaction. The response type options box will open with the default of pushbutton. Since you intend for it to be a button to record the EKG, select OK to close the box and name the icon *Record*. Drag a second map icon to the right of *Record* and name it *Hint*.

Now you will place three calculation and one animation icons that are needed to control the placement of the electrode on the patient's body. Drag the first calculation and drop it to the right of *Hint*. The new icon will assume the pushbutton response type, but we want it to be a move object, so double-click on the *untitled* icon's pushbutton response type symbol to open it. When the Pushbutton Options dialog box opens, select the Response Type button to open the Response Type dialog box. Change the response type to Movable Object by clicking on its button, and then select OK to close it and the Movable Object dialog box will appear. Close it also. You will see that the response type symbol has changed to a little arrow. This little arrow represents a target area for a movable object to be placed in it. Title the calculation *home*. After we set up all the Movable Object responses, you will graphically determine the location of the target areas and associate the electrode graphic as the movable object that will be eligible for placement within them. Within the calculation icon you will assign a variable that will be judged when the Record button is selected by the learner.

Authorware Tip: The order in which the Movable Object targets are placed on the interaction is important. These targets will be nested one on top of another, so that the smallest, innermost target must be located farther to the left on the interaction flowline than larger targets covering the same area.

You have just created one target. This exercise requires three more. Individually drag two more calculation icons and one animation icon to the right of *home*. Each will assume the Move Object response type. Title them *good, bad,* and *error trap* respectively. Figure 21.2 shows the completed EKG structure. Note that the first pushbutton, *Record*, was scrolled off the screen to the left to make way for the calculations.

Establishing the background

Because the learner will be moving objects around on the screen, you must append a variable to anchor the background. Select the *background* icon so that it is highlighted. Under the Data pull-down menu, choose Calculations. This will open a calculation window in which you should enter the expression and documentation as follows:

```
movable = false
-- Anchors the background against accidental movement
```

When you close this calculation window you will notice that Authorware does not ask for an initial value for movable. This is because Movable is a system variable. It is also not case-sensitive, so you do not have to type a capital M. Close the calculation window by selecting OK and reopen it using the same process that you used initially. You will see that Authorware has done some syntax work for you—and the text that you entered in the calculation has been changed to

```
Movable:= FALSE
```

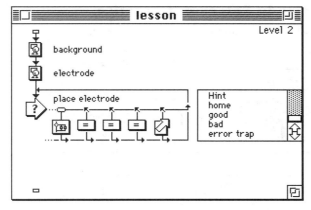

Figure 21.2 EKG Flowline

You could have typed a capital M and FALSE in all capitals, but remember our warning not to type the colon. If Authorware does ask for an initial value, it would be because you misspelled Movable.

Authorware Tip: Remember not to type the colon, except in those specific cases where it is required for an assignment instead of a comparison.

Next, you will make the background erase the welcome screen that precedes it. While the background is still selected, select Effects under the Attributes pull-down menu. Click in the Erase Previous Contents checkbox, and select an effect for the erase. We chose Mosaic. Then select OK to close the Effects dialog box.

Finally, bring in the image for the background. Use Import Graphics to import the following file:

Icon Name	Graphic to be Imported
background	**ekg_back.pct**

Center the graphic to resemble Figure 21.3. Close the *background* display to return to the Level 2 flowline, and move on.

Making the electrode work

You must have a movable object in order to set up the targets later. This is a good time to create that object. If you are beginning again after a break, open and close *background*. If you continued to this section immediately after importing the *background*, the image is in memory. All you have to do is hold down the shift key and double-click on *electrode*.

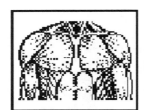
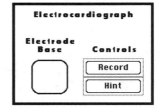
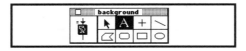

Figure 21.3 The Background Display

Create a small, round, blue object representing the electrode. Click on the oval tool in the toolbox. Now create a small circle by holding the shift key while dragging the mouse less than ¼ inch down and right. The circle should not be too large or it will obscure the patient's chest. Refer to Figure 21.4 to see the size of the circle relative to the patient's chest.

Select Fills from the Attributes menu and choose the 100% (solid black) fill. Click OK to close the Fills dialog box. Then select Color from the Attributes menu and choose a bright blue. You might take note that you are choosing from the custom palette that you imported earlier. Click OK to close the Color dialog box.

Fills

Fills are based on a foreground and a background color. On grayscale and color monitors, a foreground and a background color of a fill pattern can be controlled. In the Fills dialog box, the solid black represents a solid foreground color. The solid white represents a solid background color. Objects with a fill pattern of none will be invisible. The point to remember is that you aren't picking the colors black or white when you select the solid black or white fill. If you want to draw a white object, the correct technique is to select the black fill and select white from the Color menu choice. If you simply select the white fill, the object will not always appear white.

Now place your newly created electrode in the Electrode Base of the electrocardiograph machine. Place it exactly in the center of the white space labeled Electrode Base. Figure 21.5 shows its position.

Select *electrode* and choose the Attributes pull-down menu and select Effects. When the Effects dialog box opens, select the Freely button in the Movable section. Close the Effects dialog box to continue.

Establishing relationships

Now it is a good idea to move the buttons to their final location on the screen, so that they are not in the way when you define targets. If you are beginning again after a break, open and close *background*. If you continued to this section immediately after importing the *background*, the image is in memory. All you have to do is hold down the shift key and double-click on *electrode*.

Then, while holding down the shift key, open the *place electrode* interaction icon's display. It will show the background with the contents of all the icons that you have created. Move the Record and Hint buttons to their final positions. Now select Jump to Icons from the Try It menu to resume authoring.

Set up error trapping

Now let's move on to define the targets for the response types. Once again you must ensure that you have the *background* and *electrode* in memory by opening and closing those icons while holding down the shift key to add the second to the first. Then scroll the *place electrode* interaction's names to the bottom to reveal the *error trap*

Figure 21.4 Circle Size Relative to the
Patient's Chest

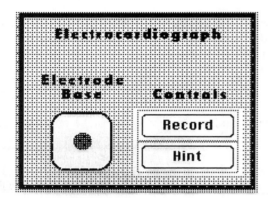

Figure 21.5 Initial Position for Electrode

animation icon. Double-click on the *error trap* icon's response type symbol (the small arrow) to open the Movable Object Options dialog box. You are prompted to associate an object with the target (the object that will move to the target). If your dialog box says "Drag object to the target position: electrode," ignore the instruction and click on the electrode anyway. The electrode, the object, may be hidden behind the Movable Object Options dialog box. If so, move the box as needed by clicking on its title bar and dragging it until you can see the electrode. Drop it there and click on the electrode. The *error trap* target, represented as a small dotted rectangle with an X in its center, located somewhere else on the screen, will center itself on the electrode.

 Authorware Tip: Opening the Movable Object Options dialog box can sometimes be confusing. The previously opened display will also open. In this case you had intentionally opened the electrode last. At other times, you may be surprised to see something you did not expect and cannot use.

Once the association has been made you can reposition the *error trap* target to its final position. As an error trap, it is a whole screen "net" that will catch all the learner's misplaced and stray placements. The error trap target must be extended to cover the screen by resizing in exactly the same way that you have previously repositioned and resized click/touch areas and the target areas in the truck lesson. One way to distinguish target areas when positioned on the same screen as click/touch areas is that the targets will have Xs in their centers.

Development Tip: The concept of error trap is important. You must always provide for the learner's unexpected response.

Leave the object destination drop-down list default of Leave at Destination. Soon you will set it up to Go Back to cause the movable object (the electrode, in this case) to return to the Electrode Base. In your lesson, when the learner makes a totally invalid placement of the electrode, such as halfway between the table and the patient, for example, the electrode will return to the electrode base. Figure 21.6 shows the screen after all the edits are complete.

Select OK-Edit Animation. The Animation Options dialog box will be displayed, for the default Fixed Destination animation type. This is the type you need.

The prompt in the dialog box says, "Drag display to destination." Carefully click on the electrode. You will see that the prompt doesn't change to provide you feedback. Beware that the Rate will reflect the duration of the time that you hold the mouse key down. Edit whatever is displayed in the Rate text field to 2. The Time will then be 2 seconds. Select OK to close the dialog box. Then use Control-J to jump to the icons.

Associate the Electrode with Targets

Now you are going to work your way to the left across the flowline as you make the associations. This will result in editing increasingly smaller targets. There are really

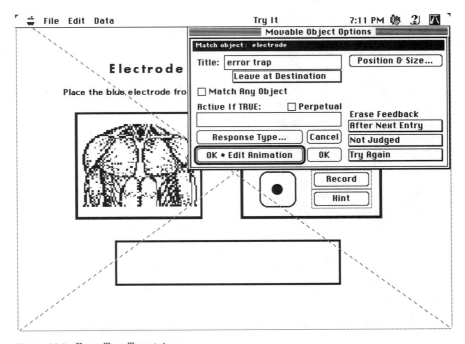

Figure 21.6 Error Trap Target Area

only two types of placements—right and wrong. The V_e location is small and located quite close to other valid positions. The issue here is that when you expect to record the V_e signal, no other will do. The *bad* target will represent all valid placements other than V_e.

Double-click the response type symbol above the *bad* calculation icon. You are again prompted to associate an object with the target. The electrode will be the object for all of the targets in this lesson. As before, it may be hidden behind the Movable Object Options dialog box. Move the dialog box and click on the electrode. The *bad* target will center itself on the electrode. Position the target as shown in Figure 21.7 and ensure that Leave at Destination is selected. In this case, the learner will have made a valid attempt to position the electrode, so you want to leave it in the spot the learner selected for judging.

Authorware Tip: Besides the targets being increasingly smaller, they are conceptually piled one on top of another. In this case, imagine the *bad* target as a piece of transparent plastic sitting on top of *error trap*, which is also a piece of transparent plastic sitting on top of the whole screen graphic. If you take a pen, for example, and attempt to touch the torso of the patient, you will always touch the *bad* target. It covers and "protects" the *error trap* from being touched in the torso area. When you go on to place the *good* target over the V_e location, it will cover and protect both the bad target and the *error trap* target from being activated within Authorware.

Close the dialog box to edit the next target. Double-click the response type symbol above the *good* calculation icon and associate the electrode with the target. After the target centers itself on the electrode, position it over location V_e as shown in Figure 21.8. The area extends from the V-shaped point of the sternum at the bottom

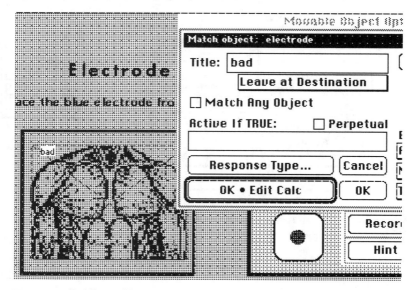

Figure 21.7 Bad Target Placement

Figure 21.8 Good Target Placement (Enlarged)

to the width of the sternum on both sides. The top is established by making the target square. Replace Leave at Destination with Snap to Center. This will provide positive reinforcement of the exact location by causing the electrode to be perfectly placed if the learner places it anywhere in the (small) target area. Close the dialog box to edit the final target.

The final target area serves yet another purpose. The home target area provides the learner with a spot not on the patient where the electrode can be successfully placed. If your learners move the electrode back to the Electrode Base, they essentially have the opportunity to try again. Double-click the response type symbol above the *home* calculation icon and associate the electrode with the target. After the target centers itself on the electrode, position it as shown in Figure 21.9 and select Snap to Center. Close the dialog box.

Judge the Electrode Placement

In this section you will enter expressions into the calculations that will be matched when the learner places the electrode into the associated target area. The values these expressions will hold will be used to provide the appropriate feedback to the learner when he or she selects the Record button.

Open the *home* calculation icon, and enter:

```
target = 0
-- Not a target
```

This expression signifies that the movable object is not in a judgeable position; thus no feedback on the electrode placement will be given. The comment will help you to remember that six months from now. Close the calculation window and give the variable target an initial value of zero (0). (Mac user select Numerical.) Enter:

```
Determines which EKG recording will be displayed
```

in the Description box.

Repeat this process for the remaining calculations, entering expressions as shown:

Calculation Icon	Expression	Documentation
home	`target = 0`	**-- Not a target**
good	`target = 1`	**-- Displays a good EKG recording**
bad	`target = 2`	**-- Displays a poor EKG recording**

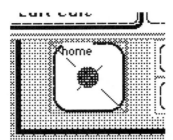

Figure 21.9 Home Target Placement

Finally, you will append the expressions shown below to the animation icon.

Animation Icon	Expression	Documentation
error trap	`target = 0`	**-- Not a target**

Select the *error trap* animation icon and then click on the Data pull-down menu to select Calculations. Enter the expression and its documentation.

Authorware Tip: You can enter the documentation on the same line as an expression. When Authorware reaches the two hyphens in a row, it knows that it should ignore the remainder of that line. When they are placed at the start of a line the whole line is ignored. Note that the next line is read afresh, so that more documentation will require its own two hyphens. Then select OK to close the calculation window.

Test drive

It is now time to run an initial test to see that the electrode performs as needed. Run the lesson and check to see the electrode's performance. Try moving it outside its base and dropping it back in the base to ensure that it snaps to the center of the base. Try dropping it anywhere on the screen other than on the patient's torso. It should return to the Electrode Base. Now drop it on the torso, away from the V_e location. It should remain where you drop it. Also, if you drop it on the V_e location it should remain there.

Now we can make clear why you used an animation icon for the error trap, instead of another calculation. If the error trap were built the same as *good, bad,* and *home* it would produce an undesirable effect that you can find in some Authorware lessons. What would occur is that, if the electrode were dropped into either the *good* or *bad* target areas and then moved again and dropped anywhere within the error trap target, it would be "Put Back." But it would be put back to the spot it was in previously, the *good* or *bad* target area, not back into its base. In effect, you are saying in the response type, "leave it at its destination." Then you use the animation icon's functionality to send it back to the proper source.

Display EKG Recordings

Next you want to provide a feedback mechanism for the learner to obtain reinforcement of the accuracy of his electrode placement. This will appear in the form of a representation of the paper recordings that EKG machines produce. When the learner selects the Record button, one of two representative recordings will animate in a window, with the appearance of being drawn or printed—like the real thing. Unlike the real thing, any bad recording will be represented by a blank strip. Learning to recognize a correct recording is a different and more difficult task that is not part of this lesson.

Open the *lesson* map icon at the Level 2 flowline, and then open the *Record* map and drag a decision icon to the flowline. Name it *target position*. Then drag two display icons to the Level 3 flowline. Label them: *good EKG* and *bad EKG*. These will both be waiting, out of the learner's sight, until one is revealed into view by the Record button.

You want to determine whether the learner has placed the electrode on the V_e position correctly. You will achieve this by reading a value that tells whether it is in the target area, and is used to determine which of the two displays to reveal.

Double-click the *target position* icon to open the decision icon dialog box. Click on the Calculated Path button under Branching. Enter

```
Target
```

in the text field. Select OK to close the dialog box.

After selecting *good EKG,* open the Attributes pull-down menu and select Effects. In the Effects dialog box, select the Effect Build to Right, and close the Effects dialog box. Repeat this process for *bad EKG*.

Next, open and close the *background* to place it into memory. Then, while holding down the shift key, import the graphics representing the recordings into each as follows:

Icon Name	Graphics File to be Imported
good EKG	**ekg_good.bmp**
bad EKG	**ekg_bad.bmp**

Carefully place each of the graphics in the feedback placeholder. They should fit perfectly.

Possibly one of the two graphics will "effect" into view. It will be better to *not* remain there when the learner makes a new electrode placement and records again. To make this clean, we want to erase the recording for a fresh start. The default of After Next Entry on the record button takes care of this. To complete the erase control process, double-click the *good EKG* display icon and change the default Erase Displayed Object from Before Next Selection to Don't Erase. This will result in the *good EKG* display remaining visible until some other interaction occurs on the *place electrode* interaction structure. Select OK to close the dialog box. Then repeat this procedure for *bad EKG*. Figure 21.10 shows the completed *Record* structure, as well as the *lesson* structure.

 Go With the Flow: Let's start at the detailed level and work our way out. The built-in erase effects for *good EKG* and *bad EKG* have been changed to Don't Erase. As a result, within Level 3, when the flow passes through the decision the

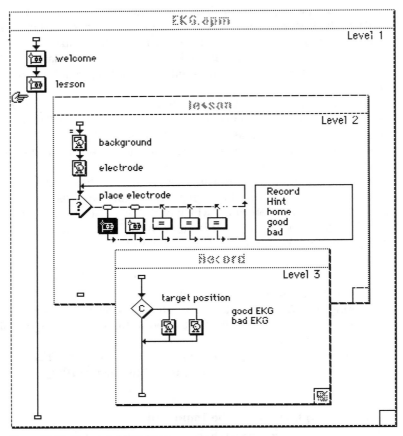

Figure 21.10 Completed Flowlines

displays will not be erased. However, when the flow falls out of the bottom of the Level 3 flowline it will return to its place in the *lesson* Level 2 flowline. It will fall out of the bottom of the *Record* map and around to the *place electrode* interaction. The erase features of the Record button (we are using the default erase setting of After Next Entry) take precedence over the Don't Erase in the nested decision structure and do erase the display whenever any of the associated icons are activated. In this case, you are using the best of built-in erase features to get exactly what you want.

Test Drive

The program is nearly complete. Take it out for a spin to see that it works as expected. If you have trouble, carefully review this chapter. You have probably missed a step.

Provide Help for Electrode Placement

It is always a good practice to provide context-sensitive help for the learner. In this case, you can help the learner see the best spot for V_e electrode placement by showing a view of it when the learner selects the Hint button.

Open the *background* and close it immediately. Then open the *Hint* map icon, drag a display to the flowline, and name it *exact location*. While holding down shift, open the display and import `ekg_hint.pct`. Place the hint graphic over the torso and close the presentation window.

Icon Name	Graphic to be Imported
exact location	`ekg_hint.pct`

Drag a wait icon below the *exact location* icon, open it, deactivate the default settings, and set the Time Limit to 3 seconds. Close the wait and close the map.

Finally, change the erase in the response type dialog box for *Hint* to Before Next Entry. The Before Next Entry selection will erase the exact location hint when the flow exits the map after three seconds.

Provide Feedback when Learner Misses Targets

Next you will set feedback to accompany the error trapping for unsatisfactory electrode placement. Previously, you created an animation icon for the error trapping called *error trap*. Now select *error trap* and use either the Control-G shortcut or Group under the Edit pull-down menu to group it, and *error trap* will become a map. Double-click the map icon to open it to Level 3.

Drag a display icon to the top of the flowline (above the animation icon). Name it *missed all targets*. This display will present a helpful message to the learner when he or she drops the electrode in a spot other than on the torso of the patient. Now open and close the *background* display icon. Then, while depressing the shift key, open the *missed all targets* display. Select the text tool and click in the recording placeholder. Type the following:

```
You must place the electrode on the correct location of the patient's torso by
dragging and releasing it when in the best position.
```

Then select the arrow tool, and use it to select Font and Style from the Text pull-down menu. Select a good-looking font, such as Arial, and give it the Bold style. The size we used is 10-point. You will have to limit your choices to a size that will fit the message within the recording placeholder. Figure 21.11 shows the screen with the text in place. When you are satisfied, close the display.

Provide Selective Access to Buttons

As it is, the program allows selection of Record or Hint at any time. Good instruction limits selections to relevant interactions. You can easily make changes that

File   Edit   Data   Libraries   Attributes   Text   Try It   7:21 PM

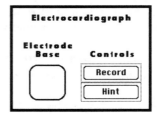

E l e c t r o d e   P l a c e m e n t   P r a c t i c e

Place the blue electrode from the electrocardiograph onto the V_e location

You must place the electrode on the
correct location of the patient's torso by
dragging and releasing it when in the best
position.

Figure 21.11   Error Trap Text Placement

will bring the EKG lesson into line with these ideas. To make this work, you will establish the condition under which each button will become active and available to the learner.

First, you will set the *Record* button to become active only when the learner drops the electrode on either the *good EKG* or *bad EKG* target area, to which you gave a value of Target=1 and Target=2 respectively.

Open the pushbutton response type symbol above the *Record* map and select the Active if True text field. Type:

```
target <> 0
```

The < and > keys are shift-comma and shift-period, respectively, on most keyboards. This expression will deactivate the *Record* button until the electrode has been placed in a valid target area. Select OK to close the *Record* Pushbutton Options dialog box.

Next, you will set the *Hint* button to become active only when the learner drops the electrode anywhere on the screen, other than the *good EKG* and *bad EKG* target areas, to which you gave a value of Target=1 and Target=2 respectively.

Now, open the pushbutton response type symbol above the *Hint* map. Select the Active if True text field and type:

```
target = 0
```

This expression will deactivate the Hint button once the electrode has been placed in a valid target area. Select OK to close the dialog box.

Provide the Quit Function

Right now, there is no way to escape from the lesson. Even the most studious EKG technician needs a break once in a while, so let's add the quit. You should be familiar with how to do this by now. If you want to try it on your own, skip to the Test Drive; otherwise read on.

Drag a calculation icon in between the *Record* and *Hint* icons. It will become a pushbutton because it assumes the characteristics of the icon to its left. Name it Quit and open it for editing. Type the quit function in directly as:

```
Quit(0)
```

and close the calculation box.

Test Drive

Your EKG practice lesson is finished! But before you round up a technician to try it, make sure that it functions perfectly. Run the lesson. Try each possible action, such as dropping the electrode on the floor, placing it poorly, and placing it perfectly. Check that the record feature works and that the proper recordings are shown when you make the poor and good placements. Look for the feedback when you drop the electrode on the floor. Try the Hint button and ensure that the hint graphic displays properly and disappears after 3 seconds. Finally, check that the Record is only available when the electrode has been placed on the patient, and that the Hint button is only available when the electrode is in its home position.

Troubleshooting

If you experience erase problems, such as the feedback does not properly erase, reread the section that describes creation of the Record structure.

If the recording just blinks on and off, look for the chosen effect (or lack thereof) in the *good EKG* and *bad EKG* display icons.

If the wrong recording is displayed, or the electrode does not "stick" to the patient, you may have misplaced the *home, good, bad,* and *error trap* target areas. The same symptom might be the result of having these icons in the wrong order on the interaction (reread Building the Lesson Structure).

Ideas for Expansion, Enhancement, and Evolution

Here are some ideas for use of this lesson in new ways:

Heartbeat

This lesson is a natural for expansion. You already know how to associate sound with your lessons. You could add location V_A and V_1 through V_7 to test the learner's ability to differentiate between each of them.

If you had recorded heart sounds you could use the recording in several ways. You could have the heart sound play when the recording animates. This would be a good exercise for you to practice programming, but we do not favor it because it is essentially a gratuitous bell and whistle. It does not add realism but creates *un*reality, since there is no sound that accompanies the EKG recording.

You could create a stethoscope to check the patient's heartbeat before placing the electrodes. This assumes that the current targets are valid. It would require additional graphics. You would replicate the *target position* structure, place sound where the animations are, and create a listen button on the *place electrode* interaction.

The whole scenario could be expanded to provide completely different diagnostic processes. For example, you could associate a whole variety of heart, lung, and bowel noises with hotspots located appropriately for each. The noises themselves could be assigned to separate patients, who have different conditions. The learner could be asked to suggest diagnoses based on the sounds heard.

EKG

The most obvious enhancement would be to create all the other electrodes and their proper placement areas.

You can provide text feedback on the placement of the electrode, telling the learner how accurate the placement is. This would be more direct than the current recording, because the learner may not recognize a good recording or may not know which way to move the electrode if it is in the wrong placement.

Customization

You could change the welcome page to welcome the learner instead of, or in addition to, claiming credit for building the lesson. If you collected the learner's name with your sign-on routine, and passed the variable holding that name (as you will do in Chapter 23) you could welcome the learner by name. It would be displayed in an embedded variable {UserName} on the screen.

Other

The whole idea of asking the learner to drag something to a specific new location is powerful. The technique works to assemble correct text, by dragging the right words to the correct blank spot. This also works for assembling a list of steps in the proper order. The learner can assemble equipment in the proper order as well as in the correct places.

We're Off in a Flash

Sound is a powerful tool and the easiest of the other media to employ in lessons. We hope you will consider using meaningful audio to support your efforts to help workers learn.

As we move on, you will tackle an area of Authorware authoring avoided by many developers—arrays. In the next chapter you will get a feel for their power by building a lesson that uses arrays. Let's address the chapter!

22

Flashcards

In this lesson you will develop a useful tool that you can immediately divert to any other topic. You will build a lesson that presents flashcards in just the way that a friendly helper would show them to you, or in the way that you would use paper flashcards to study facts about any topic.

In making the flashcard lesson you will use an array. This is an area of programming that many developers avoid, because they don't understand how to use the arrays. Authorware's array capability is not so daunting that you need to avoid it, so we lure you with a very interesting exercise as the basis for exploring it.

What You Will Learn in This Chapter

- How to use functions to display icons
- How to use arrays
- How to isolate icons from the primary flowline

Set Up the Lesson

Open a new file and call it *flshcard*. Open the File Setup dialog box to set default characteristics for the lesson. Deselect UserMenu Bar, Title Bar, and Overlay Menu Bar. Select VGA from the Presentation Window Size drop-down menu. Also, change the Background Color to black. The dialog box will look as in Figure 22.1. Now close the dialog box.

Next, you may want to edit a file we have supplied, called *flshtext.txt*. It *must* be in the same location as your new file *flshcard*. Its content is:

```
Who was the first U.S. President ?
George Washington
```

```
How many states are in the U.S.A. ?
50
What is the Capital of the U.S.A.?
Washington, DC
What is the largest state in the U.S.A.?
Alaska
How many Senators represent each state?
2
What is the smallest state in the U.S.A.?
Rhode Island
```

These will be the questions and answers that the flashcard lesson uses. The questions will be shown randomly and the learner can then choose to see the answers—exactly as with paper flashcards.

Development Tip: We have used a technique that is often used where information has a short shelf life. The content that is used by the program is stored externally, so that it can be edited or even replaced by another file of the same name, and still work. For example, species currently on the endangered species list may be changed as often as needed without editing the Authorware code. You can use this as a feature for lessons that you develop, that can have content updates done as a clerical activity by the lesson's sponsor. At a more advanced level, the contents of such a file (for example, stock prices) could be updated electronically.

Now let's create the overall structure for the *flshcard* lesson. Drag a display icon to the flowline and name it *background*. Then drag a calculation and name it *read external questions*. Finally, drag two maps to the flowline and name them *load array* and *flashcard controls*. That completes the basic structure, which looks like Figure 22.2.

Open the *background* icon and import the *flshback.pct* graphic into it. Position it nicely on the screen until it looks like Figure 22.3. Note that it has round graphical buttons on it that you will use with click/touch areas instead of Authorware buttons.

Now open the *read external questions* calculation. Go to the ReadExtFile function under the File Category (Data pull-down menu, Show Functions, File), read the Description, and Paste it into the calculation. It will be:

```
ReadExtFile("filename")
```

File Setup

Memory : 2,560K   File : 11K in 13 icons 6 variables

Title:
flshcard

Wait Button Title:
Continue

Content Search Path:

Presentation Window Size:
VGA
☐ User Menu Bar   ☐ Use VGA Palette
☐ Title Bar   ☐ Desktop Pattern

Background Color...
Chroma Key...

When User Returns:
◉ Restart at Beginning   ○ Resume

OK   Cancel

Figure 22.1 File Setup

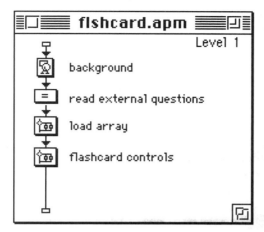

Figure 22.2 Level 1 Flowline

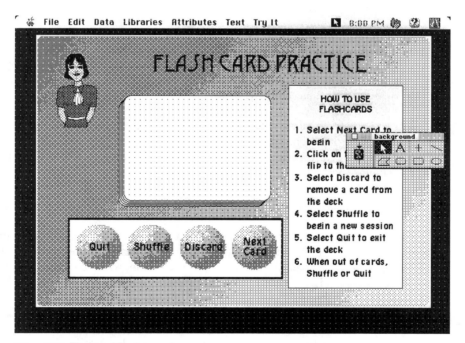

Figure 22.3 Flashcard Background

This function will read an external file—in this case, the questions. Your next step is to create a custom variable to hold the contents of the external file. You want to store the function's value in a custom variable called cardtext. Insert:

```
cardtext =
```

before the ReadExtFile. Then insert:

```
FileLocation^
```

before "filename" to tell Authorware to look for the file in the same location as the lesson. Finally, replace "filename" with:

```
flshtext.txt
```

When you have finished, the argument will be:

```
cardtext = ReadExtFile(FileLocation^"flshtext.txt")
```

Next, enter a comment to document the purpose of this calculation; on the next line type:

```
-- reads in the contents of flshtext.txt
```

The total entry will be:

```
cardtext = ReadExtFile(FileLocation^"flshtext.txt")
-- reads in the contents of flshtext.txt
```

When you have finished, close the calculation. When you are prompted for the initial value of cardtext character variable, enter "". (Mac users select text type.) Before closing the New Variable dialog box, enter documentation of its purpose with words similar to:

```
stores contents of flshtext.txt file for use
```

This is not duplicate documentation. You will refer to the comments in calculations at separate times and for different reasons than the descriptions in custom variables. One describes the purpose of the variable, while the other explains what the function does. Don't shortchange yourself on documentation!

Working with Arrays

Open the *load array* map. Drag a decision icon to the flowline and name it *count address*. Then drag a calculation to associate with *count address* and name it *address data in array*. Open the decision icon. First, change the Don't Repeat default to Until True and enter the following in the Repeat Until TRUE field:

```
RepCount >= LineCount(cardtext)
```

(Mac users will note, upon reopening the decision icon after closing, that Authorware will convert the >= to ≥. Both representations are read "greater than or equal to" and have the same meaning as each other.) Figure 22.4 shows the finished decision dialog box. Close the decision dialog box by selecting OK.

At this point *count address* should be selected. If not, select but don't open it, and select Calculations under the Data pull-down menu. Type the following into the calculation window:

```
loop_number = loop_number + 1
```

add the documentation comment:

```
-- increments the value of the variable loop_number
-- as the file is loaded into the array
```

Close the window. When you are asked for the initial value of loop_number, enter a 0 (zero) as its numeric value (Mac users, accept the Numeric default).

```
holds the number of times the loop is repeated
```

When closed, the *load array* map structure will appear as shown in Figure 22.5.

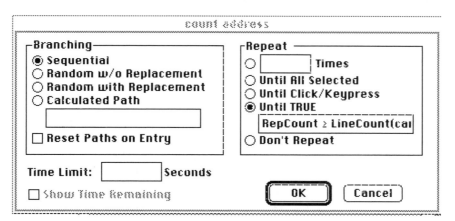

Figure 22.4 Count Address Decision Dialog Box

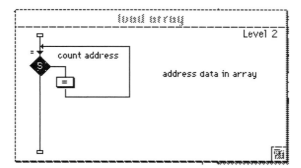

Figure 22.5 Load Array Structure

Open the *address data in array* calculation icon. The array will hold the contents of the text file. Each line of the text file will be an individual address in the array. By doing this, and because the first line holds a question and questions and answers alternate, you will end with an array with odd-numbered addresses as questions, and even-numbered answers.

Arrays

An array is an arrangement of data, usually in rows and columns. Authorware enables you to store and retrieve data by a reference number. An application can have only one array of up to 2,500 data items. Values written in an array can have more than one item, through the use of concatenation of multiple items into a string.

Now, you will create an expression that will assign the individual lines (that were originally in the *flshtext.txt* file and would have been loaded into the variable cardtext) into individual addresses in the Authorware array. Find the ArraySet function under the Math Category (Data pull-down menu, Show Function, Math), read the Description, and Paste it into the calculation. It will be:

```
ArraySet(n,value)
```

Replace n by typing:

```
loop_number
```

The loop_number becomes the array address. Next, you will replace the value at the address that loop_number represents. To do this, highlight "value" and, after reading the Description, replace it by pasting the GetLine function (found under the Character category). After you complete this action, you will have:

```
ArraySet(loop_number,GetLine(string,n [,m,delim]))
```

Delete the optional arguments [,m,delim]. Then replace "string" with:

```
cardtext
```

and replace "n" with:

```
loop_number
```

When you finish the expression will be:

```
ArraySet(loop_number,GetLine(cardtext,loop_number))
```

This completed expression will assign each line of text that originated in the *flsh-text.txt* file into an equivalent address within the Authorware array. So, line 1 of cardtext can be accessed in address 1 in the array. Likewise, line 100 of some other original source could be found in address 100 of its matching array.

Document the meaning of this expression as:

```
-- each individual line is read from cardtext
-- and stored in an array address
```

The completed entries are:

```
ArraySet(loop_number,GetLine(cardtext,loop_number))
-- each individual line is read from cardtext
-- and stored in an array address
```

Close the calculation and move on to the portion of the lesson where the flash-cards are controlled.

Controlling the Flashcards

Open *flashcard controls* to create the heart of the interface. This portion of the program will present a card with controls that dictate what will be displayed on the card. There will be questions and answers on the "flip" side of the card, the ability to put cards aside once their content is mastered, the ability to restore the full deck of cards, and a quit option.

Drag four display icons to the flowline. Each of these will hold a button that is individually selectable to control the flashcards. Because each is a clickable object that inverses when clicked, the learner will get solid feedback that a button has been pressed. Name the display icons *quit button*, *shuffle button*, *discard button*, and *next card button*. You could place the graphics into the displays by opening and closing *background* and then opening each display. Instead, you can automate the process by simply running the program. Select Run from the pull-down menu. The flow will display the background and fall as far as the first empty display icon—*quit button*. The program will pause and open the display for editing. Your indication that this has happened is the appearance of the *quit button* toolbox. Just go ahead and load the *flshquit.pct* graphic, using Import Graphic. Carefully place it over that button on the background and click in the toolbox close button. The program flow will continue, but only as far as the next icon, *shuffle button*, and will invite you to place its content. Continue as before for this and the remaining buttons. The correct files are:

File Name	Icon
flshquit.pct	*quit button*
flshshuf.pct	*shuffle button*
flshdisc.pct	*discard button*
flshnxcd.pct	*next card button*

Use Control-J or select Jump to Icons from the Try It pull-down menu after Control-spacebar to reveal the menu bar to return to the icons (Command-J and spacebar-slash, respectively, on the Mac).

Now drag an interaction icon to the flowline and name it *present flashcard*. Next drag a map icon to associate with *present flashcard*. When asked to confirm the response type, change it to Click/Touch and select OK to close the dialog box. Name the map *card stack*. Now double-click the Click/Touch response type symbol to open the Click/Touch Options dialog box. Select the Use Custom (Custom Cursor on the Mac) check box. Select Load Cursor (click on the cursor icon on the Mac) and then select the *hand.cur* cursor (move to the directory that holds Authorware, if it does not open there) and load the *hand.cur* file. Now, move the dialog box out of the way of the cards on the background. If you have been following along, you have the background showing. (If your background is black, you can restore everything to memory by Running the program again, and using Control-J to jump to the icons before double-clicking the Click/Touch response type symbol.)

In the Active if True field enter:

```
random_array_address <> 0
```

This variable, as used here, will deactivate the click/touch area when you first enter the program and after shuffling the deck. This makes the flip card idea function, by limiting it to when a card is in condition to be flipped.

Next, reposition and resize the click/touch area to cover the top card on the deck of cards on the background. Figure 22.6 shows the completed changes.

Select OK to close the Click/Touch Options dialog box. When prompted for the initial value of random_array_address, enter 0. (Mac users approve default Numerical.) Under the Description, enter:

```
contains a random question number generated whenever next card is selected
```

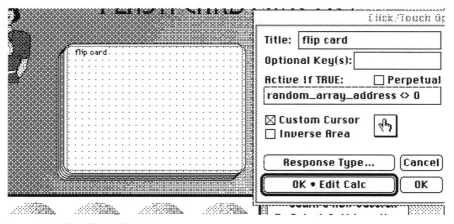

Figure 22.6 Click/Touch Settings

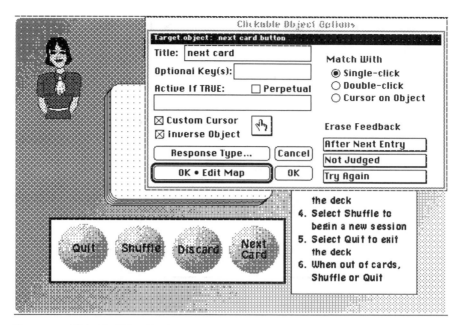

Figure 22.7 Clickable Object Settings

Now drag a map icon to the right of the *card stack* calculation icon and name it *next card*. Double-click on the response type symbol above *next card*, and when it opens select the Response Type button to change the response type to Clickable Object, and select OK to close the Response Type options dialog box and open the Clickable Object Options dialog box. Select the Use Custom (Custom Cursor on the Mac) and Inverse Object checkboxes. Select Load Cursor (click on the cursor icon on the Mac), and then select the *hand.cur* cursor and load the *hand.cur* file.

That completes changes in the Clickable Object Options dialog box, but before closing it, click on the target object as requested by the prompt line to exactly associate the Next Card button as the active object. Figure 22.7 shows the completed changes. Select OK to close the Clickable Object Options dialog box.

Then drag three calculations to the right of *next card* and name them *discard*, *shuffle*, and *quit*. Now drag two display icons below the interaction. They will resume the interrupted flowline without any connection to the present flashcard interaction structure immediately above them. Name them *question card* and *answer card*. When you finish, *flashcard controls* will look like Figure 22.8.

Go with the Flow: Now consider a flowline where there is no flowline. The icons at the bottom of the screen are useful even though they are not attached to the rest of the flowline. We're sure that you can perceive that the flow can never reach them because of their separation. This is a useful technique that you will use often as you create your own programs. You will never want to "jump" to the displays—you will access them by using them in functions. If you have a large number, we suggest

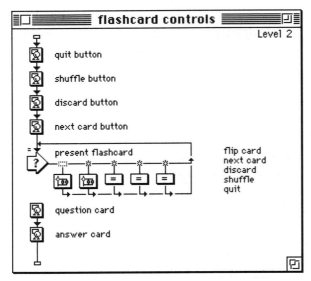

Figure 22.8 Flashcard Controls Structure

hanging them on a decision icon for convenience in viewing, and to spread them laterally rather than vertically. A programmer in our group calls them "storage lockers."

Finish the clickable object associations

The associations for the final three calculations have not yet been made. All you have to do is make the association requested by the prompt line of each by clicking on the object to associate. To do this, Run the program. It will follow the flowline until it reaches the first calculation without an associated clickable object, *discard*. The Clickable Object Options dialog box will appear with all the conditions that you established for *next card*. In the Active if True field enter:

```
random_array_address <> 0
```

In a way similar to your use of it in *card stack*, this variable will deactivate the clickable object when you first enter the program and after shuffling the deck. This makes the discard idea function, by limiting it to when a card is available to be discarded.

The prompt at the top of the dialog box is inviting you to click on the correct object. Simply click once on the Discard button and then select OK to approve your choice and close the dialog box. The next calculation without an associated clickable object will open, *shuffle*. Follow the same steps for shuffle and for *quit*. (Remember, if you select the wrong object you will be warned by its name on the prompt line. If this happens, just click on the correct object to replace it.) When you have closed the *quit* Clickable Object Options dialog box, do a Control-J to return to the icons.

Complete cards

Now you can make the cards completely functional by placing the proper graphics, embedding a variable, and selecting a draw effect. While holding down the shift key to retain the background in memory, double-click *question card* to open it and import the graphic *flshques.pct*. Place it inside the top card in the stack in the background. You must embed a variable to display the content of the various cards. Select the text tool and click on a spot near the upper left of the card. Modify the line length to conform to the card. Type:

```
{display_text}
```

Confirm selection of a pleasing font and size for the variable. Select the Centered Justification and Transparent Mode. The variable will display the updated contents of the display_text variable. When you finish, the completed embedded variable placement will look similar to Figure 22.9. When Authorware demands the initial value of display_text (Mac users select Text), enter :

```
Select Next Card button to begin.
```

and enter:

```
displays contents of card
```

as the Description.

Before closing, select Effects from the Attributes pull-down menu, and change the default display Effect to Build Up (Zoom from Line on Macs). Select OK to leave the

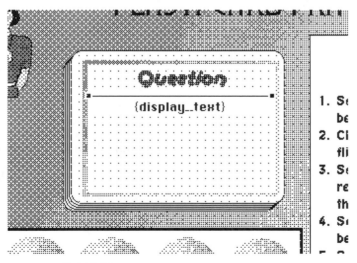

Figure 22.9 Variable Placement

Effects dialog box and select the toolbox close button to close the display. Now, while holding the shift key down, open *answer card* and import *flshansr.pct*. Carefully position the answer card graphic so that the borders of the two cards align exactly. The opposite colorization is to present the impression that the card is flipped over. Close the *answer card* display.

You will often want to place text or objects in identical locations on different displays. Use that technique here. Now open the *question card* icon (no need to hold down the shift key as you don't need the background). Use the arrow tool to select only the variable text. Copy the text to the computer's clipboard by using Control-C or Copy from the Edit pull-down menu, and close the display. Now open the *answer card* icon and immediately, without clicking anywhere on the screen, paste the contents of the computer's clipboard by Control-V or Paste from the Edit pull-down menu. A benefit of this technique is that all of the text's attributes, such as the font, size, mode, and justification, are brought with the text. Text color will also come along, an advantage in the event you had selected a color other than black. Before closing, select Effects from the Attributes pull-down menu and change the default display Effect to Build Up (Zoom from Line on Macs). Select OK to leave the Effects dialog box and close the *answer card* display. The cards are now complete, even though they are not yet functional.

Display effects

Next, to set the erase for the displays, you will establish an erase icon to erase each with the opposite effect from its draw effect. Open and close the question card display. Then, while holding down the shift key, open the answer card display to place both in memory. Double-click on the card stack map to reveal the Level 3 flowline. Drag an erase icon below *flip card* and name it *erase cards*. Open *erase cards* and the cards will be displayed. Click on each to associate them with the erase. Then select the Remove Down Effect (Zoom to Line on Macs). Figure 22.10 shows the completed changes. Select OK to close.

Make cards functional

In order to make Authorware get the card images at the right moment to display the questions and answers, you will append some expressions to the interaction that contains the controlling buttons. Which card is displayed depends on the address of the array that is used. Remember, all the odd addresses in the array are the questions.

Select the *present flashcard* interaction; then, under the Data pull-down menu, select Calculations to open the calculation for editing. When the flowline hits this calculation, the first thing you want it to do is to clear whichever card is displayed, in preparation for showing the appropriate card. To make this happen, get the Erase-Icon function from the General category, under Show Functions in the Data pull-down menu. Paste it into the calculation. It will read:

```
EraseIcon(IconID@"IconTitle")
```

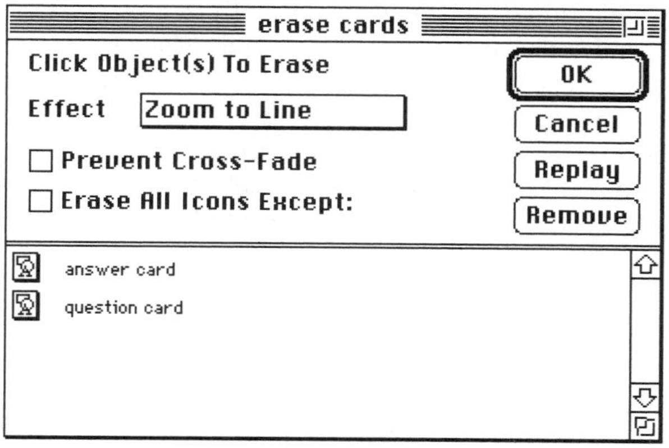

Figure 22.10 Erase Cards

Even though the Functions dialog box has closed, the EraseIcon function is still in your computer's clipboard. Strike the return key to move to a new line and paste from the clipboard, using Control-V, or Paste from the Edit pull-down menu. You will now have:

```
EraseIcon(IconID@"IconTitle")
EraseIcon(IconID@"IconTitle")
```

On the first line, select "IconTitle" and replace it with "question card." On the second line, select "IconTitle" and replace it with "answer card." Add a line of documentation, such as:

```
-- Erases both the question and answer cards
-- before displaying a new card
```

The result will be:

```
EraseIcon(IconID@"question card")
EraseIcon(IconID@"answer card")
-- Erases both the question and answer cards
-- before displaying a new card
```

Next, press the return key twice to insert a blank line before continuing. You will place an IF statement here to display the appropriate type card and content appropriate with the learner's choice of discard, flip card, or next card.

Now paste the IF function into the calculation. (IF under General in Show Functions, under the Data pull-down menu.) It will be:

```
IF(condition,TRUE expression,FALSE expression)
```

First you will set the condition to determine whether the address of the array is odd or even (remember, the questions are in the odd lines). You will use the Math function MOD to determine if the array address is even or odd. MOD returns the remainder of one number divided by another, and since there will only be a remainder when you divide an odd number by 2, you can use it for your purpose. Select condition and get MOD from the Data pull-down menu, Show Functions selection, Math category, and after reading the Description, paste it to replace the selected text. The result will be:

```
IF(MOD(x,y),TRUE expression,FALSE expression)
```

It will be (MOD(x,base) on Macs. The x will be the custom variable called random_array_address. Its value will be generated each time the learner selects the Next Card button. Replace x with random_array_address. The y (base on Macs) is the 2 that you are dividing by. Replace y with 2. Finally, after the close parenthesis that follows the y, you will establish the needed comparison to determine whether the condition is true or false. You will compare the remainder to 0 (zero), so add <>0. The result will be:

```
IF(MOD(random_array_address,2)<>0,TRUE expression,FALSE expression)
```

As it is, the lesson would start and display the initial message to the learner on the answer card. This looks awkward, so you can avoid the problem by making an exception to the condition you just established that will display the answer card whenever the value of random_array_address is an even number. You will add a second condition to display the question card whenever the value of random_array_address is zero.

To enter the second condition, you will have to use the *or* character (|). It can be found on most keyboards as the "uppercase" character on the backslash key. It may look like a straight line or like two small lines one above the other. Now type the | immediately after the zero in the expression. Then continue to type

```
(random_array_address=0)
```

immediately after the |.

Note to Our Reader

We finally have come to an argument that is just too long to print on one line of this book. This book uses the special character ⌐ to indicate that the end of the line is really artificial and that you must treat it as one line. DO NOT ATTEMPT TO TYPE THESE CHARACTERS. YOU MUST TYPE A SINGLE LINE. If you want to see it on one line for comparison, open the sample flshcard.apw (flshcard.apm for Mac users)file on your CD.

The result will be:

```
IF(MOD(random_array_address,2)<>0|(random_array_address=0),⌐
TRUE expression,FALSE expression)
```

The true and false expressions will indicate which card to display, so you will replace the TRUE expression, FALSE expression part of the IF statement with a DisplayIcon function. Select TRUE expression and get DisplayIcon (Data pull-down menu, Show Functions selection, General category). Paste it to replace TRUE expression. Then use the same technique as you did previously to paste multiple functions, by selecting FALSE expression and selecting paste again. The result will be:

```
IF(MOD(random_array_address,2)<>0|(random_array_address=0),¬
DisplayIcon(IconID@"IconTitle"),DisplayIcon(IconID@"IconTitle"))
```

Replace the true expression's "IconTitle" with "question card," and the false expression's "IconTitle" with "answer card."

```
IF(MOD(random_array_address,2)<>0|(random_array_address=0),¬
DisplayIcon(IconID@"question card"),DisplayIcon(IconID@"answer card"))
```

Place your cursor on the next line and enter the documentation for this expression. Enter something like:

```
-- Determines whether random_array_address is odd
-- Displays question card if true or answer card if false
```

The final result of all this editing will be:

```
IF(MOD(random_array_address,2)<>0|(random_array_address=0),¬
DisplayIcon(IconID@"question card"),DisplayIcon(IconID@"answer card"))
-- Determines whether random_array_address is odd
-- Displays question card if true or answer card if false
```

Close the calculation.

Program next card

Open the *next card* map and place a calculation icon inside it. Name the new calculation *get next card*. The next card structure is shown in Figure 22.11.

 Go with the Flow: You may wonder why we have placed one calculation alone inside a map, when there are three others setting plainly on the same interaction. Basically, it is a question of the GoTo statement saying GoTo myself. There will be a GoTo inside the calculation that jumps to *next card*. You have to create a different icon so that the GoTo goes somewhere (else).

Now you will instruct Authorware to pick a question at random from the array. Double-click *get next card* to open it for editing. Start by typing `random_array _address =` and then paste the Random function to its right (It is a Math function). The result will be:

```
random_array_address = Random(min,max,units)
```

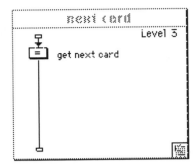

Figure 22.11 Next Card Map

Remember that the array holds the questions in odd-numbered lines. You want to access the odd-numbered lines between 1 and the end of the array. Therefore, set min to 1, then select max to highlight it. After reading the description, Paste the LineCount function, from the Character Category, to replace max. Your expression will look like:

```
random_array_address = Random(1,LineCount(string,delim),units)
```

Mac users will not get the optional delimiter. PC users, delete the comma and delim to leave (string). The string is cardtext, the text read from the external text file. Replace the word string in the expression with cardtext. Place =1 between the close parenthesis and the comma. Finally, the units we want is 2 so that, starting with 1, we will access only the odd numbered lines (e.g., 1 + 2 = 3). The completed expression is:

```
random_array_address = Random(1,LineCount(cardtext)+1,2)
```

On the next line, you will create a variable to temporarily hold the array address for the current question. This is quite straightforward. You just give the new variable, question address, the value of random_array_address. Simply type:

```
question_address = random_array_address
```

Because each new flashcard starts with a question, you will set the display text equal to the current value of the random_array_address variable. The display text variable that you embedded in the interaction's display will do the work, so start by typing on a new line:

```
display_text =
```

Then paste the ArrayGet function from the Math Category after the equals sign. The result will be:

```
display_text = ArrayGet(n)
```

To finish this expression you must tell the system what array address to display. Replace the n with the random_array_address variable that you created at the beginning of this calculation (we suggest that you copy it and paste it—one way to avoid typos). The completed expression is:

```
display_text = ArrayGet(random_array_address)
```

The next three lines work together with the discard calculation. They deal with discarding cards that the learner feels are mastered, and not allowing the user to flip the cards when there is no logical reverse side (for example, when there are no more cards). These statements look to see how many cards have been discarded. When all the cards have been discarded, the learner will be asked to Quit or Shuffle. To start this, paste an IF statement from the General Category. It is:

```
IF(condition,TRUE expression,FALSE expression)
```

Delete the FALSE expression along with its comma, as it is not needed in this case. You will create a new variable called discard. Its value is the number of cards that the learner has discarded. At this point, you are looking for the condition when the number of cards discarded is greater than or equal to the total number of questions in the array. Select condition and type discard >= (LineCount (cardtext) /2). Remember, you have recently pasted LineCount. The result will be:

```
IF(discard>=(LineCount(cardtext)/2),TRUE expression)
```

Now you can complete this expression by typing the message that will be displayed if and when the cards are exhausted. Select the TRUE expression and type:

```
display_text = "Out of cards. Shuffle or Quit"
```

At this point your work should look like this (except that all arguments must be on only one line).

```
random_array_address = Random(1,LineCount(cardtext)+1,2)
question_address = random_array_address
display_text = ArrayGet(random_array_address)
IF(discard >= (LineCount(cardtext)/2), display_text = "Out of cards. Shuffle or
¬  Quit.")
```

Copy the IF statement and paste it below itself twice. Now you can complete the second IF by editing instead of working from scratch. All you have to do is select the entire TRUE expression (display_text = "Out of cards. Shuffle or Quit."). Replace it with: random_array_address=0). The completed line will be:

```
IF(discard >= (LineCount(cardtext)/2), random_array_address=0)
```

You can also complete the third IF by editing instead of working from scratch. All you have to do is select the entire TRUE expression (`display_text = "Out of cards. Shuffle or Quit."`). Replace it with `GoTo(IconID@"present flashcard")`. The completed line will be:

```
IF(discard >= (LineCount(cardtext)/2), GoTo(IconID@"present flashcard"))
```

You are down to the last line in the calculation. It checks for a blank value in the array address. If the value is blank it looks for another address to try to display a card. Remember the IF format is:

```
IF(condition,TRUE expression,FALSE expression)
```

You will not need a FALSE expression. Modify the condition to be: display_text = "". You have done a large number of GoTo functions already. At this point you may want to just type it. Otherwise, paste it from the Jump Category. If you elect to type, enter: GoTo(IconID@"next card"). The completed expression is:

```
IF(display_text = "", GoTo(IconID@"next card"))
```

You have completed the *get next card* calculation. Check your entries against the sample below, and when you are ready, close the calculation.

```
random_array_address = Random(1,LineCount(cardtext),2)
question_address = random_array_address
display_text = ArrayGet(random_array_address)
IF(discard >= (LineCount(cardtext)/2), display_text = "Out of cards. Shuffle or
  Quit.")
IF(discard >= (LineCount(cardtext)/2), random_array_address=0)
IF(discard >= (LineCount(cardtext)/2), GoTo(IconID@"present flashcard"))
IF(display_text = "", GoTo(IconID@"next card"))
```

You will be asked for initial values. The custom variable random_array_address already has been initialized. Here are the proper ones for the others:

Variable name	Type	Initial value	Description
question_address	numerical	0	holds the array address of the current question
discard	numerical	0	contains the number of discarded cards

Troubleshooting

 Any time you type or edit text you can introduce errors. That is one reason why we continue to paste functions that are well known to us. Problems that may present themselves when you attempt to close the calculation include:

- Misspelled icon titles that are given to be jumped to will produce the message, "The icon (the bad name here) does not exist."

- If you do not have the correct number of parentheses, Authorware may report that an argument in a function is missing, or give the more straightforward, "A right parenthesis ')' is missing here."

- If you insert an extra space, you may see messages such as, "The icon title is reserved, and may not be referenced."

- If you are asked to provide initial values for variables other than those you anticipate, this may result from misspelling the name of a variable.

Program flip card expressions

Next open the *card stack* map icon. Drag a calculation to the Level 3 flowline and name it *flip card*. Double-click on *flip card* to open it for editing. You will create two IF statements so that, when the learner clicks on either a question or an answer, the display will "flip" to the other one. You have greater complexity than might have been the case because you permit the learner to flip back and forth between the front and back of a card as many times as he or she chooses. Start with the familiar IF structure:

```
IF(condition,TRUE expression,FALSE expression)
```

This time you will need the FALSE expression. The condition checks to see whether the learner has flipped the card. To do this it compares the value of the currently selected, odd-numbered line in the array (which remains constant for as long as that card is in use) with another value that would have changed if the learner had flipped the card. Type:

```
random_array_address = question_address
```

to replace the condition. If the condition is TRUE, the TRUE expression will flip the card. To do this, the embedded variable display_text displays the contents of the next higher line from the array. You can type it in. Replace TRUE expression with

```
display_text = ArrayGet(random_array_address+1)
```

At this point the partially completed expression is:

```
IF(random_array_address = question_address,display_text = ArrayGet
  (random_array_address+1),FALSE expression)
```

To complete the expression you must enter the FALSE expression. In this case, if the card has been flipped to the answer, it will redisplay the question. The FALSE expression is exactly like the TRUE expression, except that the plus sign becomes a minus sign. Copy the TRUE expression and paste it in the FALSE expression location. Don't forget to change the +1 to –1. This completes the first expression. Check it carefully against the following example to make sure your work is accurate.

```
IF(random_array_address = question_address,display_text = ¬
 ArrayGet(random_array_address+1),display_text = ¬
 ArrayGet(random_array_address-1))
```

The second expression changes the number stored in random_array_address so that later you will be able to tell whether you have displayed the question or the answer. Fortunately, the second expression is almost like the first. Copy the first expression and paste it on a new line directly below itself.

If (because the learner has clicked the card when the question was displayed) the previous expression changed the display to the answer, this expression updates the variable to record the change. Select the TRUE expression portion of the expression. It is display_text = ArrayGet (random_array_address+1). Enter

```
random_array_address = random_array_address+1
```

The FALSE expression is identical except that +1 becomes –1. Copy the TRUE expression and paste it, replacing the FALSE expression portion of the IF statement. Then change the +1 to –1. Compare your work to the following example. *Remember, the special character is only an indicator not to start a new line.*

```
IF(random_array_address = question_address,display_text = ¬
 ArrayGet(random_array_address+1),display_text = ¬
 ArrayGet(random_array_address-1))
IF(random_array_address = question_address,random_array_address = ¬
 random_array_address+1,random_array_address = ¬
 random_array_address-1)
```

You have finished the *flip card* calculation. Close the calculation window. There are no new variables so it will close without further ado.

Program discard expressions

Now open *discard* for editing. As the name suggests, this calculation activates when the learner clicks on the discard hotspot. The three expressions will deal with this whether the question or answer is displayed. It also keeps track of how many cards have been removed.

The first expression is the one that keeps track of how many cards have been discarded. Type it in:

```
discard = discard + 1
```

In the next expression, an IF statement checks to see whether the card has been flipped and, determining the correct line in the array, discards the question by replacing its line in the array with a blank. We hope you like to avoid typing as much as we do. If so, go to the first IF statement in the *flip card* calculation. It is:

```
IF(random_array_address = question_address,display_text = ¬
 ArrayGet(random_array_address+1),display_text = ¬
 ArrayGet(random_array_address-1))
```

Copy this IF statement and paste it into the *discard* calculation. The condition is correct as it is. In the TRUE expression, delete `display_text =`. Change the **G** in ArrayGet to an **S** to make ArraySet. Then delete the +1 and enter a comma and two quotation marks. The TRUE expression will now read:

```
ArraySet(random_array_address,"")
```

Similarly, the FALSE expression can be changed by editing. Delete `display_text =` and change the **G** in ArrayGet to an **S** to make ArraySet. Leave the −1 as it is and add a comma and two quotation marks after it. The complete FALSE expression is:

```
ArraySet((random_array_address-1),"")
```

Your in-progress set of *discard* expressions should look like the example below:

```
discard := discard + 1
IF(random_array_address = question_address, ¬
 ArraySet(random_array_address,""), ¬
 ArraySet((random_array_address-1),""))
```

The last line deals with the situation wherein a question has just been deleted. A new card must be displayed. What has happened is that the contents of the line in the array have been deleted, so you must jump to the portion of the program that gets a card. Type:

```
GoTo(IconID@"next card")
```

That completes the *discard* calculation. Check your work against the sample below:

```
discard := discard + 1
IF(random_array_address = question_address, ¬
 ArraySet(random_array_address,""), ¬
 ArraySet((random_array_address-1),""))
GoTo(IconID@"next card")
```

When you are satisfied with the calculation, close it. There are no new variables so it will close directly. Now, move on to the shuffle of the deck.

Program shuffle expressions

When the learner has discarded the entire deck, no cards can be displayed. The only recourse at that point is to shuffle the deck (to restore all the cards) or to quit. The program also makes provision for the learner to shuffle at any time. The learner might want to do this if an unlearned card is mistakenly discarded.

Open the *shuffle* calculation for editing. There are four expressions. The first three restore initial values to variables and the final one jumps to a spot where questions are loaded into the array. They are so simple that you can enter them all directly. Type:

```
random_array_address=0 -- to deactivate flip card and discard
loop_number = 0
discard = 0
display_text = "Select Next Card button to begin"
-- First 4 lines restore variables to initial values
GoTo(IconID@"load array") -- reload the array with the full question set
```

When you have entered the expressions, check them carefully to see that they match the example and close the calculation. It will close directly since there are no new variables.

Program quit expressions

Finally, open the quit calculation. Type the Quit function into it with the zero option to permit your learner to exit the lesson. The exact line is:

```
Quit(0)
```

Close the calculation window.

Test Drive

Finally you can give the lesson a spin. Try every combination of next card, shuffle, and discard that you can imagine.

Troubleshooting

After starting and choosing Next Card you could get the message, "Out of cards. Shuffle or Quit." If so, you have not placed the text file in the same directory as the flashcard lesson. Bring them together and the problem will disappear.

You may see that the buttons jiggle slightly as if settling into place when the lesson starts up. This is because it is quite difficult to place them perfectly, although you will likely come within a pixel or two. You can perfectly align the buttons by repeatedly running the lesson and watching the movement of a single button, selecting that button, and using the keyboard arrow keys to move the button one pixel in the direction opposite that in which it was moving. When that button does not move on startup, move on to the next button.

We would like to remind you of more extensive troubleshooting ideas for your use at this point. To make them more centrally available we placed them in Chapter 16, "Troubleshooting." If you find that your lesson does not work as advertised, we suggest that you read the section titled *Using Displayed Variables to Track Functionality* in Chapter 16 to explore how you can solidify what is happening in your program.

Also, you can make an icon-by-icon comparison with the sample lesson *flsh-card.apw,* as well as running it to be sure how it is supposed to work.

Ideas for Expansion, Enhancement, and Evolution

Here are some ideas for use of this lesson in new ways:

- The most obvious idea is to greatly expand the citizenship-type questions that are in the text file. The limit of the array is 2,500 data items, so you can have up to 1,250 sets of questions and answers.

- The next most obvious idea is to substitute an entirely different set of questions and answers on any topic of your own choosing. By doing this, you can put the lesson to immediate use at home or at work by providing drill and practice on any subject.

- Present a fixed number of cards, offer a choice of answers on screen, and report the number right out of the total.

- As above, display the score on screen as the "Best Score" and retain it when a new turn is started.

- Allow competition between two learners. Collect and display the names of each, along with the running score as each gets answers right or wrong.

- You could have the system read the content of each card, using techniques covered in Chapter 18.

Here are some ideas for the evolution of the lesson:

- We had an objective of making the structure and controlling code the same for both PC and Macintosh—something that would be a must if you were developing on one platform for later delivery on both. This lesson includes a large number of small compromises forced by differences in the way Authorware works on the two platforms. If we were to simply develop the lesson on either of the platforms, the structure and code would be different. Considering this, depending on which platform you use, you might want to consider looking at the program to find ways to optimize it for your platform.

How Can We Bring This Curriculum Together? A CMI System!

You now have quite an array (pardon the pun) of lessons. There's a mouse practice to make sure the learner is ready, a sign-on to capture the learner's name, an ADA compliant reader, and flashcards. You have a set of lessons, including lessons on crane signals, mixing concrete, distributing weight on a tractor trailer, and placing EKG electrodes.

Wouldn't it be great if you could build a CMI system to deliver pre- and post-tests to the learner, make instructional assignments based on the learner's mastery of objectives, print a diploma, and store records of everything that happened? We think so. So we've arranged for you to create all that in the next chapter! Yes, all within 50 icons. Let's go tie everything together.

23

A Training Curriculum

This chapter ties together the sign-on and lessons that you have created to learn how to use computer-managed instruction (CMI). Now might be a good time to review the CMI part of Chapter 2 and look at Figure 2.10 again.

We will imagine, for the moment, that the diverse lessons that you created have a commonality that makes them a logical fit in one curriculum. Your learner can sign on, take a test, and choose any of the lessons from a menu. You will capture the learner's name, learn how to store records of student results in an external file, and report those results to the learner and to a learning facilitator. Finally, you will learn how to print a customized diploma.

What You Will Learn in This Chapter

- How to use custom scoring to vary testing strategies
- How to run separate lessons from a central menu
- How to pass variables
- How to store student results in an external file
- How to read data from an external file
- How to send a screen image to a printer
- How to print an external file
- How to format text in a text field

The Curriculum Structure

From the point of view of programming, the whole curriculum uses two new files to work with all the files that you have created in Chapters 13 to 22. Remember the modes of CMI covered first in Chapter 2. They are testing, prescription generation, and record keeping. The new files are a test and a curriculum that will do the prescription generation and record keeping.

First you will build the test, then add the curriculum to make everything work, including printing a diploma. Using the example lessons that you have created from the chapters of this book does not really result in a coherent curriculum that would fit any real person that we can imagine. It *does*, however, provide you with good practice so that, in the future, you create entire curricula that are controlled by your (modified) CMI system. You will have to be very careful in following along, since the test uses all 50 icons permitted and the curriculum uses 49.

Building the Tests

There is really only one fully featured test. It is used by the curriculum to administer pre- and post tests. You will build it in two stages, adding the post testing capability in a simple second stage.

Build the pre-test

To get started, open a new file and name it *cu_test*. You will name all files associated with the curriculum with names that start with "cu." Pull down the File menu to access the File Setup options. Set the Presentation Window Size to VGA, deselect User Menu Bar, Overlay Menu Bar, and Title Bar. Finally, set the Background Color to a bright blue. Each part of the curriculum will have a different background color, providing navigation information to the learner. The sign-on background is yellow, the test will be blue, and the curriculum will be black. When you have completed the File Setup, close the dialog box.

Now you can begin the test structure. You will use a progressive development approach to building the test, starting simply and adding complexity as you go. Drag a display icon to the flowline and name it *background*. Open *background* and import the *cutestbk.pct* file. Do your best to place it nicely on the screen with pleasing borders all around. This is very important because you will use this placement for all the windows in the test and the curriculum. Be sure to toggle the menu bar off when doing this (Control-spacebar on PCs, Command-/ on Macs) so that you can see the whole screen. Your result should look like Figure 23.1. You may note that we have decided to downplay the testing function by calling it a progress check. Many adult learners are stressed by their memories of school and are less alarmed by a test that is called a "progress check."

When you are satisfied with the placement, close the display to return to the icons.

Add the Test Control Section

Now drag an interaction icon to the flowline and label it *test intro*. Then drag a map icon to its right. Approve the default pushbutton response type, since that is exactly what you need here. Then drag a calculation icon to the right of the *untitled* map. It will assume a pushbutton response type. Name the two new icons *Start Test* and

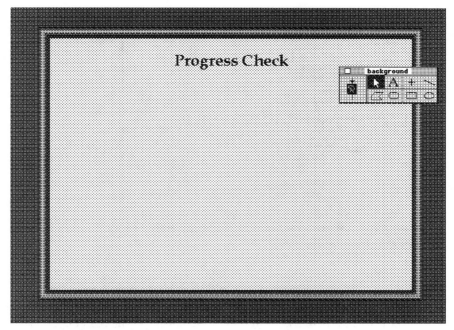

Figure 23.1 Test Background

Quit respectively. Be sure to use initial capital letters. Control-click on the branch below the *Start Test* icon to switch its branching to Exit Interaction. When you reach this point, your test will look like Figure 23.2.

To complete the *test intro*, you must place the buttons and place the Quit function in the *Quit* calculation. First, place the buttons by using the now familiar open *background* and close it, followed by shift-clicking to open the *test intro* display. When the display opens, place the buttons about one-half inch up from the bottom of the background frame. Click on the buttons to open the Pushbutton Options dialog box. Click the Position and Size button to set them to 130 pixels wide by 24 high. Repeat the process for the other button to ensure that they are exactly the same size. Make placement adjustments as necessary.

Select the text tool and click in the middle-left portion of the screen. Enter the flowing text:

```
If you are ready to begin the test, select Start Test to begin. Otherwise,
select Quit to leave.

Once you begin the test, you will not be able to quit until it is completed.
```

Select *Start Test* with your text tool. Then open the Attributes menu and select Color. Pick a bright blue. Then select *Quit* and change it to blue also. Now change to the Arrow tool (we find it easier to make most changes to text when it is an object. Using the Text menu, change the font to Arial Bold 12-point with transparent mode.

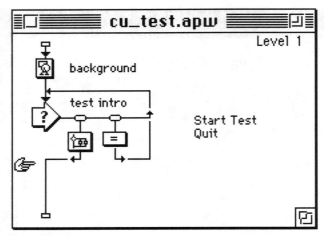

Figure 23.2 Test Intro Structure

The default left justification is fine. Adjust the size of the text object and roughly center it within the background. Figure 23.3 shows the results.

Jump to the icons. Then, open the *Quit* calculation and enter

```
Quit(0)
```

Close the calculation. That completes the *test intro*.

Complete Level 1 icons

Now flesh out the icon structure. Drag four map icons and one calculation icon to the flowline below *test intro*. Name them *text response, multiple choice, movable object,* and *multiple entry w/time limit.* Your completed flowline should look like Figure 23.4.

Eventually, the quit will automatically shut down the test when it is completed, and return the learner to the curriculum. This is the first time that you have encountered such a quit.

You can wrap up the quit right now by opening the *quit* calculation and entering

```
Quit(0)
```

Close the calculation.

Optionally, you could test drive the test right now to check out the *Quit* button and that the *Start Test* button leads to the automatic quit. We would not ordinarily test drive our work yet, because everything is pretty obvious at this point.

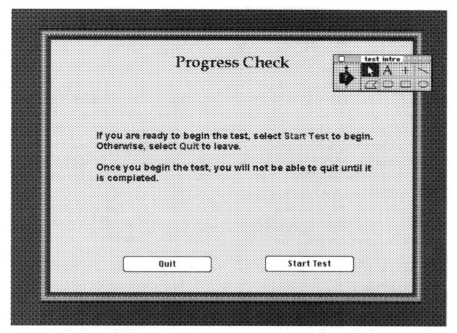

Figure 23.3 Test Intro Display

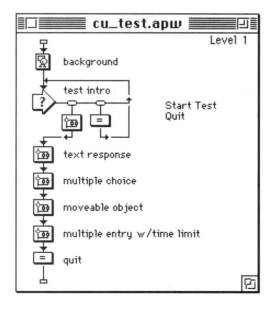

Figure 23.4 Level 1 Structure

Create the Text Response Question

The first question requires the learner to use the keyboard and type in a response to a question. You will show one of the Crane Operator hand signals and the learner will type in its name. Generally, text questions are the most difficult to judge because the learner has nearly infinite possibilities for responding. You will recall from Chapter 14 that Authorware's text response options assist you by providing the capability to ignore capitalization, extra punctuation, spaces, extra words, incremental matching, and word order. We think you will come to appreciate this capability as you test drive this question. Each icon attached to the interaction will relate to a single text entry field that the learner sees. You will have to add icons to deal with some of the possible wrong answers. To start with you will create the basic structure, check it out, and then add the additional icons.

Open the *text response* map icon to create the flowline structure for the first question. Drag an interaction icon to the level 2 text response flowline. Name it *identify hand signal*. Now drag a calculation icon to the right of the interaction icon. When the Response Type dialog box opens, select the Text response type and close the dialog box. Drag two more calculation icons to the right of the other *untitled* calculation. They will also assume the text response type attributes. Name them *boom out, 2 tries*, and * (shift-8).

Select *2 tries* response type symbol and change its response type to Tries Limit. When the Tries Limit Options dialog box opens, enter 2 in the maximum tries text field. Notice that the branching option has changed to Exit Interaction. This makes sense, because the tries limit purpose is to close the question when the tries limit is reached. Therefore, exit interaction makes the most sense. Close the response type dialog box. For essentially the same reason, change the branching of *boom out* to Exit Interaction. Control-click on the branching line just under the icon to cycle until you reach Exit Interaction. Figure 23.5 shows the identify hand signals structure at this point.

You will now create the first of four custom variables that track the learner's performance on each question. In each case, it is only associated with the correct response, changing from FALSE to TRUE if the learner answers the question correctly. In this question, *boom out* is the correct response. Double-click the *boom out* calculation to open for editing. Enter the following:

```
obj_1_correct = TRUE
-- the learner has answered the objective 1 question correctly
```

Select OK to close the calculation. When you are prompted for the initial value of the variable, make its Initial value false (logical Type on Macs) and enter the following description:

```
is updated to true when the question is answered correctly
```

Then select OK to close the New Variable dialog box.

Open and close background to load it into memory. Then double-click the *identify hand signal* interaction icon and click in the Pause Before Exiting and Show Button checkboxes. You may note that this is the first time that we have used the pause be-

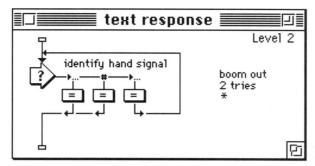

Figure 23.5 Identify Hand Signal Structure

fore exiting feature. It generates a Continue button exactly like the one generated by the Wait icon. This feature will become important later in the programming, to save the use of one icon. Figure 23.6 shows the selected checkboxes.

You can control the characteristics of the text entry field by selecting the Text Entry Options button. The interaction dialog box will expand, providing options to control the text field in which the learner types the answer to the question. Try this now. The default settings are satisfactory for this lesson. If you wanted to change the font or point size of the text field the learner typed in you could do it here with the text pull-down menu. So, after you have completed an examination of the dialog box, hold down the Shift key while you click on OK-Edit display. The display will open, showing the background and a white rectangle that is the text field in which the learner will eventually enter his or her answer.

Select the text tool and click in the top center of the screen. Type:

```
Objective 1
Crane Operator Skills
```

Now click in the middle left of the screen to create a new text field and type:

```
This is one of the seven hand signals used to direct the crane operator.
Which one is it?

Type your answer in the space provided and press the Return key on your
keyboard.
```

There are nine blank lines between the upper and lower text. For the last piece of text on the screen click in the bottom center of the screen and type:

```
feedback
```

Select all the text with Control-A. Control-A selects all objects of any kind, but that is OK. Using the Text menu, change the font to Arial Bold 10-point. Leave the default left justification for now. While the text is still selected, change the mode to transparent. If your text should come in as blue, select Color from the Attributes menu and change it to black. Use the text tool to select the words "Crane Operator Skills" and change the size to 14-point. Now change to the Arrow tool to work with

Figure 23.6 Interaction Dialog Box with Pause Before Exiting Selected

individual text objects. Select Objective 1, Crane Operator Skills, and change the justification to centered. Finally, one by one, select the text object handles for the top and bottom text objects and drag them to the edge of the frame in the background to both sides. This will guarantee accurate centering.

Import the crpsbmot.pct file. You may remember importing it previously for the Crane Operator lesson. Place it neatly centered in the space created by the nine blank lines that you entered. Figure 23.7 shows the results.

Now place curly brackets around feedback like this:

```
{feedback}
```

Jump to the icons. When you do, the New Variable dialog box will open. This is a character variable with initial value of " ". Enter the Description as:

```
contains the feedback for all answers
```

When you close the New Variable dialog box, the feedback text on the screen will disappear. That is because it contains nothing (there is nothing between the quotation marks). While the on-screen variable is still selected (even if you don't see it), choose Effects from the Attributes pull-down menu and click in the Update Displayed Variables checkbox. This will ensure that the feedback is displayed as soon as it becomes effective. This wouldn't be a problem for the wrong response, because that loops back to the interaction. You can see already that there are two icons with exit branching. Update Displayed Variables will cause their feedback to be displayed.

The next step is to place the appropriate feedback into each of the calculations, to provide feedback as the learner answers the question. Remember that *boom out* already has an expression in the calculation. Simply add to it. Place feedback as follows:

Icon	Feedback
boom out	feedback = "Correct. Two hands with thumbs outward is Boom Out."
2 tries	feedback = "That is not correct. Two hands with thumbs outward is Boom Out."
*	feedback = "That is not correct. You have 1 try remaining."

 Go With the Flow: Follow the flowline in Figure 23.5. The hierarchy of answer judging show there is important. The icons on the flowline are recognized from left to right. Let's assume that the learner makes a response. If the response is not boom out or out boom (remember that you have used the ignore word order feature), the flow moves to *2 tries*. But because there have not been two tries, it passes to the wild card *. The wild card is activated and displays its feedback message, and loops around to the interaction. Assume that the learner makes another entry. If the answer is also wrong, the flow will pass *boom out*, *2 tries* will pick it up, display its feedback, and exit the interaction. You can see that the flow can only reach the wild card on the first try, because it will always be intercepted by *2 tries* on the second try.

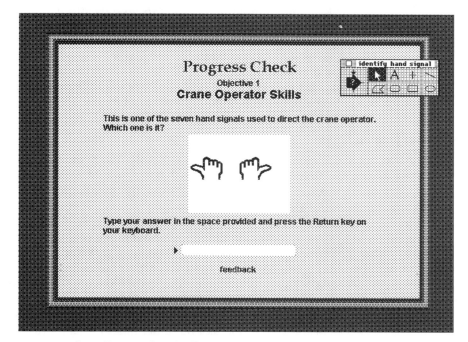

Figure 23.7 Crane Operator Question Display

Test Drive

Run your test. Select Start Test from the initial display. Run the following tests:

First Response	Second Response	Outcome
boom out	n/a	Correct feedback w/Continue button
boom out signal	n/a	Correct feedback w/Continue button
boom, out	n/a	Correct feedback w/Continue button
bOom oUt	n/a	Correct feedback w/Continue button
out boom	n/a	Correct feedback w/Continue button
any wrong answer	n/a	1 try remaining feedback w/response highlighted
any wrong answer	boom out	Correct feedback w/Continue button
any wrong answer	out boom	Correct feedback w/Continue button
any wrong answer	any wrong answer	Incorrect feedback w/Continue button

When you enter boom out the first time, the flow will exit the interaction and the Continue button generated by the Pause Before Exiting checkbox in the identify hand signal interaction will be displayed. Pause the program with Control-P and move the Continue button to the lower right corner of the background frame. If your feedback line is too close to the bottom, move it up a bit.

Enhance answer judging

Your text entry question works. It uses some of Authorware's answer judging capabilities, as you saw from your boom out signal, boom, out, bOoM oUt, and out boom responses. Let's test some additional capabilities so that you know how they work for possible use in the future.

First, let's make the *boom out* response even more flexible. Double-click on the response type symbol and click the Incremental Matching checkbox. This will recognize either 'boom' or 'out' on the first response, note that it was made, and allow the flow to pass down the flowline to the wild card. If the learner enters the other word on the second try, *boom out* will judge the answer as complete and correct, display its feedback, and exit the interaction.

The next enhancement is to establish another set of conditions for answer judging. You will enable boom out to recognize an even wider range of answers as correct. Let's assume that you want to do this because of the complete unfamiliarity with the keyboard and (possible) poor spelling skills of the learners. You will accomplish this by

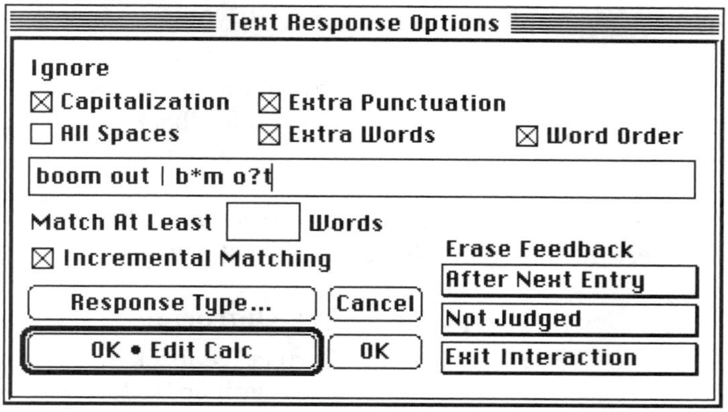

Figure 23.8   Text Response Options Dialog Box

making an additional change to the anticipated responses text field. Place your cursor after the t in boom out, add a space for legibility, and type | (shift-\ on most keyboards), the symbol for 'or.' Then complete the text field so that it looks as shown below :

```
boom out | b*m o?t
```

The or indicates that either of the two anticipated responses should be judged by this icon. Any response other than entered in the anticipated responses text field will not be matched by the learner's response, and the flow will continue out to the right of the interaction.

What do the * and the ? mean? The * is the catch-all text response. It substitutes for an entire word or any missing part of a word. The ? substitutes for any single character. Figure 23.8 shows the completed dialog box.

You can best get an appreciation of this by seeing it in action. Click OK to close the Text Response Options dialog box.

Test drive

Run your test again. Select Start Test from the initial display. Run the following tests on it to test incremental matching:

First Response	Second Response	Outcome
boom	out	Correct feedback w/Continue button
out	boom	Correct feedback w/Continue button
boom signal	oUt	Correct feedback w/Continue button

Now Run your test again to test the catch-all text response and the single character substitute:

First Response	Second Response	Outcome
boum out	n/a	Correct feedback w/Continue button
bom oot	n/a	Correct feedback w/Continue button

There is a downside to this capability. It works *exactly* as advertised. You can Run your test again to test the less desirable outcomes that can also occur:

First Response	Second Response	Outcome
bzm oxt	n/a	Correct feedback w/Continue button
babcdefghijklm	out	Correct feedback w/Continue button

 Authorware Tip: You can see that this is a powerful, but delicate, judging tool. You are responsible for the final outcome, so you have to apply finite controls. We suggest that you experiment with this feature to understand it. When you make another question with text response, establish the kind of testing that you just completed to see what the downside outcomes are. Be sure that you are satisfied that when the learner's answer is judged correct he or she was making an honest attempt to provide a correct answer.

Add context-specific feedback

You want to work with the learner to provide helpful feedback when he or she may have misread the question or made a mental transposition resulting in a predictable wrong response. First, you will improve the incremental matching. It works as it is, but when the learner enters boom or out, incorrect feedback is provided. You can change this to a more appropriate message.

Drag a calculation icon to the right end of the flowline. It will pick up the text response type from the wildcard icon. Now move it in between *2 tries* and * and name it:

```
boom | b*m
```

These are actually the first words of the two parts of the *boom out | b*m o?t* calculation icon. By entering its name you also place the same information into the anticipated responses text field. Although this icon enhances the incremental matching, it is not actually connected to it in any way and does not require incremental matching to be selected. As you saw in your test, incremental matching already works. You are only making it more user-friendly.

Now repeat the process by dragging a calculation to the right of *boom out | b*m o?t* . It will assume the text response type from the *boom out | b*m o?t* icon. Name it:

```
out | o?t
```

The next step is to place the appropriate feedback into each of these calculations to provide context-sensitive feedback. Place feedback as follows:

Icon	Feedback
boom | b*m	`feedback = "This is a boom signal, but not the one you entered."`
out | o?t	`feedback := "This is an out signal, but not the one you entered."`

Now finish the icons to deal with the learner who confuses the pointed thumbs with the travel signals. Doing this is really a design consideration. If you do, you will be helping learners who may not have adequately learned to correctly answer the question. In this case you are doing it to increase your understanding of how context-sensitive feedback works.

Drag another calculation icon to the right of *out \| o?t* and name it:

```
travel | east | west
```

Place the appropriate feedback into this calculation to provide the context-sensitive feedback. Place feedback as follows:

Icon	Feedback
travel | east | west	`feedback = "This is a different signal. Think, and try again."`

As you now know, if the learner responds with travel, east, or west, this icon will intercept the flow and provide the context-specific feedback that you just entered. Figure 23.9 shows the text response structure. Note that the wildcard response is scrolled out of sight to the right of those shown.

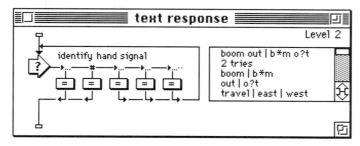

Figure 23.9 Text Response Structure

Test drive

Run your test again. Select Start Test from the initial display and Run the following tests on it to check your recent programming:

First Response	Second Response	Outcome
boom	n/a	Partial correct feedback w/ Continue button
out	n/a	Partial correct feedback w/ Continue button
any wrong answer	boom	Incorrect feedback w/ Continue button
any wrong answer	out	Incorrect feedback w/ Continue button
travel	n/a	Context sensitive feedback w/Continue button
east	n/a	Context sensitive feedback w/Continue button
west	n/a	Context sensitive feedback w/Continue button
any wrong answer	travel	Incorrect feedback w/Continue button
any wrong answer	east	Incorrect feedback w/Continue button
any wrong answer	west	Incorrect feedback w/Continue button

One try is fairly standard when you want to measure knowledge. Two tries are usually all that are permitted. But if you were to set tries limit to three tries, these results would be different. Outcomes of the first and second would be the same.

Even though this is a completely functional test question it has no mechanism to track scores. You will return to it later to provide that capability.

You have completed the most complex question. Now clear the decks to begin the next one. Drag the completed text response map icon to the bottom of the flowline, below the *quit* calculation, to clear the field for working on the *multiple choice w/ tries limit* question.

Authorware Tip: As you saw, it was very convenient to repeatedly run the program to test out the question you were working on. By placing the completed question below quit, it will not be encountered as you run the program to test the question you work on next. When all questions are completed you can restore the desired structure. This same technique can be used when questions are placed on a decision structure for random selection. By setting the decision to sequential you can always see them in the same order from left to right on the decision.

Create Typical Multiple Choice Questions

Double-click the *multiple choice* map to get to the Level 2 flowline. Drag an interaction to the flowline and title it *identify weight ratios*. Drag one calculation to the right of *identify weight ratios* and OK the pushbutton response type. Name the calculation *A*. Control-click on the branch symbol at the bottom of the *A* calculation to establish Exit Interaction branching.

Now drag three map icons to the right of *A* and name them *B, C,* and *D*. Figure 23.10 shows the completed *multiple choice* structure.

A will be the right answer. *B, C,* and *D* are finished. Often it is the design choice not to provide feedback for test questions. If there were feedback, you would need to use display icons or calculations as in the preceding question. Display icons are better for providing feedback with graphics. Using a calculation with an embedded variable probably works better for text most of the time.

Now you will place the question in the *identify weight ratios* interaction. First, place the header. To make all of the headers consistent the best technique is to copy it from the one you already formatted for Objective 1, and paste it into the *identify weight ratios* interaction. Open the identify hand signal interaction display, select the header and question objects with the arrow tool, copy them, then open the *identify weight ratios* interaction and proceed to its display, and (without clicking in that icon) finally paste them there. They will be in the exact positions they held in the original icon.

Now select the 1 in Objective 1 and change it to 2. Then select Crane Operator Skills and change it to Weight Distribution Skills. You may have wondered why you were copying the question text when it clearly will be wrong for this question. The reason is that you can avoid several formatting steps by using it with a totally replaced content. Select the entire question with the text tool and replace it with this:

```
Your rig has 80,000 pound gross vehicle weight.
Select the choice that has the best distribution of the weight among the axles.
```

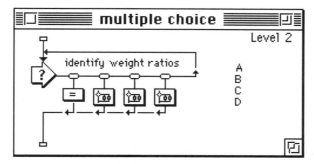

Figure 23.10 Completed Multiple Choice Structure

Select this new text using the Arrow tool, copy it, and paste it two times. This is because you will find it easier to create the text in three parts and you can again avoid several formatting steps by this copy-and-paste technique (or "trick").

Select the second of the three identical texts with the text tool and replace it with:

```
Steer Axle    Drive Axles    Trailer Tandem
```

Type a tab before each word set. Your text may not separate yet, but don't worry about it. Now select the last of the three formerly identical texts with the text tool and replace it with:

```
12,000    34,000    34,000

10,000    44,000    26,000

20,000    30,000    30,000

10,000    18,000    52,000
```

Insert a blank line between each line of text, and insert tabs before each set of numbers. Figure 23.11 shows the completed screen that you can use as a model. After you have roughly placed your text, drag the buttons to their approximate final positions.

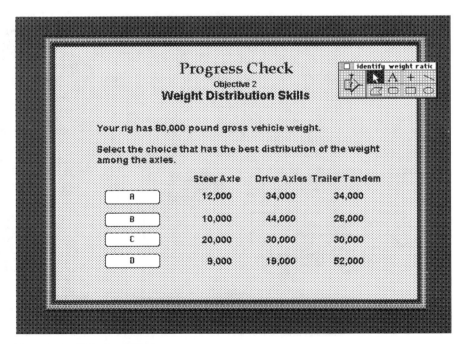

Figure 23.11 Objective 2 Display

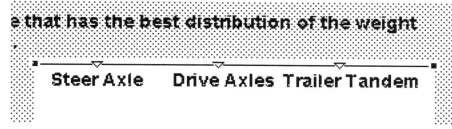

Figure 23.12 Right-Align Tabs

Steer Axle	Drive Axles	Trailer Tandem
12,000	34,000	34,000
10,000	44,000	26,000
20,000	30,000	30,000
9,000	19,000	52,000

Figure 23.13 Decimal Tabs

Using tabs in text fields

You can best achieve the results shown using tabs. Using spaces is generally a poor practice and sometime prevents precise alignment. It is simple to put the tabs that are in your text to work. When you use the text tool to select the text, you can click on the line itself. A small triangle will appear that is a left-align tab. If you click on the triangle, it will become a right-align tab, or a decimal tab for numbers. Figure 23.12 shows the tab used to right-align the first words in the header.

Figure 23.13 shows the decimal alignment based on placement of decimal tabs. Notice that 9,000 is perfectly aligned. Adjust your text and buttons until they match Figure 23.11, then jump to the icons.

Now you will add another variable, associated with the correct response, changing from FALSE to TRUE if the learner answers the question correctly. In this question, A is the correct response. Double-click the A calculation. Enter the following:

```
obj_2_correct = TRUE
-- the learner has answered the objective 2 question correctly
```

Select OK to close the calculation. When you are prompted for the initial value of the variable, make its Initial value false (logical Type on Macs) and enter the following description:

```
is updated to true when the question is answered correctly
```

Then select OK to close the New Variable dialog box. Select OK to close *A*.

Test Drive

Run your test again. Remember that you placed the question for objective 1 on the bottom of the flowline, after the quit. Thus, when you perform your test drive you will only encounter the question for objective 2. Select Start Test from the initial display and try each answer to check your recent programming.

Troubleshooting

The problem is that you can't be sure that the interaction is working properly—only that you are falling through. To make sure that your work is performing properly you can apply a simple programming trick. You temporarily set a message on a path and then see whether it is displayed. If it is, your flow followed the path. Refer to Figure 23.10. You can place a map icon on the flowline, name it *troubleshooter*, open it, and drag a display icon to the flowline, calling it *message*. Enter a text message such as:

```
I got this far!
```

in it. Place a wait icon on the flowline below *message*. To use it, drag *troubleshooter* to the Level 3 flowline of *B*, Run the program, and observe whether your message is displayed. If it is, the flow works as it should. If not, you know you have a problem. Repeat this process for *C* and *D*. To check *A*, you will have to first group *A* into a map. When you finish be sure that you have not left any icon behind, and that those you grouped are ungrouped. You can save *troubleshooter* for use in testing a later question, but will have to delete it in the end, as there are not icons to spare.

Create Moveable Object Question

Drag the *multiple choice* map to the bottom of the flowline to clear the way for eventual testing of the next question. Then double-click the *moveable object* map to get to the Level 2 flowline. First you need a display icon with an electrode. Open your EKG lesson. The electrode icon is the second one on the flowline within the *lesson* map icon. Select it, but do not open it. Copy the icon and close the EKG lesson. Now reopen *cu_test* and click on the *moveable object* Level 2 flowline. Then paste the electrode icon to it. Select Effects from the Attributes pull-down menu to deselect Prevent Automatic Erase (PC users only), an attribute of the source icon but not one you want here. The electrode is drawn first, but is needed by the user. The later graphics will cover it if you don't prevent it. The way to prevent this is to set Layers to 2. Do that now and select OK to close the dialog box. That completes the electrode except for final placement.

Next, drag an interaction icon to the flowline and name it *place electrode*. Then drag a calculation icon to the flowline to the right of place electrode. When the Response Type dialog box opens, select the Moveable Object response type and select OK to close the dialog box. Next, drag two maps to the flowline to the right of the *untitled* calculation. They will assume the Moveable Object response type. Now name the calculation *correct,* and the maps *incorrect* and *error trap* respectively.

Open the *correct* calculation to add another variable, associated with the correct responses in this test. In this question, *correct* is the correct response. Double-click the *correct* calculation. Enter the following:

```
obj_3_correct = TRUE
-- the learner has answered the objective 3 question correctly
```

Select OK to close the calculation. When you are prompted for the initial value of the variable, make its Initial value false (logical Type on Macs) and enter the following description:

```
is updated to true when the question is answered correctly
```

Then select OK to close the New Variable dialog box. Select OK to close *correct*.

In this case, the correct and incorrect answers are valid answers and will be scored without feedback to the learner. The error trap picks up totally invalid electrode placement that is probably a slip or other mistake. It will allow the learner to make another try to answer the question without penalty. To make this happen, Control-click on the branching symbol at the bottom of *correct* and *incorrect* to change them to Exit Interaction. The completed structure is shown in Figure 23.14.

Now use the same technique to copy the header and text from Objective 1. When you have copied it, open the *place electrode* interaction display for editing and (without clicking anywhere) paste it. Edit it by selecting text and retyping to replace the Objective 1 with Objective 3, and Crane Operator Skills with EKG Technician Skills.

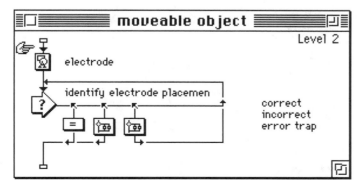

Figure 23.14 Completed Moveable Object Structure

Select the question text and replace it with:

```
Drag the electrode
to the Vₑ position
```

Use the objects handles to center it and select the Center justification from the text menu. Then, after opening and closing the background icon, and while holding the shift key down, import the graphic contained in the *cutetors.pct* file. Center it in the bottom of the screen. Adjust the graphic until it fits nicely in the bottom center of your screen. Figure 23.15 shows the question after placing the graphic.

Place target areas

Next, you will make basic question components unmovable. Then you will place the target areas and establish the electrode in its base location.

Select the *electrode* icon, but do not open it. Select Calculations from the Data pull-down menu and enter the following expressions and documentary comments. You can type it, but should look it up. If you don't type it you can Paste it from the Moveable variable of the General category, under Show Variables in the Data pull-down menu.

```
Moveable@"background" = FALSE
Moveable@"place electrode" = FALSE
-- locks the background and torso display in place
-- has no effect on the electrode
```

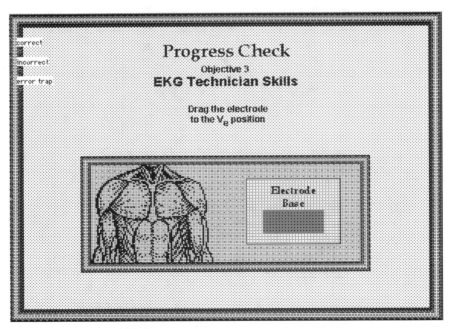

Figure 23.15 Objective 3 Display

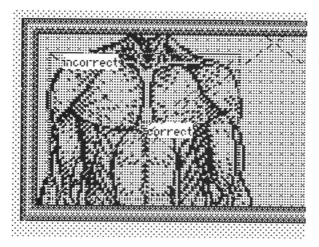

Figure 23.16 Detail of Multiple Target Areas

Now finish the electrode. To do that, open and close *place electrode* and then, while holding down shift, open *electrode*. (Mac users must select the electrode graphic.) Open Attributes and change the color of the electrode to red. Then drag it to a spot in the center of the electrode base. Close the display when you are finished.

It would be possible to Run the program to edit the targets on the fly on the PC, but to be consistent with Mac users just place them the old-fashioned way, as you did in the EKG lesson. Double-click the movable object response type just above the *correct* icon and the Moveable Object Options dialog box will appear. It prompts you to click an object to associate with the target area. Click once on the electrode. The target, which has been quietly waiting in the upper left of the screen, will jump to center on the electrode. Resize and reposition the target area as you did in the EKG chapter. Since this is the correct answer, it should be small and should fit over the end of the xigmoid process. Change the Leave at Destination default of the Object Destination drop-down list to Snap to Center. Then click on OK to close the dialog box.

Next double-click the *incorrect* response type symbol. Repeat the process of associating the electrode with the target and moving and resizing the target to cover the patient's torso. The default Leave at Destination is OK, so just click on OK to close the dialog box.

Finally, double-click the *error trap* response type symbol. Associate the electrode with the target and move and resize the target to full screen size. Change the Leave at Destination default of the Object Destination drop-down list to Put Back. This will return the electrode to its base if it is dropped totally outside the torso. Click on OK to close the dialog box.

Run the test. When the EKG Technician Skills question appears, use Control-P to pause the program. All the target areas will be revealed at once, as well as the electrode and background. Figure 23.16 shows the detail of the multiple target areas. Close the display when you are satisfied, by using Control-J to jump to the icons.

The moveable object question is finished, but to test it you should place an erase to dispose of the electrode. Later, when the program matures, it will not be needed. Drag an erase icon to the bottom of the *moveable object* flowline and name it *remove me later*. Then, open and close the *electrode*. Finally, open *remove me later* and click on the *electrode* to associate it with the erase. Select OK to close the erase.

Test Drive

Run your test. Remember that you placed the questions for objectives 1 and 2 on the bottom of the flowline, below the quit. When you conduct your test drive you will see only the question for objective 3. Select Start Test from the initial display and check your recent programming. On successive attempts, drag the electrode and drop it anywhere outside the torso, inside the torso away from the V_e location, and at the V_e location. When you are satisfied, drag the *moveable object* map to the bottom of the flowline.

Create Multiple Entry Question with a Time Limit

Double-click the *multiple entry w/time limit* map to get to the Level 2 flowline. Then drag an interaction icon to the flowline and name it *select concrete components*. Then drag a calculation icon to associate with *select concrete components*. When the Response Type dialog box opens, change the response type to Conditional and select OK to close.

At this point, Control-click to change the branching to Exit Interaction. Notice that the calculator has a blank title, similar to a wait icon. You will name it later with a system variable. Double-click the unnamed calculation to open *AllCorrectMatched* to add another custom variable associated with the correct response, changing from FALSE to TRUE if the learner answers the question correctly. Double-click the *unnamed* calculation. Enter the following:

```
obj_4_correct = TRUE
-- the learner has answered the objective 4 question correctly
```

Select OK to close the calculation. When you are prompted for the initial value of the variable, make its initial value false (Type logical on Macs) and enter the following description:

```
is updated to true when the question is answered correctly
```

Then select OK to close the New Variable dialog box. Select OK to close *AllCorrect-Matched*.

Next, drag two maps to the right of the untitled calculation (it actually has a blank name). They will pick all of the characteristics it has. The first of these will remain Conditional and, for now, will have a blank name. Click on the response type symbol of the last icon in the row and change the response type to Time Limit. When the Time Limit Options dialog box opens, enter 60 in the Time limit text box to set it at 60 seconds (durations of more than this must still be expressed in seconds). Click the Show Time Remaining checkbox to place a small alarm clock image on screen to show that "the clock is running." The default Continue Timing is correct for your use. Figure 23.17 shows the Time Limit Options dialog box after the selections have been made.

Select OK to close the dialog box and name the icon *60 seconds*. Figure 23.18 shows the structure of the icons established so far.

Create concrete component choices

The learner will be asked to select correct amounts of sand, gravel, and cement for a general purpose mix. To bring this about, next you will create nine choices that will place a checkmark next to the learner's selections. Drag a display icon to the right of *60 seconds*. Double-click the response type symbol to change it to Click/Touch, and change the erase feedback drop-down menu from After Next Entry to On Exit. Then, select OK to close. Name the icon *1 sand*. Control-click on the branching symbol to cycle it to Try Again. Open *1 sand* and import the graphic from the file

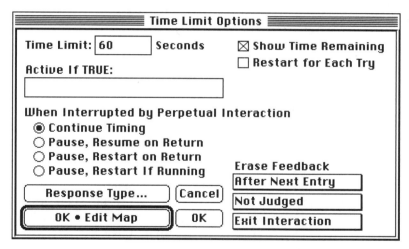

Figure 23.17 Time Limit Options Dialog Box

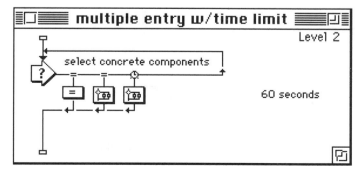

Figure 23.18 Select Connected Component Early Structure

cutestck.pct. Then close the display. The structure with the added icon is shown in Figure 23.19.

Since 1 sand has every characteristic that we want in the remaining eight icons, it will be much better to copy it and paste it than to drag the icons and have to import graphics, or even to copy and paste the graphic. Now select *1 sand*, but do not open it. Copy it and click to its own right to place the paste hand as shown in Figure 23.19, and then paste. Repeat the paste seven more times. You should have nine icons, all named *1 sand*. Scroll back to the left to the original *1 sand*. Rename the nine 1 sand icons as follows:

Icon Name

1 sand
2 sand
3 sand
1 gravel
2 gravel
3 gravel
1 cement
2 cement
3 cement

Next you will import the display for selecting the concrete components. You must align this display with the background. Open and close the background to load it into memory. Then, while holding shift, open the *select concrete components* interaction icon for editing. Import *cutesto4.pct* and position the image exactly over the background. Next you will need to copy in the heading. Close the interaction, find the *identify hand signal* interaction, open it, and copy the heading. Close *identify hand signal,* open the *select concrete components* interaction icon, and paste the heading into the display. If you didn't click in the freshly open display before the paste, the heading will appear in the exact same location from which it was copied, which is where you want it. Change the heading to Objective 4, Concrete Mixing Skills.

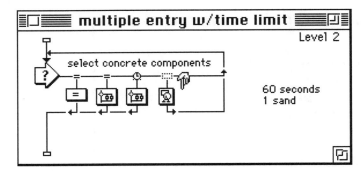

Figure 23.19 Structure with 1 Sand Icon

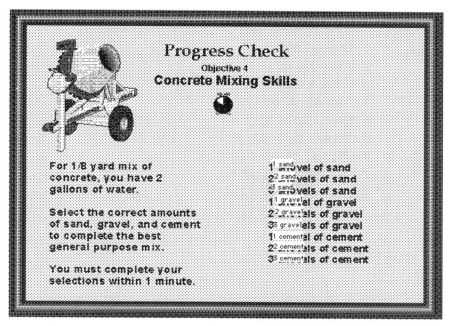

Figure 23.20 Completed Concrete Mixing Skills Display

Look around on the display and find the image of an alarm clock. Drag it to the center of the screen below Mixing.

Next, reposition and resize the nine click/touch areas to cover each of the lines of text correlated to the click/touch area name. When you have completed this task your screen will resemble Figure 23.20.

The *select concrete components* question is basically finished except for the checkmarks. Currently all the checkmarks are piled one atop the other in a single spot. If you run the program you can easily move them to appropriate locations.

Run the program. Click on 1 shovel of gravel when the select concrete components question appears. The checkmark will appear. Select it and position it in front of the appropriate answer. Repeat the process by clicking on 2 shovels of sand and so forth, until you have placed a checkmark in front of each. If the question terminates because you ran out of time, simply run the question again and pick up where you left off. Figure 23.21 shows the position of each of the nine checkmarks.

The last feature of this question is to set up the conditions to limit the responses to three, and for judging the responses to determine if the answer is correct. Double-click on the conditional response type symbol for the first unnamed calculation icon. Open Show Variable under the Data pull-down menu, and under the interaction category select the AllCorrectMatched variable. Read the description and then paste it into the Match if True text field. Change Auto-Match from the default Off to On False To True. Select OK to close.

Next double-click the conditional response type symbol above the unnamed map icon. As before, open Show Variable under the Data pull-down menu; then, under

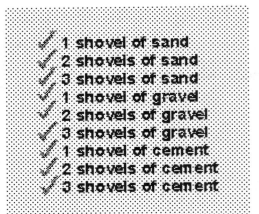

Figure 23.21 Positioned Checkmarks

the interaction category, select the ChoicesMatched variable. Read the description and then paste it into the Match if True text field. Then edit it to read:

```
ChoicesMatched = 3
```

This is how you limit the responses to three. Again change the Auto-Match from the default Off to On False To True. Select OK to close.

When you close the icon you can see that the first two calculation icons have assumed the names AllCorrectMatched and ChoicesMatched = 3.

Next control-click directly in front of each of the nine concrete component icons. On the first click a small plus sign will appear, indicating that it is a correct answer. Click again and the plus will change to a minus. A third click will restore the not-judged condition. Set them as shown below:

Icon Name	Response Judging
1 sand	−
2 sand	−
3 sand	+
1 gravel	−
2 gravel	−
3 gravel	+
1 cement	−
2 cement	−
3 cement	+

The completed *select concrete components* structure is shown in Figure 23.22.

By setting the response judging for each of the responses on the *Select Concrete Components,* you will be able to use the predefined Authorware variable to track the scoring of this question. You have already entered the necessary variables.

Here is how it works. The AllCorrectMatched condition is matched and exits the interaction if the learner gets the three correct answers. It has to be first in line to determine if the three choices are correct. The ChoicesMatched = 3 icon is waiting in line, and its condition is activated by any three. Since it is second in line it can never be activated by the three correct answers. Therefore, when its condition is matched by three choices they cannot be correct. When matched it also exits the interaction. If neither of the first two icon's conditions are met before the time limit of 60 seconds, then the Time Limit interaction response type matched and the interaction is exited.

Test Drive

Run your program to test it. Remember that you placed the questions for objectives 1 and 2 on the bottom of the flowline, below the quit. Test each branch as well as the timer, to see that they all fall through. Let the clock time out. You may use *troubleshooter* (created to test the multiple-choice question) to test that each of the other exit branches is working properly.

Now move the multiple entry w/time limit map calculation icon to the very bottom of the Level 1 flowline. This is to place the questions in the same order as the objectives. Eventually, you will deal with this in another way, but for now this move will do it. Now move quit to the bottom of the flowline. This will permit you to run all four questions of the test as they will eventually be encountered. This will suffice for now, since you can use the test as it is for pre-testing. You will create the post testing capability quite easily once you have built the CMI program itself. Figure 23.23 shows the flowline at this point.

Building the Curriculum

There are three component parts in the Authorware curriculum Level 1 structure that we have laid out. To start with, open a new file and name it *curricul.apw*. Open the File Setup menu under the File pull-down menu and de-select User Menu Bar, Title Bar, and Overlay Menu Bar. Then select black for the background color and VGA in the Presentation Window, and close the setup. Now drag three map icons to the flowline and name them *mouse literacy, registration,* and *curriculum menu.* When you finish you will have created the basic structure at Level 1 and your work will be the same as Figure 23.24.

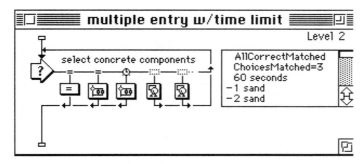

Figure 23.22 Completed Select Concrete Components Structure

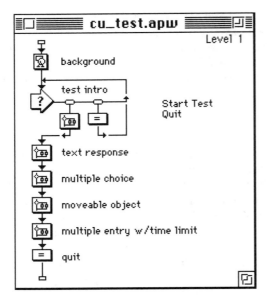

Figure 23.23 Pre-test Flowline

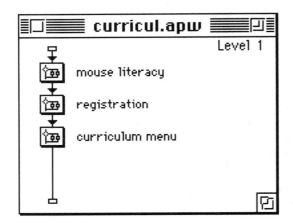

Figure 23.24 Curriculum Structure

Complete the Mouse Literacy Map

Open the *mouse literacy* map, drag an interaction icon to the flowline, and title it *want mouse practice?* Double-click on the interaction and change the erase feature from On Exit to After Next Entry. Then drag a map icon to associate with *want mouse practice?* When the Response Type dialog box opens, change the response type to Click/Touch and close the dialog box. Then open the Click/Touch Response Type dialog box. Under Erase Feedback, change the default Try Again to Exit Interaction and close the dialog box. Name it *skip mouse practice*.

Now drag a calculation icon and drop it to the right of *skip mouse practice,* and name it *Y|y*. (The | character, which represents "or" to the system, appears on the keyboard as a straight vertical line. It is Shift \ on our keyboard.) Double-click on the click/touch response type symbol, and when the Click/Touch Response Type dialog box opens, change the response type to Keypress and the Keypress Response Type dialog box will open. It will look like Figure 23.25. Note that the name of the icon that you have already entered (Y|y) automatically becomes the expected keys. You would read it "Y or y." Now close the dialog box.

To finish the mouse practice option section of the lesson you must import the content of the *want mouse practice* icon and place several arguments to provide functionality.

You will enter text in this lesson that will display on top of a colored background. If you did nothing to prevent it, the text would all display within a white (text) field. This is because text has a default setting of opaque mode. You can control this by changing the default setting. To do so you must be in a display, so open the *want mouse practice?* display. Don't worry that it is black; there is no content anyway (you can tell that you are in the right place if the text pull-down menu is not dimmed). If an object is selected, select the Text tool and then immediately select the Selection tool (arrow) to deselect all objects. Select the Attributes pull-down menu and Modes within it. Set the Mode to Transparent and select OK. Now, every time that you edit text in this lesson it will have the transparent mode.

Authorware Tip: Setting default values for all graphic objects and text fields is accomplished in the same way as just illustrated for the Transparent Mode. You select the attribute or text characteristic that you want while in an open display, with nothing selected.

Now you will place the mouse practice invitational frame. For your whole CMI system and separate test program to be consistent you must use the technique that you used earlier—but between files.

- Open *cu_test.apw*
- Open the *background* icon
- Select and copy the image
- Close *cu_test.apw*
- Reopen *curricul.apw*
- Open the *want mouse practice?* display
- Paste the image

```
┌─────────────────────────────────────────────┐
│              Keypress Options                 │
│ ┌───────────────────────────────────────────┐ │
│ │ Key:  Y|y                                  │ │
│ │ Active If TRUE:                            │ │
│ │ ┌─────────────────────┐  Erase Feedback    │ │
│ │ │                     │  ┌───────────────┐ │ │
│ │ │                     │  │ After Next Entry│ │ │
│ │ ┌─────────────────┐┌────┐├───────────────┤ │ │
│ │ │ Response Type...││Cancel││ Not Judged   │ │ │
│ │ ├─────────────────┤├────┤├───────────────┤ │ │
│ │ │ OK • Edit Calc  ││ OK ││ Exit Interaction│ │ │
│ └───────────────────────────────────────────┘ │
└─────────────────────────────────────────────┘
```

Figure 23.25 Keypress Options Dialog Box

This is the target for the new graphic's placement. Now import the graphic *cu_ mouse.pct* and carefully place it in the presentation window directly over the *test* background. When it is right, send it to the rear, click on the test graphic, and delete it. When you are pleased with the location of the mouse graphic, move and resize the *skip mouse practice* click/touch area to nicely fit around the mouse. Your completed work should resemble Figure 23.26. Close the display.

The next step is simple. You will place a function to jump out to the *mousepr* program that you created in Chapter 13. Open the *Yly* calculation icon, then open Show Functions, read the Description, and Paste the JumpFileReturn function (from the Jump Category in Show Functions). It will be:

```
JumpFileReturn("filename" [,"variable1, variable2…", "directory"])
```

 Development Tip: Authorware's JumpFileReturn and JumpOutReturn functions perform a basic activity common to most software. They permit you to execute another program from inside the program you are running. The difference between these two functions is that JumpFileReturn jumps only to another Authorware program, and returns. It is limited to jumping only from unpackaged file to unpackaged file, or from packaged file to packaged file. JumpOutReturn is used exclusively for non-Authorware files. For example, you could run Lotus 1-2-3 from Authorware, if you wanted to.

The optional arguments (variables and data directory—folder on Macs) won't be used in this argument, so delete them. Substitute "mousepr" for "filename." You

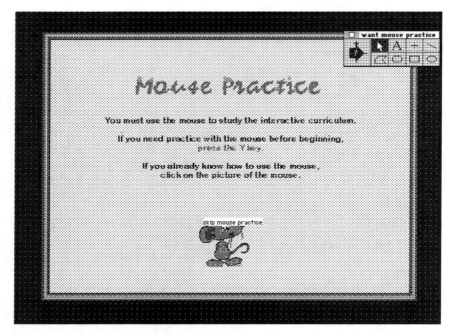

Figure 23.26 Want Mouse Practice Graphic

could simply type "FileLocation^," but we suggest that you open the File Category in the Variables dialog box and read the Description. Note that when you enter the file name of the file jumped to, that you not use the Windows file extension.

The Current Value of the FileLocation system variable is the current location of the file you are editing. This is very important to the function of your curriculum. All the files that will be jumped to, and all the files they use (such as the *mobydick.txt* file) must be in the same location. FileLocation is a nonassignable system variable, compared to all the other assignable variables you have used up to this point. Nonassignable system variables substitute for (possibly complex) code you might enter to control actions or conditions within your lesson. In this case you could type something like **c:\my_work** if your file is in that location. FileLocation is advantageous because Authorware automatically updates nonassignable system variables, and it will specify the current location even if you were to move your lessons several layers deep, such as **c:\training\my_work\empl_dev\new_curr**.

Once you have completed your editing, the argument, with comment, should read:

```
JumpFileReturn(FileLocation^"mousepr")
-- jumps out to the mousepr lesson to provide practice using the mouse
```

When it does, close the calculation window.

 Authorware Tip: If you do not place the file jumped to in the same location as the program that jumps to it, you can still make the jump. However, it will look confusing to many users, because the operating system's standard directory dialog box will appear. Once the proper file is located it will continue to run. We suggest that you avoid this confusing set of events.

This will complete the mouse literacy module, as far as we will complete it now. Later, after you work on the registration portion, you will better understand the meaning of the final expression that must be entered there.

The *want mouse practice?* interaction structure looks like Figure 23.27. Close the *mouse literacy* Level 2 map.

Test Drive

Run your lesson to verify that it performs as planned. You should be able to type Y or y and jump to your *mousepr* lesson. When you finish your *mousepr* lesson, by selecting Quit, you should return to the curriculum lesson you are currently working on. When you return, you will see only a blank black screen, for you will be past the mouse literacy map. You can use Control-J to escape from the black screen. Try the troubleshooting technique described earlier in this chapter to provide proof that you have reached the bottom of the flowchart.

 Authorware Tip: When you jump from one lesson to another, you will observe that each window closes, the lesson closes (inviting you to Save if you haven't), the other lesson opens, and any windows that were open when it was saved open. Then the other lesson runs, all creating what looks like quite a fuss on your screen. That is because you are using the Authorware Working Model and cannot package. When you package lessons, they close and open seamlessly. You can minimize the fuss by sav-

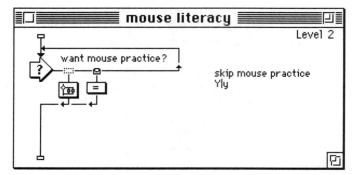

Figure 23.27   Mouse Literacy Structure

ing each file with only the Level 1 window open. The process will be the same, but there will appear to be much less to it.

Complete Registration

Now you will complete the simple *registration* portion of the curriculum. Open the *registration* map icon and drag a calculation to the flowline. Name it *jumpfilereturn to signon & pass variable*. Figure 23.28 shows the Level 2 view.

Open the *Y|y* calculation and copy the argument. Close *Y|y*, then open *jumpfile return to signon & pass variable* for editing, and paste the function. It will be:

```
JumpFileReturn(FileLocation^"mousepr")
```

Change the name of the file you want to jump from *mousepr* to *signon*, so that this calculation will take the learner to the sign-on you built in Chapter 14.

Then add the variables that you want to pass to the file being run. In this case, you want to receive the learner's name (UserName) back from the sign-on when it closes. Using JumpFileReturn, you can get back only what you send, so enter a comma after the "sign-on" followed by UserName. Then add a comment for documentation. Compare your results to:

```
JumpFileReturn(FileLocation^"signon",UserName)
-- jumps out to the signon lesson to get the new user's name
```

When you are satisfied, close the calculation and map.

Authorware Tip: You can pass multiple variables with the **JumpFileReturn**, but to do this you will need to enclose the variables within parentheses. The variables must also be separated by commas. If you do not do this, Authorware will assume that the second variable after the comma represents a third argument in the function. This third argument controls the location of the data files Authorware maintains for each lesson.

Test Drive

Try your curriculum as far as it goes now. You should be able to do or not do mouse practice as you choose, and then be taken to the sign-on to enter your name. You will return to a black screen again, something you will attend to soon.

Guarding against blanks

Right now, if your learner were to ignore entering any name at all (they are forced to type at least a space), your displays would look funny and no data file would be written. To avoid this, select the *curriculum* map on the Level 1 flowline. Open the Data pull-down menu and select Calculations. Enter the following to set the name to Jane Doe:

```
IF(UserName = " ", UserName = "Jane Doe")
-- forces name Jane Doe to UserName when only a space is entered
```

Complete the Curriculum Menu Map

Your curriculum menu is the core of the CMI system, where you offer the learner all the curriculum options. There will be pushbuttons for Pre-Test, Instructional Resources, post test Reports, and Practice Resources, besides a Quit button. To build it, you will create a structure composed of an interaction icon with one calculation and five maps. Open the *curriculum menu* map, drag an interaction icon to the flowline, and name it *menu*. Then drag a map icon to associate with menu, accept the Pushbutton response type when presented, close the dialog box, and label the icon *Quit*.

You can take a shortcut here to make all the buttons on the menu the same size. By creating the Quit button in the right size, you can copy and paste it so the other icons will have the same-size buttons. The menu itself will accommodate all the buttons nicely if they are 184 wide by 42 high. Open the pushbutton response type symbol above Quit and select the Position and Size button. Change the dimensions to 184 wide by 42 high.

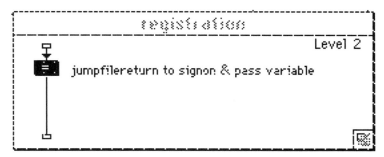

Figure 23.28 Registration

We can't tell you the placement numbers. Ours is 341 down and 365 over from the upper left corner of the screen. If you place the frame differently than we did, by as little as a single pixel, your numbers will be different. You will be able to place them by eye. Leave the Position and Size dialog box and select OK to return to the icons.

Development Tip: When you design a lesson, you can ease the programming by doing the button math. Every set of buttons will not fit evenly in a box of any size; one or two buttons cannot be the same as the others. For example, the button placeholder box on the menu is 184 pixels wide by 252 pixels high. Six buttons fit perfectly in it, but five would not. All the other button placeholders in the curriculum were precalculated in the same way.

Now copy *Quit* and paste it five times to the right of itself. Name the new versions *Pre-Test, Instructional Resources, post test, Reports*, and *Practice Resources*. Now open *Quit*. Place a calculation icon in it and close *Quit*. Now ungroup the map to reveal only the calculation on the flowline. Figure 23.29 shows the completed curriculum structure.

Complete the menu

The menu provides the learner with an easy way to select from the various services your CMI system provides. They match the icons you just created: *Pre-Test, Instructional Resources, post test, Reports, Practice Resources*, and *Quit*.

Open and immediately close *want mouse practice?* First, select the *menu* icon and pull down the Attributes menu. Select Effects and set the Effect to Mosaic, then open *menu* and pause at the interaction dialog box. Set the Erase Effect to Mosaic and change the Erase interaction from On Exit to After Next Entry. Then select OK-Edit Display for editing. Import the *cu_menu.pct* graphic and place it to match the mouse practice frame. Move the buttons to fit in the button placeholders of the graphic. Your completed work should look like Figure 23.30.

Complete Quit

This Quit is the same as many you have already made elsewhere. Open the *Quit* calculation, enter **Quit(0)**, and close it. That's it!

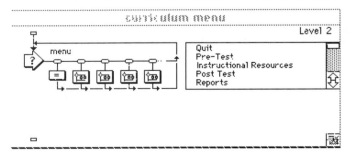

Figure 23.29 Curriculum Map Menu

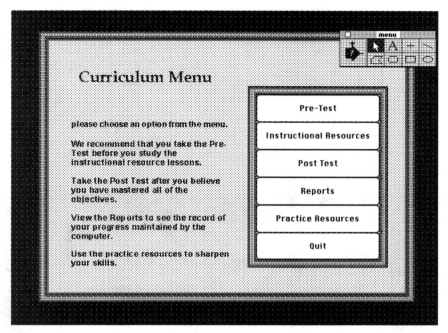

Figure 23.30 Menu

Complete instructional resources

Copy the *Quit* to preserve the button size. Then, open the Instructional Resources map, drag an interaction icon to the flowline, and name it *choose instruction*. Then paste *Quit* and rename it *Crane Operator Signals*. Then copy *Crane Operator Signals* and paste it four times to the right of itself. Name the new icons *Balancing the Load, Mixing Concrete, EKG Electrodes,* and *Return*. Then group *Return,* open it, delete the calculation to leave an empty map icon, and close it . The *Return* icon will remain blank so that, when its pushbutton is selected, the flowline will fall through it. The flow should then return to the main flowline. To make that happen, hold down the Control key and click on the branching arrow at the bottom of the icon. As you have experienced before, each click will cycle the arrow through the branching options. Stop at Exit Interaction, which is a left-facing arrowhead. Figure 23.31 shows the Instructional Resources structure as it will appear when you reach this point.

Open and immediately close *want mouse practice?* Then, select the *choose instruction* icon, select Effects from the Attributes pull-down menu, and set the Effect to Mosaic. Then open *choose instruction* and pause at the interaction dialog box. Set the Erase Effect to Mosaic. Then hold in shift, select OK-Edit Display to edit. Import the *cu_i_r.pct* graphic and place it to match the mouse practice frame. Then place the buttons to fit nicely on the button placeholder. Figure 23.32 shows the Instructional Resources menu as it will appear when you have made the placements.

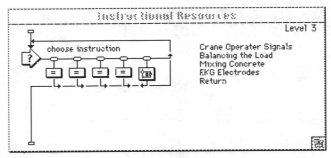

Figure 23.31 Instructional Resources

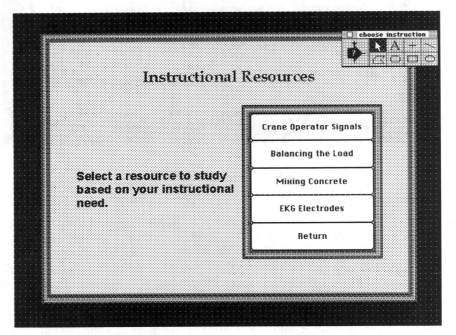

Figure 23.32 Instructional Resources Menu

Now you can gain one of the benefits that course developers use all the time. You can copy some code that you have already carefully produced. Go to the *mouse literacy* map and open it to reveal the *Yly* calculation icon. Open *Yly* to reveal its argument and documentation:

```
JumpFileReturn(FileLocation^"mousepr")
-- jumps out to the mousepr lesson to provide practice using the mouse
```

Copy the argument and comment, then return to the *Crane Operator Signals* calculation icon and open it. Now paste the argument and comment into the calculation window. It is almost exactly what you need here! Simply replace the word **mousepr** with the word **crane,** and modify the comment. The result will be:

```
JumpFileReturn(FileLocation^"crane")
-- jumps out to the crane lesson to provide hand signal instruction
```

This argument will cause the learner who selects the Crane Operator Signals pushbutton to jump out to the crane lesson you created in Chapter 15. Now you can repeat the same shortcut. One by one, open each of the remaining calculation icons and paste the same function and comment into them, and make edits as follows:

Icon Name	Change mousepr to	Comment
Balancing the Load	**truck**	**-- jumps out to the crane lesson** **-- to provide hand signal** **instruction**
Mixing Concrete	**concrete**	**-- jumps out to the concrete lesson** **-- to provide concrete mixing** **instruction**
EKG Electrodes	**EKG**	**-- jumps out to the ekg lesson to** **-- to provide electrode placement** **instruction**

Test Drive

You can give it a spin. Your lesson should perform all the options you had previously, and should also provide the ability to explore the instructional resources you have already programmed. If this is not the case, you will want to carefully review the preceding steps to look for discrepancies in your code. You can also look at the completed curriculum that we have provided on the CD, to verify what the resulting code should look like.

Complete practice resources

The flowline structure for the *Practice Resources* map is the same as the *Instructional Resources* map. Now you can save even more time in programming your curriculum by copying the entire structure from inside the *Instructional Resources* map. Open the *Instructional Resources* map and select all the icons, by drawing a rectangle around them while holding down the left mouse button. When you have all the icons selected they will be black. If you missed a few, you can easily repeat the process until you save them all. (If this proves too difficult, click on Select All from the Edit pull-down menu.) Now copy them and close the *Instructional Resources* map. Open the *Practice Resources* map and paste. Rename the interaction *resources*. Delete one of the *calculations* as it is not needed. Now rename the others *ADA Reader, Flashcards,* and *Mouse Practice.* The *Return* map is correctly named already. Figure 23.33 shows the *Practice Resources* structure as it will appear when you reach this point.

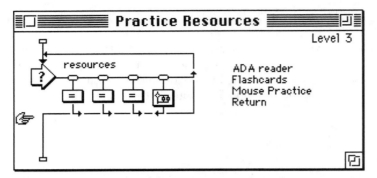

Figure 23.33 Practice Resources Map

Open the *resources* interaction and select **OK-Edit Display** to continue. *Do not* delete the previous contents of the display. Import the *cu_p_r.pct* graphic and place it exactly covering the Instructional Resources frame. When you are satisfied and while it is still selected, choose Send to Back from the Attributes pull-down menu. Then click on the Instructional Resources frame and delete it. Then place the buttons to fit on the button placeholders. Figure 23.34 shows the Practice Resources menu as it will appear when you have completed the placements.

Again you can increase efficiency by using code that you have already produced. Open the *ADA reader* map calculation icon. Its argument will be similar to our old friend mousepr . . . but it needs another word. Simply replace the name of the file with **ada**. Then modify the comment. The result will be:

```
JumpFileReturn(FileLocation^"ada")
-- jumps out to the ada reading utility
```

Now you can repeat the shortcut. One by one, open each of the remaining calculation icons and revise the function as follows:

Icon Name	Change file name to	Comment
Flashcards	**flshcard**	-- jumps out to the flashcard drill and practice
Mouse Practice	**mousepr**	-- jumps out to the mousepr lesson to provide -- practice using the mouse

Test Drive

Fun time again. Make sure the lesson performs all the options as previously, plus the new ones. Be sure to leave with Return. If the lessons are not working properly, carefully review the preceding steps to look for discrepancies in your code. Also look at the completed curriculum that we provided on the CD to review the corresponding code.

 Development Tip: It is a good practice to run your lessons often. If an error has entered your code you may see it early and find a simple solution. Otherwise, if you wait until you have larger blocks of code, it will be more difficult to debug and determine the source of the error.

Complete pre-test

Now you will create the functionality that permits the learner to try the pre-test. Eventually the pre-test will be available before the instruction, and any objective mastered on the pre-test will not be tested again on the post test.

You will also have Authorware pass variables back and forth between the curriculum and the test (actually there is only one test question bank for the curriculum; it is used by both the pre- and post test functions). These variables will allow the test to tell the curriculum which questions were answered correctly, enabling the curriculum to provide the appropriate prescription. After the post test, if all the objectives have been mastered, the curriculum will present a diploma signifying the learner's mastery.

Open the Pre-Test map and drag an interaction icon to the flowline. Name it *provide prescription* and associate three icons with it. The first two are maps that you should name *Return* and *Take Pre-Test*. Since the first icon dragged will assume the pushbutton response type you can accept it as created. The other icon is a calculation to be named *Print Prescription*.

All the associated icons have Try Again branching. Leave *Print Prescription* as it is. Change *Return* to Exit Interaction branching by using the Control-click shortcut.

Use the same technique to change the branching for *Take Pre-Test*. You could leave it as it is. However, we think that if you change it to Continue branching it will provide a visual reminder of what is occurring. Remember Continue branching is signified by small arrows that appear to enter and leave the icon at the top. Figure 23.35 shows the icon structure for Pre-Test.

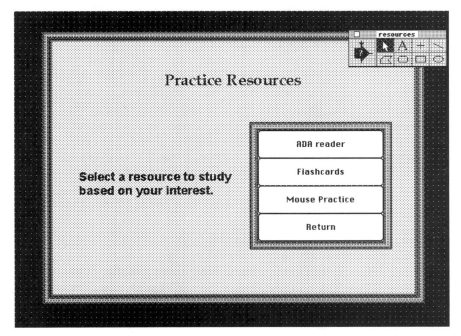

Figure 23.34 Practice Resources Menu

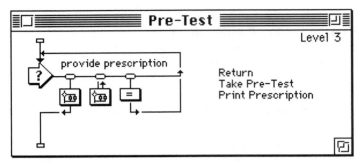

Figure 23.35 Pre-Test Map

You can confirm that the branching is changed by opening the response type symbol above Take Pre-Test. It will open the dialog box shown in Figure 23.36. You can see that the default branch of Try again has changed to Continue. In the future, you won't have to confirm such changes.

Next you will place the Instructional Prescription menu in the *provide prescription* icon. You can take a big shortcut again. Copy the *menu* interaction display of the *curriculum* map. Paste it on the Level 3 flowline of the *Pre-test* map. It will bring with it its attributes: draw effect, erase effect, and frame placement. Rename it *provide prescription* and open it to edit the display and import the *cuipmenu.pct* file, placing it accurately on the pre-existing frame. When you are satisfied, send it to the background and delete the *menu* frame. Position the Print Prescription, Take Pre-Test, and Exit buttons in the button evenly across the bottom of the screen.

Next you will embed variables in the display, as you did in the crane operator lesson in Chapter 15. Using the text tool, select a spot in the large box and click to establish the text field. Type:

```
{prescription}
```

Then stretch the text field across the box to provide space for the longer lines of text that will be displayed in it. Pick a moderate size font (12-point or so) that looks pleasing to you. If you don't like it later when the prescription is displayed, you can always change it.

When you close the text field, Authorware will require an initial value for the new variable **prescription**. (Mac users choose character.) Set an initial value of " ". Then enter a description something like:

```
recommended learner study assignment
```

Select OK to close the New Variable dialog box.

Now you will make a similar text field for the learner's name. Remember that the learner's name is held in the variable UserName, and that you have already assigned a value of Jane Doe to UserName when you built the *want mouse practice?* icon. Click below the Instructional Prescription with the text cursor. Type:

```
{UserName}
```

Now pick a pleasing font (you may want to try Times) and set a large font size so that **{UserName}** is approximately the same size as the line above it.

In this case, select Justification from the Text pull-down menu and choose Centered to center **{UserName}** in the text field. Then drag the ends of the field nearly to each side of the display to compensate for longer or shorter names. Your completed Instructional Prescription menu will look approximately like Figure 23.37.

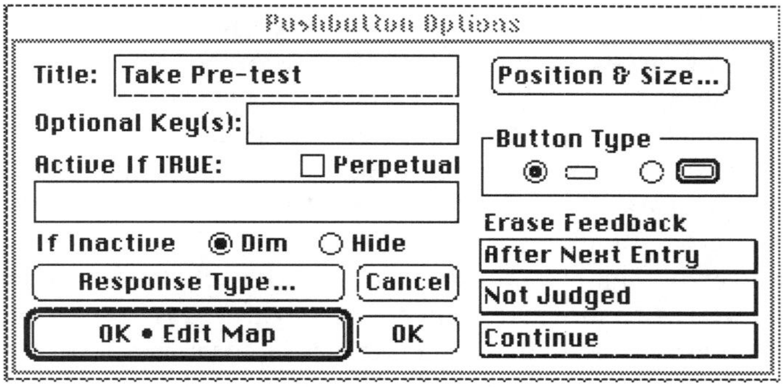

Figure 23.36 Options Box with Continue Selected

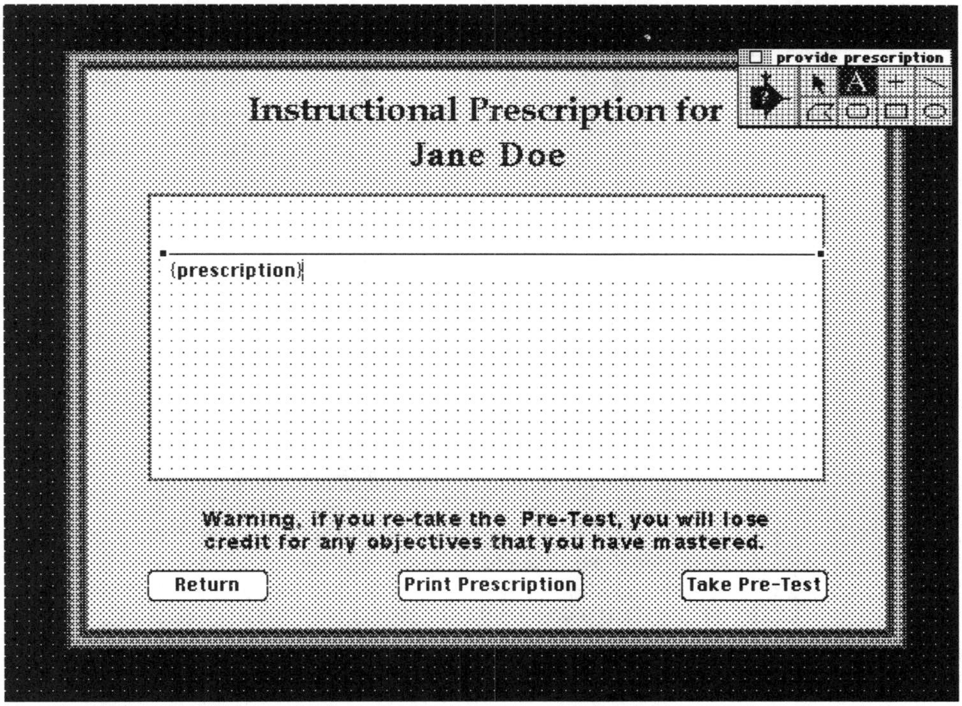

Figure 23.37 Pre-Test Results Menu

It is not possible to have two text fields open at the same time, so our example shows **{UserName}** with the initial value displayed and the **{prescription}** embedded variable revealed. Use these as guides for placement and size of the text. Close the *provide prescription* icon.

You will now arrange for the jump to the pre-test. Open the *Take Pre-Test* icon and drag two calculation icons to its flowline. Name the upper one *jumpfilereturn to pretest, pass variables* and the lower one *save data file on results*. Figure 23.38 shows these icons.

 Authorware Tip: Sometimes it is better to use separate calculations, or other type icons. This is one of those cases. Authorware will start to execute one "line" of its code and immediately start to execute the next (this is especially obvious when it starts to execute an animation and then a sound). In this case, Authorware would execute the first argument and jump. Upon return, it would begin with the next icon, causing the remaining arguments in the first icon to be missed. Therefore, you would have created two calculations.

Now you will set the initial values for the objectives that the test will measure. These variables will, when modified, generate the instructional prescription. Finally, you will set up an append file function to record the mastery of each objective. Be extremely careful in entering the arguments; a small mistake can spoil your work and may be difficult for you to find.

Open the *jumpfilereturn to pretest, pass variables* icon for editing. But you will create a set of four variables to track performance on each of four objectives. You have already created them in the *cu_test.apw* file. These same variable names must be used because you will be passing their values between the two different files. You will use long, descriptive names to make it easier to follow what is happening as you create, and possibly later modify, the arguments. Short, cryptic names would be easier to enter, but harder to interpret. You can't have it both ways. Enter the following exactly:

```
obj_1_correct = FALSE
obj_2_correct = FALSE
obj_3_correct = FALSE
obj_4_correct = FALSE
-- Sets test results to failed before test taking
```

This also provides the characteristic of setting the pre-test so that if a learner repeats the pre-test (something we would not expect or encourage) it will provide a fresh test of knowledge, regardless of previous success.

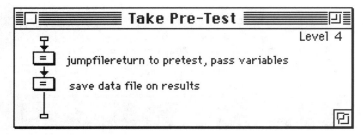

Figure 23.38 Take Pre-Test Map

Finally, you will add the **JumpFileReturn** function by pasting from the Show Functions menu. You may recall that its format is:

```
JumpFileReturn("filename" [,"variable1, variable2…", "directory"])
```

Add FileLocation and follow it with the ^ (concatenation symbol) before "filename." Delete the first bracket ([ ) and overwrite variable1, variable2… with the variables you want to pass. They are:

- UserName
- obj_1_correct
- obj_2_correct
- obj_3_correct
- obj_4_correct

Separate them by commas. Delete the final comma, quotation mark, the word directory, final quote, and bracket. The resulting argument is as shown below. However, we have come to an argument that is too long to print on one line of this book. As you may recall from Chapter 22, we will use the special character ¬ to indicate that the end of the line is really artificial, and that you must treat it as one line.

```
JumpFileReturn(FileLocation^"cu_test","UserName, obj_1_correct,¬
obj_2_correct,obj_3_correct,obj_4_correct")
-- Jumps out to test and returns
```

When you close the calculation window you will be asked about each of the new variables that you have created. The chart below indicates the variables that you should be asked about, and the initial value for each. If you are asked about any other variable, it indicates that you have made a mistake typing the arguments. If this happens, select Cancel and return to the expression to identify and edit the problem.

Variable Name	Initial Value	Comment
obj_1_correct	FALSE	**records objective 1 test results. used by the CMI system to determine which test questions to administer**
obj_2_correct	FALSE	**records objective 2 test results. used by the CMI system to determine which test questions to administer**
obj_3_correct	FALSE	**records objective 3 test results. used by the CMI system to determine which test questions to administer**
obj_4_correct	FALSE	**records objective 4 test results. used by the CMI system to determine which test questions to administer**

Now open the *save data file on results* calculation icon for editing. This is the most complex entry we will ask you to make in this book. It also is longer than the average you are likely to use in your near-future authoring. It may represent average or smaller and less complex than the average for highly skilled programmers.

You will set the initial value for prescription as blank quotes to purge any value it may have before beginning the pre-test. Then you will create four IF statements that will build the lines of the prescription, to indicate mastery or recommend an instructional resource. Next, you will append an external file that will write an external text file that will hold information about the learner's performance. Finally, the last statement checks whether all objectives are mastered. If so, the program will show the diploma. You will use a savvy programming technique on this one.

Type in the expression and comment:

```
prescription = ""
-- this will remove the previous contents of prescription
-- prior to writing the new one
```

Now find the IF statement from the General Function category. Read the Description before Pasting it into the *save data file on results* calculation window.

```
IF(condition,TRUE expression,FALSE expression)
```

Replace **condition** with:

```
obj_4_correct = FALSE
```

Next you will create the true expression. Immediately after the first comma, type:

```
prescription =
```

Then paste the InsertLine function (Character category). Read the Description and Paste it into the calculation window. It will be:

```
InsertLine(string,n,newstring ,delim)
```

Mac users will find that the paste results in :

```
InsertLine(string,n,newstring [,delim])
```

Both platform users delete the [,delim], as it isn't needed here.

Replace string with *prescription*. Set the line number n to zero and replace **new string** with the following: "Objective four not mastered. Study the Mixing Concrete lesson." including the quotation marks. This completes the TRUE expression.

It will be much easier to write the FALSE expression. Simply copy the entire TRUE expression you have just finished (NOT the condition) and paste it to replace the FALSE expression. Then delete the last sentence and the not that precedes the word mastered. Look carefully at your argument. It should look exactly like the example below, except that yours must all be on one line.

```
IF(obj_4_correct = FALSE, ¬
prescription = InsertLine(prescription,0,"Objective four not mastered. ¬
```

```
Study the Mixing Concrete lesson"), ¬
prescription = InsertLine(prescription,0,"Objective four mastered"))
```

Quality check

Time for a Quality check. Count your commas. There should be a total of six. Now compare your parentheses carefully. When you are satisfied that everything is right, close the calculation. If you have done everything perfectly, the icon will close without a complaint. If there is a syntax error, Authorware will ask you to define or clarify something. If you are asked for an initial value, cancel. If the syntax is wrong, OK will return you to editing. In either case, look careful at the expression to find and fix the discrepancy.

Once it closes you can reopen it to finish the four IF statements. Copy the IF statement that you just created and paste it three times. Then all you have to do is change the objective number and the actual prescription. Copy the prescriptions and comment from the example below.

```
IF(obj_3_correct = FALSE, prescription =  ¬
InsertLine(prescription,0,"Objective three not mastered. Study  ¬
the EKG lesson"),prescription =  ¬
InsertLine(prescription,0,"Objective three mastered"))
IF(obj_2_correct = FALSE, prescription =  ¬
InsertLine(prescription,0,"Objective two not mastered. Study  ¬
the Balance the Load lesson"),prescription =  ¬
InsertLine(prescription,0,"Objective two mastered"))
IF(obj_1_correct = FALSE, prescription =  ¬
InsertLine(prescription,0,"Objective one not mastered. Study  ¬
the Crane Operator lesson"),prescription =  ¬
InsertLine(prescription,0,"Objective one mastered"))
-- inserts four lines into prescription based on the test result
-- insert causes the line before to be "pushed down" so they are
-- in reverse order
```

Next, you will set up the Append. Get the AppendExtFile function from the File Category. Read the Description and then Paste it into the calculation. It will be:

```
AppendExtFile("filename",string)
```

First add a new system variable that's not too different from the old familiar FileLocation. It is RecordsLocation. It contains a path to the APW_DATA subdirectory located in the Windows directory (APM folder in the System folder on the Mac). Get the RecordsLocation variable from the File Category, read the Description and Paste it after the open parenthesis. Add the ^"my_data\\ "^ after RecordsLocation to combine the file name with the records location path. It will then be:

```
AppendExtFile(RecordsLocation^"my_data\\"^"filename",string)
```

You would like the remainder of the "filename" to be UserName, but you must face the DOS limitation of eight characters with no spaces and Authorware's (for Windows) requirement for a file extension. You will handle this with nested functions. By using nested functions, you will avoid creating custom variables just to achieve the metamorphosis. It will take several steps.

Mac Difference: The Mac freedom to use up to 31 characters in a file name allows you to omit stripping spaces and cutting to 8 characters. Your file name can be: *RecordsLocation^"my_data:"^UserName.*

Development Tip: When you must work with both a name and an employee number (or another identification number, such as social security number, or other identifying information) you can create the data files using the number rather than the name. Such files are much more likely to be unique among a large number of users.

Now you will nest one function inside another. The result will capture the last word contained in the variable UserName, and will join it with the FirstName to form the name of the file that holds the learner's prescription. Highlight "filename" and replace it by pasting the GetWord function (another Character function).

```
AppendExtFile(RecordsLocation^"my_data\\"^GetWord(n,string),string)
```

The n is the word count. You will replace n with the (Character) function Word-Count. Paste it to replace the n. Then fill the string in the parentheses with User-Name. The result will be:

```
AppendExtFile(RecordsLocation^"my_data\\"^GetWord(WordCount(UserName), ¬
string),string)
```

Now you are ready to work on the first string, which is the final part of the Word-Count. Replace the string portion of the function with UserName. The result will be:

```
AppendExtFile(RecordsLocation^"my_data\\"^GetWord(WordCount(UserName), ¬
UserName),string)
```

Now make provision for more than one person with the same family name (of less than eight characters). After the final parenthesis following the second UserName, enter ^FirstName. This will attach the first name to the end of the last name. The result will be:

```
AppendExtFile(RecordsLocation^"my_data\\"^GetWord(WordCount(UserName), ¬
UserName^FirstName),string)
```

Now look at the second string, which is the content of the file to be appended. Replace the string portion of the function with:

```
UserName^Return^"Instructional prescription on "^Date^Return^prescription
^Return
```

The complete function is finished. Be very careful to include a space after the word on. That will provide a space in the eventual date and the words you just entered. Note that UserName, Date, and prescription are variables that should not be enclosed in quotes. The function, with a comment, should read:

```
AppendExtFile(RecordsLocation^"my_data\\"^GetWord(WordCount(UserName), ¬
UserName^FirstName), ¬
UserName^Return^"Instructional prescription on "^Date^Return^prescription
^Return)
-- writes the prescription to an external file with filename based on
```

```
the learner's
-- last name plus first name up to a total of 8 characters
```

You will be completely finished when you add an IF statement to look for a prescription with all objectives mastered. In this special case, there will be no recommended instructional resources and the learner will branch directly to the diploma. Don't you wish all programs operated this way?

Paste an IF statement function from the General Category. You are very familiar with it by now. It will be:

```
IF(condition,TRUE expression,FALSE expression)
```

The condition will inspect the values of the four objective correct variables. You may recall that the initial values will be FALSE. If the learner achieved mastery on each objective, they will all be TRUE at this point. Therefore, if all of them are TRUE, the entire condition is TRUE, and the TRUE expression will be executed. If any of them are FALSE, the FALSE expression will be executed.

Start by deleting the second comma and FALSE expression, because if it is executed the flow will just drop down and continue. Now change the condition to:

```
obj_1_correct & obj_2_correct & obj_3_correct & obj_4_correct
```

At this point, you should have:

```
IF(obj_1_correct & obj_2_correct & obj_3_correct & obj_4_correct, ¬
TRUE expression)
```

Finally, replace the TRUE expression with a GoTo function you can paste in from the Jump Category. It will be:

```
GoTo(IconID@"IconTitle")
```

Replace the word IconTitle with diploma and then prepare to look very clever. The diploma icon doesn't exist yet. Authorware will not accept what you have just typed, but it was clearer and simpler to enter it now. What can you do?

You can put this work on hold by commenting it out. Just type two hyphens before the IF so that Authorware will ignore it in executing your program. After you create the diploma, you will come back to *save data file on results* and remove the hyphens to activate the line.

The completed IF statement, with comment, should now look like this:

```
-- IF(obj_1_correct & obj_2_correct & obj_3_correct & ¬
obj_4_correct,GoTo(IconID@"diploma"))
-- if all questions are mastered, go straight to the diploma
```

Close the *save data file on results* calculation icon.

Set the default prescription

Finally, you have to give the variable called prescription an initial value at the *want mouse practice?* icon at the very beginning of the file. Select *want mouse practice?* and open the appended calculation (Calculations under the Data pull-down menu).

You are going to enter a long string of text to provide the initial value for prescription. Now enter prescription and its entire initial value and comment as shown:

```
prescription = "Objective four not tested. Study the Mixing ¬
Concrete lesson"^Return^"Objective three not tested. Study ¬
the EKG lesson"^Return^"Objective two not tested. Study the ¬
Balance the Load lesson"^Return^"Objective one not tested. ¬
Study the Crane Operator lesson"
-- this is the default prescription for a user who has not
-- demonstrated mastery of any of the objectives
```

Test Drive

Run your curriculum and try the pre-test. Your instructional prescription page should accurately assign a prescription based on your success (or lack of it) on the test.

Troubleshooting

We suggest that you read the section titled *Using Displayed Variables to Track Functionality* in Chapter 16 now, to explore how you can solidify what is happening in your program. Figure 23.39 shows how your screen looked as you tested the passing of variables during the development of the CMI system's *curricul* program. So

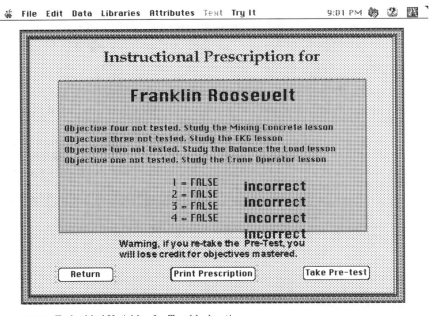

Figure 23.39 Embedded Variables for Troubleshooting

that you can appreciate the results depicted, the way we used the variables on the left of the two embedded sets were:

```
1 = {obj_1_correct}
2 = {obj_2_correct}
3 = {obj_3_correct}
4 = {obj_4_correct}
```

The screen is showing the results when none of the questions were answered correctly. On the right is an embedded variable that you created temporarily just to use in troubleshooting. We were looking at the way the questions worked in reporting their results to Authorware and ultimately being passed successfully back to the curriculum. This might look something like:

```
{troubleshooting_1 = response1}
{troubleshooting_2 = response1}
{troubleshooting_3 = response1}
{troubleshooting_4 = response1}
```

To ensure that the test collected information about the learner's success—not the same as functioning correctly on-screen—we did a similar thing in the test. Figure 23.40 shows the under-development test with embedded variables for troubleshooting.

The variables here are the same as on the left in Figure 23.39, preceded by one you have yet to create (revealing that this was captured at a slightly later stage in out testing). You will soon see how it was used.

```
objective = {objective_number}
1 = {obj_1_correct}
2 = {obj_2_correct}
3 = {obj_3_correct}
4 = {obj_4_correct}
```

Complete post test

The post test administers the same test as is used by the pre-test. Because we tracked mastery of objectives during the pre-test, we can avoid repeating the testing for these objectives. The post test reports results to the curriculum that are then used to advise that mastery has not been achieved, or to display the diploma.

Open the *Post Test* map for editing. Drag two calculations to the path and name them *jumpfile return to post test, pass variables,* and *save data file on results.* Then drag a decision icon to the flowline and drop it below *save data file on results.* Name it *mastery.* Attach two map icons to the *mastery* decision icon and name them *sorry* and *certificate.* The completed *post test* structure should look like Figure 23.41.

Start by opening the *jumpfile return to pre-test* calculation icon and copy the JumpFileReturn function with all its arguments. After you paste it, the contents of *jumpfile return to post test* should be:

```
JumpFileReturn(FileLocation^"cu_test","UserName,obj_1_correct, ¬
obj_2_correct,obj_3_correct,obj_4_correct")
-- Jumps out to test and returns
```

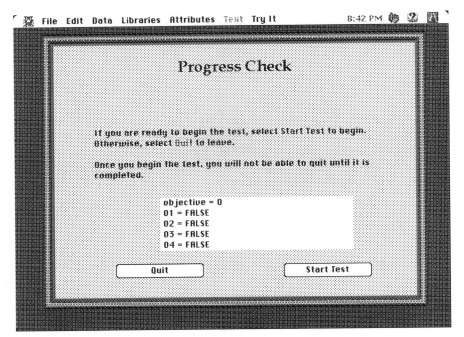

Figure 23.40 Test with Embedded Variables for Troubleshooting

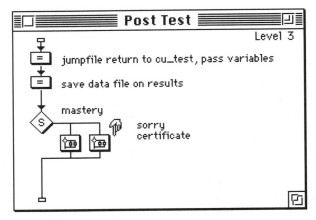

Figure 23.41 Post-Test

Close it and open the *save data file on results* calculation in the *pre-test*, copy the contents of the calculation, and paste it into the *save data file on results* calculation in the post test. (You can see it earlier in this chapter, just below the Quality Check subhead.)

You must make a change to the last expression because it is the one that writes to the learner's data file. It says:

```
prescription := ""
-- this will remove the previous contents of prescription
-- prior to writing the new one
IF(obj_4_correct = FALSE, prescription := ¬
InsertLine(prescription,0,"Objective four not mastered. Study the Mixing ¬
Concrete lesson"),prescription := InsertLine(prescription,0,"Objective ¬
four mastered"))
IF(obj_3_correct = FALSE, prescription := ¬
InsertLine(prescription,0,"Objective three not mastered. Study the EKG ¬
lesson"),prescription := InsertLine(prescription,0,"Objective three ¬
mastered"))
IF(obj_2_correct = FALSE, prescription := ¬
InsertLine(prescription,0,"Objective two not mastered. Study the Balance ¬
the Load lesson"),prescription := InsertLine(prescription,0,"Objective ¬
two mastered"))
IF(obj_1_correct = FALSE, prescription := ¬
InsertLine(prescription,0,"Objective one not mastered. Study the Crane ¬
Operator lesson"),prescription := InsertLine(prescription,0,"Objective ¬
one mastered"))
-- inserts four lines into prescription based on the test result
-- insert causes the line before to be "pushed down" so they are
-- in reverse order
AppendExtFile(RecordsLocation^"my_data\\"^GetWord(WordCount(UserName), ¬
UserName^FirstName),UserName^Return^"Instructional prescription on ¬
"^Date^Return^prescription^Return)
-- writes the prescription to an external file with filename based on ¬
the learner's last name plus first name up to a total of 8 characters
-- IF(obj_1_correct & obj_2_correct & obj_3_correct &
-- obj_4_correct,GoTo(IconID@"diploma"))
-- if all questions are mastered, go straight to the diploma
```

Now delete the last three lines, since they are not appropriate for the post test. This expression is going to add to what has already been written in the learner's record file, so you don't want to re-write the learner's name. Delete the UserName^ that appears in the AppendExtFile function. Carefully compare the corrected text below with the original above, to be sure to identify the correct one (of three) User-Names to remove.

```
AppendExtFile(RecordsLocation^"my_data\\"^GetWord(WordCount(UserName), ¬
UserName^FirstName),Return^"Instructional prescription on" ¬
^Date^Return^prescription^Return)
```

Then change "Instructional prescription on" to "Post test results on" (don't forget the space at the end). In addition, you can add a time stamp, using the FullTime variable, to show exactly when the post test was completed. You can type it in, but read its description under the Time Category. After the "^Date^ add:

```
" at "^FullTime^
```

Your efforts will yield the following changed AppendExtFile:

```
AppendExtFile(RecordsLocation^"my_data\\"^GetWord(WordCount(UserName), ¬
UserName^FirstName),Return^"Post test results on ¬
"^Date^" at "^FullTime^Return^prescription^Return)
```

Close the calculation. You may be wondering what is placed in the file. Here is the data file generated by Jane Doe. She started by taking the pre-test on December 17th. She mastered two objectives—one and three. She studied the instructional resource for objective two but skipped the study for objective four, because it was getting late. She took the post test and mastered objective two, but not four. Since it was late she went home, but returned the next day and studied the resource for objective four. When she took the post test again she mastered the final objective. Her record file looks like this:

```
Jane Doe
Instructional prescription on 12/17/94
Objective one mastered
Objective two not mastered. Study the Balance the Load lesson
Objective three mastered
Objective four not mastered. Study the Mixing Concrete lesson

Post test results on 12/17/94 at 9:18:50 PM
Objective one mastered
Objective two mastered
Objective three mastered
Objective four not mastered. Study the Mixing Concrete lesson

Post test results on 12/18/95 at 10:23:14 AM
Objective one mastered
Objective two mastered
Objective three mastered
Objective four mastered
```

Now you are ready to edit the *mastery* decision icon to tell Authorware whether to display a message saying the learner did not achieve mastery, or to display the diploma. Now open the *mastery* icon. Change the default Sequential Branching to Calculated Path. Now enter the IF statement in the field. Carefully enter the following:

```
IF(obj_1_correct & obj_2_correct & obj_3_correct & obj_3_correct &
obj_4_correct,2,1)
```

Figure 23.42 shows the completed mastery decision options dialog box. Close the dialog box.

Open and close the *menu* icon in the *curriculum menu* map and immediately close it. Then open the *sorry* map and, when the decision dialog box opens, change the Erase Displayed Objects from the default Before Next Selection to On Exit. Click OK-Edit Map to continue. Now drag an interaction icon to the flowline and call it *sorry message*. (For your information, we are using an interaction here to save icons. The same result could be achieved with a display icon followed by an erase icon.) Open it and change the Erase Interaction to Mosaic and select the Pause Before Exiting checkbox, and *while holding down the shift key*, select OK-Edit Display. Then carefully import and place the graphic *cu_msg.pct*. Then select the text tool and click in the upper left of the graphic's report box. Enter the following:

```
{prescription}
```

It should be transparent, based on your earlier selections. If not, set it now. Then open the Attributes menu to access the Effects pull-down menu. Select the Mosaic erase effect.

You are now ready to complete the *certificate*. Open the *certificate* icon, drag a display icon to the flowline, and name it *diploma*. Then drag an interaction icon to

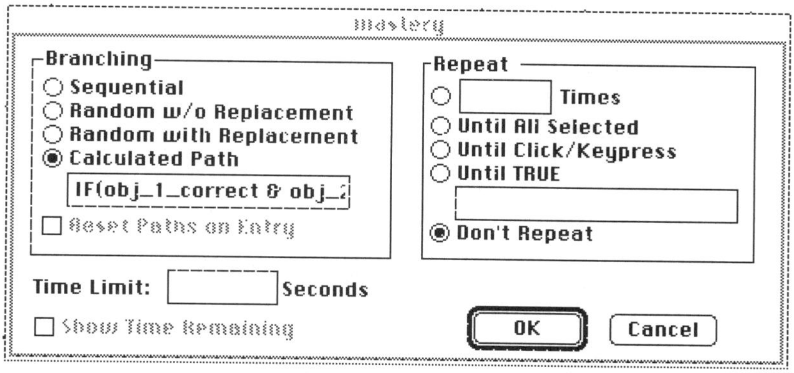

Figure 23.42 Mastery Decision Options Dialog Box

the flowline and name it *print a certificate*. There will be two buttons, offering the learner the choice of printing the certificate or not. Drag a calculation to associate it with *print a certificate*. Accept the pushbutton response type and name it *Print*. Then drag a map to the right of *Print* and name it *Continue*. Change the branching of the feedback by Control-clicking the flowline below the *Print* and *Continue* icons. Figure 23.43 shows the *certificate* structure.

The next step is to import the graphic of the certificate of completion into the *diploma* icon. The correct file is *cu_diplo.pct*. Once it is imported and placed, choose Effects from the Attributes pull-down menu and select the Mosaic effect for action on display.

You must add embedded variables for the learner's name and the date of completion. The course name doesn't fit the curriculum contents, but we wanted to provide you with something for all your efforts. If you have worked your way to this point in the exercises, you deserve it! Select the text tool and enter:

```
{UserName}
```

nicely centered in the space between competed by and In the workshop. Make sure the Font is attractive, and that you select center justification, transparent mode, and a size of approximately 18 points.

Then copy the text object to keep all its characteristics. Paste it under the Given. Change the font size to 8-point Arial Bold, and select and overwrite the text with:

```
{MonthName} {Day}, {Year}
```

Figure 23.44 shows the certificate after it has been placed in the presentation window. Close the display.

If you have just completed the editing of the embedded variables, the diploma is in memory. If it is not there, open and close the diploma icon to place it there. Then open the *print a certificate* interaction to reposition the buttons. As you do so the *print a certificate* interaction options dialog box will open. When it does, change the Erase Interaction from Upon Exit to After Next Entry. This will erase the buttons

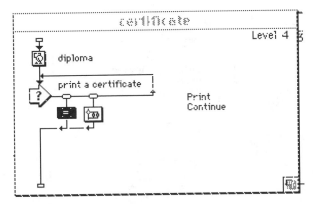

Figure 23.43   Certificate Structure

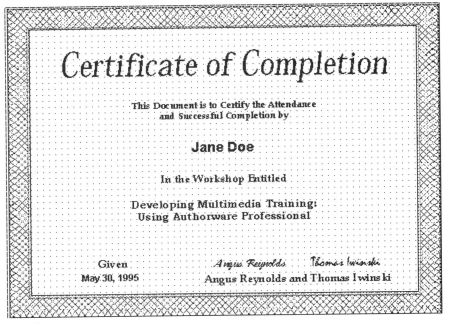

Figure 23.44   Diploma Display Icon

from the screen before the certificate prints. Figure 23.45 shows the revised *print a certificate* interaction options dialog box.

Figure 23.46 shows how we have repositioned the buttons. Place them in similar positions and close the icon.

Now open the Print calculation for editing. You could type the PrintScreen function, but if you did you would miss the Description. Open the General Category to select PrintScreen and read its Description. Then Paste it.

```
PrintScreen()
```

Now for a bit of housekeeping. Do you remember that you commented-out an expression that would GoTo the *diploma* icon if the learner achieved mastery on all objectives in the pre-test? Now is the time to undo that action. Open the *Pre-Test* map icon, and then the *Take a Pre-Test* map to reveal the *save data file on results* calculation icon. Open it and remove the hyphens which comment-out the IF expression. Close the icon.

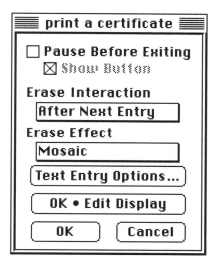

Figure 23.45 Print Interaction Dialog Box

Figure 23.46 Running Certificate Showing Buttons

Test Drive

The major difference in what you have just done is that now, if the learner gets the test completely right on the pre-test, he or she will proceed directly to the diploma. You can run the post test and see the questions, but you haven't completed the part that tracks your performance.

Troubleshooting

If the year on your learner's diploma is shown as 1,995 it is because the Number Format under the Data pull-down menu is set to Show Thousands/Millions Separator. If it is checked there, click to deselect it.

Add the post test Capability

You will change the now-linear questions into randomly selected, without replacement and offer them only if they were not previously mastered when the same learner took the pre-test or post test.

Save and close the *curricul* file, and open *cu_test*. Open the *Start Test* map and drag a calculation to its Level 2 flowline. Don't worry about its name at this point. Open the calculation .

At this point you will create four IF statements that will check the variables that were passed to the test from the curriculum. If the learner had previously mastered an objective, its variable (obj_1_correct, for example) would have a value of TRUE. If it is TRUE you want to remove the matching question from the question pool. You will create a new variable to track whether a question was mastered or offered once already in the current test session. In either case, the question will be ignored.

Carefully enter the following:

```
IF(obj_1_correct = TRUE, obj_1_complete = TRUE, obj_1_complete =FALSE)
IF(obj_2_correct = TRUE, obj_2_complete = TRUE, obj_2_complete =FALSE)
IF(obj_3_correct = TRUE, obj_3_complete = TRUE, obj_3_complete =FALSE)
IF(obj_4_correct = TRUE, obj_4_complete = TRUE, obj_4_complete =FALSE)
-- if a question has been mastered, it is set to completed
-- otherwise it is set to not completed
```

Select OK to close the calculation and you will be asked for the initial values for the four new variables. All are logical, with initial values of FALSE, and all have the same Description:

```
tracks whether to ask question when test is entered and as questions are
completed
```

Close the *Start Test* map and use Control-U to ungroup the map. The result will be the calculation named *Start Test* at Level 1.

Next you will create the structure to present the questions randomly and ignore questions once they have been presented once in the current session. If all you wanted to do is present the questions randomly, it would be simple enough to place them on a decision. What you will do is more sophisticated.

First you will make the capability to ignore previously used questions. You will nest each of the question maps one level deeper before elaborating its structure. To do this select, but do not open, *text response*. Use Control-G to group it. It will flash but look unchanged. If you didn't fumble the keys, the original *text response* map is now inside the *text response* map that you see. Rename the Level 1 icon to *objective 1*. Now repeat this process for the three remaining question maps. Name the Level 1 icons *objective 2, objective 3,* and *objective 4*. Figure 23.47 shows the structure that you are creating. The original questions are now inside maps labeled by their corresponding objective numbers.

Now open *objective 1* to edit at Level 2. Drag a decision icon to the flowline and name it *tried before?* Drag the *text response* map to the left of *tried before?* to associate it with the decision structure. Then select *text response* and pull down the Data menu to access the Calculations choice to append a calculation to the icon. You will set this icon to record that the question has already been used in a current session, by entering the following expression and comment:

```
obj_1_complete = TRUE
-- sets question 1 to complete (not to mastered)
```

Close the calculation and move to the *tried before* decision icon. Open it and change the branching from Sequential to Calculated Path. Enter the expression in the Calculated Path text field as follows:

```
SelectedEver@"objective 1" = FALSE
```

Read the description under the Decision category under Show variables. Close the dialog box by selecting OK. The completed structure looks like Figure 23.48.

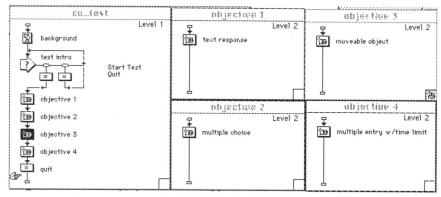

Figure 23.47 Grouped Maps

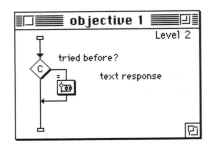

Figure 23.48 Objective 1 Structure

Now repeat this process for the three remaining objective maps. You can reuse the tried-before icon name for the decisions. The items that are different are as follows:

Icon	*multiple choice*
Appended Calculation	**obj_2_complete = TRUE**
Comment	**-- sets question 2 to complete (not to mastered)**
Calculated Path	**SelectedEver@"objective 2" = FALSE**
Icon	*movable object*
Appended Calculation	**obj_3_complete = TRUE**
Comment	**-- sets question 3 to complete (not to mastered)**
Calculated Path	**SelectedEver@"objective 3" = FALSE**
Icon	*multiple entry w/time limit*
Appended Calculation	**obj_4_complete = TRUE**
Comment	**-- sets question 4 to complete (not to mastered)**
Calculated Path	**SelectedEver@"objective 4" = FALSE**

When you complete the work on *movable object,* open the map itself. Inside you will find an erase that you placed earlier to make the test run when it was in the linear structure. The erase was needed then, but now is handled automatically. Delete the *remove me later* erase icon.

Next you will begin to set the questions to random selection from the question bank. Drag a decision icon to the flowline above *text response* and call it *objective question sets*. Now drag each of the objective maps to its right to associate with the decision. Finally, open the decision and click on Calculated path. Enter an expression as follows:

```
objective_number
```

Then select OK to close the dialog box. When you are asked for the initial value of objective_number, set it as numerical with an initial value of 0 (zero). Provide a description something like:

```
holds the value of a randomly generated number
```

Figure 23.49 shows the structure at this point.

Next, you will finish the structure essential to the randomization. Select the *objective question sets* decision icon, and all of the associated map icons. Once they are selected, use Control-G to group them. The new group will be called *objective question sets.* Change it to *random selection.* Now drag a decision icon to the flowline above *random selection,* and name it *pick a question.* Double-click *pick a question* to open it for editing. The default Sequential branching is fine. Click on the Repeat Until TRUE button and enter the following in the text field:

```
obj_1_complete & obj_2_complete & obj_3_complete & obj_4_complete
```

This expression will allow the loop, including the questions, to run until it finds that its condition is met. This can only happen if all of the objectives are set to complete by some combination of questions mastered earlier, whose objective was passed to the post test as already correct and set to complete, as well as those that were presented in the current session. (Whether they were correctly answered or not does not affect the presentation of the questions.)

Troubleshooting

Pick a question is the 50th icon. If Authorware refuses to allow you to create it, you have left a stray icon somewhere. Logical candidates are related to constructing groups (you could have doubled your Control-G somewhere, creating two groups). The best way to find them is to carefully compare the structure of the sample *cu_testfile* on your CD with your lesson, to locate a difference.

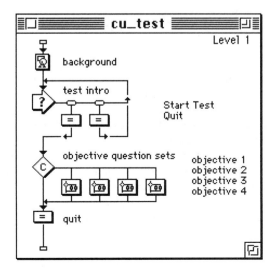

Figure 23.49 Interim Structure

This will be the end of work on the test. You will append a calculation to the *pick a question* decision. You will enter five expressions. The first generates the random number to be tried on this loop. The next four check control retesting. They see whether the objective that matches the random number has been mastered. If it has, the objective number is assigned a value of zero and the loop repeats to select a new random number. The process repeats until all objectives are complete. Select the *pick a question* decision. Select The Data pull-down menu and choose Calculations. Enter the following:

```
objective_number = Random (1,4,1)
-- selects a random number between 1 and 4 in increments of 1
```

Next, enter the IF statements that compare mastery with the randomly generated objective number. Enter the following:

```
IF((objective_number = 1) & (obj_1_correct = TRUE), objective_number = 0)
IF((objective_number = 2) & (obj_2_correct = TRUE), objective_number = 0)
IF((objective_number = 3) & (obj_3_correct = TRUE), objective_number = 0)
IF((objective_number = 4) & (obj_4_correct = TRUE), objective_number = 0)
-- if the objective was selected by the random number generator
-- and the objective is mastered, choose another number,
-- otherwise ask that objective's question
```

Test Drive

To verify your work you have to run it from the curriculum. Be sure to close your *cu_test* and then run your lesson to verify that it performs as planned. You should be able to take the pre-test and then have the opportunity to be retested in the post test on the objectives you missed. When you fail to master all of the objectives you will see a "sorry" message. If you are successful in mastering all the objectives you will be shown a diploma signifying your accomplishment. Print the diploma in the landscape orientation to frame and hang on your wall. Good job!

Complete Reports

This next section of the curriculum is for providing information on the learner's performance. You will create an interface that will access the learner's record by name, and will be able to view the individual data file kept on each learner. We would actually reserve this for a facilitator's level access to a more complete CMI system. In this book, we thought you would benefit from seeing how it works.

You will create several new variables that will control which reports are displayed. You will use some system functions to catalog the contents of a data directory in which the individual learner's files are stored. You will read the first line from each file to generate a list of all user's names. You will display subsets of 10 names on each page. The user will choose a name to see a report.

Open the *Reports* map icon. Drag a calculation icon to the flowline and title it *catalog data files*. Open the *catalog data files* calculation. You will enter eight expressions with comments as follows:

```
name_set = 0
list_number = 0
registered_data = ""
registered_users = ""
-- rests variables for initial display
```

Then continue with the four remaining expressions.

```
update_names = TRUE
-- reset value to read first 10 names

list_number = 2
-- only needed on PCs because DOS has 2 unused lines of file names
-- (. and ..) in subdirectories

directory_list = Catalog(RecordsLocation^"my_data:")
-- lists user-generated files

data_loop = LineCount(directory_list) - 2
-- decision will loop and read names for each file
-- except for the 2 DOS filenames
```

Close the calculation and set the variables as follows:

Variable Name	Type	Initial Value	Description
name_set	Numerical	0	sets of 10 names to determine which set of up to 10 names is displayed
list_number	Numerical	0	tracks the number of names appended to the list of registered users
registered_data	Character	" "	displays report data for the selected individual name from the compiled list of registered_users
registered_users	Character	" "	the summary list of collected users' names
update_names	Numerical	0	only allows names to be updated when forward or back arrow button is selected
directory_list	Character	" "	contains all user-generated files in the my_data directory
data_loop	Numerical	0	determines how many times individual files are needed to extract users' names

Next you will create a structure to read the first line of each user's file until there aren't any more. The first line contains the learners' names. Drag a decision icon to the flowline below *catalog data files*. Name it data loop and open it. The Repeat button is already set to blank times. In the blank enter:

```
data_loop
```

Select OK to close the *data loop* decision icon.

Next drag a calculation to the right of *data loop* and title it *read user files*. This icon will read individual files and create a list of names extracted from each file. Open the calculation and enter the following five expressions:

```
report_file = GetLine (directory_list,list_number +1)
-- selects the file name from the cataloged list

file_data = ReadExtFile(RecordsLocation^"my_data\\"^report_file)
-- reads the contents of the selected file (Mac uses : not \\)

name_in_file = GetLine(file_data,1)
-- selects only the first line of the file's contents which
-- contain the full user name

registered_users = InsertLine(registered_users,list_number - 2, ¬
SubStr(name_in_file,1,20))
-- places first 20 characters of user name in a list for
-- display starting on line 1

list_number = list_number + 1
-- increases the list number that determines which file will be
-- read for extracting the user's names
```

Close the calculation and set the variables as follows:

Variable Name	Type	Initial Value	Description
report_file	Character	" "	selects the file name from the catalog list, based on the line clicked
file_data			temporarily holds all the users' data extracted from each file, for later reading of the user's name from the first line
name_in_file	Character	" "	holds the user's name extracted from the first line of each file

The final part of the *Reports* structure is an interaction with initially six calculation icons associated with it. This structure controls the interface for displaying the reports. Drag an interaction to the bottom of the flowline and name it *choose a file to read*. Then drag six calculation icons to its right. When the Response Type dialog box opens, approve the default Pushbutton response type. Name the icons: *Continue, click a name, Print Report, <-, and ->*. Leave the last icon *untitled*. The arrows are just hyphens and the greater-than and less-than keys found as shift-comma and shift-period on most keyboards. Now that you created the buttons so quickly, there are a couple of changes. Change the *click a name* icon to a Click/Touch response type by double-clicking on the response type symbol. Then change the *untitled* icon to a conditional response type, set the Auto-match to When True, and enter *update-names* in the Match If TRUE text field.

Now set the branching using Control-click. Set them as follows:

Icon	Branching
Continue	Exit Interaction
click a name	Try Again
Print Report	Try Again
<-	Continue
->	Continue
update-names	Try Again

Your completed structure should look like Figure 23.50.

Now it is time to import the graphic for the background of the Performance Reports display. Open and close *menu* as you did before, to set the placement example in memory. Open the *choose a file to read* interaction icon and set its Erase Effect to Mosaic. While holding the shift key down, click on OK-Edit Display and import the *cu_rprts.pct* file. Carefully position the display. Place the buttons across the bottom of the display. Then resize and reposition the hotspot to cover the display box on the left of the graphic.

Now to create the list of learners and the report field. (PC as well as Mac users will benefit from referring to Chapter 16, for a reminder of how scrolling text is accomplished on the Mac.) You are going to make this element of the CMI system cross-platform compatible, by using similar techniques. In the smaller field, where you will display the learner's names, embed the variable

```
{names}
```

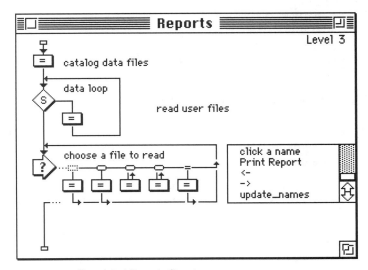

Figure 23.50 Completed Reports Structure

At the bottom of the same display field, embed

```
{page_number} of {total_pages}
```

Select Effects from the Attributes pull-down menu and set the Mosaic display effect. Before closing the dialog box, check the Update Displayed variables checkbox. As you leave each of the text fields, set the variables as follows:

Variable Name	Type	Initial Value	Description
names	Character	" "	contains a list of up to 10 names from the list of all registered
page_number	Numerical	1	for displaying page number of registered_users
total_pages	Numerical	0	pages of registered_users names in sets of 10 per page

Figure 23.51 shows the completed Performance Reports display.

Now finish the update names calculation first. Double-click to open it for editing. Here are the four expressions to enter.

```
names = GetLine(registered_users,(name_set * 10) + 1, (name_set * 10) +10)
-- holds a subset of 10 names from the list of registered_users

page_number = name_set + 1
-- page number comes from name_set and is initially 0 for the paging model

IF(MOD(data_loop,10)<>0,total_pages = INT((data_loop/10), ¬
total_pages = INT(data_loop / 10))
-- looks for a remainder when total registered users are divided by 10,
-- adds 1 to total_pages if there is a remainder

update_names = FALSE
-- only allows names to be updated when forward or back
-- arrow button is selected
```

When you close the calculation, no variables will need to be initialized, as they are all existing.

To stick with building on knowledge that you already have, skip to the *click a name* icon. The three expressions in this icon get the file that the user clicked on, read the file's contents, and display it in a ScrollEdit box. Enter them as follows:

```
report_file := GetLine(directory_list,((name_set*10)+LastLineClicked))
-- selects the filename from the cataloged list based on line clicked,
-- (+ 1) to avoid the DOS files names

registered_data = ReadExtFile(RecordsLocation^"my_data"^report_file)
-- reads the contents of the selected file for display as a report

CloseWindow("record_display")
ScrollEdit("R","record_display","260,169,561,377","","","Times",12)
SetProperty("record_display","text",registered_data)
-- displays the record for the selected name in the ScrollEdit box
```

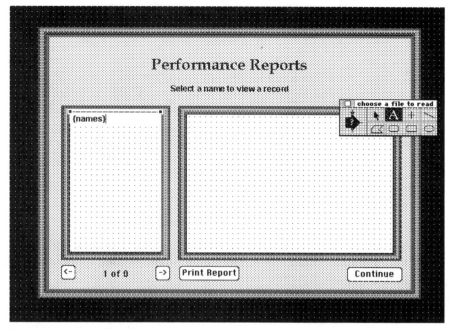

Figure 23.51 Reports Display

When you close the calculation, you will be asked where is the *scrledit.ucd*. Locate it and click on it. Then select OK. Mac users will be asked to locate *ScrollEdit*.

Next complete the paging arrows. As you might expect, there is a certain symmetry between them. Open <- and enter the following four expressions:

```
name_set=name_set-1
-- increments the set of names that are placed on pages

update_names=TRUE
-- reset value to read previous 10 names

registered_data := ""
-- removes date from record display
-- when moving to a different record

CloseWindow("record_display")
-- to remove viewed record
```

Before you close the calculation, copy the text to paste into the other arrow. Open -> and paste the contents of the first arrow. Then make only one simple edit. Change the –1 in the first line to a +1, and modify its comment. It should read like this:

```
name_set:=name_set+1
-- decrements the set of names that are placed on pages
```

Close the calculation.

Next you will enter the expressions that will control the buttons for moving forward or backward among the pages. First open the response type symbol for the ->

button. Enter the following in the Active If TRUE text field. Then select OK to close the dialog box.

```
name_set<((data_loop/10)-1)
```

The back arrow has a much simpler expression.

```
name_set>0
```

Enter it in the Active If TRUE text field of the arrow and close the dialog box.

The next step is the simple job of setting the report to print. Open the *Print Report* calculation and type in the PrintScreen function and a comment. It will be:

```
PrintScreen()
-- Prints the screen containing the report
-- If there were multiple sessions, the user will have to
-- scroll the latest report into view before printing
```

Finally, you can complete the action by placing a CloseWindow function in the *Continue* button's calculation. You can copy the needed function from the *click a name* calculation. It is near the bottom. You are looking for:.

```
CloseWindow("record_display")
```

When you find it, open *Continue* and paste it in. Add the following comment:

```
-- to remove the viewed record
```

Test Drive

You can run this test without even taking the test again, provided you have been using different names as you tried the testing earlier. You will need more than 10 records stored to test the paging of the display. Now that you can see the records, you might experiment with names of unusual length or composition, such as "W. E. B. DuBois," "G. Gordon Liddy," "George Washington," and "Englebert Humperdink." The performance reports display looks like Figure 23.52 when in use. Your display may be a bit off due to initial placement that you followed consistently. You can adjust the parameters in the *click a name* calculation.

Troubleshooting

Once again we refer you to the troubleshooting ideas in Chapter 16, and the use of embedded variables on the screen as we demonstrated earlier.

Ideas for Expansion, Enhancement, and Evolution

Here are some ideas for use of this lesson in new ways:

- You could set the prescription to print.

- You could make an eight-character family name for more than one person by using a substring to capture the first letter of their first name and joining it after the seventh character of their last name. This is similar to what you have done already, with an added layer of complexity.

- The CMI system is currently "hard-wired" for four learning objectives. You could change it to handle more.

- You could program Authorware to print out the entire learner report file using the JumpPrint/Return function.

- Place the names of all learners in a scrolling text field instead of pages.

Help!

That pretty well wraps up what we plan to do with the working model. There is a new star on the horizon, though. A new version of Authorware, version 3.0, contains changes in the interface. We have considered it carefully and feel that there is nothing that will throw you for a loop when you move to it.

One of the most important parts of your output is help to the learner. Chapter 24 looks specifically at those possibilities. Let's take a peek.

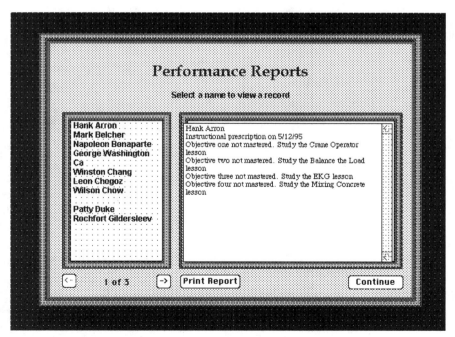

Figure 23.52 A Report

Enhancing Your Lessons

24

Helping the Learner

This chapter is about the Help function that we include in lessons. It's also about a whole lot more than that. We want to ensure that the learner sees a user-friendly lesson, and we have some ideas about how to make that happen. Some are as simple as the commonly used navigational assistance, context-sensitive help, and access to a glossary. We want to provide the kind of lesson that will enlist the support, cooperation, and enthusiasm of the learner.

You would be surprised how many lessons do virtually nothing to engage and support the learner. Nothing special is done to make the content meaningful to individual learners. Besides boredom, the problem here is that, without meaning, such efforts will be cut off from the learner's long-term memory. The learner will have a hard time assimilating and integrating the new knowledge with their already learned information and concepts.

In many lessons, where interaction is only superficial, it is due to the simplicity of the lesson's design. In such lessons, the learner is more of an observer than a participant. We want to help you to get past the pitfalls so that you don't settle for far less than is possible!

What You Will Learn in This Chapter

- Standards for providing help and how to achieve them
- Characteristics of help techniques
- How to implement help in your multimedia development

Provide Help

Basically, the help that you can provide for learners when they use a lesson falls into two categories:

- Procedural
- Informational

Procedural help

Procedural help is about the operation of the lesson, such as how to move through it. Lessons should always provide procedural help. This essential information is usually provided in a separate section of directions for the lesson. A common technique for providing procedural help is to return the learner to those directions. More recently, balloon help that identifies an icon's function when the cursor passes over it has become more common. As you can imagine, this kind of help is easy to provide. Also, once you have created the template to present such help you can reuse it in other lessons.

The downside of this help is that, when learners need help with the lesson's content, it is very frustrating to find that "help" only tells how the lesson itself works. Your design should consider both functions and how to separate them for the learner.

Informational help

The much more important help is tied to the content. Informational help assists the learner with that content. Just how you provide informational help depends on the lesson itself. Examples of informational help you might provide for the learner include:

- Additional examples
- Descriptions or explanations with greater detail
- Descriptions or explanations worded more simply
- Sample cases

We are enthusiastic over "context-sensitive help." It is the ultimate form of help. Unfortunately, for those of us who want to do a super job of providing top-notch training, doing a good job of providing context-sensitive help requires considerably more effort than doing the job less well. But it is far more valuable to the learner.

How to make help accessible

Help must be easy for learners to access. The PLATO system used a special keyboard with a HELP key to provide help. Most personal computers have 10 or more special function keys. One of these keys can be specified by the designer as the HELP key. In fact, so many software applications use the F1 key as the help key that many users already expect F1 to be the key for help. Today, the learner probably has his or her hand on the mouse already, and an on-screen Help button is probably the most convenient way to access help. The button also replaces the message, found at the bottom of the screen in older lessons, that tells what key to press for help.

When to provide help

We disagree with some practitioners, who say that you should provide options for the learner to ask for help and to leave the program whenever the learner is at a question. Their point is that the lesson's judging must recognize these efforts, not as responses but as requests for help or requests to leave. That is, of course, a programming consideration.

Our experience is exactly contrary to this and is also a programming consideration. You turned off all access to Help and Quit when the learner entered the test in Chapter 15. If a learner could access help during a test, it would be like an open-book test. The customary way to handle this in business and industry is to announce that the test is about to start in a screen that precedes it. Help and Quit are active there. Once the learner begins the test, it must be completed. In practice, this is not a burden or handicap at all.

Provide Glossary Access

It is so simple to include a glossary that we do so if the content supports such a need at all. A perpetual button, available on all screens except during a test, does the trick. Your experience in providing perpetual buttons in Chapter 15 is applicable.

We favor a glossary of one or more pages because of the simpler programming required. The learner can access the glossary simply, and if there are more terms than can fit on one screen you can use a paging model to allow the learner to page back and forth at will. We think this type of glossary is superior, because the learner will see other terms that may not be totally familiar but didn't generate the trip to the glossary.

It isn't that difficult to provide access to a specific term, using Authorware's Get-Line function. The learner can click on any term in a list and the entry for that term is displayed.

Provide Mouse Practice

Frankly, we are amazed that so many people have successfully avoided computer mice. Mac users have used them since their introduction more than a decade ago. Still, we have seen people do amazing things when presented with a mouse. This is a true story. At a demonstration of a new lesson, one of the people who were exploring the lesson held the mouse up in the air at about the height of the screen and moved it around in space. We were both there and, if we needed convincing of the need for a mouse practice utility, that did it. It is no accident that your first experience was in building a mouse practice.

The Windows mouse practice routine is nicely done, with good graphics and animation. You can provide access to it by having a button do:

```
JumpOutReturn(c:Windows "mouse")
```

A weakness of this approach is that the learner must quit the mouse practice before it turns into a complete review of Windows.

You could have done more with the `mousepr` utility if it hadn't been your first Authorware programming experience. One mouse practice has a part that tests the learner's ability to drag by directing him or her to drag a ball to a hole. When the ball gets to the hole it is seen by a target and erased, giving the effect of dropping into the hole.

You have a good start in providing mouse practice. We are fond of the little mouse activity that you have made already in Chapter 13. You might want to obtain pleasing graphics to make your `mousepr` more attractive. You could change the circles to graphics related to the training's sponsor organization. The varied colors, fills, and effects were only for the familiarization you needed at that time. Now that they have served their purpose, you could clean up the eye appeal considerably by using consistent fills and erases.

Provide a User-Friendly Lesson

Let's look at several ways that you can make your lesson more accessible, interesting, and motivating to your learner. User-friendly help is usually "faded" as the lesson unfolds. Less help is built in until, eventually, the learner isn't provided with that type of help at all. This is an example of the kind of instructional element that you would track carefully during the formative evaluation. As you try your lesson under development you may find that you have faded too quickly.

As we introduced you to Authorware, we showed each icon and dialog box the first time that you met with it. Gradually, we faded all such prompts. The principle is the same.

Don't hide your help "under a bushel." It must be noticed by the learner in order to work. Place the important information near the center of the display. Separate it from "clutter." When you need to, use attention-getting devices like arrows, animation, color, and highlighting.

Now let's examine three ideas for making your lessons more user-friendly:

- Analogies
- Hints
- Mnemonics

Analogies

One effective type of prompt is analogy. Remember, we want to help the learner connect with information already in long-term memory. Analogy uses the learner's previous knowledge to relate to the new information. For example, you could explain an electrical system's parts and functions by comparing them to the human circulatory system.

Hints

Cues, or prompts, guide the learner and provide hints. An example of a prompt is underlining important words. Another is a highlight around one (or more) particular part(s) of a graphic. Following an incorrect answer, you could provide the hint "Try again, you apparently multiplied the numbers. This problem calls for division." This redirects the learner, who may have made a mistake in choosing, rather than in learning incorrectly. A brute-force cue is to indicate that "this point is very important" to capture the learner's attention.

Mnemonics

Mnemonics are a great way to help the learner remember a list. A well-known example is the mnemonic HOMES. It is constructed from the first letters of the names of the five Great Lakes: Huron, Ontario, Michigan, Erie, and Superior. When a learner can't quite remember one of the lakes, the process of elimination provides the first letter as a hint. You'd be surprised how easy it is for you to provide a unique mnemonic for a topic you have to present. It offers the advantage of giving the learner something to take away to assist in recall when the information is needed on the job.

Make Your Instruction More Meaningful

You can make your lessons more meaningful by personalizing the instruction. You can do this in several ways. Let's look at several of the methods for personalizing your instruction to make it more meaningful for your learners.

Background information

During the analysis, you will collect information about commonalities in the background of the learners. They all might have completed the same required training, might have similar career goals, or might live in the same community. You can periodically and subtly integrate this information into your lesson.

Learner control

We have addressed learner control versus program control in several chapters. Sometimes the learner can make good decisions on which instructional activity is appropriate for them. When that is the case, we permit it. We hold that the learner should assume as much personal responsibility for successes and failures as is reasonable. As we indicated very early on, we don't permit the learner to run amuck through the content when we know sequential information is involved. Current research supports our view. We do provide as much learner control as is consistent with the lesson's objectives.

Learner's name

The ultimate, and perhaps most common, method for personalizing instruction is to employ the user's name in the lesson. In our experience, this proves difficult to do well. There was a day when, if Tom received a letter that said, "Mr. Thomas Iwinski, you are probably aware of the beautiful new aluminum siding that is being installed on homes in the `Iwinski` neighborhood. . . ." he would have been impressed. Today, even our copy of *Newsweek* includes our own name printed on an inside page. We, and most learners, have become jaded. Our name on the screen isn't enough. It must be well-integrated into the lesson.

A good opportunity is to use the learner's name in reporting results, especially when done formally. The score-reporting display in a simulation includes the learner's name. We often include an on-screen diploma, just as you did in Chapter 23. This is a perfect way to use the learner's name.

Pacing

In our experience, we find it best to use timed events only when they are relevant to instruction. For example, in a simulation, the clock is running and will have a big impact on realism. We are not as enthusiastic about timing questions. When you included a timed question in the curriculum test you built in Chapter 23, it was simply to provide you with experience in using that function.

Participation

We do not count merely pressing the space bar to move through a lesson as interaction. We suggest that you explore the full range of possibilities for involving the learner with meaningful interaction during a lesson. Use the techniques that you have already programmed into your lessons as you completed earlier chapters, in new ways to involve the learner in the learning experience.

You can also increase the range of learners who might use a particular lesson by making its information more relevant for them. When you make it relevant, you facilitate the relationships that help your learner to place the wanted information into long-term memory.

Practice

Whenever possible, provide the opportunity for the learner to practice various aspects of the lesson content. Along with providing interactivity, the learner's activities are integrated completely with lesson content. This level of activity also helps the learner to build conceptual bridges to the lesson information.

Your crane operator lesson is a good example of providing well-designed practice after basic instruction. Using the practice, your crane operator learner will become more involved with the instruction.

Previous responses

Sometimes you can remind the learner of the response they made to previously presented questions. For example, you can store an initial response in a variable, then introduce it at a later point in the lesson. The learner will feel that the lesson is treating him as an individual—and it is.

Progress-check questions

Progress-check questions test the learner's capacity to repeat the information and perform the skills, procedures, or tasks that you have been presenting. Your progress-check questions should be distributed throughout the lesson. They should also clearly relate to the preceding lesson content, should have clearly defined directions for responding, and should use the allotted screen space intelligently. This is another idea based on research.

Relevant examples

This may seem obvious, but including meaningful and relevant examples is a powerful instructional tool. We try to include relevant stimuli, including graphic elements, to fit the instruction to the learner. One of the companies we enjoy working with is a plant in Texas. The lessons made for them include armadillos, cattle brands, cowboy video scenarios, rawhide, a narrator with the appropriate accent, and the Texas flag. We use examples that are directly related to the work the learners do. For example, when we want to cover shop math, we don't use a supermarket purchase example. We take the example from the shop floor to make it more relevant to the needs of our learner.

A Challenge

Our challenge to you is to try to outdo everyone else in providing high quality, highly interactive training. When you do, true professionals will welcome you more completely than you could ever expect based on your degrees, credentials, or even years of experience. Doing good work surpasses all of these in importance.

Sound and Motion

Now that you have made everything for the learner copasetic, you can get serious about the most technical end of multimedia. The audio and video that we use to support sophisticated lessons aren't just Clem playing his harmonica softly into the old tape recorder, although it could be.

In Chapter 25 we'll work on getting our hands around the higher-scale audio and video that can make your lessons into award winners. Let's get started.

Audio and Video Considerations

You may or may not have an authoring system or the special hardware and software needed to access the sophisticated audio and video media that exist in both Mac and PC platforms. Words like *black-stripe* and *chroma-key, digital, and analog* may or may not sound strange to your ear. In this chapter we will walk the tightrope of presenting technical information while trying to hold the description to a technical level appropriate to those without previous knowledge of this area.

Also, there are marked distinctions between the file types between the delivery platforms. We will cover both and will address the differences between approaches for the necessary hardware and software.

What You Will Learn in This Chapter

- The characteristics of video formats for multimedia training
- Aspects of hardware-supported video versus software-supported video
- The platform differences for video
- Which are the directions for future video use
- Issues related to the production and use of analog video
- Issues related to the production and capture of digital video
- Use of QuickTime movies on the Mac
- Use of rmagic.Vdr in authorware
- Specific programming techniques to incorporate audio and video into your lessons
- Use of Mediadynamics *mdctrl.dll* on the PC
- Using director movies

Copyright

Let's put first things first! If you record and use copyrighted material without first obtaining the permission from the owner or publisher of the material you are breaking the law. You must always "play it safe" by making your own audio from scratch at your desk or in a sound studio, or by using sounds that have a clear and paid-for ownership and permission trail. Don't take a risk and break the law.

We recommend digitized clip sounds sold with an unlimited-use, royalty-free license. Vendors include: Passport Designs (MediaMusic), ProSonus (SoundBytes), and Voyetra (MusiClips). Beware of the Internet or a bulletin board that offers clips from such favorites as *Star Trek*, or one-liners from Clint Eastwood movies. You can bet that these sounds have been copied without permission.

This is a true story. A developer downloaded sounds from a bulletin board and placed them on the organization's LAN. Another developer later loaded one of the sounds into a project for a customer, thinking that it was from the licensed library. The project manager also thought it was from the library. When the problem was discovered it was necessary to think of a piece that would exactly replace the first sound while still fitting the graphic that had been created for the illegal audio. Don't let this happen to you.

Why Multimedia

You use the elements of multimedia for many reasons. Good instruction has the ability to reach the target audience and increase its impact when appropriate techniques are employed. In addition to its entertainment value, good multimedia can provide a complementary role in communication or, if necessary, it can provide redundancy. Multimedia can provide emphasis, moods, atmosphere, transitions, or cues. It can exemplify, demonstrate, or narrate. All these capabilities can be very powerful when used in training in specific domains of learning, such as effective or psychomotor.

Audio

On both the Macintosh and in Windows you can easily use certain sounds, based on the operating system. These sounds are quite limited, to say the least. The Macintosh features: Droplet, Indigo, Quack, Simple Beep, Sosumi, and Wild Eep. Windows 3.1 gives you: Chimes, Chord, Ding, and Tada. These sounds mark system events, such as startup and application warnings.

You can try installing the *speaker.drv* file to play sound through the internal speaker of your PC. If you do, you will find the tiny internal speaker on the PC is inadequate for any multimedia performance. Conventional audio speakers were never designed with computer users in mind. Hooking up regular speakers to a PC is OK for low-quality monophonic signals, but now, with high-quality stereo audio cards coming onto the market, you need decent speakers to do your sound justice. To play audio seriously with Windows, you must have a sound board installed in your PC and high-quality speakers. Fortunately, these often come in a package with a CD-ROM player, called a multimedia kit.

Many multimedia sound packages come with a variety of accompany .wav and .mid files for your ready use. If your PC is an MPC-level machine, check in the directories associated with the sound card and you will probably find a larger selection of audio clips. Much of this media, however, is not really suitable for training needs. You will find it is usually much easier to record and capture your own custom audio and sound effects than to spend the time and energy searching for a suitable prerecorded sound. You will shortly be introduced to this process of digitizing your own custom sounds.

Recording sound

Recording digital audio files is quite straightforward. The first step is to digitize the analog sound material by recording it onto computer-readable digital media. Generally, this means playing the sound from your tape recorder directly into your computer, using any audio digitizing card (a card may not be required on the Mac) with appropriate software. Place your focus on these aspects of preparing digital audio files:

- Set proper recording levels to get a good, clean recording.
- Set recording levels to equal with the audio in other media.
- Balance the need for sound quality with your available RAM and hard disk space.

If your computer meets the specifications for adequate RAM for the sound card, you will have the option of digitizing your audio at varying levels of playback sound quality. The range is from a thin mono, telephone-like sound quality up to the same high-end stereo you expect from commercially produced and recorded CDs. The main difference and consideration is the size of the resulting file. This will have a big impact on the source you will need to deliver your programs. A 3.5 floppy will hold only seconds of stereo CD-quality audio. On the low end of the scale the files are tiny. If you have lots of narration in your program you will find it is not necessary to digitize simple speech at the high level. You will get very acceptable sound playback quality and a much smaller file by digitizing at the lower end of the scale. For a larger program delivered on a CD-ROM this can make a major difference. Consider that you will have runtime executable files, drivers, and other graphic, animation, and video media types on the same CD. If you digitized your animation at the higher end of the scale, the volume of sound you could store on the CD would be measured in minutes because of the large file size. On the other hand, digitizing in mono on the low end of the scale will produce very acceptable playback quality, but you'll have space for hours of sound. You should always keep in mind the limitations of the final delivery medium and hardware.

 Mac Difference: You can use System 7 and newer Macintosh models with a connected microphone to record new sounds. Any Macintosh with a sound-digitizing device like MacRecorder will also work. This recording software is built into the system. Every Macintosh provides at least 8-bit audio.

However, in the PC world only MPC computers are guaranteed to have this capability. Millions of Windows-equipped PCs have no digital audio capabilities at all. Windows computers get their digital audio capabilities from the add-in sound card. Both 8-bit and 16-bit sound cards exist. There is no benefit to digitizing audio at a higher specification than can be used by the target playback device. If you produce a 16-bit file and the learning station has an 8-bit card, the file won't play. Like anything else, the movement is toward the more capable format. In the future, everything will be 16-bit or more.

Audio file formats

There are file formats for text, sounds, images, animation, and digital video clips. The sound file's format is a recognized method for organizing the digitized sound into a data file. The Macintosh uses .aif or .snd files. Windows machines use digitized sounds most often stored as .wav files. Every software program that uses digital audio will have a simple method for combining .wav files with other data. Authorware provides a sound icon to easily incorporate .wav files into the code. In this chapter you will learn another method of incorporating media, using a dynamic link library (.dll). If you follow the instructions you can't miss. The included CD contains the mdCtrl.dll.

Adding sound to your lesson

Regardless of your platform, you must follow specific steps to bring an audio recording into your multimedia project. The process, which may vary depending on your choice of sound hardware and software, goes like this:

- Decide what sound is needed and where these audio events will appear in the flow of your lesson.
- Decide where and when you want to use digital audio.
- Acquire the needed source material. Create it from scratch or buy it.
- Edit the sounds to fit your need.
- Test the sounds to be sure they are timed properly with the lessons flow.

When it's time to import your edited audio into your lesson, just use a sound icon and follow the procedure you used in Chapter 10 to tell Authorware which file to play, and when to play it.

There are also third-party vendors that provide very good and acceptable methods for incorporating audio into your programs. One such solution is a .dll. This piece of code allows your Windows Program to communicate with the media interface in the computer. Because it is a more direct method of controlling your media and can even be custom written (by a programmer of course), the .dll approach has many great benefits over the canned-icon approach. This, however, is not without liabilities. Though the .dll gives greater control, it also requires that you maintain the source files separate from the program files. You must also track the location of the .dll, for it is a separate file in the process. For the novice the sound icon is very easy, and it also embeds the sound file inside the program file so there are no external files to track and control. You should examine the Media Dynamics directory on the CD to go into depth using the provided *mdctrl.dll* to play .wav, .mid, and digital video files later in this chapter. For now, just be aware that you have options on using and controlling media.

Professional capture and compression services

Even if your organization doesn't have the skills or equipment necessary to create your own custom media, provided your budget can support it, you can use professional media services to create computer-readable files. These services can have a wide range of prices. You can typically specify the quality and data transfer rates that your program can handle.

Keep track of your audio

Make sure your tape deck has a good counter built into it, so you can mark and log the locations of various takes and events on the tape to find them quickly later. Record the counter position and tape content in a log whenever you record sounds. This is called shot-sheeting your media. You will end up with a list of your clips and their locations on your edit-master tape. Also, keep your audio files stored safely. Remember, Authorware puts the sound into its sound icon. The source file isn't used and you can't reverse the process to produce a file from the sound icon. If your project is elaborate, with many sounds, it's really important to maintain a good database of the original files.

Give your sound files memorable names. We usually key the audio file name to the script with names like *narrar21.wav* or *scene10.wav*. Avoid unhelpful names such as *snd0046b.wav* or *lsn4-6.wav*. These names won't help you remember the file's actual audio content.

 Development Tip: Avoid hyphens in the file names. Most CD-Recordable products disallow hyphens in file names. Larger development projects may require a naming convention to keep track of the many similar files.

Test, test, and test

The most serious challenges with audio and video is to ensure usefulness, and to synchronize the sound elements with the presentation of visual images on the learner's computer. This is because it is likely to be slower than the machine on which you incorporated the sound elements. Unless you plan ahead, problems will not emerge until you begin testing on different computers.

A ten-second digital audio file will play for the same time on a slow Macintosh Classic or 386SX, or on a fast PowerMac or Pentium. The difference in the power of the computer to decompress and display the file will be reflected in dropped frames and reduced accuracy of audio synchronization. However, an animation will run five to ten times faster on a 486/66 than on a 386SX, and faster still in a Pentium. If you time your separate audio clips to your animations on a slow machine, and then play them back on a faster machine, you may find that the music continues to play after the speedier animation sequences are done. You can't make a slow machine run faster, so the solution is to design your code for synchronization on all platforms. We suggest that you regularly test the sound-and-image synchronization during editing and authoring of your lesson on the slowest platform, as well as the fastest. You can resolve many synchronization problems with the SyncWait() and SyncPoint() functions in Authorware.

In professional film and video projects, sound is incorporated during a post-production session after all the film and video footage has been assembled. The same should be true of your lesson. Remember, the soundtrack can make or break your project!

Cost

A professional, mid-America narrator will charge approximately $50 per page of script, with a maximum of $400–500. As with anything else, you can pay more. Costs on both coasts will be significantly more. Also, if you want Charleton Heston to speak the part of Moses, costs will be significantly higher.

What would be the typical recording session to produce an audio track, centered around narration for a multimedia course? Here are some of the considerations. Our favorite narrator, Bob Lange, points out that, "The difference in studio price will be reflected in the quality of the potential sound. For example, the more expensive studios will use better microphones."

The needle-drop fee for music and sound effects reflects the days in which a vinyl record was the source. It refers to a fee for a single use of prerecorded music or a sound effect. Due to varying licensing requirements, sometimes the charge will allow several plays of the same musical selection as one drop, while other times it will generate a charge for each as a separate drop.

When the session is over, you must transport the recorded audio to marry up with the computer. DAT is a high quality tape format for storage and transport of the audio. You could also put the sound on videotape, if you have video facilities. Today, an increasing number of studios can now furnish the recorded sound as finished .WAV files.

Item	Cost (in $)
Studio rental	50–80 (cheap studio at 35/hr)
Narrator	400
Music	65/needle drop
Sound effects	free or 10/drop
DAT cassette	10–15
Total	**$1,145**

Video

Analog video—Interactive Videodisc (IVD)

We discussed interactive video in Chapter 9. Refer to that chapter for details.

Digital video training

Digital video also delivers motion and still video, mixed with computer text, and graphics and audio for interactive learning materials. The all-digital format offers important new flexibility and capabilities. The video, now a computer file, can be easily edited or updated. Because of their inherent advantages, these systems will eventually replace the larger and more costly 12-inch videodisc. Today, learning stations for digital video are much cheaper than for IVD. New training projects are more likely to choose the digital-video option. We would certainly recommend digital video for new development. In fact, we felt that we had seen the last new development for DVI. We were recently amazed to see one more new IVD project. Although someone has to be last, the person in charge of this effort should have known better.

Digital video is not tied to the vast storage of the 12-cm CD, but is often delivered on one. This is because an average lesson with full-motion video is often up to 50 times larger than without—swamping older hard disks. One of our desktop simulations is 250 megabytes in size. There are two more in the same curriculum, filling three-fourths of a gigabyte drive. You can see the motivation to run the lesson from CDs.

Shooting video

The greatest difference between professional and consumer camcorders is their ability to perform at low light levels, and the clarity of the image. Proper lighting, however, can make a huge difference. Use a simple floodlight kit, or just be sure that daylight illuminates the room to improve your image. Make sure that you have a steady shooting platform. Always use a tripod, or even place the camera on a rolled-up jacket on the hood of a car. A sturdy conventional tripod can do wonders. If you must use a hand-held camera, try to use a camera with an electronic image stabilization feature. Remember to apply all standard conventions to video production. Recording high-quality video is an art in itself.

Chroma key or blue screen

If your background doesn't include video, you probably don't know about video's special background. A useful tool you can use in most video editing applications is "blue screen" or "chroma key" editing.

When you see an actress chatting in front of the Trivoli Fountain in Rome or the great wall of China, it is more probable that she is actually standing on a studio set in front of a blue screen. After the actress was shot against a blue background, another stock video with the desired background was mixed with the first. All the blue in the actress' shot was replaced by the background image, frame-by-frame.

You can let your imagination run wild. Anything is possible! You can rent the studio with the necessary chroma key blue screen, so no capital investment is required.

You will also encounter the concept of chroma key when you incorporate digital video into your Authorware program. The process is the same, but it is handled automatically for you. When playing a video source file in your program, Authorware will create a chroma key color field in which the image will be displayed. But in this case, the default chroma key color is magenta. Magenta is one of the least-used colors and makes a good choice. However, you can specify a different chroma key color in the File Setup dialog box in Authorware. You will notice the color palette you use will have a "c" in the color block of the chroma key. This is to remind you to avoid its use, as it may conflict with proper playback of your digital-video files.

Analog vs. digital editing

Depending on the facilities and budget you have available, you will have to choose one or the other. The primary differences are that analog editing is typically the process of editing video tape in an on-line or off-line studio, whereas digital editing is a process of editing digital files on a computer hard drive. To perform digital editing you must first capture a typically analog video signal to an uncompressed digital file. There are already pure digital cameras and video recorders available today, but they are extremely expensive and primarily for broadcast television use. But even these digital recorders store their images on special digital tape. The more typical Betacam, U-matic, and VHS are analog signals. The primary advantage of the digital process is that, during editing, you don't experience a generation loss. This generation loss occurs with analog systems each time the signal is transferred to another tape, during editing. On low-end systems, if you edit VHS tape, the third or fourth generations become unacceptable. The images get soft and lose detail and color. Figure 25.1 illustrates the generational loss concept.

On a digital editing system there is no generation loss, because the signal is exactly reproduced from the source. This is because the signal is a series of 1s and 0s, and exact copies can be made. Analog systems store the images in radio frequency (RF) signals, which degrade rather quickly when transferred during the edit process.

Your editing decisions should take these factors into consideration. Digital editing is better but doesn't work as easily or as well with compressed files. Uncompressed file are huge and can require multiple-gigabyte hard drive arrays to hold the files until they are compressed to a more functional size for your program. Once you have compressed a digital video file you cannot uncompress that file. If extensive edit

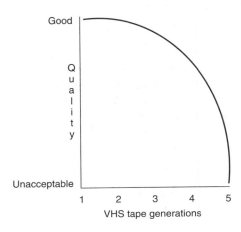

Figure 25.1 Quality Loss in Generations of VHS Tape

changes are required you will have to go back and make the changes to the original source.

If you are incorporating digital media into your program you will need to convert the signal to a compressed format signal. At what stage this occurs is based on your capabilities and needs. The earlier the better, but at a greater expense.

Another form of editing actually combines the two types. In this process, a lower-quality digital file is created from the master analog tape. The digital file is edited much more quickly, because the process is non-linear and doesn't require shuttling through video tape. From this low-quality prototype of the edit master, an edit decision list (EDL) is generated. The EDL contains all the necessary information (source tape, frame numbers, mix effects, audio tracks, etc.) about what the final edit master will look like. The EDL is then used like a software program, to control an analog-programmable editor.

Shooting video for computer use

The general rules for shooting quality video for broadcast use apply as well to video for playback from CD-ROM in a small computer window. A big factor is that, the more a scene changes from frame to frame, the more "delta" information must be transferred from the computer's memory to the screen. Remember, compression algorithms store all the frame content only for "key frames." Frames in between the key frames are represented only by information that is different from the frame preceding it.

Here are some ideas:

- Avoid wide panoramic shots. The effects of sweeping panoramas are lost in small windows, and every frame will have 100% changing content, maximizing the data transfer rate.

- Use close-up and medium shots, head-and-shoulders or even tighter.

- Consider the amount of motion in the shot. Keep the camera still instead of zooming and panning.

- Let the subject add the motion to your shot by walking, turning, or talking.

- Control the contrast of color in your image.

- Avoid the use of white.

- Avoid reds and saturated colors; they will appear to bleed.

- Avoid finer detail and patterns; they will cause a moiré effect and will probably be lost in the compression process.

Get your tape ready

- Always *pack* your new tapes to make sure that tape tension is even, from beginning to end. Unequal tape tension can cause timing and editing problems. To pack them, fast-forward your new tapes to the end and then rewind them.

- Always *black-stripe* your tape by running it through the recorder once with the lens cap on and the audio turned off. A truly black and uniform control track will be recorded. If you don't do this, blank spots in your video program will include snowy noise. This is only necessary for in-camera editing or blacking an edit master for analog editing.

Record your computer's output

There may be times when you want to display your work in other than a computer demo. You can create a videotape to show your work. If you want to transfer your project to videotape, you need an add-on board with a digital/analog encoder. This device is called a signal converter. The board converts the computer's high-quality RGB signal to an NTSC (lower-quality) signal that you can record on a VCR. This is only necessary to capture a linear output from your computer, or to capture some animation that will be compressed for faster playback.

Examples of suitable boards that produce video with graphics overlay include: Fast's VideoMachine, NewTek's Video Toaster, and VideoLogic's DVA4000, as well as others. Most boards can also digitize movies for QuickTime or AVI.

Take care of your videotapes

Your original videotapes are irreplaceable, so you should protect them. More than once we have needed an edit master—again. Always make backup copies of tapes before you begin editing. They can break, be erased, or even be chewed up by the tape drive. Also, always remove the break-off tab on the back of your original video cassettes before you begin editing. This will help you to avoid an accidental erasure or overwriting of your precious material.

Cost

Shawn Wallwork, President of Wallwork Productions says, "Budgeting shoots in itself is an art form. There never seems to be enough money to really do what you want to. So you are always having to make tough decisions. I always try to cut budgets in ways that aren't going to show up on the screen. I never cut the budget for the on-camera talent, because they are usually critical to the success of the project. However, I have been known to get my friends to work as background extras. You can also cut the budget by redesigning your storyboards to limit the number of scenes shot inside (which require extra time and equipment to light). If you can find a good Director/Cameraperson, they can help you keep your budget under control without sacrificing the quality of the finished video."

Video can be separated into three categories. They are: broadcast quality—think of what you see on network TV; industrial quality—corporate level presentations; and consumer grade. Here are the ranges of pricing for most of the people and equipment you'll need for a modest industrial-quality video shoot.

The lows are more typical for mid-America. Production on either coast will cost more. A day is 10 hours. You should expect to pay overtime after that—unless you negotiate a flat rate up-front.

The following is what a typical low-budget two-day video shoot will cost. If you really push it and there aren't very many interior shots, you can probably get ten minutes of finished video done in a day. (This varies greatly, since long scenes of a spokesperson talking to the camera produce a lot of finished minutes in a relatively short amount of time, whereas a thirty-second, fast-paced montage can take as long as two days to shoot.)

Item	Low	High
BetaSP Camera Package	$425/day	$650/day
Director/Cameraperson	300/day	750/day
Soundperson	200/day	400/day
Grip	150/day	250/day
Talent	250/day	600/day
Hair/Make-up Person	200/day	300/day
Additional Lighting	100/day	350/day
Additional Grip Equipment	100/day	350/day
BetaSP Tape Stock	50/min.	1/min.
Voice Over Talent	100/session	600/session
Audio Studio	35/hr.	125/hr.
¼" Tape Stock	8/roll	
Off-line Editing	35/hr.	100/hr.
On-line Editing	125/hr.	450/hr.
1" Tape Stock	.50/min	1.20/min.

Item	Cost
BetaSP camera package	$ 550
Director/Camera person	450
Soundperson	250
Grip	200
Additional lighting	150
Additional grip equipment	100
Talent	600
Hair/Make-up person	250
BetaSP	144
Voiceover talent	400
Audio studio	200
¼" tape stock	15
Off-line editing	500
On-line editing	1,000
1" tone stock	35
Total	**$4,844**

Video Compression

Digitizing and storing a short clip of full-motion video in your computer requires the transfer of a huge amount of data very quickly. Full-size, full-motion video requires the computer to deliver data at about 30 MB per second. Just 10 seconds of video could fill a 300 MB hard disk. The Macintosh NuBus channel can transfer data at about 13 MB per second. Typical hard disk drives transfer data at only about 1 MB per second, and double-speed CD-ROM players at 300 K per second.

Based on this analysis, you can see that full-motion video in your computer is clearly impossible! Well, not really. Digital-image compression techniques make it happen. Real-time video compression algorithms compress digital video information at rates that range from 50:1 to 200:1, greatly reducing the amount of data that must be transferred. Compression makes the whole thing possible. Let's examine some popular compression formats.

Cost

MPEG compression costs an average of $50 per minute today, when done by a compression house.

MPEG

Currently, the MPEG (Motion Picture Experts Group) standard is becoming the most popular method to encode motion images. MPEG allows compression of audio, its compression speeds are fast, and decompression occurs in real time. MPEG decompresses data at from 1.2 to 6 Megabits per second permitting CD players to play full-motion color movies at 30 frames per second.

JPEG

The JPEG (Joint Photographic Experts Group) standard was developed for use with still images. JPEG has become popular for compressing full-motion video on the Macintosh, but at higher compression rates it loses considerable image data. JPEG decompresses data at about 1 MB per second, well within the capabilities of CD players.

DVI

DVI is a proprietary, programmable compression/decompression technology based on the Intel i750 chip set. Two levels of compression and decompression are provided by DVI: Production Level Video (PLV) and Real Time Video (RTV).

PLV is a proprietary, asymmetrical compression technique for encoding full-motion color video. The cost of the relatively expensive computers needed for this process generally requires that compression be performed by encoding contractors.

RTV provides image quality comparable to frame-rate, and can be done at reasonable cost at a personal computer. RTV is a lower-quality DVI file that can be captured on your desktop PC. It is good for prototyping your video files before sending them out for high-level, and more expensive, compression.

Lack of support for the DVI standard from Intel seems to spell the death of this standard. Although we chose it initially because we feel that it offers the highest quality video available on a computer, we have switched to MPEG.

Others

Other compression systems are being developed by Kodak, Sony, Storm Technology, SuperMac, Iterated Systems, C-Cube Micro-systems, and other companies. We have not heard the final word about video formats.

Compression ideas

- Use regularly spaced key frames, 10 to 15 frames apart, to facilitate playing clips from within a file or the editing of that file.
- The size of the video window and the frame rate you specify dramatically affect performance. In QuickTime or Video for Windows, 20 frames per second played in a small window is equivalent to playing 10 frames per second in a big window. The more data that has to be decompressed and transferred from the source CD-ROM to the screen, the lower the quality of the playback will be. This is true of any software-based video format.
- If you are working with QuickTime, consider using a specialized application, such as MovieShop, to automatically optimize your digital video file for playback from CD.

CD recording ideas

A CD-R is a write-once process of creating a CD. Some CD-R writers allow for multisession recording of data, but be aware that not all playback CD readers can access multisession recorded CDs.

- Be aware that CD-Rs currently come in two sizes, 540 MB and 640 MB. If storage space might be tight, be sure that you are using the 640MB.
- *Seek time* is the time it takes the CD-ROM player to locate specific data on the CD. You might benefit from a careful layout of the files you record on the CD, to minimize seek time.
- Avoid the use of hyphens and other unusual characters in file names, as they will fall outside of the ISO 9660 standard. The standard is limited to the letters A–Z, the digits 0–9, and the underscore character.
- Get the fastest CD writer you can afford. Quad-spin and faster writers are a pleasure to use compared to single-spin.
- Use multisession capabilities to create archives for your work, but avoid their use for deliverables, because older CD-ROM drives in use may not be able to play them.

Care of CDs and CD-Rs

You will buy CDs with audio, video, or graphics. Compression houses will send you your own video on CD-Rs. Finally, the day will come when you record your own CD-Rs. CD-Rs are significantly less robust than commercially made CDs. Optical discs were originally touted as indestructible, but they aren't. Everything you know about protecting your audio CDs goes double for CD-Rs.

Clean and safely store the CDs and CD-Rs. Here are a few suggestions for the care of CDs and CD-Rs:

- Avoid getting fingerprints, scratches, or dirt on the recording surface (green side on CD-Rs).

- Do not bend CDs or CD-Rs.

- Handle CD-Rs extra gently; they can be damaged by a shock.

- Store CDs and CD-Rs in their original jewel cases when they are not in a drive caddy.

- Keep CDs and CD-Rs out of direct sunlight, because they will warp

- Do not store CDs and CD-Rs in humid places, to avoid condensation.

- Store at moderate temperatures, 40–95° Fahrenheit, 5–37° Celsius.

- Clean with a soft dry cloth or CD cleaner kit to remove dust.

- Do not use chemically treated cloths or volatile solvents, such as thinner, benzene, anti-static fluid, or LP cleaner. All of these will damage a CD-R.

- If absolutely necessary, wash them with warm water and mild detergent.

Digital-Video Technology—Today and Tomorrow

Digital-video technology is probably the single, fastest-moving area of computing today. Just three years ago, the nadir of digital-video technology on the PC was the successful marriage of digital text and graphics with analog audio and video, by means of expensive, analog laser, disc players and video, overlay boards. Today, the state of the art involves two different approaches to fully digital, full-motion video on computers; hardware-assisted delivery, and software-only solutions.

Hardware-assisted delivery currently provides very high-quality, full-motion, full-screen video. Compression technologies, such as DVI, MPEG, and True Motion, provide this delivery with modest hardware requirements. Software-only technologies initially promise no added hardware cost for delivery, but to this point they provide somewhat less video quality and reduced delivery rates. The bottleneck is that software video places significantly greater demands on the computer's CPU and video subsystem. All the video decompression is performed there, rather than in custom-designed chips as is the case with hardware-assisted video. These requirements somewhat negate the cost benefits of software video today. However, as CPUs and video systems increase in power and capability, as they inevitably will, these concerns will become moot.

Digital-video technologies are in use and, in comparison to analog IVD, are saving money today. They will have their place, today and tomorrow. If you are working on a PC, take a few minutes and explore the Media Dynamics DLL included on the book CD. The Media Device Control DLL accesses, controls, formats and displays digital video and digital audio. This allows designers and programmers of interactive multimedia to integrate audio and video simply and easily as all of the access and control issue are contained in a single dynamic link library. The benefits of this approach are substantial. There are a standards set of commands to access and play a wide variety of multimedia files. The mdCtrl Library detects and adapts to the current multimedia data type. The commands held within this DLL have been created to operate within any Windows that can load and call a dynamic link library. This includes (but is not limited to) Authorware Professional, Toolbook, Visual Basic and C/C++.

Where Do We Go From Here?

Although many of the audio and video standards and products are completely incompatible, the success of some of them will lead us to better lessons and lower prices in training. We think that, eventually, the best multimedia will run on most of the computers that workers use, and the mechanisms that make it all work will appear seamless to the learner.

Let's Get Real!

You have probably heard the quip about artificial intelligence, "I'd rather have the real thing." It might be that we'd rather have real equipment or real situations. A salesperson could probably learn a lot from trying to sell his wares to real customers; in fact, many salespeople do learn that way. But the value of one sale, and the number of potential customers that can be lost while the salesperson flounders, justify sales training. Higher-end sales training includes simulations in which the salesperson interacts with a computer until he masters the techniques of sales.

In Chapter 26 we will explore the highest and lowest ends of simulation. In many cases, simulation is better than the real thing.

26

Simulation and Simulators

Next to on-the-job training, many experts agree that simulation is the most powerful means of transferring skills and knowledge to learners. The aviation and power industries use massive, complex, costly, and highly realistic simulators to provide instruction in a variety of critical occupations. However, these simulators are only the tip of the simulation iceberg. Rarely is simulation considered for most organization's training problems. Many learning specialists never stop to consider that several different levels of fidelity in simulation are possible.

What You Will Learn in This Chapter

- Divergent characteristics of simulation and simulators
- Advantages and disadvantages of simulation and simulators
- Characteristics of simulation methods
- How to rank fidelity of simulations
- How to determine categories of simulations
- Characteristics of different types of simulated time

In this chapter we will distinguish between *simulation* and *simulators*. Simulation is a strategy. We can achieve simulation using a variety of equipment. Simulators are special-purpose hardware devices that provide simulation exclusively. There is also a broad range of simulation possible that may not come so readily to mind. Noncomputer simulation is also a useful media. Personal computers, so widely available, can support hybrid simulations. And, more especially because PCs have become progressively more robust, the chance to use personal computer-based simulation is increasingly within your grasp.

Computer Simulations and Simulators in General

Simulators resemble real equipment to a high degree. Simulations may use a variety of different learning stations or combine with other media to provide realistic instruction. Students experience highly simulated environments by combining computer capabilities with other media or equipment for instruction or testing. Simulators and simulations can control interactive self-instruction to teach operation, steps, and processes. Simulators and simulations are excellent tools to create real-world situations. Some typical examples are: simulated landing of aircraft as done by American and other airlines; docking a ship as done by SimShip; or emergency drills as done by the U.S. Department of Energy office of Emergency Management. Sometimes, models or mockups can be used to allow students to observe results. They are very useful to create real-world situations, or when used to control film or video materials.

Advantages of simulations

- Lower fidelity simulations are available at reduced cost.
- It is possible to practice events that happen rarely.
- It is possible to practice events too dangerous or damaging for practice on real equipment.
- Response time can be realistic, or faster or slower, as demanded by the instruction.
- Simulations normally have greater capabilities than simulators, providing greater flexibility in instructional methods and curriculum.
- Test results can be generated automatically.

Advantages of simulators

- It is possible to practice events that happen rarely.
- It is possible to practice events too dangerous or damaging for practice on real equipment.
- It provides the "highest quality" practice possible without real equipment.
- Response time can be realistic, or faster or slower, as demanded by the instruction.
- Simulators normally have greater capabilities than computer simulations.
- Test results can be generated automatically.

Disadvantages of simulations

- Little commercially produced courseware is available.
- Simulation is the most expensive CAI mode to develop.
- Skilled developers may not be available in the organization.
- Usually, one of the more costly computer configurations is required.

Disadvantages of simulators

- A breakdown of the simulator will prevent all the students from practicing.
- No commercially produced courseware is available.
- Normally, this is the most costly training system you could buy.

If you are contemplating use of simulators and simulations there are many complex issues involved. Consider the following:

- Are simulators or simulations necessary?
- Is damage to equipment, environment, or personnel likely in training with actual equipment?
- Do you have the development skill needed to prepare the complex programming you will need?
- Have you considered lower-cost, noncomputer simulations such as in-basket exercises, role playing, situation simulation, and business games?
- Is upper management committed to supporting simulation?

Simulation

Simulation is the representation of a situation or device, with a reasonable (or high) degree of fidelity. It allows learners to see and practice a wanted performance. Simulation provides practice in a way that, if duplicated in the real world, would be costly, inconvenient, impractical, foolish, unwise, dangerous, impossible, or "all of the above." Simulation techniques are extremely desirable for training in subjects where students must assess information and begin correct action within a short time. This is a characteristic of many high-technology occupations.

Methods of simulation

Methods of simulation include:

- Computer
- Manual
- Hybrid (combined manual and computer)

With today's advancements, computer simulation comes much closer to hands-on training. More typical organizations don't need the complexity associated with the aircraft and nuclear power industries. By taking advantage of inexpensive, desk-top computers, training groups can provide realistic simulation. Simulation done exclusively, or nearly exclusively, by PCs and other electronic devices, is called "computer" simulation.

Often, the advantages of computer simulation, such as instant reconfiguration control and automatic record keeping, will be combined with manual simulation.

Desk-top computers communicate with mechanically built simulators through simple electronic converters, to insert faults or change system line-ups at the press of a button. This combination of computer and manual simulation is "hybrid" simulation.

Of course, simulation can be done without a computer. The instructor could choose to build a model of the system to be learned, using smaller or partial components as compared to the real equipment. For example, we could mount pressure switches, gauges, a tank, and a pump on a roll-around cart to simulate the operation of a large system. This type of simulation, without computer, is considered "manual" simulation. Manual simulation offers the advantage of letting learners get their "hands-on" real hardware, even if it is scaled down or incomplete. In fact, manual simulation often uses the very same components found at the work site.

Fidelity of simulation

Simulation "fidelity" is a description of its realness or degree of accuracy, which can be low, medium, or high. Increased fidelity usually improves the rate at which advanced learners internalize new material. It may, however, impede learning in certain situations. Sometimes, complex is *not* better, just more confusing. High-fidelity training environments usually have associated prerequisites, such as basic skills in a particular discipline. The appropriate fidelity level may depend on the stage at which the learner is in the overall training program. Low-fidelity could be better for new learners, while advanced learners can cope with the distractions of high-fidelity.

Categories of simulation

Simulators will provide a learning experience as either whole-task or part-task. A whole-task simulation is one in which training is provided for the complete task to be performed, instead of providing the learning experience in stages. The massive simulators used in nuclear power are whole-task, as the operator crews complete all or most of their training in this environment. The aircraft industry, on the other hand, uses full-scale flight simulators complemented by smaller, computer-based simulations. The latter are part-task simulators.

The Simulation Model

Each of the qualities just presented; methods, categories, and fidelity, combine to define any simulation.[1] Figure 26.1 shows the methods.

Figure 26.2 shows the addition of manual and computer simulation to the complete part-whole model. There are now four possibilities.

Figure 26.3 shows the components of simulation buildup to the complete simulation model. There are 12 combinations in all.

The model illustrates the relationships of the combinations of methods, fidelity, and categories. The model is used to illustrate the full range of simulation possible: from

---

[1]The Simulation Model grew out of the work of Angus Reynolds and Cheryl Samuels-Campbell. See Reynolds, A. and Samuels-Campbell, C. "Simulations: Time to Take Another Look!" *Performance and Instruction*. Vol. 24, No. 4, May 1985, pp. 15–17.

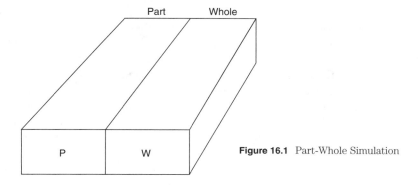

Figure 16.1 Part-Whole Simulation

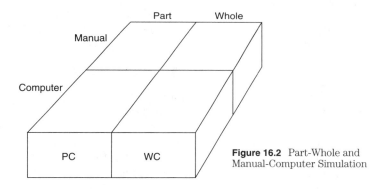

Figure 16.2 Part-Whole and
Manual-Computer Simulation

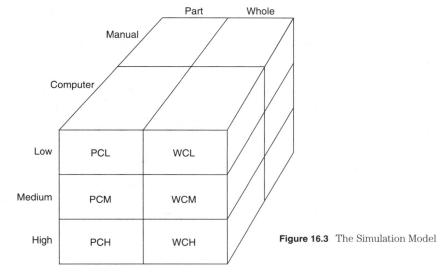

Figure 16.3 The Simulation Model

part-task—manual—low-fidelity to whole-task—computer-based—high-fidelity. The model helps raise consciousness of the range available.

For example, the front lower right cell of the model is labeled WCH. WCH represents whole-task/computer-based/high-fidelity simulation. One WCH simulation is the aircraft-specific flight simulator. A more common example is PMH, part-task/manual/high fidelity, represented by the in-basket exercise. PMH is not among the six labeled cells in the figure. It is among the six cell labels at the rear in this view. They represent the manual equivalents of the computer cells in front. For example, a whole-task/manual simulation, available in all three fidelity levels, is the mockup.

Smaller Could Be Better

One could argue that bigger may be better. However, it is clear beyond any doubt that big is not always essential. Here are some arguments for less than majestic simulation:

- Manual simulation is important in more organizations than computerized simulation.
- Low or medium fidelity is often adequate for the training at hand.
- Part-task is completely adequate for meeting most training needs.

It is important not to limit your thinking of simulator training only to psychomotor skills. While this is the type of learning traditionally associated with many simulators, cognitive and even effective goals may also be met by using simulation. Business games, situation simulation, and role playing are examples of manual or hybrid simulation often used to achieve cognitive or effective objectives. Personal computers continue to become more interactive and increasingly ergonomic. As they do, their ability to deal one-on-one with the learner in effective and cognitive tasks is limited only by the imaginations of designers and programmers.

Psychomotor skills dominate our concept of simulations. Don't let that obscure the potential for activities of other types, such as in-basket exercises, role playing, situation simulation, business games, or any other modest efforts to simulate. The availability of computers is a boon to simulations for a wide variety of training. The imaginative usefulness of small computers to enhance simulations is still largely untapped.

The level of fidelity, or degree of realism, will affect the rate of learning and the transfer of learning to the real equipment. How realistic does the simulated equipment need to be? Research has shown that high fidelity is not needed for learning procedural tasks. The reduced-fidelity, simulated environment is ideal for a beginning learner. The actual equipment may be quite intimidating. If so, it may also be significantly less conducive to learning. "Overload" is the intimidation factor caused by excessive equipment or high-fidelity simulation. Complexities and details of the real situation can overwhelm the learner. Too many new stimuli emerge for the learner to get the desired content. To summarize research into simulator-fidelity requirements, reduced fidelity can improve learning for a novice because:

- High fidelity means higher complexity that taxes memory and other cognitive abilities.

- Proven instructional techniques that improve initial learning tend to reduce fidelity.[2]

Remember, high-fidelity, or maximum job/task simulation, is only appropriate if students have prerequisite skills. For example, it would be a waste of money and time if a novice pilot began in a simulator without meeting the basic skill requirements. A simulator simulates the real flying conditions. This could create a stressful learning atmosphere and deter learning if the pilot was not ready for this degree of fidelity. In this case, more (fidelity) is not necessarily better!

Simulation—the mode

Simulation is one of the modes of CAI. However, it is linked so closely to the system and method chosen it deserves separate consideration. The combination of the hardware and software features make computer simulation an excellent choice for complex simulations. Graphics capability, combined with the tactile input screen, permit the student's learning station to function as though it were the specific equipment item. The learning experiences that result approximate the benefits of a "hands-on" practice session with the actual equipment.

Simulation can increase insight into the cause-effect relationship illustrated. The computer learning station can use special control features and feedback. This can provide the learner the opportunity to see and understand complex electronic and mechanical (or other) phenomena in a unique way.

Simulators and Simulation

In many technical occupations, some sort of practice before using the actual equipment is extremely helpful and important. Classic examples are aircraft flight crews and nuclear power reactor operators. Both industries use very costly, special, and specific simulators. One computer learning terminal can be used to integrate other learning experiences with the equipment simulation, and can simulate an "automatic pilot"—and a moment later provide another learner with a nuclear power reactor control panel. The CBL terminal is obviously more flexible and less expensive than the special simulators for either.

One guy who knows what he's talking about is Bob Vonderlin of SimShip. He says, "At the high end of the simulation spectrum are the original—and in my opinion the only—true virtual reality systems, the full-fidelity simulators. They combine computer-generated visuals motion bases, sound systems, precise replicas of the human-machine interface, and math models of the systems' behavior. Certain aircraft simulators are so realistic that a pilot can train and be certified in the simulator alone, without ever flying the real thing."

[2]See Alessi, M., and Trollip, S. *Computer-Based Instruction: Methods and Development.* Englewood Cliffs, NJ: Prentice Hall. 1985.

Simulation in the airlines

Major airlines were quick to recognize the value of computer-based learning to solve their training problems. The computer learning station does not replace the specialized simulator. It fulfills its proper role to supplement it. Extensive use of graphics and animation are common in aviation simulations. The rapid display of complex flight panels is essential to represent accurately an operation on the aircraft. The use of an interactive computer learning system provides the student input when he touches the screen. The combination of simulation with a properly developed training program can increase the quality of training in the classroom, and during full-scale simulator sessions.

The training technique illustrated here is important. The airlines recognized the advantage and developed the dual simulation-simulator method. Training on a learning station before the simulator session enables the simulator to put the trainee's knowledge to the test in a realistic way. The more costly special simulator then does not simply teach or provide experience. It tests the learner's real knowledge of the equipment. It does it in a way that other means cannot.

The success enjoyed by the airlines prompted them to make major use of computer simulation in the training the next time an entirely new series of aircraft came into service. The Boeing 767 series of aircraft provided the first opportunity to design a complete computer-based training system for an aircraft. The aircraft's flight-management system, with seven computers that replaced electromechanical devices, almost suggested computer-based learning simulation. The next series, the 777, will have complete TBL.

Simulation in nuclear power plants

Nuclear utility companies recognize the value of full-fidelity simulators to solve their training problems. Dozens of nuclear utility companies in the United States operate enormous simulators. Priced at over $1 million each, these room-size simulators are replicas of the real reactor's control rooms. The displays are identical in placement and appearance to those located in the actual control room. The simulator responds identically to the actual reactor system. They are unique and specially programmed to create situations that have occurred, or could occur, in the plant. Training is for the crews who will start up the (simulated) plant, recognize and correct plant problems, and safely shut it down several times over before operating the real thing. Why all the expense? For one, regulating agencies, always in search of the utmost in training, require simulator training. For another, imagine the incalculable costs associated with an accident of the scope of the Three Mile Island event. All this is exceptionally expensive to buy and use. But as we said, the Nuclear Regulatory Commission requires plants to have access to simulators. They test and certify reactor operators on simulators.

While most organizations don't have $2 million in the budget for a simulator this year, the concept of simulation can easily be applied to nearly any training program. The ever-increasing power of personal computers can transform your classroom desktop into an effective platform for simulation.

Its combination of hardware and software features makes the PC an excellent choice for complex simulations. The graphics capability, combined with the tactile input, permit the student's computer to function as though it were an item of specific equipment. The resulting learning experiences approximate the benefits of "hands-on" practice with the actual equipment. David C. Paquin, of Niagara Mohawk Power, says, "This often provides greater insight into the cause-and-effect relationship depicted. The special control features and feedback mechanisms can sometimes provide the student the opportunity to see and understand complex electrical, mechanical, and thermal phenomena. Learners can then see phenomena not viewable in either an actual operating unit or in the normal training simulator. Only meters, indication lights, and control switches are available there for student interaction. All this combines to enhance the training experience and results in better retention and overall knowledge of the subject material."

Simulation in the maritime arena

A less-well-known type of simulator exists to train ship's officers. The simulator appears to be the bridge of a ship, with room for several people to walk about—as we've all seen in the movies. Out the windows we see the busy Hong Kong harbor. No, wait, it's Rio de Janeiro. No, wait . . .we could go on, because it can be anywhere with different conditions of tide or current according to the simulation need.

SimShip's Bob Vonderlin again: "When the cost or risk involved with using actual equipment is extreme but extensive training and evaluation is necessary, as is the case with operators of ships, airplanes, and nuclear power plants, full-fidelity simulation is an attractive solution. The operators of these systems must train and practice in an environment that features the conditions, initiating cues, and consequences of actions that the operators will experience in the real world. Accurately simulating a complex environment can be quite costly, but in cases like those mentioned, the benefits outweigh the costs. Properly facilitated simulator training, incorporating no-risk trial and error, has proven to be more efficient than using actual equipment, without any of the danger. And there is ample evidence that, if an operator can perform a procedure correctly on a high-fidelity simulator, then that operator can be expected to perform it correctly on the actual equipment. Additionally, simulators are invaluable for practicing emergency procedures and developing new procedures, tasks that are essential but too risky to be attempted with actual equipment."

Simulating time

Computers allow us to easily simulate one of the essential elements of practice—time. Timing can be critical when the realistic timing of events is important. One of the most critical elements associated with modern-day training is timing. The nuclear plant operator must start and stop pumps in a specific sequence. Technicians often are needed to perform steps not only sequentially, but within very short time periods. Computers can obviously time events with perfection. You may have considered the benefits of doing things in "real time." The accurate representation of time is important for some things, but it is not always the most important timing possibility.

One of the great advantages of simulators over using real equipment is their ability to compress or extend time. Changed time scales present important opportunities for learning. Slowed time, stepping in small increments, permits examination of a process to understand a specific progression. Events that happen in microseconds can be frozen in time for close inspection. This is particularly useful to the beginning student, who can, without danger to personnel or equipment, cautiously weigh the alternatives before making a major decision. In some situations, you can ease learning by freezing time and events. This permits an examination of the simulated system in ways that would not be possible in the real world. It can freeze a speeding neutron as it blazes across a uranium core!

Accelerated time permits us to examine conditions that develop over hours, days, or even months. Obviously, the learner can't sit there waiting for things to develop over such a long time. Condensed time permits the learner to see the potential result of action or inaction over the event's or development's full cycle.

A simulator can stop the world or make it spin like crazy! That is no small achievement.

Look Toto, It's Kansas

You might like to think that if you have gone through the careful analysis, design development, troubleshooting, and evaluation that your course will stand up anywhere. We suspect by this time that you realize that things don't just happen by clicking your ruby slippers together. It takes much more than that.

In Chapter 27 we will take "much more than that" to a new level. There are many considerations that apply to courseware that will be delivered in another country, and you can master them too. In fact, careful analysis, design development, troubleshooting, and evaluation will suffice, because truly careful work will anticipate foreign use of your courseware. Grab Toto and stand by for liftoff!

27

Adapting Technology-Based Training for Foreign Learners

Angus can never seem to talk about his experiences working in other countries without telling the singing dog story. He never heard anyone say "I'd like one of the singing dogs please!", but as he rode to work on the train each day in Japan he often fantasized such a scene. There was a large sign on a building along the tracks near Kamakura that proclaimed, "Singing Bird and Dog Sale." Most Americans couldn't read the Japanese characters that had been translated to identify the establishment to foreigners as a pet shop. But the harmless singing dog translation pales beside a famous interpreting mistake involving President Nixon. The Prime Minister of Japan's comment was translated as "I'll take care of it." A more on-target translation would have been "I'll take it under advisement." That misunderstanding created a major problem in the relations between the U.S. and Japan.

What You Will Learn in This Chapter

- How technology-based learning differs from conventional training delivery
- What to consider when translating materials
- Considerations for culturalization
- How to identify and avoid cultural bias
- How to estimate the cost of adapting multimedia training for foreign delivery

Although important in training, correct translation is only one component of good adaptation for use by foreign users. In the late 1950s, high-quality Japanese consumer products were successfully introduced to the U.S. Gradually they were embraced by Americans who appreciated the high-quality, well-engineered, modestly priced products. Japanese penetration of the American market at that time was entirely owing to their engineering excellence, and *not* to good adaptation for use by foreigners. User training (manuals and instructions) was almost unbelievable. Few examples survive, but I have preserved a stamp pad from that period. It was a great product at a time when stamp pads had to be re-inked every few days—a messy job. The user instructions begin with the proclamation "Good for 1,000 stamp on face of abroad." But have you opened a user manual for a Japanese car recently? Times have changed!

Training, like excellently engineered products, will succeed because it is well-designed and developed. TBL materials design *must* include appropriate adaptation before export to be well-designed and developed. This adaptation is both figuratively and literally the price of success.

Why Are Automated Materials Different from Seminars?

Many companies and U.S. training organizations "export" their seminar-based training to non-English speaking countries. Somehow it seems to survive the trip. Why would TBL be any different?

Only the most naive trainer believes that the training actually does "survive" the trip. In fact, it *doesn't*. The reason it doesn't survive is that no local seminar leader wants to appear like a fool. The local national who delivers the "foreign" seminar provides more than simple translation. The local person applies a natural sense of his or her own setting and provides judicious amounts of both pre-planned and spontaneous cultural adaptation.

I once asked the Director of Training of Xerox do Brasil (the subsidiary in Brazil) how he employed training packages sent from Headquarters. Xerox packages were, and are, well-done. He replied, "We never use them as they arrive. We always have to adapt them to fit in with our own circumstances." This is typical of answers to the same question repeated all around the world.

TBL multimedia self-study packages obviously lack the local national to provide the key on-the-spot cultural adaptation. Also, in most cases local subsidiaries or customers lack the technical capability to "adapt them to fit in with our own circumstances." The only recourse is to adapt them before they go overseas. This chapter deals not only with why various aspects of automated materials must be changed, but how. The first consideration is translation.

Translation

Whether you view a gaffe by a translator (or interpreter, as the case may be) as either funny or horrible depends on its effect on you. As the Japanese singing dog shows, literal translation is rarely the best one. Good translation embodies a "sense" of the original. John Eldridge, a TBL development expert with wide overseas experience, suggests, "The problem is not to translate the words but to convey the ideas across cultures. Employ a writer from the other culture to write your idea in the local language."

Translation is an obvious need. Still, there are subtleties that sometimes elude insular Americans. For example, if you were translating a CAI program into Spanish, which dialect should the final version be in? Significant differences, if incorporated, could brand the final product as "Cuban," "Puerto Rican," or "Mexican" when "generic Western Hemisphere Spanish" might be wanted. "Translation into Chinese" leaves another unanswered question. What Chinese? The one spoken in Hong Kong (Cantonese) or the one used in Beijing (Mandarin)? Aand this doesn't even address the additional problem that written Chinese characters are not quite the same in Beijing, Hong Kong, and Taiwan.

Dean Wade, Director of Courseware Development at Soza Company, warns that maintaining the translated materials at the designed literacy level is also important. He points out that a well-educated, native translator will convert English materials with linguistic and educational pride. You must make certain that the resulting translation avoids "upgrading" the literacy level. Make certain that the new language version is at an understandable level *for the intended audience*. Dean says, "It is wise to use a revision matrix to help project management. List the factors considered and use it as a checklist before proceeding to actual revision. Depending on the number of different target populations, the matrix may be quite large, but it can be a major aid in ensuring that areas of potential concern have been appropriately addressed."

No local national would make the same mistakes an American would make. However, those suggested here, and many more, have been made by U.S. organizations. You have to test *everything* linguistic with the target audience, not just the text, audio, and video. Verification might have prevented General Motors' Nova snafu. Chevrolet sold its popular Nova in Latin America under its North American name. But in Spanish, "no va" means "you don't go." Who would buy a car with a name that suggests you can't go? (Yugo, a clever reversal, wasn't enough to make that car sell either, but that's another story!) Simple translation, even when accurate, is rarely enough.

Culturalization

Think of culturalization as total translation. Len Nadler, an experienced practitioner and observer of international training activities, likes to point out that culture and language are inextricably linked. *Experienced* international training practitioners understand the need to consider cultural as well as linguistic differences when translating a training program into another language.

To ignore the need for cultural adaptation when translating a program from English into Spanish—or Turkish, or Chinese—is to court disaster. We once worked with Abdulhamied Al Romaithy, Executive Director of the Gulf Institute in Fujairah, to identify 91 different sets of conditions that might obtain for individuals in technology-transfer situations. Competent culturalization should resolve many of them.

Ethnocentrism

Cultural adaptation is still important, even when the language remains the same. Ethnocentrism places cultural blinders upon all of us. Consider translating English into American! It's difficult to recognize the extent to which you are an "American" speaker, as opposed to an English speaker, and what that means for training materials you create. Business contacts assured us that a CAI program that taught "American" English could not succeed in India. One program was translated into British English for sale in the United Kingdom. That version didn't work in Australia and was redone a second time for use there. Mike Pellet, President of M^3, has prepared numerous video-based programs for foreign use. He tells of his experiences with a particular U.S. video. The video was first tried in Britain. It didn't work because it was too American. It was dubbed using British voices. To the developers' surprise, that didn't work either. It had become "Americans with British voices." Finally it was necessary to entirely re-shoot the video using British talent.

When you produce a TBL program of any kind, you won't be there to tell the learner what the screen really means. It will be right or wrong, effective or ineffective. The only way to make your courseware right and effective for the intended audience is to ensure good cultural adaptation. Automated materials magnify the need for cultural adaptation, in addition to straight translation.

Unfortunately, successful programs usually incorporate a high degree of creativity. It makes them come alive. Creativity helps the learner relate to the material, keeps the programs from boring American learners, and leads to success. All the best programs that we know of share this characteristic. The problem is that the creative elements tend to be highly culture-specific—to the culture of origin. Things that "turn on" the American learner are most likely to turn off the overseas learner. This includes the English-speaking foreign learner. Solving this paradox necessitates careful work and compromises.

General and Technical Considerations

As computer people say, let's take a "top down" look at the considerations essential to doing a good job. You have to get past the "mechanics" of presenting the program before you can focus on content. The suggestions that we provide are listed in ascending order of technical complexity.

Keep it simple

A simple lesson will be easier to adapt. The problem here is that sometimes simple equals boring. Also, design rules such as "keep it simple" tend to limit creativity. You will find it difficult to hold back on ideas for a lesson in English just because the lesson might someday be translated.

Anyone who designs a multimedia lesson should want it to be as effective and interesting as possible. At one point, an instructional designer colleague who must remain nameless in this case, was "cranking out" TBL lessons. In that case a tight budget and short schedule ensured simplicity. The resulting lessons were simple indeed. She wasn't happy working on that project because she had the skill to produce more stimulating learning materials. Remember, simplicity is a paradox and you must keep it in balance. Although you can't have the best of both worlds, strive to ensure that keeping it simple does not equal making it dull.

Ensure clarity

A vague English narrative will be equally obscure in French or Korean. You should totally rethink exporting anything that isn't clear in the original—which, of course, you should never produce in the first place!

Anticipate foreign use

Standardization can help to avoid difficulty. If you think your courseware may have foreign marketing potential you should act on that knowledge. Certain format standards should already exist for the designers who create the originals for any development project. We suggest them in Chapter 32. You can establish additional standards based on an anticipated foreign audience. A standard could specify the size of borders or the positioning of certain information on displays. Others might prohibit the display of specifically U.S. things, such as coins, dollar signs, and famous U.S. landmarks. "Generic" standardization can be done before any particular target country for foreign delivery has been identified. But, if you know in advance that a module might be used in Sri Lanka or Venezuela, you can make the most creative use of that knowledge.

Space will be the main evidence of such anticipation. You may not be aware that some written languages take far more space than others to convey the same information. For us, German is the most frequently encountered space-limitation example, although there are other languages with similar requirements. As a rule, German text requires about 30 percent more space than English. Foresight is more important in the adaptation of TBL than of printed texts. If you think that a program will later be translated into another language, you should pay particular attention to the potential space problems when laying out frames. This isn't a major problem in translating a printed text or manual—you can just add pages. TBL is different. In a well-conceived TBL lesson, it could ruin the entire design.

A better concept for anticipation is to produce a "modular" basic design. Provision is made for development of country, industry, and company-specific modules according to user need and demand.

Think screens vs. pages

We have tried to steer you away from "page turner" lessons. If you have to translate something bad, no one may notice. It can't get worse. In contrast, a well-designed program presents much of its information on discrete screen displays, or "frames." Creative and interesting programs often reveal much to the learner in a single frame, such as in a simulation. If the designer has to divide a uni-frame design to accommodate a different, space-consuming language, the integrity and impact of the lesson can be lost.

Undivided, the frame may become cluttered despite your best efforts to keep it simple. Equipment or other diagrams with labels or informational boxes are prime examples. A frame already crowded in English just isn't going to work in German.

Anticipate display format

Sometimes the foreign language doesn't lend itself to presentation in the pre-planned space. Common examples are the translation of English material into Arabic and Hebrew. Some frames have English text accompanying a graphic display. You might place it on the left of the related graphic or space for an answer. Languages written from right to left expect the "natural" positions for these to be the reverse. To avoid such problems, you can save space on both sides of graphics, or consistently place the text either above or below them. These standards may work, but such imposed limitations might impair your creativity.

Consider text characteristics

A worst-case illustration of the format problem arises when you try to translate TBL into Japanese or Chinese. These are character-oriented languages and require much different keyboard input and display. In 1979, Angus created one of the earliest Japanese CAI lessons developed anywhere. He planned to convert an existing program from English to Japanese. But the system he used did not yet have Japanese characters available, so he had to create those he would need, dot by dot. This was made much harder by the great number of dots needed. Sixfold more were needed to display the complex Japanese Kanji characters. A one-for-one assignment of keyboard keys can be done for Russian Cyrillic characters. It isn't possible for the large number of characters needed. He also found that the format used in the original lesson was not suitable for Japanese, for some of the reasons already discussed. Many of the displays looked "funny"; at the same time, it became clear that some of the content just wasn't right for Japanese users. Both problems led to much cultural adaptation. By the time he finished, only the concept of the original lesson remained. The program had been redesigned from the first *shoshomachi kudasai* message, that displayed while the computer was loading the lesson, to the *sayonara* page.

We suggest that, when you negotiate with a foreign buyer for a translated version of your automated training program, you remember this story. Don't commit to a price based entirely on the assumption that all you will have to do is turn the English program over to a translator. In the real world of international technology-based training, such thinking is foolish at best.

Deal with system- and application-generated messages

Imagine the familiar Microsoft Excel spreadsheet. It is "application software." You can buy special software that enables your computer to display "foreign" letters and numbers in the spreadsheet. Your Armenian customer could then type on special key caps, to display the unique Armenian language. Typing in Armenian doesn't change the spreadsheet's own software. Excel's menus and messages will still be displayed in English. Remember this example to help appreciate software considerations in TBL training development.

Today, lessons are usually created using menu-oriented development "systems" such as Authorware, as opposed to being written in a computer language. The designer does not write code but fills out menus, conceptually the same as entering information in a spreadsheet. After responses to questions, the system generates the desired program. Like the popular spreadsheet, some of these standardized menus, and the displays they generate, make things simpler in the United States. They obviously do not make things simple when the user is literate only in another language. If you haven't thought about it before, you do not *own* your Lotus 1-2-3 code, nor do you have the access needed to alter it. Typically, you will not own the code for programs such as Authorware, used to develop and deliver technology-based training. The problem for an organization that wants to present instruction in Tamil or Czech is not so much that the menus are in English. The problem is that the automatic displays will remain in English. The displays are generated by the software application. Two important questions must be answered. Is the system available in the target language? If not, can you get access to translate it?

Training a complete courseware development group in instructional design is an unusual step. Such a step provided the delightful experience of working with Kingsley Wanigasundera and his Sri Lankan courseware development team to help them generate lessons on growing spices. They then designed and developed computer and video lessons that would eventually be driven as far into rural Sri Lanka as the roads go, and then "manpacked" to remote villages for delivery on battery-powered equipment. The team created a beautiful Sinhalese character set, and were granted access to change the authoring language's automatic displays. Development involving special complex character sets always takes comparatively long because of multiple-step text entry. They did a super job!

The size problem is also operative in application-generated cases. Jim Glish, of Computer Teaching Corporation, correctly anticipated that the lesson model software he was designing would eventually be used in Germany. He planned for, and provided, thirty percent additional space. As it happened, the particular topics and lessons that were ultimately translated exceeded even the extra space that his foresight had provided.

Cultural Bias

Our family and associates assist us to thoroughly culturalize us in our own culture as we grow up. Normal people everywhere embrace a whole system of principles, concepts, and beliefs that are not obvious to people in other parts of the world. In fact, different groups may hold totally opposite views. You may recall the TV and film space traveler "Coneheads" family from the planet Remulak. Dan Akroyd advised his daughter to explain even the most bizarre behavior simply by saying, "We are from France." People readily accept the notion that those from other countries are strange.

"Ethnocentrism" is the fifty-cent word for cultural bias, which is really "clinging to your own culture." It is a thoroughly human characteristic exhibited by members of all groups. H. L. Mencken perfectly satirized linguistic ethnocentrism when he wrote, "If English was good enough for Jesus Christ, it's good enough for me." The international marketplace application of "Mencken's ethnocentrism" is the failure of U.S. manufacturers to provide foreign language instructions for the countries to which their products are exported. We often open purchases to find instructions in up to five languages. Typically, those products are not U.S.-made. You must recognize and overcome ethnocentrism's limitations in order to succeed in the international training marketplace.

A strong NIH (Not Invented Here) syndrome is in effect for training materials used everywhere. People want to feel that the people they see and the text they read in their training materials were developed specifically with them in mind. This may sound petty, but is true within the U.S. and shows up in foreign countries as well. Cultural bias in automated TBL training turns up most frequently in audio narrative material, video examples, and textual explanations.

You can spot the cultural bias by using well-established and proven formative evaluation techniques in developing your materials. You simply must try the lessons with real members of the target population! This may sound obvious, but it is probably the most commonly violated rule of developing training materials for domestic users, not to mention foreign ones. Frank Otto, Professor of Linguistics at Brigham Young University and a founder of the Computer Assisted Language Instruction Consortium, converted a series of CAI lessons for use by Spanish-speaking U.S. citizens. There were several "situations" that were obviously biased toward the predominant U.S. culture. He wisely surveyed members of the target groups, picked replacement topics, and redeveloped those portions of the lessons. Frank says, "I'm glad we did, because the interests shown by the students on the questionnaires were quite different from what we had originally planned."

Not even your instructional strategy is above suspicion. If you are adapting existing instruction for a new audience, a careful check must be made to validate all of the activities included in the lesson. Hal Christensen, Manager of Courseware Development at CES Training Corporation, says, "We New Yorkers have to be careful how we say things. When I redo an automated package for a new audience in another part of the U.S. I exhaustively reevaluate its entire design and contents. This goes double for packages destined for export." You simply can't be too careful. For example, Caroline Wai-Ying Sin, Personnel and Training Manager of the International Hotel in the New Economic Zone in Shantou, China, warns "Instructional games are usually not an appropriate strategy for use with Chinese learners. They may work in some cases, but they are a gamble if you don't try them out first." This has been reinforced by other Chinese colleagues.

In your video, body language can also give away the cultural heritage of the training materials. The so-called "spaghetti westerns" made in Italy in the 1960s were obviously linked to their origin. Gestures are especially risky. For example, at an international training meeting, a Libyan seminar participant announced that there was certainly *one* universally understood gesture. He then demonstrated a gesture that he meant to illustrate "all right." The example he used has an obscene meaning in half the world! Make no assumptions about the gestures or actions of the people shown on your video. The users in the target country will be the final arbiters of your training material's acceptability.

Half a Dozen Foreign Adaptation Alerts

Why not do the job right? Attention to the items we suggest here will make a remarkable difference.

Acronyms and initials

Initials often carry double meanings and innuendo. Those that convey a rich meaning in one culture may only confuse in another. Other initials that seem innocuous may spell an undesirable word in the foreign language or lead to confusion. At a hotel lobby meeting in Abu Dhabi, a client exclaimed loudly and enthusiastically; "I love the CIA." He meant CAI. You should have seen the heads turn! Most of us have difficulty keeping track of our own acronyms. Any courseware with "foreign" acronyms is in for real trouble.

Jargon and clichés

Jargon does not include technical terms or professional terms that are also the jargon of the foreign users. Petroleum workers in another country may have already picked up the jargon of that work. For example, the computer world is filled with universally understood jargon. It is the other guy's jargon that doesn't translate. A standard technique used on technology-transfer projects where automated courses are being adapted on a "production" basis is to establish a dictionary of "legal" words available to your lessons. You can produce quite capable courseware with a surprisingly small dictionary.

You should avoid clichés in English anyway. They simply won't survive the trip abroad. Examples might include: "We are down on our luck." "Our managers can't cut the mustard." "Our division has its back to the wall." "Now is the time to put your ear to the ground and nose to the grindstone." It could take extra lessons to explain these to foreign learners.

Numbers and money

Have you ever read a book that said something cost £35 thousand million? This "unbiased" cultural evidence can create a problem. You could get the meaning more quickly if the figure were given as $47 billion. Some math lessons have been exported with examples using "nickels, dimes, and quarters." Your lessons just can't get away with showing "foreign" U.S. currency, and we hope you won't attempt such a shallow adaptation. Inappropriate use of numbers can be remarkably distracting for the learner in ways that an American designer might not suspect. It can create what Cheryl Samuels-Campbell, a Caribbean instructional design consultant, likes to call "cultural interference." Working with Cheryl on training materials for accountants in Barbados, we found that examples of billion-dollar industries not only ran the risk of boggling the learner, but also of being dismissed as propaganda — selling a negative (U.S.) image that bigger is better.

Sports

People around the world enjoy different sports. American sports examples and metaphors often cannot survive adaptation. This illustrates the concept that what makes something fit congruently into one culture makes it a miss for another. Baseball and football interest is shared in only a few countries. "We have no other choice than to drop back and punt" communicates nothing to most of the people of the world. Neal Nadler of Vanderbilt University tells of the successful (at least in the U.S.) consultant who used a snow skiing analogy in a Middle East desert sheikdom. He applied good interpersonal skills and survived the gaffe. Your automated program can't do that.

Humor

Humor is dangerous even in our own culture. Sometimes efforts to be humorous fall flat. We dearly love the British humor exemplified by John Cleese. Other people tell us that it just doesn't work with their (American) learners. Humor is culture-related and it is often difficult to translate to another culture. All too often it leaves the foreign learner baffled, if not insulted. Generally, well-designed courseware can be expected to retain its training value in a foreign country, even without the jokes.

Sex

Gender roles vary widely in different parts of the world. You must provide native learners a chance to contribute honest input after trial use of TBL training, showing people of either gender. A scene we consider ordinary may show a person in a role considered inappropriate in the target culture. As with many other aspects of any culture, people in another area are apt to have difficulty relating to text or scenes that they find unreal—or foreign.

How Much Is All This Going to Cost?

What is the first question your management will ask? If it isn't cost-related, you work in a very interesting organization. Automated training *always* costs more to develop than instructor-led. The same delivery advantages that make it attractive in the U.S. apply in foreign cases as well. Several different kinds of cost must be considered—with radically escalating impact on the project's bottom line. The projected "rule of thumb" costs indicated are percentages of the original development cost of existing materials. Let's look at the costs of:

- Creativity
- Translation
- Culturalization
- Major modifications

General and technical considerations

Keep it simple, etc. will not cost any money. When implemented in an original design standard it may even reduce costs. Beware, however, that all limitations harbor the potential to curb creativity. They could make the lessons ordinary or boring instead of outstanding. That is the "creativity cost."

Translation

Language translation won't be expensive, totaling approximately five percent. But, if you have read this far you know that such a simple translation will only buy you trouble. If the target language uses a non-roman character set, translation cost will be the same but implementation will be more expensive. How costly depends on a variety of circumstances. Translations that involve creation of a new character set can have a heavy "front end" cost. Hopefully, you can amortize it over many lessons.

Culturalization

Culturalization costs are difficult to extrapolate because the degree of adaptation required for each training project varies. The degree to which the original developers anticipated the possibility of foreign use will affect cost proportionately. Modular design in anticipation of custom adaptation has higher initial cost, but will speed and improve adaptation. Both culture-specific graphics and text cost more to adapt, depending on the specific items. Generally, cultural adaptation adds ten to twenty-five percent to the cost of development. But eliminating jargon and clichés, acronyms and initials, sports, humor, and sex has no extra cost at all. They will be removed as a part of any competent cultural translation. Costs of culturalization of materials with heavy video component will escalate if the video must be reshot in the other culture. This extra cost can easily run from fifty to one hundred percent.

Heavy-duty adaptation includes altering display or text characteristics, or implementing system changes, or changing application-generated displays. Even if you have the ability and permission, extensive changes of this type can add one hundred percent *or more* to costs.

Reinventing the Wheel

Many of the principles and techniques listed here are "twice-told tales." They were first applied to the successful adaptation of print learning materials and for video-based technology transfer efforts. They have also been proven in pioneer courseware adaptation efforts for CAI. They work.

As an "attention gainer" Angus once started an international presentation with the statement that "there is absolutely no difference in designing instruction for delivery to a foreign audience." This is true, if you agree that a professional job *always* includes identification of and provision for relevant differences in the target population. The instructional design principles for international TBL remain the same.

The TBL adaptation business is still a new one. Frankly, it remains a bigger problem than it has to be. But we don't have to invent a new wheel. The international training wheel was discovered long ago and is now considerably improved. A tried-and-true methodology is available to those who care to do things overseas right, the first time. The big difference is that, if you want TBL to succeed, you have to apply the methodology. The day that you don't have to adapt your training, you'll be able to buy the singing dog as well!

Let's Tie It Up

Wow! The business of developing multimedia training is pretty complex. It is, but there are still a few more points that need to be made. Since you are working with the Authorware working model, you haven't encountered what it is like to "package" your courseware for delivery to its sponsor. In Chapter 28, we'll show you how that is done, and then some. Let's get the old scissors and string out and get to it.

28

Is This All There Is?

In this chapter we will go beyond what you can reasonably do with the software on the book CD. The Authorware working model packaged with the book is limited in some features. Also, some of the advanced features of Authorware are best approached by readers with a solid math background. We have not included complex mathematics in the exercises.

This chapter will describe how software is packaged prior to delivery to customers, to prevent tampering and protect intellectual property. We expect that you will use the Mac or Windows platform and present information about moving your work from one to the other. We also explore conversion of completed courses from one platform to another. Finally, we look at copyrights, trademarks, and patents.

What You Will Learn in This Chapter

- Differences between the Authorware Working Model and the full version
- Advanced features of Authorware and other authoring systems, and how they are used
- How and why to package courseware for delivery
- How to convert courseware for delivery on another platform

Mathematics

Computers were first created to do calculations. "It is in their blood" so to speak. Authorware has a fully developed set of mathematical functions that, with the exception of Random and the array functions, we have ignored in this book.

If you have the mathematical background, we invite you to explore the use of the mathematical operators. You have your choice of:

ABS	LN
ACOS	LOG10
ASIN	MOD
ATAN	Round
COS	Sign
EXP	SIN
EXP10	SQRT
INT	TAN

If you have the mathematics background you are familiar with the meaning of these function names and are probably well-equipped and ready to put them to use.

Packaging

Perhaps you can imagine why Microsoft does not provide you with the source code for their best-selling word processing software. Packaging is the name Authorware gives to preparing lesson files in a coded format that prevents unauthorized changes. It does *not* mean that they are compressed or in a fundamentally different format. Other terms for the same concept are *run-time* and *binary*.

The term for the editable files that you have been working with during the exercises in the chapters of this book is *source*. When you buy software, such as Microsoft Word, you are only buying the binary version. You have no rights to Microsoft's source code.

Why package?

The Authorware Working Model that is distributed in your book CD is limited to producing source code only. To distribute your work safely you need to consider three things. *First*, you want to protect your intellectual property. You may have worked out some clever reusable icon sets. If you distribute your source code, any user can see your work and you will lose whatever market edge you have worked to create. *Second*, the editable code works differently than the packages. It is likely to create learner confusion. It opens for edit if you make a double click where only a single click is required. If you have tried your exercise lessons with very many friends, you are very likely to have experienced this already. *Third*, your customer will eventually decide to "improve" your code. This most often results in it not working properly, if at all. Who do you suppose will be blamed for the code that doesn't work? Yes, that's right. You will. The reason Microsoft doesn't distribute its source code is the same one that provides you motivation not to do so either.

How is a lesson packaged?

Open your copy of the Authorware Working Model and pull down the File menu. In the middle section of the menu choices you will see: File Setup, Video Setup, and Package. Like Import Graphics, the Package choice is dimmed, indicating that it is not available. As you know, Import Graphics becomes available when it is an appropriate choice. Package is simply never available in the Working Model.

In the full version of Authorware, when you have a file open for editing, Package is not dimmed. If you select the Package choice, the Package Options dialog box will open. Figure 28.1 shows the Package Options dialog box.

Notice the two choices of packages format, With RunAPW and Without RunAPW (With RunAPM and Without RunAPM, respectively, in the Mac version). Authorware is really asking whether you want to include special code in the package or want to include it in a separate file.

If we choose Package File With RunAPW a complete executable file will be created; for example, *mylesson.exe*. You can distribute this single file without any other files needed on a diskette (assuming that it will fit). Your lesson will run normally. The file that was packaged with RunAPW will be bigger than the original *mylesson.apw* file. This is very convenient and, if you plan to distribute only the single lesson it is the best way to go.

If we choose Package File Without RunAPW a special nonexecutable *mylesson.app* file will be created. You must distribute this file along with a copy of the RunAPW file, which must be present to make your lesson work. If you distribute it on a diskette (again assuming that it will fit), the RunAPW must also be distributed. When RunAPW is present, your lesson will run normally. The file that was packaged without RunAPW will be about the same size as the original source file. This is the best method if you plan to distribute several lessons, as only one RunAPW is needed and the total disk space needed will be less. Storage may be an important matter in deciding which to do.

Here is a summary chart addressing the use of these two methods.

Package Method	Advantage	Disadvantage
With RunAPW (.exe)	Only one file simple for user	Larger lesson file size
Without RunAPW (.app)	Multiple file size smaller	More complex for user

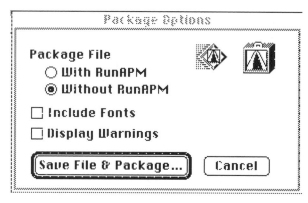

Figure 28.1 Macintosh Package Options

Inter-Platform Conversion

Not many authoring systems today offer conversion between delivery platforms—particularly between the two most popular desktop systems, Windows and Macintosh. Authorware is one that does include such a conversion capability.

Why convert between platforms?

The advantage of inter-platform conversion is that you can develop your lesson once and then deliver it twice! That is, develop it once on the Macintosh and deliver it once on the Macintosh and again on the PC, at least in theory.

In practice, there remain differences outside of Authorware that require separate actions when converting. For example, sound and video file formats are not interchangeable. In the industry segment where we do most of our work today, the PC rules! Still, in some organizations there are a significant number of Macintosh computers. Any program that can run on either platform has a strong advantage. Your ability to develop for both platforms is a big plus.

How to convert between platforms?

The inter-platform conversion on Authorware 2.0 is only in one direction today, so we will describe that method here. It is extremely simple. We suggest that you do frequent checks to ensure that the conversion is what you expect, and to identify what doesn't convert such as graphics, sound, and video, in order to be alert to create a PC version of it.

Here is how to do the conversion. If you have both platforms you can follow the process with the files on your book CD. Name any unpackaged Macintosh Authorware lesson with an 8-character filename and the file extension .APM. Although not needed on the Macintosh, it facilitates the recognition. It will then have a name such as *crane.apm*. Place a PC-formatted diskette in your computer (Mac system 7.5 includes DOS disk-recognition software). Drag the icon of your lesson to the PC diskette. Remove the diskette and place it in the PC. Open the .APM file. Authorware will recognize the file as a Macintosh Authorware program and offer to convert it. The conversion will proceed. The principal events that occur will be notifications that certain resources cannot be converted, and queries for font conversion. You can tell Authorware to use defaults for conversion, but we do not.

If you use defaults you will not be asked again for your choices. Depending on the fonts that you used on the Macintosh, the results can range from acceptable to disappointingly poor. We head this off by using fonts on the Macintosh that we know will convert well, such as Arial MT.

My files are too large

What's that? Your 12 MB lesson won't fit on a floppy? We know what you mean. It can get a bit more complicated in the middle when the files are large. Let's look at good and bad solutions.

First, the not so good. You may find, in certain cases, that to move files around you have to take them apart. Most of the lessons that you created in Chapters 13 through 22 are ideally structured for that process (by coincidence). You can take them apart, move them to different media or LAN locations, and then reassemble them. It works, but there's a price to pay. The variables will lose their associations, and when put them together, icons may be renamed. This can give you a button named **Return to Menu2**. You will have to repair the damage, and on big files it can be annoying.

You may have media that can be accepted by both platforms. If you were to go to the trouble of cutting a desktop CD, the media would be accepted by both machines. If you have a Bernoulli or Syquest-type storage device, you can follow the same route as described for the diskette. If you have both platforms connected to a file server you can upload from the Mac and download to the PC. If you don't have any of these things, you can get it done by a service contractor.

Copyright, Trademark, and Patents

In Chapter 6 we provided a warning not to include other copyrighted works, such as Mickey Mouse's image or the Beatle's music, in your lessons. Now the shoe is on the other foot. We are not lawyers and we cannot provide legal advice, so you should consult your own attorney relative to copyright, trademark, and patents. Having said that, we will tell you what we do.

Copyright

We mark our work indicating our claim to ownership with the copyright warning, a small letter c in a circle. For example:

© Copyright Angus Reynolds, 1995. All rights reserved.

The "All rights reserved" sentence is not a part of the copyright. It is an additional warning. Figure 28.2 shows how the notice might be used on an opening page of a lesson.

Also, we place a calculation icon at the top of the flowline and name it copyright notice. Inside we place the copyright notice and comment it out with two hyphens, so it will not interfere with the functioning of the program, as in Figure 28.3.

We know when we copyright a lesson that we are not protecting what it does. If we make a simulation for the pilot of a light plane, we realize that anyone else with the skill can accomplish the same thing. We don't own the idea. For example, Lotus 1-2-3 was not protected by its copyright when Microsoft brought out Excel.

We also know that we aren't protecting the look and feel of the lesson, because the courts have ruled that these things are not protected by copyright either. What then, is protected? It is our code. We may have spent days working out how we will accomplish something. In Authorware, it is our creation of unique icon structures that we hope to protect. And even though they are copyrighted, we protect them from prying eyes as well.

Trademark

Trademarks are registered words, symbols, and visual displays that belong exclusively to the owner. Coca-Cola® is a world-famous trademark. It is not just the

Figure 28.2 Opening Screen with Copyright Notice

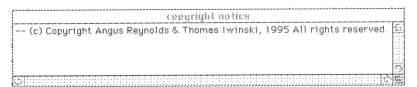

Figure 28.3 Copyright Notice Calculation

words, but the font and special "look" of the words as they are presented on Coca-Cola products. The small letter r in a circle indicates that the trademark procedure is complete. It is a *registered* trademark.

We might indicate our claim to original rights to use a trademark to describe a product. We might have based our pilot's simulation on a model that we can reuse, and possibly sell to others. We might give it the name Simu-Pilot™. The small letters TM indicate our intention to protect the trademark in the interim before it becomes registered.

Patents

Until recently, we never would have considered the possibility of applying for a U.S. patent for software we created. Recently, the courts have supported attempts to patent software. We have not patented anything to date. We will continue to study this as more is learned about the ins and outs of patenting training courseware.

What Is It Like in the (Cold Hard) Real World?

Now that you've put the cap on the technical side of development, we will turn to the world of business and industry. Chapters 29 through 31, in Part 5, explore technology-based learning at four big companies in different sectors of the economy. Let's have a look at how they do it.

7

Case Studies of Successful Applications

Rolling on with Learning at Union Pacific

In 1862, Congress chartered the Union Pacific Railroad to build a key part of the first transcontinental railway. Construction, under the direction of Major General Grenville Dodge, began at Omaha and ended with the driving of the Golden Spike at Promontory, Utah in 1869, linking the East and West Coasts. One hundred and twenty years later, in 1990, Union Pacific made a commitment to roll with multimedia training. And they've never looked back.

At that time they were struggling to improve service reliability, using a computerized Train Control System (TCS) which promised to improve communications and increase productivity by processing data from centralized locations. However, its success depended on the cooperation of a diverse network of employees—from train conductors and customer service reps to field operations managers and marketing personnel—and many of them were not cooperating. The company-wide downsizing of the mid-eighties, plus extensive restructuring and relocations, had taken their toll. The rift between management and the front-line workers was damaging the communications network and affecting service reliability.

Union Pacific (UP) looked to multimedia training to help solve these problems. They've been working to implement more than 90 hours of multimedia training— including both management and technical skills training— that will reach over 9,000 employees.

What You Will Learn in This Chapter

- Training concerns typical of the transportation industry
- The value of analysis in identifying root causes of problems

- Savings possible using technology-based learning
- Learner benefits possible using technology-based learning

Orientation to Union Pacific

As the nation's second largest railroad system, Union Pacific faces great challenges. It controls a 23,000-mile rail network, operates 3,000 of the familiar yellow locomotives, and more than 700 scheduled trains moving up to 180,000 freight cars a day, on track that stretches over 19 states from the Mississippi River to the Pacific Ocean. The stakes are high when you are moving freight such as chemicals, coal, grain, automotive products, machinery, forest products, and intermodal (truck-to-train) merchandise. The consequences of delays are devastating. If freight isn't moved on time it can mean closing down an assembly line at a large factory. Service reliability is everything.

At that time, the railroad giant faced some significant problems:

- Deregulation had led to competition
- Downsizing of over 50%
- Restructuring and relocations
- Requirement to adopt high-tech solutions
- Unhappy people

Part of the solution was to improve service by adding computers to locomotive cabs, and to train conductors to use those computers

Modernization

After Drew Lewis (former transportation secretary under President Reagan) became CEO in 1987, UP started to focus on its core businesses. In 1991, the company initiated a restructuring to increase efficiency. UP reduced its crews from three down to two on 90% of its rail lines.

To better manage and control such a massive movement of trains, and to improve their service reliability, Union Pacific has made an aggressive move toward computerization, installing state-of-the-art computer systems in their National Customer Service Center in St. Louis, Missouri, and in the Harriman Dispatch Center in Omaha, Nebraska. Many trains are now equipped with on-board computer systems that allow conductors to send and receive information on their work as it happens. This sophisticated Train Control System (TCS) promises to increase productivity by processing all work orders from a centralized location and by providing current and accurate information to conductors and customers. "What we're doing is dramatically improving our real-time data, which in turn allows us to manage day-to-day operations better," explains Dave Dwerlkotte, director of Union Pacific's human resources program development and systems training. "With this new system, we are within two hours—not 12–14 hours—of knowing where all train cars are in the system."

However, the computer technology cannot solve operational challenges by itself. It is people who make the railroad work. The ability to provide more reliable service through the new computer systems depends on the cooperation of a diverse network of employees that includes train conductors, customer service reps, field operations managers, marketing and sales personnel, dispatchers, and the customers themselves. Only when everyone in the network uses the system properly can the customer be better served—on time and on plan. Union Pacific's training challenge is to motivate employees to use the technology to its highest potential.

UP took the multimedia plunge as part of an $89 million project designed to improve its service, which had slipped during decades of railroad regulation. Its plan: Install on-board computer terminals (OBTs) in the locomotive fleet, which would interface with the Transportation Control System (TCS), to improve communications and productivity by processing data from centralized locations.

However, as noted above, because the success of the service improvement plan depended on the cooperation of such a vast network of employees, UP decided to explore multimedia solutions. They hoped to:

- Provide training consistency
- Cover wide geography
- Allow 24-hour availability of courseware
- Track performance and encourage accountability
- Increase training impact, with more retention and transfer in less training time

Time for some help

To meet this challenge, Allen Communications of Salt Lake City was called in to help UP develop the training program for the conductors who would use the on-board TCS, using multimedia technology. Before designing the actual training courseware, however, the firm conducted an employee attitude survey which showed that, in addition to its customer service problems, UP had troubles at home. After years of reorganization and cutbacks, the workforce was disenchanted and distrustful. Mike Allen, President of Allen Communications says, "They asked us to train conductors to use computers . . . and to like them! But, our analysis revealed that the problem was not only computers. Employees did not want ANY more change. They didn't trust management. They were demoralized and discouraged. They did not see how they fit in. We proposed a much broader solution, both systemic and systematic." The proposal included these characteristics:

- General Service Reliability NETWORK Course for all
- Address real problems
- Attack issues honestly
- Acknowledge cultural issue(s)
- Challenge current thinking
- Persuade learners to at least give it a chance
- Make it surprising, demanding

"These were frightening ideas for a 150-year-old culture, but they took the risk!" says Allen.

Unique Attributes of the Organization's Approach

To help heal the rift between management and front-line workers, Allen created a Service Reliability Overview course that addressed UP employees' concerns, explained what the company planned to do, and showed how workers' jobs would be affected. It taught employees at all levels how their specific roles affected a whole network of people and the overall success of Union Pacific. The overview course presented a series of honest perspectives on communication issues, including filmed interviews with a cross section of UP employees at all levels. During the three-hour overview course, the responsibilities of all employees in the service reliability network were clearly defined. In tests and interactions embedded in the multimedia course, employees were required to demonstrate their understanding of their own jobs and other employees' jobs. Employees learned what specific actions cause the network to break down and, most important, what can happen when everyone "pulls together" to meet customer needs.

Foot stompin' excitement

The overview course opens with an MTV-style music video that touches on many of the doubts and concerns that UP employees face. The song helps to prepare and motivate employees for the training that follows. The music video stimulated adrenaline and boosted morale, helping to prepare and motivate employees for the training that followed.

To deliver the technical TCS training, Allen developed courses rich in real-world scenarios. "We have eight key areas in our network that require training," explains Dwerlkotte. "The best way to get to such a widely disparate audience was interactive video."

The programs teach the employees by simulating typical work situations and problems that employees face. During the training, employees make decisions, listen to feedback, answer questions, solve problems, and vigorously test their skills.

Video testimonials and interviews help employees learn how their fellow workers and others in the network feel about issues and problems. Trainees respond to these testimonials on a graded scale. The data is stored, so later they can see how their attitudes change.

Interactivity a key

The UP courses provide high-level interactivity, focusing on real-world applications of skills rather than rote learning of rules or abstract guidelines.

"Employees' attitudes change dramatically when they discover the interactivity these courses provide," said Robert Bates, senior instructor for Service Reliability Training Design and Development at UP. "At first they try to sit back and glide, but the training demands their attention. They say, 'This course will chew me up if I don't get involved,' and soon their concentration picks up and they get to work."

Other interactions require trainees to choose between three strategies for solving a problem. They watch video segments that explain each strategy, choose an option, and then watch the consequences of their choice. This teaches them to carefully distinguish between good and bad advice from other employees.

Success Attributable to Technology-Based Learning

Union Pacific implemented the new operating mode in twelve months less time than expected. UP has implemented more than 100 hours of multimedia training—including nonmanagement and technical skills development—that will reach over 15,000 employees. So far, multimedia training has proven to be more effective and less expensive than traditional approaches, according to Dwerlkotte.

Operations improved

Delivery of cars on time/on plan is up thirty percent in the cutover area, for a net gain of many millions of dollars. The TCS courseware is used to instruct 7,000 conductors in how to use the on-board computer systems to report train movement: to show 1,000 customer service people at UP's National Customer Service Center in St. Louis how to process freight orders and work orders for conductors; to train 700 field operations personnel to work directly with conductors to carry out transportation plans; and to teach 350 managers at the Harriman Dispatching Center in Omaha how to follow TCS procedures.

Training dollars saved

The results were major savings in time and money. UP trained nearly 8,000 people for about 30,000 training days. While doing the training, they saved up to 10,000 training days, plus all related travel, per diems, time off job, facilities, and support staff.

According to Bates, multimedia courses for the NCSC service reps have reduced training time by fifty percent. "Cuts like these add up quickly," he says. "When you take someone off the job to train him, especially in a union environment, you often have to fill his job by paying someone else overtime."

Dwerlkotte estimates, "Development costs for the conductor's course is about $33 per student. Even the courses with a smaller audience, where the cost is about $600 per student, are well within industry training standards . . ."

Dwerlkotte projects that over the five-year period ending in 1994, the company will save at least thirty-five percent in training costs associated with its service reliability improvement project, because interactive video courses have eliminated the need for trainers to travel from site to site.

Learners satisfied

From a productivity standpoint, Dwerlkotte estimates that trainees are learning thirty percent faster and retaining forty percent more than in traditional training. Ninety percent score even higher after they get used to the multimedia environment.

Bates states, "No one is failing these courses. In fact the courses have helped us identify people with reading disabilities and dyslexia so we can provide the specialized training they need. We never could have identified these problems with traditional training." Dwerlkotte adds, "With multimedia we can define real performance levels. We know what they know when they leave the course."

Unions have been fully supportive of UP's efforts, Dwerlkotte continued. "They see that we're doing a good training job and making equipment available which allows workers to continually improve their skills on the job."

Rolling out more

A second multimedia course teaches train conductors how to use the on-board computer terminals to report car handling and train movement. Hundreds of conductors have already taken the course and have responded with great enthusiasm. So far, the average final score on the certification test is ninety-two percent. Only a few individuals have scored below the eighty-five percent required for certification. Although the course is designed to take four days, many have finished in less time—an estimated thirty-four percent reduction in training time. The multimedia course will eventually be administered to up to 7,000 conductors.

Lessons Learned and Challenges Remaining

The bottom line is that UP's multimedia training is on track. Union Pacific now uses multimedia courseware to train various employees in the service reliability network.

Technical training courses and on-screen simulations teach 7,000 conductors how to use on-board computer systems to report train movement through the TCS system. One thousand customer service personnel at UP's National Customer Service Center (NCSC) in St. Louis learn to produce work orders for conductors and process freight orders via the system. About 700 field operations personnel learn to work directly with conductors to carry out transportation plans according to TCS standards. Other courses teach 350 managers at the Harriman Dispatching Center in Omaha how to follow TCS procedures. An overview course on service reliability shows how the success of the TCS system depends on the cooperation of all.

Now, says Dwerlkotte, multimedia training is being further deployed. Over $3.5 million has been budgeted for course enhancements and future developments aimed at over 15,000 employees. "Our multimedia training programs have grown and blossomed," Dwerlkotte maintains.

Meanwhile, Allen also is testing a sophisticated troubleshooting simulation for UP locomotive electricians. There also is a good chance for some cross-pollination. UP is involved in a nine-member railroad consortium that is looking at developing and designing generic railroad training products which would use multimedia equipment.

Union Pacific continues to expand their multimedia training program. Leadership skills training—aimed at over 5,000 Human Resource employees at supervisory and management levels—is currently under development at Allen Communication.

Several other multimedia courses address more than 800 customer service representatives and managers who use the centralized transportation control system in

St. Louis, and approximately 700 field operations personnel—yard masters, superintendents, train managers, industry operations managers—who are located in various field sites throughout the country. Eventually, multimedia training will be provided for all UP employees in the service reliability network.

"We're committed to multimedia. We've set up a standard and we plan to stay with it," Bates said. "Once you've driven a Cadillac you can't go back to your old Chevy."

Corporate strategy and positioning benefited from the new training approach. Benefits include:

- Greater ability to quickly and effectively implement change
- Better able to meet needs of culturally diverse workforce
- Able to honestly empower employees with knowledge/skills and to work better with unions

All of which leads to a significant competitive edge!

30

Tuned to Learning at Magnavox

Despite the current demise of the Soviet Union and the Warsaw Pact, you only have to read the morning newspaper to see that America's armed forces continue to have reason to maintain their combat readiness. If American divisions are to be inactivated, air squadrons grounded, and navy ships moth-balled, as seems likely, we must place a premium on the accelerated fielding of force-multiplier capabilities. Command and control modernization programs offer an attractive cost-benefit alternative to tanks, missiles, and aircraft. It is one that has already gained the attention of our budget-conscious legislature.

One such program offers great promise in building an Army-wide command and control system to meet or exceed U.S. battlefield requirements over the next two decades. It is called the Advanced Field Artillery Tactical Data System—AFATDS. In 1984, Magnavox undertook the concept-evaluation phase of AFATDS, a major element of the Army Tactical Command and Control System. In 1991, the company was awarded a sole-source contract for the continued development and fielding of AFATDS. The program represents one of the earliest applications of Ada software in the Department of Defense, with the software development having reached 1,000,000 lines of code. Engineering design for Version 2 is in progress now.

This chapter describes how Magnavox Electronic Systems, the Fort Wayne, Indiana developers of AFATDS, produced training to be delivered on the same specialized hardware as the militarized system itself. U.S. Army and Marine Corps personnel will learn to operate the AFATDS software on the actual battlefield system.

What You Will Learn in This Chapter

- The value of rapid prototyping
- The difficulties associated with developing new software training
- Some of the aspects of very large government contract operation

Orientation to the Organization

Magnavox has been a familiar name in electronics for over 80 years. The company began as a manufacturer of loudspeakers but quickly entered the military electronics field, supplying unique noise-cancellation microphones to WW I aviators that permitted conversation between air crew members in open cockpit aircraft. During WW II, Magnavox supplied gun-firing solenoids and other electronic devices to the U.S. military, and later created the Government and Industrial Products Division to specifically address the needs of the military and industrial electronics markets.

Since WW II, Magnavox has made major contributions in a number of electronic areas. It has led the way in spread-spectrum antijam communications technology, delivering the first operational airborne antijam communications system in 1961. It developed the first mass-produced sonobuoy in 1969. Since the early 1970s, Magnavox has been an industry leader in development and manufacture of UHF communications equipment, thermal night sights, satellite navigation, and commercial satellite communications.

Today, Magnavox is a broad-based electronics company with an established reputation for excellence and a proven commitment to delivering training systems every bit as innovative and technically advanced as the electronic products they support.

Unique Attributes of the Organization's Approach

"The name AFATDS is actually something of a misnomer," says Philip J. (Flip) Millis, Magnavox's AFATDS Training Manager. He continues, "It is a total fire support command, control, and coordination system, capable of integrating all known fire systems, to include field artillery, air fire support, mortars, naval gunfire, aviation, and offensive electronic warfare. AFATDS operates on a militarized Hewlett-Packard 9000/300 series workstation and has a Unix operating system, with all software programmed in Ada."[1] That is the source of the problem. It isn't as easy to develop courseware for less common computer platforms. When Magnavox planned the proj-ect there were no compatible development tools for the HP Unix systems.

Magnavox has a sole-source contract through the Army's communications-electronics Command (CECOM) for the software development and training for the AFATDS system. With a contract to train forty instructors and key personnel, Magnavox's original intention was to conduct AFATDS training with a traditional lecture and practical exercise format. "When advised that our contract would likely be modified to train up to 400 AFATDS operators, Magnavox determined that the required number of additional instructors would be such that alternative media should be investigated in the interest of cost savings," says Millis.

---

[1]Ada is the name of a computer language. In a move intended to enforce standardization, the U.S. Department of Defense specified that all software delivered on government contracts would be developed in Ada.

Analysis pays off

They explored programmed text, video-based instruction, and computer-based instruction with the following results. Programmed text instruction, while inexpensive, offered limited hands-on opportunities and was judged inadequate. Video-based training, while attractive, was too expensive to support a two- to three-week course of instruction. Computer-aided instruction (CAI), on the other hand, seemed to offer just the mix of attributes that the project called for. CAI is cost effective, focuses on the hands-on experience and, if properly designed, becomes an integral part of the system software, requiring no additional hardware. They didn't start out to put the training on the systems, but analysis showed that way was the best choice for the project.

Rapid prototyping

Millis and his developers prepared a concept demonstration, using the Macintosh hypermedia product HyperCard. Figure 30.1 shows one of the rapid prototype screens developed on the Macintosh to make clear the project's direction. The prototype was presented to representatives of the United States Army Field Artillery School (USAFAS) at Fort Sill, Oklahoma, with the recommendation that CAI be adopted as the primary AFATDS instructional medium. Fort Sill enthusiastically concurred with Magnavox's recommendation.

It actually would have been much easier to develop the entire training project on the Macintosh. The trick was now to make the same thing happen inside the green boxes that might someday go to war.

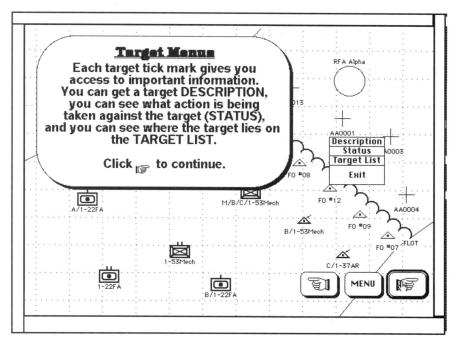

Figure 30.1 Rapid Prototype Screen

Get set!

Magnavox's initial training development team of four conducted a task analysis, interviewed prospective employees, and carefully planned for the bulk of the work. They went to Fort Sill, Oklahoma to meet with their customer's eight-member task-selection panel, identifying those tasks that were critical to AFATDS operations.

Their understanding of those tasks was put to the test when the full team set about mapping window designs to the system specifications on which the task analysis was based. The fact that most members of the development team were previously members of the target population (U.S. Army Field Artillery) facilitated the mapping analysis. It also had the added benefit of encouraging ownership of the process by newly hired training team members.

In-house tool development

The Magnavox team's initial strategy for developing the CAI lessons was to use the actual AFATDS window images and overlay dialog boxes and student instructions directly on the windows. These modified images would then be developed into storyboards for use by CECOM's reviewers. The same programmer-ready materials would also serve as the hand-off vehicle to the software engineers' implementation team. The software engineers would create draft lessons from the storyboards, pending receipt of the customer's comments.

For this strategy to work, however, they required the ability to capture bit-mapped images and then add dialog boxes and implementation instructions, as well as an audit trail. Finally, they had to print the completed storyboards. In the absence of any commercial products, Magnavox's software team elected to develop the capability in-house, with the training team serving as a beta test site.

Expert assistance

Although Millis was confident that they had a viable plan and a competent team, he realized that they were, nevertheless, novices in the CAI arena. He elected to engage the services of two leading experts in the field. "I asked them to visit with us, observe our processes, and then to comment on our strengths and shortcomings," says Millis. He got exactly what he needed at that point—reinforcements. The consultants reaffirmed the sound ISD approach that came out of the development group's Army background. They examined the development process and suggested "tweaking" some things, and introduced new ideas based on their commercial courseware development experience.

Logistical problems

"We were now, more than *ever*, confident of our plan and our team, and we were making steady, albeit painfully slow, progress," says Millis. Some lessons required up to 200 storyboards. Millis had decided that the training development team's products would be so detailed that even a junior programmer could cope with their implementation.

The problem was that the involved systems, network, and very high-resolution screens combined to drive screen print times much too high. Millis explored the idea of submitting the lesson storyboards in electronic form. Magnavox approached its customer with the idea. They discovered that any alternative to the small mountain of paper the customers were having to review would be welcome. Instead of reviewing a black-and-white paper representation of a workstation window, the government could now work with full-color screen prototypes. To make this work, however, they needed a software capability that was less a storyboarding tool than a slideshow utility.

Rapid prototyping on the military hardware

Magnavox had been interested in rapid prototyping applications for some time. Their proof of concept demonstration in Macintosh HyperCard confirmed that they were quite comfortable with this technique. Unfortunately, there were no suitable applications available to them in the HP/Unix world (although some Windows products were available in emulation mode, they were dog-slow on the powerful HP machines). Millis asked the in-house personnel to develop the next best thing, a computerized presentation that would afford government reviewers a better look at the flow of each lesson. The same product would clearly show the implementation team how the training developers wanted the final product to look and act. The company's software group immediately began work on the desired product, while the training development team continued to produce paper storyboards to meet the existing review schedule.

And a miracle . . .

Millis recalls, "It was about this time that one of those minor miracles, on which you base the contract bid and schedule, occurred." A newly hired software engineer was assigned to the human interface group and given responsibility for fully developing the capability they needed. "As luck would have it," Millis continues, "this individual had considerable expertise in hypermedia, and rather than focusing on how difficult the assignment might prove, asked 'Why Not?' and threw himself into the effort." This development proved especially timely because, as often happens with software development, it is difficult to foresee exactly how the software will roll out.

Success Attributable to Technology-Based Learning

Developing courseware at the same time that the software is being produced isn't fun. Believe us, we've been there. Software doesn't have to be completed from front to end. "Patches" of code can be developed to do various tasks. Difficulties in development may alter the look of screens. The uncertainty generates real problems for the training developers.

De-couple training development activities

Millis saw that he had to develop a software capability that allowed the training team to de-couple its development activities from those of the software team. In doing so they could both attain a measure of independence; they also significantly altered the traditional software training development cycle.

Rather than having to wait until the system software was functional, the developers could use a rapid prototyping tool to simulate system functionality, then the system programmers could convert it into the Ada language deliverable product. By de-coupling training development from software development, individual training could proceed without functional and tested software. The approach offered the added bonus of buying additional development time for the software team. The only missing pieces were baselined window designs and CECOM's concurrence.

Window baselining

The AFATDS window baselining process revolves around the system engineering team. Working with human engineers and the OSF/MOTIF style guide, they develop draft window designs. These designs are then reviewed by software engineers, who ensure compatibility with X-window functionality and expand the design to include a narrative description of the window's general use and relationship to other windows.

Upon a second review by all parties, including training engineers, the windows are considered "baselined" and are sent to CECOM for final acceptance. Meanwhile, the software engineers create the windows in Ada code and make them available for use by other programmers throughout the development network. Once these windows exist, and armed with an understanding of how they work, the training developers can produce their training windows with functionality resembling that of the final software. What the student sees on his or her training screen looks, feels, and acts like the real system. This is impressive, considering that the real system may not be functional for several weeks. In this way, operator training can take place without final tested software.

The Army buys in

"Our customer immediately saw the advantages of our proposed approach. If faced with a potential program slip due to software development delays, the Program Manager could have the option of replanning the program's production schedule, with software and training development occurring in parallel rather than in series," says Millis. Nothing, however, is free. In this case, the Program Manager and the training development team elected to accept the risk of lesson reworking that might be required due to software changes that were not foreseen when the windows were baselined. Such changes are inevitable and the Magnavox project team knew it. The Program Manager set aside one month from the production schedule expressly for the inevitable lesson rework.

A quality job

The AFATDS training development team produced draft CAI lessons at the rate of three per week, using the in-house developed tools. They completed 60 draft lessons well within the schedule. It proved necessary to rework approximately twenty percent of the total effort, an effort equivalent to producing 12 new CAI lessons.

Millis' team closely monitored the lesson implementation efforts of the company software group. Their focus was on ensuring that the lessons were properly error-trapped and tested, to ensure that they were made as "soldier-proof" as possible. Magnavox's CAI software was used first to train instructors and key program personnel, for full-scale operator training at Fort Hood, Texas, at the Fort Sill Artillery School for training Marines, and for use in the field with the delivered systems.

Lessons Learned and Challenges Remaining

Flip Millis sums it all up about as well as possible. He says, "The AFATDS training team has found that there is nothing like the urgencies of working on a tightly scheduled, high-profile defense program to focus one's attention on finding schedule-saving approaches to long-standing problems, in our case, the challenge of developing CAI lessons in the absence of mature software. Thanks to the efforts of a single, determined software engineer and a progressive program manager, we were able to establish a new relationship between software and training development, one that we feel holds great promise for our future efforts." In 1995, the AFATDS training system was judged "suitable and effective for total force use."

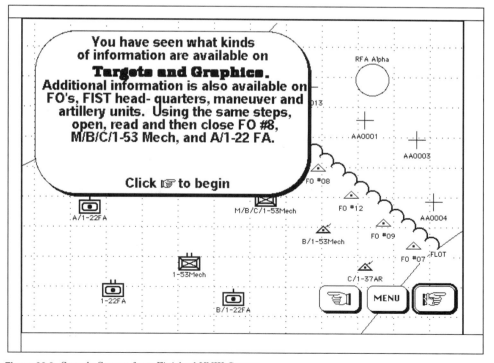

Figure 30.2 Sample Screen from Finished UNIX Course

31

Insuring High Performance at Aetna

The "tell, tell, test" model of interactive video tutorials is widely known. For many people, particularly for skeptical trainees and their managers, the model defines these technologies. To distinguish their simulations from less stimulating training, at Aetna they often introduce them as "interactive video that doesn't teach." We think that will get anyone's attention.

Aetna believes that most learning takes place in the context of performing real work. As mentioned in Chapter 8, it takes 18 months for insurance salespeople to achieve competence in their job. And, typical on-the-job training has its own limitations. It is both slow and unpredictable.

Aetna's simulations do teach, of course. They just don't "tell" in the traditional sense. In Aetna's simulations, virtually every screen requires a decision. Learning grows out of performance and any feedback, whether presented in text or video.

The simulations provide many of the benefits of on-the-job training, as we indicated in Chapter 26. At Aetna, the benefit comes without the attendant risks or the cost of waiting for the right experiences to happen to the trainee. Stan Malcolm, Aetna's Manager of Learning Technologies says, "Our solution is 'whole-job simulation,' which integrates technical, interpersonal, data processing, and administrative skills. Users in field offices across the country gain experience in technical processes in a context that stresses accuracy and efficiency, while modeling appropriate behaviors. In this way, we build competencies, such as management of resources and communications, as they are experienced on the job."

Orientation to the Organization

Started by Hartford businessman and judge Eliphalet Bulkeley in 1853, Aetna is the nation's largest stockholder-owned insurance organization, with assets of almost $92 billion. It is one of the world's major providers of insurance (life, health, and property/casualty) and financial services to corporations, public and private organizations, and individuals. Aetna also underwrites and administers group insurance and managed health care products and services and manages group pension funds.

Still a Hartford-based company, Aetna has over 200 U.S. branch and marketing offices and provides insurance and financial services in the Pacific Basin, South America, Canada, and Europe. In 1992 Aetna derived economies from 4,800 layoffs, in addition to 2,600 jobs cut since 1990.

Unique Attributes of the Organization's Approach

Insurance claim representatives are fairly typical of service industry professionals. Aetna wanted to find a way to provide new claim representatives with experiences critical to success, and to achieve this without risk of expensive errors or damage to the goodwill of customers, claimants, or agents.

For example, bodily injury claims require conversations and interviews with the parties involved. They also involve travel to the accident sites, offices, and medical facilities. It isn't surprising that they can take months to settle. Aetna applies TBL simulation to portray relationships realistically and to model behaviors. The simulation makes distance disappear and compresses time.

Claim Liability Assessment

Aetna developed a Claim Liability Assessment simulation to address one aspect of the bodily injury claims need. It centers on the investigative procedures used to determine responsibility for an automobile accident involving an injury. The simulation is installed in 22 offices nationwide. Claim Liability Assessment itself, which includes 18 minutes of video, takes an individual from 45 minutes to one hour to complete. When the simulation is presented in a small group setting, it can provide more than four hours of intense learning and experience sharing.

Claim representatives have large caseloads. It is part of efforts to minimize the costs of processing claims. The claim representatives must maintain accuracy and yet display high standards of efficiency. Aetna management recognized that inexperience among new claim representatives was costing the company more than it should. Worse, a claim representative's investigative mistake might cause a claim to be paid where the insured client was not at fault, or was only partly at fault. This could needlessly cost the company and its client money.

The Claim Liability Assessment simulation includes two main objectives. They are:

- To make the correct liability assessment
- To make it at the right moment (after conducting enough investigation to be confidently accurate, but not enough to waste time on unnecessary steps)

It also monitors the claim representatives for professional and courteous behavior toward people with whom they interact in the simulation.

Whiplash

The simulation begins at the scene of a two-car collision. Aetna's insured client's car collided with another whose driver sustained a soft-tissue injury to the neck. Such injuries are commonly called "whiplash." Through dialog, the claim representative learner suspects that the intersection's stop sign might have been missing and that Aetna's insured's brakes may have failed. That ends the motivating introduction.

It is followed by a brief text introduction and orientation to program operation that covers the buttons that control program features, such as Case File, Glossary, and Quit. Next, the learner sees a claim representative receive an assignment to the case. The learner performs in the role of that claim representative during the simulation. The simulation task is to choose the steps to investigate the case and to gather the facts necessary to determine liability.

Text reinforcement

During the simulation, most screens require the learner to choose the best investigative step(s) to follow next. Sometimes, there may be several correct choices; for example, when sequence is not critical. Every choice, right or wrong, generates a brief text response. These responses reinforce and amplify critical learning messages. These include important standards of performance; for example, the time limit before which the claim representative must have performed certain notifications. In most paths, video follows the text response.

Video interaction

The simulation uses video to present learners with the consequences of their good or bad decisions, without the obvious risk of practicing on a live case. (Remember, on-the-job training is, in fact, practicing on live cases.)

For example, a learner has the choice of asking a claimant either, "How fast were you going?" Or, "Are you sure you weren't speeding." The first choice produces a reasonable response from a cooperative claimant. The second, closed question implies that the claimant was in the wrong and provokes an irate, "Of course I wasn't speeding!" A wake-up call for a claim representative who chooses it, the learner discovers that careless interaction can jeopardize the relationship between claim representative and claimant. Simulation text reinforces the point—never ask questions that imply an answer, because they may lead to misrepresentation of the facts of a case.

The simulated case is quite complex. When completed properly, it requires interviews with the claimant, the insured, witnesses, a police officer, a mechanic, an independent brake inspector, and the town engineer, as well as a thorough review of diagrams, forms, photos, and reports. Distractions are plentiful among the simulated facts. Conflicting information is included and necessary, since people remember things imperfectly. The Assess Liability button is available on every screen. Anytime the learner feels that the investigation is completed, he or she can click it.

Case File button

Besides the usual buttons, such as Glossary and Quit, a Case File button appears on every screen. Case File mimicks the traditional paper claim file maintained for every case. The button reinforces the administrative side of the claim representative's job. It leads to a new Case File layout.

On the left is an ever-growing list of completed investigative tasks. On the right are additional buttons that lead to menus of forms, notes, and video clips that the learner might wish to review. The menus that are available grow as the simulation continues, based on the learner's actions. The learner can only review those elements that have been revealed through his decisions.

Assessment and evaluation

When the learner chooses the Assess Liability button too soon, the system provides the learner with feedback to suggest that some steps were omitted.

A too early or too late Assess Liability button flags the point in the learner's record. Failing to assess liability when it could be confidently done also provokes a forced assessment.

It might be possible for a learner to get it right, but for the wrong reasons. The simulation provides learners with feedback on their choices of who's liable, and winds up with a recap of why other parties aren't liable. At the end it offers an opportunity for users to comment on the program's design and effectiveness. These responses are periodically forwarded from regional offices to Learning Technologies in Hartford.

Claim trainers or supervisors review learner records locally. To facilitate review of errors, a "guest" feature provides trainers with access to any point in the program. It also permits reinforcement of locally significant points.

Success Attributable to Technology-Based Learning

Stan Malcolm says, "The cost of bodily injury claims is such that a savings of only two or three errors over the life of the program would more than justify the cost of development. Another measure of success is the value placed on the programs by branch office staff. After four years, the programs are still in active use."

Lessons Learned and Challenges Remaining

Aetna education advisor Kathy Izzarelli says, "Technical skills are fundamental to performance. In the end, however, they are just one part of a larger collection of interpersonal, administrative, and other less-obvious skills that contribute to the effective performance of the whole job. Developing all these skills is what whole-job simulation is about."

Good design and interesting program content are key contributors to success, but they're not the whole story. Aetna knows that the content must be relevant to a performance problem identified by its management. Also, careful consideration is given to melding it into local administration. The simulation must be integrated with other training and must be seen as an asset to the trainers who will administer it. Finally, Aetna carefully developed follow-up channels for problems, feedback, and access to additional training programs to address local needs. It is efficient in action and effectively managed.

Aetna's second simulation continues the claim representative scenario. The claim for delayed medical expenses has been filed and further investigation is required to negotiate a fair settlement with the claimant's attorney.

In the second program, Aetna strengthened the negative consequences of inappropriate choices. If the learner hasn't prepared thoroughly, the resulting negotiations won't be successful. The learner must settle within an acceptable dollar range. If not, the claim representative and supervisor discuss the situation on screen.

Other potential simulations exist in the underwriting, sales, and supervision.

Looking ahead

To avoid an expensive remake of the videodisc, the Case File is implemented entirely in software. When Aetna replaces its paper claim files with electronic ones, they can easily modify the program to mimic the new version of the file. They also simulate the mainframe system used to verify coverage, which integrates system tasks into the context of other investigative steps. Including the actual mainframe portion of the system would greatly complicate development and delivery.

People power

The simulation was designed for the individual learner, but Aetna has learned that an experienced facilitator plays a valuable role. The facilitator provides feedback to suggested actions that weren't anticipated and points out local variations on the national average procedures that the simulation follows. A facilitator can also enrich the experience with the inevitable war stories based on local and personal experience. All of this reinforces and expands the simulation content.

Also a job preview

The Claim Liability Assessment simulation serves as a realistic job preview because of its accurate portrayal of the job situation. If the learner is told that performance on the program is not judged, and that the company understands that they can't successfully assess liability without training, candidates have a chance to self-assess their suitability for Aetna careers. Each candidate who concludes that he or she is not a good fit with the claim representative's job is saved from a lot of heartache. Aetna is also saved the cost of the training.

Candidates who believe they'd enjoy the challenge of claims investigation work also realize that they could do the job for another insurance company as well. Aetna believes that technology-based learning conveys, if only subliminally, the message that the company is willing to invest more in their success than its competitors in the job market.

A performance emphasis

Simulations were Aetna's first bridge from training to job performance. Izzarelli says, "To be effective, simulations must achieve a level of difficulty that is not overwhelming. We want it to be impossible for untrained staff to successfully complete the program. We also want experienced claim representatives to achieve near-perfect scores. Finally, we want new claim representatives that have just completed our technical training program to find success in the program challenging, yet achievable. Our simulations meet all three criteria."

Stan Malcolm expands, "If we apply the notion of problem-centered learning to corporate education, we see that the entire purpose of our learning events is to produce real outcomes in the world of real work. Learning is really only a secondary outcome (albeit a desirable and likely one). Now employees are coming to the classroom—or the "classroom" is coming to them—with an expectation that before they're done they will have completed some real work task that they really care about."

The goal is that, at the end of an event, each person will walk away with a real work product, such as an actual insurance claim properly settled. And you can believe that Aetna has heard the word—from the top! Aetna's chairman, Ron Compton, says the following:

"We've been looking at learning as an outcome, when learning is only a by-product. Performance is what we want. And by providing the supports employees need to learn their jobs while they do their jobs, we'll get competent performance faster and more consistently.

"As business managers facing a tough and unknowable future, we can't afford the luxury of learning when it's not accompanied by performing. We have to radically change our organizations and our processes so that automation finally gives us the gains in productivity that up to now have been unkept promises. To achieve that, we as managers must show leadership of the most radical kind, (and be) willing to develop and use the tools that make us better workers, better listeners, and better thinkers. And we must be willing to provide the support, both human and electronic, that our workers need to perform successfully."

The Business of
Technology-Based Learning

32

Getting Up and Running

In this chapter we will present suggestions pointing you in directions to build your *own* courseware development capability. Organization is the key to successful implementation of this potentially very powerful new media. It doesn't matter whether you are working alone or inside a major organization; many considerations, such as what is a good development station, are the same. We will offer guidelines for "getting up and running" in multimedia training development, with a focus on the skills and resources you need to make this technology work.

What You Will Learn in This Chapter

- What platform is needed for commercial development
- Suggested steps in preparing for viability
- Skills and competencies needed for multimedia training development
- Comparative advantages of buying or building courseware
- How to select a development platform
- How to work within differing delivery environments
- Why you should work with a formal system for courseware development
- Why everyone uses the same system
- How to work with a formal system in a practical way
- How to employ the concept of total quality training
- How to employ "smart" development tips
- How to use effective project management techniques
- How to develop and employ programming specifications

- Advantages and disadvantages of programming specifications
- What the near-future trends in multimedia training are
- How to use the technology life cycle to predict future changes in multimedia for training
- How to cope with technological change

There is no shortage of people claiming to have found the holy grail of instruction. What seems to be in short supply is level-headed advice about how to get started and avoid the pitfalls in this field.

The First Step

Have you ever read *What Color is Your Parachute*? It is a book about finding the right career. That book, and practically all such similar books suggest, as we do now, that you conduct a self analysis. What are your strengths and weaknesses? Where are you ready, and not ready, to start? In Chapter 4 you looked at the organization and its readiness for TBL. We suggest that you get out a sheet of lined paper and write your strengths on one side, and your weaknesses on the other. One of the lines should contain a statement of your TBL competence. This is an important step. If you wind up with a huge list of competencies and capabilities, so much the better. But regardless of the outcome, you now have a formal starting point.

TBL Competencies

To effectively bring about TBL you need to possess a number of skills. You may or may not have these skills today. But whether you do or not, you can be successful. If you lack them personally, you must muster the necessary resources and have them formally committed to your TBL project for it to succeed. Diane Gayeski lists eight basic competencies for IVD development. From it, we have evolved the list below. You must, collectively, be able to:

1. Understand the basics of instructional technology
2. Identify and select appropriate hardware and software
3. Create original instructional designs
4. Use storyboarding, script writing, and flowcharting techniques
5. Generate sophisticated graphics
6. Use authoring tools to create and update your programs
7. Develop appropriate formative and summative evaluation techniques
8. Manage the hardware, software, and record keeping

Selecting Your Hardware Platforms

Certainly one of the most difficult decisions you will have to make, in order to get up and running in interactive multimedia, is the selection of your hardware system. Unfortunately, since there is no standard playback system or format, you have to make a choice similar to choosing between Beta and VHS, hoping that you pick the equivalent of VHS.

Hardware platform for digital video courseware

Courseware incorporating digital video technology requires robust delivery hardware, powerful enough to effect smooth, full-motion video and real-time program operation. Delivery system requirements differ according to delivery medium (CD-ROM or network). Storage requirements are large (on the order of at least a 500-MB hard drive) for delivery of digital-video courseware from an internal hard drive. A 200- to 340-MB hard drive is adequate for delivery of this courseware from double-spin CD-ROM. Networked workstations also require a network card. Care must be taken to choose a card that reliably provides the 300-kB transfer rate necessary for smooth delivery of networked digital-video courseware.

Our recommended delivery system components

We must say that any equipment recommendation in the multimedia field is a snapshot. We update our recommendations several times a year. With that in mind, here is a list to start from:

- 80486DX/66 or Pentium ISA/VL-bus
- Motherboard with 128-K RAM cache
- 8-MB 70-NS or faster RAM
- 200-MB to 340-MB IDE hard drive
- ISA or VL-bus IDE controller
- Quad-spin CD-ROM drive
- If networked, fast 16-bit network card
- 16-bit sound card supporting HDMA 5 setting
- SVGA Windows accelerator card
- 15-inch or larger flat screen monitor
- Mid-sized tower case with at least three 5.25-inch accessible drive bays
- 101-keyboard
- Mouse
- DOS 6.x
- Windows 3.1 (soon you must deal with Windows 95 and Windows NT)
- Amplified speakers or headphones

Cost

Systems in this configuration range in cost from approximately $2,000 to $3,000 or even more, depending on the total of higher-end choices.

Digital video

The configuration shown does not address the digital video itself, or the attendant software needed for a development station. Your authoring system could cost up to $5,000 for a single copy. If hardware-supported video is used (MPEG or DVI), an additional card will be required at a cost of $300 to $1,000.

Hardware Maintenance

It is important to establish a system for routine maintenance of your hardware and software.

- Clean your monitors, keyboards, and mice. They get dirty and drag down your productivity. You can buy special packages designed especially to clean each of these.
- Use a utility such as Norton Utilities for disk management and diagnostics. You may head off a problem before it cripples your efforts.
- Use a virus-protection program such as Norton Antivirus. You may not get a virus for a long time, but if you do it can wipe out everything you have.
- An uninteruptible power supply (UPS) will protect your computer from damage, and the prices are now reasonable. If you get a UPS, you won't need a surge protector.
- All of your files require backup on a regular basis. Use a program such as Colorado Backup. This can be a problem with massive video files, so if you already have them on CD you can back up all but video.
- Keep cables away from your feet; they could become disconnected with a resultant loss of data.
- Clean around all your equipment; it is a dust magnet, which could clog a vent and cause overheating.

Using a Development System

As we mentioned much earlier, most large organizations have a document with some form of the ISD model as their own development process. In this section, we present one such model for your consideration as you prepare to build your own.

Almost every organization is trying to improve the quality of its products. Standardization is one of the key techniques to improve quality. This fact drives organizations to build their own standard for courseware development.

Yet, if everyone went their own way, it would be chaotic. The organizational model provides the leveling influence that enables each worker to know how others in the organization will proceed.

A simple organizational model was used in the 1980s by the PLATO group at Control Data Corporation. It was in a thin, small-format booklet. Yet it told simply how each step in the process would proceed, in terms that uninitiated customers could follow. It is still a valid model for an organizational process.

A Process

Here is a simple organizational model for you to consider as the basis for your own:

Analysis

1. The **customer** identifies a performance discrepancy that may be resolved by a technology-based training course. The customer may also identify a subject matter expert (SME).

2. The **manager** assigns a project leader and selects a project team.

3. The **project leader** develops and follows a plan to gather performance data and review new or existing data. The output of the plan is an Analysis Report that includes a recommended approach for resolving the performance discrepancy.

4. The **project team** uses the Analysis Report Checklist to gather data, and summarizes the results in a draft Analysis Report. The Analysis Report Checklist is shown in Figure 32.1. The analysis and Analysis Report was also the subject of Chapter 10.

5. The **project team** revises the Analysis Report as necessary, and submits the report to the manager for review.

6. The **manager** reviews the report and provides comments. When comments have been addressed, the **manager** approves the report.

7. The **customer** reviews the Analysis Report with the project leader.

8. The **project leader** incorporates customer comments and obtains written customer approval.

Design

In the following list of steps, many internal coordinating activities and collegial consultations are not listed. In practice, the process is **not** sterile but rich in activities.

1. Based on the results of the analysis phase, the **manager** assigns a project leader and project team to carry out the design phase.

2. The **project leader**, in cooperation with **project team members**, organizes and designs a plan for each element of instruction. The plan should include these steps:
~Perform instructional task analysis
~Specify instructional objectives
~Define entry behaviors
~Group and sequence objectives
~Specify learning activities
~Specify assessment system
~Specify evaluation system
~Review and select existing materials

3. The **project team** designs the technology-based training program and documents the design in a design document. The design checklist indicates items that should be included in the design document. Figure 32.2 shows a design checklist.

4. The **project leader** arranges for a quality review of the Design Document.

5. The **project leader** directs the project team in making any necessary revisions, and submits the Design Document to the work package manager for review.

6. The **manager** reviews the Design Document and provides comments. When the comments have been addressed, the manager approves the Design Document.

7. If he/she judges that one is necessary, the **project leader** prepares a proof-of-concept demonstration of the training. Figure 32.3 shows a Proof-of-Concept Demonstration Checklist.

8. The **project leader** incorporates any changes made by the manager and returns it to him/her for approval.

9. The **project leader** submits the Design Document and, if applicable, the proof-of-concept to the customer for review.

10. The **project leader** incorporates customer comments and obtains written customer approval.

Development

1. Following customer approval of the program design, the project leader directs the project team in creating programmer-ready materials.

2. The **project leader** arranges for a quality review of the programmer-ready materials. Figure 32.4 shows the Programmer-Ready Materials Checklist.

3. The **project leader** directs the project team in making any necessary changes to the programmer-ready materials.

4. The **project leader** directs the project team in programming the courseware in accordance with the approved programmer-ready materials.

5. The **project leader** arranges for a quality review of the courseware. Figure 32.5 shows the Development Checklist.

6. The **project leader** submits the program to the manager for review.

7. The **manager** reviews and approves the program.

8. The **customer**, with input from the project leader, selects learners to participate in the small group evaluation. Figure 32.6 shows the Small Group Trial Checklist.

9. The **project leader** makes any changes resulting from the small group evaluation, and presents the courseware to the customer for review.

10. The **project leader** incorporates customer comments and obtains customer approval.

Analysis Report Checklist

Analysis conducted by _____
Date _____
Title of project _____

Background
1. Has a performance discrepancy been identified? _____

2. If so, what is the nature of the performance discrepancy? _____
   (describe the discrepancy)

3. Who is the audience for the proposal discrepancy? _____
   –Age? ____
   –Job being performed? _____
   –Previous training on this job? _____
   –Educational level? _____

4. What are the results of the survey of existing training?

5. What organizational constraints, if any, exist?
   (describe constraints, if applicable)

Methodology
6. How was the data gathered?

Findings
7. What did the data reveal? _____

Conclusions
8. What are the cause(s) of the performance discrepancy? The cause(s) may include one or more
   of the following:
   –Poor knowledge and skills (skill deficiency)? _____
   –Inability to do work (distracting obstacles or absence of potential)? _____
   –Lack of standards? _____
   –Poorly defined conditions or processes? _____
   –Lack of proper incentives or punishing consequences? _____
   –Imprecise measurement criteria? _____
   –Lack of feedback or incorrect rewards? _____

Recommendations
9. Have one or more solutions or remedies for a performance discrepancy been identified and
   described? _____

10. Do the recommended solutions include training? _____

11. Does each solution address one or more problems identified during the analysis? _____

12. Is each solution feasible? _____

13. Is each solution practical? _____

14. Is each solution economical? _____

15. Is the organization experiencing the performance discrepancy equipped to implement the
    recommended solution? _____

Additional Comments

Figure 32.1 Analysis Report Checklist

Design checklist

Design conducted by_____
Date_____
Title of project_____

Evaluated items

Design document form, content outline, overview flowchart, and treatment

1. Do the terminal performance objective(s) clearly state the measurable performance (including the conditions and standards) the learner will be able to demonstrate at the conclusion of the training?

2. Do the enabling objective(s) clearly state the measurable component actions the learner will be able to demonstrate to attain the terminal objective(s)?____

3. Are the enabling objective(s) coded and referenced to appropriate measurement (test) items and activities?_____

4. Is the overview of instructional events clear, concise, and appropriate to the program's objectives? ____

5. Are the proposed sequence and structure appropriate to the content and effective?____

6. Are resource documents and personnel identified?____

7. Is the content logically divided into topics and subtopics corresponding to a menu and submenu structure?____

8. Is the level of user control appropriate to the application, the audience, and the environment?

9. Are appropriate instructional techniques (such as drill and practice or simulation) employed to achieve the stated learning objectives of the program?____

10. Are tests provided when appropriate?_____

11. Is a clear and concise overview (treatment) of the program provided?____

12. Does the overview flowchart clearly depict the logic and structure of the program?____

13. Is a method for evaluating the user's performance detailed?____

14. Is a method for evaluating the program's effectiveness detailed?____

Comments

Figure 32.2 Design Checklist

Implementation

1. The **customer** agrees that the instructional materials are ready for implementation.

2. The **customer** installs the courseware for regular use. Figure 32.7 shows the Implementation Checklist.

Planning for Courseware Development

Almost every organization is trying to improve the quality of its products and services. You will want to develop high-quality lessons for your organization or client. In this section we will present suggestions for your consideration when you build your own courseware. We will look at the concept of total quality training, something you should consider if you work within an organization. We will also make suggestions for better development, and round all this out with attention to better management of instructional development projects. If you have responsibility for training, you can make a difference by implementing a total quality training program.

Proof-of-concept demonstration checklist

Proof of concept checked by_____
Date_____
Title of project_____

Evaluated items: Program design proof-of-concept demonstration

A. Is a proof-of-concept demonstration required?___

B. If the answer to question A is "Yes", is a paper-based proof-of-concept adequate for this program?___

If the answer to question A is "yes," and the answer to question B is "no," a computer-based proof-of-concept is required.

1. Is the information attractively presented?___

2. Are titles, headers, and text functional and attractive?___

3. Do all the screens have a consistent style?

4. Are text screens formatted for easy reading and retention?___

5. Are the screen colors attractive and not distracting, e.g., harmonious, not glaring, not overused on a single screen?___

6. Is the program's navigation logical to the user? That is, is it easy to see how to quit, repeat, move on, and get help?___

Figure 32.3 Proof-of-Concept Demonstration Checklist

Programmer ready materials checksheet

PRM check conducted by_____
Date_____
Title of project_____

1. Have changes in content since the initial design review been identified?___

2. Is it clear from the programmer-ready materials that the goals of the program will be met?___

3. Is it clear from the programmer-ready materials that the objectives of the program will be met?___

4. Has the treatment (specified in the design document) been effectively and efficiently executed in the development documentation?___

5. Is it clear from the programmer-ready materials that transitions are smooth and logical for all possible paths through the program?___

6. Are sentence length, structure, and vocabulary appropriate for the target audience?___

7. Is feedback effectively used to provide information to the learner regarding the appropriateness of his/her response?___

8. Is the audio portion written for the ear? In other words,
    -Is the phrasing smooth?___
    -Are the words easy to pronounce?___
    -Is a speaking (not reading) vocabulary used?___

9. Are the audio and special effects synchronized with the visual material?___

10. Do the special effects contribute to the program's message?___

11. Does the visual material accompany and amplify key points?___

12. Are video segments as short as possible while still achieving their objectives?___

13. Are computer graphics consistent throughout the program?___

14. Are there instances when one color is overused on a screen?___

15. Is the art pleasing to the eye?___

16. Is the style consistent throughout the program?___

17. Are the icons unambiguous?___

18. Are the screen arrangements logical and attractive?___

19. Is there a storyboard, script, or shot-list entry for every video element in the programming flowchart?
___

20. Does the authoring documentation allow authoring to be passed to another person without the need for further explanations?___

Comments

Figure 32.4 Programmer-Ready Materials Checklist

Development phase checklist

Development checked by_____
Date_____
Title of project_____

1. Does program development completed thus far include
Authoring?____
Video?____
Graphics?____
Audio?____

2. Have changes made in content since design review been documented?____

3. Have design specifications been met?____

4. Are the learning objectives clearly stated at the beginning of the lesson, if appropriate?____

5. Is a positive user attitude set from the start of the program?____

6. Is the amount of information presented in small enough increments to facilitate learning and retention?
____

7. Does the program have menu or linking structure that enables the learner to select activities?____

8. Does the program allow learners to always know where they are in the program?____

9. Does the design effectively use principles of adult learning?____

10. Is the level of difficulty appropriate for the target audience?____

11. Is feedback effectively used to provide information to the learner regarding the appropriateness of his /her response?____

12. For text screens, are words correctly spelled, and standard grammar, syntax, and punctuation used?
____

13. Is the information attractively and effectively presented:
    a. Do all the screens have a consistent style?____
    b. Are titles, headers, and text functional and attractive?____
    c. Are text screens formatted for easy reading and retention?____
    d. Are all fonts easy read?____
    e. When different fonts are used on the same screen, are the fonts harmonious and not distracting?____
    f. Are the screen colors easy to look at; for example, harmonious with each other, and not glaring?____
    g. Do the screen colors enhance, rather than detract from, the student's ability to learn and retain the information that is presented?____
    h. Are any colors over-used on a single screen?____

14. Is the video picture quality well-defined and distinct, with no bleeding, streaking, or blurring?____

15. Is the talent pleasing, appropriate, and well-suited to the role?____

16. Does the narration employ proper grammar and conventional syntax?____

17. Are all words pronounced and inflected property?____

18. Are audio tracks clear and free of distortion and extraneous noise?____

19. Is the programs navigation system logical and appropriate for the target population?____

20. Is it obvious how to quit, repeat, move on, or get help?_____

Comments

Figure 32.5 Development Phase Checklist

Small group review checklist

Small group review conducted by_____
Date_____
Title of project_____

1. Where you told at the beginning of the lesson exactly what you were expected to learn?____

2. Does the program use techniques that helped you learn what the lesson was presenting?____

3. Were you able to control the program in a way that was helpful to you?____

4. Was the amount of information presented in each segment small enough to let you learn it and remember it easily?____

5. Does the program have a menu or linking structure that lets you select activities?____

6. Does the program allow you to always know where you are in the lesson?____

7. Did the program promote positive feelings in you from the beginning?____

8. Did you find it easy to learn the information that was presented?____

9. Did you have the sense that the program "talked down" to you?____
If so, in the "Comments" block at the end of this checklist, give examples of where this happened.

10. Is it too simple to master the program?____

11. Is it too difficult to master the program?____

12. Did the feedback provide helpful information about your answers to the test questions?____

13. Is the information attractively and effectively presented:
   a. Are titles, headers, and text attractive?__
   b. Did titles, headers, and text help you learn the material?____
   c. Do all the screens have a consistent style throughout the program?____
   d. Is the text easy to read and remember?____
   e. Are all type fonts easy to read?____
   f. When different fonts are used on the same screen, do the fonts look attractive together?____
   g. Did you ever find the type fonts distracting-that is, were you thinking about the fonts rather than the information that was being presented?____
   h. Are the screen colors easy to look at?__
   i. Did you ever find the screen colors distracting? That is, did they ever make it harder for you to learn what was begin presented?____
   j. Did the colors make it easier for you to learn the information that was being presented?__
   k. Are any colors overused on single screen?____

14. Are the audio effects appropriate and helpful?____

15. Are the video effects appropriate and helpful?____

16. Was it easy to find your way around the program? That is, was it obvious how to quit, repeat, move on, or get help?____

Comments

Figure 32.6 Small Group Review Checklist

Total quality training

There is great emphasis on total quality in companies around the world. There are many flavors of total quality programs. Total Quality Training (TQT) is simply applying the principles often associated with quality programs to training. Nobody invented TQT. It is the natural extension of the quality process to training. Aramco's General Manager of Training, Ali Dialdin, first introduced us to TQT. Aramco has an exemplary companywide program that encourages employees to take part in identifying and solving problems.

Quality assurance is a system for ensuring and maintaining wanted characteristics in a process or product. Considerations in a manufacturing QA process might be input, process, output, and customer. TQT has essentially the same categories. The input is our learner. The process is the training program. The output is our graduate. Training's customer is the job.

Most organizations use the ISD (instructional systems development) process to develop instruction. You can treat TQT as part of the evaluation phase of ISD. TQT must be systematic and provide useful information about the training process, so we can maintain what's good and improve what isn't.

How do we achieve TQT?

Training must maintain a productive, nonthreatening environment for TQT to work. For example, avoid the use of the words "test" and "evaluation." Instead, use "re-

---

**Implementation
checklist**

Implement check by_____
Date_____
Title of project_____

1. Has technical information for planning and installation been obtained from the system manufacturer(s), if necessary?____

2. Is the physical plan complete for delivery of the system?____

3. Are procedures in place for collecting monitoring data for the application?

4. Are personnel trained on-site to perform maintenance, including start-up, operation, and shut-down procedures?____

Comments

Figure 32.7 Implementation Checklist

view." Solve problems at the lowest possible level by assigning a person to a problem who has both the skill and authority to solve it. Involve the problem-solvers in identifying the problem. "Ownership" is a key to lasting problem solving. Finally, place problem-solving responsibility with individuals instead of groups. You can monitor TQT effectively using only three quality functions. They are training standards, training output, and job needs.

Planning

We use instruments to make TQT happen. Planning is deciding what and where to evaluate, and who will do it. Customers can tell us where we could have better prepared our graduates. Several methods can get at this information. Send evaluation sheets to the graduate's managers 60 or 90 days after graduation as a regular evaluation activity. Also schedule and conduct a periodic field review of the output of each course taught. The tools are surveys of graduate-job match, schedules of periodic reviews, and descriptions of review procedures.

Performance

Conduct audits of instruction, learners, and graduates. Use checklists for auditing tests for validity, the curriculum for job relevance, and administration for timely and effective support. Use performance tests whenever you can, and use written tests elsewhere to measure learning. Surveys reveal the effect of training on the targeted jobs.

Tracking

Make sure that corrections and improvements are, in fact, carried out. The tools to use are implementing documents that will vary with the organization. TQT tracking charts compare items identified, corrected, and verified.

Results

The TQT process produces results in your training programs. You will have set and met standards for curriculum, instruction, testing, classroom performance, and job performance. One happy result is improved safety. Employee recommendations to change facilities, equipment, and procedures flow from TQT.

Aramco has a technique for documenting the positive side of the quality review. They circulate TQT Good Practice flyers companywide. These flyers recognize exemplary training practices and share the knowledge gained.

The Development Process

If you work within an organization, one thing to think about is potential sources of courseware. There are five that come to our minds.

- TBL system vendors
- Another company

- Software house
- Body shop
- In-house

System Vendors often provide development services. Since they know the software better than anyone they are certainly in a position to provide support. Support is something you shouldn't take for granted. They may also provide design and development services. To find out, just ask.

Another company that uses the same development tool is also a good potential source of assistance. Since they are doing development in earnest, their help will be pointed and may be the result of learning many lessons the hard way. With their help you can avoid the same errors. If your sector is not directly competitive, a company in your industry would be ideal. They face the same problems and understand your "dialect" of training. Don't be afraid to ask for generic help from any company that is willing to provide it.

A software or courseware house exists to provide you with help. This form of help may be very cost-effective, and puts the help just where and when you need it. They are not equal, however. Whenever you use an external source, ask for and check references.

The difference between a courseware house and a body shop is that the person in the courseware house who works on your lessons will probably still be there next year. A body shop hires help only for "the duration." When your project is over, the people who worked on it will go back to their consulting activities.

Finally, you can do it in-house—what this book is all about. You *can* do it if you persevere. You can build your capability from scratch, starting now. We've seen others do it with great success.

How to Develop "Smart"

Smart isn't an acronym, it's an adjective. In this section we offer a potpourri of ideas that have been learned from experience and can offer considerable bang for the buck.

CMI prescription generation rules

Here are rules for the generation of CMI prescriptions, something you did at a basic level in Chapter 22.

1. Provide resources for all measured needs.
2. Select as few resources as possible.
3. Minimize unneeded instruction.
4. Avoid reusing resources where possible.

The apparently contradictory rules presented in 2 and 4 must be applied in a balanced way. If there is only one resource you cannot avoid reusing it if you permit a second shot.

Analysis and preliminary design

This is a technique that has always worked wherever tried. The key is that the project is structured in two parts, the analysis and preliminary design and the rest of the project. This concept pertains to fixed price contracts, the most common type. The whole idea is based on the premise that any organization that wants to survive in business must have more financial winners than losers. To assure success they must insert padding into their estimate of what they actually think it will cost to do the work. That means that the customer must pay more.

On the other side, there is considerable risk for the contractor. The work must be done, and if he miscalculates it can result in a loss. You can't stay in business with many losses.

The analysis and preliminary design solves both party's problems. The risk and extra cost will be applied to an analysis and only enough design to clearly lay out the course of the rest of the project. After the analysis, the true extent of the rest of the project will be known clearly. Contracting for it can be done by both parties with their eyes open. Since the client also knows the extent more clearly he or she will look for a fair price. Figure 32.8 shows the analysis and preliminary design concept.

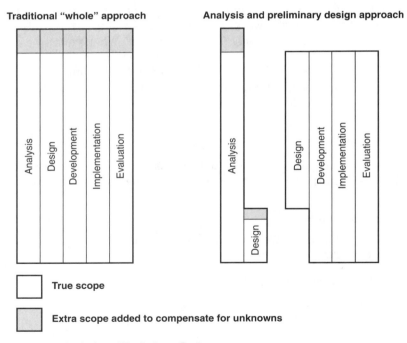

Figure 32.8 Analysis and Preliminary Design

Bell system three-step model

A very smart trainer, Dick Davis, led AT&T's efforts in TBL before the breakup. They had some of the best training found anywhere. He used a three-step method to roll out projects.

- Trial
- Develop prototype
- Full scale implementation

The courseware itself was rolled out in three steps. The trial was held to ensure that the development concept was sound and would work. The prototype development followed and was thoroughly tested. Finally, the organization rolled out the training in a full-scale implementation and the training organization wrote the general methods for implementation. Dick often referred to the "Spinnaker Effect" in dissemination. If you aren't a sailor, the spinnaker is the huge balloon-like sail (perhaps with a corporate logo) that looks so pretty. What Dick used to say is that everything is great and you are really moving out with the spinnaker. Then, you reach down in the cockpit to grab a sandwich, and when you look up the big spinnaker is *in the water*—a problem. Implementation of a training project is like that. Everything can be going along great, but when you divert your attention to something else and look back, you've got a problem.

Working together for efficient course development

If you are working with a consultant to get started there is a pattern that works best. The degree of consultant input should be the greatest on the first project, or first part of a large project. In fact, you might just assist with the first projects. The second time around do what you can do well. Eventually, taper the use of outsider to specialists only such as graphic artists, videographers, and device vendors for digital-file compression. Figure 32.9 shows the pattern.

Ratio of effort

There is another conceptually related, but different, concept. We suspect you would be amazed at how beneficial it is to spend development time *disproportionately*.

Imagine a project with ten lessons. Which should you develop first? We see inexperienced developers start with number one. Actually numbers one and ten would be the worst choices, because they are almost surely atypical for the project, probably being introductory and summary. The best lesson to develop would be the most typical lesson of all, no matter which one it is. Let's assume it is lesson seven.

That is the part of the idea that is most intuitive. The harder part comes next. You can successfully develop the entire lesson seven before turning to the other nine. In

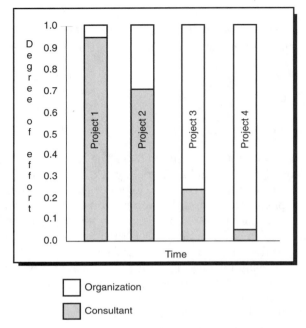

Figure 32.9 Combined Effort over Several Projects

doing so, you will create a template that can be used for all of the other lessons, greatly speeding the development of each. All your techniques will be established and new decisions won't be required. Figure 32.10 shows the ratio of effort for the lessons.

Much more important, you may discover that certain ideas didn't work well. If you had used the pattern that is most common, the poorly working ideas would have been incorporated into many of the lessons before you discovered that they did not work in this situation.

Time saving development techniques

There are three ideas that can improve your productivity. We have mentioned them as you developed the lessons in Chapters 13 through 22, and you used them to some degree.

- Models
- Templates
- Modules

Models are an Authorware capability. Under the Libraries pull-down menu you will find New Model, Load Model, and Unload Model. You find the model as you find any other file, and load it. This is a sophisticated way of achieving the same thing that you could do by copying an icon group from one lesson and pasting it into another. This permits you to "develop one and deliver many." The model is simply a file that is accessible from within Authorware (you cannot open two regular Authorware files at the same time). If you want to create a model, select the icon structure that you want to place in the model so it is highlighted. Let's say you have a tutorial sequence. Select the Libraries pull-down menu and choose New Model. You will activate your systems file selection menu and have the opportunity to select the file location and name for the model. Call it *tutorial*. Authorware will add the .MOD file extension. The Macintosh version of the model file is shown in Figure 32.11 inside a Models folder (subdirectory).

To use your model when you are already inside a lesson that you are working on, select Paste Model from the Libraries pull-down menu. It will be on a menu list of loaded models. If you had never used the Tutorial model before you would first select Load Model from the Libraries pull-down menu, find it, and load it to make it pasteable. Once a model's icons are pasted they are no different from icons that you created in the usual way.

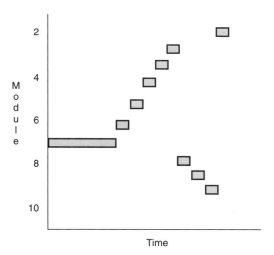

Figure 32.10   Ratio of Effort

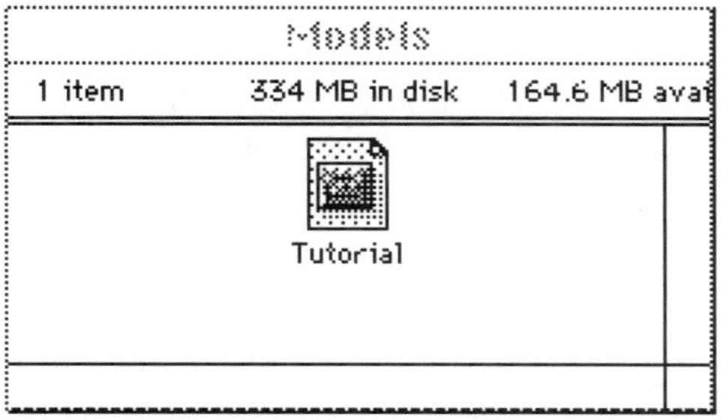

Figure 32.11   Model File Icon

Templates are whole parts of lessons or whole lessons themselves. The preexisting content is treated as placeholders and is replaced with the new content. If the original worked mechanically, the templated new lesson will work too. This can greatly speed development by eliminating the need to troubleshoot errors in newly written code.

Modules are a completely different idea. The module concept applies to developing multiple versions of a lesson. Let's say you develop lessons for a new product. The usual (but inefficient and less instructionally sound) way is to develop the principal lesson and then to make variants of it. The module concept is to structure the lessons into modules that can be assembled in various patterns. Perhaps the introductory module can be used for executives and salespeople, as well as to introduce the main module. It can also accompany the special module needed by repair people. You can extend this idea by mixing and matching modules to build each unique version of the training.

Project Management Tools

We don't think you should hold back in applying tools to help you manage the multimedia training development project.

Project management documents

We urge you to employ a whole range of project management documents. These include:

- Timeline
- Major events list
- PERT
- Gantt
- Project cost plans
- Courseware development standards
- Programming specifications
- Task assignment sheets
- Summary data (On-line or hardcopy)
- Project management document
- Project status reports

Figure 32.12 shows a portion of a PERT chart. Although Gantt charts are common and simpler to use, PERT charts provide the relationships between project activities that Gantt charts cannot display.

Activity log

The key to sound documentation evaluation is integrating data collection and reporting into the work habits of all team members. An essential instrument for this is a development activity log. Each team member accurately records his or her time

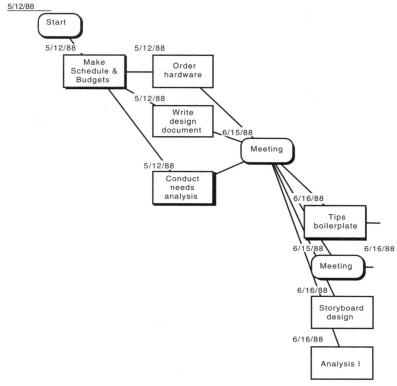

Figure 32.12 PERT Chart Detail

spent on each of the development tasks. This provides basic information on the current status of your project, enabling you to head off problems such as schedule delays or budget shortfalls. Page logs have been around for years. The log can be on a computer, but ideally it would be accessible on a LAN so that team-members could easily log in their efforts centrally. Figure 32.13 illustrates a sample log sheet.

Project diary

Jane Greiner suggests a "project diary" for documentation evaluation. You can keep a project diary in computer files using common word processing and spreadsheet programs. Some recommended components of a project diary are:

- Product development proposal and/or contract
- Development schedule
- Budget
- Project status reports
- Sign-off forms
- Anecdotal records

Emergency Simulation Project Log				
Date	Hours	Project number	Activity code	Comments
6/3/95	3.0	HKWR1201	KO1	Met with Charles Shelton to discuss application of PSS to center operations
6/3/95	5.0	HKWR1244	KO1	Completed consolidated operations staff position task list
6/4/95	2.0	HKWR1244	KO1	Worked with Charles Shelton to refine task list for center operations staff positions
6/4/95	4.5	HKWR1237	KO1	Met with Willy Vandergrift to generate narration script

Figure 32.13 Development Activity Log

Project status report

The preceding documents are project-level documents. The project status report is a brief document distributed to all project team members and management. Depending on how you complete your report, it may also be presented to the customer. These reports update everyone about the current project status and document problems, solutions, and other important events. Figure 32.14 illustrates a portion of a project status report.

Developing a technology-based learning project can be compared to a major engineering project. It yields tangible draft products at regular intervals that can and should be reviewed by clients. A sign-off form is an important documentation tool. It indicates the client's approval to proceed with the next step of the development cycle and to pay for the completion of this step, if applicable. The sign-off form is a powerful tool that will help you and the project manager keep things moving, and will prevent the client from constantly rethinking the project. See Figure 11.6 in Chapter 11 for an example of a customer-signed design document.

Now let's look at a more detailed example. The sign-off form documents client approval of a given project milestone. Figure 32.15, adapted from one used by Tom Reeves, presents a much more specific and detailed sign-off form.

Notice that the sample in Figure 32.15 also incorporates a payment action, and presumably would be attached to the invoice submitted for payment.

Project record form

Documentation of events can also be important. Here is a true story of a developer who did the wrong thing, but documented it. A prime contractor customer suddenly noticed that a project was running over budget. He called a meeting with the subcontractor, who had lent two developers to the project. Soon there was an argument because the higher cost was due to many changes to the project design (remember the importance of sign-off). The lead subcontractor developer claimed that the prime contractor had requested all of the changes. Each was small, but totally they added up. The subcontractor's lead developer was able to provide a stack of over 100 e-mail messages requesting the changes. At this point, both parties were in the wrong. The subcontractor should not have executed changes to the project without bringing it to management's attention, at least in a memo documenting that the small change was being made. The prime contractor should not have requested changes without expecting the project to cost more.

A project record form can be a useful instrument for recording the "story" of a project. An important thing to note about this instrument is that it requires the person completing it to carefully distinguish between what was observed and his/her interpretation of the observation. Figure 32.16 shows the sample project record form.

Courseware Maintenance

Since corporate training requirements and subject matter are changing with increasing speed, it's crucial to monitor your courseware to ensure that it's up-to-date.

 Z a

Zia Performance Technology
Multimedia Development

SBA TRAINING DEVELOPMENT PROJECT
Status Report for Week of January 7, 1996

Task Area	Deliverable	Issues, Requirements	Status
1. Maintenance and Harddrive back-up	10/95, 11/95, 12/95 completed. Ongoing through September 30, 1996	Training computer was relocated inside TCC	In progress
2. Repurpose three IVD modules	Basics of Communications, JVC Communications, and JCC Operations IVD modules restructured into PSSs or training modules on new JCC training computer.	Scheduled to begin 1/15/96	Review of IVD begun 1/3/96
3. Diagnostic test questions	Within the context of SBA operator certification program, diagnostic test questions developed for high priority tasks of GS-723-06, 09, and GS-688-11 jobs. Prototype certification plan for GS-432-06,09, and GS-434-11 job classifications.	Scheduled to begin 1/15/96	
4. Annotated listing of paper-based resources	Paper-based,annotated listing of SBA library that can be incorporated into Performance Support System (PSS)	None	In progress
5. Revise existing PSS components	Make changes to existing PSS components and install updated version on SCC training computer.	Time needs to be scheduled to review PSSs with operators	Completed 12/22/95
6. Develop PSS (version 2)	Version 2 of PSS	None	In progress
7. Pilot group review	Implement content changes identified by operators in the existing simulation program.	None	Completed changes 12/19/95.

Figure 32.14 Project Status Report

Project milestone approval

Project: HAZCOM refresher training lesson

Milestone: Design document

I have reviewed and approved the Design Document for the HAZCOM course, with changes, additions, deletions or corrections as annotated in the master copy.

I hereby authorize you to proceed with the HAZCOM project: creating the drafts of all of the documents for course materials based on it. I also give my approval for you to invoice my department for satisfactory completion of the Design Document milestone of this project.

I understand that further changes to the structure, objectives, or content of the course (aside from those specified in the master copy) will likely result in the final delivery date and could result in additional charges to my department and/ or costs to Bullock Industries.

_____   _____

      [signature]   [date]

Chris Bullock, VP ES&H, Bullock Industries
cc: Sheela Jackson, Training Manager

Figure 32.15 Sample Sign-Off Form

Remember, it doesn't have conversations with colleagues or read the newspaper! Be sure that the TBL systems aren't teaching outdated facts or neglecting important new information. Typically, this is beyond the expertise of instructional designers or training managers to determine, but you should set up a regular plan of evaluation by content experts.

If you've done your homework, you should have ensured that you have a means (both technically and legally) of getting into the software code to update it. You may need to license a copy of the authoring system used to create the program in order to edit the computer text or branching instructions. Generally, it's too expensive to re-shoot, edit, and master another CD-ROM, but sometimes it's viable to program around outdated material, or overlay parts of a visual with computer graphics. Just as you'll need resources to supervise and maintain the equipment, you'll need resources to update the content. This should be a part of every annual training budget.

Multimedia training is thought of as a medium when, once purchased, does not require further attention. Unfortunately, this isn't true. In order to establish an effective interactive training system, you'll need to:

- Collect feedback on lessons
- Use the feedback to adjust lessons
- Decide when lessons should be completely overhauled or retired

Programming Specifications

This section describes the process used when more than one person will contribute to the same course or curriculum for a single sponsor. We suggest guidelines for design and programming of the ultimate courseware, to ensure uniformity of external appearance and internal operation. You do the actual programming or authoring of a lesson during the development phase. However, during design and development of the programmer-ready materials you have to give fair consideration to programming issues. If you are working in a group of two or more, we strongly recommend that you agree on programming standards before beginning a project.

Project record form

Date: _6/4/95_

Title of project: _____RCRA_____

Location: _____Bldg. X201_____

Observer: _____Toni Garcia_____

Description:

After two hours of study, one of the trainees got up and left the class. I followed him out into the hall and asked if anything was wrong. He replied: "I can't waste my time sitting in the class because I don't intend to use the new system." I asked him why and he answered: "Computers don't work for me. As soon as I touch one, the program blows up. You'll be glad I won't use your system because it would just fall apart if I did. It's nothing against you or your course. I just know it won't work."

I tried to talk to him more, but he indicated that he had to make some phone calls and left.

Interpretation:

The RCRA course training is innovative and user-friendly is our eyes, but in the eyes of person with high anxiety about technology, it is just another threatening computer program. I suspect that this person strongly fears computers and that he has an unusually strong degree of "learned helplessness" with respect to "technophobia" and make special efforts to help those who express high anxiety. Also, this person indicated before the beginning of the course that he was only there because his boss insisted that he attend. We may need to clarify the enrollment procedures for this and other clients.

Comments:

None.

Figure 32.16 Sample Project Record Form

You will find that your standards will save time. The standards promote clarity and consistency and will also increase efficiency and productivity, because they will eliminate the need for modification and rework.

Our warning is not to kill the potential for creativity. Standards are *not* meant to be broken, so develop ones that are not too suppressive of future change that may be for the better.

Teamwork is easier when the team communicates. The standards will serve as mutual communication about who will do what. We have found that a good way to provide the creativity is to have two different specifications. One is overall and will apply to any course developed. Another is specific for a particular product or set of products and describes the particular way it will be handled. Here are our recommendations for programming specifications.

General Programming Specifications

General programming specifications include specifications for screen layout, questions and feedback, and other items relative to each lesson.

Screen layout

Specific location for on-screen objects:

- Cues
- Margins
- Paragraph indentation
- Pop-up windows
- Titles

Questions and feedback

- Handling of hints
- Type of learner responses allowed
  ~Dragging
  ~Pointing
  ~Selecting
  ~Text entry
- Type of feedback for each try
  ~Knowledge of result
  ~Explanation
  ~Remediation

Presentation sequence in each lesson

- Title screen
- Credits

- Opening segment
- Display objectives
- Body of instruction
- Summary
- Exercise, practice, or game
- Test

Miscellaneous

- Sign-on procedures
- Naming conventions for video and audio files
- Transition
- First-person learner references

Course-Specific Programming Specifications

Course specifications deal with size, media types, course and file structure, screen types, layout questions and feedback, input methods, learner activity, lesson organization, and end-of-course output.

Course size

- Course length
- Estimated on-line hours
- Estimated percentages of on-line instruction

Off-line media types (if any)

- Print
- Other media

Course structure

- Components (i.e., number of modules, units, lessons; which components will be presented on-line and which off-line)
- Specific sequence of learner activities
  ~Orientation
  ~Sequence within modules, units, lessons

File structure

The types of files required, and the functions each will perform:

- Data file for test responses
- Note files for learner comments

- Resource
- Driver
- Curriculum
- Models or templates to be used

Screen types

These are created first and approved by the customer before general development. The lesson is then built only of the predefined screens.

- Course/lesson/subject title screen
- Introduction/overview screen
- Instructional screen
- Inserted question and feedback screen
- Review screen
- Summary screen
- Practice/exercise screen
- Test screen
- Help screen

Screen layout

This is an overarching specification. It includes screen types and layout standards. Specific location for on-screen objects:

- Buttons
- Captions
- Color (text, background, emphasis, borders)
- Menus (structure, labels)
- Text font and size

Questions and feedback

- Presentation of questions
  ~Audio
  ~Graphics
  ~Text
  ~Video
  ~Combination
- Number of tries allowed
- Presentation of feedback
  ~Audio
  ~Graphics

~Text
~Video
~Combination

- Type of feedback for each try (knowledge of result, explanation, remediation)

Input methods

Will you use clerical help to enter the test information?

- Instruction
- Tests/answers
- Data

Learner activity

- On-line sequence of learner activities (including log-on, selecting options to read/write notes, take lesson, take test, etc.)
- Key conventions
- On-line resources for learner

Lesson design details

- Summary or number of lessons
- For each lesson
  ~Description of CAI lesson strategies

Test organization and rules

- Summary or number of test items and general description of types of feedback that will be provided
- For each test set
  ~Description of test item formats
  ~Specific description of types of feedback that will be given to learners

End-of-course outputs

- Learner test results
- Learner evaluation questionnaire response
- Reports

Development tasks

- Information needed from course developers to complete programming
- Sequenced list of programming activities that need to be performed

Additional requirements
- Materials
- Tasks

A Peek Into the Future

This whole book has described the past and present of a field that is among the fastest moving there is. In Chapter 33 we will try to draw back the curtain that hides the future and look as far as we can see.

Chapter

33

Looking at the Learning Horizon

Our view of how the future will look was well summed up by a famous psychiatrist.

> "But we cannot live the
> afternoon of life according
> to the programme of life's
> morning; for what was great
> in the morning will be little
> at evening, and what in the
> morning was true will at evening
> become a lie."
>
> —Carl Jung

Jung hit it on the head: Things change. We have seen them change, and you will see them change too.

You can think of changes as great waves pounding on the beach, *and* as the tide rising and falling at the same time. The trick is to ride the changes rather than drowning in them.

We are lucky in the multimedia field to be able to see change coming so clearly. The Pentium chip was not a surprise to anyone. It was the natural progression of a trend of long standing. The P6 chip and others will follow.

In this chapter we will describe trends for technology-based learning as we approach the 21st Century. We will also make suggestions for you to forecast changes that involve your own organization or situation.

The Computer Environment

Where are we going? A fair question, and one that can be best answered by seeing where we have been.

Our divided origins . . . our common future

Our field can be seen as the child of two disciplines, system theory and educational psychology. The two come together as shown in Figure 33.1.

The figure shows two columns, but the bottom row really represents a coming together. We expect that both will come together for the development and delivery of high-quality instruction.

The technological basis for advances in TBL

Angus has presented seminars on Computer-Based Learning (now Technology-Based Learning) since the late 1970s and Performance Support Systems since the late 1980s. The trends and future are the same today as they were then. It is a story of size and cost decreases, overall performance increases, and the concept of "threshold."

The size and cost decreases occur in the electronic chips. Chips continually get smaller, in the sense that the space for any capability is always less in a newer chip. When they get smaller, more components are squeezed into the space and the result is that they get more powerful. The transistor replaced the vacuum tube, one-for-

	Systems theory	Educational psychology
Origins	Interactive computing (24 × 80 world)	Office automation (8½ × 80 world)
Uses	Deliver instruction	Develop instruction
Future	Sophisticated terminals to deal with a broad range of human performance characteristics	Integrated workbenches of tools for trainers

Figure 33.1 The Genealogy of Technology-Based Learning

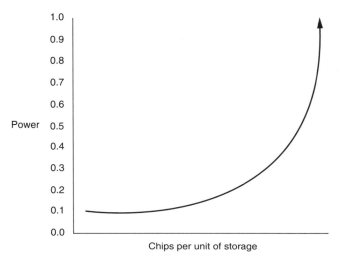

Figure 33.2 Generations of Chip Technology

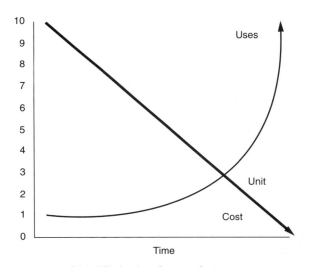

Figure 33.3 Digital Technology Impacts Society

one. A ten-tube radio became a ten-transistor radio. The next step was the integrated circuit, ten transistors on one chip. After that, it was a series of successive generations of chips with greater levels of integration. The sequence is shown in Figure 33.2.

As the chips improve there are overall performance increases in what they can be used for. The astronauts went to the moon with computing power that is ¹⁄₁₀,₀₀₀ of what you may have on your desk today. Figure 33.3 shows the increases in power available as technology advances.

Each advance is not in a steady progression. There are thresholds that, when surpassed, lead to a whole new range of possibilities. There are advances in system capabilities, and they are followed by advances in what we can use the technology to accomplish. Today, we can do sophisticated simulations on the desktop. It can make a big difference in the training that we can offer. Better yet, the trend continues . . . and will continue! Figure 33.4 shows how the economics of TBL are affected by the costs of computing power.

This is really all of the background that you need to predict the future of multimedia and training. Combine this with the life-cycle concept and you can make specific prognostications.

The Technology Life Cycle

There is the technology life cycle. We described it in Chapter 9 and illustrated it in Figure 9.2. The technology life cycle is not related specifically to electronic progress. It is a simple pattern that can be followed back into history.

As with the waves on the beach, the trick is not to drown when a technology goes away. Organizations and individuals have been punished by this effect. The Polaroid Corporation struggled mightily for decades to perfect the instant movie, and they did it. You may not recall because the new product came out at the same time as amateur video cameras.

The most recent events in this arena are the decision of IBM and Intel not to support DVI and the announcement of the DVD format as the compact disc of the future. We know an individual entrepreneur who built his whole business on DVI, was early, and paid the initial high prices. We don't know whether his business will recover.

In other cases it is obvious. IVD is at the decline phase of its life cycle. It is a smooth, normal, expected progression.

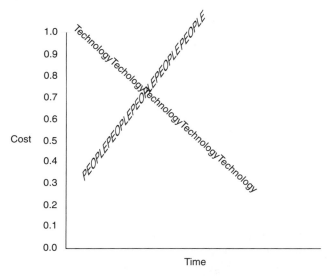

Figure 33.4 The Changing Economics of Training

The Information Superhighway

Internetworking on the information superhighway has changed the way we communicate and do business. Information is the ultimate tool for knowledge workers, and this is surely the stone age of network communicating. The Internet has been described as "a raging torrent of information" that anyone can tap with the right connection. If you aren't already connected and using the Internet to support your work you are already behind the knowledge curve. Worse, you are in danger of falling seriously behind.

We'd be the first to admit that there are some strange new terms to learn, but they aren't any worse than those you already know. RCRA may be one of yours already. Explaining the whole Internet is well beyond the scope of this chapter. In fact, we'd prefer to think that you are among the millions already on the net. Here are some very brief discussions of the features you are most likely to use in the future.

E-mail (electronic mail)

A mail system was the original motivation for the Internet network itself. Today, as an Internet user, you can exchange mail, including almost any kind of data, with anyone else who is on the Internet.

We would enjoy the opportunity to meet you, even at a distance. If you want to contact us by e-mail, try Angus at:

```
zia@rt66.com
```

or Tom at:

```
tmi107@psu.edu
```

You can follow interesting discussions on newsgroups.

Newsgroups

Internet newsgroups are forums where discussions focus around the group's theme. Several newsgroups on the Internet are devoted directly to training or closely related topics. Most of the activity is sharing of opinions and ideas and the asking and answering of questions. It is not uncommon to see a question answered by someone in The Netherlands or Australia.

On the Internet, Authorware is currently discussed in the newsgroup:

```
bit.listserv.authorware
```

Authorware topics are discussed on CompuServe under:

```
60 MACROMEDIA
```

Some questions appear repeatedly, and these questions are addressed in a document called a FAQ (frequently asked questions). In some cases, FAQs are massive documents that offer a comprehensive compilation of information.

Hang on to your hat, you ain't seen 'nuthin yet. The real action is on the Web.

The World Wide Web

The Web helps you jump from place to place, following logical links in the data. The Web has been described as a global, interactive, dynamic, cross-platform, distributed, graphical hypertext information system that runs over the Internet. We would add that it is multimedia.

This same technique can provide the branching to make interactive instruction possible. The big differences in using the WWW are the delay in transmitting graphics (and big wait for video) and the unlimited distribution possibilities.

You can sample this concept now! As far as we know, Dr. Mable Kinzie of the University of Virginia produced the first sample WWW interactive lesson. Working with graduate students, she produced the WWW version of a familiar lesson on frog dissection. The lesson works just as the older, diskette-based version did. To sample the lesson, point your Web browser to:

```
http://curry.edschool.virginia.edu/insttech/frog
```

Figure 33.5 shows the main menu. Check it out!

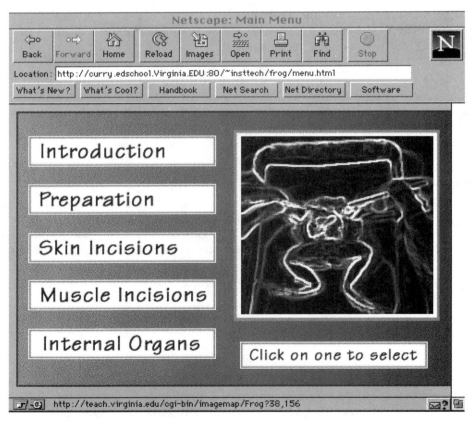

Figure 33.5 Frog Lesson Main Menu

The frog is the first of a new breed of lesson that may be useful to you. Kinzie made the lesson when setting up touch areas (called image mapping) was a black art. Now you can buy a book about it in your local bookstore. Several other lessons have been developed already. By following the principles discussed in this book, and using a knowledge of the Web, you can create interactive (but slow) training that can be accessed worldwide.

We enjoy discussions of all this, and would like to hear your ideas by e-mail. If you want to know what we are up to you can point your browser to us on the WWW at this URL:

```
http://www.rt66.com/www/zia.html
```

We look forward to an exchange of ideas.

The Evolution of Today's Technology

We are certain of one thing. You can foresee the future as well as we can. It is going to be a natural progression. The major developments will be written about long before they become available. If you take the time to read the multimedia industry press you will not be surprised when products come to market with the new technology. Sometimes you will be a little disappointed in the implementation, compared to your expectations, but you should never be surprised.

Technology-Based Learning and You As We Enter the 21st Century

At the beginning of Chapter 1 we compared you to Juan Sebastian del Cano, who completed the first voyage around the world.[1] It was completed in 1522 and took two years, eleven months, and 17 days. After almost 400 years, in 1873, Jules Verne wrote an improbable, fictional account called *The Tour of the World in Eighty Days*. We suppose it reflected what was potentially possible then. About 100 years after that, anyone could fly around the world on a routine commercial Pan American Airways flight in approximately four days. In 1961 Yuri Alekseyevich Gagarin completed a circumnavigation of the world, alone in the spacecraft Vostok, in 89.1 minutes!

All of these factors leave us poised on the brink of professional victory. You, in fact, may be today's Juan Sebastian del Cano, fixed on the rolling deck of the small, but indomitable *Victoria*. You are bravely sailing into uncharted waters. We wish you every success, great and small. When you ultimately prevail in completing today's voyage, the world will again be smaller. If you do your job well, it will also be better!

---

[1]Americans are taught about Ferdinand Magellan, who conceived and initiated the voyage with five ships and 265 men. Magellan did not complete the circumnavigation, because he was killed in the Philippines. Only del Cano, with 18 other men, completed the entire trip on the *Victoria*.

Glossary

Many special terms are used in training, particularly in technology-based learning and more so in complex systems. The terms here are among those heard frequently, which may not be familiar.

Some of these terms are taken with permission from *The Trainer's Dictionary*, published by HRD Press, Amherst, MA, 1993.

adult learning theory   Adult learning principles and practices, especially those advanced by Malcolm Knowles under the term andragogy. Adult learning considers the wants and needs of the adult learner as opposed to a child.

affective domain   The area of human learning associated with attitudes, feelings, interests, opinions, world views, and values.

affective objective   A learning objective specifying the acquisition of particular attitudes, values, or feelings. Affective objectives deal with the affective domain. Affective objectives are also called attitudinal objectives.

algorithm   Organization of any task into the exact sequence of steps needed to accomplish it. Algorithms replace continuous prose as a means for communicating complex rules and regulations, and can be used as the basis of a job aid.

andragogy   (Pronounced an´-dra-go-gee. The "gee" sounds like gee wiz.) The art and science of helping adults learn. A European term introduced into the English-speaking adult learning vocabulary by Malcolm Knowles. Andragogy is based on the Greek *andr-* (man, as opposed to boy) and *agogus* (leader). A contrast is usually made with pedagogy—teaching children. Andragogy makes specific assumptions about how adults perceive and react to learning situations. Andragogy emphasizes self-directedness, utilization of the learner's experience as a resource for learning, and involves sharing in the diagnosis of needs, formulation of objectives, building and doing of learning plans, and evaluation of the process.

animation   Objects drawn, selectively erased, and repositioned to produce apparent movement on a video or computer display. For example, liquid flow though a system or movement of the needle of a gauge.

argument   A value used with an operator or passed to a subprogram that then carries out operations using the argument.

array   A list of data values stored for later use. An element in an array can be referenced by an expression.

audio   The medium that involves words or sounds delivered to the learner's ear by a method other than voice.

author   A person who creates technology-based learning course material. Programmer is a separate role.

authoring station   The combination of computer and peripheral hardware that can be used to develop technology-based learning. The authoring station is normally more completely configured and may include more powerful components than a delivery station.

authoring system   Special type of program that eases the programming of CAI courseware by enabling a content expert to interact with the computer in everyday language. Unlike an authoring language, it does not need programming knowledge or skill. Authoring systems are also called authoring aids and authoring utilities.

author language   A computer language used specifically for creating CAI (including multimedia) courseware. For example, the learning-specific Tencore™ as opposed to a general-purpose computer language such as FORTRAN. Author languages provide greater capabilities than authoring systems, at the price of the greater effort required to learn them.

behavior   One of the three required parts of a learning objective that describe what the learner will be able to do after instruction. Behavior is also called performance. Behavior is also the third level of Donald Kirkpatrick's summative evaluation model, focusing on the learner's new or changed job performance produced by instruction. Collected by questionnaire, usually 30, 60, or 90 days after the completion of instruction. It asks the manager how well the training has enabled the employee to do what's needed to get the job done. Some HRD departments send a similar form to the trainee.

Betacam   A hand-held combination camera and recorder using a professional quality Beta videocassette recorder.

beta test   The formal test of under-development courseware and draft documentation by selected users before external testing or distribution. Users test the functionality and determine whether operational or utilization errors still exist. Beta testing is one of the last steps before release of the product. Also used to describe the testing of surveys and questionnaires. Beta test is also written β test.

Bloom's taxonomy   A taxonomy of learning objectives developed by Benjamin Bloom. He addressed affective and cognitive learning outcomes in hierarchical fashion. His taxonomy was adopted by many developers and is applied to the development of a large body of instruction today. The taxonomy cites six cognitive behaviors: knowledge, comprehension, application, analysis, synthesis, and evaluation. It cites five affective behaviors: receiving, responding, valuing, organization, and characterization. Psychomotor behaviors were not addressed by Bloom.

branching   In technology-based learning, the process of directing the learner to one of two or more paths through instructional material on the basis of replies to questions. Branching can also be responsive to learner-directed ideas, such as deciding to see a glossary.

camera ready   Copy ready to be photographed for printing.

carrel   A carrel consists of a desk-like work area and chair, or sometimes a more elaborate setup. The distinguishing characteristic of a carrel is a partition separating the learning activity of one learner from the adjacent carrel. Carrels may also have shelves, storage, and functional areas for computer or audiovisual equipment.

CD-ROM drive   The drive needed to retrieve data from a CD-ROM format disc.

clip art   Computer files that provide the same functionality as the traditional paper clip art. Electronic clip art is "cut and pasted" into the target document.

clip media   Already developed animation, sound, and motion video computer files that provide the same functionality as clip art. Clip media speeds creation of multimedia programs.

color graphics adaptor (CGA)   CGA is the low-end color video system available for IBM and compatible computers. CGA has less resolution than EGA (enhanced graphics adaptor) or VGA (video graphics adaptor). Obsolete today.

compact disc (CD)   Any of several 12-cm compact disc formats. Because of the inherent advantages of all of the smaller digital disc systems, they will eventually replace the larger 12-inch analog videodisc, just as they will be replaced by the DVD format.

compact disc-interactive (CD-I)   A compact disc format designed for interactive multimedia, usually called by its initials. A 12-cm CD-I disc holds a comprehensive mix of up to one hour of video, 7,000 still images, audio, computer text and graphics, and interaction capabilities. One competitive format for interactive multimedia.

compact disc read-only memory (CD-ROM)   A compact disc format designed to store large amounts of text or picture data usually called by its initials. A CD-ROM provides enough storage for five encyclopedias on a 4.75-inch (12-cm) disc. CD-ROMs are read by a laser. The format is not compatible with either CD-I or DVI.

computer application   Commonly used practical programs. For example, word processing, spreadsheets, data bases, graphics, and communications.

computer assisted instruction (CAI)   The use of a computer to deliver instruction, usually called by its initials. The modes of CAI are drill and practice, modeling, tutorial, and simulation. This is the preferred term. It is synonymous with CAT and CAL. CAI, along with CMI and CSLR, are the components of TBL. Unfortunately, some trainee's say "CAI" when they mean TBL.

computer assisted learning (CAL)   A synonym for computer-assisted instruction.

computer assisted training (CAT)   A synonym for computer-assisted instruction.

computer-based education (CBE)   Since technology-based learning (TBL) was originally developed in a university setting, the term education was naturally applied to it. Therefore, CBE is the oldest of the several synonymous terms in use.

computer-based instruction (CBI)   The meaning is identical to technology-based learning but is preferred by some users in industry.

computer-based learning (CBL)   Also called technology-based learning. CBL is an the umbrella term that includes all forms of use of computers in support of learning. The components of CBL are CAI, CMI, and CSLR. The meaning of CBL is identical to CBE, CBI, CBT, and TBL but is preferred by HRD people, who focus on the learner rather than the instructor.

computer-based reference (CBR)   Storage and retrieval of reference materials using a computer.

computer-based training (CBT)   The meaning is identical to computer-based learning but is preferred by some users with a training focus. Loosely used by some practitioners as a synonym for computer assisted instruction.

computer game   An instructional game that involves the use of a computer.

computer language Software with instructions used in programming.

computer managed instruction (CMI) The aspect of TBL that includes testing, prescription generation, and record keeping modes. CMI, along with CAI and CSLR, are the components of TBL.

computer managed learning A synonym for computer-managed instruction.

computer managed training (CMT) A synonym for computer-managed instruction.

computer supported learning resources (CSLR) Usually called by its initials, CSLR is any form of computer support for learning other than those that teach (CAI) or test, prescribe, or keep records (CMI). The modes of CSLR are communications, data base, hypermedia, and performance support systems. CSLR, CAI and CMI are the components of TBL.

condition One of the three required parts of a learning objective. Condition describes the circumstances under which the performance or outcome of learning will be tested. It states what items or circumstances will apply, be provided, or be withheld. It may include manuals or tools the trainee will have to work with.

cost avoidance A form of cost justification based upon eliminating or reducing existing or future costs. For example, travel and equipment costs.

cost-benefit analysis A method of evaluating the implications of alternative HRD plans. Cost-benefit analysis determines whether a project will save an amount equal to or greater than its cost and lost opportunities. It is a technique for assessing the relationship between results of outcomes of HRD programs and the cost required to produce them.

course map A document that outlines a course and shows the various relationships between the lessons and modules. A course map usually takes the form of a diagram or flowchart.

criterion One of the three required parts of a learning objective, that states the minimum competency or performance level that the student must attain by the end of instruction. A properly stated criterion allows the designer and learner to measure success. Criterion is often based on time limit, accuracy, or quality. For example, the learner must be able to assemble the gear box within ten minutes or the learner must identify seven of ten blueprint errors to pass the test. The plural of criterion is criteria. Criterion is also called standard and proficiency.

criterion-referenced instruction (CRI) Synonym for performance-based instruction.

curriculum The largest instructional component. A curriculum is made up of two or more courses.

delivery A phase in the ISD process, usually called implementation.

delivery system (delivery station) The equipment used to deliver a technology-based learning program.

design One of the phases in the ISD process. It includes preparation of a detailed plan for the learning activity. The information gathered in the analysis phase forms the basis of the design. Parts of the design process include completion of a work analysis, specification of learning objectives, definition of entry behaviors, grouping and sequencing of objectives, specification of learning activities and assessment and evaluation systems, and selection of existing materials.

designer The member of an instructional development group who specializes in design activities. In small groups this may be only one of the tasks performed by a single person.

developer The member of an instructional development group who specializes in development activities. In small groups this may be only one of the tasks performed by a single person.

development One of the phases in the ISD process. Production of instructional materials ready for trial use. Materials are produced as specified in the design phase and in accordance with the design and development strategy specified in earlier phases.

development station Synonym for authoring station.

digital versatile disc The next generation compact disc, for audio, video, and computer applications.

Digital Video Interactive (DVI) Usually called by its abbreviation, DVI is a compact disc format designed for interactive multimedia. A 12-cm DVI disc holds a comprehensive mix of up to one hour of video, 7,000 still images, audio, computer text and graphics, and interaction capabilities. One competitive format for interactive multimedia.

domains of learning The three domains into which instructional activities can be placed. They are: cognitive, psychomotor, and affective.

drill and practice A series of questions used to review and practice previously learned material. One of the most common instructional techniques. One of the modes of CAI.

educational technology A synonym for instructional technology.

embedded instruction Instruction about one or more aspects of any technology-based system available to the user within the system itself. The distinction is that the user need not quit the work problem to seek the instruction.

enhanced graphics adapter (EGA) Medium resolution video signal used in VDTs. Inferior to VGA resolution for technology-based learning. Obsolete today.

entry behavior A formal statement of the prior knowledge and skills necessary for undertaking a particular instruction.

ergonomics Synonym for human factors.

evaluation Evaluation can be considered as two separate steps. First, an important evaluation is conducted using learners before the general implementation of the program materials. It is called formative evaluation. Second, the measure of the effectiveness of the materials in solving the instructional problem identified in the analysis phase, called summative evaluation. Kirkpatrick's four-level model of summative evaluation is often used. Evaluation is one of the phases in the ISD process. The others are analysis, design, development, and implementation.

evaluator The role of identifying the impact of an intervention on individual or organizational effectiveness.

expression Any combination of identifiers, values, or operators that produces a result when evaluated by the computer program.

feedback Information presented to learners after they answer a question. Correct answers, incorrect answers, unexpected answers, and failures produce different feedback.

field trial Synonym for pilot test.

formative evaluation The evaluation of material conducted during its early developmental stages for the purpose of revising materials before widespread use. Formative evaluation is conducted during the development phase of ISD.

function Defined components of computer code that perform specific tasks. Functions operate on values or do other specific tasks. Authorware includes two kinds of functions, system (predefined and unchangeable) and custom (written by the user and imported).

generational loss The reduction in quality resulting from the copying of analog media. This is usually a description of degraded quality in videotape and laser disc.

generic courseware Courseware that is not specific to one organization. Generic courseware may appeal to a broader market, as opposed to custom courseware, which primarily meets the needs of one specific client or audience.

hardware Physical equipment. Hardware excludes the instructions to the equipment called software, and the instructional software and supporting physical materials called courseware.

heterogeneous Learners with different work experiences. This is the most common situation.

high resolution In industrial technology-based learning, resolution greater than the best television screen (such as 480×640 or 512×512 pixels per inch) is desirable. True high resolution (2400×2400 pixels per inch) is beyond the usual needs of technology-based learning.

human factors Generally anything that influences the design of equipment or processes based on the human body, so that people are comfortable working. The term also includes those aspects of technology-based learning courseware that were included to make it easy for learners to use.

hypermedia A program that links different media under learner control in a way similar to hypertext linkage of text. Hypermedia links media such as text, graphics, video, voice, and animation. For example, the learner can choose video (when available), see a related video sequence, and then return to the program.

hypertext A program that links nonlinear text. Hypertext allows flexible, learner-directed browsing to seek additional information by moving between related documents along thematic lines, without losing the context of the original inquiry. For example, the learner chooses a word such as *gear*. The program links to text that says, "This equipment has *helical* gears." Further exploration of *helical* is possible.

icon A symbol that looks like an object. An icon can represent any function or task. In icon-driven systems, the learner chooses the icon with a tactile device, such as a mouse, instead of pressing function keys or typing commands.

implementation One of the phases in the ISD process. It involves delivering the learning activities to the target population of learners in the intended environment. All instructional materials are reproduced and distributed during the implementation phase.

individualized instruction An instructional technique in which the instruction is designed to be used by individual learners being. The learner is taught only the material that is not already known, instead of taught everything in a specified curriculum, as is true with traditional instruction. This is more than learners simply working on materials without regard to the activities of other learners in the same class. All individualized instruction is self-paced instruction. But not all self-paced instruction is individualized.

instructional development The process of producing learning activities.

instructional game One of the modes of CAI. The dividing line between amusement and education is not always easily discernible, because learning by playing is still learning. Despite the instructional legitimacy and value of instructional gaming, it has not been well-accepted by some organizations. A game is a rule-governed activity involving some conflict that obstructs the players from reaching a specific goal. Instructional games usually, but not always, include some form of competition.

instructional prescription An assignment given to a learner in individualized learning situations to provide needed learning. Instructional prescriptions are often based on a pre-test given to participants to determine what level of knowledge, skill, or aptitude they bring to the instruction.

instructional system An integrated combination of resources, including students, instructors, materials, equipment, and facilities; techniques; and procedures performing efficiently the functions required to achieve specified learning objectives.

instructional systems development (ISD) Usually used in abbreviated form, ISD is a term for a variety of related systems that organize the development of instruction. ISD should be a deliberate and orderly, but flexible, process for planning and developing instructional programs that ensure personnel are taught in a cost-effective way the knowledge, skills, and attitudes essential for successful job performance. The phases of ISD are analysis, design, development, implementation, and evaluation. ISD depends on a description and analysis of several integral instructional factors, such as the tasks necessary for performing the job, and learning objectives. Tests are clearly stated before instruction begins. Evaluation procedures are carried out to determine whether the objectives have been reached, and methods for revising the process are thus based on empirical data.

instructional technology Technology that enables the systematic practice of designing, carrying out, and evaluating the total learning process, employing a combination of human and nonhuman resources to bring about more effective instruction.

instructor-led training Any learning activity dependent on an instructor or facilitator. Instructor-led training is a relatively new term for an old activity, occasioned by the development of alternatives such as CAI.

interaction A reciprocal interchange between the learner and the instructional medium. In CAI an interaction is never simply pressing a key to advance the display. A complete interaction is a question or problem, directions, expected correct and incorrect answers, and feedback for each possible answer. The interaction may be followed by branching, contributing to individualized instruction. The interactivity of courseware is sometimes judged by counting the frequency of interactions.

interactive multimedia (IM) Essentially, CAI carried to its logical conclusion. IM is a somewhat redundant term that has grown in popularity, primarily because of marketing efforts.

interactive videodisc (IVD) Video images linked with a computerized learning program that are learner-controlled through the use of a computer. Depending on the learner's response to a question, the learner may be shown any one of several video sequences. Technically, IVD is CAI controlling an added 12-inch laser-read player. IVD usually includes motion video, audio, and a touch panel. Sequences can be still, regular, slow, or fast motion. Videodiscs hold 54,000 video images, or about one hour. Never spelled videodisk.

learning objective Learning objectives are the key part of the instructional system. Carefully written objectives will identify the sought-after behavior for trainers as well as for learners. They must communicate in clear and precise language. In the system developed by Robert Mager, a well-written objective contains three elements: (1) the condition, (2) the performance, and (3) the criterion.

learning station A location for a person to study. A learning station may feature a video player, computer, and any associated input or output devices based on the particular learning need.

learning style Each individual's unique approach to learning. The learner's psychological traits determine how that person will perceive, interact with, and respond to any environment. Specifically, it includes the ways an individual behaves, feels, and processes information in learning situations. Experts do not agree how to categorize these styles.

lesson   Any block of learning designed around a specific skill. A curriculum is composed of lessons. A lesson may be made up of a number of units, each covering one learning objective.

levels of interactivity   Derived from interactive systems levels. Does not relate to the quality, relative value, or degree of sophistication. Three standards of videodisc system interactivity proposed by the Nebraska Videodisc Design/Production Group have been widely accepted. They are
  1. Level One system: Usually a consumer-model videodisc player with still/freeze frame, picture stop, chapter stop, frame address, and dual-channel audio, but with limited memory and limited processing power.
  2. Level Two system: An industrial-model videodisc player with the capabilities of Level One, plus on-board programmable memory and improved access time.
  3. Level Three system: Level One or Two players interfaced to an external computer and/or other peripheral processing devices.

life cycle costs   The costs of an HRD project over its entire lifetime.

log-in   Process that must be performed in order for a computer system to recognize an authorized user. This is also termed "sign-on" or "log-on."

manipulation   The learner moving objects on the screen through tactile interaction.

Maslow's hierarchy   A classic theory of motivation developed by Abraham Maslow and often used in management development. The theory names five specific needs, arranged in priority order: (1) physiological, (2) safety, (3) love and belongingness, (4) esteem, and (5) self-actualization. They are often represented as successive levels of a pyramid. The theory suggests that until lower needs are satisfied, higher needs cannot be addressed, and that a satisfied need no longer is a motivator.

master performer   An employee who has the highest skill level. In the analysis phase of instructional development, this person is observed to determine how the task(s) should be done.

mastery learning   A principle of evaluating learning based on mastery of material according to a predetermined criterion. Mastery learning is also called criterion-referenced instruction (CRI), or performance-based instruction. This is in contrast to norm-referenced learning, in which the learner is compared to other learners instead of to a fixed standard.

menu-driven   The types of authoring or learning systems in which actions or topics are selected from a list of choices.

metaphor   A term that implies a different meaning than the one which it ordinarily signifies. Metaphors are often used in technology-based learning.

modeling   One of the modes of CAI. The others are drill and practice, instructional games, simulation, and tutorial. Use of the CBL system to represent a system or process, permitting the learner to change values and observe the effects of the change on the system. An example is a model of population.

module   An arbitrary unit of instruction. Usually, a module is constructed to teach one specific thing and can be taught, measured, evaluated for change, or bypassed as a whole. Modules can be assembled to form complete courses and curricula.

multimedia   Use of any two or more instructional media together. Multimedia usually simulates person-to-person or person-to-machine dialogue. Technically, examples include any two media, such as tape-slide. In practice, this term has come to represent optical disk technology combined with computer power.

norm-referenced learning   The traditional grading scheme. The principle of grading based on each learner's success compared to other learners.

NTSC video   The video standard used in the United States, Canada, and most other countries where 60 Hz. power is used. NTSC video is 525 scan lines.

one-on-one trial   Review of an evolving instructional package by an instructional developer, conducted with one member of the target population at a time. A one-on-one trial evaluates the then-current effectiveness of the under-development instructional product and provides for improvements, which are made before another such trial. The acquisition and analysis of data from selected members of the target population is used to identify and correct weaknesses. A formative evaluation step.

part-task simulation   A technique for the use of computer-based learning in the simulation mode. A learning station may not be able to simulate an entire situation at once. By simulating only one of several parts, effective learning can take place. For example, simulation of a system on an aircraft instead of the entire aircraft.

performance   One of the three required parts of a Magerian learning objective. What the learners must demonstrate to prove that they have grasped the task. These action words state the main intent of the objective. The performance should match the job task, describe the simplest and most direct behavior possible, and be stated clearly. Observable and measurable action words should be used, such as choose, describe, write, identify, or solve. To be useful, performance statements must tell plainly how the trainee's learning will be observed. Certain words should be avoided, such as "to know" or "understand." Poor performance statements include "understand the Operator's Manual" and "know Ohm's Law."

performance-based instruction   Learning activities designed to provide the specific on-the-job knowledge and skills required to perform the task to be learned. These are determined in a task analysis and expressed as learning objectives. Often includes performance-based evaluation. Performance-based instruction is also called criterion-referenced instruction (CRI).

performance objective   The new capability the learner must demonstrate on the job. The instruction is intended to enable this performance. The learning objective can be satisfied in the classroom, but the performance objective must equal the task at the job site.

performance support system   An integrated computer program that provides any combination of expert system, hypertext, embedded animation, CAI, and hypermedia to an employee on demand. Performance support systems allow employees to perform with a minimum of support and intervention by others. Examples include help systems, electronic job aids, and expert advisors.

pilot test   The acquisition and analysis of data from outside the formal instructional environment to evaluate the instructional product in the operating environment. A formative evaluation step. In a pilot test, an instructional program is presented in final form to a portion of the target population.

platform   A particular computer setup. For example, a combination of hardware and software capable, or not, of supporting a particular instructional package.

positive reinforcement   Any favorable consequence or recognition directed at the learner. Positive reinforcement is provided upon the learner's demonstration of a desirable behavior. Learners are more likely to repeat activities for which they receive positive reinforcement.

post test   Any assessment of learners after they complete an exercise. Post tests are often used to measure the learner's mastery of the course objectives. The post test is sometimes compared to the pretest to determine learning gained.

pre-mastering   In videodisc production, when the master tape is checked and prepared for final transfer onto the master disc. All delivery discs will be pressed from the master disc.

pre-production   In video production, all design tasks that lead up to the actual shoot. For example, storyboarding and scriptwriting.

prerequisite   Any knowledge or skill that must be acquired by the learner before other new knowledge or skills can be learned. When these are taught in a specific course, that course may become the prerequisite.

prescription generation   The process of matching a learner accurately with the instructional materials actually needed by that individual, based on the results of a test. One of the modes of CMI.

programmer   The person who codes computer programs, including TBL.

programmer ready materials (PRM)   In technology-based learning, the output of the designer-developer during the development process. The programmer can completely program the instruction, based solely on the content of the materials and without the need for further collaboration. Storyboards are the major component of PRM.

progress check   A question used to verify participant's progress and understanding. Sometimes called a double-check question.

psychomotor objective   A learning objective that specifies muscular coordination and movement, manipulation of materials and objects, or an act which requires neuromuscular coordination.

random test item   In computer-based testing, a test question drawn from a test bank for presentation to a learner. Structured, non-random methods of test item selection are also used.

rapid prototyping   In technology-based learning design, the early development of a small-scale prototype used to test key features of the design.

reaction   The first level of Kirkpatrick's model of summative evaluation. Learners indicate opinions, attitudes, or feelings of satisfaction or dissatisfaction with the learning experience. Data are collected with reaction sheets. Reaction evaluation is used in a majority of training situations.

readability (level)   A measure of the level at which a sample of text is written. Readability level specifies the education level required of the reader (learner). Readability level may be calculated to produce a Flesch Reading Ease Score (number represents a percentage of American adults who can read the material), Flesch-Kincaid index (Flesch score converted to a grade level), or Gunning-Fog index (also a grade level).

record keeping   Computers can capture more data about a learner than can be reasonably used. Typically, the CMI system will record success on pre- and post tests. One of the modes of CMI.

repurposing   Modifying the content of an existing program to accomplish a task other than the one for which it was originally designed. Level One consumer videodiscs are often repurposed for Level Three use.

resolution   The degree to which detail can be displayed. On a video monitor, resolution is measured in dots (pixel elements), vertically and horizontally. High resolution is necessary to display graphics. Low resolution is adequate for text. The best resolution of which an NTSC television screen is capable is low resolution. Overall size of the display does not alter the resolution. Resolutions are CGA (Color Graphics Adapter) 320×200 four color, 640×200 monochrome; EGA (Enhanced Graphics Adapter) 640×350 16 color; VGA (Video Graphics Adapter) 640×480 16 color. Only VGA is suitable for TBL.

self-paced instruction   Any method of instruction in which the learner determines the actual speed of progress within predefined limits.

sign-on   The act of entering one's identity into the technology-based learning system to begin work or study.

simulation   Any representation of an item of equipment, device, situation, system, or subsystem in realistic form. Simulation enables the learner to experience the operation of the target equipment without possibility of destruction of the equipment. The simulation may focus on a small subset of the features of the actual job-world situation. Technology-based (usually part-task) simulation contrasts with the very costly, single-purpose special simulators typified by aircraft simulators. Each has a proper role. Simulation allows users to learn the operation of equipment without damaging it or harming themselves or others. Simulation is one of the modes of CAI.

situation simulation   Essentially, a CAI action maze. Learners choose from alternatives at decision points. After a decision, the learner is provided with the consequences of the decision, more information, and further choices. Often, a score is accumulated for comparison against a norm or the self.

small group trial   Use of an instructional package by a limited number of members of the target population. A trial by a small group, usually under the supervision of an instructional developer, evaluates the effectiveness of the development instructional product to ensure market readiness. Weaknesses are corrected before release for use in the field. A formative evaluation step.

software   Programs that make computers work. Computer programs that deliver content are part of courseware, not software.

special effects generator   In video production, a device to add various optical effects to video images.

stimulus   The event, situation, condition, signal, or cue to which a response must be made.

storyboard   Documents used for film, video, and computer display planning. A series of sketches resembling a cartoon strip that help visualize the sequence of scenes or views to be presented. Plot, character, and action are all subjects of storyboards.

student disk   A diskette with technology-based lessons on it. The diskette may also require a presentation system.

subject matter expert (SME)   A person thoroughly knowledgeable of the content of instruction to be developed, who works with others on the design of instruction. The SME acts as advisor to the instructional designer. (Is pronounced by its initials—S-M-E—not as a single word, "smee.")

summative evaluation   Instruction conducted during and after delivery, for the purpose of assessing the instructional environment, learning, on-the-job use, and return on investment. Summative evaluation is conducted during the evaluation phase of ISD.

surrogate travel   One multimedia application in which physical travel is precisely simulated using videodisc and computer. Surrogate travel allows the user to control the path taken through the virtual environment. For example, a tour of a nuclear power plant. Also known as vicarious travel.

tactile input   Interaction with a technology-based program by use of touch, as compared with keyboard input. May be achieved by use of a light pen, mouse, digitizer, stylus, or touch panel screen. Experience shows that categories of users who never use a keyboard strongly prefer tactile input. The learner's status may also be involved. For example, doctors and pilots.

target population   The group of people for whom a behavior change is intended, usually defined in terms of age, background, and ability. Samples from this population are used in evaluating instructional materials during their development. Sometimes called target audience.

task   A set of skills performed to accomplish a specific objective. A subset of a job. A unit of work activity or operation which forms a significant part of a duty. A task constitutes a logical and necessary step in a performance, and usually has a logical beginning and end.

task analysis   A process of arriving at a step-by-step description of all the performance elements (tasks) that make up a job. Task analysis applies whether the steps of the task are mainly cognitive or psychomotor. Task analysis is done by questionnaires, observations of performance, and interviews with incumbents and supervisors. A term coined by Robert Gagne, it is also referred to as skills analysis. Task and skills analysis are subsets of the complete job.

technology-based learning   Also called computer-based learning. TBL is the umbrella term that includes all forms of use of computers in support of learning. The components of CBL are CAI, CMI, and CSLR. TBL was defined by Donald Bitzer as, "any time a person and a computer come together, and one of them learns something." The meaning of TBL is identical to CBE, CBI, and CBT, and CBL but is the preferred term, in order to decrease the emphasis on the computer itself.

templates   Instructional models that are frequently built into authoring systems. Templates offer increased productivity. For example, there may be a multiple-choice template. The author fills in the question, choices, answers, and feedbacks. The disadvantage is decreased flexibility.

testing   One of the modes of CMI. In technology-based learning, testing is used to determine the gaps in a particular learner's knowledge. The information will be used to generate an appropriate instructional prescription.

touch screen or panel   A special panel fitted in front of a display screen that permits the learner to indicate choices by touching a screen location directly, without use of a mouse or keyboard. The touch panel does not interfere with vision.

unit   The smallest instructional component. A unit covers one learning objective. A lesson is composed of one or more units.

user-friendly   A desirable attribute for any computer system. Implies that the user need not be an expert to use the system and that mistakes are easily overcome or avoided by the system.

user interface   The integration between technology and its user.

validation   Ensuring that a learning activity, instructional product, measurement instrument, or system is capable of achieving its intended aims and functions. For example, validation of instruction includes developmental testing, field testing, and revision of instruction to ensure that the instructional intent is achieved. Validation allows instructional designers to guarantee specified results.

validity   The extent to which a test is a worthwhile measure for its intended purpose. Tests that are valid yield essentially true results. The degree to which a test performs this function satisfactorily is usually called the relative validity. Actions taken to make the test instrument valid are called *defending* the validity of the instrument.

variable   A representation of a value that can change—it varies. Authorware includes system variables that are predefined and unalterable, and a custom variable capability permitting you to define your own.

video compression   Any technique used to reduce the bandwidth required for the transmission of the video signal.

videodisc   A medium based on video accessed from a laser disc. Videodisc is the principal form of video combined with CAI to constitute interactive video. The spelling with a "c" is preferred by video and HRD professionals over the spelling with a "k" (videodisk), which is also seen. Never spelled "videodisk".

video display terminal (VDT)   The preferred term for computer display, commonly referred to in its abbreviated form, VDT. VDT is preferred, since it accurately describes a monitor using any display technology, such as CRT, LCD, or plasma panel.

video graphics array (VGA)   A very high resolution signal used in personal computers. VGA graphics are adequate for technology-based learning.

virtual reality (VR)   An experience in a computer-generated simulated environment. Virtual reality is particularly used to simulate conditions that do not actually exist, but may also be used to simulate actual potential conditions. Immersive virtual reality uses special peripherals, particularly data gloves and special, close-to-the-user's-eyes computer graphic displays, called head-mounted displays (HMD). Immersive VR gives the user the feeling of being present in a scene and able to move around in it. Desktop virtual reality is based on standard desktop computers.

whole-task simulation   The most difficult level of simulation to achieve. Whole-task simulation requires provision of all of the relevant elements of a work environment. For example, a simulator for a particular aircraft.

wide area network (WAN)   A network composed of local area networks (LANs).

workstation   A work location, sometimes confused with a learning station. A workstation may feature a computer and any associated input or output devices, based on the particular job need.

Index

Illustrations are indicated by **boldface.**

procedures, 151-152
product, 84
product expectations, 151
purpose, 151-152
structure, 152, **153**
design
 checklist, 544
 phase, general, 83-84
 process, 541-542
 tips, 164-166
development, 84
 checklist, 547
 planning, 545
 process, 542, 550-551
 ratio of effort, 554
 time-saving techniques, 554
Dialdin, Ali, 549
diary, project, 557-558
digital video
 analog comparison, 472-473
 evolution, 70
 future, 478
 cost, 540
 training, 129-131, 471
digital versatile disc (DVD), 126-127, 570
digital video interactive (DVI), 129-130, 476
digital video technology, 478
documentation, 179, 223-224
 Authorware, 223
 courseware development, 7-8
 rationale, 180, 223
 untitled icons, 219
 using comments, 256
domains of learning, 64-65
drag and drop, 207
drill and practice, 22
 mode defined, 18
 simulation use, 20
Dwerlkotte, David, 514-518

E

E-mail, 571
Eastman, George, 35
edit decision list (EDL), 473
editing, analog vs. digital, 472-473
Eldridge, John, 126, 492
electric power, 49
electromagnetic fields, concerns, 48
erase icon, 261-262
erasing, 265-266

ergonomic, 47-49
 courseware, 49
 tips, 48
 user-friendliness, 460-463
error trapping, 227, 351-353, **311, 353, 360**
ethnocentrism, 493-494, 497
evaluation, 93-99, 269-276 (*see also* tests and testing)
 alpha tests, 271
 beta tests, 272-273
 costs, 99
 data collection, 273-274
 data examination, 274-275
 definition/description, 93
 expert reviews, 270-271, **272**
 field trial, 96-97
 formative, 94, 270-271
 market, 98-99
 on-line course, 273
 on-screen questions, **275**
 one-on-one trials, 95
 phase, 84
 plan, 273, **274**
 procedures, 94
 questions to ask, 270, **270**
 small group trials, 95-96
 summative, 97-98, 273-275
 supervisor involvement, 271
 tips, 99
example practice test, 165
exercises
 analyzing objectives, 80-82
 behavior identification, 80
 computer applications, 4
 envisionsing a TBL system, 5
 individual project definition, 59, 73
 project justification, 119
 understanding your own project (and organization), 34, 45-46
 WOMBAT delivery requirements, 59-61
expert reviews, 270-271
expert systems
 CSLR use, 31
 training support use, 33

F

facilitator, capacity, 39
FALSE variable, 264-265, 377, **265**
Federal Aviation Administration, 45
feedback, 164
 context-sensitive, 398-399, **399**

ABOUT THE AUTHORS

Dr. Angus Reynolds, an internationally known expert on technology-based training, has worked in the field for more than 15 years, acting as a consultant for more than 75 leading companies in the United States and abroad. He is Multimedia Program Manager at AlliedSignal Aerospace. Formerly he was a professor of instructional technology and associate dean of the graduate programs in training and development at New York Institute of Technology.

Thomas Iwinski is an instructional designer/multimedia producer and has worked for EG&G Energy Measurements and Allied Signal AeroSpace. He currently is pursuing a doctorate at Pennsylvania State University in Distance Education.

DATE DUE L.-Brault

Bibliofiche 297B